CW01500008

PREFACE

This *Companion* is a labor of love by 14 scholars to whom Ovid has become over the years a faithful friend, characterized by boundless energy, a sheer love of language, and the ability to renew himself and others, continually enriching our understanding of the ways of the Roman poet and his world. The goal of this effort has been consistent throughout: to make Ovid's distinctive gifts to the Western literary tradition available and accessible to all who read him, whether as newcomers or as old and familiar companions—thus the title of this book. The arrangement of the book is straightforward: opening chapters on Ovid's life and poetic style offer an orientation to two essential aspects of our poet, and establish a basis for what will follow by taking account of the common elements unifying a poetic corpus produced over a 30- to 40-year period. The next nine chapters are arranged chronologically, in terms of the dates of composition and/or publication of each of Ovid's extant works. Readers will find in each chapter when appropriate more specific consideration of controversies and consensus (where either or both exist) regarding chronology. The concluding three chapters of the *Companion* offer an inviting introduction to Ovid's posthumous survival—in the new poetry of ensuing centuries, up to the *aetas Ovidiana*, and in the precious manuscripts which preserved and transmitted Ovid's poetry from antiquity. These chapters also offer the opportunity for a synoptic view of Ovid's poetry, considered now not only as a series of individual works but also as a the legacy of a variable but singular poetic voice from the past. Having escorted our poet to the dawn of the printed page, we leave him there to be entrusted to the care of others—as indeed he has been attended to in much recent work on Ovid's legacy since the Renaissance.

As editor, I have invited each of the contributors to seek out a balance between a comprehensive overview of a particular topic and a focused analysis of some aspect of it. In each case, the contributors and I have attempted to focus on a feature of the work under consideration that in some way typifies or captures a crucial aspect of the experience of reading Ovid. Readers will find that Ovid's text is pre-eminent here; but the close focus of each individual chapter combines with that of the others to provide what I hope will be an extended and complex meditation on the essential Ovid. It will also be clear to readers that, in spite of this volume's ample size, it cannot hope to contain everything worth saying about Ovid; and I have not attempted to have it do so. Rather, it is to be hoped that this book can contribute to the launching of a new millennium of Ovid studies, by inspiring scholars and readers to think again about an old friend. I therefore invite our readers to find the gaps, so to speak, and to help to fill them, with the inspiration and energy of this book as their guide.

This book would not have been possible had it not been for the good will, hard work, and enthusiastic support of each of the contributors, particularly as I struggled to impose a sense of order on the volume in its final stages. I extend my heartfelt thanks, therefore, to each of them: Michael Dewar, Elaine Fantham, Ralph Hexter, E.J. Kenney, Alison Keith, Peter Knox, John Miller, John Richmond, Gianpiero Rosati, Garth Tissol, Pat Watson, Peter White, and Gareth Williams, all *amici Ovidiani*. I am also indebted to a number of colleagues in the field who made valuable suggestions along the way, including Denis Feeney, Nicholas Horsfall, and Danuta Schanzer, as well as to Richard Tarrant, who corresponded with several of the contributors regarding textual matters in the *Metamorphoses*. I have had wonderful support for this project at Bowdoin, from the untiring staff of the Hawthorne-Longfellow Library, who tracked down countless interlibrary loan requests for me (*inter alia*), to the timely and cheerful intervention of Ruth Maschino, word-processing teacher and troubleshooter extraordinaire. I am deeply indebted to two people in particular for patient, efficient, and benevolent assistance on an almost daily basis: the Classics Department coordinator, Tammis Donovan Lareau, and my inestimably talented student assistant (and budding Ovidian), Rebecca Sears. I also want to acknowledge the supportive and efficient staff at Brill Academic Publishers, in particular the editors with whom I have worked, especially Julian Deahl, Job Lisman, and Michiel Klein Swormink. And last but not least, I owe a profound debt of gratitude, and more, to Michael Boyd and Rachel E.W. Boyd, without whose love and support none of this would have been possible.

Barbara Weiden Boyd
Brunswick, Maine (USA)
April 2001

Brill's Companion to Ovid

Brill's Companion to Ovid

Edited by

Barbara Weiden Boyd

BRILL

LEIDEN • BOSTON
2012

Library of Congress Control Number: 2002282461

This paperback was originally published in hardback under ISBN 978 90 04 12156 0.

ISBN 978 90 04 22676 0

Copyright 2002 by Koninklijke Brill NV, Leiden, The Netherlands.
Koninklijke Brill NV incorporates the imprints Brill, Global Oriental, Hotei Publishing,
IDC Publishers, Martinus Nijhoff Publishers and VSP.

All rights reserved. No part of this publication may be reproduced, translated, stored in
a retrieval system, or transmitted in any form or by any means, electronic, mechanical,
photocopying, recording or otherwise, without prior written permission from the publisher.

Authorization to photocopy items for internal or personal use is granted by Koninklijke Brill NV
provided that the appropriate fees are paid directly to The Copyright Clearance Center,
222 Rosewood Drive, Suite 910, Danvers, MA 01923, USA.
Fees are subject to change.

This book is printed on acid-free paper.

ET DOCTIS ET DISCIPULIS

D · D · D

CONTENTS

LIST OF CONTRIBUTORS

Barbara Weiden Boyd is Henry Winkley Professor of Latin and Greek at Bowdoin College. She is the author *of Ovid's Literary Loves: Influence and Innovation in the Amores* (1997), and numerous articles on Virgil, Ovid, and Latin literature. She is currently working on narrative patterns in the *Fasti* and *Metamorphoses*.

Michael Dewar is Professor of Classics at the University of Toronto. In addition to a number of articles on Latin poets from the first to the fifth centuries, he has published commentaries on the ninth book of the *Thebaid* of Statius (1991) and the *De Sexto Consulatu Honorii* of Claudian (1996).

Elaine Fantham taught at the University of Toronto and at Princeton University, where she was Giger Professor of Latin until her retirement in 1999. Author of commentaries on Seneca's *Troades* (1982), Lucan's *de Bello Civili II* (1992), and Ovid's *Fasti IV* (1998), she has also published *Roman Literary Culture from Cicero to Apuleius* (1996), and many articles on post-Virgilian poetry.

Ralph Hexter is Professor of Classics and Comparative Literature at the University of California, Berkeley. His publications include *Ovid and Medieval Schooling* (1986), *Innovations of Antiquity*, coedited with Daniel Selden (1992), *A Guide to the Odyssey* (1993), and articles on topics from Virgil to Goethe. He is currently serving as Dean of Arts and Humanities in the College of Letters and Science at Berkeley.

Alison Keith is Associate Professor of Classics and Women's Studies at the University of Toronto, and a Fellow of Victoria College. Her publications include *The Play of Fictions: Studies in Ovid's Metamorphoses, Book 2* (1992) and *Engendering Rome: Women in Roman Epic* (2000). She is currently completing a commentary on the fourth book of Ovid's *Metamorphoses*.

E.J. Kenney is Emeritus Kennedy Professor of Latin in the University of Cambridge, and was a Fellow of Peterhouse, Cambridge, from 1953 to 1991. His publications include a critical edition of Ovid's amatory works (1961; 2d ed. 1995); editions with commentary of Lucretius's *De rerum natura III* (1971), Apuleius's *Cupid & Psyche* (1990), and Ovid's *Heroides XVI–XXI* (1996); a translation with introduction and notes of Apuleius's *Golden Ass* (1998); and *The Classical Text* (1974; Italian translation by A. Lunelli, 1995). He is at present working on a commentary on Ovid, *Metamorphoses VII–IX*.

Peter Knox, Professor of Classics at the University of Colorado, is the author of *Ovid's Metamorphoses and the Traditions of Augustan Poetry* (1986) and a commentary on a selection of Ovid's *Heroides* (1995). He has published many articles on Latin literature and Hellenistic poetry.

John F. Miller is Associate Professor and Chair of Classics at the University of Virginia. He is the author of *Ovid's Elegiac Festivals: Studies in the Fasti* (1991) and numerous articles on a wide range of Latin poetic subjects.

J.A. Richmond is Professor Emeritus of Greek at University College, Dublin, and was a pupil of the late Otto Skutsch. His publications include an edition of the pseudo-Ovidian *Halieutica* (1962), *Chapters on Greek Fish-lore* (1973), and an edition of Ovid's *Ex Ponto* (1990).

Gianpiero Rosati is Professor of Latin Literature at the University of Udine. He is the author of *Narciso e Pigmalione* (1983), an edition with commentary of Ovid's *Heroides XVIII–XIX* (1996), and other publications on Ovid. He is now working on a commentary on *Metamorphoses IV–VI* for the Fondazione Valla.

Garth Tissol, Associate Professor of Classics at Emory University, is the author of *The Face of Nature: Wit, Narrative, and Cosmic Origins in Ovid's Metamorphoses* (1997). He has also published on Virgil and on John Dryden's translations of Latin poetry. He is currently working on Ovid's exilic elegies.

Patricia Watson is Senior Lecturer in Classics at the University of Sydney. Her publications include *Ancient Stepmothers: Myth, Misogyny, and Reality* (1995) and numerous articles on Roman poetry and Latin poetic language. She has just completed a commentary on selections from Martial, co-authored with her husband Lindsay Watson.

Gareth Williams, Associate Professor of Classics at Columbia University, is the author of *Banished Voices: Readings in Ovid's Exile Poetry* (1994) and *The Curse of Exile: A Study of Ovid's Ibis* (1996). He is currently working on an edition with commentary of selected *Moral Dialogues* of the younger Seneca.

Peter White is Professor of Classics at the University of Chicago, where he has taught since 1968. He has published *Promised Verse* (1993) and various articles about the interrelationship of Latin poetry and Roman society, and he is currently at work on a book about the pragmatics of Cicero's letters.

CHAPTER ONE

OVID AND THE AUGUSTAN MILIEU*

Peter White

Although Ovid left a more copious body of work than any other
Augustan poet, no manuscript carries an ancient biographical sketch
of the sort transmitted with the poems of Virgil, Horace, and Tibullus.
Almost everything we think about his life depends on first-person
utterances in his poems. The difficulties of weighing this sort of tes-
timony are by now familiar. No formula has yet been found that
graphs the relationship between the imaginative "I" who speaks in
poems and the life experience of poets who write them. Even when
a poem seems to gesture most transparently toward external reali-
ties, it is prudent to suspect that it discloses not so much facts as
factoids. The details may not fit the Ovid of history but an imagi-
nary alter ego projected by a self-aggrandizing, evasive, and incon-
sistent informant.

On the other hand, relatively little in poets' testimony or in other
lore about their lives is ever decisively discredited. Since details can
rarely be checked against an independent record, the criterion of
truth comes down to one of fit. A given detail either fits or does
not fit an understanding built up from other details. But a changed
understanding always has the potential to vindicate details hitherto
dismissed. Furthermore, while the *persona* strain of criticism has taught
us to interpret the rhetorical slant of first-person utterances more
acutely, it has not seriously shaken belief in the grosser information
that poets impart about their lives. *Persona* criticism that is true to
its creed makes no claim about the external world, after all. And so
with rare exceptions, even critical readers still believe that Horace's
father was a freedman, that Virgil worked on the *Georgics* in Naples,
and that Ovid was sent into exile by Augustus.

* I wish to thank Robert Kaster and Barbara Weiden Boyd for their comments on
an earlier version of this chapter.

In any case, for Ovid's life we have little choice but to make the best of the testimony we have, with the caveat that the name "Ovid" in what follows refers for the most part to a figment of his poems.

1. *Early Ovid (43 to 13 B.C.)*

According to *Tr.* 4.10.3–14, Ovid was born in Sulmo about ninety miles east of Rome on March 20, 43 B.C. In this poem and others (*Am.* 3.8.9–10, 3.15.5–6, *Pont.* 4.8.17–18), much stress is laid upon the pedigree of his family: Ovid says that they had belonged to the equestrian order for generations, unlike the knights created during the recent civil wars.[1] At the same time, there is no hint in all of his work that his family had suffered in the civil wars. He is the only Augustan poet whose background does *not* feature an episode of handicap or deprivation resulting from the period.

How the Ovidii of Sulmo negotiated the twisting course of the struggle is not recorded, but as leading citizens (see *CIL* 9.3082), they are likely to have played a part in the town's decision to declare for Julius Caesar at the very beginning (Caes. *BC* 1.18.1–2). At the end of it, the young Ovid shared in the favor that lifted up many families of municipal Italy during Augustus's reign. His affinity with other municipal elites comes into view at later points in his life. One of his three marriages (*Tr.* 4.10.69–74) was to a woman from Falerii (*Am.* 3.13.1–2), and Ovid later allied himself with a family from Fundi (*Pont.* 2.11).[2] That wife brought Roman connections which were even more important. She was a protégée of Augustus's aunt Atia and cousin Marcia, and she frequented the house of Paullus Fabius Maximus, the blue-blood whom Marcia married.[3]

Ovid's daughter was eventually to complete the family's ascent to senatorial status by marrying a Roman senator (*Tr.* 1.3.19 and Sen. *Dial.* 2.17.1); a step-daughter was also married to a senator (*Pont.* 4.8.11–12). But Ovid had had the opportunity to achieve senatorial

---

[1] As Millar (1993) 6 notes, this claim cannot be strictly true, since Sulmo did not share in the Roman citizenship until the first century B.C.

[2] About the origin of one of his three wives nothing is known. Ovid's municipal connections also included a long-time *hospes* at Carseoli (*F.* 4.687).

[3] For Ovid's wife's connections with Marcia and Maximus, see White (1993), Appendix 2B, nos. 18 and 32.

status in his own right many years before. As a boy he was brought from Sulmo to Rome and sent to school with the city's best-known teachers (*Tr.* 4.10.15–16). Then at the age of about 16 when he celebrated his majority, his father arranged for him to begin wearing in public the garb which identified young men of senatorial family (*Tr.* 4.10.27–29). Later in the principate and probably already at this date (Ovid reached his sixteenth birthday in 27 B.C.), a young man who lacked senatorial antecedents was required to obtain the emperor's permission before he could appropriate the laticlave tunic.[4] By putting it on, he launched himself in public life: it signified that he courted recognition and support and that he intended eventually to stand for senatorial office. The emperor's bestowal of the *latus clauus* helped to even the chances of newcomers in their canvass against the scions of senatorial families.

Ovid says that he carried his pursuit of office as far as service on the Board of Three (*Tr.* 4.10.34), one of the minor elective posts that preceded the senatorial cursus proper. He does not specify whether he was one of the three mintmasters or one of the three officials charged with punishing infractions of public order. But since the mint was almost exclusively the preserve of senators' sons, while the *tresuiri capitales* tended to be newcomers to the establishment, it is likely that Ovid occupied the latter post.[5] It would have involved him in the repression of offenses like murder, theft, and arson and sometimes in the jailing or execution of offenders (a reminiscence of which perhaps survives at *Pont.* 1.6.37–38).

After this taste of office, Ovid retreated to his originary status as a knight. He claims that he was neither physically nor mentally fit for the stresses of a senate career (*Tr.* 4.10.35–38). One imminent stress he could anticipate was the military service so often decried in his poems. Equestrians seeking entry to the senate normally toured as junior officers in the army first. And if Ovid had managed to bypass the army and advance directly to a quaestorship, he would have faced a strong likelihood of having to serve abroad in that capacity.

---

[4] On the *latus clauus* see Levick (1991). Sen. *Epist.* 98.13 seems to indicate that, contrary to current orthodoxy, it was in the emperor's gift as early as the time of Julius Caesar.

[5] On recruitment to the vigintivirate, see Birley (1954) and McAlindon (1957). For the functions of the *tresuiri capitales*, see Mommsen (1887) 2:594–601 and Robinson (1992) 174–79.

Later on, Ovid would again hold one of the minor city magis-
tracies, serving this time in a judicial capacity on the Board of Ten
(*F.* 4.383–84). Since it was unusual to repeat posts at this level, he
may have been drafted the second time, as happened to other knights
when willing candidates were scarce during the middle years of
Augustus's reign (Cass. Dio 54.26.5). Activity in the courts of Rome
was to be a continuing and formative part of Ovid's life, however.
Although he did not plead cases, from the age of 25 or 30 until his
exile he regularly took part in judging them. He alludes to sitting
on the large jury panels of the Court of One Hundred and to arbi-
trating in private suits (*Tr.* 2.93–96, *Pont.* 3.5.23–24). In these venues
he heard litigation regarding property disputes, inheritances, and the
like, but there is no reason to doubt that he was sometimes called
to serve on juries in the criminal courts as well.

Ovid's experience as a *iudex* is noteworthy for two reasons. First,
the jurors in every public trial at Rome and many of the arbitra-
tors were drawn from a select roster of upper-class citizens which
Augustus reviewed and approved.[6] Ovid's visibility in the courts there-
fore accredited him in his own eyes and in the eyes of contempo-
raries as an adherent of the establishment. His decision to forgo a
senatorial career did not mean that he disdained to play an active
civic role in the Augustan state. The retention of his name on the
juror list also gave some color to a defense he made when he was
denounced for the *Ars Amatoria* many years after having written it,
which was that nothing about his life had ever prompted the emperor
to question his fitness to serve (*Tr.* 2.89–96). The second reason
Ovid's experience in the courts is significant is that it provided a
rich fund of conceits in his poetry. In range and frequency, Ovid's
exploitation of legal imagery far exceeds that of other Augustan
poets.[7]

At one point or another, Ovid studied in Athens, visited the his-
toric cities of Asia Minor, and accompanied a senatorial or eques-
trian friend on a tour of administration in Sicily.[8] But the impression
he creates overall is that his activity was rooted in the capital. Two

---

[6] For the courts and the qualifications of those who served in them, see Crook
(1967) 68–97 and Mommsen (1887) 3:527–39. For Augustus's attention to the jury
lists, see Suet. *Aug.* 29.3, 32.3, and Pliny *HNat.* 33.30.

[7] See Kenney (1969b).

[8] *Tr.* 1.2.77–78, *Pont.* 2.10.21–42; for the identity of Macer in the latter passage,
see White (1992).

vignettes bracket his career in poetry. He describes how he launched himself in public just as the generation of Horace, Virgil, and the elegists was disappearing (*Tr.* 4.10.41–56), and in the last poem of his last book he recollects the names of all the poets he consorted with before his banishment (*Pont.* 4.16). The sense of Rome as a literary hub is pervasive in Ovid. The landmarks his poems most consistently evoke are her poets.[9]

Although Ovid dates his first endeavors in verse to his teens or earlier (*Tr.* 4.10.19–30), we have no poem by him that we can place with certainty before his thirties.[10] His early activities are therefore a matter of speculation. Ovid encourages us to speculate that during this period he was writing love poetry, and indeed, the very poems which after revision and triage would emerge in the extant books of the *Amores*. At *Tr.* 4.10.57–60 he recalls that he gave the first recitation of his poetry at about the time he began to trim his beard (in his late teens, by Roman convention),[11] when "Corinna had stirred my talent." The Corinna we know is the beloved of the *Amores*, still fueling Ovid's talent in about 8 B.C.[12]

That the *Amores* were a work in progress for a decade and a half or more is plausible enough. Given Ovid's subsequent productivity, however, it is not plausible that work on this collection was all that occupied him in his twenties. Besides, the reminiscence he offers on this point is complicated by a revisionary undercurrent. Immediately

---

[9] As witness the many catalogs of Latin poets which Ovid offers, for example *Am.* 1.15.19–30, 3.9.59–66, *Ars* 3.333–38, *Rem.* 763–66, *Tr.* 2.359–60 and 423–66.

[10] The arguable exception is the lament for Tibullus (*Am.* 3.9), who died in 19 when Ovid was 24. But although Ovid's poem may have originated as a funeral piece, it is certainly not typical of that genre. Ovid does not write as a personal acquaintance of the deceased (see *Tr.* 4.10.51–52) or for any of Tibullus's family or friends, and the poem does not describe a funeral that takes place in the real world. *Amores* 3.9 is through and through a literary memorial to Tibullus. It is addressed to the goddess of Elegy, it imagines a solemnity attended by Cupid and Venus, and it evokes only those details of Tibullus's life which Tibullus had himself celebrated in his poetry.

[11] See Wheeler (1925) 12–17.

[12] The firmest date in the *Amores* is the reference to a triumph over the Sygambri at *Am.* 1.14.45–50, in a passage which is integral to the Corinna story. (Although Corinna is not there identified by name, the subject of hairdressing links the poem with 1.11.1–6, where she is named.) According to Ovid's conceit, the triumph holds the solution to a problem of sudden hair loss, because Corinna will now (*nunc*, 45) be able to buy a blonde wig in place of her own hair. The triumph is evidently imminent, and must be that earned by Tiberius in 8 B.C. and celebrated in January of the following year (Cass. Dio 55.8.1–2).

after declaring that Corinna was the theme of his early work, he backtracks, adding, "to be sure, I wrote many things, but what I thought defective, I consigned to the fire" (*Tr.* 4.10.61–62). Such statements are so common in Ovid and other writers of the period that critics have tended to discount them as mere pretence. But Ovid's claim to have suppressed some early writings is supported by another text. An epigram prefacing the transmitted text of the *Amores* informs readers that the three books which follow have replaced a larger five-book series. Ovid could not have achieved this condensation without cutting material. And there is a second area in which he seems to have dissociated himself from work that he had written, at least as far as the general public was concerned. Although he sometimes mentions having composed commemorative pieces for this or that occasion, he never includes them in listings of his oeuvre and they do not survive with the rest of his poetry today.[13]

Ovid was unique among the Augustan poets in periodically recasting his poetic canon.[14] He is the only one who testifies to having suppressed poems and to having reissued books in new formats. Poems he decided to disown he eased out of view. In the reminiscence offered in *Tristia* 4.10, we must bear in mind that the mature Ovid is censoring the youthful Ovid's output. The poems of the *Amores* were all he cared to acknowledge from his twenties, but perhaps not all that he produced.

Under the casual procedures by which ancient books were produced and disseminated, it was not unheard of for an author's work to circulate even against his wishes. If writings which Ovid disowned have survived, however, it would be apart from any collection which he authorized and the texts themselves would carry the stigma of being authorial rejects. Both circumstances would make it difficult to distinguish them from completely spurious texts. Such complications may be resolved if specialists in intertextual analysis begin to apply their expertise in this direction. In the meantime, two texts within the Ovidian penumbra invite a glance here.[15]

One is the *libellus* of six elegiac pieces transmitted under the name of Lygdamus in Book 3 of the Tibullan corpus. These poems are

---

[13] See Citroni (1995) 460–61.
[14] See Barchiesi (1997b) 262.
[15] On doubtful works of Ovid, see Richmond (1981) and (for Lygdamus) Duret (1983) 1461–67.

not ascribed to Ovid in any ancient source or manuscript and they sound unlike his poetry, but they unmistakably evoke it. The author declares that he—like Ovid—was born in 43 B.C. and in discourse about himself he produces lines or half-lines that recur in bona-fide poems of Ovid.[16] Moreover the plot of the Lygdamus romance has a curious resonance with Ovid's life. Unlike every other love cele-brated in extant Latin poetry, it seems to involve not a liaison but a marriage. "Neaera" is depicted as a woman of respectable family whom Lygdamus had married but who has left him, in circumstances that call to mind Ovid's report of his marital history at *Tr.* 4.10.69–70. The most widely accepted view of Lygdamus now is that he is a pseudonymous but real coeval from whose poems Ovid later bor-rowed several lines. But the coincidences between them make it much likelier that Lygdamus is either the youthful Ovid or a later writer impersonating the young Ovid.[17]

The second text falls outside the period of Ovid's youth, but is more conveniently dealt with here than later. The *Consolatio ad Liviam* purports to be a funeral piece occasioned by the death of Livia's son (Augustus's stepson) Drusus in 9 B.C. It is attributed to Ovid in the Renaissance manuscripts and editions which are the earliest wit-nesses to the text and, unlike the Lygdamus elegies, it is very much in Ovid's manner. Among modern scholars, however, a consensus exists that it is not only inferior to Ovid's best work but contains anachronisms which preclude its having been written in Ovid's life-time. The second issue is evidently more crucial than the first. In respect of quality, the *Consolatio* would fit a category of occasional verse that Ovid is known to have produced but not to have taken into his canon. A recent reexamination of the *Consolatio* comes to the conclusion that there is no reason to doubt the ostensible date of 9 B.C.[18] If that argument holds up, the possibility of Ovidian authorship would have to be considered afresh.

Ovid's social attachments are as nebulous as his poetic output dur-ing the first half of his life. Apart from claiming an early and con-stant association with other poets, he says little about the circles in

---

[16] [Tib.] 3.5.15–20 is the most densely Ovidian passage in Lygdamus, with par-allels to Ov. *Ars* 2.670, *Tr.* 4.10.6, and *Am.* 2.14.23–24. But Ovidian phrasing is found throughout the *libellus*.

[17] The fullest statement of the case for thinking that Lygdamus is Ovid was made by Gruppe (1838) 105–43; the case was later rearticulated by La Penna (1951).

[18] See Fraschetti (1995), with references to earlier discussion.

which he moved when young. He does not mention what his con-
temporary Seneca the Elder reports, that Ovid participated in the
performances of improvisational oratory regularly put on by profes-
sional and amateur declaimers.[19] But it thus appears that in contrast
to Virgil and Horace, he could and did avail himself of a lively insti-
tutional culture from the start of his career. The public poetry recital
and the declamation came into vogue at Rome during his boyhood,
and although both media were organized or popularized by the elite,
they offered access to a more diversified public than the entourage
of any individual socialite. Ovid never dissembled his desire to appeal
to a broad audience or his pride in being able to.

Ovid names only two of his attachments among the city's elite
during his early years. One was to Tuticanus, a senator (or possibly
a knight) and a fellow poet about whom little else is known.[20] The
more important one was to Messalla Corvinus and, through him, to
his sons Messalinus and Cotta.[21] Roughly twenty years older than
Ovid, Messalla was an aristocrat who initially chose the side of the
Liberators and then of Antony during the civil war that followed
Caesar's death. But after going over to Octavian in the mid-30s, he
allowed himself to be refashioned into a pilaster of the new regime.
At the same time he became, like Maecenas, a promoter of young
poetic talent. Although it is not certain that Ovid had already formed
a connection with him in the 20s, one had obviously developed by
the next decade, and the poet's friendship with the family lasted into
the period of exile.

That we know only two of Ovid's early connections may not seem
surprising. Most of his statements about himself are made in poetic
epistles that he wrote to friends late in life and they naturally tend
to illuminate relationships still current at that point. Some of his
early friends will have died by then, like Messalla himself, or drifted
away, and in addition, Ovid complains, many friends broke with
him when he incurred the emperor's displeasure.[22] But this expla-
nation for his silence only conceals another problem: why are the

---

[19] Sen. *Cont.* 2.2.8–12. In that passage Seneca incidentally names Arellius Fuscus
and Porcius Latro as two preceptors with whom Ovid studied rhetoric, perhaps as
early as the 20s.
[20] *Pont.* 4.12.19–28; for sources on Tuticanus, see White (1993) 247, no. 57.
[21] Syme (1978) 114–34.
[22] *Tr.* 1.9.19–20, 2.87–88, 3.5.5–6, *Pont.* 1.9.15, 2.3.25–30, 3.2.7–16, and 4.3.

early friends not named in his pre-exilic poetry? Ovid recalls that both Tuticanus and Messalla encouraged and helped launch his youthful work (*Pont.* 2.3.77–78, 4.12.23–25), yet neither man is celebrated in the *Amores* or elsewhere, as supporters of Virgil, Horace, Propertius, and Tibullus were celebrated in their early poems.[23] How Ovid's poems represent his milieu is the issue to be considered next.

2. *Ovid's Prime (13 B.C. to A.D. 8)*

Ovid's biography dwindles to little more than the facts of literary output from the time the extant books begin to appear until the year he is banished. The contraction of data has at least the advantage of shifting attention from his life to his poems and to the spirit in which they address the Augustan milieu. But a detailed study is not here in view. I want only to draw attention to certain panoramic features of his oeuvre while keeping out of the way of close-ups offered by other contributors to this volume. For the sake of comparing works, it will be best to keep my focus on the surfaces they present. But limitations of space would make it impossible in any case to sound for Ovidian under-meanings here, or to try to recuperate a likely reader response on the part of Augustus.

The year 13 B.C. is a somewhat arbitrary point from which to plot a time-line of the extant books. Although Ovid's latest works can be dated to within a year or so, the chronology of the early ones is tangled and uncertain.[24] Since I am concerned with the profile presented by books overall rather than with individual poems, I emphasize the dates of books, and of books in the form in which we have them, which it must be assumed is their latest form. Thus while some and even many of the *Amores* may have been carried over unrevised from books published in Ovid's youth, all we really know is that they appear in books produced to satisfy public taste in or after 8 B.C. If we wish to allow for a period of writing or

---

[23] The paucity of references to friends is the more curious because at *Tr.* 3.4.67–68 Ovid seems to imply that he often paid compliments to them in pre-exilic poems. Yet he passes up opportunities to name them even where they make appearances at *Rem.* 663, *F.* 4.687, and 6.226 (with 2.27).

[24] The clues available for dating different components of the Ovidian corpus are reviewed by Syme (1978) 1–47, though debate about chronology has continued to be lively.

rewriting, we must count back a few years from that point, and a terminus of 13 will serve as well as any. It allows sufficient lead time for preparation of a new edition of the *Amores*. It should even accommodate publication of the *Heroides*, which are mentioned in the *Amores* but cannot be shown to be earlier than 13 B.C.[25] And it has the symbolic advantage of coinciding with Ovid's thirtieth birthday and Augustus's return to Rome from his last lengthy residence abroad.

To relate the work that Ovid produced between 13 B.C. and A.D. 8 to an Augustan discourse known from parallel texts is all but impossible. There are no Latin prose works extant from this period and—apart from Ovid's—few in verse.[26] For lack of external comparanda, I will try to describe Ovid's engagement of the Augustan regime as it develops within his corpus from one work to the next.

Augustus is the focus of fewer than 20 out of 2400 lines in the collection of *Amores* which Ovid published in about 8 B.C. There is one allusion to the German wars (1.14.45–50) and one to the cult of Caesar (3.8.51–52), but nothing else that touches specifically on Augustus's family or his enterprises. Yet Ovid's reticence in this regard is only one aspect of a topical spareness evident throughout the collection. Although the *Amores* unfold within a contemporary urban chronotope like earlier elegiac poetry, they contain little scenographic detail. Apart from his glance at a victory over the Germans, the one historical event which Ovid mentions is Tibullus's death (*Am.* 3.9). He names only four of his society friends, writes no occasional pieces for them, and does not depict his relationships with them.[27] Few of the poems evoke specific locations in Rome and they rarely advert to its characteristic cults or institutions.[28] Even where Ovid

---

[25] The *Heroides* will not come into this discussion because they do not obviously implicate the Augustan milieu. But it is possible to read a political engagement even in these: see Arena (1995).

[26] The books which Livy composed during these years have not survived. Horace's last book of *Odes* came out in about 13 B.C. and two of his long literary epistles may have appeared soon after, but all other verse texts which might date from this period are suspect, like the *Consolatio ad Liuiam* and poems from the *Appendix Vergiliana* such as the *Elegiae in Maecenatem*. Manilius's astronomical poem did not come into circulation until after A.D. 8.

[27] Friends are named in *Am.* 1.9 (Atticus), 2.10 (Graecinus), and 2.18 (Macer and Sabinus).

[28] Sites mentioned are the Via Sacra (*Am.* 1.8.100), the Atrium Vestae (1.13.19, where the text is disputed), the Palatine Temple of Apollo (2.2.3–4), unspecified theaters (2.2.26, 2.7.3), the Forum (1.15.6, 2.17.24, and 3.8.57), the Circus (3.2), the Temple of Divus Caesar and unspecified shrines of Quirinus, Liber, and Hercules

could easily have lent his material a topical coloring, as with the paradigm of the soldier in *Amores* 1.9 or the lament for Tibullus in 3.9, he prefers to import embellishments from the realms of myth and literature.

The suppression of topical details may reflect a deliberate effort on Ovid's part to efface personal relationships and circumstances and to direct attention instead to his literary engagement with poetic predecessors.[29] But whatever the explanation, the treatment of Augustus in the *Amores* fits the same pattern. Too many opportunities of celebrating him are passed by for us to imagine that the poems are driven by a panegyrical program. Ovid alludes to a famous painting in the Temple of Caesar (1.14.33–34) while skirting mention of either Caesar or temple; he points to the Palatine Temple of Apollo (2.2.3–4) without naming its builder; he puts the circus races described in 3.2 under the presidency of a praetor rather than of Augustus; and the point of his reference to the Sygambrian triumph at 1.14.45–50 is not the glory of empire but the fresh availability of wigs. Worse, his aside about Caesar's temple at 3.8.51–52 seems not just not complimentary but derogatory: Ovid mocks at human vanity for presuming to transform Quirinus, Liber, Hercules, and Caesar into gods.[30]

His few direct references to Augustus, however, are formally encomiastic.[31] A light wash of fealty was evidently all that Ovid sought to impart. Late in life he claimed that he had made a point of paying homage to Augustus in all his books (*Pont.* 1.1.27–28), and his punctiliousness is evident in the *Amores*. One compliment occurs in the middle of three introductory poems which open the collection

---

(3.8.51–52), the Curia (3.8.55), and the Campus Martius (3.8.57). The cults are women's cults identified with the poet's girlfriend: Isis (1.8.74, 2.2.25, 2.13.7–16), Cybele (2.13.17–18), Ilythyia (2.13.19–22), and Ceres (3.10). The contemporary institution which Ovid most vividly evokes is the world of the Roman courts: 1.10.37–40, 2.17.24, 3.8.55–58. The only other area in which Roman institutions contribute significantly to imagery in the *Amores* is that of the triumph, where Ovid follows Propertius's lead: 1.2.23–52, 1.7.35–40, 1.11.25–28, 1.15.26, 2.9.16, 2.12.1–16, 2.18.18.

[29] Boyd (1997) relates Ovid's "lack of concern for extraliterary discourse" (66) in the *Amores* to his literary aims, and Citroni (1995) 435–40 has argued that Ovid downplayed attachments to particular individuals in order to appeal more directly to the reading public.

[30] This passage will seem pointedly anti-Augustan if it is read as a critique of the dynasty, less so if read in the context of other free-thinking sallies regarding the divine in book 3: 3.3.23–26, 3.6.17–18, 3.9.32–36, 3.12.19–44.

[31] *Am.* 1.2.51–52, 2.14.17–18, 3.9.63–64, 3.12.15–16.

(1.2.51–52) and a *recusatio* motif is sounded near the close (3.12.15–16). That they are slight is a quality they share with all other background features.

By the time Ovid published the *Ars Amatoria* some six or seven years later, his scenography had altered markedly.[32] The *Ars* exudes urban hipness and its references to specific sites and institutions are a part of the effect. In the first book alone, Ovid points to the Theater of Pompey and the Theater of Marcellus, the Portico of Livia, the Palatine Temple of Apollo, the Temple of Isis, and Caesar's Forum. He alludes to the Matronalia and the Sigillaria and to city cults of Adonis, Cybele, and the Jews. He conjures up races in the Circus, gladiatorial matches in the Forum, a naumachia, and a triumph. As features of the Roman backdrop come into focus, the presence of Augustus becomes more distinct as well. This time Ovid pauses to inform the reader that such-and-such a monument commemorates a victory of Augustus or was erected by his wife or sister or son-in-law (3.389–92). The naumachia is a spectacle which Augustus had staged only a few months earlier (1.171–76) and the triumph is the triumph to which all look forward when his son Gaius returns from campaigning in the East (1.177–228).

The three books of the *Ars* devote more than five times as many lines to Augustus as the *Amores* and the range of reference is wider. Ovid now takes note of the emperor's family, entertainments, foreign policy, and building program. His exaltation of Rome as the capital of the world (*Ars* 1.51–66 and 3.113–28) can be considered a tribute to what Augustus had wrought, if not directly to the man himself. Ovid could declare in perfect truth that "I described the times as happy under his governance" (*Tr.* 1.2.103).

Augustus cast a long shadow over Ovid's poem, however. The *Ars* in its present form came into circulation only months at most after

---

[32] The *terminus post* for the enlarged, three-book edition of the *Ars* that has come down to us is late 2 B.C. Preparations for the send-off of Gaius Caesar to the East, which is the latest datable element mentioned (1.177–204), belong to the end of that year or the beginning of the next. A *terminus ante* of A.D. 2 seems to be established by the *Remedia Amoris* which is a sequel to the *Ars*. At the time it was written, Gaius had arrived in the East but not yet effected a settlement with the Parthian king (*Rem.* 155–58 and 224). Murgia (1986a and 1986b) downdates the three-book version of the *Ars* to A.D. 8 on the basis of verbal parallels between the *Metamorphoses* and *Ars* 3. But his argument posits an analogy between intertextual influence and manuscript stemmatics which I do not believe is valid. (On the relationship of *Med.*, *Ars*, and *Rem.*, see also Watson, ch. 4 below.)

the discovery and punishment of Julia's adulterous intrigues in 2 B.C.[33] Until then, although Augustus's adultery law had stood on the books for a decade and a half, his own conduct might have encouraged doubts that it was to be taken seriously.[34] Ovid at least had not shied from joking in the *Amores* that adultery was one of Rome's hallowed traditions (3.4.37–40). But with the execution or exile of Julia's lovers he shifted into reverse. The *Ars* is posted with repeated warnings that it is off limits for the respectable women whose behavior the law had in view.[35] Its argument is punctuated by asides dissociating the relationships treated in the poem from marital relationships.[36] And Ovid half-heartedly attempts to sanitize his material. Among the erotic scenarios he had dramatized in the *Amores*, several had involved triangular relationships in which the third party was a fatuous or jealous husband. When he recycles them in the *Ars*, however, the husband figure is bleached into a mere *rivalis*.[37]

Ovid's tinkering reveals plainly enough that, however impervious he was to the spirit of Augustus's moral legislation, he was anxious about its letter. He warns off matrons rather than husbands because the law was essentially concerned with the behavior of women, and specifically of those women who enjoyed some standing in Roman society. What men did was regulated only when it affected a woman in that category. The law did not prohibit a man from enjoying sexual relations with slaves, prostitutes, or non-citizens whether he was married or not.[38] Having brought the *Ars* into compliance with the law, Ovid was satisfied that he had rendered it unobjectionable.[39]

---

[33] Syme (1984) 923.

[34] On the notoriety surrounding Augustus's own affairs in this period, see Cass. Dio 54.16.3 and 54.19.3. Between passage of the law and the Julia scandal, only two prosecutions are recorded. In one, Augustus let the defendants off (Cass. Dio 54.16.6); in the other, the defendant was represented by Augustus's cousin and by Maecenas, and he was aided by an intervention on the part of Augustus himself (Cass. Dio 54.30.4).

[35] *Ars* 1.31–34, 2.599–600, 3.57–58, 3.483, and 3.613–16, plus a reminder at *Rem.* 386.

[36] *Ars* 2.153–56, 2.388, 2.545–46, 2.597–600, and 3.585–86.

[37] Ovid's most ostentatious removal of husbands from the *dramatis personae* occurs at *Ars* 3.611–16. As Stroh (1979) points out, language implying adultery is confined to sections dealing with mythical exempla, where Ovid could count on its being non-controversial.

[38] McGinn (1998) 140–215.

[39] It is possible that Ovid's accommodations to the adultery law belong to the second edition of the *Ars* and were one goal of it. If *artes teneri profitemur amoris* at

Nevertheless, shortly afterward he turned from erotic themes to two projects which were more ambitious, more erudite, and more politically engaged, though the meaning of that engagement has been vigorously contested.[40] Ovid's most lavishly Augustan work was to be the *Fasti*, which remained unfinished and unreleased at the moment of his death, where I will return to it. The other was the *Metamorphoses*, an intricate chain of tales about creaturely and cosmic transformations in fifteen books. Augustus takes up a relatively small amount of space in it. Except for one allusion at a significant juncture in Book 13 (line 715), he is not evoked at all between the first book and the last. But structurally he has a more salient role than in any previous Ovidian work, as the end point of an arc that joins the framing books.[41] The first human metamorphosis described in the poem is inflicted on Lycaon who "laid a plot" (198) against Jupiter when the god walked the earth in human guise. Jupiter reports the attempt before a council of the gods which Ovid likens to a gathering of Roman senators, and they clamor for punishment "even as when an unholy gang sought madly to drown the Roman name in Caesar's blood" (200–201). The punishment of Lycaon is followed by a world-wide flood that is sent to destroy his wicked race.

After being thus previewed in Book 1, the assassination of Julius Caesar is treated at length in the last book, where it initiates the climactic metamorphosis of the poem (746–870). Ovid recreates the atmospherics of the Lycaon story. The plot against Caesar unfolds amid portents of cosmic disorder and is the subject of anguished discussion among the gods. Olympus again takes on a strong likeness to Rome: the Fates staff a record-office that is modeled on a public *tabularium* (808–15). Although the mortal Caesar succumbs to the plot

---

Am. 2.18.19 indicates that Ovid was already at work on the *Ars* six years earlier (as is widely believed), the Julia scandal in 2 B.C. may have been what prompted him to revise. Book 3, which certainly belongs to the second edition, contains three of the five warnings to matrons in the *Ars*.

[40] For an orientation to recent writing about the politics of the *Fasti*, see Fantham (1995a); for the *Metamorphoses*, see Bretzigheimer (1993). The question of Ovid's subservience or resistance to the Augustan regime has a striking parallel in the current debate over the music of Shostakovich—with the difference that in Ovid's case there is no purported deposition from the principal.

[41] Ovid adumbrated his design in a letter to Augustus: *prima surgens ab origine mundi/ in tua deduxi tempora, Caesar, opus* (*Tr.* 2.559–60). Buchheit (1966) 89 and Davis (1980) note the structural relationship between the Lycaon and the Caesar narratives.

against him, his soul survives to be transformed into a watchful and beneficent comet, and his son Augustus then takes charge of bringing order back to earth. After praising Augustus's performance as warrior, legislator, reformer, and establisher of a dynasty—it is the most comprehensive encomium in all the poems—Ovid draws the analogy which has been implicit throughout: "Jupiter rules the citadel in heaven and the world's three realms, while earth is in Augustus's power. Each is father and ruler" (858–60). The comparison works to the advantage of Augustus, who has been able to redress crime on earth by less drastic means than Jupiter.

The *Metamorphoses* had just begun to circulate in draft when Ovid received the shock that ended his career in Rome. By every index he had been a success until that point. He owned a town-house on or near the Capitoline (*Tr.* 1.3.29–30), a villa in the hills on the northern outskirts of Rome, and a family estate near Sulmo (*Pont.* 1.8.41–48).[42] His third marriage had strengthened his ties with the Roman aristocracy and opened a channel of influence to the emperor's wife.[43] Copies of his work were collected in the new state libraries (*Tr.* 3.1.65 and 71) and his poems had enough popular appeal that some had been adapted for balletic performance in the theaters (*Tr.* 2.519–20). By his own estimate, his literary reputation now equaled that of the great poets of his age (*Tr.* 2.119–20, 4.10.125–28). Some of his long-time friends would soon reach the peak of distinction and influence in Roman society: Fabius Maximus was to become consul in 11 and Pomponius Graecinus in 16.[44] Ovid himself, by virtue of his marriage and his talent, had amassed the social capital to organize a salon in his own right (*Tr.* 1.9.17–18 and 4.10.55).

---

[42] *The Times* of London recently reported that Italian archaeologists have unearthed what they believe to be Ovid's villa (21 September 2000).

[43] Marcia, whose protegée Ovid's wife was, was in her turn a confidante of Livia: Tac. *Ann.* 1.5.2.

[44] Servius Cornelius Lentulus Maluginensis, consul in A.D. 10, may be another of Ovid's aristocratic friends from the pre-exilic period. At *F.* 6.226–34 Ovid quotes from a conversation he had with the wife of the *flamen Dialis*. Maluginensis was the incumbent of that office when he died in 23 (Tac. *Ann.* 3.58 and 4.16.1) and he may already have been serving at the time of Ovid's consultation two decades earlier.

3. *Ovid in Exile (A.D. 8 to 17)*

In the latter half of A.D. 8, just after Ovid had turned 50, Augustus banished him to the Black Sea port of Tomis in present-day Romania.[45] The circumstances remain obscure because our sole informant is Ovid, who did not wish to be explicit about them.[46] Possibly Augustus sentenced him after a formal hearing that would be one of the first exercises of the independent judicial power which the emperors acquired under the principate. Yet Ovid does not indicate that he was tried, only that he was expelled, and Roman legal historians have voiced increasing skepticism that the criminal jurisdiction which emperors exercised in the Severan Age was already in vigor under Augustus.[47] Augustus may have acted simply by fiat.

As for the offense, Ovid reports that it was twofold (*Tr.* 2.207). His *Ars Amatoria*, which had been in circulation for eight or nine years, was at this late hour denounced as a provocation to adultery. To this charge Ovid replied within the year in an open letter to Augustus nearly 600 lines long (*Tristia* 2). For all its swerves into self-abasement, it is one of the most outspoken manifestos addressed by any subject to any emperor during the principate.

The other charge, which Ovid considered more pernicious (*Pont.* 3.3.72), concerned an incident he refuses to specify. He insists repeatedly that his own part in it amounted to a fault or a mistake rather than a crime, but does admit that he witnessed serious wrongdoing (*Tr.* 3.6.25–36). Whatever Ovid did or failed to do on that occasion, Augustus considered his behavior a personal injury (*Tr.* 2.209–10).

Ovid's hints about his misdeed stop there. But a majority of modern readers believe that he was banished in consequence of a scandal

---

[45] The year is fixed by a number of statements Ovid makes. He says that the catastrophe befell him after ten *lustra* or fifty years (*Tr.* 4.8.33, 4.10.95–96), which dates it after March 20th of the year 8. In *Epistulae ex Ponto* 4.13 he describes a poem he has composed about Augustus's apotheosis and mentions that he is writing during his sixth winter in Tomis. Since Augustus was made a *diuus* in September of 14, Ovid's sixth winter should be that of 14/15, putting his arrival in Tomis after the spring of 9, which is consistent with his having left Italy in December of the year before (*Tr.* 1.11.3–4).

[46] The fullest collection of Ovidian statements on the subject is Owen (1924) 1–19. The fullest repertory of modern hypotheses is Thibault (1964), but speculation has continued.

[47] See Kelly (1957) 37–46 and Bleicken (1962) 66–78. That Augustus already exercised a criminal jurisdiction is however accepted by Millar (1977) 523–24.

surrounding Augustus's granddaughter Julia. This episode too is poorly documented, but known details mesh with Ovid's information.[48] Both events can be dated to the same year. The allegations of adultery against Julia would help explain the renewed topicality of the *Ars*. Ovid characterizes his injury to Augustus in language colored by the contemporary discourse about treason (*laesa maiestas*), which was also made an issue in the Julia affair. And in one place he lets it be known that connections with the palace family had something to do with his catastrophe.[49]

Augustus issued public notice of Ovid's expulsion (*Tr.* 2.135–38) and had the *Ars* and perhaps the rest of his books cast out of the public libraries (*Tr.* 2.8, 3.1.65–68). He allowed him to retain his citizen status and his material assets (*Tr.* 5.2.56–57, 5.11.15), but interned him—on purpose, Ovid believed (*Tr.* 1.2.90)—in an outpost that exquisitely revenged the glamorization of swinging Rome in the *Ars*. "No one who has been banished has had a more remote place assigned to him than I" (*Tr.* 2.194). In December, leaving his wife to be his advocate at home, Ovid embarked on a journey by sea and land that brought him to Tomis in the following spring.

Unlike Cicero, who could produce nothing during periods when his enemies barred him from Rome, Ovid wrote constantly in exile. Leaving doubtful works out of the reckoning, during his eight or nine years in Tomis he published the five books of the *Tristia*, the four books of *Epistulae ex Ponto*, the *Ibis*, and two pieces in honor of the imperial house, and he began to rework the *Fasti*. As striking as his productivity is his ability to publish at such a distance from the capital, and that after having been publicly excoriated by the emperor. Until the second century, Latin literature remained almost entirely the product of writers domiciled in Rome. Yet Ovid was able to sustain a literary presence there for nearly a decade after his enforced departure.[50] It can be assumed that his wife and unmentioned members

---

[48] See Syme (1978) 219–21.

[49] In *Tristia* 3.4 Ovid cites his own sorry experience in support of an admonition to others to avoid *nomina magna* (4), *praelustria* (5), *potentes* (7), and *nimium sublimia* (31). This is not how he speaks of any of his other society friends, and as if to emphasize that he means denizens of the palace, he adds that, brilliant though they are, they have a singular potency for harm: *uiue tibi, quantumque potes praelustria uita:/saeuum praelustri fulmen ab arce uenit./nam quamquam soli possunt prodesse potentes,/non prosit potius, siquis obesse potest* (5–8).

[50] Despite occasional passages like *Pont.* 1.5.71–86 in which Ovid despairs of

of his household were important intermediaries in that operation and other agents can also be glimpsed. The Brutus who receives *Ex Ponto* 1.1 and 3.9—apparently the end-pieces of a collection of exilic verse— is thought to be Ovid's publisher, while the anonymous addressee of *Tristia* 3.14 seems to be a bookseller.[51]

Most of the exilic poems are cast in the form of letters into which Ovid pours out his lamentations or his pleas to friends with influence at court. He says himself that the utilitarian aim of the *Tristia* and the *Epistulae ex Ponto* gives them a different quality from his earlier poems (*Pont.* 3.9.55–56). They also present an optic that is new. They display a profusion of similes and other images that occur nowhere else in Ovid's work (and in some cases, nowhere else in Latin literature). There is a strong visual element also in his reports of life at Tomis, for many aspects of which he is a unique though suspect eyewitness.[52] Vignettes of Rome are even more frequent, as Ovid practices the calisthenics of visualizing all he can remember of his old life.

Rome impinges in another way as well: for the first time, topics relating to Augustus proliferate freely in Ovid's poems. In the *Amores*, the *Ars*, and the *Metamorphoses* they were progressively more prominent, but they were integrated into poetic schemes that were independent of them. In the exilic poems, however, Augustus is a constant preoccupation and all manifestations of his hegemony engage Ovid's attention.[53] A clear sign of the shift is that these poems are filled with references to Augustan military enterprises, a topic from which Ovid had earlier sought to keep his distance (*Am.* 3.12.15, *F.* 1.13–14, *Tr.* 2.529–30).

---

being read in Rome, it is clear that he was sending material to be published there, that he thought it was circulating, and that it was in fact circulating: *Tr.* 3.14.25–26, 5.1.1–2, 5.12.65–66, *Pont.* 2.5.9–10 and 33–34, 3.4.3–6, 3.9.1–2 and 51–56, 4.6.17–20, 4.9.131–34, 4.16.1–4. At *Pont.* 3.1.49–56 he claims that exile had made him more renowned than ever.

[51] Kaster (1995) 212 has offered compelling reasons to doubt the usual view that the recipient of *Tr.* 3.14 is Augustus's librarian C. Iulius Hyginus. The whole tone of lines 5–18 (especially *conficis* in 5 and *palam* in 18) suggests a bookseller.

[52] Over the last thirty years scholars (mainly from eastern Europe) who have compared Ovid's picture of Tomis with archaeological and other data about the region have been pointing out elements of stylization if not fiction in the former; the sources are conveniently assembled by Williams (1994) 3–8.

[53] See Millar (1993).

One reason for the change of orientation toward Augustus is that the epistolary format does not impose a distinct thematic of its own. As letters to contemporaries, the *Tristia* and the *Epistulae ex Ponto* were bound to absorb more of a contemporary imprint than a poem like the *Metamorphoses*. It is also relevant that many of the persons to whom Ovid is writing have close attachments to Augustus: it is because they are in a position to intercede that he writes to them. What he says on the subject of Augustus is not only a reflection of his own concerns but is also intended to broadcast their loyalism. Yet surely the most important explanation for his obsession with Augustus in the late poems is autobiographical. An unlooked-for connection with Augustus late in life finally impelled Ovid into occasional verse, though it was his own life that supplied the all-important event.

When Ovid published the letters comprised in the *Tristia*, he suppressed the names of the recipients because he feared that they might feel compromised to be associated with him. But four years into his exile, he was sufficiently emboldened to identify most of the addressees in a second set of verse epistles he produced. Twenty-one correspondents are introduced in the *Epistulae ex Ponto* and letters to them provide details about four further connections. This one collection reveals more about Ovid's place in Roman society than we know for any other Augustan poet except Horace.[54]

No Latin poetry book, however, gives an unfiltered impression of a poet's friends. In Ovid's case, we must bear in mind that the mass of his correspondence in this period was conducted in prose (*Pont.* 4.2.5–8) and that the prose letters were not published. His verse letters were almost certainly reserved for the more privileged among his friends. Yet not even they are represented in the strength in which they mustered before his disgrace. What we perceive in reading the *Epistulae ex Ponto* is a severely damaged network under repair. As noted earlier, Ovid complains that many old friends abandoned him when he ran afoul of Augustus. Another part of his network must have been liquidated when the younger Julia and her satellites fell, if it is true that Ovid was linked with them. In neither case can we expect letters documenting these relationships. At the opposite

---

[54] On Ovid's social connections see Syme (1978) 76–93 and White (1993) Appendix 2B.

extreme, there are many letters which show Ovid grappling for new connections. He reaches out to relatives of his family and friends, to intimates of the poet-prince Germanicus (with whom he had somehow failed to strike up an acquaintance before his exile), and even to notables of purely local influence in the region where he was interned.

There remains a core of some fourteen correspondents whose friendship appears to have carried over from the period before his exile. A little over half of them receive entreaties to intercede for him, and not surprisingly these include the rising senators Cotta, Fabius Maximus, Sextus Pompeius, and Pomponius Graecinus. But there are also some whom he does not press for aid and to whom he does not offer the penitent rehearsals of his fall that are so common in other letters. These friends—Albinovanus Pedo, Atticus, Cornelius Severus, Junius Gallio, Macer, and Rufinus—are less eminent than the first group. Only Gallio and perhaps Macer were senators. More significant is they they are mostly fellow poets (though Gallio was a rhetorician). It appears that Ovid was still able to count on the sympathy of friends in the literary community and that with them he felt no need to excuse himself.

The sequence of the *Epistulae ex Ponto* can be traced down to approximately the spring of 16.[55] In the following year, according to Jerome's chronicle (p. 171 g Helm), Ovid died and received burial in the region where he had languished. He left behind the first half of a poem on the Roman year which he had begun a decade and a half earlier and with which he was still (or again) occupied in the years just prior to his death.

Of the major Ovidian works, the *Fasti* most openly invites a reading in terms of Augustan ideology, whether with or against the grain. Its stimulus to both political and poetic analysis explains in part why it has elicited some of the most intelligent writing on Ovid in recent years. Yet in contrast to some poems of Virgil, Horace, and Propertius, it has rarely if ever been perceived as an officially inspired work. Ovid nowhere hints that Augustus encouraged him to write the *Fasti* and critics have been loath to imagine a rapprochement between them after the *Ars*. The calendar poem appears instead to be a spon-

---

[55] *Pont.* 4.9 was written to hail Pomponius Graecinus on his inauguration as suffect consul in that year.

taneous response to Augustus's remodeling of an institution that
ordered the activities and molded the consciousness of every Roman.[56]
Awareness of the calendar had been heightened not only by the
addition of many new festivals honoring Augustus but also by his
supervisory interventions as pontifex maximus. Just a decade before
Ovid began the *Fasti*, Augustus executed an important correction of
the calendar and took title to the month now named for him.[57]

By noting in the proem that he would sing about "the altars of
Caesar and holydays he has added to the year," Ovid encouraged
readers to discover a panegyrical tendency in the *Fasti*.[58] His choice
of material would have pointed that way in any case. A treatment
of Rome's annual festivals offered many more cues for paying homage
to Augustus than the plan of any previous work.[59] But numerous as
the Augustan anniversaries were, they did not engross the entire cal-
endar,[60] and they do not fill Ovid's poem about it. More often than
not, Ovid skips mention of Augustus when declaring the theme of
his work, as in the opening couplet, "I will sing of the arrangements
of time across the Latin year and the reasons thereof, and of the
constellations as they rise and sink beneath the earth."[61] Moreover,
as has often been pointed out, the lore about constellations to which
Ovid alludes here played no part in official versions of the calen-
dar. The decision to include it further diluted the Augustan mater-
ial in the *Fasti*. Ovid thus seems to have adhered to the strategy
evident in his earlier work, which was to integrate Augustus into a
poetic design without putting him at the center of it.

In the counterpoint between Augustan and non-Augustan parts of
the *Fasti* and between what Ovid articulates and what he leaves
unsaid critics have detected a subversive edge which is crucial to

---

[56] See Beard (1987).

[57] Suet. *Aug.* 31.2, Cass. Dio 55.6.6, Macr. *Sat.* 1.14.14. Wallace-Hadrill (1987)
takes the *Fasti* as a response to Augustus's systematic inscription of himself in Roman
schemes of recording time, from the official calendar to the triumphal fasti on the
Parthian arch and the great sundial on the Campus Martius.

[58] *F.* 1.13–14, similarly *F.* 2.15–16. But it is outside the poem, in a verse letter
to Augustus, that Ovid makes his broadest claim for the Augustocentrism of the
Fasti: *id... tuo nuper scriptum sub nomine, Caesar/et tibi sacratum... opus* (*Tr.* 2.551–52).

[59] See the table of Augustan holidays in Herz (1978) 1148–49.

[60] For the limits of Augustus's appropriation of the calendar, see Rüpke (1995)
396–416.

[61] *F.* 1.1–2, repeated in varied form at 4.11–12. Other passages which charac-
terize the *Fasti* without reference to Augustus are 1.101, 2.7, 3.177, 6.8, and 6.21–24.

most current interpretations of the poem. Rather than scrutinize the
text from this perspective, however, I want to redirect attention to
the surface panegyric and to make two points about it. The first is
that Ovid handles Augustan material in the *Fasti* with the same free-
dom and ingenuity as other components of the poem. He has com-
posed entries regarding Roman festivals, rites, foundations, and
anniversaries for about 75 days out of the six-month period he covers.
Seventeen of those days commemorate events involving Augustus or
his kin, the entries for which vary greatly in scale. Some have been
worked up into elaborate set-pieces, like *F.* 1.589–616 (January 13th)
and 5.549–98 (May 12th), while others are despatched in a couple
of lines, like *F.* 4.347–48 and 627–28 (April 4th and 13th respec-
tively). On two occasions, Ovid does not bother to spell out the
Augustan connection of anniversaries he registers, and there are days
that could be linked to Augustus which he skips over altogether.[62]
Still, he often opts to deselect or deemphasize non-Augustan anniver-
saries in the same way, and that suggests that when he downplays
Augustan material, his reasons may have as much to do with poetic
economy as with politics.

In any case, Ovid's freedom to manipulate what the calendar pre-
sented was not limited to making cuts. Often he imports mention
of Augustus and his house into contexts where the calendar did not
call for it, establishing a regular tempo of praise even though the
Fasti does not notice every relevant anniversary.[63] Book 6 on the
month of June provides the clearest illustration. Ovid found no major
feast in honor of Augustus in June and turned a dedication by Livia
on the 11th into his only entry concerning an Augustan anniversary
(*F.* 6.637–48). But he also contrived to work in references to Augustus
at five other points during the month.[64]

---

[62] For March 30th (*F.* 3.881–82) and April 13th (4.623–24) the Augustan link is
specified by sources other than Ovid; see Bömer, *F.* For Augustan anniversaries
which Ovid opted not to include, see Syme (1978) 23–29, with the response of
Herbert-Brown (1994) 215–33.

[63] The Sementiva in January (*F.* 1.697–704), the dedication of the temple of Juno
Sospita on February 1 (2.63–66, on which see Herbert-Brown (1994) 33–43), the
Cara Caristia on February 22 (2.635–38), the dedication of the temple of Minerva
on March 19 (3.848), Ceres' feast in early April (4.408), and the Parilia on April
21 (4.859–62).

[64] *F.* 6.91–92, 455–58, 465–68, 763–70, and 809.

The build-up of Augustus in the *Fasti* rests on more than a simple accumulation of compliments. It is partly an effect of the way he is presented in relation to others. Because he and relatives of his are the only living persons noticed in the poem, he completely eclipses all contemporaries. He is often made to overshadow Romans of times past as well. In describing the cult of the Great Mother, for example, Ovid notes that a temple built by Metellus has since been replaced by a new one which Augustus built (*F.* 4.347–48). Under the calendar entry for June 9th he recalls Crassus's defeat and death in Parthia[65] and credits Augustus with having avenged the loss (*F.* 6.463–68). A passage commemorating Caesar's assassination on March 15th segues into a celebration of Augustus's political debut (*F.* 3.697–710). The anniversary of Augustus's recognition as "Father of the Fatherland" serves to launch an extended comparison extolling Augustus over Romulus (*F.* 2.127–44). Although the surface panegyric is necessarily communicated by less subtle means than any undercode, it is a carefully plotted feature of the poem's design.

One of the most intriguing things about the Augustan panegyric in the *Fasti* is that Ovid began to alter it when he was part-way through.[66] That brings me to the second point, which is that the poem presents concurrent strategies of praise in operation at the same time. Ovid claims that twelve books were already written down in some form at the time of his catastrophe in the year 8.[67] Yet the version that has survived comprises only six books, parts of which were not composed until after the death of Augustus six years later.

---

[65] Ovid never refers to Augustus's own sorrows or setbacks in the *Fasti*—not, for example, to the anniversary of his son Gaius's death in February, or to the military alarms on which the exilic letters harp so often.

[66] On Ovid's revisions to the *Fasti*, see especially Fantham (1986) and Herbert-Brown (1994) 173–214.

[67] At *Tr.* 2.549 Ovid tells Augustus *sex ego fastorum scripsi totidemque libellos*, where *sex totidemque* appears to be a metrically workable paraphrase for *duodecim*, as it certainly is at *F.* 6.725. While it is possible either to tease a different sense from Ovid's words or to think that he was fibbing in order to impress Augustus, it is not impossible to accept his statement as it stands. Ovid could have drafted a full treatment, even a metrical treatment, of all twelve months, but unless the later books adhered to the same format as the earlier books, they would have been awkward to combine in the same edition. Broadly speaking, extant books of the *Fasti* follow a three-part recipe comprising introduction, official anniversaries, and star-myths. Although the core of the poem (as of the calendar) consisted of the anniversaries, if the last six books contained *only* those, they would have seemed deficient in comparison with the first six.

With the change of regime, Ovid evidently undertook a revision which he did not live to complete. And not only did he not finish work on the second half of the poem. He did not fully revise the first six books, since some parts now presuppose that Augustus is dead while other parts presuppose that he is alive.

It is impossible to determine exactly how much of the existing text predates Ovid's exile and Augustus's death and how much was rewritten afterward. What no one disputes is a minimum: that a series of indications in the first book and one in Book 4 guarantee at least their immediate contexts as post-exilic.[68] If that evidence can fairly be interpreted to mean that the first book was substantially revised but the other five books underwent little or no change, then the thrust of Ovid's revisions would be clear. He was in the process of converting the praise of Augustus into a more broadly targeted panegyric of the imperial house.[69]

This shift of strategy emerges right at the opening of the *Fasti*, which in its revised form is addressed to Germanicus (Augustus does not appear as dedicatee until Book 2). But the new plan accommodates Tiberius and Livia as well. Ovid has shoehorned two compliments to Livia into Book 1, including a famously malapropos prediction of her deification.[70] He spotlights Tiberius four times in the course of the book and promises that the *Fasti* will often mention him.[71] Yet Tiberius is not mentioned in any other book—not even on the anniversary of his adoption by Augustus in June—so this emphasis must have been absent from the original conception.[72]

As Ovid began to write in compliments to other members of the family, he also downgraded Augustus's importance in the book. Passages about him have been turned into praise of the dynasty, in

---

[68] Demonstrably late passages include Ovid's addresses to Germanicus at 1.1–26, 63, 285–88, 590, and 701, his references to the succession of Tiberius at 1.533–36 and 615–16, his account of the Temple of Concord at 1.637–50, and in Book 4, the lament on his exile in lines 79–84. However, it would be unwise to assume that Ovid tagged every revision he introduced with an indication of its lateness. Revisions are likely to be more numerous than those we can prove.

[69] This inference is the more likely to be correct in that a parallel progression can be seen in the exilic letters.

[70] The prophecy is at *F.* 1.535–36. For the incongruity of Livia's appearance at 1.649–50, see Herbert-Brown (1994) 165–71.

[71] The promise is made at *F.* 1.9–12, after which Tiberius is introduced at 1.533–34, 613–16, 645–48, and 707–8.

[72] See Syme (1978) 28–34.

the same way that in the first version passages about others were often made the foil for praise of Augustus. The anniversary of the day on which he received the name "Augustus," for example, is used not to celebrate him but to advertise an honorific which Tiberius is now assumed to bear (*F.* 1.591–616). In an entry which commemorates the dedication of the Altar of Augustan Peace, Augustus is not mentioned. Instead Ovid praises the *domus* as the guarantor of peace (*F.* 1.709–22). "There is not one anniversary in January, in fact, which lauds Augustus purely in his own right."[73] The deemphasis is so consistent that one is bound to wonder whether Ovid might not have suppressed entire sections about Augustus when he revised Book 1. Four of the anniversaries which Syme noted were missing from the *Fasti* fall in January.[74]

It is rare to find a Latin poem which is so tangibly a composite of different states and intentions, and more remains to be done with the opportunity we have been given. For one thing, the complications that Ovid's rewrite poses for subversive readings of the *Fasti* have not been completely sorted through. Rather than a surface at odds with its undermeaning, the poem presents *two* surfaces, one of which in some degree undoes the other. How does a strategy of subversive reading proceed when it is applied to a surface which is itself subversive of another surface? The *Fasti* also provides a valuable reference point for thinking about the problem of second editions in Ovid. As the one case study we have of a revision in progress, it can help illuminate other parts of the corpus where Ovid revised but left no traces.

---

[73] Herbert-Brown (1994) 219.
[74] January 7th, 8th, 11th, and 17th, for which see Syme (1978) 23–29.

CHAPTER TWO

OVID'S LANGUAGE AND STYLE

E.J. Kenney

Lingua Latina apud eum metro dactylico, cui natura repugnat, adeo videtur aptata, ut levissimos ac facillimos Ovidi versus legentes plane obliviscamur illud metrum primo tam fuisse alienum ab ingenio linguae Latinae, et paene audeamus dicere Romanos exempla Graeca arte vicisse.

Bednara (1906) 604 = 120

In Ovid the Latin language seems to be so well adapted to dactylic meter, though resistant to it by nature, that as we read his smooth and easy verses we quite forget that this meter was originally so foreign to the natural character of Latin, and we almost dare to say that the Romans have excelled their Greek models in technique.

The Elegiac Poems

I

"Nihil quod tetigit non transformauit." Ovid was from first to last a worker of metamorphoses. The first transfiguration in his poetic oeuvre occurs in the opening lines of the *Amores*, where he tells how Cupid transformed his hexameters into elegiacs by docking every second verse of a foot.[1] It may seem obvious that what differentiates

---

[1] The technical implications of this conceit deserve attention. Ovid's readers would have been well aware that the change could not be effected simply by docking the hexameter of its last foot. What it entails is the removal of a hypothetical compound foot made up of the second elements of the third and sixth feet. That postulates a metrical scheme for the hexameter corresponding to one of the two alternative analyses of the pentameter attested by the ancient grammarians (Mar. Vict. *GLK* 6:109.29–110.16, Ter. Maur. *GLK* 6:377.1753–1800). This lends point to Ovid's pained expostulation to Cupid: what business has he to meddle in this

elegy from epic is the pentameter, but it is precisely Ovid's handling of the pentameter that is central in any discussion of the style of his elegies. Ovid himself, in this witty conceit of Cupid's hijacking the role of Apollo, has slyly and allusively identified this crucial technical point.

But there is more to it than that. The words *arma graui numero uiolentaque bella* create expectation of an epic; and the distribution of consonants and the sequence of vowels specifically invoke the first and second proems of the *Aeneid*.[2] Virgil's poetic progress had been "from relatively small to ever greater compositions . . . a model for many poets and writers to come."[3] Ovid's ostensible claim to have started with epic and abandoned it for elegy reverses this canonical sequence and implies a deliberate promotion of this comparatively humble genre. Though he did eventually write an epic which, indirectly but unmistakably, challenged the *Aeneid*, it was with elegy, when the crunch came, that he found his poetic identity to be bound up;[4] and his claim to have done for elegy what Virgil did for epic (*Rem.* 395–96) if anything understates his achievement as poetic empire-builder. As Virgil had reshaped the hexameter that he had inherited from Ennius, Catullus, Lucretius, and Cicero,[5] so Ovid, no less masterfully,[6] remolded the distich as he found it in Gallus, Propertius, and Tibullus into a uniquely flexible and adaptable instrument, giving it what was to prove its definitive form through twenty centuries.[7]

---

highly specialized field? Metrical technicalities are the province of the Muses (cf. Hinds (1987a) 16–17).

[2] McKeown 2:11–12.

[3] von Albrecht (1997) 1:702; cf. Clausen (1987) 1.

[4] For reasons of space no examples from the exile poetry figure in this article, but the omission is not to be construed as a reflection on their technical quality: see, e.g., Kenney (1992a) xxi–xxi, Williams (1994) 50–99, and chapter 11 below.

[5] Cicero's role in the evolution of Latin verse technique is too often undervalued: see von Albrecht (1997) 1:539, Clausen (1982) 178: "Neither as a poet nor as a critic of poetry is Cicero to be ridiculed: he was . . . as good a poet as a highly intelligent man who has never experienced the sacred rage can be."

[6] "[T]he Roman attacks the problems of the transfer of Greek metrical forms to Latin with great determination. One cannot help admiring the dexterity with which Ovid lightened the Roman elegiac, even if in doing so he overworked his scanty supply of iambi" (Gildersleeve *ap.* Miller (1930) 354). Ovid had once been Gildersleeve's favorite poet (Miller (1930) 401).

[7] Cf. Wilamowitz (1924) 1:240. Generations of English schoolmasters and classical dons have demonstrated the versatility of the Ovidian couplet, none more brilliantly than B.H. Kennedy and W.H.D. Rouse: the former in, for instance, his rendering of the summons to a committee meeting called to consider a proposal

The ease and fluency of Ovid's writing is highly deceptive. To reverse Sheridan's dictum, "easy reading's damned hard writing." What Macaulay said of the *Metamorphoses* applies with equal force to everything Ovid wrote: "in . . . the art of doing difficult things in expression and versification as if they were the easiest in the world, Ovid is incomparable."[8] Macaulay's "as if" betokens the literary artist's awareness of what Ovid's critics have often failed to grasp,[9] that—as with another deceptively fluent writer who has much in common with him, P.G. Wodehouse[10]—this apparent ease is grounded on an Alexandrian bedrock of love and respect for language (tempered always with readiness to take liberties in a good cause) and sheer hard work: *philologia* and *agrypnia*.[11] The straightforwardness and indeed ordinariness that scholars identify as his stylistic trademarks[12] are the product of innumerable discreet manipulations of meter, diction and syntax. In the words of Gilbert Murray, writing at a time when Ovid was distinctly unfashionable, "He was a poet utterly in love with poetry . . . with the real face and voice and body and clothes and accessories of poetry."[13] It is a modern fallacy that preoccupation

---

for laying down gas-pipes (How (1904) 120–21); the latter in his versions of newspaper advertisements such as the following, reproduced by kind permission of the Master and Fellows of Christ's College, Cambridge (Christ's College Post-Medieval MSS and Papers, Misc. notes by W.H.D. Rouse, Box 113 (1), x):
A fortunate purchase enables Fortnum & Mason to offer Havana cigars (mostly Upmann's) of the 1922 crop, at less than cost price. Write for list.
Fumiferos herbae quos mittit Havana cylindros,
    conficis in fabrica quos, Opimanne, tua,
quadrimam messem nos emimus omine fausto:
    quanti stent, quales, quotque, rogare licet.
sic Fortnos Fortuna iuvat, Fortuna Masones:
    nam minus est pretium quam prior ille dedit.
[8] Macaulay *ap.* Trevelyan (1923) 2:725, cit. Stroh (1969) 112 (not quite correctly).
[9] Even Dryden: "[A]s his Verse came easily, he wanted the toyl of Application to amend it" (cit. Stroh (1969) 67).
[10] See Kenney (1992b).
[11] See Stroh (1968) on the critics' misunderstanding of *Tr.* 4.10.25–26; and cf. Tissol (1997) 5–7. That Ovid did indeed on occasion have second thoughts about his work we know from the preliminary "epigram" to the *Amores*; we are not bound to believe, what seems inherently unlikely, his assertion that he limited his revision to selection. Comparison of the elegiac and epic versions of the same story or of the reuse of the same material in a new setting demonstrates the care that went into his rewriting: see, e.g., Thomas (1969), Jäger (1970), Hinds (1987a). If, as I have tentatively suggested, our text of *Heroides* 16–21 is an uncorrected first draft (Kenney (1996) 25, (1999a) 413), it is instructive to speculate how he might have revised it for publication.
[12] McKeown 1:32, Booth (1991) 12.
[13] Murray (1921) 116. See his analysis of *Her.* 2.1–2 ((1921) 120–21), concluding

with technique necessarily inhibits or displaces creativity. Ovid wrote with seeming facility not because his mind was facile but because he had consciously shaped a medium of expression that rapidly became second nature to him: *ars adeo latet arte sua.*

II

Discussion of Ovid's style must begin with his meter, with which the effects that particularly distinguish him, his fluency and his wit, are inextricably bound up.[14] His treatment of the elegiac couplet has come in for some adverse criticism. Axelson quotes with approval a description of it which he attributes to Wilamowitz as a "Klappermühle;"[15] and Ernest Harrison, rather unexpectedly, given the English tradition in these matters,[16] contrasted the limitations of the Ovidian pentameter unfavorably with the greater freedom and expressivity of Catullus's treatment.[17] The facts are indeed striking. The "rule" dictating that the last word of the verse must be a disyllable at a stroke radically differentiated the Latin elegiac distich from its Greek forebear by checking the free flow of construction and sense from couplet to couplet and so changing the whole ethos of the meter. The leader in this development was Tibullus, whose example was followed by Propertius in his Books 3–4.[18] The reasons for this technical revolution are a matter of dispute among scholars, but it must have been motivated by something more essential than personal whim

---

"That is *Poesis.* That is the way to build your line if you work in an inflected language"—a juster appraisal than that of Kirfel (1969) 89–90. It is both interesting and significant that "Hellenists," as they are generally termed, such as Murray and Wilamowitz should have appreciated Ovid at his true worth at a time when "Latinists" were apt to disparage him. It may not be amiss to recall that he was a favorite with Sir Denys Page.

[14] Booth (1991) 14.

[15] Axelson (1958) 135 = (1987) 273. He ascribes the expression to Wilamowitz, "if I remember rightly." Wilamowitz does indeed refer to Ovid's distichs as "in the long run monotonous" (Wilamowitz (1924) 1:240), but I have failed to run "Klappermühle" to earth in his writings. Cf. Gildersleeve's reservations *ap.* Miller (1930) 401–2. For a demonstration that there is nothing mechanical about Ovid's metrical virtuosity see von Albrecht (1992) 182–85.

[16] Well exemplified by Rouse (1899), who bases himself exclusively on Ovid. No arguments are advanced for this preference; in the Preface it is baldly stated that the *Ars, Amores,* and *Heroides* "form the most perfect models of elegiac verse."

[17] Harrison (1943).

[18] Figures at Wilkinson (1940) 38. For Tibullus as "the Waller of Latin Elegy" who "paved the way for Ovid, its Pope," see Wilkinson (1940) 40–41 = (1955) 31.

or literary fashion; there must have been something about the poly-syllabic ending which was at odds with native linguistic habits. That was evidently also the case with the hexameter, on the ending of which analogous limitations had been imposed at a considerably earlier date.[19] It is unnecessary to explore the question here: the most plausible explanation remains that advanced by Wilkinson, that it was the influence of the Latin stress accent on the metrical structure that was the determining factor.[20]

In the longer perspective the Catullan treatment of the pentameter must probably be regarded, *pace* Harrison, as an aberration, a metrical Grecism imposed against the grain of the language. The remains of early Latin elegy are too scanty for statistics to be pressed, but it is worth noting that of the pentameters attributed to Ennius four out of five end with disyllables,[21] whereas with Valerius Aedituus, Porcius Licinus, and Lutatius Catulus the figure is three out of ten.[22] Their poems, like the similar group of epigrams found inscribed on a wall at Pompeii,[23] testify to the penetration of Italy by Hellenistic epigram from the late second century B.C. onwards,[24] foreshadowing the close engagement with Alexandrian poetry of Catullus and his contemporaries. The Catullan way with pentameter endings was firmly Greek, only 39 per cent being disyllabic.[25] With Gallus, so far as his exiguous fragments take us, the balance can be seen tilting, with four out of six.[26] That figure, for what it is worth, is broadly in line with the 61 per cent of the first book of Propertius;[27] it was Tibullus, with 93 per cent of disyllabic endings in his first book,

---

[19] Already in Ennius 75 percent of his hexameters "end in the classical Latin manner, the last two feet consisting of a dactylic word or word-end followed by a disyllable, or a trochaic word or word-end followed by a trisyllable" (Skutsch (1985) 49).

[20] Wilkinson (1940) 41–43; cf. Allen (1973) 186–88. For Wilamowitz it was the conflict of ictus and accent that constituted "the charm" of Ovid's pentameters (Wilamowitz (1972) 6:155).

[21] Courtney (1993) 39–43. It seems *a priori* improbable that, given Ennius's evident disinclination to treat the end of the hexameter *à la grecque* (above, n. 19), he would have felt differently about the pentameter.

[22] Courtney (1993) 70–78.

[23] Ross (1969a) 147–51, (1969b): one out of four surviving pentameters ends with a disyllable.

[24] Cf. Hutton (1935) 10–13.

[25] Wilkinson (1940) 38.

[26] Courtney (1993) 263.

[27] Wilkinson (1940) 38.

who, Hellenizer though he was,[28] in this particular at least[29] called
his countrymen, phonologically speaking, to order.[30]

Of the technical consequences of this development the most obvi-
ous is the drastic restriction which it imposed on the choice of words
with which to end the line. The supply of Latin disyllables is lim-
ited, and since the end of the couplet now necessarily tended to
coincide with the end of a clause or sentence, the elegists naturally
preferred a noun or verb as the last word. Ovid was somewhat freer
than Propertius and Tibullus in promoting adjectives and adverbs to
this position, but his usage is still broadly in line with theirs.[31] The
most important exception is his predilection for ending the pen-
tameter with unemphatic words, especially possessive pronouns and
parts of *sum*.[32] Axelson's analysis of the Ovidian pentameter ends
with an unfavorable comparison between "the technical superficiality
of the superelegant verse-virtuoso" and Tibullus's "finer perception
of the fact that the pentameter should end in pregnancy, not in
something metrically convenient but empty of content such as *habet*
or *erat*."[33] That judgement appears to be tacitly predicated on prin-
ciples which apply to Latin *Kunstprosa* but which are not necessarily
valid for this quite different medium. Ovid's treatment of the end of
the pentameter must be assessed in the context of the structure of the
couplet as a whole and its function in connected elegiac discourse.

As has been noted, the most important effect of the disyllable
"rule" was to mark off the couplet as a discrete semantic and rhetor-
ical entity. The reduction in metrical weight and impact on the ear
of the last word of every other verse, accentuated in Ovid's case by
a higher proportion of unemphatic words in that position, had the

---

[28] Cairns (1979a).

[29] He is, on the other hand, found in Book 1 maintaining the Alexandrian obser-
vance of "Hermann's Bridge," which forbids a trochaic caesura in the fourth foot of
the hexameter; his single breach at 1.9.83 may be specially motivated (Ross (1969a)
129). In Book 2 he abandoned this restriction, and Propertius and Ovid exploited
with increasing freedom a rhythm that, uncongenial to the Greek ear, evidently did
not displease the Roman (Wilamowitz (1924) 1:240, Knox (1986a) 87).

[30] Wilkinson (1940) 38.

[31] Platnauer (1951) 40–48.

[32] Figures at Wilkinson (1940) 39; but cf. Axelson (1958) 132 = (1987) 270, point-
ing out that his use of personal pronouns in this *sedes*, as distinct from pronominal
adjectives, is not out of line with that of his predecessors.

[33] Axelson (1958) 135 = (1987) 273. Contrast Gildersleeve's more forbearing
judgement, quoted above, n. 6.

effect of, so to say, throwing the metrical and semantic center of gravity back to the earlier part of the pentameter and so concentrating the reader's attention on it.[34] So in an unexpected source, a handbook of 1835 for English schoolboy composers:

> Finally, let us not forget to point out the peculiar merit of Ovid's elegiac verse, in that fine variety of modification, *apparently but little appreciated*, which distinguishes his pentameter.
>
> On that line, as always winding up an exact portion of sense, Ovid had to bestow his principal care; and in doing this he has with such nicety of skill avoided monotony from caesural division, that, generally speaking, two successive pentameters will seldom be found constructed on a similar plan, in the words and arrangement of words, of which they are composed.[35]

The writer of these words seems to have grasped instinctively[36] an essential truth about the Latin form of the elegiac couplet: that the pentameter is no longer subordinate but stands on a level with its heroic partner. Where it particularly comes into its own is as a vehicle for wit and epigram.[37] Additional point can be lent by the kind of verbal patterning that had become a characteristic feature of the Latin hexameter from Cicero onwards, most evident in the "enclosing" type of word-order, in which an adjective at (frequently though not invariably the main) caesura agrees with a noun at the end of the verse.[38] As in the hexameter,[39] this was a specifically Latin development, as emerges from consideration of the fragments of Gallus. Scanty though these are, it seems unlikely to be due to pure chance that of his six surviving and decipherable pentameters five have an

---

[34] "It is especially in the pentameter . . ., which rounds off the unit of composition, where O. focuses the attention of the reader" (Knox (1995) 32). Cf. McKeown 1:109: "Often, it is the pentameter which bears the main emphasis."

[35] Tate (1835) 26–27 (my italics). It may be noted in passing that Tate's discussion of Ovid's hexameters is in contrast perfunctory (28–30) and is vitiated by similar prejudices to those mentioned below. Hilberg's ponderous monograph (Hilberg (1894)) is an elaborate demonstration of the futility of any attempt to reduce Ovid's manipulations of language and meter to a system of "rules" without reference to their function in a connected utterance.

[36] But his perceptions must have been sharpened by his own attempts to compose in the Ovidian manner: there is more to be said for this now neglected art (cf. above, n. 7) than its critics are disposed to allow.

[37] Wilkinson (1955) 35–36: "the hexameter . . . sometimes seems to exist only to compère its brilliant young partner."

[38] See Pearce (1966), Knox (1995) 33 and nn. 85, 86.

[39] See Pearce (1966) 298–303.

adjective-noun or noun-adjective pair articulating the verse. The most striking case is that of the line preserved by Vibius Sequester describing the river Hypanis: *uno tellures diuidit amne duas.*[40] This is a classic "quasi-Golden" structure of the form aBVAb.[41] In sharp contrast Valerius Aedituus and co. have no such pentameters.[42] In fact, the incidence of this kind of structure in the Ovidian pentameter is somewhat lower than in either Propertius or Tibullus and approximately equal to that in Catullus.[43] That finding may surprise at first, but it confirms that Ovid's handling of the couplet is less mechanical than Axelson's analysis purports to show. He had indeed many other devices up his sleeve to provide the "heavy spicing" that Wilkinson thought was required to vary the often predictable subject-matter of his elegy.[44]

The most immediate impression made by Ovid's elegiac writing is one of fluency and speed. The means by which this is achieved are evident at a glance: more dactyls and fewer and lighter elisions. The statistics are on record and need not be reproduced here,[45] but something can usefully be added to what has been said by others on Ovid's cultivation of the dactyl. Latin is not as naturally rich in short syllables as Greek, and poets very early on resorted to such expedients as the free use of the "poetic" plural of neuter nouns for metrical convenience: already Ennius's *caeli caerula templa*[46] demonstrates awareness of this resource, which Ovid, as might be expected, exploited to the full.[47] Commentators, however, have not always appreciated the subtlety and dexterity with which he manipulated these possibilities.

Since we have spoken of manipulation, it is, appropriately enough, in his handling of hands that his skill in this area can be most strik-

---

[40] Courtney (1993) 263.

[41] Cf. Wilkinson (1963) 215–17, Kenney (1984) xliv–xlv, lxi–lxiv, Knox (1995) 33 n. 85, remarking that discussion has largely concentrated on hexameters. However, *mutatis mutandis*, the picture in the elegists is not markedly different. Cf. Kenney (1996) Index s.v. "patterned" verses.

[42] Courtney (1993) 70.

[43] Catullus (poems 65, 66, 67.1–24, 68) 34 per cent; Propertius (1.1–1.6.24, 4.2–4.4.64) 57 per cent; Tibullus (1.1, 1.4, 2.1, 2.3) 46 per cent; Ovid (*Am.* 1.8.1–100, *AA* 1.1–100, *Her.* 6.1–100, *F.* 1.1–100) 32 per cent.

[44] Wilkinson (1955) 34–43.

[45] Platnauer (1951) 36–38, 72–90.

[46] 1.33 Sk.; see Skutsch (1985) 201, *OLD* s.v. *templum* 4.

[47] Bednara (1906) 540–52 = 56–68, 554–62 = 70–78, Herr (1937). On the broader linguistic implications Löfstedt (1942) 27–65 remains the classic discussion.

ingly illustrated. To render "hand" he had at his disposal four words: *manus* itself, *digiti*, *pollex*, and *unguis*. What particularly invites notice is his use of the poetic *singular* to engineer a desired dactylic rhythm. *Manus*, no doubt predictably, tended in the singular to gravitate to the end of the pentameter.[48] What is perhaps unexpected is that *manibus* is relatively rare: only 24 instances out of nearly 400 occurrences of the word in the elegies. However, when an anapaest for either "hand" or "hands" was wanted, *digiti* was also at hand to stand in for *manus*. So at *Her.* 11.20 we have *feminea teneo non mea tela manu* and at *F.* 2.102 *non haec sunt digitis arma tenenda tuis*.[49] What has gone unremarked by lexicographers and (until recently) commentators is that when a dactyl was wanted in such expressions Ovid habitually drafted in *pollice* as an equivalent to "hand" or "fingers,"[50] an example of the "formulaic economy" remarked below as a feature of the *Metamorphoses*. He uses *pollex* 28 times, 27 of these in the ablative singular;[51] in only two cases is the sense "thumb" required (*Met.* 9.79, *F.* 5.433), while elsewhere the most natural interpretation is "fingers and thumb," "hand."[52] When finger*tips* are in question, as in the act of plucking, then *unguis* also comes into play. Again formulaic economy can be seen at work: *pollice* and *unguibus*, both dactyls, are in terms of the metrical properties of their first and last syllables mirror-images. So we have at *F.* 5.255 *decerpsi pollice florem* and at *Met.* 8.800 *unguibus et raras uellentem dentibus*[53] *herbas*; and *ungue*

---

[48] See Nagle (1987) for an interesting discussion of this "mannerism." One or two other words which fitted this position were apt to be overworked. A good example is *ops*: of 203 instances in the elegiac poems 150 end a pentameter. The figures for *opus* are less striking but still noteworthy: 112 out of 206. Most remarkable of all is *aqua* with 343 out of 367, but here Ovid was following the example of Propertius and Tibullus (Axelson (1958) 126–28 = (1987) 266–68).

[49] Exploiting also the ambiguity of *arma*, which can mean "(ship's) tackle" (*OLD* 10c) as well as "weapons."

[50] See Booth (1991) 116, Kenney (1996) 145, McKeown 3:76.

[51] Cf. McKeown 3:76, remarking that "*pollex* occurs some fifty times in hexameters in the period from Catullus to Juvenal, always in the form *pollice* and in this [sc. the penultimate] line-position, except at *Met.* 9.79 *pollicibus* and at *Met.* 11.170, *Laus. Pis.* 177 and Mart. 14.167.1."

[52] The thumb is after all a specialized finger, as was recognized by Isid. *Etym.* 11.1.70, *primus* [sc. *digitus*] *pollex uocatus, eo quod inter ceteros polleat uirtute et potestate* (Maltby (1991) 482). This usage, if a grammatical pigeonhole be wanted for it, may perhaps be classified as an extension of the *geminus Pollux* construction (Bell (1923) 3–8).

[53] *dens* was also available in the collective-poetic singular, as at, e.g., *AA* 1.20, *Her.* 10.84, 18.18, *Met.* 10.704, 11.23 (*TLL* s.v. 537.50–55).

adds a useful trochee for good measure, as at *Her.* 4.30, *tenui primam delegere ungue rosam* and *F.* 4.438, *papauereas subsecat ungue comas.*

Ovid deploys his linguistic resources to secure metrical fluency and smoothness so deftly that it is easy to label his technique mechanical. The juxtaposition of variant prosodies was a device familiar in Greek poetry from Homer onwards, and it was taken up by Latin poets, by none more readily than Ovid.[54] Its metrical utility is obvious, especially with such words as *mihi, tibi, sibi,* or with alternative forms such as *siue* and *seu,* but it cannot be dismissed out of hand as a pure expedient.[55] When Ovid writes at *AA* 1.84, *quique aliis cauit, non cauet ipse sibi,* the triple variation of tense, quantity, and ictus drives home the point. At *AA* 3.578, *et sit in infida proditione fides,* the paradox is reinforced by the paronomasia and further underlined by the variation in quantity and ictus. At *F.* 2.489–90, *Iuppiter adnuerat: nutu tremefactus uterque/est polus,* the device can be seen operating on several levels. The syllabic anaphora serves as grammatical connection, the etymologizing juxtaposition signals cause and effect, and the heavy *nutu* following immediately on the rapid *adnuerat* underscores the inevitability of Jupiter's decision.[56] The Homeric commonplace has been, so to say, naturalized and invested with Roman authority and *dignitas.*

III

Ovid's elegiac style is in general simple and unaffected, but not therefore "prosaic" *tout court.*[57] In the hierarchy of genres elegy ranked

---

[54] Hopkinson (1982) 173.

[55] As it is by Nisbet and Hubbard (1970) 364 on Hor. *C.* 1.32.11.

[56] Other Ovidian examples at Hopkinson (1982) 173–77. Cf. Bömer (1982) 356, commenting on *Met.* 13.607–8, *et primo similis uolucri, mox uera uolucris/insonuit pennis.*

[57] On the distinction between the prosaic and the colloquial in poetic style see Mayer (1994) 16–17. Ovid did not go out of his way to avoid words avoided by other poets if they expressed his meaning precisely, if no other word for the thing was readily available (a good case in point being *auditor*), and if they did not impede the smooth flow of the verse. So with, e.g., *notitia* (11x), otherwise only in prose, Terence, the *Culex* and the *Nux,* and Lucretius, in whom it has a specific technical sense = πρόληψις; Ovid uses it over a wide range of meaning (*OLD* s.v. 1, 2, 4, 6). The case of *materia/-es* is even more striking: this is a predominantly prose word and likewise a Lucretian technical term, which Ovid uses 47 times (McKeown 2:13 on *Am.* 1.1.1–2). On his exploitation of legal terminology see Kenney (1969b). A technical nuance is missed by the commentators on *Am.* 1.5.21, *quam castigato planus sub pectore uenter!,* where *castigato* means "disciplined," i.e., "correct" (Quint. *IO* 10.1.115

well below epic, and colloquial diction and idiom were evidently felt
to be, in moderation, appropriate to it.[58] Ovid's use of ordinary dic-
tion—ordinary but not therefore necessarily inexpressive—to facili-
tate the smooth and fluent style of writing that he made his own
can be conveniently exemplified from two classes of word: 4-sylla-
ble nouns in *-itas* and 5-syllable adjectives in *-iosus*. Both these are
peculiarly well suited for fitting into the pentameter, the first in the
genitive and ablative singular, the second in the cases ending in *-us*,
-e, and short *-a*.[59]

(1) 4-syllable nouns in *-itas*.[60] *anxietas* (2 *Met.*) (Juv., prose); *asperitas*
    7 (1p, nom. + *-que*) (2 *Met.*) (Lucret., Hor. *Ep.*, Sil., prose); *cal-
    liditas* 3p (Ter., Mart., prose); *commoditas* 3p (Plaut., Ter., Manil.,
    prose); *credulitas* 7 (4p) (4 *Met.*) (Phaedr., Mart., prose); *ebrietas* 4
    (1 *Met.*) (Hor. *Ep.*, prose); *fertilitas* 2p (2 *Met.*) (*Nux* (1p), prose);
    garrulitas (1 *Met.*) (Manil., Mart., prose); *impietas* (2 *Met.*) (Plaut.,
    Acc., Sen. trag., *Culex*, prose); *improbitas* 1 (Manil., Phaedr., Juv.,
    prose); *mobilitas* 2 (1p) (Lucret., Virg., *ES*, prose); *nobilitas* 23 (18p)
    (4 *Met.*) (common); *posteritas* 9 (6p (1 nom. + *-que*)) (Prop., Lucan,
    Juv., Mart., prose); *proximitas* 1p (2 *Met.*) (*Nux* (1p), prose); *rustic-
    itas* 5 (1p) (Calp. Sic., Mart., prose); *sedulitas* 6 (4p) (1 *Met.*) (Hor.
    Ep., Calp. Sic., prose); *simplicitas* 10 (4p) (1 *Met.*) (Lucret., *Eleg.
    Maec.*, Juv., Mart., prose); *strenuitas* (1 *Met.*) (Varro);[61] *uirginitas* 11
    (7p) (7 *Met.*) (common).

(2) 5-syllable adjectives in *-iosus*. The eclectic character of Ovid's
    poetic vocabulary[62] is well illustrated by his use of adjectives in
    -osus. This way of forming adjectives was characteristic of the

---

and Peterson (1891) 113 ad loc.). Corinna is appraised as a work of art which con-
forms to the highest technical standards. Martinon (1897) 221 glosses "beau, par-
fait;" Barsby (1973) 68 comments "literally 'disciplined'" but does not pursue the
implications. Cf. *Met.* 7.555, the first instance of *indicium* in the technical sense of
"symptom." Syntactical prosaisms include, e.g., forms such as *estote*, favored for met-
rical reasons rather than as imparting solemnity (cf. N–W 3:150–51, 216–23; Bömer
(1976) 62 on *Met.* 4.154), and the "double" pluperfects of the type of *Her.* 17.23,
si delenita fuissem = si d. essem (Kenney (1996) 127 ad loc.).

[58] Tränkle (1960), Watson (1985).

[59] Cf. McKeown 2:223–24 on *Am.* 1.8.43–44, Kenney (1996) 91 on *Her.* 16.52.

[60] p = occupies penultimate *sedes* in pentameter. The figures for the *Met.* are also
included. In his use of words of this shape and of 4-syllable words + *-que* Ovid is
more restrained than Tibullus, in whom it verges on a mannerism, less so than
Propertius.

[61] *LL* 8.15; otherwise only in late authors (Bömer (1977) 374 on *Met.* 9.320).

[62] See Knox (1986a) 42, (1986b) 100.

sermo plebeius,[63] but that does not brand them as "unpoetic"; as McKeown has pointed out, "the nuance of such formations ranges from the colloquial to the highly poetic."[64] Ovid's attitude to language is catholic: "a major aspect of his originality lies in his intelligent use of forms taken from everyday speech and employed with precision in the exposition of character."[65] This can be seen especially clearly in the case of *formosus*.[66] Many of these words had the additional attraction of metrical convenience, as emerges with especial force in the case of those listed here:[67]

ambitiosus 8p (2 *Met.*) (Lucret., Hor.,[68] Mart., prose); *desidiosus* 3p (Lucan, Mart., prose); *ingeniosus* 18 (17p) (1 *Met.*) (*ES*, Mart., prose); *insidiosus* 5p (2 *Met.*) (*ES*, Hor. *Ep.*, Phaedr., Stat., Mart., prose); *inuidiosus* 15 (8p) (10 *Met.*) (*Cons.*, Lucil., Prop., Lucan, Mart., prose); *litigiosus* 3p (Hor. *Sat.*, prose); *luxuriosus* 4p (Lucan, Juv., Mart., prose); *officiosus* 10p (*Nux*, Hor. *Sat. Ep.*, Mart., prose); *perniciosus* 2p (Hor. *Sat.*, Juv., Mart., prose); *prodigiosus* 1 (2 *Met.*) (Stat., Juv., Mart., prose).

The authors of the *Epistula Sapphus*, the *Nux*, and the *Consolatio ad Liviam* evidently recognized Ovid's use of such words as one of his trademarks;[69] and it is not surprising that Martial, the only Latin poet who rivaled and occasionally even bid fair to outdo Ovid in the virtuosity of his management of the elegiac couplet, appreciated their metrical convenience.

Ovid has had some difficulty in living down the charges of Seneca

---

[63] Knox (1986b) 97–98.

[64] McKeown 2:18 on *Am.* 1.1.9–10; cf. on Ovid's "adventurous" use of *spatiosus* McKeown 2:366 on 1.14.3–4.

[65] Knox (1986a) 42.

[66] "Nur teilweise unpoetisch ist *formosus*" (Axelson (1945) 60). The figures are illuminating: Virg. *Ecl.* 16, *G.* 1; Prop. 35; Tib. 6; Ov. eleg. 21, *Met.* 23 (*pulcher* 26) (Knox (1986b) 100). Virgil did not altogether exclude -*osus* adjectives from the *Aeneid* (28x), but Ovid was distinctly freer in his epic (53x) (Knox (1986b) 99–100).

[67] It is restricted to those scanning $-\cup\cup-\cup$, since these offer the most obvious exemplification of Ovid's readiness to tailor the language to the verse medium, but the discussion could be extended: e.g., it is notable that of his 13 instances of *studiosus*, a predominantly prose word, 9 are in the penultimate *sedes* in the pentameter. Cf. below, n. 69.

[68] For Horace's enterprising use of this word see Nisbet and Hubbard (1970) 406 on *C.* 1.36.20.

[69] In addition to the instances noted in the list cf. *ES* 1 *studiosae*, 41 *formosa*, 124 *formoso*; *Nux* 23 *formosa*, 57 *operoso*; and most strikingly in the *Consolatio* 15 *latebrosas*, 105 *umbrosis*, 109 *plumosa*, 207 *generosa*, 251 *spatiosas*, 259 *generosa*, 265 *operosa*, 269 *speciosus*, 445 *nebulosum*, 464 *generosa*.

and Quintilian that he never knew when to stop and made no effort to discipline his genius.[70] These strictures certainly do not apply to his diction, in the choice and creation of which enterprise and restraint are nicely balanced. In the formation of compounds, as is noted below in regard to the *Metamorphoses*, his innovations were on traditional lines. One class of words that deserves mention in the elegiac context is that of compounds in *semi-*. Of the 19 such words used by him, 5 are *hapax legomena* and 6 first occur in him.[71] Here we may particularly note *semiadapertus*‡,[72] *semicrematus* (Mart.), *semireductus*‡, *semirefectus*‡, *semisepultus*‡, *semisupinus* (3) (Mart.), all except *semisepultus* in the penultimate position in the pentameter.[73]

It may be allowed that words like these, when all is said and done, do tend to draw attention to themselves and to that extent offer ammunition to Ovid's detractors. Most of his characteristic compounds are more discreetly formed. An example with interesting metrical implications is that of verbs compounded with *re-*.[74] These and other compounds with a short first syllable were metrically useful, especially in the second half of the hexameter. Mention has been made of the disregard of "Hermann's Bridge" evident in elegy from Tibullus Book 2 onwards,[75] and compounds of this type lent themselves to the exploitation of this now sanctioned rhythm. Thus, all four examples of *recandesco*‡ (*Met.*) are of the form *recanduit* following a trochaic caesura in the fourth foot of the hexameter; and so also with *recalfacio*‡, *recolligo* (*Met.*), *relanguesco* (+ *Met.*),[76] *remollio* (*Met.*), *resaeuio*‡, *resanesco*‡, *resemino*‡ (*Met.*), *resuscito* (*Met.*),[77] and *retexo* (*Met.*).

---

[70] Sen. *Contr.* 2.2.12, 9.5.17; Quint. *IO* 10.1.8, 98.

[71] McKeown 2:125–26 on *Am.* 1.6.3–4.

[72] ‡ = *hapax legomenon* or occurring only in Ovid, as the case may be. For full listings of such words see Dräger (1888), Linse (1891).

[73] One other word particularly favored for this position deserves mention. *sanguinulentus* is securely attested in poetry before Ovid only at Tib. 2.6.40; Ovid uses it 15 times, always in the "p" position. Formulaic economy can be seen at work here too: the alternative *sanguineus* (preferred in *Met.*, where generic considerations evidently also played a part) is found in 10 out of 11 instances, as its scansion dictates, in first or second position in the verse. A similar demarcation can be observed with other pairs of equivalents such as *puluereus* and *puluerulentus*; cf. *nemorosus* and *nemoralis* (on adjectives in *-alis* found first or only in Ovid see McKeown 3:142 on *Am.* 2.6.57–58), alternative words for "hair" (*capillus, coma, crines*) in, e.g., *Am.* 1.14.

[74] For a list of such compounds occurring first or only in Ovid see McKeown 2:241 on *Am.* 1.8.75–76.

[75] Above, n. 29.

[76] See McKeown 3:184–85 on *Am.* 2.9.27–28.

[77] It is interesting that we should apparently owe such a commonplace word as "resuscitate" to Ovid.

Several other types of compound slot neatly into this position. In
in-:[78] *inattenuatus*‡ (*Met.*), *ineditus*‡, *ineuitabilis* (*Met.*), *inexcusabilis* (*Met.*),
inexpectatus (*Met.*), *inexperrectus*‡ (*Met.*), *inexpugnabilis* (+ *Met.*), *inobrutus*‡
(*Met.*), *inobseruatus* (*Met.*). In *bi*-:[79] *Bicorniger*‡, *binominis* (+ *Met.*), *bipen-
nifer*‡.[80] Other: *puerperus* (*Met.*),[81] *salutifer* (*Met.*), *tridentifer*‡ (*Met.*). Non-
compounds, some of them *hapax legomena* or first attested in Ovid,
are also exploited in this way: e.g., *aquaticus* (+ *Met.*, *ES*), *cacumino*
(*Met.*), *crepuscula* (+ *Met.*), *forabilis* (*Met.*),[82] *piabilis*‡ (*Met.*), *piamina*‡, *son-
abilis*‡, *uolatilis* (+ *Met.*).

The lavish employment of (mostly Greek) proper names that char-
acterizes the *Metamorphoses* is only sporadically evident in the elegies.[83]
Here we may limit ourselves to noticing changes which Ovid rings
on adjectival forms of the same name to suit the verse:[84] *Argeas fran-
gite, Troes, opes* (*Am.* 1.9.34, al.), *Argolico . . . Orestae* (*Am.* 2.6.15, al.),
Argolides . . . puppes (*Rem.* 735, al.); *albis, Cephei, placebas* (*AA* 3.191),
Cepheia uirgo (*Am.* 3.3.17, *ES* 35), *Cephea . . . arua* (*Met.* 4.669); *Cnosias
uxor* (*AA* 1.556, al.),[85] *Cnosi relicta* (*AA* 3.158, al.), *Cnosia . . . humus* (*Her.*

---

[78] On Ovid's penchant for compounding participles with *in-* see below on *Met.*
For a list of privative adjectives with *in-* found first or only in Ovid see McKeown
3:195–96 on *Am.* 2.9.51–52.

[79] For other adjectives compounded with *bi-* found first or only in Ovid see
McKeown 3:269 on *Am.* 2.12.9–10.

[80] This word also exemplifies the fact that compounds and forms of compounds
of the metrical shape ◡–◡◡(–), of which there are many in Ovid, are equally use-
ful in the oblique cases for filling the hexameter effectively between an initial trochee
and the penthemimeral caesura. So with *Met.* 4.22, *Penthea tu uenerande bipenniferumque
Lycurgum*, compare *Tr.* 5.3.39, *ossa bipenniferi sic sint male pressa Lycurgi*. Cf. *Chimaerifer*‡,
colubrifer, corymbifer‡, *laborifer, odorifer, oliuifer, papyrifer*‡, *racemifer*‡, *sagittifer, salutifer, soporifer,
uenenifer*‡; *securiger, tridentiger*‡; *aenipes*‡ (*Her.* 6.32, 12.93 ex corr. Heinsii; *et aeripedes*
codd.), *draconigenus*‡, *gemellipara*‡; and the compounds in *in-* and *re-* already noticed.

[81] *OLD* registers *puerpera* as a noun and for adjectival *puerperus* records only *Met.*
10.511, *uerba puerpera*. Clearly the word is an adjective, though for obvious reasons
unlikely to be used in the masculine or neuter; Ovid's use of it in all three instances
in *Met.* is adjectival: 6.337, 9.313, 10.511 (cf. Bömer (1976) 98 on 6.337).

[82] On adjectives in *-abilis* attested first or only in Ovid see McKeown 2:153–54
on *Am.* 1.6.59–60.

[83] E.g., the catalogue of rivers at *Am.* 3.6.25–44 and some effective clusters in
the *Fasti*, as at 2.39–44 (see Wilkinson (1955) 278), 3.81–86, 3.105–8, 4.467–80 (cf.
Fantham (1998) 46–47), 5.81–92.

[84] Only cases of three or more variants are recorded (otherwise the list would
be inordinately long), and overlap with the complementary list given below for *Met.*
is avoided.

[85] On names in *-ias* in Ovid see Kenney (1999b) and Δειπνιάς Callim. fr. 87 Pf.,
Iphias Ov. *Tr.* 5.14.38; also (*per* Professor J. Griffin) Ἀκτιάς Callim. fr. 63.12,
Ἀνιγριάς Moero *AP* 6.189.1, Ἑλλεσποντιάς Archestr. *SH* 166.14, Δρακοντιάς Nicand.
fr. 73.1.

4.68, al.), *Cnosiacas . . . rates* (*Met.* 7.471, al.);[86] *Cresia regna* (*Her.* 16.301), *Cressa Corona* (*AA* 1.558), *Cretaea . . . sub Ida* (*Am.* 3.10.25, al.), *nymphae . . . Cretides‡* (*F.* 3.443–44); *testudine Cyllenaea* (*AA* 3.147), *Cyllenia proles* (*AA* 3.725, al.),[87] *Cyllenide . . . harpe* (*Met.* 5.176); *Dardana sacra* (*Her.* 7.158, al.), *Dardanides . . . nurus* (*Her.* 17.212, al.), *Dardanias . . . per urbes* (*Her.* 16.333, al.); *Italidas matres* (*F.* 2.441), *Itala regna* (*Her.*7.10, al.), *litore in Italico* (*Met.* 14.17, 15.9); *causas . . . Latinas* (*F.* 2.359, al.), *uulneribus Latiis* (*AA* 1.414, al.), *populi Latialis* (*Met.* 15.481);[88] *rapuit Minoida Theseus* (*Her.* 16.349, al.), *ne forte parum Minoia credar* (*Her.* 4.61, al.), *Minoo nata Thoante* (*Her.* 6.114, al.); *motis Pallantias‡ astris* (*F.* 4.373, al.), *Pallantide‡ . . . eadem* (*F.* 6.567, *Met.* 15.700), *Pallantius‡ heros* (*F.* 5.647), *Palladiae . . . coronae* (*AA* 1.727, al.); *Pelopeidas . . . undas* (*F.* 4.285), *Pelopeius Atreus* (*Her.* 8.27, al.), *Pelopeiades . . . Mycenae* (*F.* 3.83, al.); *Phasiacae . . . terrae* (*Rem.* 261, al.), *Phasias Aeetine* (*Her.* 6.103, al.), *Phasida‡* (*AA* 3.33, al.); *Pittheidos‡ Aethrae* (*Her.* 10.131), *Pittheia‡ regna* (*Her.* 4.107, al.), *prope Pittheam‡ . . . Troezena* (*Met.* 15.296, 506); *Thessalis ara* (*Her.* 13.112, *Met.* 12.190), *hospes . . . Thessalus* (*Her.* 6.23, al.), *Thessalico . . . ueneno* (*Am.* 3.7.27, al.).

The Latin poets were sparing in their use of parts of speech other than nouns, adjectives, and verbs, and were selective in what they did admit. Prepositions, conjunctions, and particles, which took up room in the verse while contributing little to content or emphasis, were often dispensed with. Some prepositions were evidently felt to be prosaic and were avoided altogether;[89] others might be omitted when, most commonly in expressions of motion, the sense was sufficiently defined by case.[90] Coordination (parataxis) was regularly preferred to subordination (hypotaxis) to obviate the need for conjunctions and particles.[91] By none was this tendency more brilliantly

---

[86] *Cnosiacus* 4x in *Met.* (not in elegies), Sen trag., Stat. Editors and lexicographers are still all too apt to spell these names *Gn-.*

[87] *Cyllenius* = Mercury 4x in *Met.*

[88] *Latinus* is the ordinary word (13x; not in *Am., AA, Rem., Her.*); *Latius* (26x) only in Varro before Ovid; *Latialis* (1x) first in Ovid (*varia lectio Latiaris*).

[89] Axelson (1945) 77–81.

[90] Maurach (1995) 44. Conversely Ovid frequently uses *ab* + abl. instrumentally for the sake of the extra short syllable, as at *Am.* 2.4.30, *tenerum molli torquet ab arte latus*; see McKeown 3:77 ad loc., Guttmann (1890), Tränkle (1960) 87.

[91] Cf. Janssen (1941) 26 [= Lunelli (1980) 110–11], Maurach (1995) 181–82. Even in prose it is observable that, where Greek would almost invariably insert a connecting particle, Latin writers will often work through word-order, achieving connection and emphasis by the positioning of a key word or phrase. Thus, when

exploited than by Ovid: his elegies abound in points enhanced or
conveyed by paratactic sentence-structure, shaped and accentuated
by the couplet-form itself.

In one respect his usage in this area differs appreciably from that
of other Latin poets, his treatment of adverbs. These were often
expressed in poetry by predicative expressions, as at *Her.* 17.107, *ad
possessa uenis praeceptaque gaudia serus*; or adjective-noun phrases, as at
Am. 2.14.23–24, *quid. . ./poma . . . crudeli uellis acerba manu?*; or the
Grecizing use of neuter adjectives, as at *F.* 2.703–4, *hortus. . ./sectus
humum riuo lene sonantis aquae.* In particular, adverbs in *-e*, *-o*, and
-(i)ter were evidently felt to be beneath the dignity of poetry and
were generally avoided.[92] This aversion Ovid did not share;[93] indeed,
he sometimes seems to go out of his way to flout propriety, as with
the otherwise exclusively prosaic *dissimulanter* (*AA* 1.488, *Her.* 20.130).
In both these cases the word occupies the second half of the pen-
tameter, and metrical smartness was clearly a factor, as with, e.g.,
fideliter, *inaniter*, and *tenaciter*, which slot in neatly after a fourth-foot
trochaic caesura in the hexameter, and with comparative forms in
-ius, of which Ovid makes free use.

These examples, however, are less remarkable than one which has
apparently gone unnoticed, his extraordinary predilection for the very
ordinary word *bene*, a useful pyrrhic, which he uses 211 times against
Virgil's nine.[94] The figures for *male*, which often serves as a synonym
for *non* or the equivalent of a negative prefix,[95] are almost equally
striking: Ovid 124, Virgil 7.[96] Proportionately no less remarkable is
paene: Ovid 68, Virgil 1.[97] Other such unpretentious adverbs pro-
ducing a serviceable quota of short syllables are *denique*, *inde*, *magis*,

---

Propertius fills the entire first half of a hexameter with the majestic *quandocumque
igitur* (2.1.71, 2.13.17), in both cases to herald the day of his death, the effect is
doubly arresting. Parataxis was not a specifically poetic device; it was characteris-
tic of ordinary speech (Mayer (1994) 25; cf. H–S 527–33). To pursue the implica-
tions of these facts for the evolution of Latin syntax would take us too far afield.

[92] Axelson (1945) 62–63.

[93] Kenney (1996) 106 on *Her.* 16.174 (add 16.169 *stulte*, 227 *artius*, 17.129 *aegre*);
cf. Bednara (1906) 599–600 = 115–16.

[94] Other poets: Lucret. 21, Catull. 17, Hor. lyr. 10, Hor. hex. 29, Prop. 11, Tib.
13, Lucan 10, Sen. trag. 18, Val. Fl. 0, Sil. 3, Stat. 11, Juv. 6, Mart. 48.

[95] E.g., *Am.* 2.18.23, *male gratus* = *ingratus*, 3.7.77, *male sane* = *insane*; *OLD* s.v. 6
(but "quasi-neg." understates the case), *TLL* s.v. *malus* 243.18–58, H–S 455.

[96] Lucret. 7, Catull. 10, Hor. 38, Prop. 2, Tib. 4, Lucan 6, Sen. trag. 11, Val.
Fl., Sil. 0, Stat. 11, Juv. 4, Mart. 21.

[97] Lucret. 1, Catull. 1, Hor. 10, Prop. 1, Tib. 0, Lucan 6, Sen. trag. 5, Val.
Fl. 0, Sil. 2, Stat. 12, Juv. 3, Mart. 8 (McKeown 3:259 on *Am.* 2.11.49–50).

minus, nimium/nimis, prope, protinus, satis, scilicet, semel, simul. The individual statistics are not as arresting as those quoted above and may be forborne; but there is one particle which in this department may be said to sweep the board, namely *tamen*: Ovid 830, Virgil 64.[98]

IV

From diction to its employment. Some of the syntactical ploys which characterize Ovid's style are discussed and illustrated below as they figure in the *Metamorphoses*.[99] Of hyperbaton (artificial dislocation of word-order), as is there noted, his use in his hexameters is relatively restrained. In his elegies license in this area has to some seemed to shade into abuse. When, however, his practice is seen in the larger perspective it is not so extreme as it appears simply by comparison with Propertius and Tibullus, who made no use of the device.[100] It had in fact been a feature of Latin poetic style since Lucretius,[101] and not infrequently it is editorial punctuation rather than the order of words itself which constitutes the real stumbling-block.[102] Confined, as Ovid's invariably are, within the limits of the individual couplet, such departures from the expected or "natural" order of the elements of the sentence often serve to focus the reader's attention and sharpen the point that the Ovidian couplet is so well adapted to express.[103] So at *Her.* 3.19, *si progressa forem caperer ne nocte timebam*, "the dislocation of *nocte* together with its juxtaposition with *timebam* lends emphasis to [Briseis's] fears of getting lost in the dark."[104] At *Her.* 17.109–10,

---

[98] Lucret. 170, Catull. 18, Hor. 60, Prop. 49, Tib. 14, Lucan 61, Sen. trag. 59, Val. Fl. 44, Sil. 36, Stat. 171, Juv. 87, Mart. 120.

[99] For double enallage (cf. below, nn. 264, 265) in Ovid's elegies cf., e.g., *Am.* 3.7.21–22, *sic* **flammas** *aditura* **pias aeterna sacerdos**/*surgit et a* **caro fratre uerenda soror** and Bertini (1983) 234 ad loc., Thomamüller (1968); *Her.* 16.107, 18.133 and Kenney (1996) 98–99, 158 ad loc.

[100] Platnauer (1951) 108.

[101] Housman (1972) 140–41. On Hellenistic and earlier Greek precedents see Fordyce (1961) 331 on Catull. 66.18, Hollis (1990) 14 and n. 12.

[102] Cf. below for instances in *Met.* For an example of divergent views on the punctuation of hyperbata see McKeown 3:98 on *Am.* 2.5.38. Editorial commas sometimes have the effect of impaling a modern reader on one horn of a syntactical dilemma which the native Latin speaker would not have recognized. Cf. for instance the superfluous commas in some modern texts of the *Fasti* at 5.16, 183.

[103] Barsby (1973) 25–26.

[104] Knox (1995) 31; cf. n. 82 on *Her.* 3.56, "where the dislocation of *mecum* adds to Briseis' tone of indignation."

> ut tamen optarim fieri tua, Troice, coniunx,
>   inuitam sic me nec Menelaus habet

> But though I might desire to be your wife, Trojan, it is by no means
> against my will that Menelaus holds me,

Ovid could no doubt have written *sic non inuitam me Menelaus habet.*
Instead he chose to position *inuitam* more emphatically, and by asso-
ciating the negative (*nec = ne . . . quidem*) with Menelaus to impart a
significant nuance to Helen's attitude to the two men: "yes, I find
you attractive, but then Menelaus too is far from disagreeable to
me."[105] It is true that there are some instances of this figure for
which it is difficult to detect a plausible motive other than metrical
convenience, but even in these cases it is rarely that a reader with
a sensibly punctuated text whose Latin is good enough to take in
the sense of a two-line sentence *as a whole* will feel that the language
has been put under excessive strain.[106]

The question of how far in fact Ovid can perhaps be seen to
strain the language at times arises in an interesting way in connec-
tion with his innovatory treatment of the conjunctions *-que* and *nec.*
It may well be significant that in the latter case at least his lead was
not followed by later poets. We meet the first of these mannerisms
in the very first poem of the *Amores* (1.1.23–24):

> lunauitque genu sinuosum fortiter arcum
>   'quod'que 'canas, uates, accipe' dixit 'opus.'

> And manfully bending his curved bow against his knee[107] he said "Take
> this, poet, as something to sing about."

This trick of inserting the connective *-que* into the quoted speech
recurs throughout Ovid's work; it does not appear to have been
extensively imitated by his successors.[108] More idiosyncratic and pecu-

---

[105] Kenney (1996) 134 ad loc.

[106] It must not be assumed that the Latin poets were slaves to meter (Housman
(1972) 823).

[107] The operations of stringing and drawing the bow are conflated, a point not
made altogether clear by commentators; Martinon (1897) 206 ad loc. has a useful
note. On *opus* in this position (often in hyperbaton) see McKeown 2:26 ad loc., and
cf. above, n. 48.

[108] "The usage recurs occasionally in later Latin poets, perhaps most frequently
in Valerius Flaccus" (McKeown 2:26). Credit for first drawing attention to this
device belongs to Haupt ((1875–76) 3:510–12); cf. Marouzeau (1958) 104–5, Bömer
(1977) 305 on *Met.* 9.109.

liar to Ovid is what Housman described as "a natural sequel,"[109] the apportionment of the copulative and negative functions of *nec/neque* and *neu(e)* between narrative and quoted speech, as at *Her.* 16.83–84:

dulce Venus risit 'nec te, Pari, munera tangant
   utraque suspensi plena timoris' ait,

Sweetly Venus laughed and "Do not be moved, Paris," she said, "by either gift, full as it is of anxious fear,"

where *nec* stands for *et* "*ne.*" This usage is not only unique to Ovid but occurs only in *Heroides* 16 and 21,[110] the *Metamorphoses*, and the *Fasti*.[111] These particular divagations from normal or expected usage are significant as illustrating Ovid's quietly masterful way with Latin and its potentially flexible character (something to which conventional grammars often fail to do justice). However, as the very restricted take-up of them by later poets demonstrates, even such potentially useful contributions as these[112] to the economy of the Latin verse line could not be guaranteed to appeal to Ovid's successors.[113]

Ovid's exploitation of the figures of thought and speech in the classical repertory was, as might be expected, extensive and enterprising.[114] One in particular calls for notice as having evidently held a special attraction for him: "that quick-witted figure of speech,"[115] syllepsis. This is a form of expression in which the literal and the figurative are joined in syntactical wedlock, as in Horace's *iam galeam Pallas et aegida/currusque et rabiem parat* (*C.* 1.15.11–12), where the

---

[109] Housman (1972) 413.

[110] For its bearing on the date and authorship of the "double" epistles see Kenney (1979) 396, (1996) 21.

[111] *nec/neque: Her.* 16.83, 21.222, *Met.* 5.414, 9.131, 10.569, 11.263, *F.* 4.598; *neue* (an extension in effect of the common use of *neue = et, ne*): *Met.* 11.136. It appears that the idiom was first correctly explained by van Lennep (1812) 265; cf. Loers (1829) 395, Haupt (1875–76) 3:512, Housman (1972) 413–14. The further extensions at *Her.* 12.201–2 and Mart. 10.4.8 detected by Housman (1972) 414, 726 are respectively doubted and disallowed by Shackleton Bailey (1989) 142.

[112] They "jump[s] the gap between narrative and speech" (Fantham (1998) 44), so promoting the speed and flow of the verse.

[113] On other syntactical usages unique to Ovid see Kenney (1999a) 400 and n. 2; add, e.g., *attinet* + subj. at *Her.* 1.2 (Housman (1972) 1052–55, Knox (1995) 88), a construction which the copyists sank without trace in Ovid's MSS and which Housman rescued from a grammarian's citation.

[114] It is, predictably, Virgil who figures most prominently in Quintilian's examples of poetic rhetoric in action; his Ovidian examples are mostly from *Met.* Frécaut (1972) well illustrates the range and variety of Ovid's technique in this area.

[115] Fränkel (1945) 197.

abstract *rabiem*, as Nisbet and Hubbard note, imparts an unexpected edge to the expression.[116] Virgil's employment of syllepsis, as in *pariter . . . oculos telumque tetendit* (*Aen.* 5.508), is infrequent and relatively colorless;[117] he is rather given to a related figure, the more grammatically licentious zeugma, in which one part of an expression must be supplied from the other part, which is different, and may be actually opposed, in sense.[118]

Ovid made this figure peculiarly his own: "Syllepsis is pervasive in Ovid's writings."[119] In exploiting the ambiguities and imprecisions of language Ovid was doing what all poets do; the wit with which he mined this particular vein of rhetorical ore was unique to him, and his way of doing so reflects his way of viewing the physical world.[120] These are not tacked-on embellishments: "Il est impossible de relire les lettres de Didon, de Léandre et d'Héro, les épisodes de Callisto, d'Anna, et d'autres passages, sans être sensible à la valeur de ces zeugmas ou attelages, qui ne sont pas purs enjolivements surajoutés."[121]

We first encounter this figure in the *Amores*, in a form that he was to return to and vary repeatedly (*Am.* 1.7.15–16):

> talis periuri promissaque uelaque Thesei
> fleuit praecipites Cressa tulisse Notos.[122]

This was how Ariadne looked when she wept that the headlong south wind had carried off the sails and the promises of perjured Theseus.

Phyllis makes the same point but drives it home by alliteration (*Her.* 2.25–26):

---

[116] Nisbet and Hubbard (1970) 194, terming it zeugma: see below, n. 118. Their comment that "later the figure became chiefly mock-heroic and finally facetious" fails to do justice to Ovid's use of it.

[117] See Tissol (1997) 19 for the contrast with Ovid.

[118] For the distinction see Kenney (1971) 160, (1972) 40; and for a helpful discussion of the terminology see Frécaut (1969) 28–31. It was not observed by the ancient grammarians (Tissol (1997) 18–19, 219–20), but it is unfortunate that their successors continue to blur a practically useful differentiation (e.g., H–S 831–34). Instances of true zeugma in Ovid are elusive (Knox (1995) 30 n. 77): a possible instance at *Met.* 7.348–49, *cum uerbis guttura/abstulit.*

[119] Tissol (1997) 221 (with many examples), 220 (bibliography).

[120] Tissol (1997) 18–26, an enlightening discussion.

[121] Frécaut (1969) 41.

[122] See McKeown 2:172 ad loc., drawing attention to "an interestingly close precedent" at Callim. *AP* 7.272.1–2 (*HE* 1219–20): "Lycus of Naxos (N.B.) . . . saw his ship and his life destroyed together."

Demophoon, uentis et uerba et uela dedisti;
uela queror reditu, uerba carere fide.[123]

Demophoon, you gave both your words and your sails to the winds;
I complain that your sails have not returned and that your word has
not been kept.

An especially effective twist is imparted when one component, the
odd man out, is sandwiched, as in Ariadne's terrified reaction to the
epiphany of Bacchus (*AA* 1.551), *et color et Theseus et uox abiere puel-
lae*, or Apollo's reception of the news of Coronis's infidelity (*Met.*
2.600–602), *laurea delapsa est audito crimine amantis,/et pariter uultusque
deo plectrumque colorque/excidit.*[124] This is emphatically not cleverness for
its own sake. The phrasing is designed to convey the simultaneity
of these events, focusing attention on the central and significant detail:
the instant usurpation by Bacchus of Theseus's place in Ariadne's
world, the immediate substitution in Apollo's hand of the death-deal-
ing bow for the pleasure-giving plectrum. "O[vid]'s manner inspired
many imitators among later Latin poets, but rarely were any able
to approximate his wit in harmonizing thought and expression."[125]
Similarly with the figures of speech involving repetition: what may
at first sight look like a mere mannerism usually proves to serve a
poetic end.[126] The definition and function of the figure technically
termed polyptoton or *traductio*, the repetition for effect of differing
forms of the same word, was in practice flexible.[127] Here again Ovid
was freer than any other Latin poet, with an average of one instance
in 36 verses.[128] What is characteristic of him is the way in which
this is combined with other rhetorical devices, as in the celebrated
comment on the women at the games (*AA* 1.99): *spectatum ueniunt,
ueniunt spectentur ut ipsae*, where it is the joint effect of polyptoton,
anaphora, antithesis, and chiasmus that, with inimitable economy

---

[123] See Knox (1995) 30. Further variations on the theme at *Her.* 7.8, *Rem.* 286,
Tr. 1.2.17–18, *Met.* 8.134–35, *ES* 209.

[124] Cf. Galinsky (1975) 143 and n. 37. On Ovid's use of *excido* cf. Bömer (1969)
385 ad loc., *TLL* s.v. 1238.57–70 (this passage not in *OLD*).

[125] Knox (1995) 31 and n. 79. Cf. McKeown 2:172, contrasting Ovid's relatively
conservative use of this figure with Seneca's.

[126] Frécaut (1972) 58.

[127] Cf. Quint. *IO* 9.3.37, H–S 707–8; and for a comprehensive discussion see
Wills (1996) 188–268.

[128] Lucret. 1/41, Virg. 1/84, Tib. 1/98, Prop. 1/110 (H–S 708); cf. Kenney
(1993) 461.

and precision, points up the conceit.[129] This is then glossed and dri-
ven home by the following pentameter: *ille locus casti damna pudoris
habet.* The girls (well, perhaps) simply want to be admired; to the
poet and his predatory disciples all are fair game. One more example
may be taken from an embarrassingly copious supply (*Her.* 20.227–28):

> appeteres talem uel non iurata maritum;
>   iuratae uel non talis habendus erat.

> Even unsworn you should have sought such a husband; once you were
> sworn you should have accepted even a husband who was not such.

Anaphora, polyptoton, and chiasmus accentuate Cydippe's logical
and ethical dilemma as hammered home by her unscrupulous wooer.[130]

These last two examples illustrate what has been well described
as "the way in which the form of an elegiac couplet can impose its
personality on the rhetoric of a passage."[131] The first of them forms
the conclusion of a passage that has been admirably analyzed by
J.F. Miller. As he ends by remarking, "the intricate network of struc-
tures" which he maps out "is hardly unique either in [the *Ars*] or
in Ovidian elegy."[132] His analysis complements an excellent discus-
sion by McKeown of the many variations of structure in the cou-
plets of the *Amores*, and of the way in which within those structures
the meter is exploited for specific effects. Thus even in a potentially
monotonous passage such as the catalogue of rivers at 3.6.25–44,
Ovid is never predictable.[133]

V

From earliest times the elegiac couplet had been the vehicle *par excel-
lence* for epigram; and, as was noted above, the limitations imposed
on the couplet form by the Roman elegists, and by Ovid in partic-
ular, enhanced its tendency to lend itself to "effects of balance and

---

[129] Frécaut (1972) 48, Wills (1996) 393. The one word in the verse that does not
pack a punch, the grammatically essential but colorless *ut*, is neatly sandwiched
between its verb and the concluding *ipsae*; cf. *AA* 1.253, *proxima consiliis dominae sit
ut illa uideto.* On the postponement of subordinating conjunctions and relative pro-
nouns in the poets cf. Marouzeau (1949) 121–36.
[130] Kenney (1996) 214 ad loc.
[131] Hinds (1987a) 119.
[132] Miller (1997) 339.
[133] McKeown 1:108–23.

antithesis"[134] and to crisp, pointed, and sententious expression. For the didactic and admonitory mode in which much of Ovid's amatory poetry is couched it was tailor-made. Some examples from his swan-song in that genre, the *Remedia Amoris*:

> principiis obsta: sero medicina paratur,
> cum mala per longas conualuere moras (91–92).

> Resist it at the outset: it's too late to call in the doctor when diseases have had time to gain strength.

Hackneyed proverbial wisdom,[135] neatly and pointedly glossed: *sero . . . moras* enclose a sentence articulated by "the dispersed alliteration of the three key words *medicina, mala, moras*"[136] and fetching up on the paradoxical idea of a disease's "convalescing."

> dum furor in cursu est, currenti cede furori:
> difficiles aditus impetus omnis habet (119–20).

> While the frenzy is in full career, yield to it: to approach a violent impulse is never easy.

Syntactically the hexameter divides tidily into two at the main caesura; a double polyptoton with chiasmus simultaneously integrates it on the rhetorical level. The explanatory pentameter is a remarkable example of Ovid's way with words; *difficiles aditus* is lifted from Horace's encounter with the pest on the Via Sacra, where it is used to describe Maecenas as initially difficult of access, *difficiles primos aditus habet* (*Sat.* 1.9.56). The phrase and the emphasis of the couplet are transposed into the medical mode by *impetus*, whose meanings include both "(irrational) mental impulse" (*OLD* s.v. 5) and "attack" of disease (3b). The traditional description of the passion of love as *furor* (*OLD* 3) takes on the characteristics of a medical diagnosis.[137]

Ovid can be deceptively simple:

> nam quoniam uariant animi, uariabimus artes;
> mille mali species, mille salutis erunt (525–26).

> For since minds vary so much, we shall vary our methods; many are the sorts of disease, many the remedies.

---

[134] Du Quesnay (1973) 15.
[135] Cf. Theognis 1122–24, Otto (1890) s.v. *principium* 1.
[136] Henderson (1979) 53 ad loc., *OLD* s.v. *conualesco* 1b, 2.
[137] Cf. Pinotti (1988) 78 ad loc., comparing line 10 *quod nunc ratio est, impetus ante fuit* as the first hint of the metaphor of love that is the connecting thread of the *Rem.*

The elegiac couplet particularly lends itself to the device of "theme and variation,"[138] of which this is a typical example, the pentameter restating and giving a fresh twist to the sentiment of the hexameter. The ostensibly straightforward symmetry of each verse, with none of the interlocking structures that often articulate Ovid's couplets, is subtly diversified by the change from intransitive to transitive *uario* and the play of alliteration and assonance in the pentameter. Theme and variation can be seen at work on a slightly larger scale in

> quisquis amas, loca sola nocent: loca sola caueto;
>   quo fugis? in populo tutior esse potes.
> non tibi secretis (augent secreta furores)
>   est opus; auxilio turba futura tibi est (579–82).

> If you are in love, solitude is harmful; beware of solitude. What is the point[139] of running away? You are safer in a crowd. Seclusion is not what you need; that only increases passion. It is mixing with others that you will find[140] a help.

Ovid's point is, as often, underlined by repetition of the key words *loca sola*,[141] taken up and varied by *secrétis . . . secréta*, as *populo* is taken up by *turba* and *tutior* by *auxilio*. The precise correspondence in placing and meter of *in populo . . . potes* and *auxilio . . . tibi est* is offset by the variations in sense-pauses and metrical effects which lead up to the first-foot diaereses of the pentameters.

From Antimachus onwards the elegiac couplet had also been a vehicle for narrative poetry. In what was projected as Ovid's elegiac *chef d'oeuvre*, the *Fasti*, a poem which had it been completed would have matched the *Metamorphoses* in its scale and pretentions, narrative, as in his precursors in the genre, Callimachus's *Aetia* and the aetiological elegies of Propertius's Book 4, played a prominent part. Indeed for most readers it is probably the narrative element that comprises its chief attraction. The elegiac couplet as developed and perfected by Ovid was not on the face of it ideally suited to continuous story-telling, and its large-scale deployment in the *Fasti* presented him with a formidable technical challenge.[142] Inevitably the

---

[138] See below, n. 268.

[139] *quo* = "to what end" (*OLD* 2) rather than "whither?" (1). Cf. Prop. 2.30.1, *quo fugis a demens?* eqs., cit. Pinotti (1998) 261 ad loc.

[140] For this idiomatic use of the future indicative by Ovid cf. McKeown 2:37 on *Am.* 1.2.7–8, Kenney (1996) 107 on *Her.* 16.186.

[141] Henderson (1979) 113 ad loc.

[142] Cf. Miller (1997) 333. On the style and versification of the *Fasti* see Fantham (1998) 42–49 and Miller, chapter 6, below.

stories had to be told in a series of discrete or semi-discrete units of identical length. Single couplets could be combined into larger structures, but the subtle interplay of end-stopping and enjambment that distinguishes the hexameter as Ovid inherited it from Virgil was not available to the elegiac composer: "the fetters of the couplet allow the *Fasti* to succeed fully in one kind of narrative only, the swift and exciting."[143]

What could be achieved within these inherent limitations by way of variation in structure and tempo can be seen from analysis of a famous story, that of Lucretia (*F.* 2.721–852).[144] Of its 66 couplets 37 are singletons, i.e., are generally followed by an editorial full stop and are complete in sense and construction. Of the rest 18 are in two-couplet structures, 6 in three-couplet, and one in a four-couplet; the odd man out is 743–44, introducing a sequence of singletons. Continuity within these blocks of couplets is managed in various ways: the divide is straddled by the grammar (841–44) or by direct speech (734–35, 782–83, 808–9), by a subordinating structure (727–30, 775–78), by anaphora (763–66, 771–74), and by simple coordination (793–96, 797–800, 813–18, 825–28, 837–40). These variations notwithstanding, the total effect is inescapably staccato; the narrative unfolds in a series of stills, so to say, rather than in a continuous sequence.

Some of these vignettes are wonderfully effective. A particularly brilliant example is the quatrain in which Tarquin's lust is inflamed by his recollection of Lucretia at home (2.771–74):

> sic sedit, sic culta fuit, sic stamina neuit,
> iniectae collo sic iacuere comae,
> hos habuit uultus, haec illi uerba fuerunt,
> hic color, haec facies, hic decor oris erat.

That was how she sat, how she was dressed, how she spun the yarn, how her hair hung down her neck; that was how she looked, how she spoke; that was her complexion, her appearance, the beauty of her face.

---

[143] Wilkinson (1955) 280. On Ovid's "elegization" of *Aen.* 8.31–35 at *F.* 5.637–38 cf. Newlands (1995) 64 n. 33; for a comparison of his treatments of the Daedalus and Icarus story at *AA* 2.17–98 and *Met.* 8.152–259 see von Albrecht (1977) 63–77.

[144] Here a text will be required, but it should be noted that the punctuation on which what follows is predicated is not that of any one edition. On "the swift economy" of Ovid's treatment see Wilkinson (1955) 280–84.

Tarquin's obsession is vividly conveyed by the anaphora of *sic* and *hic*, with polyptoton and elegant alternation of gender. The couplet structure is skilfully varied: 771 articulated by phrases of 3, 5, and 6 syllables (tricolon crescendo), with assonance and interplay of ictus (*sédit . . . fúit . . . néuit*), 772 a flowing verse with enclosing word-order centered on *sic*, 773 a spondaic line with a more deliberative feel, divided at the main caesura, 774 again breaking out into obsession in the insistent *hic . . . haec . . . hic*, with another tricolon crescendo of 3 + 4 + 8 syllables.

There was no room in this style for the expansive descriptions proper to epic.[145] The scene of Proserpine's abduction, lovingly depicted at some length by Cicero (*Verr.* 2.4.107), which occupies 7½ lines in the *Metamorphoses* (5.385–91), is here polished off in two couplets (4.427–30); it is the catalogue of flowers (435–42) on which Ovid, in true Alexandrian fashion, spreads himself.[146] The couplet form lends itself especially to the playfulness which is never far below the surface, coming to the fore in passages such as that in which Numa pits his wits against Jupiter's and comes off best.[147] Chloris/Flora's account of her rape by Zephyr takes hardly less time to tell than it can have taken to happen (5.201–2):

> uer erat, errabam; Zephyrus conspexit, abibam;
>   insequitur, fugio; fortior ille fuit.

> It was springtime and I was rambling; Zephyrus caught sight of me, and I tried to get away; he pursued, and I fled; he was the stronger.

The accelerating tempo of events is neatly mirrored by the variations of tense[148] and the interplay of ictus in *errabam . . . abibam, insequitur, fugio . . . fuit*, the coincidence of the last three plus alliteration lending speed, insistence, and finality to the denouement; the understated *fortior ille fuit* almost connotes a shrug of semi-humorous res-

---

[145] See, e.g., Newlands (1995) 96–102 on the description of the Temple of Mars in the Forum Augustum.

[146] See Fantham (1998) 177 ad loc.

[147] Cf. Wilkinson (1955) 272.

[148] Cf. von Albrecht (1968), though his discussion perhaps understates the factors of metrical convenience and pure love of variety; it is, for instance, not easy to detect a consistent rationale for the kaleidoscopic alternations of imperfect, preterite, and present tenses at *AA* 1.103–30 (Livy 1.9.6–12 is perceptibly more restrained). It is interesting and perhaps surprising that Ovid does not affect the historic infinitive even in *Met.* (Maurach (1995) 62).

ignation. Similarly Mars, seeing Rhea Silvia asleep, wastes no time (3.21): *Mars uidet hanc uisamque cupit potiturque cupita*; and when she woke up she was, all unknowingly, pregnant—with Romulus (23–24):

> somnus abit, iacet ipsa grauis; iam scilicet intra
> uiscera Romanae conditor Vrbis erat.

Sleep left her, and she lay there feeling weighed down[149]—as well she might, seeing that already within her womb was the founder of the City.

Pregnant writing indeed. The episode is rounded off by an impish parenthesis (39–40):

> dixerat, et plenam non firmis uiribus urnam
> sustulit (implerat, dum sua uisa refert)—

She finished and feebly took up her full urn—for she had filled it while she was speaking—

—just in case you thought I'd forgotten![150] The almost insolent virtuosity of Ovid's handling of the couplet is perhaps at its most striking in the thirty-odd variations that he imparts to the familiar "dawn and dusk" topos.[151]

The "conciseness and concentration"[152] that distinguish the style of the *Fasti* did not greatly favor the cultivation of the affective, and there are no passages of sustained pathos in its narratives.[153] For examples of that we have to turn back to the *Heroides* and the monologues of Ariadne (10.7–58) and Hypermnestra (14.21–84). Both are too long to reproduce here, but the opening lines of the first offer a particularly fine example of the "delicacy and gentle effectiveness"[154] of Ovidian pathos at its best:

> tempus erat, uitrea quo primum terra pruina
> spargitur et tectae fronde queruntur aues.
> incertum uigilans ac somno languida moui
> Thesea prensuras semisupina manus—

---

[149] Bömer (1958) 142 ad loc. makes heavy weather of *grauis*. She feels "heavy," oppressed (*OLD* s.v. 7a), as well she might (*scilicet*), being gravid (2b) with Romulus, no less.

[150] For such "footnoting" parentheses cf., e.g., 4.517–18, 521.

[151] Cf. Fantham (1998) 123–24 on 4.165–66; in Book 4 alone we have 165–66, 179–80, 373–74, 389–90, 629, 679, 713–14, 721, 943–44.

[152] von Albrecht (1997) 1:805.

[153] Odd touches, it may be granted: cf., e.g., Fantham (1998) 43 and n. 83.

[154] Jacobson (1974) 218.

nullus erat! referoque manus iterumque retempto
    perque torum moueo bracchia: nullus erat! (*Her.* 10.7–12)

It was the time when the first glassy frost of morning is sprinkled over
the earth and under the leaves the birds begin their plaintive cheep-
ings. Between sleeping and waking I turned drowsily over and stretched
out my hands to embrace Theseus—he was not there! Again I stretched
them out[155] and again I tried, running my arms over the whole bed—
no Theseus!

Theseus's desertion of Ariadne was a favorite theme of poets and
painters; Ovid's treatment inevitably challenged comparison with that
in particular of Catullus in the *Peleus and Thetis*.[156] The comparison
is by no means to his disadvantage:

Ovid evokes, while Catullus ignores, the sense of situation, the atmos-
phere and mood of a place, the relationship between circumstances
and person, the reality of the inanimate, indeed, the reality of noth-
ingness, of alone-ness.[157]

It is this specificity that makes it easier to identify with Ovid's char-
acters than with those of any other Latin poet and that helps to
explain why he has always been the poets' poet.

When he wrote the *Fasti* Ovid's art was at the peak of its tech-
nical perfection; that the elegiac couplet could rise to real nobility
is demonstrated by the apologia for astronomy which makes a curi-
ously abrupt, and indeed anomalous,[158] appearance towards the begin-
ning of the poem (1.295–310):

Quid uetat et stellas, ut quaeque oriturque caditque,
    dicere? promissi pars sit et ista mei.
felices animae, quibus haec cognoscere primis
    inque domos superas scandere cura fuit!
credibile est illos pariter uitiisque locisque
    altius humanis exseruisse caput.
non Venus et uinum sublimia pectora fregit
    officiumque fori militiaeue labor,
nec leuis ambitio perfusaque gloria fuco
    magnarumque fames sollicitauit opum.

---

[155] *refero* here = "redirect" (*OLD* s.v. 14) rather than "draw back," as the trans-
lators have it. Planudes, interestingly, renders ἐπαναφέρω.
[156] Jacobson (1974) 213–27, Knox (1995) 233–35.
[157] Jacobson (1974) 221, in a rewarding appraisal.
[158] For the possibility that it was written at Tomis as part of the revision of the
poem begun there cf. Fantham (1985), Barchiesi (1997b) 177–80.

admouere oculis distantia sidera nostris
    aetheraque ingenio supposuere suo.
sic petitur caelum, non ut ferat Ossan Olympus
    summaque Peliacus sidera tangat apex.
nos quoque sub ducibus caelum metabimur illis
    ponemusque suos ad uaga signa dies.

Why should I not also tell of the risings and settings of the constellations? That too must be part of my undertaking. Blessed souls, who first took it on themselves to seek out these things and ascend to the home of the gods! We may well believe that they lifted their heads above this flawed human world. Their sublime spirits were not enfeebled by love or wine or public office or military duty; neither vain ambition nor gaudy glory nor hunger for great wealth ever troubled them. They brought the distant stars close to our sight,[159] and made the heavens subject to their intelligence. That is the way to reach heaven, not by piling Olympus on Ossa and Pelion above them for its peak to touch the highest stars. I too shall measure out the heavens under their guidance and allot their proper days to the wandering signs.

The richly allusive literary texture of this passage has been well discussed by Newlands.[160] Its structure is elegantly symmetrical: 1 + 1 + 4 + 1 + 1 couplets, with ring-composition:

295–96 Why not tell of the stars?
   297–98 Happy they who first climbed the heavens.
     299–306 Their virtue and achievements.
   307–8 That is the right way to climb to heaven.
309–10 I too then shall follow in their footsteps.

Within this framework the construction of the individual couplets is discreetly varied, but the overall tempo is measured and dignified.

---

[159] I.e., made us look at them more carefully; but E.H. Alton's *mentis* for *nostris*, "brought them into their mind's eye," is more pointed, making the couplet another example of theme and variation.

[160] Newlands (1995) 32–41. A little may be added. At line 309 *metabimur* may also = "shall traverse" (*OLD* s.v. 4), recalling Epicurus, who *omne immensum peragrauit mente animoque* (Lucret. 1.74); for the presence of Lucretius and Virgil in the passage see Newlands 34. One Virgilian echo is seemingly missed by the commentators: *felices animae* (297) is a literal quotation from the Sibyl's questions to Musaeus in the Underworld (*Aen.* 6.669). Virgil's heroes are located in a region *alta terra et caligine mersa* (6.267), whereas Ovid's ascend *in domos superas*. His *sic petitur caelum* thus implicitly confronts Virgil's *sic itur ad astra* (9.641) and his celebration of the triumphs of the intellect refutes Anchises' ranking of conquest and empire above art, oratory, and astronomy (6.847–53)—pointed indeed, if these words were written in exile. Cf. Barchiesi (1997b) 179–80.

If this is, as has been argued, a generic *prise de position* as well as an attempt to enlist the support of the astronomer-prince Germanicus,[161] it is a far cry from the slick Callimacheanism of the *Amores*.[162]

Metamorphoses

VI

Judgements on Ovid's style have tended to exemplify something of the facility which they purport to expose. Often he has in effect been criticized for not being Virgil. So Mackail speaks of "the tripping movement . . . into which [the hexameter] was metamorphosed . . . by the facile adroitness of Ovid."[163] Similarly Green's verdict that Ovid's verses are "under-enjambed" and "over-dactylic"[164] can only mean "compared with Virgil's."[165] Glover called them "often only elegiac couplets in disguise,"[166] a sentence echoed by Wilkinson,[167] though with an important qualification: for having duly quoted the famous criticism of Dryden that "Ovid with all his sweetness, has as little variety of Numbers and sound as [Claudian]: He is always as it were upon the Hand-gallop, and his Verse runs upon Carpet ground,"[168] he goes on to add the rider "Yet may not Ovid perhaps have been right, for the purpose in hand?"[169] That surely is the crux of the matter.

What was that purpose? Much ink has been spilt on the question whether the *Metamorphoses* is or is not an epic. von Albrecht's careful analysis of the surprisingly brief proem shows that Ovid's declared pretensions are those of an epic poet;[170] and Herter has rightly insisted

---

[161] Newlands (1995) 33–40, Barchiesi (1997b) 179.

[162] McKeown 1:32–37.

[163] Mackail (1950) lxxvii. Mackail's brief but trenchant discussion of Virgil's hexameter fails to receive due acknowledgement from Worstbrook (1965).

[164] Green (1960) 130.

[165] Green (1960) 129.

[166] Glover (1932) 191.

[167] Wilkinson (1955) 150.

[168] Now conveniently accessible, together with many other such verdicts, in the useful and entertaining compilation of Stroh (1969).

[169] Cf. Wilkinson's comparison of Virg. *G.* 4.463–69 with *Met.* 10.11–16 and his pertinent comment: "Virgil is concerned to create atmosphere by his rhythm, Ovid to get on with the story" (Wilkinson (1963) 131–32).

[170] von Albrecht (1961).

on the significance of the word *perpetuum* (1.4), with its oblique but unambiguous anti-Callimachean implication that the *Metamorphoses* was a single poem intended for continuous reading, and not merely a collection of epyllia.[171] There is of course in this attitude a touch of deliberate paradox, perhaps verging on defiance, since when all is said and done, the resemblance to the *Aetia*, meter apart, is immediately obvious; and whatever thematic architecture Ovid's ingenuity might devise or the percipience of modern critics detect, the poem is bound to appeal to most readers as a collection of stories. It is indeed, as von Albrecht has said, "an epos *sui generis*,"[172] and that uniqueness is, as he has also said, the decisive point. In setting out to write the *Metamorphoses* Ovid was attempting something for which, as he envisaged the undertaking, no precedents existed; and those readers who instinctively sense in the first four words of the poem, *in noua fert animus*, read autonomously, a proclamation by the poet to that effect are, I think, following a hint intended by him. However that may be, precisely what was he attempting? What is the special *genus* of which the *Metamorphoses* is sole representative? To this question very various answers have been returned. One critic sees the poem as an example of "Kollektivgedicht,"[173] another as an "anti-epic" protest,[174] another as a playful variation of epic,[175] another as an epic of love,[176] yet another as an epic of rape;[177] and I have myself elsewhere offered epic of *pathos*.[178] The search for a label may or may not be a profitable exercise;[179] the diversity of labels suggested at all

---

[171] Herter (1948) = (1968). Cf. Otis (1970) 332–34, Kenney (1976), Gilbert (1976), Myers (1994a) 1–5, Wheeler (1999) 8–30.

[172] Haupt-von Albrecht (1966) 1:486.

[173] Little (1970) 72. Little may have somewhat underrated the fundamental unity of the *Met.*, but he is right to insist (69 n. 6) that the style of the poem is dictated by a "difference of intent."

[174] Coleman (1971).

[175] Bernbeck (1967) 130: "spielerische Abwandlung des Epos." Bernbeck stresses (130–31) that the poem is a unity. Cf. Wilamowitz (1924) 1:243, "sein komisches Epos."

[176] Otis (1966) 334, 345; but see the new concluding chapter of (1970), interpreting the poem as a blend of "anti-epic" and "un-epic," of "iconoclasm and human sympathy" (374).

[177] Segal (1969) 93: "one may wonder if it is not rather an epic of rape. Its very subject, metamorphosis, implies violence." This of course raises the question whether or in what sense metamorphosis *is* the subject of the poem; cf. Kenney (1967) 51–52 on Viarre (1964), and see below, *sub fin.*

[178] Kenney (1968) 58. See now Hughes (1997) ix: "Above all, Ovid was interested in passion."

[179] On the fallacy of attempting to pin down *Met.* in terms of genre see Tissol (1997) 151–52.

events serves to emphasize the special character of the poem. However, there is one point on which the interpreters seem to be unanimous, and that is the dominant importance of narrative in the *Metamorphoses*, its status as what has been called "the very soul of the work."[180] To describe Ovid's verse medium as "a comfortable, well-sprung, well-oiled vehicle for his story"[181] is perhaps to relegate it to too subordinate and separate a role: the medium and the message can hardly be distinguished in quite the way suggested by this metaphor. Nevertheless, the idea of a vehicle is helpful as a reminder of the necessity for keeping this long poem moving and for sustaining its character as a *perpetuum carmen*. The reader of the *Metamorphoses* is always being carried on; the ingenious transitions from episode to episode, abused by Quintilian and variously criticized or justified by later critics,[182] are fundamentally a functional device (whatever extravagances Ovid may have committed in the application of it) to ensure a steady progress through the poem. Smoothness and speed are likewise the salient characteristics of Ovid's hexameter. Critics who merely miss in Ovid the weight, sonority, and expressiveness of Virgil are failing to recognize the great difference, not only between the two poets, but between their two undertakings.[183] The comparison with Virgil is by no means misguided; but it is illuminating precisely as it directs attention to this difference.

The existence and instant canonization of the *Aeneid* confronted all subsequent aspirants to epic honors with a most intractable problem. Of surviving Latin epicists only Ovid and Lucan can be said to have tackled it with originality and anything approaching success. It is relevant to bring in Lucan at this point because the very different nature of his attempted solution and of the stylistic means by which he executed it helps to illustrate the originality of both the *Metamorphoses* and the *Bellum Civile*. Both poems were brilliant essays in a modern, or contemporary, style of epic which might legitimately challenge comparison with Virgil, not on his own ground (which Ovid, who obviously admired him, must have seen to be impossible),[184] but on

---

[180] Little (1970) 71.

[181] Wilkinson (1963) 202.

[182] Quint. *IO* 4.1.77; Wilkinson (1958) 231–44, Frécaut (1968), Wheeler (1999) 122–25. Even their sometimes apparently arbitrary character is functional, reflecting the insecurity of Ovid's Heraclitean universe.

[183] Cf. Duckworth (1969) 73 on the "Greekness" of Ovid's meter compared with Virgil's.

[184] Lucan's challenge was to this extent on Virgil's own ground, that the *Bellum*

a new and independent footing. In material, structure, and intention Ovid's independence from Virgil is almost complete. In language it seems at first sight to be otherwise: for all Ovid's work is shot through and through with Virgilian reminiscences.[185] Closer analysis, however, shows that this is not a matter of straightforward borrowing and adaptation, but rather that what might be called a consistent and calculated process of denaturing has been at work. It is important to distinguish in Virgil's Latinity between its base, the "common style," as Quinn has called it,[186] which relates directly to the medium itself, the dactylic hexameter,[187] and what is specific and original to Virgil himself: his *callidae iuncturae*[188] and his management of the verse-period.[189] Virgil's penchant for "coining . . . expressive original phrases out of extremely elementary words,"[190] as seen in lines like *sensit laeta dolis et formae conscia coniunx* (*Aen.* 8.393) is something more than a trick of style; it is part and parcel of the allusive, ambiguous, and allegorical mode in which the *Aeneid* was composed. Ovid's diction is on the whole no more and no less plain than Virgil's; his use of it is infinitely more straightforward, because that straightforwardness was what the mode in which he was writing called for. Bömer's careful and perceptive analysis of this problem[191] perhaps fails to do full justice to its complexity when it speaks of the *debasement* of Virgil's diction by Ovid.[192] It would be more proper to say that Ovid restored to common currency what Virgil had temporarily taken out of general circulation. When, however, Bömer speaks of Ovid's "profaning" his original[193] the term may be accepted if it is understood in the sense of making generally available. Ovid's adaptations of Virgilian diction and phraseology (which are of course not confined to the *Metamorphoses*) are best seen as a

---

Civile best makes sense if read as in some measure an answer to the *Aeneid*, an "anti-*Aeneid*" in fact. Cf., e.g., Braund (1992) xlv–xlvi.

[185] Zingerle (1869–71) *passim*.

[186] See Quinn (1968) 375–84.

[187] Worstbrock (1963) 148: "Die Syntax der Poesie ist eine metrische Syntax." The remark, as was illustrated above apropos of Ovid's elegy, can be extended to cover diction.

[188] See Quinn (1968) 384–91, Wilkinson (1959) 181–92.

[189] Worstbrock (1963) chapter 3 "Vers und Syntax" (122–67).

[190] Camps (1969) 63; cf. Quinn (1968) 385.

[191] Bömer (1959) 268–88 = (1968) 173–202.

[192] "So schnell sind innerhalb einer Generation die Worte der hohen Dichtersprache abgenutzt, abgesunken" (Bömer (1959) 277 = (1968) 185).

[193] Bömer (1959) 279 = (1968) 158–59.

deliberate *vulgarization* (in the strict French sense) by a poet who was himself a master-craftsman. His contribution to the subsequent development of Latin poetry may be described as the perfection of a poetic *koine*,[194] a stylistic instrument which was freely manageable by writers of lesser genius. The Ovidian manner, as generations of clever English schoolboys have discovered, is imitable; Virgil's is not.[195]

Similar considerations apply to the management of the verse-period. The average length of Ovid's periods in the *Metamorphoses*, mechanically measured, probably does not differ significantly from that of Virgil's.[196] However, the important considerations here too are not quantitative but qualitative. Worstbrock's analyses have shown that the Virgilian sentence and period look forward to a concluding "Schwerpunkt."[197] The total effect is not thereby discontinuous, for Virgil always provides the necessary insurance against loss of momentum,[198] but it is (allowing for many designed variations in tempo) on the whole deliberate and measured. Ovid achieves his continuity and a markedly higher overall speed by a more even distribution of emphasis over his sentences; his periods less commonly build up in the Virgilian manner. Whereas, for instance, Virgil's "golden" lines always have a clearly observable climactic function, occurring at pauses in the action or exposition,[199] Ovid's are more usually in the nature of casual decoration.[200] His method may perhaps be described as one of reliance on a succession of small surprises and detours: the main thread of the narrative or argument is never lost sight of, but the reader is constantly entertained by unexpected changes of subject, parentheses, adversatives, antitheses, all illuminated and sus-

---

[194] On Ovid's role in shaping the diction of Silver Latin poetry see Galinsky (1989), Tarrant (1989); cf. Kenney (1998) 312, Dewar, chapter 11 below.

[195] Pighi (1959) 16: "tutta la dizione epica latina, dopo l'inimitabile Virgilio e l'imitabile Ovidio, è più ovidiana che virgiliana." Cf. Marmorale (1956) 199.

[196] Worstbrock (1963) 131 gives three verses as the average in Virgil's narrative, three to four verses elsewhere. My own rather crude count of *Met.* 3 (using the text of G.M. Edwards in Postgate (1894) 401–93 and simply counting the lines between the editor's full stops) gives an average of about 3.5 verses for the Ovidian period.

[197] Worstbrock (1963) 147, 150.

[198] Worstbrock (1963) 147–48.

[199] Worstbrock (1963) 162.

[200] This is not invariably the case, as some of the examples discussed below demonstrate. In Book 1 the golden lines at 100 and 112 are both obviously functional, but by Virgilian standards this is overdoing it. Cf. 1.528, 929, discussed in the text; also, e.g., 147 (not at the end of its period), 165, 265, 484.

tained by a verbal wit that from time to time broadens into a full-scale *tour de force*.[201]

VII

Virgil's vocabulary in the *Aeneid* has been exhaustively analyzed by Cordier,[202] and whatever reservations may be necessary about particular features of his discussion, it clearly emerges from it that the poet set himself to follow a *via media* between ordinary speech and cultivated literary diction.[203] Such innovations as were made by Ovid on the stock of epic diction inherited from his great predecessor were in the main unobtrusive, but appear to be designed to adapt it to the purposes of the "modern" epic, as I have described it, that the *Metamorphoses* was intended to be. Archaisms, of which Virgil himself had made extremely sparing use,[204] had little or no place in this type of poetry, and genuine archaisms, as distinct from poeticisms—i.e., old words that had won acceptance as part of the stock poetical vocabulary[205]—are very rare in the *Metamorphoses*. It is not always easy to decide how to classify certain isolated words or, what is more important, how to assess their intended effect. Ovid uses the word *actutum* (quickly) twice only, at *Her.* 12.207: *quos equidem actutum . . .* (in aposiopesis), and *Met.* 3.557, there in conjunction with two elisions, both unusual: *quem quidem ego actutum . . . cogam . . . fateri*. As a glance at *TLL* will show, *actutum* is an old word, frequent in Comedy and occurring also in the fragments of Republican Tragedy; it is used once by Virgil (*Aen.* 9.255). If, as is at least possible, Ovid's treatment of the Pentheus story owes something to Pacuvius,[206] *actutum* may have been intended as *color tragicus* quite as much as *color epicus*. It is difficult to guess how much impression a single word can have

---

[201] A good summary characterization at Bernbeck (1967) 78. On surprise as an important element in the narrative of *Met.* see Tissol (1997) Index s.v. narrative, disruption of.

[202] Cordier (1939).

[203] Cf. Wilkinson (1959) 185–56.

[204] Quint. *IO* 8.3.24.

[205] Such as, for instance, *extemplo*, used by Ovid ten times, only in *Met.* and thus marginally more strictly than by Virgil, who uses the word once in the *G.* as well as fourteen times in the *Aen.* (cf. Austin (1971) 54 on *Aen.* 1.92). Contrast Livy, with 370+ instances.

[206] D'Anna (1959) 220–26, Otis (1970) 400–401.

made even on an alert reader, but this would not be the only instance in Ovid of such an allusion.[207] What is clear is that his use of "poet-icisms" is extremely restrained: using as a convenient basis Cordier's catalogue of what he (somewhat loosely)[208] classifies as Virgilian archaisms we find:

(1) Some obviously useful and not obtrusively "poetic" words avoided by Ovid for no very clear reason: examples are *celero* (6 times[209] in the *Aeneid*), *fluentum* (3), *loquella**,[210] *pauperies*.[211]

(2) Some more obviously "poetic" words not used by him: *cernuus*, *flictus*, *illuuies*, *intempestus*, *obnubo*, *pernix*.

(3) Some "poetic" words used once only in *Aeneid* and *Metamorphoses* by both authors: *dius*,[212] *incanus*, *properus*, *sentus*, *suboles*, *tremebundus*; cf. *uirago* (once in *Aeneid*, twice in *Metamorphoses*).

These are no more than straws in the wind. A clearer picture of Ovid's policy as regards specifically poetic or epic diction can be obtained from studying his use of compound adjectives. That this class of word was recognized as posing a particular problem in Latin is evident from the well-known discussion of Quintilian (*IO* 1.5.65–70). If Cordier's lists are again taken as a basis[213] we find:

(4) Some compounds used by both poets in *Aeneid* and *Metamorphoses*: *aeripes*,[214] *alipes* (2, 3)*, *armiger* (6, 5), *arquitenens* (1, 2), *bicolor* (2, 3), *bicornis* (1, 3)†[215]*, *biforis**, *biformis* (2, 5)*, *biiugus* (8,[216] 1), *bimembris* (1, 2)*, *caelicola* (8, 2), *corniger* (1, 6)*, *fatidicus* (3, 2)*, *fatifer* (2, 2)*, *grandaeuus* (1, 3)†*, *horrifer* (1, 3), *indigena* (2, 7)*, *laniger* (4, 4)†*,

---

[207] See, e.g., Jacobson (1968), White (1970) (Ennius); Hollis (1970) xxiv (Accius).

[208] Sandbach (1940) 198.

[209] Where no figure is given in these lists, the word occurs once only.

[210] * = occurs in Ovidian corpus outside *Met.*

[211] *paupertas* is not used by Virgil, three times (once in *Met.*) by Ovid.

[212] Accepting Heinsius's conjecture at *Met.* 4.537.

[213] For this purpose I have conflated the two lists at 40–41 ('archaisms') and 46 ("coinages"). Defects in Cordier's classification (Sandbach (1940)) are of no moment for our present purpose.

[214] At *Her.* 6.32, 12.93 read, with Heinsius, *aenipedes*. See above, n. 80.

[215] † = occurs in Virgilian corpus outside *Aen.* Comparison of the respective incidence of † and * (above, n. 210), when due allowance is made for the difference in bulk, offers some guide to the "purity" of the attitudes of the two poets to epic diction.

[216] Including *biiugis* at 12.355; the variation in declension can only be ascribed to the demands of euphony.

letifer (2, 5)*, *longaeuus* (14,1)*, *magnanimus* (12,4)†*, *nauifragus, nubigena* (2, 2), *odorifer, pacifer, pestifer* (1, 5)*, *quadriiugus* (2,[217] 1)†*, *quadrupedans* (2, 1), *saetiger* (3, 3)*, *sagittifer, semianimis* (5, 4)*, *semifer* (2, 2), *semihomo, seminex* (5, 1)*, *semiuir* (2, 1)*, *septemplex* (1, 2)*, *somnifer* (1, 2), *soporifer, terrificus* (3, 1), *trisulcus*†*, *uulnificus* (1, 2).

(5) Some compounds used by Virgil in *Aeneid* but not by Ovid in *Metamorphoses: aequaeuus* (2), *aliger* (2),[218] *Appenninicola, armipotens* (5)*, *armisonus, auricomus, bellipotens, bifrons* (2), *bilinguis, bilix, bipatens* (2), *biremis* (2), *biuius,*[219] *caelifer, centumgeminus, caprigenus, conifer, cornipes* (2)*, *fumifer* (2), *Graiugena* (2), *horrificus* (3), *horrisonus* (2), *ignipotens* (7), *legifer*, *luctificus, malesuadus, malifer, mortifer*, *noctiuagus, oliuifer*, *omnigenus, omniparens, Phoebigena,*[220] *pinifer* (2)*, *primaeuus* (3), *quadrifidus*†, *regificus, septemgeminus, siluicola*, *sonipes* (3), *tergeminus* (2)*, *tricorpor, trifaux, trilix* (3), *Troiugena* (3), *turicremus**, *turriger* (2)*, *ueliuolus**, *uersicolor**, *uitisator, umbrifer, unanimus* (3).

(6) Some compounds used by Ovid in *Metamorphoses* but not by Virgil in *Aeneid* (except where otherwise noted these appear for the first time in Ovid):[221] *amnicola*‡, *anguicomus, anguifer* (Propertius), *anguigena*‡, *anguipes, Appenninigena, armifer* (2)*, *aurigena, bifidus, bifurcus* (Livy), *bimaris* (4)* (Horace), *bimater, binominis** (Plautus?), *bipennifer* (2)*‡, *bisulcus* (2) (Lucretius, al.), *caducifer* (2)*‡, *centimanus** (Horace), *Chimaerifer*‡, *circumfluus* (3), *circumsonus, clauiger* (3)*,[222] *colubrifer, consonus* (2)* (Cicero), *falcifer** (Lucretius), *faticinus* (2)‡, *Faunigena, flammifer* (4)* (Ennius), *flexipes*‡, *florilegus*‡, *frugifer** (Ennius, Cicero, Livy), *frugilegus*‡, *fumificus* (Plautus), *gemellipara**‡, *glandifer* (Lucretius, Cicero), *granifer**‡, *herbifer**‡, *Ianigena*‡, *ignifer* (2)[223] (Lucretius), *ignigena*‡, *imbrifer* (Virgil†), *Iunonigena*‡, *laborifer* (2), *lanificus** (Tibullus), *Latonigena*‡, *Lemnicola*‡, *lentiscifer*‡, *liniger**, *luctisonus*‡, *magniloquus, mellifer, monticola*‡, *multicauus*‡, *multifidus* (2), *multiforus, nubifer**, *opifer* (2),

---

[217] Including *quadriiugis* at 10.571; see preceding n.

[218] *aliger uaria lectio* at *F.* 4.562 (*alifer*); cf. below (6) s.v. *armifer*.

[219] In the phrase *in biuio* also at *Aen.* 9.238, Ov. *Rem.* 486.

[220] Ovid affects *Phoebeius* (4x), not used by Virgil. On his predilection for proper adjectives ending in *-ius* and *-eius* cf. Linse (1891) 24–25; so far as those in *-eius* are concerned, metrical considerations were clearly paramount.

[221] Cf. Linse (1891) 39–40, 42–47, Draeger (1888) 4–6.

[222] In *Met.* = "club-bearing;" at *F.* 1.228 (of Janus) = "key-bearing."

[223] But at 2.392 there is a strong case for reading *ignipedum* (so Tarrant in OCT, forthcoming). The evidence of Stat. *Theb.* 1.27, *ignipedum frenator equorum*, can admittedly cut both ways (Tarrant (1989)) but the form of the gen. pl. *igniferum* is very improbable for Ovid.

palmifer* (Propertius), *papyrifer**‡, *penatiger*‡, *pinniger** (Lucretius),
portentificus, puerperus (adj.), *racemifer* (2)*‡, *ruricola* (4)*, *rurigena*‡,
sacrificus (3)*, *salutifer* (3)*, *saxificus**, *securifer*‡,[224] *semicaper**‡, *semicre-*
mus‡, *semideus* (subst.) (2)‡,[225] *semilacer*‡, *semimas* (2)* (Varro), *septemfluus*
(2)‡, *serpentigena*‡, *sexangulus, spumiger*[226] (Lucretius), *squamiger* (Lucretius,
Cicero), *terrigena* (4)* (Lucretius), *triceps* (Cicero), *tricuspis*‡, *tridenti-*
fer‡, *tridentiger*‡,[227] *trifidus, triformis* (3) (Horace), *uaticinus* (Livy), *uelifer*
(Propertius), *uenefica* (adj.) (?),[228] *uenenifer*.

These lists provide the material for some simple but enlightening
deductions of general relevance to Ovid's lexical choices in the
Metamorphoses. The proportion of identifiably "poetic" or "epic" words
in his vocabulary does not seem to differ substantially from that in
Virgil's. He does not go out of his way to avoid compounds already
used in the *Aeneid* and therefore, so to say, sanctified, but he also
innovates on his own account with moderate freedom. His innova-
tions are in the main themselves traditional in so far as they conform
to types already well established in poetic usage, with a predominance
of verbal suffixes in *-cola, -gena, -ficus, -fer, -ger*, etc. and numerical
prefixes in *bi-, tri-, centi-, multi-, semi-*, etc. Formations on the model
of *anguicomus, anguipes, flexipes*, etc. are in a small minority.[229] In a
poem of some 12,000 verses this relatively small number of poeti-
cisms cannot impart any very marked coloration, and (especially if
one takes into account other features of Ovid's vocabulary, discussed
below) it is probable that their metrical convenience was at least as
important to him as their expressive value. Both prefixes and suffixes
were a valuable source of short syllables and helped in the unob-
trusive production of dactyls. Strategically placed, the longer com-
pounds also contribute to the smoothness, fluency, and speed that
was necessary to Ovid's narrative, as was noted above apropos of
those of the metrical shape ∪–∪∪, which yield a rapid rhythm affected

---

[224] *securiger* at *Her.* 4.117 and later poets.

[225] *semideus* (adj.)* and in later poets.

[226] *Varia lectio, spumifer*, cf. Stat. *Achill.* 1.59.

[227] *Varia lectio, tridentifer*.

[228] *Varia lectio* at 14.365; *preces . . . precantia*, though the modern vulgate, is difficult
to swallow. The adjectival use of *uenefica* is analogous to that of *puerpera* (cf. n. 81)
above.

[229] In this respect he does not follow the example set by his admired Lucretius,
who compounded with great freedom (Bailey (1947) 1:133–34), but shows himself
an Augustan of the Augustans. Cf. Austin (1971) 88 on Virg. *Aen.* 1.224.

by Ovid much more than by Virgil,[230] or, when used in oblique cases, after a trochaic caesura in the first foot, so filling out the first half of the verse and creating "tension," i.e., the expectation of a noun in agreement to follow, and hence again contributing rapidity.[231]

These metrical considerations are relevant to another class of compound words in the formation of which Ovid exercised some freedom, that of verbs and participles (or words of participial form).[232] For instance, the compound *defrenatus*‡ was clearly coined by Ovid to fit the verse in the scene in which Neptune unleashes the rivers to flood the earth: *fontibus ora relaxant/ et defrenato uoluuntur in aequora cursu* (1.281–82). Here however there are other factors at work besides the purely metrical: the development of an image of racing horses begun at 1.280 (*totas inmittite habenas*) and expressiveness in the spondees of *defrenato*, suggesting a pause while the mass of waters builds up before sweeping resistlessly on to the sea in the following dactyls. Even more remarkable are the double compounds, of which one perhaps deserves particular notice. Into his account of the metamorphosis of Ceyx and Alcyone, one of the most poignant passages of the poem, Ovid inserts a short *ecphrasis*, skilfully positioned so as to offer the least possible obstruction to the current of the narrative:[233]

> adiacet undis
> facta manu moles, quae primas aequoris iras[234]
> frangit et incursus quae praedelassat aquarum (11.728–30).

Right by the waves was a man-made breakwater, which took the first shock of the angry sea and wore out beforehand the oncoming waters.

The unique *praedelasso*‡[235] is finely descriptive in itself and also contributes to the idyllic atmosphere of calm after storm in which the sufferings of the tormented pair find release:

---

[230] See Lee (1953) 36; cf. above, III and nn. 74–82.

[231] Cf. above, n. 80.

[232] Cf. Linse (1891) 48–51, 52–56.

[233] It is worth pausing to point out how this result is achieved: note (*a*) the change of subject at the bucolic diaeresis of 728; (*b*) the closeness of the enjambment between 728–29, 729–30; (*c*) the change back to the original subject at the beginning of 731; (*d*) the placing of the verbs *ait, adiacet, insilit*. Such techniques are fundamental to Ovid's use of parenthesis: see below, n. 273.

[234] *iras* recc., Heinsius: *undas* codd. The repetition *undis ... undas* is quite pointless and cannot be ascribed to Ovid: cf. above, n. 228.

[235] *delasso* does not appear to have been an especially "poetic" word: it was used before Ovid by Plautus and Horace (*Sat.*), after him by Manilius and Martial.

tum iacet unda maris: uentos custodit et arcet
Aeolus egressu praestatque nepotibus aequor (11.747–48).

> Then [sc. during the "halcyon days"] the waves are at rest, for Aeolus keeps the winds close, forbidding them to emerge, and provides for his descendants a level ocean.

The rarity of such formations in Latin (for so far as I am aware this possibility was not much exploited by later poets) must have enhanced their effect on the Roman ear.

An especially rich category of Ovidian coinages and *hapax legomena* is that of participles compounded with the negative prefix *in-*.[236] Like many of the other compound words discussed these are often long, but they do not merely serve to fill up the line: they can be used with widely differing effect. One may contrast the contributions made to the movement of the verse by *inobseruatus** and *indeuitatus*‡ in the same story. The first occurs in a piece of fast-moving, relatively colorless "linking" narrative:

> pulchrior in tota quam Larisaea Coronis
> non fuit Haemonia: placuit tibi, Delphice, certe,
> dum uel casta fuit uel inobseruata, sed ales
> sensit adulterium Phoebeius *eqs.* (2.542–45).

> In the whole of Thessaly no girl was more beautiful than Coronis of Larissa: you certainly, Apollo, thought so, as long as she was faithful—or unwatched. But the bird of Phoebus discovered her infidelity...

There is enjambment between lines 542–43 and 544–45, and only the lightest of pauses at the end of 543 (since *certe*, though pointed, is not strongly emphatic); and the placing of *inobseruata* ($\smile$–––$\smile$) in the penultimate position in the line is managed so as to convey a characteristically Ovidian point while not impeding the movement of the verses. That point depends for its effect, not only on the sense, but on the greater length of the word that complements *casta*; but the word itself, like the diction of the whole passage (at least as far as 549) is colorless, as its function in the context requires it to be. Clearly Ovid coined *inobseruatus* to perform a specific function in this passage, which it does with extreme efficiency. The second word occurs in a narrative sequence which is also fast moving, but in this case "pathetic," with a more colorful vocabulary effectively deployed:

---

[236] Cf. Linse (1891) 49–50 and above, n. 78.

laurea delapsa est audito crimine amantis,
et pariter uultusque deo plectrumque colorque
excidit, utque animus tumida feruebat ab ira,
arma adsueta rapit[237] flexumque a cornibus arcum
tendit et illa suo totiens cum pectore iuncta
indeuitato traiecit pectora telo (2.600–605).

His laurel wreath slipped from the god's head as he heard of his
beloved's offense,[238] and in one moment his expression changed, he
dropped his plectrum, and his face went white. His heart swelling with
rage, he snatched up his familiar weapon, strung his bow, and into
the breast that so often had been pressed to his he sent deep the arrow
that cannot miss.

Ovid sketches in the god's reaction to the news by focusing atten-
tion on externals: and his consternation is neatly conveyed in his
favorite figure, syllepsis.[239] There is enjambment between lines 601–2,
603–4 (note the position of the verbs *excidit, tendit*), and 604–5; and
the single subordinate clause in 602 retards the narrative just enough,
and no more, to emphasize that Apollo's consternation is instantly
succeeded by a new emotion, anger. This swift period, packed with
emotion and incident, is suddenly slowed down and, so to say, stopped
in its tracks by the four-word[240] last verse with its enclosing word-
order (cf. 282 quoted above): **indeuitato** *traiecit pectora* **telo**. Apollo's
precipitate action, which he is immediately to regret (612, *paenitet
heu! sero poenae crudelis amantem*), is finished and irrevocable. Again, if
Ovid had been content to use existing epic diction, the phrase *non
euitabile telum*, which he does in fact use later in the poem (6.234),
or some similar variant (cf. 3.301, *ineuitabile fulmen*), lay ready to hand
on the model of Virgil's *ineluctabile tempus* (*Aen.* 2.324) or *inexorabile
fatum* (*G.* 2.491).[241] Instead he chose to coin the strong and majestic
indeuitatus for the particular effect that he wanted.

Other features of Ovid's diction may be reviewed more briefly.
In general it may be said that they were all directed to extending,
within the limits of linguistic and literary propriety (i.e., without

---

[237] *rapit* recc., Heinsius: *capit* codd. The tempo of the narrative imperatively
demands the more violent verb.

[238] In spite of *amantem* at 2.612 I believe that the older interpreters were right in
taking *amantis* here as referring to Coronis and not to Apollo.

[239] Cf. above, nn. 115–121.

[240] An effect of which Ovid is fond: Winbolt (1903) 228.

[241] Cf. Zingerle (1869–71) 2:112; on Ovid's predilection for adjj. in *-ilis* cf. below.

substantially trenching on either the colloquial or the archaic or the
hyperpoetic resources of Latin) the poetical *koine* that in his amatory
works he had already gone a long way towards establishing as what
might be called a standard literary dialect of Latin.[242] Most of his
predilections are obviously dictated by the desire to make his verse
more smooth and dactylic: e.g., adjectives in *-ilis*, neuter nouns in
-men,[243] and above all Greek proper names. As a source of new poet-
ical vocabulary borrowings from Greek had been ruled out by the
common consent of the Augustan poets (Horace's remarks on the
subject are sufficiently well known), and in the *Metamorphoses* Ovid
shows himself predictably restrained.[244] With proper names, in con-
trast, he is extremely lavish. This, in a poem which takes a wide
sweep through Greek mythology, was of course to be expected; and
Ovid was as sensitive as any of his predecessors or successors to the
emotive or purely musical effects of names.[245] What particularly
deserves remark is the way in which, as with the compounds already
discussed, his diction is engineered to smooth and accelerate the
verse. Thus his evident preference for adjectival forms in *-is, -idis/os*
over the alternatives available must be largely due to the metrical
utility of the endings *-ida, -idis/os, -ide, -ides, -idas*.[246]

    As in the elegies, adjectival forms of the same name are freely
and innovatively varied to suit the meter:[247] *per Achaeidas‡ . . . urbes*
(3.511, al.), *Achaica dextera* (12.70), *inter Achaeiadas‡ . . . matres* (*Her.* 3.71);
Acheloiadum . . . Sirenum (14.87–88), *Acheloides* (5.552), *Acheloia . . . Calliroe*
(9.413–14, al.); *arma Aetola* (14.528, al.), *Aetolide‡ Deianira* (*Her.* 9.131),
Aetolius heros (14.461); *Cephisias‡ ora* (7.438), *Cephisidas‡ undas* (1.369),

---

[242] See Bednara (1906) *passim*.

[243] Ovid's freedom in coining such words (Linse (1891) 31–32) is reminscent of
Lucretius: cf. Bailey (1947) 1:134–35.

[244] Of the instances collected by Linse (1891) 8–14 (most of which are taken from
the *Halieutica*, which is not by Ovid) only a handful merit remark: *canna* (8) (but cf.
Adnot. super Lucanum p. 184 Endt); *harpe* (569, 170), *vox propria* of Perseus's weapon;
moly (14.292); and some names of plants and animals such as *morus; ciris, echidna,
epops, haliaeetos, hyaena*.

[245] See, e.g., Wilkinson (1955) 235–36 quoting *Met.* 2.217–26; and cf. also, e.g.,
11.194–98, *ultus abit Tmolo liquidumque per aera uectus/angustum citra pontum Nepheleidos
Helles/Laomedonteis Letoius adstitit aruis:/dextera Sigei, Rhoetei laeua profundi/ara Panomphaeo
uetus est sacrata Tonanti*. On *Tonans = Iuppiter* see Bömer (1969) 78.

[246] Cf. the almost "formulaic" use of *Asis‡* in *Asida terram* (5.648), *Aside terra* (9.448);
and cf. Kenney (1996) 250–51.

[247] As in the corresponding list for the elegies (above, III), only cases of three or
more variants are recorded. For additional examples see Bömer (1976) 303–4 on
Met. 5.303.

Cephisius‡ (3.351); *Cytherea* (10.640, al.), *Cytheriacis . . . aquis* (*Her.* 7.60, al.), *Cythereiadas*‡ *. . . columbas* (15.386), *Cythereide natum* (4.288), *Cythereius heros* (13.625, al.); *proles Letoia*‡ (8.15, al.), *Letoidos . . . arua* (7.384, al.), *Letois . . . aris* (6.274, al.),[248] *Latonia* (1.696, al.); *Minyeia*‡ *proles* (4.389), *Alcithoe Minyeias*‡ (4.1), *Minyeides*‡ (4.32, al.); *Sidoniae comites* (3.129, al.), *Sidonida nomine dicunt* (2.840, al.), *Sidonis inque pyra . . .* (14.80, al.), *Sidonius hospes* (3.129, al.);[249] *Symaetheas*‡ *. . . aquas* (*F.* 4.472), *nympha . . . Symaethide*‡ *cretus* (13.750), *Symaethius heros* (13.879); *Titania* (1.395, al.), *Titaniacis*‡ *. . . draconibus* (7.398), *Titanidos . . . Circes* (13.968, al.); *Tritonia* (2.783, al.), *Tritoniaca*‡ *. . . harundine* (6.384, al.), *Tritonida . . . arcem* (2.794, al.).

In spite of this apparent profusion of forms it becomes clear when the manner of their employment is considered that a principle something like that of formulaic economy is here at work. The same principle can be detected in Ovid's employment of some common nouns and adjectives. Thus his favored formations in *-men*, previously referred to, are used for choice in the ablative singular and accusative plural, where they provide a dactyl ending in an open vowel.[250] Similarly his abstract fourth declension substantive formations in *-us*, of which he is a fancier in a small way,[251] occur mostly in the dative and ablative plural, providing a dactyl ending in *-s*.[252] When variant forms of the same word are employed we have in effect a composite declension: *conamine* but *conatibus*, *hortamine* but *hortatibus*, *compagine* but *compagibus*.

Such devices as these for enlarging the compass of the poet's linguistic resources were not invented by Ovid or practiced only by him; what is new and peculiar to him is the unobtrusive efficiency[253]

---

[248] Ovid will have followed the Greek spellings (cf. Kenney (1996) 234 on *Her.* 21.153); his editors usually represent him as unable to make up his mind between *Le-* and *La-*.

[249] The prosodic variations are Virgilian.

[250] The figures for *Met.* (of instances, not of individual words) are: nom. sing. 2, acc. sing. 6, gen. sing. 1, abl. sing. 23 (of which *uelamine* accounts for 2); nom. pl. 5, acc. pl. 26 (*uelamina* 11). Note the variant forms *solacia* (*saepius*), *temptamenta* (2), *irritamenta*, *uelamenta*; cf. Hollis (1970) 128 on *Met.* 8.729, Austin (1971) 198 on *Aen.* 1.649.

[251] Linse (1891) 28–29; Lucretius is much less restrained (Bailey (1947) 1:135, Perrot (1955)).

[252] Dat. *conatibus, cruciatibus, narratibus, saltatibus, uenatibus, uictibus* (+ *uictu*); abl. *adflatibus* (+ *adflatu* 3), *hortatibus* (2), *iactatibus, latratibus* (4) (+ *latratu* 3, *latratus* acc.), *suspiratibus, uenatibus* (2) (+ *uenatu* 2), *ululatibus* (5) (+ *ululatu* and note 11.17, *Bacchei ululatus*).

[253] More material in Linse (1891); the examples quoted here may suffice to make the point.

with which he applied them to the creation of the copious and limpid style—a transmitting rather than, as with Virgil, a refracting medium— which he saw as appropriate for the *Metamorphoses*. In his exploita- tion of these possibilities he resembles (though he is more restrained) Lucretius more closely than any of his other predecessors. This is perhaps not surprising, for Ovid, intelligent and impatient of the obscure, was temperamentally equipped to respond to the magnificent and unequivocal clarity of the Lucretian message,[254] to appreciate the masterful handling of the language which made that clarity pos- sible, and to adapt the lessons learned from Lucretius to his own purposes.

VIII

Ovid was termed by R.S. Conway "a chartered libertine in Gram- mar."[255] This summary judgement may be allowed to stand if it is understood to refer to the ordering of words in the sentence. Ovid does not seem to me to strain the Latin language as, in their different ways, do Virgil or Propertius or Lucan: his case-usage, for instance, though flexible and versatile, cannot be called either difficult or markedly licentious.[256] So too his use of "poetic" singulars and plu- rals, given that the latter especially offer an easily available source of extra short syllables, rarely amounts to abuse;[257] where it may seem to verge on doing so, the motive is plain, to assist rapidity. So within the space of three verses Hyacinthus's wound is now plural, now singular (10.187–89). That most readers of the *Metamorphoses*, unless they happen to be grammatical lepidopterists, with net and killing-bottle at the ready as they read, do not notice such things is the best possible index of Ovid's linguistic mastery. The same is for

---

[254] Boyancé (1963) 213.

[255] Conway (1900) 358.

[256] Cf. Hau (1884). His usage is in general bolder in *Met.* than in his other works (Hau (1884) 141–42). Some idea of the respective freedom of the Latin poets can be obtained from comparing entries in the index of that great museum of syntac- tical specimens, Bell (1923).

[257] Herr (1937) 30: "the nominative and accusative cases of neuter plural nouns are not the chief source of Ovid's . . . additional short syllables;" and cf. above, III *sub fin.* Consideration of a verse such as 1.181, *talibus inde modis ora indignantia soluit,* shows that a purely mechanical approach does not reveal anything like the whole truth.

the most part true of his use of hyperbaton. His most striking instances, as has been noted above, occur in the elegiac works;[258] those which are found in the *Metamorphoses* are not usually disturbing "provided," as Postgate remarks, "that the words are read and not simply surveyed;" indeed a reader who is moderately well accomplished in Latin is unlikely to notice, unless halted and admonished by (superfluous) editorial commas, that he is confronted with hyperbaton in

non mihi quae duri colerent pater arua iuuenci
lanigerosue greges, non ulla armenta reliquit (3.584–85).

My father left me no land to be tilled by patient oxen, no sheep, no cattle.

The commentators, displaying it may be unusual tact, in fact offer no remarks on the word-order, which is in a sense a compliment to the poet; but in a discussion such as this it does deserve remark for its unobtrusive functional efficiency. In their context, in which of course they must be read, the verses emphasize that the family's only resource was fishing: this is done by using the familiar technique of negative enumeration. What comes of this technique when it is used heavy-handedly can be seen in Lucan;[259] here the touch is as light as is consistent with making the point. Grammatically the sentence is articulated by the repeated *non* (anaphora = copula), and the combined effect of the word-order and the meter is that the two cola, though disparate in length, are equivalent in weight. The rapid dactyls of 584–85[a] carry the reader on to the slow spondees of 585[b], and the first *non, pater*, and *arua* all look forward to the verb *reliquit* which completes both syntax and utterance. Conversely, *ulla* must be read *apo koinou*, qualifying the first *non* and and also connoting *ullos* sc. *greges* (cf. 2.109, cited below). Dissected in this laborious way, the structure sounds complicated and difficult; but read as a single syntactical grouping[260] it offers no impediment to understanding because the relationship of the syntactical elements, which is independent of the order in which they occur, cannot be in doubt. Occasionally in

---

[258] Two especially distinguished by Postgate (1916) 145–46 belong not to Ovid but to the unknown poet of the *Somnium* (*Am.* 3.5).

[259] *BC* 2.350–80; cf. Heitland's remarks at Haskins (1887) lxxii, Marouzeau (1946) 259–60, but see also Bramble (1982) 544–57 on the "negation antithesis" as a cardinal element in Lucan's poetic strategy.

[260] Cf. Postgate (1907–8) 167.

the *Metamorphoses* we may encounter a hyperbaton seemingly of the
forced "elegiac" type, such as becomes habitual to Martial:

> nam graue respiciens inter duo lumina ferrum
> qua naris fronti committitur accipis imae (12.314–15).

> . . . for as you look back you receive a heavy spearpoint between the
> eyes, where nose and forehead join.

or (if my interpretation is correct):

> hac agit ut pastor per deuia rura capellas
> dum uenit abductas et structis cantat auenis (1.676–77).

> With this [i.e., the *caduceus*], disguised as a shepherd, he drove through
> unfrequented ways the goats which he stole as, playing on his reed
> pipe, he came along.

The editor who prints these passages with commas around *accipis*
and *abductas* is no doubt doing his duty as a grammarian, but the
signpost that he thinks to offer the traveller is more apt to behave
as stumbling-block or stile:[261] ancient readers did not need it, nor
should a modern reader who is conscious that Latin is not English
or French or German and who has trained himself to go on until
the poet tells him, by providing the awaited syntactical/rhetorical
dénouement, that he may stop:

> qua naris *fronti* committitur accipis *imae*;

> dum *uenit* abductas *et* STRVCTIS *cantat* AVENIS.

But are these two instances in fact as purely "elegiac" as they seem?
It is at least worth asking the question whether the positioning of
accipis and *abductas* is deliberate, to emphasize that the spear struck
in the middle of the face, that the thefts were accomplished *all the while*
the god strolled and played. It does not do to underrate Ovid or
any other *doctus poeta* in even the smallest points of technique, and
if all he had wanted was to make his verses scan he could have
done so in numerous other ways.

---

[261] In such cases as 1.458, *qui dare certa ferae, dare uulnera possumus hosti* (copiously
illustrated by Housman in his note on Manil. 1.269–70), the anaphora dictates a
comma after *ferae*, but a second after *possumus* would simply trip the reader up.
With practice the ear is conditioned by the movement of the verse to accept these
distributions. They continue to lead the unwary critic into error (Kenney (1998)
311–12).

Mention has been made of the so-called *apo koinou* word-order, in which part of the second member of an utterance modifies the first member as well.[262] It becomes unnecessary to embark on an elaborate classification of this usage once it is grasped that it is essentially a special type of ellipse, the figure in which part of an utterance is suppressed for the sake of economy and effect, being readily "understood" from the context. Not only words but cases may be treated in this way, e.g., *per iuga chrysolithi positaeque ex ordine gemmae* (2.109), i.e., *per iuga ex ordine positi chrysolithi et (aliae) gemmae*, or *ut limbus totumque appareat aurum* (2.734), i.e., *ut totus appareat limbus totumque aurum*, or rather, since hendiadys too is at work, *ut totus appareat aureus limbus*.[263] The principle that sentences should be read as wholes and that each word should be understood in relation to the entire context is fundamental to a correct reading of Latin poetry and a good deal of Latin prose. In their light even Ovid's more apparently wilful games with syntax ought not to impede comprehension: *fluminaque obliquis cinxit decliuia ripis* (1.39). As has been pointed out by Bömer,[264] the attributes proper to rivers and their banks have changed places. Double enallage, as this is termed, was already known to Ovid's readers from Virgil and earlier poets,[265] and both words were familiar enough in their proper senses for an accomplished reader to grasp and relish what Ovid was up to. But, once again, is this pure play? May there not be a deliberate stroke of wit, a hint of the chaos from which order was emerging and a suggestion of a period during which the rivers were still learning their place in the new order of things and in which, for the moment, stream and banks were as yet not clearly distinguished? It is at least a piquant thought. The main point to be made, however, is that identification and classification of the various syntactical figures to be found in Ovid's Latinity, though an entirely praiseworthy occupation, is not essential

---

[262] The definition adopted by H–S 834. For further discussion see Eller (1938) 1–7; and cf. Kenney (1958a) 55, Leo (1960) 1:77–81, Mayer (1994) 25–28.

[263] The following further instances have been casually culled from a single book: 2.231, *cineres eiectatamque fauillam*; 406, *fontes et non audentia labi/flumina*; 438, *odio nemus est et conscia silua*; 490, *ante domum quondamque suis errauit in agris*.

[264] Bömer (1967) 223–26; cf. Bömer (1969) 51 ad loc., 149–50 on 1.466, and to the literature cited by him add Bell (1923) 317–21. Both adjj. would be felt as predicative in sense.

[265] E.g. Lucret. 3.972–73, *anteacta uetustas temporis aeterni*, exactly equivalent in sense to 1.558, *infinita aetas anteacti temporis omnis*.

to intelligent comprehension of his poetry; indeed, there is a danger that such exercises may encourage the disposition to see an abnormality, deserving defense or at least palliation, in what is really the acquisition by Latin of a flexibility which, compared with Greek, it lacked in its rude and inartificial state.[266]

IX

We may now turn from grammar to rhetoric, from this necessarily partial and fragmentary review of Ovid's linguistic resources and expedients to consider how he employed them in action, i.e., in the continuous utterance of the poem. That Ovid's style is "rhetorical" his critics all agree; not all trouble to define adequately what they mean by the term. Most good Latin poetry is rhetorical in the sense that it is engineered to produce a particular effect on the reader; the artistic success of the result depends principally on whether the poet observes a due proportion between ends and means. For Ovid, writing the sort of poem that the *Metamorphoses* was intended to be, two principal ends had to be kept in view if the reader's attention was not to flag: the need to keep the poem moving continuously, and the need to vary the tone and tempo according to the character of the episodes themselves. It is the first of these needs that dictated a fundamental characteristic of his style, the contrast between the elegiac (as one might term it) brevity and terseness of individual members (clauses, cola) and the flowing amplitude of the sentences as a whole. Nims, I think, puts his finger on this point when he remarks that "Ovid . . . has been found long-winded, even if musically so, but the general effect of his writing is one of conciseness."[267] One of the devices by which he achieves this effect is not peculiar to him, the so-called "theme and variation."[268] Sometimes, it is true, this amounts to little more than saying the same thing twice: *sed te decor iste, quod optas,/esse uetat, uotoque tuo tua forma repugnat* (1.488–89) differs essentially very little from

---

[266] For further discussion of certain Ovidian figures see my reviews of Bömer's commentary, Kenney (1972–88) *passim*.

[267] Nims (1965) xxii. The whole of Nims's introduction is excellent value.

[268] See Henry (1873–78) 1:206–7, 745–51. For its use by Lucretius see Kenney (1971) 25. It is, as Henry remarked, "almost inseparable from poetry." The Psalms of David are a supreme example.

nequitiam fugio, fugientem forma reducit;
    auersor morum crimina, corpus amo (*Am.* 3.11.37–38).

> I flee from your infidelity, but as I flee your beauty brings me back;
> I hate your character, I love your body.

These indeed might be called the hexameters of an elegist; yet the
emphasis on Daphne's beauty as the cause of her undoing is after
all at the center of the story. More clearly disciplined and functional
is the creation of Man:

> pronaque cum spectent animalia cetera terram,
> os homini sublime dedit caelumque uidere
> iussit et erectos ad sidera tollere uultus (1.84–86).

> . . . and whereas the rest of the animal creation go on all fours and
> look down at the earth, to man he gave an uplifted face and bade
> him gaze on the heavens and raise his eyes aloft to the stars.

The contrast between man and the other animals (a commonplace
of ancient thought, as Bömer's note shows) is pressed home by the
tricolon structure and the progressive amplifications *sublime* > *caelum*
> *sidera*: the divine element in man's composition is *en rapport* with
the stars, themselves divine. The triple structure of 1.85–86 responds
to that of the opening verses of the paragraph:

> sanctius his animal mentisque capacius altae
> deerat adhuc et quod dominari in cetera posset (76–77).

> There was as yet no animal more godlike than these, more capable
> of receiving lofty intelligence,[269] and such as might rule over the rest.

A pathetic effect is evident in

> sternuntur segetes et deplorata coloni
> uota iacent, longique perit labor irritus anni (1.272–73).

> The crops are laid flat, the farmer's prayers lie given over for dead,
> and the long year's toil has gone for nothing.

Here variation combines with imagery, diction (the effect of the
stately *deplorata*), and interlocking word-order (1.273: aBbA) to empha-
size the peasants' despair. Grandeur is the note struck in

---

[269] Bömer's suggestion ((1969) 43) that *mentis capacius altae* stands by enallage
for *mentis capax altioris* seems to be mistaken. *mens alta* is an attribute of divinity, of
which man was enabled, as the beasts were not, to receive a share (cf. Lee (1953)
79 ad loc.).

sed regina tamen ‖ sed opaci maxima mundi ‖
sed tamen inferni pollens matrona tyranni (5.507–8).

... but yet she (Proserpine) is a queen, the greatest in that dark world,
powerful wife of the lord of the underworld.

Here the tricolon structure is formally articulated and spaced by the
repeated *sed*, and the splendor of Proserpine's position emphasized
by the "golden" line 508 (abBA). This technique can also be effective
in narrative:

Lydia tota fremit, Phrygiaeque per oppida facti
rumor it et magnum sermonibus occupat orbem (6.146–47).

All Lydia is in turmoil, the news of the deed goes through the towns
of Phrygia and fills the whole world with rumor.

Here variation is accompanied by extension: the words connoting
rumor, *fremit, rumor, sermonibus*, act as a sort of semantic anaphora
articulating the account of the spread of the news from Lydia through
Phrygia and out into the wide world. The dactyls of 146 and the
enjambment *facti/rumor* add speed, and the enclosing word-order *mag-
num . . . orbem* rounds off the picture and emphasizes how completely
the news filled the world, vast as it is. In the same way, on a slightly
larger scale, the different phases of an action are brought out both
pictorially and conceptually in

his, ut quaeque pia est, hortatibus impia prima est
et, ne sit scelerata, facit scelus; haud tamen ictus
ulla suos spectare potest, oculosque reflectunt
caecaque dant saeuis auersae uulnera dextris (7.339–42).

(Pelias is murdered by his daughters at the instigation of Medea.) At
her bidding each daughter, the more she loved her father, the more
eagerly she struck, and to avoid the reproach of wickedness did a
wicked deed. Yet none could bear to look at the blows she dealt, all
averted their eyes and turning away inflicted with cruel hand wounds
they could not see.

This is a fine example of Ovid's extreme verbal dexterity in the
exploitation of paradox, conveyed through a sort of double theme
and variation. The idea of the first occurs more than once in the
poem, varied with Ovid's habitual ease:

incipit esse tamen melior germana parente
et consanguineas ut sanguine leniat umbras,
impietate pia est (8.475–77).

However, the feelings of a sister began to prevail (in Althaea) over those of a mother, and to placate with blood the ghost of a blood-relation,[270] she is undutifully dutiful;

and, more succinctly,

> ultusque parente parentem
> natus erit facto pius et sceleratus eodem (9.407–8).

(Themis on the killing of Eriphyle by Alcmaeon to avenge the death of Amphiaraus) . . . and his son, avenging parent on parent, shall be by the same deed dutiful and wicked.

This idea is then exploited in the second theme and variation by being, so to say, translated into action; as in other cases the period is completed by a verse with interlocking word-order (abAB; but for the position of the verb a golden line). There is a tendency here towards what in later poetry, especially in Juvenal, becomes a mannerism, the rounding off of a train of thought with a self-contained and quotable *sententia*. So in

> nec tam
> turpe fuit uinci quam contendisse decorum est,
> magnaque dat nobis tantus solacia uictor (9.5–7).

It was less shameful to be beaten than it is honorable to have fought, and it is a great consolation to have succumbed to so mighty a victor (Achelous on his wrestling defeat by Hercules).

There is in fact a concealed tricolon structure here, for line 6 falls into two portions of unequal length, linked and contrasted by the two pairs of verbs in different tenses, whereas the interlocking word-order of line 7 welds it into a single whole:

turpe *fuit* VINCI || quam CONTENDISSE decorum *est*,

magnaque dat nobis tantus solacia uictor.

---

[270] "A forced and almost pointless word-play" is the comment of Hollis (1970) 91 ad loc. I am not so sure. Ovid can scarcely have had in mind the old idea that a mother was not related by blood to her offspring (cf. Kenney (1971) 178–79 on Lucret. 3.743). The shedding of blood called for a bloody expiation, and in this case the victim was related to both avenger and avenged: in other words *sanguine* at 1.476 is felt in the context (after **con**sanguineas; cf. Kenney (1971) 110 on Lucret. 3.261) as = not merely "blood" but "kindred blood." I do not know exactly what Hollis means by calling the oxymoron *impietate pia est* "not very pleasing." What are the criteria which an oxymoron must satisfy in order to please?

The quality of Ovid's technical achievement in the *Metamorphoses* is not fully grasped unless the reader has trained himself to be consciously aware of the enormous range of variations which the poet imparts to these basic poetic structures. It is because of this variety that he is not monotonous as, say, Lucan is monotonous. Lucan provides an instructive contrast precisely because, though his techniques are in many respects essentially Ovidian, he lacks Ovid's versatility and flexibility in applying them.

X

It is convenient to use the device of theme and variation to illustrate the application of Ovid's techniques on a small scale. To extend these illustrations and this style of analysis on a larger scale would involve the discussion of whole books and episodes, which space does not allow and which is perhaps rather the province of the commentator.[271] I shall therefore conclude this essay by reviewing a number of slightly longer passages which seem to me to exemplify certain other aspects of Ovid's art, without pretending to completeness or even system. In a poem of such immense variety and of a richness sometimes verging on indiscipline (though never anarchy) random, or perhaps more accurately capricious, sampling is perhaps as good an approach as any. All my examples (and the same, I suspect, would be true of any others that might be preferred) are in fact essentially making the same point: they all illustrate the (on the whole, barring certain isolated *tours de force*) unobtrusive efficiency (I have used this phrase before, but make no apology for the repetition) with which Ovid keeps his poem moving and holds continuously the attention of his readers.

I have said that Ovid is never monotonous as, for instance, Lucan is monotonous. He was aware of the need for continual slight variations in tone and tempo in such a long poem. So in the account of Jason and the fire-breathing bulls (7.100–119):

> postera depulerat stellas Aurora micantes;   100
> conueniunt populi sacrum Mauortis in aruum
> consistuntque iugis; medio rex ipse resedit
> agmine purpureus sceptroque insignis eburno.

---

[271] An attractive discussion of 13.750–897 (Acis, Galatea, and Polyphemus) by West (1970) 8–14.

ecce adamanteis Vulcanum naribus efflant
aeripedes tauri, tactaeque uaporibus herbae 105
ardent; utque solent pleni resonare camini
aut ubi terrena silices fornace soluti
concipiunt ignem liquidarum adspergine aquarum,
pectora sic intus clausas uoluentia flammas
gutturaque usta sonant. tamen illis Aesone natus 110
obuius it; uertere truces uenientis ad ora
terribiles uultus praefixaque cornua ferro
puluereumque solum pede pulsauere bisulco
fumificisque locum mugitibus impleuerunt.
deriguere metu Minyae; subit ille nec ignes 115
sentit anhelatos (tantum medicamina possunt)
pendulaque audaci mulcet palearia dextra
suppositosque iugo pondus graue cogit aratri
ducere et insuetum ferro proscindere campum.

As soon as next day's dawn had banished the bright stars, the people
assembled at the sacred field of Mars and took their stand on the sur-
rounding hills. In their midst sat the king, purple-clad and resplendent
with his ivory scepter. Now, breathing fire from their adamantine nos-
trils, came the brazen-footed bulls, and the grass shrivelled as their
breath touched it. As a well-stoked furnace roars or as baked lime
burns when slaked with water, so the chests of the bulls and their fiery
throats roared with the flames within. Nevertheless the son of Aeson
went to meet them. They menacingly swung their fearful heads and
iron-tipped horns to face him as he came, pawed the dusty earth with
their cloven feet, and filled the place with their smoky bellowings. The
Minyans were rigid with terror, but Jason approached without feeling
the fiery breath (so powerful were the charms) and with daring hand
stroked their dewlaps, yoked them, and constrained them to draw the
heavy plough and cleave with the share the unaccustomed soil.

Ovid presents the scene, in contrast to his model Apollonius, as an
amphitheatral set-piece,[272] with the bulls in the center; for Jason's
victory is such a walk-over as scarcely to merit description. This con-
centration on a particular moment of the action and the taking of
the rest for granted is of course Alexandrian and characteristic of
Ovid's procedure in many episodes of the poem. Down to 112 the
narrative moves swiftly, only 100 and 103 being heavily endstopped,
and enjambment being frequent (102–3, 104–5, 105–6, 107–8, 109–10,

---

[272] The bulls appear (104 *ecce*) as if released from the *caueae*; in Apollonius
(3.1288–92) Jason has to track them down to their murky lair, and Aeetes is not
formally enthroned as in Ovid but simply stands or strolls by the river (1277; see
Fränkel (1961) 162 for the textual variants). Professor Boyd draws my attention to

110–11, 111–12). Similarly with 115–19, where enjambment (115–16, 118–19) and parenthesis[273] help to polish off the actual accomplishment of the feat in very short order. Between these lively passages intervenes the description of the bulls: static and so menacing. Their initial reaction to Jason's appearance is conveyed by the (enjambed) *uertere truces . . . uultus*, but that is the only movement in the scene. Each of the three succeeding verses is self-contained: the bulls stand staring, horns at the ready (112), pawing the ground (113; note the alliteration) and bellowing (114; are the onomatopoeic and metrical effects slightly overdone?). All this, as the reader knows perfectly well, is a sham. The Minyans of course are not in on the secret, but Jason, as Ovid tells the story, is not called upon (or possibly lacks the wit?) even to simulate anxiety or effort.[274] This brief static interruption in the brisk current of the episode (which continues in what follows) is not an unmotivated descriptive excursus but a subtle stroke of wit. By pausing to call attention to the appearance and behavior of the bulls Ovid is reminding us how the whole encounter has been "set up" by Medea—who is of course the figure that he and we are really interested in. The bulls *look* alarming—to the outsider and those not in the know—but they do not actually *do* anything; they just stand, stare, fume, and bellow.

In this passage the variations in tempo are directly connected with the incidence of enjambment (among other things); and we may now recall the criticism mentioned earlier, that Ovid's hexameters are "under-enjambed." In the *Aeneid* it has been calculated that Virgil enjambs on an average about forty per cent of his verses, a higher

---

the possibility that Ovid may also have had in mind the setting of the *Romuli auspicium* as described by Ennius, *Ann.* 72–91 Sk.

[273] On Ovid's use of parenthesis see von Albrecht (1963) and Kenney (1964). von Albrecht's discussion shows that Ovid employs parenthesis for more than one effect, but one characteristic is constant: it is always so incorporated, beginning and ending with the verses themselves or their main caesuras and unambiguously signposted (cf. above, n. 233), as to interrupt the flow as little as possible. The text printed above is as punctuated by the old editors and some of their successors; the punctuation of, e.g., Magnus and Ehwald, who begin the parenthesis at *nec*, contravenes the ambiguity principle, which requires that a parenthesis should not be deemed to begin before it has to.

[274] In contrast to Apollonius's Jason, who at least braces himself for the encounter and holds a shield in front of himself (3.1293–96), and actually has to exert himself when it comes to the yoking (3.1306–8). Did Emily Dickinson have Ovid in mind when she wrote "Jason—sham—too?" (Reference due to Professor R.G. Mayer.)

proportion than in any other hexameter poetry.[275] Taking *Metamorphoses* 7 as a representative book I have estimated that the corresponding figure for Ovid is in the region of thirty-five per cent: not exactly a low figure when compared even with the *Aeneid*, let alone with the twenty per cent of the *Eclogues*. But just as with Virgil,[276] considerable variations occur, especially in speeches: to look no further than the beginning of Book 7, the proportion of enjambed verses rises sharply towards the end of Medea's soliloquy, at 46–71; for other examples see also 59–62 (swift "linking" narrative), 188–91 (preliminary to prayer), and 406–15 (parenthetic explanation). Nor do the types of enjambment used by Ovid seem to differ appreciably from those of Virgil;[277] the main and substantial difference is in overall frequency of employment.[278] In such matters Ovid's practice seems to represent an instinctive compromise. If enjambment were to exceed the Virgilian figure, more frequent and stronger pauses in the interior of the verse would be necessary to prevent it from accelerating into a breathless gallop, but too many such pauses would unbalance the relationship between hexameter and sentence. Ovid's practice represents what his ear told him suited the general narrative pace that he wished to maintain.

---

[275] Worstbrock (1963) 156.

[276] Worstbrock (1963) 157.

[277] Worstbrock (1963) 159–62.

[278] To maintain comparability I have interpreted "enjambment" in a fairly strict grammatical sense, applied to lines whose syntax is completed by what follows. Ovid makes much use of what might be called "quasi-" or "semi-enjambment": that is, a structure which, while it does not disallow, certainly discourages a pause at the end of the line in reading. So, for instance, in (e = strict, q = quasi-enjambment):

> o cui debere salutem (e)
> confiteor, coniunx, quamquam mihi cuncta dedisti (q)
> excussit*que* fidem meritorum summa tuorum (7.164–66)

or

> constitit adueniens citra limenque foresque (q)
> *et* tantum caelo tegitur refugitque uiriles (e)
> contactus statuitque aras e caespite binas, (q)
> *dexteriore* Hecates, at laeua parte Iuuentae (7.238–41).

The close connection is very often achieved by *et* or *-que*; but other devices are used, as in the second quotation, where the unemphatic *binas* does not invite the reader to pause (as the order *binas . . . aras* would have done) and is at once picked up by *dexteriore*, which in turn looks forward to its complement in *laeua*. Examples could be multiplied; the upshot is that the overall speed of the verse is greater than the figures quoted for enjambment proper would lead one to suppose.

To illustrate the speed at which Ovid can, when he wishes, make his verses move, we may consider the description of Myrrha's sleepless night:

> noctis erat medium, curasque et corpora somnus
> soluerat; at uirgo Cinyreia peruigil igni
> carpitur indomito furiosaque uota retractat   370
> et modo desperat, modo uult temptare, pudetque,
> et cupit et quid agat non inuenit, utque securi
> saucia trabs ingens, ubi plaga nouissima restat,
> quo cadat in dubio est omnique a parte timetur:
> sic animus uario labefactus uulnere nutat   375
> huc leuis atque illuc momentaque sumit utroque.
> nec modus et requies nisi mors reperitur amoris;
> mors placet; erigitur laqueoque innectere fauces
> destinat a zona summo de poste reuincta
> 'care uale Cinyra causamque intellege mortis'   380
> dixit et aptabat pallenti uincula collo (10.368–81).

It was midnight, and all around minds and bodies lay relaxed in sleep. Only Cinyras' daughter was wakeful, tormented by the flame she could not subdue, as she went over in her mind again and again her frenzied prayers. Now she despaired, now she was for the attempt; shame and lust alternated in her, but she could not tell what to do. As a great tree, mortally stricken by the axe and awaiting the final blow, inspires fear on all sides as men wait to see which way it will fall, so her purpose, undermined by conflicting assaults, wavered unsteadily now this way and now that and moved in alternate directions. The only end and rest for her passion that she could find was death, and death she decided upon. She rose, determined to hang herself, and tying her girdle to the lintel and murmuring "Goodbye, dear Cinyras, and understand why I die," she was, deathly-pale, in the act of adjusting the noose about her neck.

Having already in 9.454–665 dealt very fully with the rather similar story of Byblis, Ovid had necessarily to vary his treatment of Myrrha—and no doubt embraced the opportunity of doing so.[279] Myrrha is given one, by Ovidian standards relatively brief, soliloquy (320–55), and once her state of mind has been established, the trans-

---

[279] The Byblis episode contains little narrative and is mostly taken up with the soliloquies (in which her letter must be included) in which the heroine's warring states of mind are analyzed. Cf. Tränkle (1963), stressing the similarities with the *Heroides* (but see also Otis (1970) 221–22). With the description of Myrrha quoted above compare 9.523–28. On elegiac elements in the vocabulary of *Met.* see Knox (1986a) 31–39.

lation of her feelings into attempted action (to be thwarted by the Euripidean figure of the Nurse) is speedily accomplished in the passage under review. Ovid is here ultimately indebted, *via* Virgil (*Aen.* 4.522–52), to the famous night-scene in Apollonius (3.744–69), but his treatment is compressed and summary, representing or rather recalling (for 320–55 are still in the reader's mind) Myrrha's successive mental states by a rapid succession of verbs. It is redeemed from dryness by the effective simile,[280] which moves almost as fast as the surrounding narrative but yet manages momentarily to arrest attention by concentrating all Myrrha's vacillations into one powerful and original image.[281] Here, it may be remarked, enjambment is well up to the Virgilian norm, with six strong (368, 369, 372, 378, 379, 380) and three weaker (370, 371, 376) instances in fourteen verses. Its employment is, as already emphasized in other passages, strictly functional.

No writer on the *Metamorphoses* has failed to pay tribute to Ovid's powers of description. "There is a plastic quality about his work. He catches the significant moment or attitude or gesture and imprints it on our mind."[282] That there is usually more to this than embellishment for its own sake has been emphasized by recent investigation.[283] Not all Ovid's descriptions, of course, are symbolic, but very few if any are otiose. Wilkinson's pertinent comment can be illustrated best from one or two descriptions of characters in action; for a landscape, after all, is static and, given the care lavished on such technical problems in formal rhetorical instruction and the existence of

---

[280] A treatment of Ovid's similes in *Met.* is outside the scope of this article: see Washietl (1883), Brunner (1966), Wilkins (1932), Owen (1931), Galinsky (1975) 125–29, 163–66, 189–90, Solodow (1988) 55–57, 211.

[281] The idea goes back to Homer and Apollonius (Bömer (1980) 136 ad loc.). In spite of the usual descriptive elaboration of the tree their application of the image is very simple. Virgil enlarges its scope and grandeur enormously when he compares the fall of Troy to that of a great tree (*Aen.* 2.626–31; cf. Austin (1964) 240 ad loc.). Ovid applies it differently again, to the psychology of the situation: Myrrha is not compared to the tree; it is the painful moments, that seem to last for hours, while the tree totters, that resemble her plight, always on the verge of making up her mind but not quite able to do so. But just as the tree must fall once it is cut through (cf. the wound image of 375), so must she decide.

[282] Wilkinson (1955) 172. Cf. H. Stephanus, in the preface to his *Poetae Graeci Principes* (1566): "Poetis autem penicillum quum tribuo, cum ad alios multos multorum poetarum locos, tum ad complures Ovidianarum metamorphoseon locos respicio." See also the literature cited by Stroh (1969) 159.

[283] Segal (1969).

good models, relatively easy to depict competently in its salient details.[284] Figures in violent motion present a less tractable assignment. Ovid's method is essentially to suggest rather than to describe,[285] as three examples will show. The first is Daphne, running from Apollo:

> plura locuturum timido Peneia cursu
> fugit cumque ipso uerba imperfecta reliquit,
> tum quoque uisa decens: nudabant corpora uenti
> obuiaque aduersas uibrabant flamina uestes
> et leuis impulsos retro dabat aura capillos,
> auctaque forma fuga est (1.325–30).

> He would have continued, but the daughter of Peneus fled in alarm leaving the god alone with his unfinished speech, beautiful also in her flight. The wind bared her body, her clothes and hair streamed behind her in the breeze, and running enhanced her loveliness.

Ovid describes the girl as she appeared in the eyes of her pursuer, with her graceful body made to seem even more desirable by her flight; his method is impressionistic, concentrating on the effects of the wind on her hair and clothes and using theme (*uenti . . . flamina . . . aura*) and variation with two golden lines of identical "shape" (528–29 = abAB) to fix the moving picture for a short moment. If, as their construction suggests they should be, these two verses are read as a combined whole, the reader receives a compound impression: the girl's clothes were partly pressed against her body (*obuia . . . aduersas*), partly waved and streamed in the breeze (*uibrabant . . . retro dabat*), as also did her hair. Ovid takes care to end his description in the middle of a verse so as to preserve narrative continuity, and to make it last for just so long a time as may allow the god to recover from his surprise (note the witty *fugit* || *cumque ipso* eqs.) and take off in pursuit. The same focusing on similar details (of which Ovid was fond)[286] is seen in the depiction of Europa:

---

[284] A good example is Virgil's description of the Trojan landfall in Africa (*Aen.* 1.159–69), which, unlike its Homeric prototypes (on which see Williams (1968) 637–44), is clearly organized by the poet so as to lead the mind's eye of the reader from point to point in a certain order. It is also, however, organized so as to bring out the symbolism of the landscape (cf. Pöschl (1977) 172–75), which prefigures both the repose and the subsequent danger that the Trojans will find in Africa— and in the cave of the nymphs (168) are we not intended to sense that other, more fateful, cave?

[285] "Un trait seul, un grand trait, abandonnez le reste à mon imagination; voilà le vrai goût, voilà le grand goût. Ovid l'a quelquefois" (Diderot, cit. Stroh (1969) 85).

[286] Bömer (1969) 165 ad loc.

> pauet haec litusque ablata relictum
> respicit et dextra cornum tenet, altera dorso
> imposita est; tremulae sinuantur flamine uestes (2.873–75).

In terror she looked back at the shore from which she was being carried off, holding a horn with her right hand and resting the other on the bull's back; her clothes fluttered and waved in the breeze.

The pose is a classic one, often represented in ancient art and a favorite with poets.[287] Ovid has exercized great restraint in his depiction, singling out three features only, the turned-back head and body (implied by *respicit*), the position of the hands, and the robe fluttering in the breeze.[288] Moschus (*Europa* 125–30) is much more elaborate and, though extremely pretty, not more effective.

The description of Europa just quoted occupies the concluding lines of Book 2. When Book 3 opens the rape has been accomplished and the ravisher's identity disclosed. The technique is reminiscent of the cinema: a fade-out on a carefully posed shot, followed by a complete change of tempo and mood in the next scene. This "cinematic" characteristic of Ovid's descriptive technique (which is not peculiar to him) has been acutely remarked by Viarre[289] and deserves study. A striking instance is that of Phaethon attempting to control the chariot of the Sun:

> tum uero Phaethon cunctis e partibus orbem
> adspicit accensum nec tantos sustinet aestus
> feruentesque auras uelut e fornace profunda
> ore trahit currusque suos candescere sentit
> et neque iam cineres eiectatamque fauillam
> ferre potest calidoque inuoluitur undique fumo
> quoque eat aut ubi sit picea caligine tectus
> nescit et arbitrio uolucrum raptatur equorum (2.227–34).

And now Phaethon saw the world on fire everywhere, and the heat was more than he could bear. He breathed in air hot as the blast of a great furnace far below and felt the chariot growing white-hot. Now he was overcome by the shower of cinders and glowing ash and found himself enveloped in hot smoke. Shrouded in pitch-black darkness he could not see which way he was going or where he was, and he was swept along at the will of the swift horses.

---

[287] Haupt – von Albrecht (1966) 1:145–46 ad loc. An especially charming instance is a Coptic bronze of the 5th–6th century A.D. (in private possession), in which the pose and the girl's robe have been reduced to a design of hieratic simplicity (Mitten and Doeringer (1968) no. 316).

[288] So too at *F.* 5.607–9, but there the effect is more crisp than decorative.

[289] Viarre (1964) 99–100.

As with Daphne, the description is presented from the point of view
of a protagonist—in this case *the* protagonist. The impression of over-
whelming heat is conveyed by a succession of key words: *accensum,
aestus, feruentes, fornace, candescere, cineres, fauillam, fumo, caligine* (a remark-
able display of Ovidian *ubertas* and *copia uerborum*), with the empha-
sis gradually shifting from heat, *via* cinders and ash, to smoke and
obscurity, as Phaethon finally loses, not only control of, but all touch
with his situation. His increasing helplessness is conveyed by the
verbs which provide the syntactical articulation of the picture: *adspicit,
nec . . . sustinet, ore trahit, neque . . . ferre potest, inuoluitur, nescit* and finally
the emphatic frequentative *raptatur*. There is in fact very little actual
description in the way of pictorial epithets and the like, and much
is left to the reader's imagination to supply; but the stimulus is
adroitly applied, as, for instance, in *profunda*, with its hint of the great
gulfs below.[290] The effect is that of a series of shots of the flames
and smoke alternating with close-ups of Phaethon's face as it regis-
ters horror, bewilderment, and despair. The syntactical structure
enforces rapidity of reading: even editors who habitually over-punc-
tuate are sparing with commas in this passage, but it seems to me
that Ovid's Latin here requires no punctuation at all, and I have so
printed it.

A special class of descriptive problem is posed by the metamor-
phoses themselves. As with the transitions, variety was of the essence,
especially in the numerous cases of persons who were changed into
birds. Clearly it gave Ovid pleasure to rise to this technical chal-
lenge, and he delighted to lavish on these descriptions all that clev-
erness which has so much annoyed some of his critics.[291] On occasions
they constitute what might be called set-pieces of *enargeia*. Are they
anything more? In this sort of writing Ovid has been praised by
Addison and blamed by Adam Smith;[292] and in this remarkable dis-
agreement I find myself siding with the great economist's apparently
prosaic objection that these descriptions "are so very much out of
the common course of nature as to shock us by their incredibility."

---

[290] The comparison itself, as Bömer observes ((1969) 299 ad loc.), is conventional;
it is the choice of epithet that lifts it out of the ruck.

[291] "Sometimes Ovid is indeed too clever. He was told so in his own time, and
his ghost has been hearing it ever since" (Nims (1965) xxvii).

[292] *Spectator* no. 417 (28 June 1712); *Lectures on Rhetoric and Belles Lettres*, ed.
M. Lothian (1963) 61–62 (both passages cit. Stroh (1969) 71, 86).

However far-fetched the premises of Ovid's *ethopoeia*, he never parts company completely with the fundamental humanity of his characters: into whatever excesses of speech and behavior their passions may carry them, the reader is never quite out of touch with the real world, and the Callimachean rule of poetical credibility, "so to lie as to persuade one's hearer,"[293] is not broken. With what might be termed the *ethopoeia* of material phenomena Ovid is less successful. For him, this was essentially an extension of the rhetorical exercise "Imagine the words of so-and-so in such-and-such a situation" (τίνας ἂν εἴποι λόγους ὁ δεῖνα). He handles such themes like the great rhetorical artificer that he was, and it is impossible not to admire the versatility with which he varies the "basic" transformations into birds, trees, and rocks.[294] An especially elaborate example is the metamorphosis of Cyane into a spring:

> at Cyane raptamque deam contemptaque fontis   425
> iura sui maerens inconsolabile uulnus
> mente gerit tacita lacrimisque absumitur omnis
> et quarum fuerat magnum modo numen, in illas
> extenuatur aquas: molliri membra uideres,
> ossa pati flexus, ungues posuisse rigorem,   430
> primaque de tota tenuissima quaeque liquescunt,
> caerulei crines digitique et crura pedesque
> (nam breuis in gelidas membris exilibus undas
> transitus est), post haec umeri tergusque latusque
> pectoraque in tenues abeunt euanida riuos,   435
> denique pro uiuo uitiatas sanguine uenas
> lympha subit, restatque nihil quod prendere possis (5.425–37).

But Cyane, as she mourned the rape of the goddess and the insult to the rights of her spring, cherishing deep in her heart a wound that could not be assuaged, dissolved away in tears and was rarefied into the very waters whose great godhead she had lately been. One could have seen her limbs softening, her bones becoming limp, her nails losing their hardness. First it was the thinnest parts of her that liquefied, her blue-green hair, her fingers, toes, feet, and legs (for the thinner members are easily changed into cool water); next her shoulders and back, flanks and breast melted away into liquid streams. Finally into her softened veins instead of living blood clear water flowed, and there was nothing left of her that one could grasp.

---

[293] *Hymns* 1.65: "Let me lie so as to persuade the ear of the listener."
[294] See Lafaye (1904/1971) 245–49, Quirin (1930) esp. 118–19 on Ovidian *variatio*.

From the purely technical aspect this is first-rate writing, able to give much intellectual pleasure to a sophisticated reader.[295] It obeys the principles of *enargeia*. The reader is invited to witness the transformation (429, *uideres*) and to test it for himself when it is complete (437, *quod prendere possis*). The introductory passage is heavily enjambed and moves fast; the start of the description proper is signalled by the molossus *molliri* (429), with alliterative reinforcement. First come theme and variation to convey the notion of softening; then the graduated list of parts of the body in order of their susceptibility and disappearance; finally the inner structures and the blood within. The articulation of the description is clear, with a hint of pedantry that is made explicit in the sly parenthesis[296] in which the order of events is explained. The whole is rounded off by antithetical responsion with chiasmus: 428–29, *magnum modo numen . . . aquas* ~ 437, *lympha . . . nihil*. All very efficient; but we cannot suspend our disbelief so as to share emotionally in Cyane's experience in the sense that we can share the experiences of Byblis or Phaethon. The reader cannot feel sympathy with her. In the metamorphoses the method of leaving things to the reader's imagination, so effective in descriptions of the real world and of familiar phenomena, does not come off: for the imagination has nothing to work upon, nothing that it recognizes and can use as a starting-point.

We may perhaps discern in the arch semi-pedantry of this particular description the hint of a realization of this fact on the poet's part, an implicit acknowledgment that the reader's pleasure must here be, as has been said, intellectual rather than emotional. Perhaps this should be seen as in some sense a confession of failure. By that I mean that the pleasure felt by the reader of a poetical description, if it is to amount to anything at all, must be essentially emotional and sympathetic; and that by using the suggestive and impressionistic methods appropriate to real descriptions in the composition of unreal or fantastic scenes such as few, if any, sane readers could envisage, Ovid can be seen failing to relate his stylistic means successfully to his ends.[297] The distinction that I have in mind between

---

[295] It is the first transformation into water that we encounter in *Met.*, and by far the most elaborate: cf. Quirin (1930) 106–8.

[296] Editors have not usually printed *nam breuis . . . transitus est* as such, but this is obviously what Ovid intended: so, rightly, von Albrecht (1963) 52 and Tarrant in OCT (forthcoming).

[297] The poem has a rich iconographical tradition, but artists on the whole have preferred not to illustrate the actual moment of metamorphosis: cf. Kenney (1967) 52.

what it is and is not reasonable to expect from a reader of poetry may emerge more clearly if we consider Ovid's great allegorical set-piece descriptions of Hunger, the Cave of Sleep,[298] and so forth; there is grotesque detail and to spare in these, but the best of them succeed because what is enlarged or diminished or distorted remains fundamentally recognizable and part of human experience. It is the difference, perhaps, between Dürer and Hieronymus Bosch. If there is anything in these criticisms of Ovid's transformation-scenes, it should not be allowed to weigh heavily when set against the stylistic excellences that I have tried to illustrate and, partially, to account for. In the *Metamorphoses* descriptions of the act of metamorphosis could hardly be lacking, and it can be argued that it functions as a symbol of the human condition in a universe in which no identity is ever wholly secure. But it is not what the poem is, essentially, "about." It posed a technical problem which he solved adroitly, on occasions brilliantly; but the scenes of metamorphosis are not what linger in the reader's mind. It was in the depiction of *human* actions and emotions—and what could be more human than the gods of the *Metamorphoses?*—that Ovid displayed the full range of his poetic powers.

Sections VI–X of this article reproduce, with occasional corrections and some modest amplification, my contribution, "The Style of the *Metamorphoses*," to J.W. Binns (ed.), *Ovid* (1973), 116–53, and appear here by permission of the publishers, Messrs Routledge Ltd. Sections I–V on the elegiac poems are new; here and there they provide some additional data relating to the *Metamorphoses* which it was not practicable to attempt to integrate into the earlier piece.

---

[298] Inuidia 2.760–82; Fames 8.788–808; Somnus 11.392–623; Fama 12.39–63.

CHAPTER THREE

THE *AMORES*: THE INVENTION OF OVID

Barbara Weiden Boyd

Contemporary discussions of the *Amores* have tended to start from one of a number of premises or concerns, which may roughly be classed as of two general types: literary and historical. For convenience's sake I shall use these two categories to provide a framework for the discussion that follows, although it will be readily apparent to my readers that the divisions thus implied are much tidier than what reality presents us with. My readers should also be acquainted with the critical perspective that would find even these categories misleading, since, as the argument goes, there can be no separation between the shape of poetic discourse and the political matrix in which it is modelled.[1] I shall return to this approach near the close of the chapter; meanwhile, I intend to look at how Ovid invents a poetic identity for himself in the *Amores*.

1. *Literary Approaches*

Under this heading I consider a variety of interrelated matters, chief among which are questions of literary influence, imitation, and parody; generic considerations (themes, motifs, topoi); Ovid's style; and the structure and organization of the three books of *Amores*. Limitations of space suggest that the most efficient way to address all of these topics—as well as to suggest possible future directions—is to look carefully at one poem in the collection in which they all raise a particular concern or merit renewed consideration, and to use the insights thus gleaned to establish an interpretive context for other poems in the collection. I shall suggest in the following discussion that this poem, while not chosen entirely at random, does in many of its

---

[1] For the now-classic discussion, see Kennedy (1992).

particular features serve as a sort of window onto the *Amores* as a whole. Meanwhile, readers seeking an interpretation of the *Amores* that works from the general to the particular rather than the reverse are referred to McKeown's invaluable edition with commentary of the *Amores* and his bibliography.

Even the numbering and possible division of the poem to which I shall now turn remain topics of lively discussion: Kenney's *Amores* 2.9 and 2.9b are believed to be one elegy by many scholars, and are printed as such by McKeown.[2] The inconclusiveness of the manuscript tradition and the character of the debate since Lucian Müller first proposed the division of 2.9 into two separate poems in 1856 are fully discussed by Damon, who proceeds to argue that a strong case for the division of 2.9 (as well as of 3.11) into two separate but paired elegies can be made by a comparison of these pairs with the uncontroversial pairs in the collection, 1.11–12, 2.7–8, and 2.13–14.[3] On the basis of her persuasive argument, I shall proceed to consider 2.9 and 2.9b as two separate but paired poems; it should be clear from the outset, however, that the consensus on this question, while growing, is not universal,[4] and I can only hope that my discussion will help to support its plausibility.

The two poems may be summarized briefly as follows: in 2.9, the lover, addressing Cupid, asks the god why he will not leave the defeated lover alone. It is typical, after all, for love to abandon lovers once captured; why, then, does Cupid linger now (1–14)? After all, there are many men and women yet to be conquered by love; if Rome had been as sluggish as Cupid is now, it would never have gone on to conquer the world (15–18). Nature and custom both mandate that humans, animals, and even inanimate objects be allowed to retire once they have been worn out; the weary lover, too, deserves to be put out to pasture (19–24). With the opening of 2.9b, however, the lover does an abrupt about-face: the thought of living with-

---

[2] McKeown 1:91–92 and 3:28–29 and 169. Cairns (1979b) builds his discussion of the relationship between *Am.* 2.9 and 3.11 on the foundation of the unity of 2.9; cf. also Lörcher (1975) 18–23. Booth (1991) 52–55 gives a judicious review of the scholarship, finally opting for division.

[3] Damon (1990) offers ample bibliography. On the relationship of 2.2 and 2.3, see also the cautious discussions of McKeown 3:28–29 and Booth (1991) 30–33; on the editor's responsibility generally, see Heyworth (1995b).

[4] The text referred to here is Kenney's (1995); McKeown prints the pair as one continuous poem.

out love is laughable, since however he may try to shake it off, it always returns (1–10). Indeed, the lover positively wants Cupid to keep doing what he does best; after all, if a lover is going to sleep at night, he might as well be dead (11–22). Even Mars has been conquered by Cupid and follows the love-god's example (23–26); so with the lover, Cupid is welcome to stay permanently, so long as he brings women with him (27–30).

The two-sidedness of 2.9 and 2.9b should be apparent from this summary, with the pair of elegies divided by a dramatic emotional reversal. In fact, 2.9b in both placement and theme enacts the emotional turmoil described by the lover as part and parcel of the elegiac love affair: moments after declaring his desire to leave love behind, the *amator* finds himself eager to be back in the throes of emotional upheaval again, and so in effect negates the plea to be retired that had given 2.9 its theme. Ovid's sophistic use of rhetoric—negating a position already successfully argued—works well in a number of paired poems, the most notorious of which are probably 2.7 and 2.8, addressed to Cypassis (and immediately preceding the pair discussed here).[5]

The most basic structural components of Ovid's elegiac book, juxtaposition and opposition, are techniques which Ovid also uses with poems that are less clearly to be considered pairs[6] or thematic clusters. Thus, the three poems with which Book 1 opens are clearly linked programmatically; and each of the three books both opens and closes with a poem or poems concerning Ovid's poetic calling.[7] Other pairs or groupings of poems serve a more subtle structural role, sometimes uniting the three books almost as if they were to be read as three dramatic acts:[8] thus, as I have shown elsewhere, 1.15, 2.6, and 3.9, on the poet's immortality, the death of Corinna's parrot, and Tibullus's death, respectively, all approach the theme of poetic immortality from a different perspective, and with each poem we see an increasing awareness on the poet's part of the irony

---

[5] See Watson (1983b).

[6] Davis (1977) uses the term "diptych," borrowed from the visual arts.

[7] On 1.1–3 as Ovid's program, see Boyd (1997) 147–53; cf. also Moles (1991) and Keith (1992b). On 1.1 and 1.15, 2.1 and 2.18–19, and 3.1 and 3.15, cf. also Holzberg (1997b) 13.

[8] Holzberg prefers the imagery of a "Liebesroman," but *mutatis mutandis* his interpretation bears many similarities to mine: (1997a) 42, (1997b) 12–13.

inherent in his position as successor to a long line of inspired poets.[9] In 2.19, Ovid advises the *puella*'s husband to take better care of his wife, since the harder she is to reach the more desirable she is to her lover; in 3.4, we discover that the husband has been doing his job all too well. Again, in 1.4, the *amator* advises his *puella* on how to flirt with him at a party while escaping her husband's notice; in 2.5, she has learned how to do so so well that now she deceives Ovid, too. The two elegies with which I opened this discussion, 2.9 and 9b, are reprised in 3.11 and 11b,[10] the first another attempt to free himself from his love, the second a recognition that his love endures in spite—or perhaps even because—of her betrayal.[11] While not so closely linked dramatically as before-and-after scenes, 2.11 and 2.16 likewise play upon a basic elegiac conceit—the separation of lovers—by imagining two different scenarios which can arise in consequence.[12] The first is a propemptikon in which the *amator* laments Corinna's departure, and the second, a poem in which he urges her to hasten to him in Sulmo. As a final and more complex example of how a number of these structuring devices can be linked to effect marked juxtaposition, contrast, and/or dramatic irony, I note 2.4 and 2.10, both reflections on the *amator*'s seemingly endless interest in (and proven virility regarding) a variety of women, although even as these two poems work together the first is undercut by the second, in which Ovid moves from praising all *puellae* to a focus on two in particular. The first of these, 2.4, is humorously juxtaposed to the diptych 2.2 and 2.3, addressed to the effectively degendered custodian of the lover's *puella*, the eunuch Bagoas; and the boasts of both 2.4 and 2.10 are in turn undermined by the lament of 3.7, on the lover's inopportune impotence.[13]

The current shape of the *Amores* as a collection in three books, apparently published together after the revision of a first edition (on which, see further below), also invites us to see the collection as a

---

[9] Boyd (1997) 165–89.

[10] This division, like that of 2.9 and 2.9b, was first proposed by L. Müller: see Kenney ad loc., Damon (1990), McKeown 3:28–29. Cairns (1979b) reads these also as a single poem.

[11] McKeown 1:95.

[12] McKeown 3:223 and 329–30. On both poems considered separately, see Boyd (1997) 20–30 and 53–66.

[13] See McKeown ad loc.; on 3.7, see Sharrock (1995). For other discussions of structural patterns in the *Amores*, see, e.g., Lorcher (1975).

whole functioning on at least two levels: as a narrative describing the "discovery" of the poet Ovid and his first effort to carve out an identity for himself as elegist,[14] and as a narrative of a love affair, described in perhaps the most complete detail offered by any of the elegists from its origins until its imminent departure from Ovid's life (and he from it).[15] Read in this fashion, the three books can be seen to be subtly but effectively united by the interconnectedness of many of the individual elegies, a few examples of which have been mentioned here: from the opening intervention of Cupid and the forced invention of Ovid the erotic elegist in 1.1 to the poet's heralding of a "greater work" (*grandius opus*, 3.1.70; cf. *area maior*, 3.15.18) to come in Book 3, we see the working through and out of all the conventions of the genre as exemplified most fully by Propertius. With the discovery of a new love in 1.2, Ovid embarks upon a poetic exploration of what it means to be an elegiac lover. The triumph of love and the lover's enrollment in *militia amoris*; the pleasures and pitfalls, even traumas (e.g., abortion; impotence), associated with an intense physical relationship; the game of seduction, the risk of discovery, and the pain of betrayal; the hyperbolic violence of passion and the melodrama of separation—all these themes and emotions are not only treated by Ovid, but are explored and varied, even inverted, as the poet approaches them from a variety of different perspectives. Ovid thus claims "subjective" elegy for himself, pushing the genre to its very limits by exposing its workings.[16] Paired poems like those under consideration here, 2.9 and 2.9b, are an important part of the techniques Ovid uses to incorporate this double narrative into the *Amores*—while in the first of these elegies we see the abject lover, beaten both by Cupid and by his own emotional turmoil, the second

---

[14] Boyd (1997) 136; see also Holzberg (above, n. 8). McKeown 1:93–96 resists a reading of the three books as a narrative by arguing that, e.g., the roughly datable historical event alluded to in 1.8, Rome's encounters with the Sygambri between 16 and 8 B.C., and the allusion to an apparently dead Tibullus in 1.15 suggest that at least some of the poems in Book 1 were written after the event commemorated in 3.9, the death of Tibullus. On the dating and publication of the *Amores*, see further below.

[15] Keith (1998) 149–50.

[16] Given Ovid's relationship to his theme, it should perhaps not be surprising that the motif of *servitium amoris* is of far less interest to Ovid than it had been to the earlier elegists. The elegiac *domina*'s role as such in the *Amores* is far diminished from what we see in Propertius and Tibullus; rather, it is divinities like Cupid and Elegia with whom Ovid's relationship is most dynamic.

restores to center stage a poet who controls his material admirably, even if—and because—it is by nature wild and unmanageable. Ovid thus uses the genre to explore and expand upon the oxymoron already developed in verse by Propertius and Tibullus (and, presumably, Gallus):[17] controlled, even analytical passion. Consequently, it is little surprise that the two other Ovidian works most closely connected to the *Amores* in terms of likely date of composition and of theme develop many of the same concerns: the *Heroides* put a name and a virtual face on the *amator's* beloved, as each of the heroines who speaks in these elegies becomes a female counterpart to the lover/poet of the *Amores*; and the first two books of the *Ars Amatoria* (not to mention their sequels) give us the poet now using his earlier experience with love and love poetry as a fertile source of instructive advice addressed to others.

The subject of elegy as a genre, its limits, and its range in turn calls for a consideration of two other related topics, the influence of earlier poetry on Ovid and his response to it. In his discussion of 2.9 (including what I here call 2.9b as well), McKeown has collected a large group of earlier examples of the *renuntiatio amoris*, from both Hellenistic epigram and earlier Roman love poetry; he also suggests that Propertius 2.12, the description of a playfully destructive Cupid, is an important source for Ovid.[18] The clichéd character of the theme itself should make us wonder why Ovid would take it on—but then, this same question writ large has dogged criticism of the *Amores* as a whole until very recently.[19] Yet when we turn from the general theme to its particulars as developed by Ovid, there is ample indication in both poems of this pair that Ovid is using this cliché as an opportunity to experiment with elegy.

To return to 2.9, then, let us consider the address to Cupid with which the poem opens. Its stylistic elevation suggests (to Cupid and reader alike) that Ovid is about to launch into a prayer, mock or serious, to the god (1–8):

> O numquam pro me satis indignate Cupido,
>   o in corde meo desidiose puer,
> quid me, qui miles numquam tua signa reliqui,
>   laedis, et in castris uulneror ipse meis?

---

[17] On the likely character of Gallus's *Amores*, see Ross (1975) esp. 39–50.
[18] McKeown 3:169–70.
[19] Boyd (1997) Introduction.

cur tua fax urit, figit tuus arcus amicos?
> gloria pugnantes uincere maior erat.
quid? non Haemonius, quem cuspide perculit, heros
> confossum medica postmodo iuuit ope?

O Cupid, never despised enough in proportion to my situation, o boy lazy in the case of my heart, why do you harm me, who as a soldier in your service has never abandoned your standards, and who am myself wounded in my own camp? Why does your torch burn your friends, your bow and arrow strike them? There would be greater glory in conquering those who fight you. Well then—did not the Haemonian hero later aid with medical assistance the wounded one whom he had struck with his spear?

The fact that the first couplet does not end with a complete pause is noteworthy, given Ovid's usually tidy handling of the elegiac distich;[20] equally striking are the two epithets for Cupid with which Ovid sets the tone here, *indignate*[21] and *desidiose*. While the precise meaning of the first of these is problematic, the general sense is not entirely opaque: as Bömer suggests,[22] *indignatio* is more often felt by deities against humans than vice versa; here, the inversion of this relationship, i.e., the despising of a god by a human, sets the tone for the reproaches to follow. *Desidiose* underlines the sense of ironic inversion in this couplet: *desidia* is precisely the thing Ovid had foresworn in 1.9, when after demonstrating through a long series of exempla that military and amatory campaigns are equally strenuous, he declares (31–32): *ergo desidiam quicumque uocabat amorem,/ desinat: ingenii est experientis Amor.* The physical rigor associated with *amor* is emphasized again in the final verse of 1.9, when the poet defines love as the very opposite of *desidia* (46): *qui nolet fieri desidiosus, amet.*[23] In fact, the relationship between *desidia* in the opening of 2.9 and its status at the end of 1.9, while inverted, is simultaneously reinforced by the accumulation of military imagery in the two couplets that follow: *miles . . . tua signa* (3), *in castris uulneror . . . meis* (4), *gloria pugnantes uincere maior erat* (6); and the exemplum provided by Achilles

---

[20] On the infrequency of run-on couplets in the *Amores*, see McKeown 1:108–12; Kenney, chapter 2 above, discusses the integrity of the typical Ovidian couplet.

[21] Following Kenney; McKeown 3:170–71, "hesitantly" following Goold (1965) 35, prefers the alternate reading *O numquam pro re satis indignande Cupido*; see also Booth (1991) ad loc.

[22] Bömer, *Met.* 1 on 1.181, noted by McKeown 3:171.

[23] See McKeown 2:280 and 3:172; Booth (1991) ad loc.

(*Haemonius . . . heros*, 7) parallels the featuring of Achilles in an exemplum at 1.9.33–34 meant to illustrate that even the greatest military heroes have experienced the rigors of love. In 2.9, however, Cupid is behaving in what is both an extremely novel and extremely annoying way: he does not move on, once having vanquished Ovid, but lingers lazily and allows his victim no escape.

In the couplets to follow, the lover as poet decides to offer Cupid himself some advice in the form of exempla: both in war and in hunting, the victors generally move on to new conquests, so Cupid should follow their lead (9–16). In fact, Rome herself is the perfect embodiment of the right attitude; had she not actively extended her reach around the world, her inhabitants would still be living in thatched huts (17–18). Ovid closes this part of his argument with a new series of exempla,[24] serving to illustrate that retirement is appropriate for worn-out objects, animals, and people alike (19–24).

Poem 2.9 thus concluded, we can see that by itself it neatly responds to and inverts in an unexpected way the lesson of 1.9: it is indeed not the lover who is lazy, but Love himself. The exertion expended by the lover is all well and good, but ultimately pointless, at least in Ovid's case: and so the general wisdom I have already cited from 1.9.31–32, *ergo desidiam quicumque uocabat amorem,/desinat*, is not only of absolutely no use, but also wrong. Cupid is the embodiment of *desidia*.

The radical revisionism of 2.9 would seem to be the final word on the subject—until, that is, we turn to 2.9b, and consider its opening lines (1–2): '*Viue*' *deus* '*posito*' *si quis mihi dicat* '*amore*',/*deprecer: usque adeo dulce puella malum est.* As in 2.9, so in this elegy the first verse is not immediately perfectly clear: is the speaker of the imaginary advice given at the opening of the poem a god (*deus . . . si quis*), or is *deus* in apposition with the subject of the advice, i.e., '*Viue deus posito . . . amore*'?[25] The latter alternative would imply that some unnamed person, presumably a (misguided) friend, has advised Ovid that a loveless (and presumably, therefore, painless) existence is what separates gods from mortals. My own preference is to imagine that "some god" is the speaker, presumably a god other than Cupid, and that having overheard the lament of the preceding poem he rec-

---

[24] Reminiscent, McKeown notes, of the exempla at Prop. 2.25.5–8.
[25] The second of these was proposed by Fliedner (1975), cited by McKeown 3:183.

ommends to the poet a life free of love. But we are in for a sur-
prise with the opening of the second verse: *deprecer: usque adeo dulce
puella malum est.* Yet again the lover is back, having changed his mind
upon the discovery that the pain of love brings pleasure, too. Ironic-
ally, the lover realizes that he will have better control over his love
if he abandons himself to it—in fact, it is when his passion has sub-
sided that he is most at risk of losing control, for then he can lose
his love.

One could indeed call this a fundamentally Ovidian paradox, not
very different in its essentials from the one to be played out in
extended form in the *Metamorphoses.* Movement and change, both
emotional and physical, give the lover, like the poet, a purpose and
meaning: without love there can be no lover, just as without change
there can be no poet. Ovid underlines this lesson with an extended
simile,[26] the character of which calls for our attention. Just when he
thinks his *ardor* has faded, reports the lover, he is overpowered again
by a *turbo* of some sort: *cum bene pertaesum est animoque relanguit ardor,/
nescioquo miserae turbine mentis agor* (3–4). Because the origin of this
emotional upheaval is not precisely clear, the lover uses two com-
paranda to describe the effect: it is like a horse racing out of con-
trol as his master tries in vain to control the reins (5–6), or like a
sudden breeze which blows a ship off its course just as it is about
to enter the harbor (7–8). Thus, says the lover, does the "uncertain
breeze of Cupid" (*incerta Cupidinis aura,* 9) often carry him back to
his love.

I have discussed elsewhere Ovid's liking for the extended simile,
especially of the compound sort, i.e., with more than one com-
parandum. This important feature of the style of the *Amores* is one
thing which sets off the collection from its elegiac predecessors, as
it allows Ovid to open up elegiac imagery to incorporate vistas from
beyond the elegiac horizon, including the range of epic. Because
Ovid tends to use the extended simile to analyze and intellectualize
his love, this stylistic device also serves to remind us that we are
witnessing at one remove Ovid's poetic love affair. The artifice of
verse transforms experience, so that the lover's abandonment to his
passion becomes a paradoxical way of controlling it.[27]

---

[26] See Boyd (1997) 90–93 on this term, and for an extensive bibliography on
Ovidian and other similes.
[27] Boyd (1997) 141–42.

The extended similes of the *Amores* have not always been seen as among the more successful features of the collection; in fact, because of their obvious association with epic from Homer onward, critics of Ovid have often found his elegiac similes overblown and distracting, indeed, wholly inappropriate to the intimate and closed world of elegy. I have demonstrated elsewhere that it is a more practical sort of criticism to look at these passages as moments in which we can see Ovid attempting to expand the embrace of the genre, to open up its borders to influences from outside the small world of love elegy.[28] His success at doing so can best be evaluated by looking at how Ovid creates these similes, and by observing how these similes function within an individual poem. It should not be surprising to find, given the traditions which nurtured extended similes in ancient poetry, that Ovid uses the imagery they provide both to acknowledge and to transform this inheritance. For the sake of clarity I quote the passage under consideration (2.9b.5–8):

> ut *rapit in praeceps* dominum spumantia frustra
> frena retentantem durior oris *equus*;
> ut *subitus*, prope iam prensa tellure, carinam
> tangentem portus uentus *in alta rapit*—

As a horse too hard of mouth pulls headlong its master, while he tries in vain to restrain the foaming reins; as a sudden wind, when land is just now come within grasp, pulls onto the deep seas the prow at the moment of its reaching the port—

Ovid uses a balanced structure, much as seen also in his exempla, with each couplet encompassing one image and the anaphora of *ut* in asyndeton. The first hemistich of each pentameter is marked by the vivid use of a present participle (*retentantem, tangentem*) to characterize the vain effort expended, by rider and ship, to control the forces working against them. A chiastic pattern links the two similes: *rapit in praeceps* begins 5, and has as its subject *equus* at the end of the first couplet; a nominative epithet, *subitus*, opens 7, while *in alta rapit* ends the second couplet. In addition to contributing to the structural balance of the pair of similes, the repetition of *rapit* also serves to tie together the two similes thematically: Ovid is as much the unwitting victim of his own passion as is the master of a runaway horse or a ship blown back out to sea as it heads for shore.

---

[28] Boyd (1997) 90–103.

The two separate images are also linked by the use of language in the first which also belongs to the range of imagery in the second: The reins (*spumantia . . ./frena*) held in vain by the horse's master are foaming, much as is the sea when it hosts a raging storm.

The aptness of the imagery used by Ovid here may at first distract us from the fact of its being "borrowed" imagery. In fact, however, two very similar images are used as closings for the two halves of the first *Georgic*.[29] At *G.* 1.201–3, Virgil uses a simile describing a rower who, should he slacken even momentarily, would lose control of his boat because of the river's strong current:

> non aliter quam qui aduerso uix flumine lembum
> remigiis subigit, si bracchia forte remisit,
> atque *illum in praeceps* prono *rapit* alueus amni.

> Not otherwise than the man who, if he by chance has released his arms, scarcely pushes his rowboat with oars against the river, and the river-bed pulls him headlong with its rapid stream.

The image is used by Virgil to illustrate the relentlessness of *labor* in the world of the *Georgics*. As Thomas comments: "This is not a passing touch of pessimism, nor is it embellishment, it is the very heart of the poem."[30] The same pessimistic note is struck at the close of *Georgics* 1, as Virgil uses the image of a chariot out of control to illustrate the current condition of the world as he knows it (1.511–14):

> saevit toto Mars impius orbe,
> ut cum carceribus sese effudere quadrigae,
> addunt in spatia, et *frustra retinacula tendens*
> *fertur equis auriga* neque audit currus habenas.

> Ruthless Mars rages throughout the world, as when four-horse chariots have thrown themselves forth from the gates, increasing their speed from lap to lap, and the charioteer holding the reins in vain is carried along by the horses, and the chariot does not hear the reins.

Ovid's double simile, then, recalls the pessimistic doublet from *Georgics* 1, to illustrate in this case not the ineluctability of *labor* or the madness of war, but rather the emotional struggle raging within him. This reference is not in itself, however, entirely unmediated or straightforward. Rather, Ovid adds to the two couplets features drawn from

---

[29] Thomas, *G.* 1.512–14; cf. Farrell (1991) 167–68.
[30] Thomas, *G.* ad loc.

other similes, again but not exclusively Virgilian. Lines 7–8, *prope iam prensa tellure,* **carinam/tangentem portus**, use similar language but reverse the image found in a third simile from *Georgics* 1, at 303–4: *ceu pressae cum iam* **portum tetigere carinae,**/*puppibus et laeti nautae imposuere coronas.*[31] Propertius clearly has the Virgilian phrasing in mind (though in a broadly metaphorical sense, rather than as a simile), in describing his own restoration to sanity and well-being upon his escape from the emotional turmoil caused by Cynthia (3.24.15–16): *ecce* **coronatae portum tetigere carinae,**/*traiectae Syrtes, ancora iacta mihi est.*[32] In fact, Ovid's use of the Virgilian image in a scene that closely recalls the setting of Propertius's poem but restores the image to a simile acts as a type of "window"[33] reference, in which two models are openly acknowledged at once.

Let us return now to the *tertium comparationis* for Ovid's two similes: as we saw, the fickleness of Cupid (*incerta Cupidinis aura*, 9) has taken Ovid by storm, as it were, and has driven him into a state of emotional confusion. The phrase *incerta aura* is capable of being understood in two different ways: it suggests both a particularly volatile breeze, the direction and source of which keep changing, and a breeze the nature of which is hard to define. Immediately before breaking into his extended simile, Ovid had described the source of his confusion as a *turbo* in his mind, likewise of unknown character (**nescioquo** *miserae* **turbine** *mentis*, 4). The two epithets *nescioquo* and *incerta* which frame the simile effectively provide a rationale for a simile built of two comparanda: in an attempt to describe a feeling he cannot quite comprehend, the lover is driven to use two images to make the sensation thus described as vivid as possible. On a metapoetic level, however, Ovid's repeated emphasis on the indeterminate source of his emotions—what sort of mental *turbo* is this, exactly?—pushes his reader to seek other explanations, and in doing so opens up a new range of *turbines*, all of which are likely to have been a part of the "poetic memory"[34] informing the *Amores*.

---

[31] The context is a description of midsummer; as Mynors (1990) comments ad loc., "The sailors have brought a valuable cargo safe home; hence their joy." The image itself—of safe harbor regained—has a long history in Latin poetry: cf. *Aen.* 4.418 and Pease (1935) ad loc.

[32] Propertius's heralding of the *Aeneid* at 2.34.65–66 indicates that he already had seen (or heard) at least some of the poem before it was published.

[33] Thomas (1986) 188.

[34] The term is Conte's (1986) 35–36: see Boyd (1997) 27–30.

The word *turbo* (and its uncommon variant, *turben*)[35] has an unusually broad range of meanings, developed from its basic association with a whirling or spinning movement. It can denote both natural phenomena, like whirlwinds, violent storms, and whirlpools, and man-made spinning tools and toys, like spindles, fly-wheels, and tops (*OLD* s.v.). Thus, *turbo* can be used to describe both something that whirls of (what at least to the naked eye seems to be) its own accord, like a strong wind, and something that is spun by the application of an external force, like a spindle or top. The imagery of Ovid's *nescio-quo miserae turbine mentis agor* in fact seems to combine the two aspects of *turbo*—he both is driven (*agor*) by a *turbo*, which acts upon him as an alien force of sorts, and imagines it as a metaphor for the turmoil within himself (*miserae turbine mentis*).[36]

The expressive range of *turbo* appears to have been exploited first in Latin poetry by Catullus, in a poem of unparalleled formative importance to several generations of poets following him: *turbo* appears three times in the so-called epyllion 64. DeBrohun has recently discussed Catullus's play with *turbo*, noting a duality or ambivalence in its meaning for the story of Ariadne's abandonment by Theseus.[37] Its first use is by the narrator of 64, in a simile describing the way in which Theseus overwhelms the Minotaur in the labyrinth (105–10):

nam uelut in summo quatientem bracchia Tauro
quercum aut conigeram sudanti cortice pinum
indomitus turbo contorquens flamine robur
eruit (illa procul radicitus exturbata
prona cadit, late quaeuis cumque obuia frangens),
sic domito saeuum prostrauit corpore Theseus...

...for just as an untamed whirlwind, twisting timber with its blast, uproots the oak shaking its limbs on lofty Taurus or the cone-bearing pine with its sap-oozing bark (and the tree falls forward at length, removed by force from its roots and breaking everything in its path far and wide), so did Theseus lay low the savage beast with its tamed body...

---

[35] Murgatroyd (1980/1991) ad loc. and Critical Appendix 310. Interestingly, Servius on *Aen.* 7.378 notes that this unusual alternative form was used by Catullus. Although *turben* does not appear in the extant Catullan corpus, it should perhaps come as no surprise that Servius associates Catullus with this word and its connotations; see my discussion below.

[36] The ambiguous character of the top's propulsion—driven from without or generated within?—made it an appealing subject in Stoic debates of causality and responsibility: see Rabel (1981); cf. Horsfall (2000) on Virg. *Aen.* 7.378.

[37] DeBrohun (1999) esp. 424–26.

DeBrohun observes multiple ambiguities in this simile, only one of which we need recall here: Catullus marks the thematic centrality of the word *turbo* by repeating its sound in the word *exturbata* (108),[38] simultaneously complicating its interpretation by linking the second word not to the whirlwind but to the uprooted tree, torn out of the ground in a whirling blast.[39]

The complication grows with the next appearance of *turbo* in 64, this time in Ariadne's monologue: she is the one responsible for saving the treacherous hero from certain death, '*certe ego te in medio uersantem turbine leti/eripui*' (149–50). Here, the word *turbo* is not applied to Theseus himself, nor to the Minotaur, but apparently to the labyrinth or the violent confrontation experienced within it. Thus, she locates the violent movement associated with this image not in Theseus himself, but in the external forces which, without her help, would have overwhelmed him.

Ariadne's intervention gives Theseus only temporary reprieve from destruction, however, for after he abandons her and she calls down a curse on him, we learn from the narrator how the Parcae resume their handiwork, one of them spinning out the thread of destiny: *libratum tereti uersabat turbine fusum* (314). With this instance of *turbo*, Catullus exploits its concrete application to the drop-spindle used for making thread; simultaneously, of course, the imagery of spinning associated with the Parcae has a metaphorical dimension, and this *turbo* takes on the character of fate, spun outside of Theseus's control but destined to overcome him. In the course of this poem, then, Catullus has exploited the range of *turbo* as both concrete object and metaphor, as both a violent force within an agent brought to bear upon another and an external agency of doom. "Was Ariadne, then, an agent of fate, or one of its victims (or both)?"[40]

---

[38] And perhaps by anticipating it as well in *Tauro* (105): DeBrohun (1999) 425 n. 18.

[39] Is it possible that Catullus is engaging in an interlingual wordplay here as well? The simile of a tree torn by its roots from the ground has obvious Homeric antecedents, including the scene in *Iliad* 14 when, struck by a rock thrown by Telamonian Ajax, Hector falls to the ground in a coma, "like a tree..." Homer precedes this extended simile with a much briefer comparison, saying that Ajax strikes Hector "like a top" (στρόμβον δ'ὣς, *Il.* 14.413). In using the word *turbo* at 64.107 to describe the force that uproots a tree, Catullus may be conflating the two Homeric similes.

[40] DeBrohun (1999) 426.

Lest I seem to have roamed rather far afield in this discussion of Catullus's use of *turbo*, let me emphasize why I think it is relevant to Ovid's use of *turbo* in *Amores* 2.9b: I do not mean to suggest that Ovid is "imitating" Catullus here, or even that he is "alluding" to him for any particularly significant purpose. Rather, my goal is to demonstrate first of all how the imagery of *turbo* has become, long before Ovid "discovers" it, a valuable part of the Latin poetic vernacular, particularly because of its broad and suggestive range and profound ambiguity; and secondly, how with the single word *nescio-quo* Ovid can evoke this range and ambiguity, confident that at least his thoughtful readers will appreciate the gesture. A third goal is the one to which I shall now direct attention again: the power of similes to introduce both a certain clarity and a blurring ambiguity into the contexts in which they occur.

This phenomenon is clearly captured by Virgil's use of *turbo* in two very different similes in the *Aeneid*,[41] two similes which also move us closer to the range of meanings exploited by Ovid. At *Aen.* 2.416–19, Virgil uses *turbo* in a simile to describe the onslaught of the Greeks:

> *aduersi rupto ceu quondam turbine uenti*
> *confligunt*, Zephyrusque Notusque et laetus Eois
> Eurus equis; stridunt siluae saeuitque tridenti
> spumeus atque imo Nereus ciet aequora fundo.

> As when opposing winds collide, when once a whirlwind has burst forth, the West Wind and South Wind, and the Southeast Wind, rejoicing in the horses of dawn; the forests resound with harsh creaking, and foaming Nereus rages with his trident and stirs up the seas from the very depths; . . .

Virgil's imagery in this simile parallels that used by Ovid: the winds are headed in many directions at once, and the calm waters are stirred to their depths. All of this turmoil, blasting sea and sky, is the result of a whirlwind; agency and outcome are virtually identical. Similarly, the Greek attack, provoked by the temporary loss of Cassandra (*ereptae uirginis ira*, *Aen.* 2.413), is a demonstration of wrath born of wrath, violence leading to violence.

---

[41] Rabel (1981) observes the play on meanings of *turbo* in Virgil.

Another sort of *turbo* is envisioned by Virgil later in the poem, however, when he uses the image to illustrate the frenzy of Amata when inflamed by Allecto (*Aen.* 7.378–84):

> ceu quondam torto uolitans sub uerbere *turbo*,
> quem pueri magno in gyro uacua atria circum
> intenti ludo exercent—ille *actus* habena
> curuatis fertur spatiis; stupet inscia supra
> impubesque manus mirata uolubile buxum;
> dant animos plagae; non cursu segnior illo
> per medias urbes *agitur* populosque ferocis.

> As once a top, flying beneath the twisted lash, a top which boys, intent on their game, drive in a great spiral around the empty halls—that top, driven by a whip, is carried through winding spaces; unknowing, the youthful band gapes from above, amazed, marvelling at the spinning boxwood; their blows give it energy to move. No more slowly than that top's course is Amata driven, through the midst of cities and fierce peoples.

The Virgilian image is unusual both in its content and in its development of material seemingly extraneous to the major comparison. As West has shown, however, the wealth of detail in this simile is best understood as contributing to the multiple correspondences between simile and narrative. West draws attention in particular to the repetition of forms of the verb *agere* both in the simile and around it, and to the description of the top's movement, so like that of the Bacchants whom Amata will presently provoke to dance. Both of these points bear emphasizing, because they focus our attention on the nature of the agency acting upon the spinning top: Virgil compares Amata to a *turbo* driven at first from without, as a toy by playful children, but gradually becoming self-propelling and a source of provocation for others. Ovid, on the other hand, says that he is driven by a *turbo*; we might go so far as to put Cupid in the role of playful child, but Ovid does not explicitly do so. Rather, he invites us to think about the difference between the two sources of energy suggested by Virgil even as he implies a similarity through the use of the verb *agor* (28), which in various forms appears several times in the Virgilian passage: *actus* (380) and *agitur* (384), as seen above, and later in the description of Amata, *agit* (393 and 405).[42] Are we,

---

[42] On the repetition of *agere* in this passage, see West (1969) 49.

then, to think of Ovid as out of control and driven by forces out-
side himself, like Amata-as-top? Or might Ovid expect us to recall
as well that, immediately after Virgil compares Amata to a top, he
describes how she herself becomes in turn an agent of chaos and
unrest, provoking the Italian *matres* to leave their homes and join the
ecstatic following of Bacchus (7.385–405)? The *turbo* which had begun
by exerting itself upon Amata externally has now taken up residence
within her, thus confronting us with a Virgilian reversal from victim
to aggressor.[43] We may well wonder whether the *turbo* experienced
by Ovid may not in fact have a similar outcome.

We would of course expect to find that Ovid's questioning of the
origins and implications of his inner turmoil is much more lightly
handled than what we have seen in the *Aeneid* (or in Catullus, for
that matter); indeed, with his concluding description of the *turbo* as
incerta Cupidinis aura, Ovid pulls back from the ambiguity of the pre-
ceding lines and "chooses" a definition, so to speak. The *turbo* inflicted
upon him is in fact a whirlwind "out there," not within him; it has
a divine source, Cupid; its very ambiguity is in fact a familiar sen-
sation (*sic me saepe refert*, 9), and the weapons used to inflict it are
well known (*nota . . . tela*, 10). "That old, familiar feeling" is the stuff
of elegy, after all; and in exerting the power of language and poetic
imagery to express this feeling, Ovid demonstrates that, after all, this
lover controls his love, rather than the other way around.

Ovid's exploration of the meaning of *nescioquis turbo* through alter-
native similes concludes with what I have suggested is a clarification
of its meaning; his linking of *turbo* with *aura* also suggests a "tam-
ing" of the imagery, so to speak—*aura* is generally used to describe
a much weaker and less overwhelming phenomenon than is *turbo*.
In fact, the one other appearance of *turbo* in Catullus besides those
I have already noted juxtaposes *turbo* and *aura* as two very different
types of air movement, the first dangerous and destructive, the second
soothing and restorative. We should not be surprised, I think, to find
that the context is one of Catullus's most elaborate similes (it con-
stitutes in fact a simile within a simile), in poem 68: *hic uelut* **in
nigro** *iactatis* **turbine** *nautis*/**lenius aspirans aura secunda** *uenit . . .*
(63–64). Catullus is describing the relief he experienced as a result
of Allius's support of his love affair; for him, then, *turbo* symbolizes

---

[43] See Horsfall (2000) ad loc. throughout this passage; and cf. Rabel (1981).

the state of being separated from his beloved, while *aura* represents the intervention of Allius. The strong contrast in Catullus is muted in Ovid—while Catullus had emphasized the difference between *turbo* and *aura*, Ovid draws on their similarities. But both lovers are, at least by implication, the storm-tossed sailors of these similes, saved to weather the storm of love again.

The range of Ovid's play with *turbo* is made fully apparent when we turn to Tibullus, who like Ovid uses a simile featuring a *turben*[44] to describe the emotional turmoil of being in love, a condition he has attempted repeatedly to abandon but which he finds himself drawn to again and again: *namque* agor **ut** *per plana citus sola* **uerbere turben,**/*quem celer adsueta uersat ab arte puer* (1.5.3–4). Tibullus's *turben*, the toy of a playful boy, drives him about like the *turbo* by which Ovid describes himself as being overwhelmed—but Tibullus has chosen to describe in very precise terms the same phenomenon left vague by Ovid. Tibullus is evidently looking to a Callimachean description of boys and their tops for the imagery of his simile. In *Epigram* 1 Pf., Callimachus reports that Pittacus, when asked for advice about choosing a wife, pointed to some boys playing with tops and indicated that they had the answer (7–12):

> . . . ὁ δὲ σκίπωνα γεροντικὸν ὅπλον ἀείρας·
> 'ἠνίδε κεῖνοί σοι πᾶν ἐρέουσιν ἔπος.'
> οἱ δ' ἄρ' ὑπὸ πληγῆσι θοὰς βέμβικας ἔχοντες
> ἔστρεφον εὐρείῃ παῖδες ἐνὶ τριόδῳ.
> 'κείνων ἔρχεο,' φησί, 'μετ' ἴχνια.' χὠ μὲν ἐπέστη
> πλησίον· οἱ δ' ἔλεγον· 'τὴν κατὰ σαυτὸν ἔλα.'

> And raising his staff, an old man's weapon, [Pittacus said]: "Look, those [boys] will tell the whole story to you." For the boys were spinning swift tops by blows at a broad crossroad. "Go," he says, "in their tracks." And he stood by; they were saying, "keep to your course."

The apparent κληδών convinces the enquirer to stay with a woman of his own class; as the boys seek to control their tops, so should he control his desire. Callimachus's depiction of the spinning of tops by boys at a broad crossroads (εὐρείῃ ἐνὶ τριόδῳ) is clearly echoed by Tibullus's *per plana . . . sola*; but whereas there is a group of boys in Callimachus, Tibullus focuses in on one. Even more striking, however, is the reversal of meaning that results from the use of the boys-and-tops similes by both poets: Callimachus chooses to

---

[44] See above, n. 35.

emphasize the desirability of control, while Tibullus uses the image to describe his own loss of control. Ovid in turn makes the same point as Tibullus—the on-again, off-again character of love—even as he rejects the meaning given to *turbo/turben* by the earlier elegist. Inspired by the conflation of Virgil's two *turbo* similes, Ovid's "correction" of Tibullus is substantive as well as stylistic: not only does Ovid complicate the simile by offering alternative images, but he also ultimately chooses a definition for *turbo* different from that used by Tibullus. In simultaneously including the Tibullan simile in and excluding it from his frame of reference, Ovid recognizes that the poems of both elegists address the plight of indecision aroused by amatory *furor*; he also, in passing, offers a rereading of a curious and disturbing moment in the *Aeneid*, when Amata sets out to bring chaos among the Latin women, driven by Allecto.[45] The *furor* that drives her is not the same, or at least it appears not to be, as the amatory *furor* of an indecisive lover; yet, as Ovid's reader knows, Amata's *furor* is disturbingly suggestive (cf. *Aen.* 7.344–45),[46] and may well not be neatly separable from erotic passion. Even the variability noted earlier in the imagery surrounding the two kinds of *turbines*, one internally driven and the other externally pushed, advances the two-sidedness of Ovid's evocation of the nature of love in 2.9 and 2.9b—his lack of emotional control is captured and controlled through the language of emotion in Latin poetry. And in a final typically Ovidian gesture, the paradox of controlled *furor* that teases its way through the poem receives redefinition—and clarification—in ironic closure at the end of the elegy, as the generically tantalizing *nescioquis turbo* gives way to a disorderly but ultimately far more manageable phenomenon: *nimium vaga* **turba**, *puellae* (29). Ovid's *amator* acknowledges that he has been bested by Cupid—but then, so have all those wayward girls who, in their very number, universalize the experience and make love elegy familiar territory after all. Simultaneously, Ovid acknowledges that the lesson of the Callimachean epigram has been learned, too: just as Pittacus uses the example of the playing boys to make the punning point, "Stay in your course," so Ovid returns in *Amores* 2.9b to the literary theme—and love-life—we know best.

---

[45] See now also Bleisch (1996), who develops an argument at length for the relevance of the Callimachean epigram to Virgil's top-simile; and see the full discussion of Horsfall (2000) ad loc.

[46] Cf. Lyne (1987) 13–16, 116–17.

2. Historical Questions

As the preceding discussion has illustrated in passing, questions of
influence and relative priority are not automatically and easily answered
by readers of the *Amores*. It would be much easier to be certain about
the role played by Tibullus and Propertius, e.g., not to mention by
Virgil, in Ovid's early poetic development if we were able to fix on
a date for the publication of the *Amores*; but we cannot. We simply
do not have a definitive indication, either in the work of Ovid him-
self or in references to Ovid's work made by contemporaries or later
writers, when the poems were begun, when they were finished, when
published, when revised. From exile, Ovid himself refers to these
poems only as a work of his youth (*Tr.* 4.10.57–58)—but there is a
period of about 20 years, between Ovid's twentieth and fortieth birth-
days, more or less, about which he tells us even less. It is only at
the end of this period that most scholars would locate the approx-
imate age at which he may well have published the first two books
of the *Ars*.[47] A logical, though not essential, *terminus post quem* for the
start of the *Amores* would appear to be Ovid's eighteenth birthday
in 25 B.C.; but again, this tells us nothing about the actual facts of
publication, which may have taken place as little as a year or two
or as much as 20 years (or more) later.[48] A further question con-
cerns the relative timing of the composition of the *Heroides* and the
first two books (at least) of the *Ars Amatoria*: the notoriously prob-
lematic *Amores* 2.18[49] indicates that at least some of the *Heroides* had
already been written by the time of this poem's appearance, and the
mention of *artes Amoris* at 2.18.19 suggests that the *Ars* are in progress,
too. We thus have, at least potentially, not one but three major early
collections attributable to the period c. 25–c. 2 B.C.; and, given the
clear indications that, later in his career, Ovid was inclined not to
limit himself exclusively to work on one project at a time,[50] it may

---

[47] See Watson, chapter 5 below; cf. McKeown 1:74–89 for a summary of what
we do and do not know, or suspect, about the relative chronology of Ovid's early
works, and Holzberg (1997a) 41–48 and (1997b) 10–15 for an alternative (and much
simpler) chronology.

[48] Cameron (1968); McKeown 1:84–85.

[49] See the relevant discussions of Knox, chapter 4 below, and Watson, chapter 5
below; McKeown 1:86–89 provides a summary of opinion and a cautious approach;
Holzberg (1997b) reopens the debate.

[50] E.g., Hinds (1987a) *passim*.

well be anything but daring to suggest that his earlier career witnessed the first manifestations of this tendency.

Uncertainty regarding the dating of the *Amores*' composition is further complicated by the (presumably) separate matter of their publication. The witty epigraph with which three of the four earliest manuscripts for the *Amores* open the collection raises the question squarely:

> Qui modo Nasonis fueramus quinque libelli,
> > tres sumus: hoc illi praetulit auctor opus.
> ut iam nulla tibi nos sit legisse uoluptas,
> > at leuior demptis poena duobus erit.

> We who had just recently been the five books of Naso are now three: the author preferred the present collection to the previous one. Although you may now get no pleasure in reading us, at least, with two books removed, your suffering will be lighter.

In the first couplet, Ovid's "talking books" report that, though once five in number, they have now become three; and the phrasing of the final pentameter (*demptis . . . duobus*) is explicit—or so it first appears; it remains to be asked whether the poet has indeed removed some poems that had originally appeared in the collection, and if so, whether he has supplemented them with others, or simply cut away; whether he has rearranged the remaining elegies, or left them in virtually the same configuration as that in which they had appeared earlier, but now with different book divisions; and to what extent if any the poems as we currently have them show signs of an earlier and a later edition. The facts, such as they are, are well known, and I shall not rehearse them here;[51] but it is worth noting that the frustratingly aporetic nature of all enquiries into the circumstances of the *Amores*' publication has recently been met head on by the suggestion, from varied quarters, that the epigraph itself is a bit of metapoetic fun, and that there really was no "earlier" edition than that which we have now: Ovid is simply announcing to all who may be about to embark upon a reading of the *Amores*, the very first words of which (*arma graui numero uiolentaque bella parabam/edere*, 1.1.1–2), if taken by themselves, herald—ominously—an epic undertaking, that this is no anti-Callimachean "big book" after all.[52]

---

[51] Cameron (1968), McKeown 1:76–82, 90–102.

[52] For three voices raised independently in support of this view, see Barchiesi

Whatever we conclude, the fact remains that, as we have it, the collection appears to consist of 50 poems, neatly arranged in three books as 15 + 20 + 15—so long as we agree with the poem divisions discussed above, and acknowledge the apparent inauthenticity of 3.5.[53] This tidy arrangement invites comparison with the most self-consciously Alexandrianizing publications of the 30s and 20s B.C., chief among them the *Eclogues*, the Propertian *Monobiblos*, and Horace's three books of *Odes*. Appearing as these did at a formative time in Ovid's literary education, they are likely to have made a lasting impression; but whether this impression first bore fruit in the late 20s or at any other point in the next two decades B.C. has not been, and is not likely soon to be, conclusively answered. What is clear, as we have already seen, is that at least in its present configuration the collection works as a planned unit, with three dramatic acts, so to speak, in the progress of Ovid's literary love affair captured by each of the three books.

When we turn elsewhere for clues to the earliest publication history of the *Amores*, the necessary imprecision of the picture already sketched is only reaffirmed. Corinna in role and in name clearly follows in a long line of literary mistresses, beginning with Catullus's Lesbia and continuing to Gallus's Lycoris, Propertius's Cynthia, and Tibullus's Delia; but unlike these other women, whose real identities are evidently concealed behind poetically apt pseudonyms, Corinna is not unmasked by any ancient commentator.[54] We can therefore not link her or her husband to a social circle known from other sources; and indeed, as I have suggested elsewhere, she may be as fictive as is the erotic drama Ovid creates around her.[55] Even more curious, perhaps, is the fact that Ovid mentions no great and powerful friend as dedicatee or intended recipient of the collection; there is no Pollio, no Messalla, no Maecenas here, and only three of the poems (1.9, 2.10, 2.18) have named addressees.[56] Any number of

---

(1997c [1988]) 101–3; Boyd (1997) 142–47; and Holzberg (1997a) 41–43, (1997b) 10–14.

[53] On the history of 3.5's association with the collection, see Kenney (1969a); Richmond, chapter 14, below; and McKeown's discussion, forthcoming, in the final volume of his commentary.

[54] For Lesbia, Cynthia, and Delia, Apuleius *Apol.* 10; for Lycoris, Servius on *Ecl.* 10.1.

[55] Boyd (1997) 133–34.

[56] McKeown 1:25; Boyd (1997) 134; White, chapter 1 above.

scenarios may be imagined to explain this absence—and, if provable, might be used to narrow the likely timing for the collection's publication. As it is, however, the sparse links to real people and events offered in the *Amores* only serve to emphasize the unusual "weightlessness" of the collection in the Augustan cultural universe.

Most interesting in this regard is the overarching absence of extended political or historical references in the poems. Aside from an allusion to the Sygambri at 1.14.45–50,[57] no historical events are explicitly mentioned in the *Amores*. 3.9 eulogizes the dead Tibullus, whose passing is generally believed to have taken place around 19 B.C., and in 1.15.25–28 the deaths of both Virgil and Tibullus are taken as facts.[58] In this regard the *Amores* are far closer in feel to the *Heroides*, which exist almost entirely in the timeless (albeit changing) world of myth, than to the *Ars*, which locates itself and its poet squarely in the streets, buildings, and public spaces, and among the people, of Augustan Rome.

There is on the other hand and more broadly speaking a distinctively (though not necessarily pro- or anti-)Augustan cast to the collection, seen chiefly in Ovid's engagement with subject matter reflective—or subversive?—of Augustan family values. Thus, Barchiesi has pointed to Ovid's clever and complex transformation, at *Am.* 3.11.39, of the truism "women—can't live with them, can't live without them" as observed by the censor Q. Caecilius Metellus Macedonicus in his speech *de prole augenda*, delivered in 131 B.C. and repeated before the senate by Augustus, most likely in 18/17 B.C., in support of his pro-marriage agenda.[59] Mediated through an Ovidian re-reading of Catullan questioning of Roman values, this cliché takes on new pointedness, simultaneously echoing the political discourse of the age and establishing an aesthetic distance from it. Whether we are to see and interpret this as a precise indication of impending social repressiveness by Augustus, and of Ovid's undermining of the paternalistic authoritarianism of the Princeps, or as part and parcel of the very essence of amatory elegy—and of the elegist himself who, by definition, rejects political limitations upon his identity—is however less clear, as both intent and intensity on the part of Ovid

---

[57] See above, n. 14.

[58] See McKeown 1:79–80 for possible interpretations of references to other poets in the *Amores*.

[59] Barchiesi (1997c [1988]); see also the companion piece by Badian (1997 [1988]).

are as difficult to define here as ever. Even with the abortion-poems 2.13 and 2.14, sometimes viewed in the context of Augustan family legislation,[60] we should not lose sight of the fact that the melodramatic excess found in them is cut from the same cloth as that found in a poem like *Amores* 1.14, where Ovid's solitary reference to the Sygambri is made not as a criticism of Roman military endeavors *per se*, but in the context of an ironic solution to Corinna's traumatic baldness—now she will have to buy a wig made from the hair of a Sygambrian woman.

We may look back at the pair of poems discussed earlier in the chapter to test this view. In *Amores* 2.9 and 2.9b, Ovid incorporates (or reflects) what might both properly and imprecisely be termed Augustan political discourse. In the first poem, as part of his complaint that it is time for Cupid to let him be and to move on to new conquests, Ovid draws an analogy between what Cupid should be doing and the way in which Rome herself has agressively promoted her own global authority: *Roma, nisi immensum uires promosset in orbem,/stramineis esset nunc quoque tecta casis* (2.9.17–18). Ringing yet another change on the topoi of Cupid's triumph and the lover as soldier (cf. *Amores* 1.2 and 1.9), Ovid suggests that Rome provides a good role model for Cupid: just as the Romans have progressed from the primitive Romulean huts in which they first lived (and which witnessed the first Roman battle waged for love, the rape of the Sabines) to world prominence through aggression, so can—and should—Cupid move outward and away from the modest triumph represented by Ovid to bigger and better prey. In 2.9b, Ovid again uses Cupid's military accomplishments, now even trumping those of Cupid's step-father Mars, to explain his own willing resubmission to the on-again, off-again life of love: *quod dubius Mars est, per te, priuigne Cupido, est,/et mouet exemplo uitricus arma tuo* (2.9b.23–24). Ovid's clever inversion of "every lover is a soldier"—here, the soldier par excellence becomes a lover, too[61]—seems to flout the very glorification of military accomplishment urged upon Cupid in the earlier poem. Each poem engages, however momentarily and lightly, the fabric of its world, creating a way to find humor in what is otherwise the serious

---

[60] E.g., Gamel (1989).
[61] Cf. Ovid's similar treatment of Mars in *F.* 3.1–10, introducing Mars's rape of Silvia, and see Hinds's discussion of the episode, (1992) 88–105.

and deadly business of war. These poems thus offer an ironic take on Ovid's times, as well as on his love; but whether we are therefore invited to go further, and to see this as a political statement, intended or otherwise, on Ovid's part is a leap we are not I think invited by Ovid to take. To those readers more keenly driven than I to find the stirrings of a political subversive in Ovid's first poems, I would point to the delicate balancing-act between social and political critique on the one hand and escapism into the worlds of Greek myth and Roman antiquarianism on the other achieved by Ovid and for so long negotiated by readers of the *Fasti* and *Metamorphoses*. It should come as little surprise to find the same poet experimenting in his early work with the same delicate balance, even as he focuses most of his energy and talent on the more immediate, and immediately rewarding, project of establishing a literary identity.

3. *Concluding Remarks*

The poetry of the mature Ovid has garnered much of the critical limelight in the past two decades: his quixotic changes of mood and style, his lightly-worn but profound learning, his combination of political skittishness and social nicety, and the sheer audacity of his subject matter make his later work the single most extended virtuoso performance of the age (aside, perhaps, from Livy's history—but that is an altogether different matter). And our fascination with his work grows the closer we get to the time of his exile, not because we are expecting to discover any new factual "clues" to its cause but because of a conviction that Ovid is in the details, and that something in those details can lead us to a better understanding of how this brilliantly clever man was caught short by Augustus. It is worth remembering in this regard that on at least one other occasion Augustus tolerated a long wait between the time of making a promise and that of seeing its fulfillment—I refer to his vowing of the temple of Mars Ultor in 42 B.C., as a monument to the vengeance he swore after the battle of Philippi. It is a familiar but controversial fact that the building itself of the temple did not begin when Augustus came to power in 31 B.C., or when he received his *imperium* in 27 B.C. Instead, the temple and its enclosing forum were dedicated in 2 B.C., 40 years later, the temple itself not yet quite finished; and as we

know from a number of sources, including Ovid,[62] Augustus sup-
plemented his original vow to the Avenger with a more recent (though
by no means fast-breaking) reason for celebration, the retrieval of
the Parthian standards in 20 B.C. When we consider the possible
causes for Ovid's *relegatio* in A.D. 8, therefore, we are well advised to
remember that the Princeps was not necessarily driven to action in
haste, and that the seeds of his displeasure with Ovid are likely to
have been planted long before our poet saw Rome for the last time.
Already in the *Amores*, I suggest, we see the preparation of fertile
ground to receive that seed, and the earliest evidence for the sort of
poet that Ovid not only would become but already was—pushing
the limits (of convention, genre, discretion) and refusing to be bound
to or by anything other than his own genius. Even in his earliest
literary incarnation, Ovid manages to elude our most earnest attempts
to make him fit easy definition. Instead, he gives us *Ouidius poeta*, the
Amores' greatest, most versatile, and most dangerous invention.

---

[62] *F.* 5.551–96; see Bömer *F.* ad loc. and Fantham, chapter 7 below.

CHAPTER FOUR

THE *HEROIDES*: ELEGIAC VOICES

Peter E. Knox

It may have been his reading of the third poem in Propertius's final book that sparked Ovid's imagination and inspired him to compose the *Heroides*. Propertius 4.3 takes the form of an imaginary letter from a woman named Arethusa to her lover Lycotas, a soldier who is away on campaign. It is a very different kind of poem, however, from Ovid's series of imaginary epistles by figures from literature. Since at least the ninth century, the reading public in the West encountered these poems in a collection of 20 epistles,[1] known generally as Ovid's *liber epistularum* or *liber heroidum*. The earliest citations of these poems (Priscian, *Inst.* 10.54 [= *GLK* 2:544.4] and the scholia to *Ibis* 357, 589) refer to a collection called *Heroides* and this was probably the title by which the poems were known in antiquity.[2] Ovid himself refers to an individual poem in the collection as an *epistula* (*Ars* 3.345), and this designation was probably extended to the entire collection once it included the paired epistles, numbered 16–21 in modern editions, half of which are assigned to male protagonists.

Whether it was Ovid himself who was responsible for this extension of the collection is a longstanding problem associated with these poems. So, too, is the question of the relationship to the rest of the collection of the epistle of Sappho to Phaon, which owes its position as the fifteenth poem in modern editions to Ovid's seventeenth century editor, Daniel Heinsius.[3] Finally, Ovid's authorship of several

---

[1] For the most part, the medieval tradition knew only poems 1–14 and 16–21 in the modern numeration. See Richmond (chapter 14 below) for the transmission of the collection. In this chapter, the text of the *Heroides* is cited from the second edition of Showerman's Loeb, revised by Goold (1977).

[2] Thus, e.g., Martini (1933) 18, Kraus (1968) 89, Horsfall (1981) 107. Many modern editors, such as Rosati (1996a) and Dörrie, have adopted the composite title, *Heroidum epistulae*. Heinze (1997) 26–27 prefers the more common medieval title, *Epistulae*. See also Kenney (1996) 1 n. 1.

[3] Heinsius's edition appeared in 1629. He may have been anticipated in placing

epistles has been disputed by scholars since the nineteenth century. Critical appreciation of the collection, however, is little affected by the question of authorship. In the third book of the *Ars amatoria*, Ovid appends an assertion of his originality to his recommendation of these poems as reading material for his female readers (3.345–46): *uel tibi composita cantetur Epistula uoce:/ ignotum hoc aliis ille nouauit opus.* This much at least is certain: no other work like this collection is known to us before Ovid, though his innovation attracted imitators, probably even in his own lifetime.[4] With the exception only of the *Metamorphoses*, the *Heroides* have been Ovid's most influential work from antiquity until very recent times.

1. *Authorship*

No reader since antiquity, indeed, some would argue, no reader even in antiquity, encountered the *Heroides* in the form in which they are found in modern editions. Some medieval manuscripts that include a title refer to the collection as a *liber*, but that designation cannot be ancient, for the 3,976 verses that make up modern editions could not have been accommodated in a single papyrus roll.[5] The earliest witness to the collection is Ovid himself, in an elegy of the second book of the *Amores* addressed to a friend, the poet Macer, who is writing epic verse. This prompts Ovid to describe some of his own poetic endeavors (*Am.* 2.18.19–26):

> quod licet, aut artes teneri profitemur Amoris
>   (ei mihi, praeceptis urgeor ipse meis),
> aut quod Penelopes uerbis reddatur Vlixi
>   scribimus et lacrimas, Phylli relicta, tuas,

---

the *ES* in this position by the twelfth-century *Florilegium Gallicum*, which includes excerpts of the *ES* between selections from *Heroides* 14 and 16. See Richmond, chapter 14 below.

    [4] Ovid's report in *Am.* 2.18.27–34 that his friend Sabinus composed "replies" to some of the single *Heroides* is indicative of one kind of response to the epistles. No major poet of antiquity attempted to duplicate Ovid's achievement, but the type did attract minor imitators, like the author of *Anth. Lat.* 71 SB, an epistle of Dido to Aeneas. Some might also include the authors of the allegedly spurious poems in the collection in this category as imitators of Ovid. For imitations in later periods, cf. Dörrie (1968), Trickett (1988).
    [5] Cf. Knox (1995) 11–12.

quod Paris et Macareus et quod male gratus Iason
   Hippolytique parens Hippolytusque legant,
quodque tenens strictum Dido miserabilis ensem
   dicat et †Aoniae Lesbis amata lyrae†

I do what I can: I either teach the arts of tender Love (and, alas, I am harrassed by my own precepts!) or I write what might be conveyed to Ulysses in Penelope's words and your tearful lament, forsaken Phyllis; what Paris and Macareus might read, and ungrateful Jason and Hippolytus and Hippolytus's father; and what pitiable Dido might say, holding the drawn sword, and the Lesbian, loved of the Aonian lyre.

Interpretation of this passage is bedeviled by several issues on which scholarly opinion is divided: first, the date of composition of this poem and the question of whether it formed part of the original five-book "edition" of the *Amores* or was added to the reduced second edition; second, whether the work described in 19–20 (*artes . . . Amoris*) is the *Ars Amatoria*, completed in ca. 1 B.C.E., or the *Amores*; and finally, whether this passage refers to a completed collection of *Heroides* that included also poems not mentioned here.

Most scholars today agree that 2.18 appeared for the first time in the second edition of the *Amores*.[6] This dating is closely tied to the identification of the *Ars Amatoria* as the work described in 19–20, for if Ovid is referring to the composition of the *Ars*, presumably Books 1–2, then this poem must be at least contemporaneous with it. On this hypothesis the composition of the *Heroides* would be placed sometime between 10 and 1 B.C.E. Some scholars are skeptical of this chronology for a number of reasons. In the epigram prefixed to the revised edition of the *Amores*, for example, Ovid only remarks on the removal of two books (*demptis . . . duobus*) from the first version,[7] without any indication of fresh compositions.[8] If, then, all the poems in our surviving edition formed part of the original five-book version, *artes profitemur amoris* has a more general reference to Ovid's love

---

[6] A survey of earlier scholarship can be found in Martini (1933) 11–14. Most recent scholars have generally held that this poem was composed for the second edition: cf., e.g., Jacobson (1974) 300–318, Hollis (1977) 150–51, Syme (1978) 6–7, McKeown 1:74–89 and 3:384–85. See also Boyd, chapter 3 above.

[7] Cf. *Tr.* 4.10.61–62, *multa quidem scripsi, sed, quae uitiosa putaui/emendaturis ignibus ipse dedi*, a reference to Ovid's early career that may in fact refer to this revision of the *Amores*.

[8] To the assertion of Syme (1978) 6 that "nothing precludes the addition of several poems" it might be objected that nothing requires it.

elegies and not a specific reference to the *Ars*.[9] On this interpreta-
tion, the *Heroides* must be an early work, contemporary with the ear-
liest *Amores*. A further consequence of this argument is an increased
likelihood that the paired epistles (16–21) are separated from the rest
of the collection in date and conception.

These conclusions are also affected by judgements concerning the
list of *Heroides* contained in this poem. The epistles listed here cor-
respond to nine epistles in the surviving collection: in the modern
numeration, 1 (Penelope to Ulysses), 2 (Phyllis to Demophoon), 5
(Oenone to Paris), 11 (Canace to Macareus), 6 (Hypsipyle to Jason),
10 (Ariadne to Theseus), 4 (Phaedra to Hippolytus), 7 (Dido to
Aeneas), and 15 (Sappho to Phaon). Beginning with Karl Lachmann
in 1848, some scholars have questioned whether ascription to Ovid
of any epistle not found in this list (3, 8, 9, 12–14, 16–21) is secure.[10]
While the absence of any particular epistle from this list is not proof
of a non-Ovidian origin in and of itself, it has been held that this
may constitute sufficient grounds for considering whether anomalous
features in these poems have sufficient weight to justify ascription to
an anonymous imitator. This line of argument has been rejected by
a number of scholars on the grounds that this list of *Heroides* has the
characteristics of an "Alexandrian poetic catalog," from which "it is
perverse to expect comprehensiveness."[11] Against this position it might
be argued that in fact this list is not a catalog at all, at least as the
term is generally understood in literary terms.[12] As a feature of epic
poetry the catalog stems from the Homeric "Catalog of Ships" (*Il.*
2.484–877) and the use of such lists becomes a standard feature of
ancient epic, eventually to be parodied by Ovid in the *Metamorphoses*.[13]

---

[9] Thus Cameron (1968), Knox (1995) 3–4. Cf. also the summary in McKeown
3:382–87.

[10] Lachmann (1848). Cf. Knox (1995), Tarrant (1981). Some scholars, e.g., Hinds
(1993), contend that the reference to *male gratus Iason* in 2.18.23 includes *both Her.*
12 (Medea to Jason) *and* Hypsipyle's epistle; cf. McKeown 3: ad loc., and contrast
Booth (1991) on the same passage.

[11] Hinds (1993) 30. This assertion has often been echoed in recent scholarship:
e.g., Casali (1996–97) 305, Casali (1995) 228–30, Bessone (1997) 19 n. 17, Williams
(1997) 133 n. 9, Heinze (1997) 53. This is actually a restatement of an earlier gen-
eration's reaction to Lachmann's argument, samples of which can be found at, e.g.,
Birt (1877) 310–11 and Rand (1907) 288. In neither generation do Lachmann's
critics buttress this assertion with evidence.

[12] On the literary catalog in Greek epic, see Kühlmann (1973).

[13] On Ovid's use of the catalog in the *Metamorphoses*, see Reitz (1998). Bernhardt

One function of such a list is, indeed, to conjure an image of completeness by way of suggestive selection. But the "catalog" of *Amores* 2.18 is very different from other Ovidian catalogs, for example, of hunting dogs (*Met.* 3.206–25) or faithful wives (*Tr.* 5.5.49–60). This list of Ovid's own poems has more in common with Alexandrian library catalogs. Such a self-identifying reference by an author, known as a *sphragis*, aims at specificity and completeness.[14] In any case, it cannot be asserted with certainty either that this list deliberately excludes genuine *Heroides* or that it includes all that Ovid ever wrote.

Many scholars who do not question the Ovidian authorship of the rest of the collection nonetheless find grounds to question the ascription of the *Epistula Sapphus* to Ovid.[15] The circumstances of its transmission, separate from the rest of the collection,[16] aroused suspicions when the poem first came to light in the fifteenth century,[17] but it was generally assumed to be Ovidian until the nineteenth century. After considerable debate, a consensus was again established around the judgement in favor of attributing the poem to Ovid that was outlined by L.C. Purser.[18]

The position of the paired epistles 16–21 within the collection has long been considered a problem by scholars. Unlike the *Epistula Sapphus*, they were an integral part of the medieval corpus, even though the main stream of the tradition contained significant gaps in this group of poems, with 16.39–144 and 21.15–250 missing in most manuscripts.[19] In addition to the external evidence, these poems

---

(1986) focuses on the exile poetry, but also has apt observations on the catalog in Ovid's other works.

[14] On the literary *sphragis*, see Fraenkel (1957) 362–63, with reference to earlier literature. Chaucer's *Legend of Good Women* offers an instructive parallel on the tenuous relationship between a poet's list of his poems and a surviving corpus.

[15] E.g., Hinds (1993) 44–45. McKeown 3:398 believes that the extant poem somehow replaced a genuine *ES*. The most complete case against Ovidian authorship is Tarrant (1981); cf. also Murgia (1985), Knox (1995) 12–14. Ovidian authorship is supported, by, e.g., Courtney (1990), Rosati (1996b).

[16] See Richmond, chapter 14 below.

[17] Commentaries on the poem were first published in 1471 at Venice by Giorgio Merula and in 1476 by Domizio Calderini in Brescia. The substance of the lectures delivered on the poem by Angelo Poliziano in 1481 are preserved in his notes, published in Lazzeri (1971).

[18] Purser's defense of the attribution to Ovid appears in Palmer (1898) 419–24 as the introduction to Palmer's notes on the poem and was written on Palmer's instructions. Earlier monographs supporting Ovidian authorship include Comparetti (1876) and de Vries (1885).

[19] See Richmond, chapter 14 below.

present a number of metrical and linguistic anomalies that have led many scholars to subscribe to Lachmann's judgement on this part of the collection.[20] That view has also shifted in recent years, with the publication of vigorous arguments in favor of assigning the poems to Ovid by Kenney.[21] Defenders of the ascription of the poems to Ovid regularly concede that the accumulation of inconsistencies with Ovid's practice in his amatory elegies combines with other factors to make composition at a later stage likely. Most settle upon a date shortly before Ovid's exile in 8 C.E. or not long after.[22] Subjective judgements of quality also enter into the debate. Many who accept the attribution to Ovid as author by the medieval tradition echo the assessment of these poems expressed by Rand: "If [they] are not from Ovid's pen, an *ignotus* has beaten him at his own game."[23] Scholars who dispute this attribution often argue from the contrary position that not only do the poems deviate from Ovid's manner, they fall below his high standards.[24] In the debate over authorship, however, as Courtney reminds us, it is indeed not impossible that a successful imitator of Ovid could remain anonymous.[25] And the question that should exercise scholars interested in the question of authenticity is not whether the author possessed literary merit, but the independent question of whether the author was Ovid.

---

[20] Palmer (1898) 436, against Ovidian authorship, has been influential among anglophone readers until recently, in spite of the protest by Purser in his introduction (xxxii) and defenses of Ovidian authorship mounted by Clark (1908) and Tracy (1971).

[21] Esp. Kenney (1979), (1995a), (1996) 20–26, (1999a). Cf. Rosati (1996a) 27.

[22] Thus, e.g., Kraus (1950–51) 77, Tracy (1971), Hintermeier (1993) 190–95.

[23] Cf., e.g., Kenney (1996) 20, Reeve (1973) 330 n. 1.

[24] Beck (1996) is the most recent and extensive argument against the authenticity of the paired epistles. He frequently attempts to expose the deficiencies of their author. In spite of many serious flaws this is an important work: cf. Kenney (1998), Knox (2000).

[25] Courtney (1997–98). Courtney (1965) set the fuse that ignited the late twentieth-century debate about the authenticity of the paired epistles. Published in the same year, Goold (1965) 43 reflects the prevailing sentiment in assigning all of *Heroides* 1–21 to Ovid. A dramatic shift in his views is evident in Goold (1974) 484, where he accepts only 1–7, 10, 11, and 15 as Ovidian. But in Goold (1983) he returns to his earlier acceptance of 16–21 as Ovid's work.

2. *Background and Genre*

We know of no other collection of fictional verse epistles in Greek or Latin: Ovid's *Heroides* are unique.[26] Innovation is the hallmark of every stage of Ovid's career.[27] But each innovation is firmly rooted in tradition. The originality of the *Heroides* consists primarily in the combination of features from other literary forms, and in this respect they may represent the most interesting example in Roman poetry of innovation in genre.[28] Detailed study of the *Heroides* uncovers elements traceable to different branches of ancient rhetorical and literary traditions, no single one of which can account for Ovid's achievement in the *Heroides*.

There used to be a consensus among critics that the *Heroides* were little more than versified rhetorical set pieces, composed in the manner of the school compositions.[29] Like other attempts at identifying a single source for the *Heroides*, this approach is now generally regarded as misguided, but it would be equally misguided to dismiss entirely the influence of rhetorical training and declamation. As Ovid tells us himself, his parents saw to it that he and his brother benefited from study with the leading professors of rhetoric in Rome (*Tr.* 4.10.15–16): *protinus excolimur teneri curaque parentis/ imus ad insignes urbis ab arte uiros*. Ovid's decision not to pursue a forensic career would not have implied rejection of the intellectual underpinning of his education. On the contrary, everything that we know about his career suggests that he continued to cultivate associations with leading rhetoricians of the day. The elder Seneca, for example, tells of Ovid's relationship with the rhetor M. Porcius Latro (*Contr.* 2.2.8): "He was an admirer of Latro, though his style of speech was different. He had a neat, seemly, and attractive talent. Even in those days his speech could be regarded as simply poetry put into prose. Moreover, he was so keen a student of Latro that he transferred many epigrams

---

[26] The *epistulae amatoriae* attributed to Tibullus in the manuscript *Vita* are probably a mirage.

[27] As remarked by Kenney (1982) 455. For earlier discussions of Ovid's innovativeness, see, e.g., Jacobson (1974) 319–22.

[28] Questions of genre are central to critical inquiry into the *Heroides*; cf. Conte (1991) 163, Farrell (1998).

[29] Cf. Martini (1933) 17, Wilkinson (1955) 5–10, Maurer (1990) 49–76. Jacobson (1974) 322–30 provides a judicious summary of earlier literature.

(*sententias*) into his own verse." Seneca adduces a number of exam-
ples of rhetorically inspired *sententiae* in Ovid, and it is not difficult
to identify more.[30] Seneca goes on to characterize Ovid's taste in
declaiming, observing that he "rarely declaimed *controuersiae*, and only
ones involving portrayal of character (*non nisi ethicas*). He preferred
suasoriae, finding all argumentation tiresome." Modern critics have
not been reluctant to take this remark as the starting point for char-
acterizing Ovid's style in the *Heroides*, arguing that they derive their
content and structure from the style of the *suasoriae*.[31] It is true that
in a number of the epistles Ovid's heroines aim at persuading their
addressees to adopt some particular course of action, and compari-
son with the *suasoria* can be instructive in analysis of the structure
of the argument. But Seneca's more important observation is the
identification of character portrayal as Ovid's primary interest.

The closest parallel in the rhetorical schools for the kind of exer-
cise of character portrayal that we find reflected in the *Heroides* is
the deliberative speech, known as *prosopopoeia* or *ethopoeia*.[32] As Quintilian
(*IO* 3.8.52) notes, this type of exercise is closely related to the *sua-
soria*; the difference chiefly resides in the requirement that the stu-
dent represent a figure from history or literature soliloquizing on his
particular dilemma.[33] It is not difficult to trace the impact of this
kind of schooling on Ovid's treatment of his heroines in the single
epistles. In the paired epistles, as Kenney notes, "Ovid gets the best
of both worlds, continuing his exploitation of *ethopoeia* but adding the
new dimension offered by the *controuersia*, the clash of opposing char-
acters and viewpoints."[34] As an imaginary speech suited to a char-
acter's circumstances, the *ethopoeia* clearly has special relevance for
the fictional epistles of the *Heroides*, adapted to the crises in which
the heroines find themselves.[35] But it is also possible to find close
analogies in many other types of poetry.

---

[30] E.g., Bonner (1949) 152–56.

[31] E.g., Dörrie (1967) 45–46, Sabot (1981) 2553–55.

[32] Nicolaus (*Rhet. Gr.* III 489) offers the standard definition of *ethopoeia* in antiq-
uity: ἠθοποιία ἐστὶ λόγος ἁρμόζων τοῖς ὑποκειμένοις; cf. Aphthonius, *Progymn.* 11
Rabe, Bonner (1949) 53. Comparisons between the *Heroides* and *ethopoeiae* date back
at least to Bentley (1699) 83.

[33] Cf. Bonner (1977) 267–70.

[34] Kenney (1996) 2.

[35] Jacobson (1974) 325–30 offers a survey of the rhetorical affiliations of the
Heroides; cf. Kraus (1968) 90–91; Maurer (1990) 66–70.

The monologues of Greek drama are an obvious focus for comparison, especially since some of Ovid's heroines are taken directly from celebrated tragedies.[36] The epistles of Phaedra, for example, and of Canace interact directly with well-known plays of Euripides. Such models were important for Ovid, of course, and not only in the epistles drawn from characters in drama, but other genres also exerted an influence. The poetry of Hellenistic Greece is replete with compositions in which the poet masks as a character, usually one taken from everyday life, but sometimes from myth or literature.[37] A number of poems in the Theocritean corpus can be included in this category, such as the second *Idyll*, which represents the lament of a woman who has been betrayed by her lover. Other examples in Theocritus include monologues by pastoral characters on amatory themes (e.g., 3, 12, 23), while in *Idyll* 11 the poet composes a song for the lovelorn Polyphemus. A lyric poem of the late Hellenistic period, the so-called "Fragmentum Grenfellianum" (*CA*, pp. 177–80), contains the lament of an unidentified woman in love. Another fragment (*CA*, p. 185), preserved on a papyrus of ca. 100 B.C.E., may represent a lament by Helen of Troy after being abandoned by Menelaus.[38] It is not out of the question that Greek poets adapted this conceit to elegy as well. Fragments of Greek elegiac verse survive from the early empire that seem to include the monologue form familiar to us from Roman elegy.[39] A plausible argument can be made that these fragments represent a lost category of Greek elegy that may have played a role in the development of Latin love elegy.[40] And it is not inconceivable, although of course in the current state of our knowledge it is not provable, that some Greek elegist represented the laments of a fictional woman from myth. Indeed, all of these Greek antecedents contain many of the distinctive features of Roman love elegy—references to mythological examples, the identification of the poet and the speaker—but none combines all of these elements in the manner familiar to us from Latin elegy, and none makes use of the epistolary form.

---

[36] Cf. Wilkinson (1955) 86, with references to earlier discussions.

[37] This tradition is discussed by Jacobson (1974) 343–44, who also calls attention to the role played by such poetry in the development of subjective Latin elegy.

[38] Both fragments are discussed by Jacobson (1974) 344.

[39] For example, *SH* 962, 964, and *P.Oxy.* 54 (1987) nr. 3723.

[40] Cf. Parsons (1988).

In all likelihood it was Propertius who introduced this innovation
in the fourth book of his elegies, where he casts one poem (4.3) in
the form of a letter from a woman whom he calls Arethusa to her
lover Lycotas, a soldier who is away on campaign. In the opening
verses of her epistle, Arethusa sounds a note that becomes familiar
in Ovid's *Heroides* (Prop. 4.3.1–6):[41]

> haec Arethusa suo mittit mandata Lycotae,
>   cum totiens absis, si potes esse meus.
> si qua tamen tibi lecturo pars oblita derit:
>   haec erit e lacrimis facta litura meis:
> aut si qua incerto fallet te littera tractu,
>   signa meae dextrae iam morientis erunt.

> Arethusa sends these instructions to her Lycotas, that is if you can still
> be mine in spite of your frequent absences. But if when you read this
> some part is smeared and missing, this smudge will have been caused
> by my tears; or if some writing is hard for you to make out because
> the tracing is uncertain, this will be a sign that my hand was already
> failing.

So similar to Ovid's manner is this epistle and so unique in the body
of Propertius's work, it has sometimes been thought that Ovid must
have preceded him.[42] It is more likely, however, that Ovid took this
experiment by Propertius as his inspiration for a more ambitious
project. The extension of this experiment to use the epistolary form
to represent characters from literature is, so far as we know, Ovid's
distinctive achievement. The distinguishing feature of Ovid's *Heroides*
is their inspiration from works of literature: the Dido of *Heroides* 7
is not a character recreated anew by Ovid from mythology, but quite
specifically the heroine of Virgil's *Aeneid* 4. A similar relationship
between Ovid's heroines and the literary background can be distin-
guished in all of the epistles for which the principal sources are still
extant.

---

[41] Cf. Knox (1995) on *Her.* 11.1.

[42] The suggestion that Propertius imitated Ovid in the fourth book of elegies was
apparently first made by Heinsius in his introductory note to *Heroides* 1. It has been
argued sporadically since, e.g., by Bürger (1901) 27–29; Pohlenz (1913) 14–17;
Mersmann (1931). Of course, the possibility that some of the *Heroides* antedate the
composition of Propertius 4.3 cannot be dismissed, but there is no convincing evi-
dence to that effect: cf. Reitzenstein (1936) 17–34, Becker (1971) 469–70. Most
scholars accept as the more likely scenario that Ovid, the younger of the two, took
Propertius's example of an elegiac epistle as a springboard for a new poetic ven-
ture. For the idea of drafting a love letter in verse, as Maurer (1990) 38–45 has
argued, Propertius might have drawn on traditions of narrative in Hellenistic verse.

Each of the epistles in the collection, including the paired epistles with male correspondents, refers self-consciously to a specific source in earlier literature. The opening epistle from Penelope to Ulysses may be read as programmatic in that respect. It becomes clear to the reader that the timing of Penelope's writing accords with the events of Book 19 of the *Odyssey*. We know from Homer that Penelope has just had an interview with a recently arrived stranger who tells her much about her absent husband. Ovid fills the gap in Homer's account with this letter that Penelope, as is her wont (59–62), will hand to none other than the disguised Odysseus himself.[43] Even though Ovid alludes to other sources for the story,[44] the central text against which this poem is read is always the *Odyssey*. The Homeric background provides the material for an ironic interplay between texts. In the course of reading the seventh epistle from Dido to Aeneas, we become aware of its setting in Virgil's epic in the terrible moments before dawn when Dido knows that the Trojans are departing. Ovid's use of literary models represents a very different approach to the process of allusion or imitation observable elsewhere in the mythological narratives of Roman poetry. Ovid begins with his characters as they have already been constituted in the works of his predecessors and explores the interpretative possibilities not explicit in the original works. In the following sections devoted to the major portions of the collection, we will pursue the ways in which the relationship of the *Heroides* to the literary tradition is exploited by Ovid.

3. *The Single Epistles*

Heroides 1–15, as numbered in modern editions, consist of imaginary letters from figures of myth and literature to their absent lovers or husbands: Penelope to Ulysses, Phyllis to Demophoon, Briseis to Achilles, Phaedra to Hippolytus, Oenone to Paris, Hypsipyle to Jason, Dido to Aeneas, Hermione to Orestes, Deianira to Hercules, Ariadne to Theseus, Canace to Macareus, Medea to Jason, Laodamia to

---

[43] For this approach to the *Heroides* as "episodes set in the interstices of the literary tradition" (Knox (1995) 18), see Kennedy (1984), whose discussion of *Heroides* 1 has been influential in subsequent analyses, e.g., Barchiesi (1987), Williams (1992a), and Knox (1995) 18–25.

[44] See Knox (1995) 86–87.

Protesilaus, and Hypermestra to Lynceus. Each of the heroines writes within a framework established by an important literary treatment of the myth. For example, Briseis's epistle is set within the *Iliad* in the aftermath of the failed delegation to Achilles in Book 9. In the fourth poem Ovid provides us with the text of the letter sent by Phaedra to Hippolytus in Euripides' tragedy. In the sixth epistle, Ovid picks up at the conclusion of the *Argonautica* of Apollonius of Rhodes to represent Hypsipyle writing to Jason after his safe return to Iolcus. The fourth book of the *Aeneid* provides the setting for Dido's futile attempt to prevent Aeneas's departure in *Heroides* 7. Most often, the reference is implicit in the relationship of the epistle to the earlier model, but on several occasions there are more explicit signposts in the text.

In the epistle of Briseis, for example, the relationship between this poem and its model is evident in the treatment of the story throughout, including details which can only have been known to Briseis from a reading of Homer and no other known source.[45] But there is also a more overt signal of the intertextual play in this poem. A clear example is Briseis's use of the example of Meleager in her attempt to persuade Achilles to give up his anger (91–93): *nec tibi turpe puta precibus succumbere nostris;/ coniugis Oenides uersus in arma prece est./ res audita mihi, nota est tibi.* The story of Meleager was recounted to Achilles by his old tutor Phoenix as a cautionary tale in *Il.* 9.529–99. That is how the exemplum became known (*nota*) to Achilles, but Briseis was not present at that scene and can only have heard of it (*res audita mihi*) from someone else: not from Phoenix, however, who remained with Achilles, nor, one would imagine, from Odysseus. Her best source, so to speak, would have been the *Iliad*.

Likewise, in the epistle of Dido to Aeneas, Ovid incorporates a number of references designed to direct the reader to the source in Virgil. She recounts how she heard the voice of her dead husband call to her, whereupon she exclaimed (7.105–6): *da ueniam culpae! decepit idoneus auctor;/ inuidiam noxae detrahit ille meae.* In this context the most obvious reference is to Aeneas, the *auctor* of her fault. But the phrase *idoneus auctor* most readily denotes a trustworthy literary

---

[45] Cf. *Her.* 3.145–48, where Briseis exhorts Achilles to turn on her the sword which he almost used to kill Agamemnon. As Homer represents the moment (*Il.* 1.188–222), only Athena had knowledge of Achilles' intent, so Briseis's knowledge can only be attributed to a "reading" of the *Iliad*; cf. Knox (1995) 19.

author,[46] and it is likely that Virgil is thereby implicated in this reference as well.

Detailed analysis often reveals several levels of influence at work in the *Heroides*. In the tenth epistle of Ariadne to Theseus, for example, the influence of Catullus's narrative of her abandonment on Naxos in Poem 64 has always been recognized. Indeed, Ovid signals his allusions to that text in a number of ways now familiar. In verses 17–22 of her epistle, Ariadne describes to Theseus how she went mad with grief when she realized that he had sailed away without her:

> . . . specto, si quid nisi litora cernam.
> quod uideant oculi, nil nisi litus habent.
> nunc huc, nunc illuc, et utroque sine ordine curro;
>   alta puellares tardat harena pedes.
> interea toto clamaui in litore 'Theseu!':
>   reddebant nomen concaua saxa tuum.

> I look to see if there was anything there but shoreline. As far as my eyes could see, they find nothing but shore. Now this way, now that way, I run, and always at random. The deep sand slows my girlish feet. And all the while along the entire shore I called out "Theseus," and the hollow rocks echoed your name.

This description reprises the scene in Catullus 64, where we are told that Ariadne went to the shore to scan the horizon and call out to Theseus (124–27):

> saepe illam perhibent ardenti corde furentem
> clarisonas imo fudisse e pectore uoces
> ac tum praeruptos tristem conscendere montes,
> unde aciem <in> pelagi uastos protenderet aestus.

> Often, they say, in the fury of her burning heart she poured forth piercing cries from the depths of her breast; and now she would sadly climb the rugged mountains from which to extend her gaze over the vast swells of the ocean.

In this poem, as in other poems in the collection, it is not unlikely that Ovid refers, as Catullus surely did, to other sources for the story now lost to us.[47]

---

[46] Cf. Knox (1995) ad loc.

[47] In this instance, Catullus's allusion to other sources is suggested by *perhibent* in 64.124. Comparison of this and other passages in Catullus, Ovid, and Nonnus leads

It is reasonable to assume that similar intertextual play is at work even in the epistles for which the apparent models do not survive. For example, the second epistle from Phyllis to Demophoon almost certainly is based on a work by Callimachus that was apparently quite famous, to judge from the familiarity of late antique sources with the myth.[48] Likewise, we have enough information about Euripides' lost tragedy *Aeolus* to be certain that it provided the backdrop for *Heroides* 11.[49] The evidence is more scanty for two other epistles, *Heroides* 5 and 10, and does not allow us to identify a specific source, although it is highly likely that the characters of Oenone and Ariadne had been developed in some lost narratives of the Hellenistic period.[50] The eighth epistle perhaps exploits Sophocles' lost *Hermione*, while it is most likely that Hypermnestra's epistle draws on Aeschylus's trilogy on the myth of the Danaids. Medea's epistle is set within the context of Euripides' famous play, though it also exploits other treatments of her story, including perhaps Ovid's own lost *Medea*.[51]

The epistle of Phaedra to Hippolytus, another poem in which Ovid takes his starting point from Euripides, offers a clearer example of how Ovid alludes to more than one stream of the tradition. The intertextual affiliations of this poem are complicated by the fact that Euripides produced two versions of the play, the first of which is lost, but was probably known to Ovid.[52] Ovid's epistle certainly exploits the ironies accessible to readers familiar with the surviving play. Phaedra represents herself as an elegiac figure writing to her lover (1–2): *quam nisi tu dederis, caritura est ipsa, salutem/ mittit Amazonio Cressa puella uiro.* Like Penelope (1.3), Phaedra sees herself as a *puella*, emphasized by the pointed juxtaposition with *uiro.* The risks latent in this situation are amplified by her next, apparently rhetorical ques-

---

some scholars to infer the existence of an influential account of the myth earlier than Catullus: see Knox (1998), with reference to earlier literature.

[48] Knox (1995) 111–13.

[49] See Williams (1992a) for ironies in Ovid's allusions to the lost play.

[50] For Oenone, see Knox (1995) 140–41. For Ariadne, see Knox (1998).

[51] This has sometimes been seen as evidence against Ovidian authorship of this epistle, e.g., by Knox (1986c). For a different view of the relationship with earlier models, one that is consistent with the epistle's authenticity, see Hinds (1993), Heinze (1991–93) and (1997) 51–55, and Bessone (1997) 11–41.

[52] See Barrett (1964) 32 n. 4 on Ovid's source for *Met.* 15.500–546 and *F.* 6.737–45. It is highly likely that Seneca follows the lost *Hippolytus* in his *Phaedra*, but the precise extent of his reliance upon it is much debated. Cf. Coffey and Mayer (1990) 5–6 and Halleran (1995) 25–26.

tion (3): *perlege, quodcumque est—quid epistula lecta nocebit?* For the reader who knows that she will write another letter implicating Hippolytus, however, this question has a clear response not "intended" by Phaedra.

But as with the other heroines, Ovid's allusions to the primary source are sometimes filtered by material from other traditions, in this instance probably Euripides' earlier play. This is particularly the case where Ovid is depicting Phaedra as justifying her emotions. Thus, her declaration that in making her approach to Hippolytus she follows a god's mandate (10–12, *dicere quae puduit, scribere iussit amor./quidquid Amor iussit, non est contemnere tutum;/regnat et in dominos ius habet ille deos*) has no parallel in the extant play. But it is very close to a fragment of the first *Hippolytus*:[53]

> ἔχω δὲ τόλμης καὶ θράσους διδάσκαλον
> ἐν τοῖς ἀμηχάνοισιν εὐπορώτατον,
> Ἔρωτα, πάντων δυσμαχώτατον θεόν.

> But I have as an instructor of boldness and daring Eros, most resourceful in impossible circumstances, and the hardest god of all to fight against. (trans. Halleran (1995))

The virtuous Phaedra of Euripides' second play is complicated by references to the character of the first, who makes a conscious attempt at seduction.[54] Subversion of the text of the extant play also highlights the development of Phaedra's character. Euripides' virtuous character from the first never ventured to speak her passion (*Hipp.* 393–97):

> ἠρξάμην μὲν οὖν
> ἐκ τοῦδε, σιγᾶν τήνδε καὶ κρύπτειν νόσον·
> γλώσσῃ γὰρ οὐδὲν πιστόν, ἣ θυραῖα μὲν
> φρονήματ' ἀνδρῶν νουθετεῖν ἐπίσταται
> αὐτὴ δ' ὑφ' αὑτῆς πλεῖστα κέκτηται κακά.

> So I began with this, to keep quiet about this disease and conceal it; for nothing can be trusted to the tongue, which knows how to admonish the thoughts of others, but itself possesses the most evils by its own doing. (trans. Halleran (1995))

---

[53] Fr. 430 N (= C Barrett).

[54] Other correspondences between *Heroides* 4 and *Hippolytus* I can be found, e.g., at 4.113–28, where Phaedra blames her love for Hippolytus on Theseus's wrongs: cf. Plut. *Mor.* 27f–28a (= B Barrett) τὴν ... Φαίδραν καὶ προσεγκαλοῦσαν τῷ Θησεῖ πεποίηκεν (sc. Εὐριπίδης) ὡς διὰ τὰς ἐκείνου παρανομίας ἐρασθεῖσαν τοῦ Ἱππολύτου. Cf. also fr. 433 N (= P Barrett) with *Her.* 4.129–34.

Not so Ovid's Phaedra (7–8): *ter tecum conata loqui ter inutilis haesit/ lingua, ter in primo restitit ore sonus.*[55] Her letter supplies the approach only because words failed her earlier. Ovid's portrayal of Phaedra is deepened by the appropriation of a range of literary texts.[56]

Another important aspect of the single epistles is the effect achieved by depicting epic or tragic themes in elegiac coloring.[57] It is perhaps most prominent in the ninth epistle from Deianira to Hercules. In this epistle, the poet probably relies less upon interplay with a model text than in other epistles in the collection. The epistle deals with the subject of the *Trachiniae* of Sophocles.[58] After capturing Oechalia, Hercules sends Iole, the daughter of its slain king, to Trachis. Deianira knows that she comes not as a captive only, but as Hercules' latest paramour. Consumed by jealousy, she sends him a cloak dipped in the blood of the centaur Nessus, thinking it a love-charm to win him back. The setting of this epistle is the immediate aftermath. In fact, the poem here departs from the plot of Sophocles' play, in which Deianira is denounced by her son, to picture her receiving a message while in the act of writing (143–44): *sed quid ego haec refero? scribenti nuntia uenit/ fama, uirum tunicae tabe perire meae.* This is the only instance in the *Heroides* in which an event external to the epistle is represented, and it does not, as external logic might suggest, bring the writing to a close: Deianira continues for 22 more lines.[59] In a sense, then, this epistle not only refers to dramatic action, it incorporates it. This serves to highlight the contrast with the representation of its heroine in elegiac mode.

Critics have detected this note from the poem's opening distich: *gratulor Oechaliam titulis accedere nostris;/ uictorem uictae succubuisse queror.* In *queror* modern readers have seen an allusion to elegy's supposed association with lamentation.[60] Deianira represents herself as aban-

---

[55] The point is underscored by allusion to Medea as represented at Ap. Rhod. 3.654–55.

[56] Contrast Palmer in his introduction to this epistle: "He [sc. Ovid] has accurately caught the Euripidean conception of the character of Phaedra." Yes, but which?

[57] For this approach, cf. Spoth (1992), Casali (1992), and Barchiesi (1987) 67–71. It is also applied fruitfully to the paired epistles by Rosati (1991) 103–14.

[58] Cf. Casali (1995) 11–17.

[59] Casali (1995) on 143–68 sees here a deliberate reversal of important motifs in *Trach.*, but if so, there are hardly any lexical markers.

[60] Thus, on this passage, Casali (1995) 12. Cf. Hinds (1986) 103–7, Barchiesi (1987) 76.

doned by her husband, whom she represents as captive of yet another love affair. To illustrate her condition, she refers to his past pursuit of Omphale, her choice of this exemplum being motivated by the parallels between Hercules' embarrassing behavior then and—as she sees it—now (73–74):[61] *inter Ioniacas calathum tenuisse puellas/ diceris et dominae pertimuisse minas* In *diceris*, Deianira signals an allusion to earlier treatments in literature, though not Sophocles'.[62] The motif is familiar in love-elegy, the *seruitium amoris*. Propertius, for example, makes use of this same exemplum to justify his own voluntary subjugation to a woman (3.11.17–20):

> Omphale in tantum formae processit honorem,
>   Lydia Gygaeo tincta puella lacu,
> ut, qui pacato statuisset in orbe columnas,
>   tam dura traheret mollia pensa manu.

> Omphale, the Lydian girl who bathed in Gyges' lake, achieved such renown for her beauty that the man who had set up his pillars in the world he had pacified spun her soft wool with his rough hands.

This alternative tradition about Hercules' three years of servitude at the court of Omphale is not part of Sophocles' treatment.[63] In the Greek tradition it is not attested until late, and its origins appear to be Hellenistic.[64] Lexical markers are insufficient to secure a reference to Propertius here, but the affiliation with the background of love-elegy is clearly evoked.[65]

This method provides Ovid with a framework for developing serious issues raised by his models from an entirely new perspective. Until recently critics have not generally recognized the extent to which in the *Heroides*, Ovid has reconfigured his heroines so as to invite the readers to respond to his models as literary critics. Ovid's Dido poses questions about Virgil's treatment and simultaneously suggests answers to ambiguities in her representation in the *Aeneid*.

---

[61] Cf. Jacobson (1974) 238–39.

[62] Thus, rightly, Casali (1995) ad loc.

[63] Contrast *Trach.* 69–72, 248.

[64] See Fedeli (1985) on Prop. 3.11.17–20 and Pianezzola (1991) on *Ars* 2.217–22.

[65] This passage *is* intrinsically connected to *Ars* 2.218–22: *ille, fatigata praebendo monstra nouerca,/ qui meruit caelum, quod prior ipse tulit,/* **inter Ioniacas calathum tenuisse puellas**/ *creditur et lanas excoluisse rudes./ paruit imperio* **dominae** *Tirynthius heros*. Deianira's epistle appears to allude to this passage, both here and at line 17, but such a relationship would pose difficulties of chronology (*Heroides* 9 later than the *Ars*) and raise doubts about Ovidian authorship.

Throughout the *Heroides* Ovid seizes upon moments in which his abandoned women may re-assemble the components of the original narratives in new and sometimes arresting combinations. In these moments Ovid causes the reader to separate his reactions from the original model and to question the values represented there. He effects this separation by endowing his heroines with a new voice fashioned out of his experience as an elegist.

In this respect the epistle of Sappho to Phaon (*ES*) stands apart from the other single epistles in the collection. In all of these epistles, including those whose authenticity has been disputed, a character is taken from an earlier narrative and depicted at a crucial juncture of her story. That does not appear to be the case with the *ES*, although the state of the evidence does not allow us to assert this as a certainty, since it is possible that the epistle draws on some lost work in which Sappho figured as a character in narrative. For example, there were at least six comedies produced in Athens with the title *Sappho*; other sources are also possible.[66] But none of these works seems to have achieved the notoriety that would encourage a reading of this epistle as an intertextual play in the manner of the other single *Heroides*. The author of the *ES* clearly knew Sappho's poetry and in places alludes to extant fragments of her work, and other passages in the poem may be plausibly traced to Sappho.[67] The narrative setting of this poem, however, is not drawn from any work of literature, but from ancient biographies of Sappho and the later traditions surrounding her life.[68] This was an ingenious idea, allowing the poet to play off the reader's assumptions about the poet, formed both from a reading of her verse and from biographical speculation about her life. The finished product is a fascinating portrait of the lyric poet in elegiac mode, but the effect is very different from the other poems in the *Heroides*.

4. *The Paired Epistles*

In many respects the paired epistles (16–21) represent a logical extension of the underlying conceit of the single epistles. Like them, these

---

[66] Comedies called *Sappho* are attested for Diphilus, Amipsias, Amphis, Antiphanes, Ephippus, and Timocles. For details see Knox (1995) 278.

[67] Again, see Knox (1995) on, e.g., *ES* 9–10, 17–18, 63–8, 154, or 199–202.

[68] Cf. Knox (1995) 278–29.

epistles are embedded in the narratives of earlier literature. The idea that Ovid's epistles might elicit "responses" from their fictive addressees was probably nearly contemporaneous with the dissemination of the first examples. Ovid reports that his friend Sabinus composed replies to some of the single poems (*Am.* 2.18.27–34):

> quam cito de toto rediit meus orbe Sabinus
>   scriptaque diuersis rettulit ille locis!
> candida Penelope signum cognouit Vlixis;
>   legit ab Hippolyto scripta nouerca suo.
> iam pius Aeneas miserae rescripsit Elissae,
>   quodque legat Phyllis, si modo uiuit, adest.
> tristis ad Hypsipylen ab Iasone littera uenit;
>   dat uotam Phoebo Lesbis amata lyram.

How quickly my friend Sabinus returned from his journey all around the world and brought back letters from distant places. Fair Penelope has recognized the seal of Ulysses, and the stepmother has read a letter from her Hippolytus. Pious Aeneas has already written back to poor Elissa, and there is a letter for Phyllis to read, provided she is alive. An unhappy letter has come for Hypsipyle from Jason, and the woman of Lesbos, accepted in love, is dedicating to Phoebus the lyre she vowed.

But there is a profound difference between the conception of the six paired epistles and Sabinus's responses to the single epistles. The latter were set in specific circumstances that did not allow for the possibility of a reply, a circumstance slyly alluded to by Ovid when he points out that Phyllis is likely to be dead before a response could arrive from Demophoon. The paired epistles were conceived as units, with each poem anticipating or reflecting upon its mate.

Even in the fragmentary state of our knowledge, it is possible to draw conclusions about the sources for the three exchanges of correspondence. For Paris and Helen, the poet drew upon early epic, but this time not primarily from Homer. Ovid's sources for their story included a lost play by Euripides and the early Greek epic *Cypria*, also lost.[69] But his characters retain their Homeric accents and Ovid plays off the reader's familiarity with the sequel to their courtship as it played out in the *Iliad*. As with the other two pairs of letters, the man's comes first, with Paris urging that Helen has

---

[69] On Ovid's use of Euripides' *Alexandros*, Ennius's *Alexander*, and the Epic Cycle, see Kenney (1996) 6. The sources for this pair probably also included the same used by Ovid in Oenone's epistle.

no choice but to return to Troy with him. His justification is based in his life's story, which gives Ovid the opportunity to incorporate a lengthy narrative of the events that set the story in motion. All of this is only to provide a backdrop for Helen's reply. In the paired epistles it is the women who are most fully characterized. Ovid's Helen has evidently already made up her mind to go with Paris before she set reed to papyrus: she is not fooled by Paris's plea, but is the willing accomplice of his scheme. Consistent with his technique in the single epistles, Ovid transforms the heroic lovers into recognizable human beings operating in accordance with the "norms" established in elegiac love poetry.

The second pair of correspondents, Leander and Hero, is taken from a lost Greek poem, the date and authorship of which we can only guess. The broad outlines of the story in this lost work can only be surmised from what Ovid and the late Greek poet Musaeus made of it.[70] The hypothesis of a Hellenistic original rested upon the evidence of only these texts until the publication in 1982 of a fragmentary papyrus containing parts of 50 hexameters in which many of the significant details of the story are present: the sea, a lover, a tower, and a lamp.[71] Whether or not this is part of the lost poem known to the Roman poets, as some speculate, it is further evidence for the diffusion of the story in Greek literature, the backdrop against which Ovid's epistolary drama is played.[72]

Like Paris and Helen, figures drawn from epic, Leander and Hero are portrayed in the softer tones of elegy. And so, Leander, "like Narcissus in his celebrated soliloquy in the *Metamorphoses* (2.446–53) . . . dwells on the paradoxes of his position, and like Narcissus he resorts to elegiac cliché"[73] (18.177–78): *quo propius nunc es, flamma propiore calesco,/ et res non semper, spes mihi semper adest.* The imagery of the fire of love is as old as love poetry; Leander's formulation is the more cliché because he elaborates it with a proverbial antithesis in the penta-

---

[70] A common source for Ovid and Musaeus seems a necessary inference, since Ovid can be ruled out as a source for the later poet and the story was certainly known to Virgil: cf., e.g., Kost (1971) 17–23. Recent treatments of the problem of these epistles' source can be found in Hintermeier (1993) 58–60, Kenney (1996) 9–11, and Rosati (1996a) 15–26.

[71] The papyrus, now *SH* 901A, was first published by Maehler (1982).

[72] Another fragment of the first century B.C.E. (*SH* 951) has little chance of coming from that poem; cf. Lightfoot (1999) 207–8.

[73] Kenney (1982) 426.

meter.[74] Likewise when Hero responds to Leander's complaints about the narrow strait that separates them, she does so in familiar elegiac terms (19.141–42): *parce, ferox, latoque mari tua proelia misce!/seducit terras haec breuis unda duas.* Hero's phrasing evokes a fragment of the first Roman elegiac love poet, Cornelius Gallus, perhaps also writing of his separation from his lover: *uno tellures diuidit amne duas.* That famous pentameter refers to another body of water that, according to some in antiquity, also separates Europe from Asia, the river Hypanis. For the ancient reader who recognized the context, the allusion would probably have been particularly pointed.[75]

The final pair of epistles was drawn from the story of Acontius and Cydippe which became famous in antiquity in the version narrated by the Hellenistic poet Callimachus in his elegiac narrative poem, *Aetia*.[76] The fragments of Callimachus's treatment are extensive enough to allow us to form a more complete impression of Ovid's relationship to his sources here. The more expansive format of Ovid's epistolary exchange imposes a focus on character, and Ovid's Acontius and Cydippe are more complex, more fully developed than their relatively passive Callimachean counterparts. Acontius, for example, in contrast with the pretty boy of Callimachus, is a coldly calculating man, obsessed in his pursuit of his beloved. Ovid exploits the fact that the entire situation turns on a quasi-legalistic interpretation of Cydippe's obligation to abide by the oath that she unconsciously swore. Acontius argues his case, employing the language and the logic of a Roman rhetorical education.[77] The difference from Callimachus is highlighted by specific intertextual markers.

In the *Aetia*, Acontius is an inexperienced boy, lacking native cunning, who is instructed by Eros (fr. 67.1–4 Pf.):

αὐτὸς Ἔρως ἐδίδαξεν Ἀκόντιον, ὁπότε καλῇ
ἤθετο Κυδίππῃ παῖς ἐπὶ παρθενικῇ,
τέχνην—οὐ γὰρ ὅγ' ἔσκε πολύκροτος—ὄφρα λέγοι[το
τοῦτο διὰ ζωῆς οὔνομα κουρίδιον.

---

[74] Cf. Kenney (1996) ad loc.

[75] For this fragment, see Courtney (1993) 263. For speculation about its context in Gallus and the echo here, see Knox (1985).

[76] Our knowledge of Callimachus's treatment derives from fragments (fr. 67–75 Pf.) and from Aristaenetus, *Epist.* 1.10, which is based on it. For useful introductions to the *Aetia*, see Hopkinson (1988) 85–91, d'Alessio (1996) 36–43.

[77] For a full development of this interpretation, cf. Kenney (1970a), (1996) 15–18.

> Eros himself taught Acontius the art, when the boy burned for the beautiful maiden Cydippe (for he certainly was not clever), so that he might be called her lawful husband for all his life.

Ovid's Acontius is also not naturally gifted: in the first instance it is the girl that inspires him to cleverness (20.25–26): *non ego natura nec sum tam callidus usu; / sollertem tu me, crede, puella facis.* Acontius asserts that he has learned that lesson, in terms that suggest that for him Callimachus's τέχνη is legal training. Addressing Cydippe, he notifies her that she is bound to him by the marriage vow that he composed with Amor's guidance and vaunts his legal prowess (20.27–30):

> te mihi compositis—si quid tamen egimus—a me
>   adstrinxit uerbis ingeniosus Amor.
> dictatis ab eo feci sponsalia uerbis,
>   consultoque fui iuris Amore uafer.

> It was ingenious Love who bound you to me with words that I drew up, if indeed I played any part in the matter. It was at his dictation that I betrothed us and by consulting Love I became cunning in the law.

As Purser notes,[78] *iuris* is probably to be taken both with *consulto* and *uafer* by the figure of amphibole, thus yielding "Love being my Counsel learned in the law I became cunning therein." *callidus, sollers,* and *uafer* immediately evoke a recollection of πολύκροτος,[79] the quality that Acontius lacks in Callimachus. Acontius is now the cunning lawyer, trained by his jurisconsult, Amor.

In the paired epistles, as in the single epistles, the poet effects the portrayal of character by consistent reference to a literary background familiar to his readers. Allusion, subversion, and contradiction of this background are all part of his repertoire. Ovid's special achievement in the *Heroides* is to have recognized the application of an elegiac perspective to the exploration of character in settings beyond the subjective portrayal of the poet-lover. When one considers the broad sweep of the narrative settings of the *Heroides*, the consistency with Ovid's amatory elegies in style, diction, and theme is remarkable. Some degree of similar innovation may be discerned in Propertius,

---

[78] In Palmer (1898) ad loc.; cf. Kenney (1996) ad loc.

[79] For πολύκροτος, cf. d'Alessio (1996) ad loc. The genitive with *uafer* would be unique, but is justified by analogous constructions, and it conjures up associations with legal craftiness; cf. Hor. *Serm.* 2.2.131, *uafri inscitia iuris.*

particularly in the elegies of his final book, but it was Ovid who advanced to the next stage and successfully negotiated the transfer of the elegiac voice to representations of other characters. In this respect, the *Heroides* can be viewed as an important stage in Ovid's development as a narrative poet, culminating eventually in the *Metamorphoses*.[80] Some sense of their role in this development lies behind his claim to originality in these poems. Ovid's innovative reformulation of the heroines' voices in the *Heroides* provides us with a unique perspective on his reading of the Greek and Roman traditions of narrative verse. It was not an altogether surprising step for this poet then to move from a critical commentary on those traditions to a retelling on a larger scale in the *Fasti* and the *Metamorphoses*.

---

[80] Byblis's epistle to her brother Caunus, which is incorparated into the narrative at *Met.* 9.530–63, is an acknowledgement of this progression. Her epistle is a vehicle for Byblis to offer a commentary on her own situation, as do the women in the *Heroides*. In the *Metamorphoses*, however, Ovid embeds this commentary in a narrative of his own making, which is similarly cast in the tradition of elegy. On this aspect of the *Metamorphoses*, see Knox (1986a).

CHAPTER FIVE

PRAECEPTA AMORIS: OVID'S DIDACTIC ELEGY

Patricia Watson

1. Introduction

The *Medicamina Faciei Femineae* is usually[1] regarded as the first of Ovid's didactic elegies. Whether it was composed early in Ovid's career or immediately prior to the *Ars* is unclear; all that we know for certain is that it predates Book 3 (*Ars* 3.205–6).

Books 1 and 2 of the *Ars Amatoria* were originally published together, Book 3 being brought out later, either separately[2] or as part of a second edition comprising all three books.[3] The "table of contents" (*Ars* 1.35–40) makes no reference to the third book; even more telling is the concluding couplet of Book 2 (745–46) alluding to the women's request for instruction, which spoils the closure and was clearly added later after the composition of Book 3. The conventional dating for Books 1/2 is late 2 B.C. or 1 B.C., the latter being the year when Gaius Caesar set out on his Parthian expedition, which Ovid talks about (*Ars* 1.177–212) as imminent.[4] Book 3 and the second edition of 1 and 2 followed within the space of a year or two.[5]

The final poem in the group was the *Remedia Amoris*. Allusion to a possible military triumph of Gaius Caesar over the Parthians (*Rem.* 155–58) fixes A.D. 2 as the *terminus ante quem*, the sentiments being rendered irrelevant by Gaius's diplomatic agreement with the Parthians in that year.[6]

---

[1] For the argument that it was written between *Ars* 1/2 and *Ars* 3, see Rosati (1985) 42–43.

[2] Hollis (1977) xiii.

[3] See Murgia (1986).

[4] See Hollis (1977) 65–73.

[5] For a radically different view, see Murgia (1986), dating Book 3 and the second edition of 1/2 to A.D. 8: this rather too conveniently explains the gap, on the conventional dating, between the publication of the *Ars* and the date of Ovid's exile.

[6] Henderson (1979) xi–xii argues for mid-A.D. 1, others for A.D. 1–2. See also Pinotti (1988) 13.

The *Ars Amatoria* has been the focus of a great deal of scholarly attention in recent years, though commentaries in English are still lacking for the second and third books.[7] The best overall treatment of the poem is Myerowitz's monograph (1985). On the *Medicamina Faciei Femineae* there is an excellent Italian commentary by Rosati (1985), but as yet none in English. The *Remedia Amoris* is well served by commentaries in English (Henderson (1979)), Italian (Pinotti (1988)) and German (Lucke (1982), Geisler (1969)).

2. *The* Medicamina Faciei Femineae

Ovid's earliest didactic elegiac poem, the *Medicamina Faciei Femineae*, is interesting both in its own right and in the ways it anticipates the *Ars* and the *Remedia*. The poem as we have it contains only 100 lines, and is clearly a fragment of a longer work.[8] It falls into two sections: an introduction, in which the use of cosmetics is justified as part of the *cultus* of contemporary Rome (1–50) and a highly technical passage giving five recipes for skin-care preparations (51–100).

Scholarly attention has been focused on several issues: 1) the length of the original, 2) the technical material, 3) whether or not the piece was intended as a serious handbook, and 4) the prooemium.

1) The poem must have been of a reasonable size; otherwise, the introduction would be out of proportion with the rest. On the analogy of the *Ars* and the *Remedia*, Toohey[9] has suggested that the complete poem may have contained up to 800 lines. But this ill suits Ovid's description of the work as *paruus* (*Ars* 3.206). A better comparison would be the first book of Virgil's *Georgics*, which Ovid certainly had in mind (see below): this is 514 lines long with a preface of 42 lines. If the *Medicamina* was around 500 lines it could have accommodated a lengthy introduction, while still being able to be described as *paruus*, especially in comparison with Ovid's other didactic elegies.

---

[7] For Book 1 see Hollis (1977). A major German commentary on Book 2 has recently appeared (Janka 1997); Brandt's complete edition (1902) remains invaluable.

[8] The poem was published (cf. *Ars* 3.205), but not in its extant form, given the abrupt ending and the absence of any formal closure.

[9] Toohey (1996) 162.

2) A detailed and interesting investigation of the technical material (51–100) has been undertaken by Green.[10] Ovid probably obtained his information from a technical treatise on cosmetics, like those mentioned by Galen.[11] In versifying a prose treatise, Ovid followed in the tradition of Alexandrian "metaphrasts" like Nicander. The poem also has an affinity with the sub-genre of frivolous didactic poems (*artes*) which were popularly composed for the Saturnalia (*Tr.* 2.491); the subject of cosmetics is specified by Ovid in his list of such pieces (*Tr.* 2.487).

In the extant fragment, there is a disjunction between the two halves. Whereas the prooemium has much in common with Ovid's later didactic elegies, the technical section is for the most part in the dry impersonal style of the "metaphrasts." Though Ovid's style is perhaps as "poetical" as the subject matter allows,[12] it nevertheless lacks the embellishments—similes, mythological exempla, and digressions—that characterize the later didactic elegies.

3) Having demonstrated that Ovid's recipes would actually work, Green suggested that the poem was designed as a practical textbook.[13] Certainly there is no reason to suppose that the female addressees of the poem were not accustomed to mixing cosmetic lotions for themselves; they may even have availed themselves of the poet's advice. But Ovid's primary motivation was surely less a desire to be of service to women than the poetic challenge of turning into verse highly intractable technical material. Like Virgil, he wrote for a wider audience, who would appreciate his efforts to rise to such a challenge.

4) The prooemium is the most interesting part of the fragment, in several respects anticipating the *Ars Amatoria*.[14] It begins as follows:

> Discite quae faciem commendet cura, puellae,
>   et quo sit uobis forma tuenda modo.
> cultus humum sterilem Cerealia pendere iussit
>   munera, mordaces interiere rubi;

---

[10] Green (1979).

[11] See Rosati (1985) 46.

[12] A sprinkling of phrases recalls the *Georgics* (*nec tu . . . dubita* (69), *profuit et . . . addere* (91), and *uidi quae . . ./contereret* (99–100)): these were to become part of Ovid's didactic style in the *Ars* and *Remedia*.

[13] Green (1979) 391–92.

[14] For a detailed discussion, see Heldmann (1981).

cultus et in pomis sucos emendat acerbos,   5
    fissaque adoptiuas accipit arbor opes.

Learn, women, what care enhances your appearance and how you
may preserve your beauty. Cultivation bids sterile ground produce the
gifts of Ceres and devouring brambles are destroyed; cultivation also
changes the bitter juices in the fruit and a tree, engrafted, receives
adopted bounty.

The lines clearly recall Virgil's *Georgics* and so foreshadow the didac-
tic parody developed more fully in the *Ars*. In the opening couplet,
a summary of the theme in the manner of didactic prooemia, the
indirect questions recall the first five lines of the *Georgics*, while *cura*
is a favorite Virgilian term.[15] The examples of *cultus* (3–8) suggest
Virgilian themes: remedying unfertile soil (3; cf. *G.* 1.84–93), remov-
ing weeds (4; cf. *G.* 1.150–59), and grafting (6; cf. *G.* 2.82, *miratastque
nouas frondes et non sua poma*: Virgil's personification is mirrored in
Ovid's *adoptiuas*).

At the same time, the prooemium, like the *Ars* and the *Remedia*,
bears a close relationship with the elegiac tradition. In purely for-
mal terms, the use of the elegiac meter is a notable departure for
a didactic poem, and thus a significant generic marker. Moreover,
the argumentative style is essentially that of elegiac didactic.[16] Finally,
a number of themes are derived from elegy, such as the attack on
magic (35–42) and the warning about the ravages of time on beauty
(45–50). The exemplum of the Sabine women (11–16), who repre-
sent an outdated austerity, recalls *Am.* 1.8.39–40. Most important,
female adornment is placed in the context of eroticism when con-
temporary *cultus* is justified on the grounds that the men whom the
women hope to please are similarly elegant (23–24).

In eulogizing *cultus*, Ovid both recalls and distorts the elegiac tra-
dition. The elegists had condemned luxurious female adornment (*cul-
tus*) because of its association with immorality—in particular, infidelity
to the lover.[17] In both the *Medicamina* and the famous passage in the
Ars which it foreshadows (3.101–28), *cultus* is recommended, in keep-
ing with the poet's role as teacher of women, though in the latter
it is redefined as simple elegance (*munditiae*).[18] In the *Medicamina*, Ovid

---

[15] 19 occurrences in the *Georgics*.
[16] See further discussion of *Ars* 1.41–60 below.
[17] Especially Propertius 1.2 and 4.5.
[18] Given Ovid's *persona* of poor lover/poet in the *Ars*, it is not in his interest to
advocate expensive luxuries, for which the lover would be expected to pay.

defends women's desire for bodily adornment by pointing out that *cultus* is not in itself immoral, but only if a woman uses it in order to attract a lover rather than to please herself (27–32);[19] the prooemium also concludes (43–50) by emphasizing that good character will last longer than physical beauty.

The apology is especially necessary because Ovid has included married women among the poem's addressees (25–26).[20] Given the traditional link between *cultus* and *impudicitia*, Ovid's theme invites the potential criticism that he is teaching immoral conduct to *matronae* in the face of the Augustan adultery laws; hence the attempt to dissociate *cultus* from sexual promiscuity.

Whether this is to be taken seriously, however, is another matter, especially after Ovid's irreverent treatment of those cherished Augustan icons, the Sabine women, whose austerity is contrasted unflatteringly with the finery adopted by modern women (11–16). The reader would here recollect *Am.* 1.8.39–40, where an explicit link is made between the lack of *cultus* of the Sabine women and their lack of promiscuity.[21] Ovid's efforts, then, to counter the possible charge that in teaching *cultus* he is also teaching immorality may well be just as disingenuous as his statements in the *Ars* (discussed further below) that he is writing not for married women but for courtesans.[22]

3. *The* Ars Amatoria

The *Ars Amatoria* is both an elegiac and a didactic poem: a striking example of generic mixing. It was to some extent, if not principally, the cause of Ovid's exile, and in its cynical presentation of love it has been blamed by many for the virtual demise of the elegiac genre. While most would acknowledge that it contains many examples of brilliant Ovidian wit, the degree of seriousness of the work has been the subject of much debate, as has its precise relationship to the elegiac genre. Scholarly appraisal of the poem has ranged from the morally disapproving, to the simplistic (*Ars* = *Amores* reduced to

---

[19] On these lines see Rosati (1985) 67.

[20] For the *cultus* of *matronae*, see Wyke (1994) 141–44.

[21] *Forsitan immundae Tatio regnante Sabinae/noluerint habiles pluribus esse uiris*: cf. *Med.* 11, *forsitan antiquae Tatio sub rege Sabinae*.

[22] For a more extended discussion of the *Medicamina*, see Watson (2001).

theory), to the highly sophisticated.[23] The first two approaches tend
to judge the work as inferior to the *Amores*, while the third, more
recent line of scholarship has led to a more positive evaluation of
the poem because it presupposes that Ovid is successful in achiev-
ing his poetic goals—whatever these might be.

Scholars have focused on a number of aspects of the work. These
include 1) the relationship of the *Ars* to the didactic tradition; 2) the
Ars as an elegiac poem; 3) whether the poem has a serious moral
purpose; 4) Ovid's didactic *persona*; 5) the use of myth; 6) Ovid's
treatment of Augustan themes and the extent to which the *Ars* was
the reason for his exile; 7) the sexual material; and 8) Ovid's atti-
tude to women, particularly in Book 3. In the following discussion,
I will use these topics as headings, summarizing the state of schol-
arship on each question and where appropriate offering my own
contributions.

a) *The Relationship of the* Ars *to the Didactic Tradition*

Ovid's debt to didactic poetry, especially the *De Rerum Natura* and
the *Georgics*, has been thoroughly investigated[24] and needs no repe-
tition here. But though the *Ars* has been demonstrated to be replete
with stylistic and thematic reminiscences of Lucretius and Virgil, the
reason for this intertextuality is open to question. Some have argued
that Ovid is making a serious point, e.g., that he recalls Lucretius's
history of early man in order to highlight the importance of love in
the development of civilization,[25] or invokes the *cultus* of the fields
in the *Georgics* to elevate love to a similar cultural importance.[26] A
different approach views the didactic borrowings as purely parodic,
though there is disagreement regarding the purpose of the parody.[27]
It may be intended simply to amuse by its cleverness, or there may
be a more sinister intent: subversion of the underlying ideology of
the *Georgics*, and thus by extension, of Augustan ideology.[28] Alternatively,

---

[23] For the last, see especially Sharrock (1994a) and Downing (1993). Holzberg
(1981) gives a good overview of modern scholarship.

[24] E.g., Kenney (1958b), Krókowski (1963), Leach (1964), Hollis (1973) 89–93,
Steudel (1992).

[25] Krókowski (1963) 149.

[26] Solodow (1977).

[27] On parody, see Dalzell (1996) 147–48, Steudel (1992).

[28] E.g., Scivoletto (1976), Pianezzola (1972). For arguments against the "subver-
sive" approach see Labate (1991).

Ovid's use of "georgic" imagery may be seen as part of a misogynistic stance.[29]

Of relevance here is Sharrock's recent study (1994a), which breaks new ground in making extensive use of two forms of modern critical methodology: reader response criticism and intertextuality. With the first, the relationship is investigated between the speaker of the poem and the addressee(s)—a relationship integral to didactic poetry. The second approach involves not merely identifying "sources" but discussing through a close reading of the text the way in which the poet utilizes these. In the case of the didactic tradition, Sharrock's work, confined to Book 2 of the *Ars*, points the way for similar close readings of the relationship between Ovid and the earlier didactic poets.

b) *The* Ars *as an Elegiac Poem*

Wheeler's early articles[30] demonstrated the presence in elegy of a strong didactic element, not just in the obviously paraenetic *lena* poems (Propertius 4.5 and *Amores* 1.8) and Tibullus 1.4 (Priapus's teaching on pederastic relationships), but in a general tendency for the elegists to offer advice to others on the basis of their personal experience. To some extent the *Ars* is a full-length extension of this trend. Moreover, the basic argumentative style of the poem bears close similarities to the elegies mentioned above, especially *Amores* 1.8.[31]

Much of Ovid's subject matter derives from elegy, though there are relatively few extensive borrowings. A notable exception is the passage (1.135–62) on finding a girl at the races, which is a reworking of *Amores* 3.2. Simple comparisons of the two passages have invariably resulted in a verdict in favor of the latter, outstanding in the *Amores* collection for its lively spontaneity and humor. More recent critics, accepting that the *Ars* version is by comparison a dry and derivative series of precepts, view this not as failure on Ovid's part but a deliberate way of adapting elegiac material to the didactic mode.[32]

---

[29] Leach (1964).
[30] Wheeler (1910), (1910–11).
[31] See Romano (1980).
[32] See Dalzell (1996) 141–42, Boyd (1997) 204–10, Downing (1993) 27–39, who also argues that the passage is meant to demonstrate that the "lifeless and mechanical" is *not* preferable to the "natural and spontaneous"; Sharrock (1994a) 3–4 on the relation of the *Ars* to earlier elegy in general.

The most interesting aspect of the relationship between the *Ars* and earlier elegy is Ovid's transformation of the elegiac concept of love. Whereas in the elegists *amor* is is an overpowering *furor* resulting inevitably in misery, the aim of the art of love is to enable the practitioner to enjoy the experience by remaining in control: love becomes a pleasurable game.[33] The idea is expressed metaphorically in the prooemium through the image of the *praeceptor* taming Cupid, the god who in elegy inflicts passion on the unwitting lover. Although this may be viewed merely as a witty playing with elegiac motifs, many have viewed the poet's attack on Amor as an attack on the genre of elegiac poetry itself. By presenting the behavior of the elegiac lover as a set of rules which can be learned, Ovid not only holds this behavior up to ridicule, but effects the virtual demise of the genre with the result that it is no longer possible to take this sort of love seriously. On this topic, Conte's discussion (1994) is particularly useful: he argues that Ovid goes some way towards undermining elegy in the *Amores*, while still ostensibly maintaining the stance of suffering lover: in the *Ars* this stance is dropped and the *Ars*, together with the *Remedia*, is the ultimate outcome of a trend already begun.

c) *Does the* Ars *Have a Serious Moral Purpose?*

Few would disagree that Ovid's irreverent treatment of his predecessors is an important source of humor in the poem. The majority of recent critics, however, have felt uncomfortable with taking the *Ars* as simple parody of the didactic and/or the elegiac traditions. Somehow, they feel, this devalues the work, and Ovid must have some more serious point to make.[34] Exactly what point has been the subject of much discussion. Ovid's use of Cicero's *De officiis* has been seen as giving a serious philosophical basis to the poem.[35] Many have focused on Ovid's attitude to *cultus*, in the wider sense of the sophisticated culture of Rome. Ovid's lover, applying *cultus* to the natural impulse of love, becomes a "cultural ideal,"[36] or as

---

[33] For love as play see Myerowitz (1986).

[34] Or at least his underlying "humanity and psychological insight" must absolve him from the charge of mere frivolity: Barsby (1978) 23; cf. Hollis (1973) 113.

[35] E.g., Labate (1984) 121–74.

[36] Solodow (1977).

Myerowitz puts it: "the *Ars Amatoria* represents the wide-ranging spirit of play which sees play as the proper, indeed the only valid, option for the man of culture."[37]

I come down on the side of those who view the poem as essentially playful and parodic in tone.[38] Moreover, as my comments below will suggest, I would question the common assumption that the poem's merit is compromised if it lacks a serious message.

d) *Ovid's Didactic Persona: The* Praeceptor Amoris

A useful way of evaluating the way Ovid's humor works has been through the concept of the *persona*, in other words, the speaker of the poem (commonly referred to as the *praeceptor*) as opposed to the "real" Ovid. The character of the *praeceptor* is derived from both the elegiac and didactic traditions. Like the didactic poets, he exhibits an evangelistic desire to teach an *ars* in which he claims personal expertise. As a lover and a *pauper poeta*, he is to some extent a continuation of Ovid's *Amores persona* grown older[39] and able to offer younger lovers the benefit of his own experience. Finally, as a self-proclaimed expert who offers systematic instruction to his pupils with an air of self-confidence frequently tinged with pomposity, he is reminiscent of elegiac teachers, in particular Tibullus's Priapus (1.4).

The way we view the *praeceptor* depends to some extent on what sort of *amor* we think he is teaching. The question ought to be straightforward, but as has often been noticed, there is an inconsistency in Ovid's presentation of love, which seems to vacillate between elegiac passion, e.g., 1.165–66 (a reference to the elegiac concept of love as a wound)[40] and mere role play, e.g., 1.611, *est tibi agendus amans, imitandaque uulnera uerbis.* Some of the *praeceptor's* teachings presuppose pretence, for instance the advice that the lover must attend his girl on her sick bed in order to furnish proof of his devotion (2.315–36). On the other hand, the precepts on enduring a rival

---

[37] Myerowitz (1986) 39. For a list of others who approach the work seriously, see Dalzell (1996) 133.

[38] E.g., Hollis (1973), Dalzell (1996), Holzberg (1997a).

[39] Cf. the comparison between the *praeceptor* and the *senex* Chiron (1.14), and the recommendation of older women (2.663–82) and men (3.565–76) as lovers. The seniority of the *praeceptor* is one of several respects in which the *persona* and the "real" Ovid coincide.

[40] Cf. 1.83, 176, 257–58, 615, 2.520.

(2.535–600) suggest some sort of emotion on the part of the lover:
if he were totally indifferent, would he be affected by jealousy?

It has become fashionable to solve this difficulty by emphasizing
those places where the lover is represented as engaging in pretence.
The *Ars* is not, then, teaching elegiac love at all, but the art of
courtship, in which the lover plays a part but is completely devoid
of emotional commitment. But this approach fails to take due recog-
nition of the close relationship of the poem with the elegiac tradition.

To distinguish between "real" elegiac love and seduction involv-
ing only a pretence of "real" passion is, however, misleading. Of
course the lover of the *Ars* who is urged to "*be* miserable" or to "*be*
pale" is different from the elegiac lover who needs no such prompt-
ing, but the difference is one of intensity rather than of kind. On
the one end of the scale are unhappy elegiac lovers like Propertius,
whose passion is imposed upon him and is outside his control. At
the other end of the spectrum is the sort of lover whom Ovid aims
to create: one who is happy in a long-term sexual relationship (cf.
Ars 1.38, *ut longo tempore duret amor*) because he retains his freedom.
But there is a thin dividing line between sexual attraction which is
sufficiently strong to initiate a relatively long-lasting affair and over-
whelming "Propertian" passion. As Ovid himself says (1.615–16):
saepe tamen uere coepit simulator amare,/ saepe, quod incipiens finxerat esse, fuit.
And therein the irony of attempting to teaching the art of love. It
is an art which is virtually unteachable, because by simulating mad
passion, the pupil may easily become a "genuine" lover unable to
exercise the necessary control.

The *praeceptor*, then, in attempting to turn elegiac love into an art,
is an intentionally mock-serious creation.[41] One of the ways this is
brought out is by self-referentiality: on occasion the *praeceptor* alludes
to personal "experience" to demonstrate that he is unable to follow
his own advice. At 2.535–46, for instance, he enunciates the all-
important precept that a rival must be borne with patient endurance.
The authority of the teaching is however undermined by the unex-
pected admission of its ineffectiveness in the *praeceptor*'s own case: *hac
ego, confiteor, non sum perfectus in arte;/ quid faciam? monitis sum minor ipse*

---

[41] Downing (1993) argues that Ovid succeeds in turning love into an *ars*, but
thereby makes it much less interesting than the irrational passion which it seeks to
replace, and so demonstrates that *ars* is not after all preferable to *natura*.

meis (547–48).[42] There follows (549–52) a reminiscence of an incident in the *praeceptor*'s past "life," i.e., *Amores* 2.5; the undercutting effect is compounded by the suggestion that this was not an isolated instance of failure (553, *non semel hoc uitium nocuit mihi*).

The passage also illustrates a second factor in the creation of the mock-serious persona, namely, exploitation of the incongruity between the serious didactic stance and the essential banality of the subject matter. This incongruity underpins the *Ars* as a whole, a result of Ovid's choice of *amor* as a subject for didactic poetry. But it is especially emphasized in those passages where the figure of the *praeceptor* is self-consciously in the foreground. So for instance the passage that begins: *quid moror in paruis? animus maioribus instat;/magna canam: toto pectore, uulgus, ades.* (535–36). The mock-elevated style parodies both epic and didactic poetry;[43] it continues in similar vein for a further couplet but dissolves into bathos as the nature of the "greater themes" is revealed—"patiently endure a rival" (*riualem patienter habe*, 539).

e) *The Use of Myth*

In purely structural terms, Ovid's use of myth illustrates the way elegiac and didactic elements are combined in the poem. Short *exempla* used to corroborate an argument or as paradigms of behavior are a feature of elegy, especially elegies in didactic mode.[44] The longer mythological episodes are incorporated into the text by being made to illustrate a point, and in this sense are extended *exempla*. There is some elegiac precedent for this, such as Propertius 1.20 and 3.15, and *Am.* 3.6.49–82. Mythological narrations are also of course a feature of didactic poetry, e.g., the Aristaeus "epyllion" which forms the second half of *Georgics* 4.[45]

In the case of the longer myths, since they are narrated at a length which is strictly unnecessary merely to reinforce an argument, they

---

[42] Compare Tib. 1.4.79–84, where the image of the poet as successful teacher is deflated by the lament that his art fails in the case of the boy Marathus.

[43] For *quid moror*, cf. Virg. *Aen.* 2.102, 4.325, 6.528; *animus maioribus instat* recalls *Aen.* 7.44–45, *maius opus moueo*. For *ades*, cf. Lucret. 1.499 and Manil. 3.36–37.

[44] E.g., Tib. 1.4.23–26, 37–38, Ov. *Am.* 1.8.47–48, Prop. 1.2.15–24; see Watson (1983a) 117–18.

[45] Ovid emphasizes this by using didactic formulae of transition, e.g., *ergo age* (1.343, 2.143), *sed repetamus opus* (3.747).

are usually labelled "digressions." They may be simply viewed as part of Ovid's parody of didactic poetry; nevertheless, the label "digression" "suggests the criticism of self-indulgence and irrelevance"[46] and many scholars have consequently attempted to find a more subtle meaning in the episodes than mere formal imitation of didactic style. In particular, the Daedalus and Icarus narrative (*Ars* 2.21–96) has generated much discussion.[47]

Ovid's use of myth is also a major source of humor in the *Ars*. Many of the myths come from a heroic context and thus are strictly inappropriate to elegy; they are often adapted to their new erotic milieu by changes in character and motivation, with a resultant deflating of epic heroes and heroines to the level of contemporary lovers. The effectiveness of the exempla in reinforcing an argument is thereby called into question, and their frequent employment by the *praeceptor* substantially undermines his authority as a teacher.

To illustrate how this sort of humor works, I shall discuss one of the longer mythological narrations, the rape of the Sabine women (1.101–30). The episode has been viewed as a burlesque of a Callimachean *aition*[48] or as a parody of the ancient preoccupation with inventors.[49] It also plays with Livy's version of the story, in which an incident in the story is an *aition* for part of the Roman marriage ceremony.[50] For Ovid, by contrast, the legend is an *aition* for the conduct of a contemporary love affair.

In Livy, the myth is about marriage, with Romulus a prototype Roman husband and the abducted Sabine women later to become paradigms of chaste *matronae*. The transferral of the story into the novel context of love elegy, however, involves a radical change of characterization.[51] Romulus becomes not merely the prototype of a contemporary lover, but a sexual πρῶτος εὑρετής, the discoverer of one of the arts of love. Moreover, the Sabine women are viewed implicitly as the forerunners of modern *puellae*.

---

[46] Sharrock (1994a) 89.

[47] For a detailed analysis and summary of the scholarship, see Sharrock (1994a) 87–195.

[48] Wilkinson (1955) 123.

[49] Hollis (1977) on 101. Inventors have a prominent place in didactic poetry.

[50] The ritual cry *Thalassio*: Liv. 1.9.12.

[51] For a different interpretation, see Myerowitz (1985) 62–67, who sees Romulus as instituting marriage by rape in a public context and suggests that Ovid implicitly criticizes Augustus for trying to exercize public control over marriage.

A comparison with Livy's account highlights how this effect is achieved. In describing the rape, the historian makes no mention of erotic feelings: Romulus and his men, in need of wives to increase their population, simply fall upon the assembled *uirgines*, each seizing any girl at random (1.9.11). By contrast, Ovid depicts the men as lovers planning their moves in advance; as they sit in the theater each looks back and picks out the girl of his choice (109–10). Such behavior is nothing less than a practical demonstration of the maxim *tu praecipue curuis uenare theatris* (89), itself an adaptation of an elegiac theme.[52] The erotic orientation continues in 115–16: *protinus exiliunt, animum clamore fatentes,/uirginibus cupidas iniciuntque manus. Animum clamore fatentes* suggests not merely "revealing their intentions" but "confessing their love,"[53] the idea being restated in the next line by the epithet *cupidus*; contrast Livy's bland statement *iuuentus Romana ad rapiendas uirgines discurrit* (1.9.10).

Furthermore, in keeping with the function of the myth as an *aition* for marriage, Livy's Romulus emphasizes in his speech of conciliation to the women the benefits they will obtain as a result of the rape—marriage, Roman citizenship, and motherhood. In the *Ars*, by contrast, the erotic element is to the fore, emphasized by the focus on a single couple and by the words of the man ('*quid teneros lacrimis corrumpis ocellos?*,' 129), which sound like an elegiac lover's address to his mistress.[54] And Livy's statement that husband will compensate for loss of parents becomes '*quod matri pater est, hoc tibi . . . ero*' (130): the parent-child relationship has faded out of sight and stress is transferred to the sexual relationship of the parents, which is to be repeated in the case of the newly-joined couple.

Romulus and his men, then, are portrayed as elegiac lovers. More controversial is the depiction of the Sabine women, but there are indications that they are viewed as potential elegiac mistresses. First, the women, termed *uirgines* by Livy, are referred to twice by Ovid (109, 125) as *puellae*, a word heavily laden with erotic connotations. Second, the emphasis is on fear rather than flight. In 118–19 (*utque fugit uisos agna nouella lupos,/sic illae timuere uiros sine lege ruentes*), the simile of the lamb fleeing wolves is somewhat surprisingly followed

---

[52] Cf. Prop. 4.8.77, Ov. *Am*. 2.7.3–4.

[53] For *animus* in this sense, cf. 2.250, *Am*. 2.19.24, Catull. 45.20. For *fatere* of acknowledging a secret passion, cf. *Ars* 1.573, *Her*. 4.156, 11.38.

[54] Cf. *Am*. 3.6.57, *quid fles et madidos lacrimis corrumpis ocellos?*

by *sic timuere*,[55] and in the following static tableau (121–24), only one woman is shown fleeing. The idea that their resistance is half-hearted is also suggested by 127, *si qua repugnarat nimium comitemque negarat*: as Hollis remarks, it was an elegiac commonplace that "it was right and proper to put up a show of reluctance, but not to carry their opposition too far."[56]

Once again, Ovid's methods are set in relief by a comparison with the account of Livy (1.9), where the reactions of the women are expressed in terms of strong moral disapprobation (*indignatio* §14, *irae* §15, *iniuria* §15). When they finally acquiesce in their fate they are persuaded by *blanditiae*, certainly, but the marriage is already a *fait accompli*, whereas *Ars* 1.127–30 suggest the seduction by an elegiac lover of a reluctant mistress prior to the sexual act.[57]

f) Ovid and Augustus

Ovid's own specification of the *Ars Amatoria* as one of the two causes of his exile (*Tr.* 2.208, *perdiderint . . . me duo crimina, carmen et error*, "two charges brought me ruin, a poem and a mistake") has inevitably generated widespread scholarly debate. Two major questions have been addressed: (1) to what extent was the *carmen*, as opposed to the *error*, responsible for Ovid's banishment?, and (2) granted that the *Ars* was in some way implicated, what was it about the poem that caused offense?

The nature of the *error* has given rise to much futile speculation. Perhaps Ovid was somehow involved in a dynastic scandal involving Julia the Younger and her lovers.[58] All attempts to gauge the relative importance of the *carmen* and the *error* are frustrated by Ovid's secrecy about the nature of the latter, and more recently the focus

---

[55] One might have expected *sic fugere*: cf. Hor. *C.* 1.15.29–31, *quem tu, ceruus uti uallis in altera/uisum parte lupum . . ./. . . fugies.*

[56] Hollis (1977) ad loc. The verb *negare* is also common in elegy of a girl refusing a lover's overtures. For a different reading, which views Ovid as misogynistically enjoying the women's fear, see Richlin (1992) 166–68.

[57] For an argument that Livy's Sabine women are abducted but not sexually molested, and that their agreement, attained through *blanditiae*, foreshadows the consent of the bride which was a necessary part of later Roman marriage, see Vandiver (1999), who provides a convenient list of recent scholarship on the episode in Livy.

[58] See Syme (1979) 216–22; cf. also White, chapter 1 above and Williams, chapter 11 below.

has been placed, quite correctly, on the second question—the rôle of the *Ars*—which more readily rewards investigation. This is not to say that earlier generations did not address the problem: Wilkinson's discussion, for instance, remains valuable.[59] A major difference, with some exceptions, between earlier and more recent scholars is that the former view Ovid as playfully irreverent, but essentially apolitical, the innocent victim of a vindictive emperor; the latter tend to regard Ovid as consciously mocking, if not subverting, the Augustan ideology.[60]

There is any number of elements in the *Ars* which could have offended Augustus. To some, Ovid's elevation of the frivolous pursuit of love to the level of conventionally respectable *artes* like farming is a subversion of the Augustan moral ethos.[61] Then there are allusions to Augustan monuments or to public events, such as the imagined triumph of Gaius Caesar, which in Ovid's world are useful primarily as convenient venues for love affairs. Likewise, the irreverent treatment of Augustan icons like Venus and Romulus might have annoyed the Princeps.

In the cases just mentioned, the degree of imperial displeasure would have been in inverse proportion to Augustus's sense of humor. There was one area, however, in which the emperor would not have been amused. In his defense, Ovid focuses on the charge that married women learned adulterous behavior from his teachings (*Tr.* 2.347). If this were true, the Princeps' indulgence would have been particularly tested, especially as the publication of the *Ars* coincided with the banishment for adultery of his daughter Julia. The relation of the poem to the adultery laws has, indeed, received the most emphasis on the part of recent scholars,[62] who argue—correctly, in my view—not only that Ovid's female lovers included married women, but that his disclaimers to the contrary (e.g., 1.31–34) are purposely disingenuous, a way of drawing attention to the role of *matronae* in the poem.

At *Tr.* 2.255–56 Ovid acknowledges the possible criticism that despite his statements that he was not writing for *matronae* but for

---

[59] Wilkinson (1955) 294–98. See also Rudd (1976).

[60] See especially Sharrock's excellent "anti-Augustan" reading of the *Ars* (Sharrock 1994b).

[61] Cf. note 28 above.

[62] E.g., Sharrock (1994b); see also Stroh (1979) who however views Ovid's intentions as humorous but not political.

courtesans, married women might nonetheless learn from reading a poem addressed to others. In defense, he argues that he cannot be accused of corrupting *matronae* because it was not his intention to instruct them. But this supposes that didactic teaching is directed solely at the addressee of the poem. The Readers (addressees) of Book 3 are *meretrices*, but the wider circle of intended readers must have included Roman *matronae*.[63]

There are many indications that Ovid had *matronae* in mind. For instance, allusions to activities such as wool-making (2.686) and frequent childbirth (3.81–82) are more appropriate to married women than to courtesans. The use of the famous Mars/Venus love affair—an unequivocal case of adultery—as an exemplum has been commented on.[64] Finally, the dependence of the *Ars* on the elegiac tradition is important. As in elegy, the deception of the *uir* by the *puella* is a prominent theme (e.g., *Ars* 1.579–88, 602, 3.483–84). The status of this character in elegy is unclear: he could be a husband, a reigning lover, or the *patronus* of a freedwoman courtesan. The vagueness of the terminology, however, allows for the inference that elegiac love—and likewise the *Ars*—is about adulterous relationships. If Ovid did not mean his poem to be taken in this way, he surely would have underplayed the role of the *uir* rather than emphasizing it.

But Ovid was guilty of something worse than merely promoting adultery. His pupils, both male and female, are imagined as coming to him voluntarily for instruction: Ovid's role is to teach them how to achieve what they themselves already desire. The implication is that adultery is a universal practice, i.e., that Augustus's marriage laws are ineffectual. Ovid's offense, then, was to present Roman sexual *mores* as they really were rather than as Augustus would like to pretend them to be.

Whether or not Ovid deliberately set out to attack the regime, his treatment of the marriage laws is so provocative that it is difficult to see how he could have expected the emperor to believe that he was writing only for courtesans, or to regard the whole thing as a joke. Perhaps the poet calculated that he would be safe because Augustus, if he denounced a popular poet for reflecting what every-

---

[63] I use here Sharrock's distinction (1994a 5–20) between the Reader (addressee) and the reader (implied audience).

[64] E.g., Sharrock (1994b) 113–22.

one knew to be the truth, would not only look foolish but would draw greater public attention to the unpalatable truth that his adultery laws were having little or none of their desired effect on the *mores* of the Roman upper classes.[65]

g) *The Sexual Material*

It has been customary to dismiss as unimportant the two passages on sexual technique (2.703–32, 3.769–808): they make up only a small percentage of the poem and are seemingly tacked on apologetically at the end.[66] But though the *Ars* is certainly concerned less with sex than with seduction, it might be argued that the prominent closural position of the sexual material makes up for the brevity of its treatment. And Ovid's hesitant tone may be a disingenuous means of drawing attention to subject matter which is intended to shock.

Recent discussions have largely been undertaken in the context of Roman attitudes to sexuality and to women.[67] In particular, the different character of the advice offered to men and to women has been noted: the former are assumed to have a certain knowledge by nature; what they can learn from *Ars* is the refinement of pleasure, primarily in the control and timing of the orgasm. In Book 3, by contrast, the precepts are designed to show women how to fashion themselves so as to be most attractive to men.

Let us return to the *pudor* affected by Ovid in introducing explicitly sexual material, especially in Book 3, where he begins: *ulteriora pudet docuisse, sed alma Dione/'praecipue nostrum est, quod pudet' inquit 'opus'* (3.769–70).

Such apologies were of course standard when dealing with sexual matters, and here especially necessary because of the breach of generic decorum.[68] But there is more to these lines than a stock apologia

---

[65] McGinn (1998) 245–46 argues that the Augustan laws were not as ineffective as has been supposed, but allows that "adultery may have been tolerated in some sectors among the elite."

[66] Hollis (1977) xvii–xix, for instance, makes no mention of the sex manuals among Ovid's sources for the *Ars*; see also Hollis (1973) 84–85.

[67] See Parker (1992), Myerowitz (1992), and, for a detailed discussion of the *schemata*, Ramírez de Verger (1999).

[68] Although following elegiac practice by employing euphemisms rather than basic obscenities, Ovid deals in detail with matters that are merely glossed over in elegy.

for introducing obscene material. I suggested above that Ovid's self-conscious coyness is a means of drawing attention to the sexual material, with the purpose of scandalizing, as well as titillating, the reader. It is not simply that such material was disreputable.[69] In the *Remedia*, where sexual techniques are again treated, this time in a prominent position in the center of the poem (*Rem.* 397–440), Ovid offers an extended apology (*Rem.* 357–96). Not only does he argue for the inclusion of explicit sexual matter on the clearly disingenuous grounds of generic appropriateness, but he also introduces the well-worn theme that he is not writing for *matronae*. In Ovid's mind, then, the question of the intended audience is closely linked not just to the charge that he was teaching adultery, but to the use of explicitly sexual material.

It is in this respect that the end of Book 3 might have been regarded as especially outrageous. Granted, as argued earlier, that *matronae* were among the audience of the poem, Ovid is here teaching them not merely adultery, but a whole range of sexual techniques which were considered the province of courtesans. The use of *improba uerba*, for instance, recommended by Ovid at 796, was regarded as unseemly for *matronae*,[70] while lascivious movements (3.802) were used by prostitutes both to pleasure the male and to "divert the seed": for both reasons they were not recommended for use by married women (see Lucret. 4.1268–77).

h) Ars *3 and Ovid's Attitude to* Women

Ovid's attitude to women has been viewed in two opposite ways: (1) he is the closest thing in ancient Rome to a feminist,[71] or (2) he shares the misogyny of the average Roman male. The second view seems justified in the first two books, in which Ovid, taking the side of his male pupils, teaches them techniques which could be construed as hostile to women, such as breaking promises and using force. And though Ovid attempts to defray the potential offensiveness of such behavior by noting that women are themselves deceivers

---

[69] For the bad reputation of the erotic handbooks on which Ovid drew especially for the section (3.771–88) on sexual positions (*schemata*), see Parker (1992).

[70] See, e.g., Mart. 3.68, 5.2, 10.68, 11.15.1–2, Juv. 6.196–97.

[71] Most recently Martin (1999) 198.

(1.645–46) or that they enjoy rape (*grata est uis ista puellis,* 1.673), such remarks display a cynical attitude to women which is not entirely engendered by the immediate context. Leach (1964) and others have pointed to the imagery depicting women as prey, or as the *materia* upon which the male lover can exercise his *ars*[72]—part of a general attitude, common in the ancient world, that sees women as belonging to the realm of wild nature, over which man must exercise his controlling *cultus*. A striking instance is the Pasiphae episode in Book 1 (289–326), surrounded by a prolonged series of mythological exempla to illustrate, at unnecessary and inappropriate[73] length for the argument that "all women can be caught," the violence and destructiveness of female lust.

More contentious is Book 3, where Ovid betrays his male pupils by offering advice to the "enemy." Some have regarded the writing of the book as evidence of an ability on Ovid's part to see things from a feminine perspective; others argue that for all his protestations Ovid remains on the side of the male. The latter view seems more persuasive: the poet's decision to undertake a third book addressed to women doubtless arose from the delight of a rhetorically-trained mind in presenting the same theme from the opposite perspective. And although there are times when the advice given to *puellae* is designed for their sole benefit, for instance when they are warned to avoid dubious "dandies" (433–52), on the whole Ovid's precepts are presented with the advantage of the male lover in mind.

One passage which has commanded attention is the advice that the woman too should enjoy sex (3.793–94, *sentiat ex imis Venerem resoluta medullis/femina, et ex aequo res iuuet illa duos*). To those who consider Ovid a feminist, this is evidence of an unusual concern for female welfare, but surely Ovid is interested not so much in the woman's enjoyment as in the extra excitement that her pleasure gives the lover. The surrounding context reinforces this reading: in the preceding lines, sexual positions are recommended with a view to maximizing the woman's appeal to the man, rather than her own enjoyment, and in the succeeding lines frigid women are advised to fake orgasm—surely for the benefit of their lovers.[74]

---

[72] Myerowitz (1985) 129–49.

[73] The description of the horrifying results of women's lust might deter lovers rather than encouraging them.

[74] See Myerowitz (1992) 135–36, Holzberg (1997a) 113.

On the other hand, this advice is immediately followed by the poet's own comment: *infelix, cui torpet hebes locus ille, puella,/quo pariter debent femina uirque frui*—a rare but unequivocal case where the poet displays a genuine empathy with the female sex.

I conclude with a discussion of a passage, from Book 1, chosen both to illustrate Ovid's didactic manner, and to bring together many of the themes treated above.

> dum licet et loris passim potes ire solutis,
>   elige cui dicas 'tu mihi sola places.'
> haec tibi non tenues ueniet delapsa per auras;
>   quaerenda est oculis apta puella tuis.
> scit bene uenator, ceruis ubi retia tendat;   45
>   scit bene, qua frendens ualle moretur aper.
> aucupibus noti frutices; qui sustinet hamos,
>   nouit quae multo pisce natentur aquae.
> tu quoque, materiam longo qui quaeris amori,
>   ante frequens quo sit disce puella loco.   50
> non ego quaerentem uento dare uela iubebo,
>   nec tibi ut inuenias longa terenda uia est.
> Andromedan Perseus nigris portarit ab Indis,
>   raptaque sit Phrygio Graia puella uiro:
> tot tibi tamque dabit formosas Roma puellas,   55
>   'haec habet' ut dicas 'quicquid in orbe fuit.'
> Gargara quot segetes, quot habet Methymna racemos,
>   aequore quot pisces, fronde teguntur aues,
> quot caelum stellas, tot habet tua Roma puellas:
>   mater in Aeneae constitit urbe sui.   60

While you are allowed, and you are able to wander at random with reins loosened, choose a woman to whom you can say "you alone please me." She will not come to you gliding down through thin air: you must search out with your eyes a suitable girl. The hunter knows very well where to stretch out his nets for the deer, he knows very well in what valley the boar with gnashing teeth lingers; copses are well-known to bird-catchers; the fisherman knows what waters many fish swim in: you too, who are looking for the object of a long-lasting love affair, learn first what places girls frequent. I will not tell you to set sail in your search, nor do you have to tread a long road in order to find a girl. Perseus might have transported Andromeda from the dark-skinned Aethiopians, and the Greek girl might have been carried off by the Trojan hero, but Rome will give you so many girls and such beauties that you'll say "This city contains all the girls in the world." As many as the crops of Gargara, the vine clusters of Methymna, the fish that lurk in the sea, the birds in the trees, as many as the stars in the sky, so many girls does your Rome contain: Aeneas's mother has taken up residence in the city of her son.

Stylistically, the passage is a characteristic blending of elements from elegy and didactic poetry. The basic paraenetic form is elegiac, recalling in particular Propertius 4.5, *Amores* 1.8, and Tibullus 1.4. A precept is enunciated in a single couplet (41–42) and elaborated in the next (43–44). This is then reinforced by a series of analogies (*similitudines*) joined by anaphora (45–48), followed by a couplet linking the foregoing list to the argument. There follows another precept presented in a single couplet and backed up by two contrasting mythological exempla. After another series of *similitudines* the passage concludes with a sententious utterance in the final pentameter. To this basic format are added touches in the manner of the didactic poets, e.g., *ante . . . disce* (50) and *iubebo* (51).[75] Didactic subject matter is also recalled in the analogies from hunting (45–48) and agriculture (57), while the statement that all the lover's requirements are catered for in Rome without need of foreign imports parodies in particular the famous *Laudes Italiae* at *G.* 2.136–76. The hunting imagery, common in elegy and other erotic contexts, combines both elegiac and didactic motifs.

In addition, a number of important themes and attitudes are adumbrated in the passage. Lines 41–42, for instance, are a neat summary of Ovid's adaptation of elegiac love in the *Ars*, the pupil being advised to use the words of an elegiac lover,[76] but as a result of conscious choice (*elige*). Lines 49–50 illustrate the way in which women are viewed as the raw material on which the male lover exercises his *ars*.

The passage also testifies to the centrality in Ovid's scheme of things of the city of Rome, which is the proper setting for love. The analogies from rural life, parodying the *Georgics*, emphasize this reversal of Virgilian and Augustan values.

The exempla at 53–54 are typical of Ovid's witty use of myth. The motivation for Perseus's and Paris's journeys is changed to suit a new context, and the pair thus become by implication the prototypes of young lovers forced to journey abroad to acquire a woman because of a shortage at home.[77]

---

[75] See Hollis's notes ad loc.

[76] *Tu mihi sola places*: cf. Prop. 2.7.19; [Tib.] 3.19.3.

[77] In the Perseus story, he accidentally comes across Andromeda on his mission

The last line is an instance of Ovid's irreverent treatment of Augustan symbols. On the one hand, by alluding to Venus as the mother of Aeneas, he adverts to the Venus Genetrix of Augustan iconography, whose sexuality is subsumed in her role as ancestress of the Julii and patroness of fertility.[78] At the same time, however, by placing Venus at the climax of a section on the availability of *puellae*, Ovid deliberately calls to mind her identification with the Greek Aphrodite, the patron goddess, as it were, of extra-marital love[79]—an association which Augustus would hardly have been pleased to see underlined.

4. *The* Remedia Amoris

Discite sanari per quem didicitis amare: so Ovid addresses suffering lovers near the beginning of his last didactic elegiac poem, the *Remedia Amoris* (line 43). The neat jingle makes it sound as if the poem is simply a reversal of the *Ars Amatoria*, and to a certain extent this holds true. Inevitably, many[80] of the precepts given in the *Remedia* are clever inversions of those recommended by the *praeceptor amoris*, for instance,

> turgida, si plena est, si fusca est, nigra uocetur;
>   in gracili macies crimen habere potest.
> et poterit dici petulans, quae rustica non est;
>   et poterit dici rustica, si qua proba est (*Rem.* 327–30)

> If she is full figured let her be called fat, if dusky, black; in a slender girl skinniness can be reproached. And she who is not unsophisticated will be able to be referred to as forward, and unsophisticated if she is honorable

—reverses *Ars* 2.657–62 where the lover was advised to turn a girl's faults into assets by the use of euphemistic terms such as *fusca, gracilis*, and *plena*.

Although the subject matter of the *Ars* is of necessity repeated to some extent in the *Remedia*, the latter is not a straightforward inver-

---

to kill Medusa, while Paris is sent after Helen by Aphrodite. See further Watson (1983a) 123–24.

[78] See Zanker (1988) 195–201.

[79] And the mother of Aeneas by an adulterous liaison. Her role as adulteress is also emphasized in the Mars/Venus episode in Book 2.

[80] See Henderson (1979) xvi for a list.

sion of its predecessor, or a palinode, as it has sometimes been described.[81] The *praeceptor* of the *Remedia* is not just an expert teacher who advises on how to be rid of love rather than how to find it. Making extensive use of the common metaphor of love as a disease or wound, Ovid creates a *persona* who is also a doctor, a healer of love, in the same way that Nicander is a healer of snakebites or poisons. This is underscored by the invocation to Apollo, god of healing (75–78), and by the frequent use of imagery from medicine. However, this aspect of the poem, important as it is, should not be overstated. The doctor is also a lover (8) who calls on his personal experience in the course of the poem.[82] It should not be forgotten, as well, that there is elegiac precedent for the poet/lover playing the rôle of healer as well as teacher.[83]

Second, the subject matter is derived not only from the *Ars* but from a variety of sources, including Lucretius's fourth book.[84] In keeping with Ovid's pose as doctor, there are frequent references to medical writings, which are also mirrored in the structure of the argument.[85]

A major area of debate concerns the tone of the poem, with recent critics tending to see a serious side to the work. Toohey,[86] for instance, finds that the use of negative exempla such as Circe and Phyllis, where the emphasis is on the suffering caused by love, adds a pessimistic tone—a private voice of Ovid to counterbalance the *praeceptor*'s frivolous pose as a healer of love. In a more extended discussion, Davisson,[87] also focussing on Ovid's use of myth, argues that the exempla, as often in the *Ars*, fail to serve their ostensible illustrative function, the overall effect being to make the serious point that love cannot easily be cured, and that attempts to do so may even cause further suffering.

I agree with Davisson that the effectiveness of the *praeceptor*'s teaching in the *Remedia* is constantly undercut, but whereas she separates

---

[81] See Conte (1994) 57.

[82] E.g., 311–22.

[83] E.g., Prop. 1.10.17; cf. also Theocritus *Idyll* 11.

[84] Cic. *Tusc.* 4.74 has also been compared, e.g., for the advice (135–50) to seek other pursuits.

[85] See Henderson (1979) *passim*, Pinotti 15–24. Jones (1997) 69–87 discusses the argumentative form as part of the *persona* of the healer.

[86] Toohey (1996) 169–73.

[87] Davisson (1996).

this from the witty aspects of the poem, seeing a "coexistence of parody and warning,"[88] I would view Ovid's intentions as more consistently humorous. As in the *Ars*, the *persona* is a mock-serious creation. Moreover, the *Remedia* casts retrospective light on the *Ars*. In its prooemium, Ovid claims that his teaching is directed not at successful lovers but whoever suffers the tyranny of an unworthy girl (*male fert indignae regna puellae*, 15–16). But the *Ars*—which the latter is presumed to have read (44)—had taught lovers to endure with equanimity a girl's infidelity. The fact that a scenario is imagined in which some readers of the *Ars* have fallen into an elegiac passion beyond their control undermines the *praeceptor*'s boast to have turned love into an art.

I would like to discuss briefly a passage which nicely illustrates the tone of the *Remedia*. At 136 the love-smitten pupil is advised to avoid *otium* above all. He should engage, rather, in those conventionally respectable pursuits which are elsewhere antithetical to *amor* in Ovidian elegy—law (151–52), warfare (153–68), and agriculture (169–98). The last of these is a logical consequence of the presentation in the *Ars* of *amor* as an exclusively urban activity, the farmer being specifically contrasted with the lover (*Ars* 1.725–26). Ironically, Ovid recommends agriculture as a serious activity only when *amor* is no longer desired. To emphasize the irony, the passage parodically recalls the *Georgics* in many places, eulogizing the farmer's life not for its own sake but merely as antidote to love.[89]

As has often been remarked, the passage recalls not just the *Georgics* but the whole literary tradition of the idealization of the country and the simple rustic life. More important, it also glances at pastoral poetry. For instance,

> ecce, petunt rupes praeruptaque saxa capellae:
>   iam referent haedis ubera plena suis.   180
> pastor inaequali modulatur harundine carmen,
>   nec desunt comites, sedula turba, canes.

Lo, the goats make for the crags and the steep rocks, presently they will bring back their full udders to their kids. The shepherd plays a song on his pipe of unequal reeds, nor does he lack company in the form of dogs, a faithful crowd.

---

[88] Davisson (1996) 258.
[89] For instance, with 173–74 compare *G.* 1.223–24; with 185 cf. *G.* 4.230.

The lines recall several passages in Virgil's *Eclogues*.[90] A little further on, there are reminiscences of Tibullus's first elegy, with its pastoral setting.[91] But although these allusions to pastoral themes are subtly woven into Ovid's description of the farmer's life, they are in fact entirely inappropriate. First, the pastoral world, with rustics playing on their pipes, is one of *otium* rather than hard work. Second, their *carmina* are largely on the topic of love—and unhappy love at that (e.g., the song about Daphnis dying of unrequited love in *Eclogues* 5). This is hardly the sort of world where the lover could escape from love by occupying himself with strenuous rural activities. The same inappropriateness applies to the reminiscence of Tibullus because in 1.1 the idyllic farmer's life which the poet imagines himself leading is also a setting for love. The passage then both parodies didactic poetry and also by the incongruous introduction of pastoral elements undermines the efficacy of the *praeceptor*'s advice.

Taken as a group, Ovid's didactic elegies have much in common. They share the same meter, adapting elegiac subject matter to didactic mode, while at the same time there is a constant tension between the frivolousness of the subject matter and the seriousness of the didactic stance. Clearly there is an enormous gap between the *Medicamina*, with its limited theme, and the later elegies, but much of the style of the later poems is adumbrated in the former, especially in the prooemium. Also present in Ovid's earliest didactic elegy is a cavalier attitude to Augustan ideology. Ovid's didactic persona undergoes a development, from the teacher/metaphrast of the *Medicamina* to the elegiac lover/teacher of the *Ars*, and finally in the *Remedia* there is the added dimension of the poet as healer. Within this basic framework more serious messages may be discerned, but Ovid's didactic persona is essentially mock-serious, and it is the sophisticated humor and the play with literary traditions which continues to make a lasting impression.

---

[90] Cf. Virg. *Ecl.* 1.75–76, 4.21–22, 5.14, 6.8, 10.51, and for the "interlocking appositional structure" typical of Virgilian pastoral see Henderson (1979) on 182, Solodow (1986).

[91] With 187–88 cf. Tib. 1.1.47–48, with 189 cf. Tib. 1.1.7–8.

CHAPTER SIX

THE *FASTI*: STYLE, STRUCTURE, AND TIME

John F. Miller

1. *Introductory*

Long neglected, Ovid's elegiac calendar-poem, the *Fasti*, has been voluminously recognized by recent scholarship as a literary master-work.[1] The poet himself calls it "greater" (2.3, 4.3) than his earlier poetry, no doubt in reference to its grand scale as well as the august central topics—Rome's religious feasts, national legends, and the Emperor. The plan called for twelve books but we have only six—January through June—totaling 4,972 verses (this outstrips the 4,755 lines of *Aeneid* 1–6). Speaking to Augustus from his exile at Tomis, Ovid claims that he has written twelve books of *Fasti* (*Tr.* 2.549, *scripsi*), but most now agree that he is overstating the achievement for apologetic purposes. Although the calendrical narrator on three occasions explicitly anticipates *sacra* of the year's second half (3.57–58 and 199–200; 5.145–48), no trace of the last six books survives. Strong intratextual links between Books 1 and 6 (among other things) suggest to some that Ovid finally designed the calendrical fragment which we possess as an integrated work.[2] Even the poem's incompleteness has been interpreted as part of its meaning, as Ovid's refusal to surrender his identity to the Emperor and the state[3]—just ahead lay the months of Julius and Augustus. However, Book 6 ends with straightforward praises of the imperial family (6.801–10), and the closely knit structures of the first six months hardly rule out a balancing final half.

---

[1] Surveys of much recent work: Fantham (1995a) and (1995b); also Miller (1992a).

[2] E.g., Newlands (1995) 124–45 and Holzberg (1995) 353–62.

[3] Feeney (1992) 19, Newlands (1995) 26 ("[Ovid] resisted the subsuming of his poetic identity in the powerful, controlling myths of his age by leaving his poem unfinished"); cf. Barchiesi (1997b) 262. Fantham (1983) 210–15 concludes that Books 5 and 6 reflect that Ovid's available material "was drying up" (215).

In *Tristia* 2 Ovid notes that he dedicated the *Fasti* to the Princeps and that his exile (in A.D. 8) interrupted the poem (*Tr.* 2.552, *tibi sacratum sors mea rupit opus*). The work as we have it opens with an address to Germanicus, adopted son of Tiberius and grandson of Augustus (1.1–26). Nearly everyone takes this discrepancy to point to revision of the "interrupted" *Fasti* in exile:[4] after the death of Augustus in A.D. 14, Ovid changed the dedicatee to another member of the imperial house,[5] added references to Tiberius and Germanicus in Book 1, and one direct allusion elsewhere (4.80–84) to his own sad Tomitan plight. Recent scholarship has argued for additional revisions at Tomis,[6] and Ovid's exile colors many contemporary readings of the *Fasti*, whether the critic aims to demonstrate how the banished poet seeking recall updated his encomia[7] or tries to uncover his subtle protests against the regime.[8]

The poem's "political" stance has dominated recent criticism. By incorporating into the *fasti* new *feriae* celebrating anniversaries of his achievements and honors, Augustus, like Julius Caesar before him, firmly fixed his mark on the calendar, as on everything else in Rome's public life. Many of these feasts Ovid scrupulously includes in his calendar, and he also weaves the imperial family into some tradi-

---

[4] But see now Holzberg (1995) 351–53, who argues that the evidence would suit a poem begun shortly before exile and continued (rather than revised) at Tomis: nothing in Book 1 assumes the death of Augustus; *tibi sacratum* at *Tr.* 2.552 can be interpreted indirectly—compare Virgil's opening address to Octavian's intimate associate Maecenas in the *Georgics*, a poem concerned in essential respects with Octavian himself.

[5] Many have taken the proem to Book 2, addressed to Augustus, to be the whole work's original preface, but see below, n. 56.

[6] Lefèvre (1976), (1980) shows that the discussion of the origin of animal sacrifices (1.335–456) and the sections on the Fabii—from exile Ovid approached P. Fabius Maximus as a potential advocate for his recall to Rome—likely date from the later period. Fantham (1986) 266–73 argues that the proem to Book 5 reflects the atmosphere of the early Tiberian age; Fantham (1992b) considers how much of the Evander-Carmentis story in Books 1 and 6 was the product of the years at Tomis (in both cases similarities with Ovid's exilic poems form an important part of the argument). Herbert-Brown (1994) 159–62 suggests that the whole section on Carmentis in Book 1 (1.461–542) was written after the death of Augustus. Courtney (1965) 63–64 identifies metrical grounds for Ovid's work on the *Fasti* in exile. 6.666, *exilium quodam tempore Tibur erat* calls Ovid's banishment to mind, even without reference to *Pont.* 1.3.82, *exulibus tellus ultima Tibur erat*.

[7] Lefèvre (1980), Fantham (1986), Herbert-Brown (1994).

[8] Barchiesi (1997b) starts his analysis of the *Fasti* from the vantage point of the exilic elegies; Newlands (1995) prefaces her study by quoting *Pont.* 2.6.4, *et si non liceat scribere, mutus ero.* Cf. Feeney (1992) and Johnson (1978).

tional festivals. Not a few contemporary scholars take imperial ideology to be the principal focus of the *Fasti*. In today's *mentalité* of the zero-sum game the essentially apolitical Ovid of previous generations has all but vanished. "No poet could be unpolitical."[9] Sharp differences have emerged, however, over this poem's political orientation. Some take Ovid at his word, that the *Fasti* is his "service" (2.9, *militia*) to Augustus, that he is "versifying the calendar to honour the contemporary ruler."[10] An ever increasing number, however, sees the poet's engagement with the Princeps in agonistic terms: "When Ovid adopted the Roman calendar as the subject of his poem the *Fasti*, he implicitly engaged in a contest with Augustus over control of time."[11] From this perspective Ovid's characteristic wit ironically undermines the fulsome praise of Augustus, while Greek star-myths and traditional festal merrymaking are set in opposition to the imperial refashioning of Roman state cults, and the narrator's fragmented voice is designed to resist Augustanism's totalizing force.

However we judge its precise political significance, Ovid's kaleidoscopic persona is a signal feature of the poem's grand ambitions. We encounter in the *Fasti* a broad sweep of topics, ranging from Roman legend and imperial anniversaries to traditional rituals and antiquarian *aitia* and to Greek myth, weather signs, and astronomical data. The narrator who guides us through this varied menu frequently changes his mode and his tone of presentation. The instructor in ritual performance gives way to the hymnist or the aetiological narrator or the panegyrist; the speaker is by turns matter-of-fact, playful, or solemn. In the long entry for the Parilia (4.721–862), for instance, the poet opens with a lively prayer to the attendant deity Pales, reminding her that he has often dutifully performed her rites. Then, filled with her inspiration (729–30), he authoritatively orders both the urban population and shepherd folk to complete the requisite rituals, unfolding the pastoral rites in great detail. At the close of the directions, his inspiration has apparently run dry: the multitude of possible explanations for the rituals' origin leaves him in doubt (784). After this comic moment several alternative *aitia* are posed as questions, listed in handbook style—one he rules out as

---

[9] Wallace-Hadrill (1987) 223.

[10] Herbert-Brown (1994) 27; cf. earlier Williams (1978) 83–99 on Ovid's participation in the construction of Augustan ideology.

[11] Newlands (1996) 320.

unworthy of belief (793, *uix equidem credo*). Next follows a breezy narrative of Rome's foundation—the Parilia marks the City's birthday—at the head of which the poet asks again for divine support, this time from the divinized founder Quirinus (808); in a hymnic close to the City itself he wishes for continued Roman world-rule under the Caesars (859–62).

The shifts—or clashes—of perspectives within the narrating persona often have a deconstructive quality, calling presuppositions into question. The speaker's authority is frequently ruptured, then quickly restored. He can be naive one moment, and incredulous the next. The constantly changing voice hardly corresponds to what we would call a well integrated personality, but the fractured persona in fact embodies the variegated approach of educated Romans to religion, by turns prayerful and exegetical, performative and skeptical. The *Fasti* at once encompasses the Romans' differing, sometimes contradictory, views on religion and accents the fissures in the "balkanized" system of thought.[12]

The present chapter emphasizes important formal aspects which have attracted recent scholarly attention and would benefit from further research. The formalist orientation does not mean to suggest that literature and society exist as separate worlds, or that issues of style and structure can be detached from the work's ideological puzzles and complex treatment of Roman festivals. The limited focus aims rather to make way for the companion chapter in this volume to concentrate on Augustus and religion.

2. Intertextuality

i. Fasti/Liber Fastorum

As the word *fasti* suggests, Ovid takes as a template for his poem the Roman religious calendar. The inscribed or painted calendars which in his day one could consult in sanctuaries or other public areas recorded the character of each day of the year—what official business was or was not permissible—and noted the traditional fes-

---

[12] See Feeney (1998) 14–21 on "brain-balkanisation."

tivals, "birthdays" of temples, and the newer imperial feasts. Just so does the poet at the outset promise "the order of the calendar throughout the Latin year" (1.1, *tempora . . . Latium digesta per annum*— contrast the jumbled chronological sequence of "days" enumerated by Hesiod, *Erga* 765–821 and Virgil, *G.* 1.276–86), "sacred rites" (1.7, *sacra*; cf. 2.7), and "the days that Caesar added to the religious observances" (1.14, *quoscumque sacris addidit ille dies*). At the same time, Ovid ambitiously incorporates moveable feasts like the feriae Sementivae (1.657–704) and Fornacalia (2.513–32), a private magical rite (2.571–82), and a broad array of astronomical and meteorological notices seen only rarely in the remains of contemporary or older calendars.[13]

Strictly speaking, its detailed descriptions and exegeses make Ovid's poem a commentary on the calendar, akin to prose antiquarian treatises on the topic. Varro's *Antiquitates Diuinae* contained three books *de diebus festis* (Aug. *Civ. Dei* 6.3), and related post-Ovidian calendrical researches like Masurius's and Cornelius Labeo's *Fastorum libri* (Macrob. *Sat.* 1.4.6; 1.16.29) and Nisus's *Commentarii fastorum* (Macrob. *Sat.* 1.12.30) reach back to a much older scholarly tradition. Note in this connection that the elegiac researcher on occasion speaks of the calendar(s) as a source (1.289, 657), and that the poem's full title was *Liber Fastorum*, that is, a book *about* the calendar.[14] On the other hand, learned annotations had long ago accreted to the carved and painted *fasti* themselves, so that one may properly call Ovid's *Fasti* "a calendar in book form."[15]

Much attention has recently been directed at the principles of exegesis which Ovid shares with the extant calendars' notations, in particular, the habit of enumerating multiple explanations for a given name or cultic practice, often without deciding among them.[16] In

---

[13] See *Fasti Venusini* (between 16 B.C. and 4 A.D.) on May 18 (*Sol in Geminis*) and June 19 (*Sol in Cancro*). The rarity of such notices in the *fasti* gives point to Ovid's question when he takes up the topic of the stars in earnest: *Quid uetat et stellas . . . dicere?* (1.295–96).

[14] Rüpke (1994) 125–36; (1995) 71–73.

[15] Scheid (1992) 119. The *fasti* attached to M. Fulvius Nobilior's Temple of Hercules Musarum, erected in the early 180s B.C., is the first calendar known to have included such scholarly commentary (see Macrob. *Sat.* 1.12.16; Rüpke (1995) 331–68); Ovid features this temple without mention of its *fasti* at 6.778–812. On Roman antiquarianism during the Republic, see Rawson (1985) 233–49.

[16] Porte (1985) 220–30 ("L'étymologie double"); Beard (1987) 1–15; Miller (1992b) 11–31; Scheid (1992) 122–24; Loehr (1996) esp. 192–365; Feeney (1998) 127–31.

the extant fragmentary *fasti* one first encounters such information on
a large scale during Ovid's own lifetime, in the calendar which M.
Verrius Flaccus, tutor to Augustus's grandsons and resident in the
Emperor's Palatine compound, erected in his home town of Praeneste.
For instance, Verrius's lacunose note on January 9 shows that he
treated the various etymologies of the feast Agonium. Ovid's entry
for that day enumerates, in clipped catalog-fashion reminiscent of
the antiquarians, no less than six possible explanations for the name
(1.317–34).[17] Elsewhere the calendrical poet expatiates in narrative
form on variant *aitia* (e.g., 2.283–380 on nakedness at the Lupercalia;
3.543–674 on the identity of Anna Perenna) and even constructs
two dramatic scenes around competing etymologies (prologues to
Books 5 and 6). Ovid thus simultaneously spins poetry from prose
in Alexandrian fashion and participates intelligently in a discourse
on Roman religion. Of course he infuses antiquarian speculation (like
so much else) with his familiar ludic spirit, but then such ancient
exegesis was itself at root "a sport without limits."[18] Antiquarian prac-
tice makes it difficult to read the poem's multiple explanations as a
de facto destabilizing element.[19]

The extent to which Ovid directly engages with specific antiquarian
works is often unprovable, given the fragmentary state of most such
treatises. He will certainly have reflected upon his contemporary
Verrius Flaccus's researches, although in what form must remain
uncertain. We need not assume that Ovid studied the calendar of
Praeneste on site, which was anyway only fully set up after he was
banished to the Pontic wild.[20] The commentary of the *Fasti Praenestini*
was probably abridged from a separate monograph by Verrius on
the calendar;[21] and many of the great scholar's observations on sacral
aetiology will have been repeated in his important work *De uerborum
significatu*, which we know in Festus's epitome. Assuming a basic com-
monality among these Verrian works, one might venture an inter-
pretation of Ovid engaging Verrius Flaccus as an intertext, not just

---

[17] Degrassi (1963) 113 and 393. See further Paulus-Festus 9 L., Varro *LL* 6.12;
Miller (1992b) 14–22.

[18] Scheid (1992) 123.

[19] See most recently the corrective observations of Pasco-Pranger (2000) 288. For
a different view, see Martin (1985) 264–67 and Newlands (1992) 38–39 and 47.

[20] On the chronology see Degrassi (1963) 141–42, who dates the calendar to 6–9
A.D., with additions over the following two decades.

[21] Mommsen, *CIL* I ed. 2 p. 285.

as a source.[22] On the etymology of April, for instance, Ovid sharpens the (apparently—the text is mutilated) even-handed Verrian presentation of alternative explanations into a polemical contrast: the month's name derives from Aphrodite; those who argue for *aperire* are envious people who would begrudge the goddess her due.[23] Where the *Fasti Praenestini* explains abbreviations for the character of the days (F, C, EN, etc.) when these first appear (Jan. 2—actually the second day marked "F," Jan. 3, Jan. 10), the antiquarian poet introduces these and other preliminary data in a preface (1.45–62), likewise treating them once and for all (1.61, *semel*). The first time that the narrator tells us that he consulted "the calendar itself" on a specific point (as opposed to the divine authorities to whom he frequently turns), informed readers can profitably compare Verrius's calendar with Ovid's (*Fasti Praen.* on Jan. 1; 1.289–94):

[Aescu]lapio, Vedioui in Insula

Quod tamen ex ipsis licuit mihi discere fastis,
    sacrauere patres hac duo templa die.
accepit Phoebo nymphaque Coronide natum
    insula, diuidua quam premit amnis aqua.
Iuppiter in parte est: cepit locus unus utrumque
    iunctaque sunt magno templa nepotis auo.

Feast for Aesculapius and Vediovis on Tiber Island

But here is what I have been allowed to learn from the calendar itself. On this day the senate dedicated two temples. The island which the river surrounds with its parted waters welcomed the son of Apollo and the nymph Coronis. Jupiter too has a share. One place took in both, the temples of grandson and grandfather joined together.

The anniversaries of Aesculapius and Vediovis on January 1 had been recorded in earlier *fasti* (Ant. Mai. and probably Mag.), but among extant almanacs the Praenestine calendar alone draws attention to the two temples' topographical relationship: both are situated on Tiber Island. Ovid glosses Vediovis as Jupiter,[24] but he accents

---

[22] For the latter approach see Winther (1885) and Franke (1809); also Merkel (1841) xcv–xcvii.

[23] *Fasti Praen.* on Apr. init.; 4.61–62; 85–90. For discussion see Herbert-Brown (1994) 90–92.

[24] Cf. 3.437; also (with reference to this temple) Vitr. 3.2.3, Livy 34.53.7; Latte (1960) 82 n. 1.

the same idea of local correspondence, first with enjambment of *insula* at 292, then through explicit statement (*cepit locus unus utrumque/ iunctaque sunt...*). Echoing phraseology (*accepit... cepit*) and similar word patterning in successive pentameters (292, 294) further highlight parallelism between the neighboring monuments. From the buildings' temporal and spatial coincidence Ovid teases forth an additional link, the familial relationship between the deities resident in the temples: Jupiter is joined to his grandson Aesculapius, who was introduced in terms of his parents Apollo and Coronis. Meanwhile, the various junctions have a foil in the image of the island parting the waters of the Tiber (*dividua... aqua; iuncta... templa*). Verrius's four-word notice sparks a rich Ovidian meditation, albeit likewise in brief compass, on the shrines and their divine inhabitants.

ii. *Callimachus Romanus*

If the *Fasti* is Ovid's most Roman poem, it also exudes an Alexandrian spirit. Its combined focus on calendar, cult, local legend, aetiology, constellations, and weather signs distills several facets of the *doctrina* at the heart of Hellenistic literature. One calls to mind Simias of Rhodes's *Months*, Eratosthenes' *Katasterismoi*, Aratus's *Phaenomena*, and above all else the *Aetia* of Callimachus. The Augustan poets' engagement with Callimachus which has occupied scholarship in the past few decades finds its fullest expression in Ovid's *Fasti*, a quintessentially Callimachean work.[25] In announcing his aetiological theme in the first verse (*Tempora cum causis*) Ovid hints at an affinity with the *Aetia*. Very quickly thereafter emerges the Ovidian persona of an eager searcher into antiquities clearly adapted from Callimachus's elegiac masterwork. In the entry for January 1 the speaker first (1.71–88) unfolds the consular rituals like a master of ceremonies (as he will often do later) in the manner of Callimachus's "dramatic" *Hymns* (2, 5, 6); then he questions the god Janus at length about various aetiologies (89–288) in the first of many such dialogues patterned after one of the *Aetia*'s most distinctive features. Throughout *Aetia* 1 and 2 in a scene on Mount Helicon the poet talked with several individual Muses about miscellaneous religious arcana, while

---

[25] Thomas (1993) 205. On Callimachus and the *Fasti*, see especially Heinze (1919) 91–99; Miller (1982) and (1983); Barchiesi (1997b) Index s.v. "Callimachus."

at least once in the latter pair of books Callimachus depicted himself questioning a god about his own cult (fr. 114: Delian Apollo). Ovid's interrogations of Roman deities fall mostly into the latter category, though the Muses directly inform him too about various matters (1.657–62; 4.191–372; 5.1–110). The Ovidian antiquarian's interviews with human authorities likewise follow a Callimachean paradigm of exploiting chance encounters to gather aetiological information.[26]

In the *Fasti* we can recognize only a small handful of direct allusions to the Callimachean texts,[27] given the fragmentary state of the *Aetia* today, but some of these display a rich intertextual dynamic. Like Lycian Apollo in the *Aetia*-prologue (fr. 1.21–22), Janus appears to the poet who is holding his tablets (1.93). Reference to the famous divine Callimachean literary advisor in introducing an aetiological dialogue with a deity prompts us to recognize a commonality between the two Callimachean types, and alerts us to the programmatic dimension of the interview with Janus, the first of many such encounters. The god in a sense authenticates the poet's status as aetiological poet both with the epiphany and by addressing Ovid as *uates operose dierum* (1.101). The double question put to Janus (1.89–92) has Callimachean precedent (cf. *Aet.* fr. 7.19–21 Pf.), as well as a wit imparted by the intertexts: "What god are you, who have no Greek equivalent (except for Callimachus's Lycian Apollo and Delian Apollo and the Muses)?"[28] Similarly, Ovid's *envoi* to the charming Flora (5.377–78, *floreat ut toto carmen Nasonis in aeuo,/sparge, precor, donis pectora nostra tuis*) echoes the end of the *Aetia*'s first *aition*, a prayer to the Graces for the long life of the poet's elegies (fr. 7.13–14 Pf.). Callimachus's programmatic moment enhances Ovid's—this is the only time in the *Fasti* that he mentions himself by name. The allusion also underscores the connection between Flora and the Charites which Flora herself mentioned

---

[26] At a banquet in Alexandria Callimachus and a man from Icos discuss the latter's native customs (*Aet.* fr. 178 Pf.). The Roman antiquarian poet likewise learns from a host at Carseoli (4.679–712), the flamen Quirinalis (4.905–42), flaminica Dialis (6.219–34), and a couple of old people whom he encounters in the City (4.377–86, 6.395–416). See Miller (1982) 402–4.

[27] *F.* 1.93 > Callim. *Aet.* fr. 1.21–22 Pf.; 1.327 > fr. 75.10–11 Pf.; 5.377–78 > fr. 7.13–14 Pf.; 6.176 > fr. 1.14 Pf. Also 4.133–62 > Callim. *Hymn* 5, on which see Floratos (1960) 208–16 and Miller (1980) 210–13. See most recently Barchiesi (1997b) 22–23 on Battus at 3.569–78 evoking Callimachus Battiades, son of another Battus; and Harrison (1993) on 3.661–74 and the *Hecale*.

[28] Cf. 1.103: Janus opens by directly identifying himself with the Hesiodic deity Chaos.

in her autobiography (5.219–20), and which Botticelli's "Primavera"
will famously elaborate in a visual rendering of Ovid's Flora/Chloris.

Recent studies of the *Metamorphoses* have investigated the Callima-
chean heritage of Ovid's narrative style.[29] Barchiesi has discussed in
the light of Callimachus's *Hymn to Zeus* how the *Fasti* interrogates
the authority of the traditional gods.[30] Two areas in particular await
fuller exploration against the Callimachean background: structure
and panegyric. Pfeiffer[31] claimed that the aetiological narratives of
Aetia 1–2, loosely linked in the continuous conversation with the
Muses, offered the basic pattern for Ovid's similar *Kollektivgedicht*—in
the *Fasti* the calendar is the unifying strand. But the discrete nature
of the calendrical "entries" also makes them resemble the discon-
nected elegies of *Aetia* 3–4. The types of thematic correspondence
between various parts of the *Aetia* which recent scholarship has uncov-
ered—frames, pairings, instances of ring-composition—are also amply
paralleled in the *Fasti*.[32] Likewise, the panegyrical dimension of the
Aetia (as also of the *Hymns*), about which we know so much more
since the first appearance of the "Victoria Berenices" (see now *SH*
254–68),[33] may shed light on the contentious issue of Ovid's treat-
ment of Augustus.[34] Does the *Fasti* ironize this aspect of its princi-
pal Greek model? Or were Ovid's ambiguous praises of Augustus
inspired by such a Callimachean approach to the Ptolemies? Or does
his Callimachean poem's embrace of imperial panegyric revise the
meaning of Callimachus for Ovid and the Augustan poets?

iii. *Contemporary Literature*

"No ancient poet, not even Virgil, can have read more poetry and
given back in his own work more of what he read and so made his

---

[29] Tissol (1997) 131–66 on certain disruptive features of style; Myers (1994a)
61–94 on framed aetiological narratives.

[30] Barchiesi (1997b) 181–213.

[31] Pfeiffer (1953) II.xxxv.

[32] Important recent work on the structure and narrative techniques of the *Aetia*
by Harder (1988), (1990), and (1993). N. Krevans has work in progress on the struc-
tural legacy of the *Aetia* in Roman poetry (including the *Fasti*). For brief but sug-
gestive remarks on the topic, see Barchiesi (1997b) 79.

[33] Cf. Thomas (1983) on the relevance of this section of the *Aetia* to Roman
poetry.

[34] Cameron (1995) 454–83 (esp. 470 and 476–82) demands elaboration and
response in regard to the *Fasti*.

own."[35] No elegy illustrates this Ovidian trait more abundantly than the *Fasti*. While most of the sources to which the antiquarian narrator explicitly refers—like annals and stage plays—are irrecoverable,[36] we can trace allusions to a multitude of surviving literary works. A couple of Ovid's references to earlier Latin literature have acquired paradigmatic status in recent discussion of ancient intertextuality: the quotation of Ennius, *Ann.* 1.33 Sk. at 2.487 (where the speaker Mars's quotation of Jupiter mirrors the manner of alluding) and Ariadne's memory (*memini*) of her lament when abandoned by Theseus (3.473–75), underscored by the echoes of that experience as "lived" in Catullus 64 (130–35 and 143–44).[37] Ovid's references to his contemporaries' works are particularly plentiful, and run the gamut of allusive functions. He engages the historian Livy's first book in relating tales from Rome's regal period,[38] and Tibullus in his depiction of popular festivals.[39] The start of the last poem in Horace's fourth book of *Odes* undergoes a typical if puzzling Ovidian reversal at (appropriately) the very end of the last (extant) book of the *Fasti:* the admonitory clang of Phoebus's lyre (*C.* 4.15.2, *increpuit lyra*) is softened into Hercules' assenting stroke upon the same instrument (*F.* 6.812, *adnuit Alcides increpuitque lyram*), when both poets strike a panegyrical stance vis-à-vis the Emperor. On the Ides of May (5.663–92) parts of *Odes* 1.10 are refashioned into the narrator's solemn hymn to Mercury, which is immediately set opposite a shady businessman's audacious prayer to the same divinity; then a suppressed portion of the intertext surprisingly emerges to upset the balance and validate the merchant's petition.[40] Propertius 4.1 reverberates throughout the *Fasti*, with the tour of Augustan Rome against the background of the City's humble beginnings (Prop. 4.1.1–38; cf., e.g., 6.401; ironized at 1.197–226), the characterization of certain rites (cf. Vesta at 6.311 and Prop. 4.1.21) and places (cf. Bovillae at 3.667 and Prop. 4.1.33), and above all else the program of Latin

---

[35] Kenney (1970b) 764.

[36] 1.7, 4.326; on the latter source see Wiseman (1998) 23–24 and 64–74 with further bibliography.

[37] Conte (1986) 57–67; on the larger relevance of the latter example to Ovidian allusion, see Hinds (1987b) 17–18; Miller (1993) 153–64.

[38] See Bömer (1957–58) 1.26 and most recently Fox (1996) 182–228.

[39] Miller (1991) 110–16, 119–20, 125, 130–31, and 135.

[40] Miller (1991) 100–105. For the type of procedure at work in Ovid's initial oversolemnification of Horace's hymn, see Hinds (1998) 123–29 on "Do-it-yourself literary tradition."

aetiological elegy inspired by Callimachus. Ovid's elegiac confrère promised *sacra diesque canam et cognomina prisca locorum* (4.1.69), an utterance which the *Fasti* appeals to at its start no less for authorization than to differentiate its grander, calendrical project from Propertius's "Roman elegies" (1.1–7, *Tempora cum causis Latium digesta per annum . . . canam . . . sacra recognosces annalibus eruta priscis*). On the lighter side, Ovid responds to that elegy's last verse in an unexpected context: the astrologer Horos had warned Propertius to beware of the ill-omened constellation of the eight-footed Crab (4.1.150, *octipedis Cancri terga sinistra time*); the first star notice in the *Fasti* recalls this verse when recording Cancer's setting (1.313–14, *octipedis frustra quaerentur bracchia Cancri:/praeceps occiduas ille subibit aquas*), thereby literally following Horos's advice (i.e., Ovid avoids the star by speaking of it only as absent).

The poet who elsewhere referred to himself as the Virgil of elegy (*Rem.* 395–96) gives ample play to Virgilian intertexts in the *Fasti*. The introductory praise of astronomy (1.297, *felices animae, quibus haec cognoscere primis*) alludes to a famous movement in the *Georgics*, the juxtaposed blessings of the philosopher (2.490, *felix qui potuit rerum cognoscere causas*) and the rustic, which Ovid collapses into the advantages of a single honorandus, the astronomer.[41] The *Aeneid* makes itself felt here, too, as Ovid "corrects" Apollo's injunction to Ascanius on how to win immortality through martial deeds (9.641, *sic itur ad astra*) with a summarizing remark, *sic petitur caelum* (1.307), which substitutes the implicitly peaceful pursuit of astronomy for epic warfare (cf. Ovid's earlier programmatic choice of *aras* over *arma*, 1.13). The *Fasti* is shot through with references to the *Aeneid*, one of its major models. Already a classic, the *Aeneid* was for the *Fasti* an exemplar of intermingling Roman legend, antiquarianism, and contemporary politics, of a poem with grand scope—Ovid too originally planned 12 books—and of epic style and content. The traces of Virgil's great epic in the *Fasti* (in the senses of Barchiesi's *La traccia del modello*) both reveal the heritage of its occasional experiments with an epic register—no matter how much Ovid has denatured or leveled off Virgil's style[42]—and possess a dialogic power always engaging the new Ovidian, elegiac context.

---

[41] See Fantham (1992a) for a broader perspective on the engagement with the *Georgics*.

[42] Kenney's remarks (1973) 118–19 on the Virgilian background of the *Metamorphoses* are apposite; further Bömer (1959) and Kenney, chapter 2 above.

Ovid tends to look for gaps in Virgil's narrative. At the end of his sketch of Latian pre-history in *Aeneid* 8, Evander says that he was driven from Arcadia to his present home by fate and his mother Carmentis's prophetic warnings: *matrisque egere tremenda/ Carmentis nymphae monita et deus auctor Apollo* (*Aen.* 8.335–36). In commemorating the Carmentalia in January with the story of Evander and Carmentis, Ovid notes that the mother had previously prophesied troubles for her son and herself (1.475, *dixerat haec nato motus instare sibique*), and then puts into the seer's mouth the speech that convinced the hesitant Evander to leave his native land. She does not, however, impart "dread warnings" but rather (more appropriately for a character living in an elegiac atmosphere) consoles her son, buoys his spirit (1.497, *uocibus Euander firmata mente parentis*). As they head up the Tiber, the mother's role as adviser reemerges: *iamque ratem doctae monitu Carmentis in amnem/ egerat* (1.499–500). Again, this time explicitly, Ovid rewrites the Virgilian Carmentis's *monitus*, now into simple travel directions for the son, who has taken over the role as "driver." The future reflexive allusion[43] points ahead to the moment in *Aeneid* 8 even as it revises that moment. Likewise, the immediately ensuing prophetic speech delivered by Carmentis upon landing at their new home (1.509–36) is a prequel[44] to the moment that immediately follows the aforementioned verses in *Aeneid* 8: Evander points out to Aeneas— will point out in Ovidian time—the altar and gate set up in honor of the nymph Carmentis, *uatis fatidicae, cecinit quae prima futuros/ Aeneadas magnos et nobile Pallanteum* (8.340–41). Ovid's Carmentis utters just such prophecies, extending to the imperial descendants of Aeneas who will inhabit Augustan Rome, much in the manner of Jupiter's detailed predictions in *Aeneid* 1.

Elsewhere the *Fasti* evokes Virgil in reflecting on the aftermath of the *Aeneid*. On February's festival of the dead, Aeneas's gifts to Anchises' shade are said to have originated the Roman practice of honoring the familial spirits: *hunc morem Aeneas, pietatis idoneus auctor,/ attulit in terras, iuste Latine, tuas./ ille patris Genio sollemnia dona ferebat:/ hinc populi ritus edidicere pios* (2.543–46). Ovid's calendar grounds the Virgilian hero's most famous quality in a specific cultic context. The passage alludes to Aeneas's wish (at *Aen.* 5.59–60) that his father

---

[43] See on this manner of allusion, Barchiesi (1993) 333–65.

[44] For the term used in the context of intertextuality, see Hinds (1998) 96 and 116.

accept a yearly renewal of the funereal sacrifices then being offered. Ovid's imperfect *dona ferebat* suggests that Aeneas made good on his promise of regular future honors once he had settled in Italy. That that phrase too picks up Virgil's text—5.101, *dona ferunt*, the Aeneadae sacrificing *manibus Anchisae*—intertextually accentuates that the Sicilian rites for Anchises inspired the specific Roman feast called the Feralia (cf. *Aen.* 5.60, *ferre*, and Ovid's etymologizing at 2.534 and 569). Ovid's unusual term *patris Genio* (= *manibus patris*) seems to respond in mock pedantic fashion to the Virgilian Aeneas's doubt when he renewed the offerings to his father after a snake interrupted: *incertus geniumne loci famulumne parentis/esse putet* (5.95–96). It was after all the genius of the parent!

The extensive Virgilian sequel on the Ides of March aims at more broadly humorous effects. The obscure goddess celebrated that day, Anna Perenna, is at one point identified with Dido's sister Anna. Critics differ on the lengthy *aition*'s ideological implications,[45] but Ovid clearly travesties the *Aeneid*. After Dido's death—she had burned with passion, then literally burned on the pyre (3.545–46, *arserat . . . arserat . . .*)—her scorned suitor Iarbas controls Carthage, pointlessly boasting that he enjoys the queen's marriage chamber (3.553, *thalamis*). The Tyrians compared to industrious bees while they built Carthage at *Aen.* 1.430–36 now scatter like bees wandering about after their king's death (3.555–56; this last detail, from *G.* 4.213–14, shows Ovid reading the *Georgics* in the light of the *Aeneid*).[46] Anna flees, looking back at her native city's walls just as had the departing Aeneas (3.566, *moenia respiciens* = *Aen.* 5.3), whose story hers begins to parallel: e.g., fearful amidst a storm at sea, Anna for the first time calls her (dead) sister blessed (3.597, *felix*; cf. *Aen.* 1.94, *o terque quaterque beati* and Dido's standing epithet *infelix*, e.g., 1.749, 4.596). A heroine essentially replaces the hero. Aeneas's own first appearance shows that he has been cut down to less than Virgilian dimensions. He spots Anna newly arrived in Latium while pacing with Achates on "the beach got with his dowry" (3.603, *litore dotali*), not from the heroic conflicts featured in the *Aeneid*. His wife Lavinia blazes with jealousy at the newcomer, raging (3.637, *furialiter*) like her mother

---

[45] Contrast McKeown (1984) 169–87 (the fullest study of the *imitatio*) and Newlands (1996) 329–30.

[46] Fine analysis of this simile by Hinds (1987b) 14–17.

Amata in Virgil's epic. The threatened Anna is warned in a dream by Dido's ghost (cf. Hector to Aeneas at *Aen.* 2.270–97), and makes a comic escape by leaping out a window.

3. *Genre*

Besides its orientation toward the Princeps, no other feature of the *Fasti* has aroused such intense interest as its generic identity. Taking as his point of departure Ovid's two extended narrations of the story of Proserpina in the contemporary *Fasti* and *Metamorphoses*, Heinze long ago notoriously attempted to define an elegiac as opposed to an epic narrative technique: e.g., sentimental emotions vs. solemnity, humanized vs. majestic divinities, subjective vs. objective presentation, truncated and frequent vs. long and infrequent speeches.[47] Because these categories do not entirely fit the evidence, subsequent scholars attempted to emend or jettisoned Heinze's schema. Hinds[48] has recently rescued Heinze's basic approach by attempting to excavate the metaliterary dimensions of both poems. He affirms, for instance, that the emphasis on *querimoniae* in the elegiac version of Ceres' search for her daughter properly accords with elegy's traditional association with lament (e.g., *Am.* 3.9.3). Further, Hinds has refocused Heinze's question by interpreting genre as a dynamic principle rather than as a static category, and by demonstrating how Ovidian generic play involves creative transgressions as well as observances of expected norms. Ovid characterized the *Fasti* as a "greater" sort of elegy (2.3, 4.3, 6.22)—in scope, in length, in its sacral, national, and Augustan topics—but it nonetheless continues to define itself, as did love elegy, in opposition to heroic epic's martial subjects: *Caesaris arma canant alii: nos Caesaris aras* (1.13). Hence the poet's systematic disarming of Mars in *Fasti* 3: e.g., 3.8–10, *invenies et quod inermis agas./tum quoque inermis eras, cum te Romana sacerdos/cepit.* On the other hand, in addressing a topic like the Emperor's title *pater patriae* (2.119–26), Ovid acknowledges the strains that his poem's weighty content sometimes places on his verse, and that his elegies are flirting with epic grandeur.

Given the doubts in some quarters that genre resonates much in

---

[47] Heinze (1919).
[48] Hinds (1987a) 115–34 sketches the approach, exemplified more fully in the practical criticism of Hinds (1992).

Augustan literature's extensive "crossing of genres," it is surprising
that no one has mounted a sustained counter argument.[49] Much sub-
sequent literary analysis of the *Fasti* has taken Hinds's method firmly
in hand. Thus (to cite but a very few of many possible examples),
Newlands reads Ovid's Arion (2.79–118) as an elegiac poet and the
narrative of Chiron (5.379–414) in terms of the elegiac code—the
prioritizing of Achilles' grief and a corresponding calling of *arma* into
question; Barchiesi sees in the word-play at 1.260–61 (*protinus Oebalii
rettulit arma Tati,/utque leuis custos armillis capta . . .*) the diminutive noun
elegiacally rewriting epic *arma*. He argues that when Ovid refers to
the Virgilian Aeneas as the *auctor* of the Parentalia (see above), the
small offerings demanded for that festival (2.534, *parva*) pointedly
scale down the grander "epic" sacrifices in *Aeneid* 5.[50] For all three
of these scholars this generic interplay in the *Fasti* closely parallels
its political tensions, its critical commentary on an Augustan ideol-
ogy ultimately configured as "epic."

4. *Structure*

The calendrical arrangement of the material informs it with a superficial
structure akin to the loose argument of a didactic poem like Ovid's
Ars amatoria. In fact, stylistic markers of didactic verse like gerundives
and imperatives frequently help move from one section to the next
(e.g. 2.685, *Nunc mihi dicenda est regis fuga*; 4.630, *pontifices, forda sacra
litate boue*). However, the daily entries—sometimes portions thereof—
are more discrete than segments of the *Ars*, often amounting to care-
fully crafted elegies.[51] Add to this the ever shifting variety of topics—

---

[49] Some reviewers of Hinds (1987a) registered skepticism, e.g., Anderson (1989),
who speaks of "the generic fallacy" (357) and Thomas (1990). Most recently Gee
(2000) 21–65 has argued that astronomy in the *Fasti* does not resonate in elegiac,
but rather in didactic terms. The didactic genre she sees embracing Ovid's princi-
pal Greek models, Callimachus's elegiac *Aetia* and Aratus's hexameter *Phaenomena*.
Gee aims to complement Hinds's approach to Ovid's epicizing elegy, and sees didac-
tic defining itself, like elegy, in opposition to heroic epic.

[50] Newlands (1995) 179–88 and 115–22; Barchiesi (1997b) 21 and 67–68.

[51] Three examples from among many: Ovid and Janus (1.63–288)—for instance,
note the triple ring composition at the close (283–88): deity surveying the world (cf.
85–86), Germanicus (cf. 63), and the request that Janus bless Rome's peace-bring-
ing leaders (cf. 67–68); on the overall structure see Hardie (1991) 47–64; Lupercalia

festival, temple dedication, catasterism—and presentational modes—
narrative, instruction, hymn—and the vast range in length among
sections—from very brief epigrams to 200-line "panels"—and we
begin to appreciate the structural uniqueness, the hybrid status, of
the *Fasti* among poetic collections in Latin literature. Each of Ovid's
months we might call a didactic poetry book.

While each book adheres to a sequential review of the month's
days, Ovid everywhere exercises selectivity. He was free how, and
how much, to elaborate a given festival or constellation, or which
portion to highlight, or whether to include a given event at all. The
Regifugium in February (2.685–852) receives lavish treatment, more
than three times the length of the adjacent Terminalia (2.639–84).
On the Ides of March a brief, hesitant approach to Julius Caesar's
assassination (3.697–710) follows the long, comic disquisition on the
earthy popular feast of Anna Perenna (3.523–696). Dedications of
temples usually earn fleeting notice, but on the Kalends of February
the now ruined shrine of Juno Sospita prompts (ironic?) praises of
Augustus as restorer of temples (2.55–66). Ovid includes the anniver-
saries of Thapsus (4.377–84) and Mutina (4.627–28), but passes over
the battle of Munda on March 17 (included in the *Fasti Caeretani*
and *Farnesiani*) to concentrate on the festive Liberalia (3.713–90) and
a catasterism (3.793–808). In late January he treats the moveable
agricultural feast Sementivae (1.657–704) but omits the Compitalia,
another *feriae conceptiuae* often celebrated in this month (perhaps keep-
ing it for its alternate month of December). The Megalesia is fea-
tured on the festival's opening day (4.179–372), the dies Parentales
at their close (2.533–70). Both days of the Carmentalia in January
are treated (1.461–583 and 617–36). The anniversary of the name
Augustus on January 16 is conflated with that of Octavian's return
of the provinces on the Ides (1.587–616). Ovid briefly records the
opening of the Floralia in late April (4.943–48) but expansively fea-
tures Flora's *sacra* on their penultimate day, May 2 (5.183–378), the
final day being given over to the tale of the Centaur's stellification
(5.379–414). Risings and fallings of constellations are noted, and star-
myths told, at will.

The exuberant variety both among and within individual elegies—
if we may call them that—has seemed a jumble to some, and in

(2.267–452), on which see Littlewood (1975) 1060–72; Ides of May (5.663–92)—cf.
Miller (1991) 100–105.

fact constant change of pace lies at the heart of the Ovidian aes-
thetic. Yet recent scholarship has also revealed various artistic pat-
terns at work. Braun's[52] charting of each book in terms of the length
and general topic of the entries (e.g., temple dedication, catasterism)
shares the reductive quality of many studies of poetry books. Without
considering deeper thematics, as does especially Newlands,[53] many
of Braun's alleged connections hardly resonate as such. In the first
half of Book 2, for instance, while the four catasterisms do draw
attention to themselves as a group (Arion, Callisto, the cluster Raven,
Snake, and Bowl, and Pisces), each separated from the next by
another self-contained section, it is the nexus of narrative parallels
and verbal echoes which prompts us to read one myth in the light
of another. The correspondences are chiastically arranged: in the
first the initially fearful Arion (2.103, *ille, metu pauidus*) defiantly leaps
into the waves, where "they say that the dolphin put itself under
the strange burden with its back" (2.114, *se memorant . . . subposuisse*)
and was therefore bidden by Jupiter "to have nine stars" (2.118, *stel-
las . . . habere nouem*); in the last, the frightened Venus (2.467–68, *illa
timore/pallet*) with her son Cupid jumps in desperation into another
body of water, the river Euphrates, where "they say that you and
your brother (Pisces) supported two gods on your backs" (2.459–60,
te memorant . . . tergo sustinuisse), for which service the fish too now "have
stars" (2.472, *pro quo nunc . . . sidera nomen habent*). The framed pair of
star-narratives are foils for one another: Callisto, unjustly expelled
from Diana's sacred spring and transformed by jealous Juno, and
the deceitful raven whom Apollo justly punishes. The angry god tells
the bird that it will drink water from no spring until the time when
figs are ripe (2.263–64); Callisto is once more excluded from a watery
domain when the still raging Juno asks Tethys never to wash the
Bear constellation with her waters, that is, never to let it set (2.191–92).

Overarching structural schemata are as unlikely to convince every-
one as those posited for the *Metamorphoses*, but Ovid clearly devel-
ops certain themes through stretches of the poem. Much of Book 5
is preoccupied with *pietas*.[54] Book 1 is dotted with motifs of imper-
ial peace (67–68, 285–88, 697–704) to anticipate the anniversary of

---

[52] Braun (1981).
[53] Newlands (1995) passim; see earlier Drossard (1972).
[54] Cf. the different analyses of Newlands (1995) 97–122 and Boyd (2000).

the Ara Pacis at month's end, while the book's three lengthy "panels" concern origins and beginnings (Janus, animal sacrifices, Evander and Carmentis at the site of the future Rome).[55] Likewise in Book 2 the five tales of rape, not one of them demanded by the calendar, set up the climactic narrative of Lucretia on the Regifugium. The panegyrical accents in the first part of the same book constitute a series: the poet quickly fulfills the proem's promise that his "greater" elegiac verse (2.3, *uelis . . . maioribus*) will celebrate Caesar specifically for his *nomina* and *titulos* (2.16) by digressing on Augustus as *templorum positor, templorum sancte repostor* (2.63) on the month's first day before commemorating the Emperor's title of *pater patriae* on the Ides; there Augustus is again addressed as *sancte* (2.127), and Ovid revisits in tongue-in-cheek fashion the idea that he is tackling a "greater" topic than his elegies are accustomed to (2.123, *maioraque uiribus urgent*).[56]

Connections proliferate, inviting complementary reflections on, or striking revisions of, heroes, gods, ideas. Some reach beyond the book. The six proems are paired: 1 and 2 directed to members of the imperial family; 3 and 4 addressed to Mars and Venus, respectively, in terms of their relation to Ovid's poetry; in 5 and 6 a trio of deities offers competing etymologies for the month's name. Prophetic Carmentis in *Fasti* 6 (529–48) recalls in detail her appearance in Book 1 (472–538). We are invited to read the two festivals of the dead (Feralia in February, 2.533–616, and Lemuria in May, 5.419–92) in the light of one another.[57] Romulus's story is fragmented into many pieces throughout the poem.[58] Juxtapositions of calendrical notices often resonate. At the close of February 24 a logically unrelated weather sign seals the long narrative of Lucretia: Procne the swallow heralding springtime and Tereus joyful at his metamorphosed wife's shivering cold (2.853–56) refract the Roman legend of rape and conjugal *pietas*. At 5.693–94 occurs a rare clever transition (a

---

[55] For the latter thematic grouping see Holzberg (1995) 355.

[56] For further links between the proem to Book 2 and the Ides of February, see Fränkel (1945) 239–40 n. 8, who argues that the proem was written for its present position, not to introduce the entire work as many think; on this see further Miller (1991) 16 and 143–44.

[57] See Miller (1991) 105 and 170 n. 25.

[58] On the effect of Ovid's pattern, see Stok (1991) and Barchiesi (1997b) 154–64 and 167–77.

technique more typical of the *Metamorphoses*), in which the *uates oper-
osus dierum* asks Mercury, who just previously ratified a proverbially
unscrupulous businessman's prayer, for an answer to "a much better"
astronomical question about the constellation Gemini (*At mihi pande,
precor, tanto meliora petenti*). The request alerts us to the more momen-
tous discrepancy between the god's ensuing heartfelt tale of Pollux's
devotion to his brother Castor and Mercury's own theft of his sib-
ling Apollo's cattle, which a moment ago in the previous entry play-
fully emblematized Roman commercial trickery (5.681–92).[59] Elsewhere
the "syntagmatic tensions" (to use Barchiesi's term) are more subtle.
In January the celebratory association of Augustus's name with bound-
less increase (*augere*, 1.612–13) is in the following entry (January 15)
countered by the legend of a mass abortion with which Roman
matrons protested the loss of a certain privilege (1.621–24).[60] Some
readers will resist such ideological dissonance, preferring to privilege
the resumption of the Carmentalia on January 15, especially after
the full stop of the hymnic closing to "Augustus" on the Ides. But
verbal cues seem to foster the clash of motifs: the Emperor should
assume the burden of the world (1.616, *suscipiat . . . orbis onus*) and
three pentameters later the women expelled the growing burden from
their wombs (1.624, *crescens excutiebat onus*); the phrasing of Augustus's
exclusive honor (1.592, *contigerunt nulli nomina tanta uiro*) echoes in the
reportedly inclusive nature of the matrons' protest (1.622, *ingratos
nulla prole nouare **uiros***). Of course not every verbal echo is significant,
but in a poem of such myriad internal correspondences we should
be wary of prematurely shutting down the text.

    When reading the *Fasti* in linear fashion we experience a constant
interplay between apparent randomness and shared concerns in the
succession of days, a dialectic between rhetorical closure and the-
matic continuity. Editorial conventions may encourage one sort of

---

[59] Ovid frequently uses star-myths for such counterpoint, although critics differ
on the thematic effect overall: Martin (1985) sees the astronomical notices offering
an aura of stability against the arbitrary, confusing nature of the Roman calendar.
Phillips (1992) argues the opposite, the rational universe of the Roman *fasti* vs. the
irrational Greek stellar myths with their random immortality. Newlands (1995) 31
is closer to the mark: the Greek star-narratives "often embody different codes of
value and offer further perspectives upon the Roman themes . . . the myths interact
with the Roman material, occasionally confirming but more often challenging or
undermining the points of view encoded there."
    [60] Barchiesi (1997b) 93–96.

reading or the other. In texts of the *Fasti* there is a long tradition of graphically indicating divisions between days, whether with the marginal marks of medieval manuscripts, the large initial letters in the editions of N. Heinsius and Burman, or more recent editors' calendrical notations and paragraphing. It is most likely, however, that ancient readers held a text lacking such visual markers.[61] Consider 1.307–18 in such a format:

> sic petitur caelum, non ut ferat Ossan Olympus
>   summaque Peliacus sidera tangat apex.
> nos quoque sub ducibus caelum metabimur illis,
>   ponemusque suos ad uaga signa dies.
> ergo ubi nox aderit uenturis tertia Nonis,
>   sparsaque caelesti rore madebit humus,
> octipedis frustra quaerentur bracchia Cancri:
>   praeceps occiduas ille subibit aquas.
> institerint Nonae, missi tibi nubibus atris
>   signa dabunt imbres exoriente Lyra.
> quattuor adde dies ductos ex ordine Nonis,
>   Ianus Agonali luce piandus erit.

Thus does one climb to the sky, not by piling Ossa on Olympus and making Pelion's peak touch the topmost stars. I too will mark out the sky under those leaders and will appoint the appropriate days to the wandering constellations. And so, when the third night before the coming Nones has arrived and the ground is wet, sprinkled with dew from the sky, one will search in vain for the arms of the eight-footed Crab. Headlong he will sink beneath the western waters. When the Nones are present, rain pouring from black clouds will give you the sign, while the Lyre is rising. Add four days in a row to the Nones, and on the Agonal day Janus must be appeased.

The spacing in contemporary editions would immediately show that these lines belong to four separate sections: the end of the astronomical proem (307–10), followed by the entries for January 3 (311–14) and 5 (315–16) and the start of January 9 (317–18). And each specific naming of a day does start a new movement, abetted by stylistic variation (from hypotaxis to parataxis, from statements to command). The two central epigrams have internal structural coherence. The

---

[61] Such punctuation of sections is absent from the oldest surviving manuscript of the *Fasti*, Vaticanus Reginensis 1709 (tenth century), to judge from the sample page in Chatelain (1894–1900) pl. 99. Reproduced are 2.845–3.2, where editions divide after 2.852 and 2.856. The manuscript marks only the division between the books. See also Richmond, chapter 14 below.

astronomical notice for January 3 (311–14) hangs together with a chiastic alternation between the rhyming word patterns in the first and last verses and the verbal frames of the intervening lines. Its two couplets offer a parallel shift of gaze, from the sky where dew originates to the earth, from the sky to the sea's waves. Likewise, the single, condensed distich on the Nones (315–16) elegantly punctuates with caesurae its threefold report of name, weather sign, and constellation.[62] On the other hand, several connections knit these discrete parts into a continuous flow of text: *ergo* at 311, the falling and rising constellations paired in the poem's first two star notices (cf. 1.295, *oriturque caditque*; and 1.2), the verbal repetition *caelum . . . caelum . . . caelesti* (307, 309, 312), future tenses throughout, and the thrice repeated reference to the Nones (311, 315, 317). The artistic effect is partly that of distinct epigrams and elegies, partly that of a didactic tour through the calendar not unlike Virgil's brief Hesiodic run of "days" at *G.* 1.276–86.

5. *Narrative*

For all the illuminating observations on individual passages in his pioneering monograph *Ovids elegische Erzählung*, Heinze grossly overstated the basic differences between Ovid's narrative technique in the *Metamorphoses* and that in the *Fasti*. Ovid conceived his project of elegiac narrative on a large scale to some extent as a rival to epic narrative, but Heinze's definitional categories would better suit a contrast of all Ovidian narration with Virgil's narrative manner. The distinction between a solemn tone in the *Metamorphoses* vs. a sentimental atmosphere predominating in the *Fasti* collapses upon close scrutiny; the narrator's tone constantly shifts in both works. The asymmetrical design which Heinze correctly identified in Ovid's elegiac narrative also lies at the heart of his hexameter poem's narratological orientation, as do wit, abrupt transitions, indirection, and other sorts of narrative surprise—what one might summarize as a fundamental instability in the narrative.[63]

---

[62] On this entry see Santini (1975) 16.
[63] For an anatomy of these destabilizing features in the *Metamorphoses*, see Tissol (1997).

On the micro-level nonetheless these effects operate somewhat differently in elegiacs than in continuous hexameters. It is often remarked that the couplet poses severe limitations for extended story-telling, most notably because of the fixed form of the pentameter's second half, the comparatively limited range of caesurae, and especially the increasing tendency towards end-stop.[64] More productive is the effort to appreciate Ovid's achievement in elegiac narrative, since he imported so many of its features to the hexametric *Metamorphoses*.[65] Out of the "limited" structural possibilities in elegiacs Ovid spins a narrative aesthetic aimed at keeping the reader constantly on guard. His pentameter, for instance, either fills out the meaning of the hexameter and thereby advances the action, or repeats or otherwise comments on the hexameter, which retards the progress of the story. But the reader is never sure which of these effects to expect, rapidly stated action or a pause to paint the scene or identify a character. To complicate matters further, Ovid may impart to either type of pentameter the force of a punch line. The staccato rhythm of successive distichs—the constant starting and stopping—likewise provides Ovid with the basis for a jerky narrative style, one full of abrupt shifts via apostrophe, flashback, joking, and so forth. The narrative develops through a network of correspondences between one couplet and the next, sometimes verbal repetitions, at others antitheses or thematic variations. Not infrequently these correspondences simultaneously serve as building blocks linking the distichs and introduce new and surprising perspectives.

Let us illustrate such narrative at work. Here is the start of Hercules' encounter with Cacus (1.543–52):

> ecce boues illuc Erytheidas adplicat heros
>   emensus longi clauiger orbis iter,
> dumque huic hospitium domus est Tegeaea, uagantur
>   incustoditae lata per arua boues.
> mane erat: excussus somno Tirynthius actor
>   de numero tauros sentit abesse duos.
> nulla uidet quaerens taciti uestigia furti:
>   traxerat auersos Cacus in antra ferox,
> Cacus, Auentinae timor atque infamia siluae,
>   non leue finitimis hospitibusque malum.

---

[64] See Heinze (1919) 75–76; Wilkinson (1963) 133–34.
[65] See especially Tränkle (1963) and Knox (1986a).

Look, the club-bearing hero drives the Erythaean cattle here, having made a long journey across the world. And while he enjoys hospitality in the Arcadian's home, his unguarded cattle range over the wide fields. Morning had arrived. The drover from Tiryns, roused from sleep, perceives that two bulls are missing from the count. He searches but sees no traces of the silent theft. Fierce Cacus had dragged them backwards into his cave, Cacus the terror and shame of the Aventine forest, no minor annoyance to neighbors and strangers.

The first two distichs form a block: journeying from the faraway land of Geryon, Hercules drives the captured cattle to the Arcadian settlement, where they roam while he is entertained by Evander. In Alexandrian manner Ovid obliquely identifies the hero, his point of departure, and destination. He has also greatly lowered the tonal register from that of the Virgilian scene on which this episode is obviously based.[66] There the hero enters magnificently as the proud avenging victor over Geryon (*Aen.* 8.201–3, *maximus ultor . . . spoliisque superbus . . . uictor*); here we have him stopping over on a romantic odyssey. The present heroic status, such as it is, the second couplet explodes by paralleling Hercules' travels with the wandering of his cows. His stature is further deflated with the detail that the cows were "unguarded," which imputes to the driver some blame for the ensuing loss—this Hercules is judged by pastoral values. Note how the correspondences between the two distichs effect the deconstructive dynamic at the same time that the action keeps moving ahead: in the pentameters the "long" (*longi*) journey of the hero is set opposite the "wide" (*lata*) fields through which the cattle wander; the word *boues* frames the whole narrative block, rising in prominence from grammatical object at the start to subject at the close; the enjambment at 546 enhances the deflationary surprise of *incustoditae*, while its spondaic meter preserves rhythmical continuity with the previous pentameter.

The next movement (547–52) changes the scene but links up to the previous one by again specifying the hero at the start (cf. 543, *heros*, same sedes). Hercules wakes up and looks for the missing cattle. Those actions are only indirectly expressed by participles (*excussus, quaerens*), while the main verbs in historical present pointedly oppose what the hero saw to what he did not (*sentit, nulla uidet*). In

---

[66] For comparison with Virgil see Otis (1970) 31–36.

glossing Hercules' limited vision, the second pentameter is full of surprise: the theft which precipitated the whole crisis is briefly tossed off in parenthetical flashback; Cacus's famous ruse is obscurely expressed (*auersos*; cf. *Aen.* 8.208–10, *auertit... atque hos, ne qua forent pedibus uestigia rectis, cauda in speluncam tractos*); the first two pentameters' acoustic word patterning ends with an anticlimax (*tauros//duos/auersos//ferox/*). The narrator is less interested in the theft than in describing the monster and his lair, on which he dilates for the next eight verses. After the narrative is yanked backwards with the pluperfect, the next distich (551–52) commences the ogre's elaborate introduction, with elegantly arranged appositives, framed by a bilingual etymological word play on his (repeated) name (*malum* = κακόν). His hostility to visitors (*hospitibus*) picks up an earlier motif, already pitting him against Evander's guest-friend (545, *hospitium*).

When the narrative resumes, Hercules is leaving (1.559–68):

> seruata male parte boum Ioue natus abibat:
>   mugitum rauco furta dedere sono.
> 'accipio reuocamen' ait, uocemque secutus
>   impia per siluas ultor ad antra uenit.
> ille aditum fracti praestruxerat obice montis;
>   uix iuga mouissent quinque bis illud opus.
> nititur hic humeris (caelum quoque sederat illis),
>   et uastum motu conlabefactat onus.
> quod simul euersum est, fragor aethera terruit ipsum,
>   ictaque subsedit pondere molis humus.

Having poorly protected part of his herd, the son of Jupiter was departing, when the stolen cattle bellowed hoarsely. "I heed your call," he said, and following the sound, came through the woods to the wicked lair, intent on vengeance. Cacus had blocked the entranceway with a piece of broken-off mountain; ten yokes of oxen could hardly have moved that mass. Hercules pushed at it with his shoulders (the sky, too, had once rested on those shoulders) and toppled the immense burden. As soon as it was turned aside, the crash frightened the very heavens, and the shocked earth sank under the weight of the crag.

Note the lively movement of tenses,[67] from the imperfect which frequently marks a new stage in narrative (*abibat*) through the aoristic perfect sounding the alarm (*dedere*) to historical presents for the hero's

---

[67] On tenses in Ovidian elegiac narrative see von Albrecht (1968).

reactions (*ait, uenit*); then background intruded with pluperfect (*praestrux-erat*), resumption of the action with Hercules dislodging the barrier in historical present (*nititur, conlabefactat*—momentarily interrupted by more background in the pluperfect: *sederat*), before the consequences of his action unfold in perfect tense (*euersum est, terruit, subsedit*). Once more the two initial couplets constitute a unit: from the hero's imminent departure (*abibat*) to his arrival at the monster's den (*ad antra venit*). Again a new phase starts by carefully identifying the hero in the nominative (cf. 543, 547); here the lofty epithet *Ioue natus* clashes in juxtaposition with the failure of Jupiter's son to master the mundane matter of guarding cattle (cf. 546, *incustoditae*). The most important actions, stated in the pentameters, are carefully phrased to recall the previous portion of the narrative. The stolen property, *furta* (560), cry out, thereby undoing Cacus's "quiet theft," *taciti . . . furti* (549). Hercules arrives *ad antra* (562) to win back the cattle that the monster dragged *in antra* (same sedes in 550; cf. 562, *siluas*, 551, *siluae*).

At 563 the narrative continuum freezes for a full distich to flash back to Cacus blockading his lair's entranceway (*aditum*, picking up *ad antra uenit* from the previous verse) with a giant piece of crag, and to exclaim pseudoepically that ten yokes of oxen could scarcely have budged it. Then Hercules' counter push (565, *nititur hic humeris*) is immediately interrupted at the caesura by a parenthetical comment reminding us that the sky once rested on his shoulders (in the famous exchange of duties with Atlas). The whole spasmodically advancing section is held together thematically by a nexus of verbal echoes. On the more pedestrian level, the pentameters rhyme (*opus, onus* [which really = *opus* in this context], *humus*). More significant, Hercules' brawn moves (566, *motu*) what many oxen could not (564, *uix mouis-sent*, same sedes in the preceding pentameter). The crashing sound, *fragor* (567), arises from the overturned piece of broken-off (563, *fracti*) mountain; the ground is struck, *icta* (568), by the loosened barrier derived from that verb (563, *obice*). Hercules' heroic support of the heavens' weight in the logically extraneous parenthesis (565, *caelum . . . sederat*) echoes in the narrative, as earth sinks beneath the heavy boulder (568, *subsedit . . . humus*).

The fitful progress and associative links of Ovidian storytelling have their counterparts in the didactic portions of the *Fasti*. In his instructional mode, too, the calendrical poet displays tonal complexity and indirection. Consider the very start of the poem proper, where he holds forth on the original, ten-month year (1.27–44):

Tempora digereret cum conditor Vrbis, in anno
    constituit menses quinque bis esse suo.
scilicet arma magis quam sidera, Romule, noras,
    curaque finitimos uincere maior erat.   30
est tamen et ratio, Caesar, quae mouerit illum,
    erroremque suum quo tueatur habet.
quod satis est, utero matris dum prodeat infans,
    hoc anno statuit temporis esse satis;
per totidem menses a funere coniugis uxor   35
    sustinet in uidua tristia signa domo.
haec igitur uidit trabeati cura Quirini,
    cum rudibus populis annua iura daret.
Martis erat primus mensis, Venerisque secundus;
    haec generis princeps, ipsius ille pater: 40
tertius a senibus, iuvenum de nomine quartus,
    quae sequitur, numero turba notata fuit.
at Numa nec Ianum nec auitas praeterit umbras,
    mensibus antiquis praeposuitque duos.

When the founder of the City was arranging the calendar, he decided that there would be ten months in his year. To be sure, Romulus, you understood weapons better than the stars; your greater concern was to conquer your neighbors. Yet there is a reason which may have moved him, Caesar, and he has grounds to defend his error. The time that suffices for a child's emergence from its mother's womb, this he decided was sufficient for a year. For so many months after her husband's funeral a widowed wife maintains the signs of sorrow at home. These things, then, king Quirinus had in view, when he ordained the year's rules for his primitive people. The first month went to Mars, the second to Venus; she originated the race, he was Romulus's father. The third was named for elders, the fourth for young men. Numbers marked the following group of months. But Numa overlooked neither Janus nor the ancestral shades; he added two more to the original months.

In the poem's first line Ovid promises to sing *tempora cum causis Latium digesta per annum*. The first paragraph after the proem situates that structured Roman time in an historical context: **tempora digereret cum conditor Vrbis in anno**. . . . In question is not the calendar of the Augustan era, but the year constructed by Romulus: *anno . . . suo*. The final possessive climaxes the initial distich with rhyme and by cleverly revising the meaning of the hexameter—a first reading would take *in anno* with the subordinate clause and in the pentameter expect something like *satis* to be coming at the end. The clinching word also signals that the aetiological poet is here concerned with Rome's founder as much as with his foundation of the Roman calendar.

No sooner has Ovid reported that the *conditor Vrbis* decided on a ten-month year than he breaks off into a censorious apostrophe to Romulus (29–30). The pentameter's usual variation of the hexameter (*magis . . . maior*) intensifies the critique: not only did Romulus's astronomical acuity pale next to his understanding of military science, but he anyway cared more for conquest than for matters like calendrical calculations. In effect, the esteemed figure of city-founder seen a mere couplet ago has been demoted to the status of outsider in the world of Ovid's elegy. In the proem the poet has just disclaimed war as a topic (1.13, *Caesaris arma canant alii*) and embraced the stars among his subjects (1.2, *signa*—though the *Fasti*'s notorious astronomical errors make Ovid as deficient in this area as was Romulus!).[68] The next distich (31–32) alters direction yet again. Our antiquarian narrator once more abruptly changes addressees, this time to an insider, whether we understand *Caesar* to be the learned Germanicus (1.19–20, *docti . . . principis*), whose stellar concerns were reflected in his *Phaenomena*, or Augustus, who "added days to the calendar" (1.14). The perspective also shifts from blaming Romulus to explaining his calendrical error. Yes, the founder was clearly wrong (*erroremque suum*), "but there is also a reason which motivated him." One should not be too harsh. There is a certain awkwardness in the fact that the poet inaugurates his vaunted program of calendrical aetiologies (cf. 1.1–2, *tempora cum causis . . . canam*) by clarifying a rather significant *mis*calculation in the legendary history of Roman culture. The first of the many *causae* in the *Fasti* (*ratio* = *causa*) turns out to be an excuse. If this fact ironizes the speaker, it does not diminish his effort to soften and qualify (cf. *tamen*) his criticism of Romulus.

The Romulean year, we next learn, took its number of months from the time for human pregnancy (33–34). The rhetoric strongly suggests that this was the sole criterion: the couplet's encapsulating frame (*quod satis est . . . hoc . . . esse satis*) and resumptive echo of the opening statement (*anno statuit . . . esse*; cf. 27–28, *anno constituit . . . esse*) clinch the explanation. The speaker has in any case specified a singular *ratio* (31). But Ovid is momentarily deceiving us with false clo-

---

[68] Hinds (1992) 117 locates the passage in the larger context of stereotyping Romulus in epic terms.

sure, for an unforeseen second reason (35–36) unfolds to balance the first neatly. Romulus patterned the Roman year on two *tempora* central to a woman's life, the time that nature demands for her child's birth, and that imposed by custom for her to mourn her husband's death. The overarching sweep makes this an impressive argument. The fact that the antiquarian narrator is accounting for an error has all but fallen from view. When he next (37–38) summarizes more definitively—now with an explicit logical marker (*igitur*), plural *haec* more accurate after *ratio* above, and repeating the syntactic structure of the opening (*uidit . . . cum . . . daret*; cf. 27–28, *digereret cum . . . constituit*)—the figure of Romulus himself has been rehabilitated. Initially the ten-month year seemed like a cockeyed idea sprung from the astronomically deficient brain of one without much interest in calendrical matters. But he did have such *cura* (cf. 30) after all. The archaic Roman population's lack of sophistication (*rudibus*) perhaps recalls the ignorance imputed to Romulus earlier, but here he himself is a towering figure, proleptically divine (*Quirini*), outfitted in kingly garb (*trabeati*), administering laws to his people (*iura daret*); the epic periphrasis *cura Quirini* helps to elevate the stylistic register. Unless one reads these features sarcastically, the aetiologist's justification and summary have restored to the *conditor Vrbis* the dignity which the same speaker stripped away in his critical apostrophe to Romulus.

This matter seems settled as the poet moves from why to how the founder arranged a year of ten months (39–42). Pride of place went to his father Mars and to Venus as originator of the Roman race, then to elders and youths, after which bare numerical markers filled out the rest of the calendar. Then suddenly (43, *at*) an urge for completion prompts mention of the months added later to yield the current twelve, which returns us to Romulus's error and another destabilizing argumentative maneuver: his successor Numa placed two months before the Romulean decade in recognition of Janus and the ancestral spirits. In a poem about *sacra* this correction casts the founder in the darkest light yet. Here not his knowledge (cf. 29, *noras*) but his *pietas* was defective. Romulus did demonstrate devotion to his father and the divine ancestress of Rome but he neglected honors for another god, Janus, and for the dead. It took Numa to remedy the situation—*nec . . . nec . . . praeterit*, especially forceful as the only negative expressions in the entire paragraph—to prefix the Romulean year with honors for those previously passed over (*nec . . .*

praeterit . . . praeposuit). The serious blame implicitly attaching to Romulus yet again sharply revises his status, after Ovid has metamorphosed the grand founder into the astronomical illiterate, then into the noble Roman lawgiver. "Reading Ovid is a contract that can be renegotiated at any moment."[69]

---

[69] Barchiesi (1997b) 262.

CHAPTER SEVEN

OVID'S *FASTI*: POLITICS, HISTORY, AND RELIGION

Elaine Fantham

The year before Ovid was born, Rome's highest religious authority, the Pontifex Maximus, was savagely murdered in a council-room in the temple complex of Venus Victrix. The assassination led to popular riots and irreversible political change, because this priest was a political figure even more important than the spiritual leader Martin Luther King, or Thomas à Becket, the Archbishop of Canterbury assassinated on behalf of Henry II of England. Like King or Becket, the dead leader would be celebrated in his nation's calendar.[1] Just as Becket would be declared a saint by the church he represented, so Julius Caesar, the dead Pontifex Maximus, would be declared a god by his adopted son Octavius and by others who stood to gain politically from association with him.[2] The double role of Rome's *dictator perpetuus* and her chief priest, like the meeting of the Senate in a ritually authorized *templum* in Pompey's temple-cum-theater complex, reflects the entanglement of religious with political authority which would only be systematically enhanced by Octavius as he became first Octavianus Caesar, then Imperator, Princeps, and Augustus. These two sides of authority at Rome were inextricably fused by Augustus's constant supplementation of the *Fasti*, Rome's calendar of holy days, with anniversary celebrations of his own and his father's *res gestae*. As Wallace-Hadrill has shown, Augustus was taking over Roman time itself and making it Augustan.[3] The political affirmation

---

[1] The feast of St. Thomas of Canterbury is 29 December in the Roman Catholic calendar. Martin Luther King Day, on the other hand, is not a fixed feast, but a movable celebration held on the third Monday in January, e.g., Jan. 17, 2000.

[2] Thus divine honors were voted by the senate on the proposal of Mark Antony as consul (Cic. *Phil.* 1.13, 2.110) and the temple of Divus Iulius on the site of his cremation in the Forum was decreed by the triumvirs in 42 B.C.E. On the treatment of his divinity by and under the Princeps Augustus see White (1988).

[3] See Wallace-Hadrill (1987), (1997). White (1988) notes that the new festivals included five *feriae* in honor of Caesar's victories (cf. Thapsus, *F.* 4.377–87), his birthday on July 12 and the *Ludi Victoriae Caesaris* for ten days at the end of his month, July.

of these Julian anniversaries is equally prominent in Ovid's *Fasti*, and adds a diplomatic or panegyric element to his literary motivation in composing his Roman counterpart to the *Aetia* of Callimachus. Just how straightforward this element was can best be judged after we have reviewed the evidence of Ovid's text.

Everyone knows that Caesar was murdered on the Ides of March: the Ides were one of the original days of ritual marking the progress of the lunar month (and honored by the sacrifice of a ewe-lamb to Jupiter, cf. *F.* 1.56). In March the Ides were celebrated as the feast day of Anna Perenna, perhaps originally a personification of the year's renewal, but in Ovid's time treated as a deity and variously explained.[4] Indeed, it is only after Ovid has provided a choice of identities and histories for Anna herself that he approaches the death of Caesar: "I had intended to pass over the swords plunged into the leading citizen" (*gladios in principe fixos*, 3.697), "when Vesta spoke forth from her chaste hearth":

'ne dubita meminisse: meus fuit ille sacerdos;
      sacrilegae telis me petiere manus.
ipsa uirum rapui simulacraque nuda reliqui:
      quae cecidit ferro, Caesaris umbra fuit.'
ille quidem caelo positus Iouis atria uidit
      et tenet in magno templa dicata foro.
at quicumque nefas ausi, prohibente deorum
      numine, polluerant pontificale caput,
morte iacent merita: testes estote, Philippi,
      et quorum sparsis ossibus albet humus.
Hoc opus, haec pietas, haec prima elementa fuerunt
      Caesaris, ulcisci iusta per arma patrem. (3.699–710)

"Do not hesitate to speak of it, for he was my priest, and those sacrilegious hands were aimed at me. It was I who rescued the hero and left a bare phantom; it was only Caesar's shade that fell to the sword." He himself is set in heaven and sees Jupiter's halls, and occupies a great temple dedicated in the forum. But all those who dared this abomination and polluted my priest, against the prohibition of the gods, lie dead as they deserve. Be Philippi my witness and those whose scattered bones whiten the earth there. This was Caesar's loyal achievement, his first conditioning, to avenge his father in just warfare.

---

[4] See Horsfall (1974) 191: "On the Ides, more varied and abundant information survives, I believe, than on any other day in Greek and Roman history." Horsfall speculates that the feast of Anna Perenna was seen by the conspirators as favoring their plans, because it would draw most of the common folk away from the city. On the popular picnic celebration, see Miller (1991) and Wiseman (1998).

What is the poet's tone here? Must we read the *praeteritio* as casual, almost flippant? Nothing else in this passage is flippant, least of all the careful choice of *princeps*, the republican word for a leading citizen which was now becoming a unique imperial title, or the shock effect of its combination with *gladios . . . fixos*. Couldn't the poet be implying reluctance to linger over a black moment, a shameful violation? For that is how he treats it, and how he treats the murder at far greater length as he approaches the climax of his *Metamorphoses*. There Julius Caesar is introduced as a truly Roman god (**in urbe sua deus**, *Met.* 15.746), turned into a new star by his listed military (752–57) and domestic achievements, and by his son Caesar.[5] In contrast with the imaginative trope of Vesta's intervention on behalf of her priest in *Fasti*, it is Venus, mother of Aeneas, the now deified ancestor of the *gens Iulia*, who appeals to Jupiter to rescue the priest (763), her descendant, and spare the sacred fires of Vesta (777–78). After the gods have manifested their grief by the well-known celestial portents, Jupiter answers with a prophecy that continues into Ovid's own present: Julius has completed his fated time of living but it is now time for him to become a god and for his statue to be set in the temples. This Venus herself will achieve, along with his son, who will fight as avenger with the gods' support (816–21). The living Augustus, hailed for his piety in declaring Caesar a god and destroying his enemies, will himself come to rule the whole earth and bring it peace and justice. And as he contemplates his descendants in future ages he will bid the child of his chaste spouse to bear his name and his responsibilities, until in ripe old age he too reaches the heavens as a god. Reassured, Venus unseen snatches Caesar's soul before it can dissolve, and bears it to the stars, where it catches fire and becomes a brilliant comet, gazing down benevolently on his greater son's achievements.[6]

What corresponds in *Fasti* to the epic elaboration of *Met.* 15.745–854 is not just the single notice on the Ides of March. Instead, the various panegyric elements are distributed across a series of Augustan anniversaries, but the religious element will be maintained. Even in

---

[5] On the relationship constructed by Ovid in *Met.* 15 between the deification of Caesar and of his son, see Hardie (1997).

[6] Hardie (1997) notes that this prophecy looks to Jupiter's prophecy to Venus about the future of her son Aeneas and his descendants in *Aen.* 1.257–96: there Vesta plays a role in 292.

Metamorphoses, the descendant of Venus is Vesta's priest, and the cult of Vesta, like that of Mars Ultor, will be prominent in *Fasti*. Julius Caesar becomes a god, as Aeneas and Romulus have done before him, and his son too will in the fullness of time and old age become a god.

Ovid had brought the epic to an end before he was relegated by the seventy-year-old Augustus in 8 C.E., but he returned to work on at least the first month of *Fasti* after Augustus died in 14: his proem is clearly addressed to Germanicus Caesar, Livia's natural and Augustus's adopted grandson. To Germanicus he promises a poem that adds to the occasions of the year with their causes (*tempora cum causis*) and the natural cycle of constellations, Germanicus's family celebrations (*domestica festa*, *F.* 1.9), and Augustus Caesar's altars, with whatever days he added to the public rites (*Caesaris aras/et quoscumque sacris addidit ille dies*, 1.13–14). Yet it was only in the last years before Ovid's relegation that a successor, Tiberius, had been found within the family to take on the principate. Tiberius was now recognized as the son and partner of Augustus, and had adopted the young Germanicus, however reluctantly, as his own future successor.

Days both religious and political soon appear: on the Ides of January, 27 B.C.E., Octavianus had restored all the provinces of his military command to the senate and people of Rome, and received an entirely new title. The day was marked in the calendar,[7] and Ovid honors the name of Augustus as no mere honorific derived from conquered peoples, but a religious title shared with Jupiter himself (*F.* 1.589–616). This ancient epithet, whose Greek equivalent was *Sebastos*, "all holy," had been used by Ennius, in language recalled by Ovid elsewhere,[8] for consecrated temples and the signs of augury. The didactic poet reminds his addressee (and public) of the association of the Princeps' new name with *augere*, and deftly turns his instruction into a prayer for the increase of the leader's empire and his years (613, *augeat imperium nostri ducis, augeat annos*). Three days later comes the anniversary of a "family celebration," the dedication of the temple of Concordia, by Livia, "she who alone was found

---

[7] For a sequence of Augustan calendar entries see Syme (1978) 22. The *feriale Cumanum* (Degrassi (1963) #44), though incomplete, provides a list of festivals of the imperial house from May 24 to mid-August.

[8] The adjective *augustus* is attested in Enn. *Ann.* 4.5 Skutsch, *augusto augurio postquam inclita condita Roma est* ("since Rome was founded by revered augury").

worthy to share the bridal bed of great Jupiter" (650).[9] With this equation of Princeps and Jupiter we meet a level of hyperbole beyond the earlier lyric praises of Horace, and matched only by the poet's language in writing of Augustus from exile.[10]

The last day of the religious calendar in January brings Ovid to another dynastic monument, the great altar of Augustan Peace, vowed by the Princeps in 13 B.C.E. and dedicated on this date, Livia's birthday,[11] in 9 B.C.E. The family of Augustus can be seen in procession with the pontifices and flamines on the long exterior sides of the great altar,[12] but Ovid does not attempt to describe it. The poet has made Peace, supposedly achieved by Germanicus's triumphs, into a running theme throughout January, and thus can end the month with instructions to the priests to offer incense and a white victim, that the Augustan family may be ever renewed in the peace they have guaranteed to Rome.

Let me illustrate the political or Augustan element of the poem from three more titles or aspects of the emperor's career. Three times in February Ovid praises Augustus, first in a general proem that offers this celebration of sacred rites as his form of military service to the Princeps (2.7–18). Next, the poet uses a temple anniversary, the dedication of the new shrine to Juno Sospita on February 1, to praise the living Augustus as Builder and Restorer of temples, whose house the gods should guard even as he has rebuilt their dwellings.[13] But the most important entry comes on February 5, the anniversary of the day in 2 B.C.E. when Augustus finally agreed to accept the title "father of his country."[14] How does Ovid develop this theme?

---

[9] Note that this is not the first reference to Livia. At 1.531, the climax of Carmenta's prophecy, comes a celebration of the passing of empire into the hands of the Augusti, and the time when Iulia Augusta shall become a new godhead (*numen*). The nomenclature dates the passage as an insertion after 14 C.E., when Tiberius became Princeps and Livia received her new title by the will of Augustus. For a detailed discussion of Ovid's tributes to Livia, see the chapter "Livia" in Herbert-Brown (1994).

[10] Again the praise of Livia, coming in a passage that addresses Germanicus, must belong to Ovid's revision of the poem after the death of Augustus in 14.

[11] This too would be made a festival in the calendar, to honor her as Augusta after the death of Augustus (cf. Herbert-Brown (1994) 130 n. 2).

[12] For illustrations see, e.g., Simon (1967, 1968) plates 13–15.

[13] Augustus proudly records his building and restoration of temples in *Res Gestae* 19 and 21. But (*pace* Miller, chapter 6 above) does Ovid's reference need to be ironical?

[14] *Res Gestae* 35: he had been repeatedly offered this honor until he felt it opportune to accept it in the year marked by his second grandson's consulship (Suet. *Aug.* 58).

There was much to suppress in this connection, for the Princeps had disowned and exiled his only natural child for promiscuous adultery in the very year that he had accepted the title and honored her two sons. What Ovid does is to set up a comparison between Augustus and Rome's first king, Romulus, father of his country (2.137–44), deified as Quirinus and so celebrated at the Quirinalia twelve days later (2.475–508). There are easy contrasts to be made—between Romulus's small primitive city and its vulnerable wall, and the glorious modern city of Augustus, between Romulus's rape of the Sabines and the laws of Augustus reinforcing the chastity of marriage, and other more delicate comparisons. The Princeps is known to have considered taking the title "Romulus" before he decided against it and settled for the unprecedented "Augustus," and it is most likely that he decided against it because of Romulus's murder of his brother and rival to found the city—a story barely extenuated by Ovid (F. 4.812–56 and 5.451–480) and by Livy before him.[15] The "crime of a brother's killing" had long been seen as the model for the civil wars which Augustus wished to forget. So is Ovid's belittling of Romulus an indirect blow at the Princeps? There will be no criticism of Romulus on his anniversary as Quirinus, or on the other national occasions when Ovid needs more favorable evaluations of the same national figure.[16]

In due course, on March 6, 12 B.C.E., Augustus added the title of Pontifex Maximus to his secular honors, and Ovid seizes the anniversary to do homage (3.417–28). But if we are concerned with Roman religious thinking we should first ask why Augustus had taken over 30 years to achieve the supreme office held by his father Julius. Julius had won election at great financial cost, when he was not yet consul.[17] Why, then, had his son waited so long after he had been awarded every recognized secular office? The problem was the survival of Lepidus, the failed triumvir who had been stripped of all

---

[15] In both *Fasti* and Livy's preferred account Remus is killed in a riot (*in turba ictus*, Livy 1.7.2) without Romulus's knowledge: Ovid follows Dionysius in attributing the killing to a hasty subordinate who misunderstands Romulus's protest at his brother's violation of the wall.

[16] This refers only to the tradition of fratricide, not to criticism of Romulus as primitive, bellicose, or ignorant of astronomy: as Hinds (1992) has shown, Ovid mocks the first king's lack of sophistication from the first reference in 1.29–30.

[17] The date cannot be determined, but Weinstock (1978) 29–34 puts it in 63. Suet. *D.J.* 13 describes his candidacy and expenditure on buying votes as a daring risk that succeeded.

secular power after a supposed conspiracy twenty years earlier, but who could not be deposed from his sacred office of Pontifex Maximus. But Lepidus had lived away from Rome in enforced retirement. So who was performing the all-important duties of the Pontifex Maximus? According to Plutarch (*Numa* 9–10), the chief priest had the responsibility of interpreting divine will and directing sacred rites, supervising both public and private ceremonies to ensure there was no departure from established custom; he also supervised the Vestal Virgins, who conducted the cult of the goddess.[18] Can it be that Augustus had supervised these duties without holding the title? Certainly Ovid now rejoices that the descendant of Aeneas is at last protecting the undying fires of Troy.

> Ignibus aeternis aeterna numina praesunt
>   Caesaris; imperii pignora iuncta uides . . .
> ortus ab Aenea tangit cognata sacerdos
>   numina: cognatum, Vesta, tuere caput. (3.421–22, 425–26)

> The everlasting divinity of Caesar presides over the everlasting fires; you see the guarantees of empire combined. . . . The priest descended from Aeneas handles his kindred divinity: Vesta, protect your kinsman's life.

Augustus Caesar, then, has become a pledge of Rome's lasting empire (cf. *imperii pignora*) equal to the undying fires of Vesta which he now supervises, and he now handles his kindred deity.[19] He and Vesta are *numina* on equal terms and kindred through his descent from Aeneas.[20] Yet it is only nine days to the Ides of March. No wonder the poet ends with an urgent prayer to Vesta to protect her kinsman and keep him safe, as *inextinctus* as Vesta's sacred flame (3.426–28).

But surely no mortal man was allowed to approach the temple of Vesta: certainly this will be the poet's claim when he celebrates the traditional Vestalia in June (6.254, cf. 6.450). There are two explanations; the weaker one is supplied by the traditional responsibility of the Pontifex Maximus for the Vestals' discharge of their duties.

---

[18] Ovid's handling of the religious institutions ascribed to Numa will be considered in more detail below.

[19] Is there any improper suggestion in the use of *tangit* to denote his concern with the virgin goddess? A modern reading would want to suggest this.

[20] The concept of Augustus's *numen* or divine nature provided a bridge during his lifetime to outright recognition of his divinity at Rome. On his supposed kinship with Vesta through Jupiter himself see Bömer (1987).

This is legitimized, as Ovid himself reports (6.437–54), by the precedent of the third-century Pontifex Metellus urging the Vestals to rescue the goddess when her temple caught fire.[21] The other, stronger, answer lay in the superhuman nature of the Princeps himself, as Ovid will again stress just after the story of Metellus, at 6.455–56. And Augustus had asserted this responsibility by his own actions. As newly elected Pontifex Maximus he created a second shrine of Vesta, within his Palatine precinct: this may have been a new structure outside his house, but was more likely combined with his own domestic shrine to the Penates, which he had made public property: the sacred aspect of his house was now no longer private.[22] This is confirmed by the invocation to Vesta that ends the month and book of April, repeating language we have already met:

> Aufer, Vesta, diem! cognati Vesta recepta est
>   limine: sic iusti constituere patres.
> Phoebus habet partem, Vestae pars altera cessit:
>   quod superest illis, tertius ipse tenet.
> state Palatinae laurus, praetextaque quercu
>   stet domus: aeternos tres habet una deos. (4.949–54)

> Claim the day, Vesta: Vesta has been welcomed into her kinsman's home. So the just Senate resolved. Phoebus occupies a third part, and a second part fell to Vesta's lot. What remains, Caesar himself occupies. Flourish, Palatine laurels and house adorned with oak-wreath. A single house contains three everlasting gods.

The three couplets honor three gods, not two, because this is Ovid's first opportunity to introduce the famous Palatine temple of Apollo, god of prophecy, healing, and poetry, adopted as patron by Octavian even before the victory of Actium. Earlier poets had celebrated this temple. Virgil had even modified history in order to show Octavian seated in the temple to review his triple triumph of August 29 B.C.E., before the temple was dedicated,[23] and Propertius claims to have

---

[21] The story is reported by Cicero and was alluded to by Varro in the *Antiquitates rerum divinarum*, according to Augustine in his criticism of Varro in *Civ. Dei* 6.2. Ovid gives the Pontifex every caution, as he begs the goddess's forgiveness and receives a sign of it.

[22] See Dio Cass. 54.27.3 for Augustus's de-privatization of his household shrine, and Fantham (1998) 274–76 on the disputed architectural form of his homage to Vesta. The calendar record is damaged but clearly commemorates the consecration of an altar to the goddess on the Palatine on April 30, 12 B.C.E.

[23] On the shield of Aeneas, at *Aen.* 8.720–22. For the vowing of the temple and its architectural innovation see Zanker (1988) 49–51, 67–70, 84–86.

been late for his mistress after attending its inauguration, and composing the descriptive elegy 2.31. But the temple anniversary in October postponed any formal account of the monument beyond the six books of *Fasti* that Ovid completed. Only this skilful conception of a new triad—not Jupiter with Juno and Minerva, or Apollo himself (between Latona and Diana in the new temple), but Augustus *ipse* with Apollo and Vesta, enables the poet to evoke the house of Augustus adorned with the laurel bushes of the *triumphator* and the oak wreath of the savior of his fellow-citizens.[24]

But neither we nor Ovid can forget the murder of Julius Caesar which opened this survey, or his son's role as Ultor. Augustus created a compelling symbol of his positive powers for peace and national reconstruction on the Palatine, but he also devoted over twenty years to creating, as his own gift to the people, the Forum Augustum, centered around the temple of Mars Ultor.[25] Ovid attributes the god's new title to a vow taken by Caesar's son on the field of Philippi to ensure the punishment of all participants in Caesar's murder,[26] but it also fulfilled a second more obviously national commitment—to avenge the fifty-year-old defeat of Crassus and capture of his legionary standards by the Parthians at Carrhae. Mars had originated primarily as a god of agricultural fertility, but he was also a divine ancestor, being father of Romulus and god of war. Augustus planned a great forum and temple complex to honor the new aspect of Mars, but during its construction he housed the standards which had been diplomatically recovered from the Parthians in a small temple on the Capitoline dedicated on May 12.[27] A fire-wall was constructed

---

[24] Cf. *Res Gestae* 34.2.

[25] On the Forum Augustum and temple of Mars Ultor, see Zanker (1988) 108, 110–15, and 194–96 (with plan). On the statuary of the forecourt Zanker remarks upon, "this fully integrated set of images . . . [the] didactic arrangements and constant repetition and combination of a limited number of new symbols," and their powerful effect in conveying a visual message to the people of Rome. Millar (1993) 7 notes, however, from Suet. *Aug.* 31.5 that Augustus had reinforced his visual message by an edict declaring that he had set up the images of these national leaders so that he himself, while he lived, and the Principes of subsequent generations would be required by the citizens to match their example. Ovid's description too converts this didactic message into words, enriching it with the religious history of the temple and precinct.

[26] A vow taken in 42 could hardly have gone neglected for so long; the story was probably circulated by Augustus when the temple was already under construction; see Weinstock (1971) 130 and Herbert-Brown (1992) 98.

[27] On the existence of this temple, which has been disputed, see Scheid (1992).

to protect the future temple and its precinct, and the new Augustan
Forum, that is, the forecourt of the new temple, had as its central
focus the Princeps and Imperator aloft on a triumphal *quadriga*. This
was flanked by two lines of Roman heroes, the Julii, set before and
behind Aeneas, and Rome's other military heroes set around Romulus.
Inaugurated on August 1, 2 B.C.E., the new temple of Mars Ultor
was to be the site of all embassies and senate meetings concerned
with the declaration of war and peace. But when Ovid comes to
May 12, he seizes the opportunity to offer an elegy of fifty lines cel-
ebrating the new Forum Augustum and temple, combining pane-
gyrical motifs with a physical description (559–68), an account of
Octavian's youthful vow (569–78), and an extended celebration of
the recovery of the standards. As Scheid (1992) has shown, Ovid is
not writing in ignorance of the correct anniversary of the new tem-
ple. Once the new temple was built, Romans would associate the
ludi in circo which honored Mars Ultor on the old fixed holiday with
this great monumental complex. There were positive reasons for the
poet to evoke it now, adding grandeur to May. There may also have
been other motives; Scheid mentions the association of the new tem-
ple's official anniversary with the conquest of Alexandria and defeat
of Antony—another act of vengeance, perhaps, but not necessarily
welcome subject-matter. It is also possible that by the time Ovid was
composing the book of May he had decided not to continue into
the second half of the year, an additional motive to anticipate what
he would not honor in its official season.[28] He presents the occasion
as an epiphany of Mars and shows the whole precinct focalized
through the god's eyes:

> Vltor ad ipse suos caelo descendit honores
>   templaque in Augusto conspicienda foro.
> Et deus est ingens et opus: debebat in urbe
>   non aliter nati Mars habitare sui . . . (551–54)
> spectat et Augusto praetextum nomine templum
>   et uisum lecto Caesare maius opus. (567–68)

The Avenger descends in person from heaven to his own honors, and
the brilliant temple in the Augustan Forum: the god is mighty and so
is the monument: Mars should not live in any lesser style in his own

---

[28] There are other possible anticipations, such as the women's midsummer celebra-
tion of Proserpina which is anticipated by the narrative of the rape at the Cerialia in
April, and the Vinalia of August, apparently absorbed into the Vinalia of April 23.

city. . . . He also sees the temple adorned with the name Augustus, and the monument seems even greater when he has read Caesar's name.

Here are the topoi of panegyric; the immensity of the architectural ensemble is understood as more immense when the name of Augustus is read upon the temple pediment. The name and epithet *Augustus* frames the description, first in its regular application to the Forum, then revalued as the religious title explained to Ovid's readers in Book 1 and neatly continued by *Caesar* in the same syntactical case. Echoing a theme of Hellenistic panegyric Ovid compares this achievement to the victories of Jupiter and the Olympians over the Giants, and celebrates Rome's domination extending from the rising to the setting sun, yielding trophies from the entire world (*ab Eoo orbe . . . ab occiduo sole*, 557–58; *armaque terrarum*, 562).[29] Even Mars himself, as onlooker, is overawed by the name of Caesar Augustus.

At the center of the episode is the young Octavian's own imagined speech at Philippi (unnamed on this occasion but clearly invoked in 3.707). Even in this military context, Ovid again cites the authority of his father Julius as priest of Vesta (*bellandi pater . . . Vestaeque sacerdos/auctor*, 573–74) in Octavian's battlefield appeal to Mars, as he vows the god a temple and title of Avenger in return for victory.

This recall of the civil war was difficult to handle, and recent critics have seen implicit criticism in the bloodthirsty language of 575, *satia scelerato sanguine ferrum*, "sate the steel with criminal blood," but there is a very close precedent: Aeneas's protest to Turnus.[30] The same critics can fairly fault Augustus for converting a diplomatic settlement into an international triumph, but hardly find instability of tone in Ovid's own account. Mars himself, not content with one victory, avenges another blow, the shameful defeat of Crassus at Carrhae.

---

[29] For this kind of totalizing geographical figure in Augustan panegyric see White (1993) 159–66.

[30] *Aen.* 12. 947–48, *Pallas te hoc uulnere, Pallas/immolat et poenas scelerato ex sanguine sumit* ("It is Pallas who makes you a sacrificial offering and claims the penalty from your criminal blood.") For the controversy over the moral status of Aeneas's last action in the *Aeneid*, see literature cited by Hardie (1998) 100. Galinsky (1988) should now be supplemented with Gill (1998) reviewing the reactions of the different philosophical schools. Ovid's echo is surely deliberate, but our own recent reception of this final act of Aeneas in the epic has been largely negative. Thus Boyle (1997) 14 reads both passages as critical of the violence involved. Here I would support Galinsky's stance.

The captured standards are Rome's honor (*decus belli*, 585), their loss
a source of shame (*pudor*, 594; *longi dedecus aeui*, 589). But the Parthian
has gained nothing from his treacherous archery: he has surrendered
the standards and is laying down his defeated bows. Twice now the
god has given vengeance and earned the honor vowed to him—that
is, he has paid his debt to Augustus.

I have lingered over this excerpt both because it bears out the
continuity from the original murder of Caesar to the dedication of
Mars's temple, and because it has none the less been read by subtle
and learned critics as imbued with distaste for war and its violence.[31]
How certain can we be of reading Ovid's tone, and what evidence
have our samples provided for a poet not entirely serious about pay-
ing homage to his Princeps? The recurring confrontation of Poet
and Princeps involves more than one issue. There is the ideological
question: clearly we should distinguish modern attitudes to autoc-
racy, or to this autocrat in particular, from those of Augustus's own
age. We should also recognize that Augustus himself changed, as did
the reaction of the Romans to him, between 30 B.C.E. and 14 C.E.
Virgil and Horace's early work expresses the spontaneous enthusi-
asm for the young general who had put an end to civil war: even
Horace's fourth book of *Odes* reflects an older, more established
emperor—and an older poet. As Syme has noted, the atmosphere
around the Princeps and his family began to change for the worse
around 4 C.E.[32] But there is also the question of literary genre. Like
Callimachus, his model, Ovid was writing a form of aetiological and
didactic elegy that included panegyric. And panegyric implies hyper-
bole, even requiring an increase in hyperbole with repetition: the
criterion of success is not credibility but originality and the freshness
of word-play, even wit. There is wit in Callimachus's third book of
Aetia, both in the commemoration of Berenice's vow of a lock for
her husband-brother's safe return and in the encomium of Berenice's
victory in the chariot race, at least from the humorous coloring of
Molorchus's humble entertainment of Heracles which led to the
founding of the Nemean Games.

---

[31] By Newlands (1995); cf. Barchiesi (1994). Hinds (1992) finds elements of absur-
dity in Ovid's presentation of Mars in Book 3, but is more concerned with Romulus.
He does not discuss this passage.

[32] Syme (1978) 34: see now Millar (1993), whose interpretation of the political
climate and Ovid's response to it I endorse.

Wit and humor do not have to be negative. They, more than anything else, depend on the reader. And this is the third and most powerful element in the problematics of Ovid's non-erotic elegies. If we accept that Ovid intended his calendar poem to please Augustus, can we also argue that he consciously and systematically wrote negative subtexts into his praises, deconstructing the panegyrics even as he set them up? Given Ovid's congenital lack of seriousness and compulsive wit, secondary implications will find their way into this as into his other poetry. And there will have been readers ready to seek them out, then as now. Of the major critics who have written extensively on *Fasti*, Barchiesi (1994) is more cautious than Hinds (1992), Newlands (1995), or Boyle (1996). Boyle, indeed, reads *Fasti* as "a discourse necessarily and overtly always political," and finds Barchiesi too "circumspect." Harries (1989) and Hardie (1991) have written interpretations of specific episodes that point to Ovid's questioning of the regime's authority and the "golden age" of peace and prosperity,[33] and Feeney has fairly brought out Ovid's indirect forms of protest at shrinking freedom of speech, as much in *Fasti* as in other late Ovidian poetry.[34] These scholars have matured in the age of deconstruction dominated by the influence of Barthes, Derrida, and Foucault, and the constant exposure of political corruption in all our societies has done little to discourage skepticism. Among English-speaking critics a subversive reading of *Fasti* has almost become the new orthodoxy. Older, but not necessarily wiser, critics tend to be more positive either about Augustus or about Ovid's intentions in this poem. Some are historians starting from their own perspective on Augustus and the early principate, several are European and familiar with (constitutional) monarchy: I would name here Millar (1993), Herbert-Brown (1992), and Galinsky (1996), in particular. The author of the preceding chapter, John Miller, approaches Ovid from his knowledge of Callimachus and aetiological elegy: the focus of *Ovid's Elegiac Festivals*, as of his many articles, is primarily literary and narratological, and his expertise in religion makes his work particularly valuable for the direction in which we should now move

---

[33] This is not the main point of Hardie's reading of Janus (1991), but his final section on the two voices of the gods' two mouths points to a dissonance between the boast of Augustan (or Tiberian) peace through victory and the greed for gold that disfigures present society.

[34] Feeney (1992). For a more conservative reading consult McKeown (1984).

the discussion. Together with Feeney's recent *Literature and Religion at Rome*, his work offers a discriminating literary assessment of the religious events and themes in *Fasti* that we shall be discussing.

Let us make a new start, then, by looking at some ancient and modern ways of classifying aspects of Rome's religious life. Two generations before Ovid, both Cicero and Varro had written extensively on Roman religion. Approaching national religion from the point of view of a traditionalist and augur, but one early trained in philosophy, Cicero had written the dialogue *De natura deorum* illustrating Stoic, Epicurean, and sceptic points of view, and two further books, *De divinatione* and *De fato*, on the issue of divine communication with human beings and its bearing on fate and predestination. The work of M. Terentius Varro comes closer to the kind of interest in religion reflected in *Fasti*. Two of his later works are particularly relevant: the *Antiquitates rerum divinarum*, dedicated to Caesar, and probably composed in 46 B.C.E., and the near contemporary *De gente populi Romani*.[35] Although only fragments survive, many embedded in hostile Christian citation, the disposition of materials in Varro's larger work provides a useful framework. According to Augustine (*Civ. Dei* 6.5), Varro's introductory book is the source for the famous tripartite division of religion opposing the civil "theology" or religious system of the community to the systems of poets (*mythikon/fabulosum*) and of philosophers (*physikon/naturale*). Varro followed with five topics, each treated in three books: first the men of religion, divided into the three priestly colleges of Pontifices, Augurs, and Quindecimviri; next, sacred places (*loca: sacellae, sacrae aedes, loca religiosa*); then the three books on *tempora* mentioned in the previous chapter, divided into *feriae*, *ludi circenses*, and *ludi scaenici*, holidays, circus games, and stage performances. After places and times, he dealt with dedications and private and public rites (*res: consecrationes, sacra privata*, and *sacra publica*). Last of all come the gods themselves, distinguished as *di certi, di incerti*, and *di praecipui atque selecti* (Aug. *Civ. Dei* 6.3).

If we compare Feeney's carefully chosen categories in *Literature and Religion*, it is striking how little overlap is to be found in this latest analysis of Roman religion. No concern with priesthoods as such—

---

[35] On the probable dating of Varro's *Antiquitates rerum divinarum* and *De gente populi Romani* to 46 B.C.E., see Horsfall (1972), (1982).

and rightly, for neither the Roman calendar nor its poetic literature is much concerned with the politicized priesthoods. (They are barely found in *Fasti* beyond the special Caesarian offices we have surveyed.)[36] Instead Feeney starts with the modern category of Belief, in order to demonstrate its irrelevance to Roman thinking, then proceeds to Myth and Divinity, as separate categories. These were probably treated together, if Varro and others incorporated an element of myth into the treatment of *the di certi*: the *incerti* such as the *numina* listed as *indigitamenta* had no mythical experience. Feeney's last category is Cult, which draws on time, place, and ritual *res*, and constitutes the major part of Ovid's calendar poem. This was seen by thoughtful Romans like Cicero as itself the best form of piety, when the worshippers concentrated on the gods.[37] Given the critical acumen of Feeney's chapter, based on *Fasti* itself, how can this essay usefully supplement his treatment?

First let me stress the relationship between annual cyclic time, the ostensible determinant of Ovid's calendar poem, and linear historical time. As Beard points out, the Roman calendar defined Roman power, history, and national identity "by evoking events from different chronological periods of the Roman past and arranging them in a meaningful sequence of time, but not a sequence defined by linear narrative history."[38] To some extent the contents of the calendar excluded treatment of major religious events out of season, but it by no means determined Ovid's contents. He needed variety, but also to be representative of the calendar itself. There were recurring elements, Kalends, Nones, and Ides in the monthly lunar calendar, which the poet introduces early (1.55–58), and other undatable but recurring types of ritual. Thus in January Ovid seizes on the first large sacrifice, the Agonalia (1.317–36), to dilate on animal sacrifice in its Roman and barbaric variations (1.337–456); in February, the

---

[36] See however 2.21–28 discussed below, 4.910 for the Flamen of Robigo, and 6.226–32 for the Flaminica and Flamen Dialis and a relevant taboo.

[37] Cf. Cic. *De leg.* 2.22; 2.24; 2.40.

[38] Beard (1987) 1. Indeed, Ovid goes beyond the calendar, for example narrating Romulus and Remus's exposure and suckling by the she-wolf (2.383–420) immediately before the death and deification of Romulus (2.475–515), and the infertility of the new Sabine wives (2.425–52) before the conception of Romulus and Remus, their rescue by Faustulus (3.25–58), and the actual narrative of the rape and ensuing armistice (179–228). Only the apotheosis and the Matronalia were required by the calendar. Ovid's chronological interlacing could hardly be more complex.

month of mourning at the old year's end, he explains *februa* and the
various forms of purification, Roman and also Greek (2.19–46).

There were many anniversaries of temple foundations, more indeed
than Ovid could usefully include, and shrines and altars could be
celebrated either on the day they were vowed or the date of dedi-
cation. *Fasti* first mentions dedications in general, *templa sacerdotum rite
dicata manu* (1.610), then the temple of the Dioscuri on January 27
(1.702), whereas the dedication of the Ara Pacis which follows imme-
diately is implied rather than spelled out. Other named dedications
are that of the temple of Divus Iulius (3.704), of the Bona Dea by
Livia on May 1 (5.155), and of Concordia, again by Livia, at 6.637.
But more commonly Ovid honors the occasion of the vow: Augustus's
vow of the temple of Mars Ultor (5.569, 578, and 595), Camillus's
vow of a temple to Moneta (6.184), and other vows, not necessarily
of temples. Aeneas vows the wine harvest of Latium to Jupiter at
4.893–95; the senate vows a festival to Flora in 173 B.C.E (5.327–30,
dated by the consulship of L. Postumius and Popilius Laenas).

The major feast days recorded in capital letters in all the Calendars
could not be omitted, but the poet could choose to honor a festival
on its first day, or its last.[39] Major gods had more than one holy-
day (my spelling plays on the religious and recreational aspects):
Venus, for example, was honored twice in April. Ovid could have
chosen to pass over one occasion with a mere couplet, but he pre-
ferred to use both festivals to contrast the different needs for assist-
ance from Venus of respectable ladies and street walkers.[40] Since the
month was also believed to have been named after her, in her Greek
form Aphrodite, Ovid can begin his fourth book with an apology to
Venus as the former patroness of his love poetry, and include com-
peting etymologies, recalling the Greek myth in which her birth arose
from the sea-foam of Uranus's severed genitalia (4.61–62) and reject-
ing the rival derivation of Aprilis from *aperire* (85–90). Most impor-
tant, he could both honor her as Genetrix, the ancestress of the Julii

---

[39] For the festivals of the traditional republican calendar see Warde Fowler (1908),
Scullard (1981). Thus the Cerialia of April 12 to 19 are treated on both days, with
the main entry on April 12 (4.393–620) and a special *aition* for a ritual in the cir-
cus on April 19 (679–712), after separate commemoration of the Fordicidia (dis-
cussed below).

[40] I have had to pass over in this discussion the various important women's cults,
which I have treated in my contribution to a volume of essays on *Fasti* edited by
Geraldine Herbert-Brown and forthcoming from Oxford University Press.

(4.27–60, 117–24), and hymn her in Lucretian terms as promoter of animal and human fertility and patroness of the arts—including, of course, love poetry (4.91–114).

On occasions Ovid lingers over a major festival, providing a balanced selection of etymological and aetiological explanations, Roman and Greek myth, and details of ritual actions and diet. Variety or internal symmetry could be obtained by the inclusion of star myths associated with the rising and setting of constellations, often miscalculated. (Or did he know this?) But these have been well treated by Newlands (1995) and Gee (1999) and can be omitted from consideration here.[41] What was very important to Ovid was something outside the calendar: the places of Rome and to some extent of his native Italy. Propertius had proposed to tell of *sacra diesque . . . et cognomina prisca locorum* (4.1.69), and *loca* were important, not least because Romans associated gods and demi-gods like Egeria or Thybris with particular places: Thybris (the divine identity of the Tiber) was as important to Ovid as he had been to Virgil.[42] Places enabled the poet to travel through time, offering a nostalgic contrast between the old and new Palatine, and even the ancient marshes that preceded the drainage of the forum; a brief vignette unmotivated by its calendar context reports Ovid's encounter with a matron walking to the forum barefoot.[43] An old lady sitting nearby recalls to him the

---

[41] Note, however, that Newlands (1995) and Boyle (1997) 9 focus on "syntagmatic tensions," or "the semiotics of juxtaposition," as indirect subversion of Augustan passages. Are allusions to Aquarius as Ganymede or the bear as Callisto to be read as reproaches against the lustfulness of Jupiter, briefly compared with Augustus in 2.131? Ganymede was a Trojan prince, and his role as celestial cupbearer is normally seen as an honor. Ovid simply names him and moves on.

[42] The Tiber is twice named in connection with the rites in the grove of Helernus (2.67–68; 6.105); it received the basket containing Romulus and Remus at 2.385, and is recalled unnamed at 3.60. Its sacred and secular names are discussed at 4.47–48 and 68; it receives the Argei at 5.621 and even appears to Ovid (as Tiber had to Aeneas in *Aen.* 8.31–65) at *F.* 5.638–60. In Book 6 the Tiber receives the *purgamina Vestae* at 227–28, echoed in 713–14, and it is evoked for the etymology of Vertumnus without need to name it in 401–2. The river is recalled for the last time as the site of the temple of Fortuna in 6.776, less than 50 lines before the end of the book.

[43] Claims of autopsy like this are quoted as evidence of Ovid's researches by Frazer (1927) 1:12–14, but were part of the apparatus of Callimachean aetiological poetry (Horsfall (1974) 196). Ovid watched the crowd come back tipsy from the feast of Anna Perenna (3.274), saw the Flaminica ask for *februa* (2.27), took part in leaping bonfires at the Parilia (4.725–28), and witnessed the prayers of the *flamen quirinalis* to Robigo (4.909–42).

Tiber's flood pool, the old lacus Curtius, before the construction of
the fountain, the Velabrum, and the coming of the Etruscan god
Vertumnus (6.401–15). Ancient, barely understood deities like Ver-
tumnus (also celebrated by Propertius 4.2) and their statues or shrines
were revered from nostalgia and patriotism, in the belief that they
were associated with Rome's origins. Time was clearly a powerful
element, beyond mere reference to seasonal dates, in the evocation
of both history and pre-history.

And *Fasti* began with prehistory and made a principle out of going
back before the foundational epic of Aeneas. As *Metamorphoses* begins
with creation so *Fasti* launches into an epiphany of Janus on the first
day of the year. Here is a Roman god without genealogy or Greek
equivalent, traditionally named first in the divine litany of cult.[44] And
this deity *sacer ancipiti mirandus imagine* ("marvellous with his two faced
form," 1.93) identifies himself with the pre-cosmic void, with Chaos
(1.103–4), and as if a poet himself, asks Ovid's attention for the
immensely long age whose events he can chant: *aspice quam longi tem-
poris acta canam*, 1.104.

The spirit of the New Year offers many opportunities for witty
play on his two-faced and double-mouthed speech, which Hardie
has noted as a possible guide to a double reading of Ovid's text.
We should not overlook Ovid's own stress on priority. Janus settled
at Rome on his Janiculum before Saturn came to hide in Latium,
expelled by Jupiter, at a time when Rome was still primary forest,
and a little pasture, and the Tiber was the identifying feature
(1.235–46). And Saturn reigned long before the rustic village of
Romulus (1.199–208):[45] this sweep of past history provides an instant
contrast with the golden temples of Augustan Rome, a grandeur
proper to a god (224–26). While *Fasti* articulates the life of Romulus
from conception to apotheosis over a series of episodes mostly trig-
gered by festivals, and while it gives due respect to Aeneas, it also
celebrates Evander, but in his youth, more than a generation before
the coming of Aeneas.[46] Roman history is given new parameters,

---

[44] Like all other gods Janus is treated by Wissowa (1912), but for the conve-
nience of English-speaking readers I shall refer to the 1970 translation of Dumézil's
La Religion Romaine Archaïque; comprehensive religious and linguistic annotation based
on Dumézil is now provided by Woodard in Boyle and Woodard (2000).
[45] On Saturn, see now the chapter in Parker (1997).
[46] Evander's significance in *Fasti* is discussed by Fantham (1992).

and Romulus is balanced as well by recurring attention to his successor Numa, the king who traditionally created Rome's fundamental religious institutions.

But before considering the religious institutions of the mature Republic traditionally credited to Numa, it will be useful to gather together from across Ovid's poem the more scattered evidence for the earliest forms of Roman religion, corresponding roughly to Dumézil's "Ancient Theology." Many of these are essentially defensive, and some are closer to magic than to the orthodox rituals of prayer and sacrifice. In his account of purifications (*februa*) from which the name of February was derived, Ovid lists both the ritual housekeeping of various priesthoods and special expiatory purifications for those who have incurred pollution and offended the gods (2.21–28). The list reveals a hierarchy in which the *pontifices*, generic *sacerdotes*, and *flaminica* (wife of the *flamen* or priest of Jupiter) have to ask for purifying materials, for wool, the branch of an unidentified pure tree, and a pine branch, from the Rex Sacrorum. Again, these sacred officials and the secular lictor too must obtain the *mola salsa* and pine branch from others. But these actions are undated, and can be imagined as repeated at intervals through the calendar. Ovid also alerts his readers to specific occasions on which such ritual housekeeping must be performed: the removal of the old year's laurel branches by the *flamines* on March 1, the first day of the ancient New Year, to be replaced by the new green branches in front of the Regia and the Curiae: the Vestals too provide fresh laurel for the temple.[47] In April he lists the *lauatio* (washing and redressing) of Venus's image at the Veneralia of April 1,[48] and describes the *lustratio* of the sheep and cleansing of their pens with sulphur and laurel by the shepherds at the Parilia (4.735–43). And at the same festival all the people purify themselves with the compound *suffimen* (4.731–34) prepared by the Vestals from sacrificial ashes and bean-straw.[49] Twice Ovid stresses the importance of June 15, when the

---

[47] 3.135–41. Ovid adds more problematically that the Vestals even start a new fire to reinforce the old.

[48] This rite is not otherwise attested and may be an invention calqued on that of Callimachus's fifth hymn: see Miller (1980) 204–14 and Fantham (1998) on *F.* 4.135–38.

[49] This was prepared by the Vestals from the sacrificial victim of the Fordicidia (discussed below) and the tail of the sacrificed October Horse. See Fantham (1998) ad loc.

Vestals cleared out the *purgamina* from the forum temple (6.227–28, 713–14). This day was uniquely marked on the calendar, according to Varro *LL* 6.32, as Q. ST. D. F., *Quando stercus delatum fas*: only when the ordures were removed, did the day become correct for public business.[50]

But the times before such cleansing might be dangerous. The cleansing of Vesta's temple occurred after her festival, but it was inauspicious to marry from June 6 to 15. For a different reason, fear of the dead, it was equally inauspicious to marry during the Parentalia of February 13–21 (*F.* 2.557–62) or in May, the month of the Lemuria (*F.* 5.490). Fear of the angry dead motivated the private rituals which Ovid describes: at the Parentalia, simple offerings and prayers before the hearth (2.536–42),[51] and at the Lemuria, something closer to magic: the worshipper is to rise after midnight, wearing no knotted sandals or clothing, make the averting sign, wash, turn around, and throw black beans behind him, saying nine times, "I cast these beans; with these I ransom me and mine." He must then wash again, clash bronze cymbals, and drive the shades from the house, saying nine times, "begone, ancestral spirits" ('*manes exite paterni*,' 5.443). But we should treat this with caution. Ovid does not usually echo precise prayer formulae, and the *uetus ritus* was probably no longer practiced. In connection with the Parentalia Ovid describes the unofficial performance of a more obviously magical rite for the goddess Tacita by an old hag who safeguards the household by burying beneath its threshold three lumps of incense, and threads wrapped in a sheet of lead. Although this rite is attached to the time of Parentalia, however, Ovid reports its purpose as protecting the household against hostile tongues: was this preventive medicine anticipating the hazards of the next day's family reunion, the Caristia?

This piece of magic is linked through the similar myths of Tacita and Carna to another protective ritual performed on June 1. *F.* 2.583–616 describes how the talkative nymph Lara (originally Lala, 599–601) informed Juno of Jupiter's pursuit of Juturna. As punish-

---

[50] Dumézil (1970) 317 cites confirmation from Festus 434 L., and points out that since there were no animals within the temple, and it would have been kept clean throughout the year, it is difficult to understand what was done, i.e., what was the dung (*stercus*) removed on this occasion.

[51] Dumézil (1970) 366–67 takes Ovid too literally: his examples of garlands, grain, *mola salsa*, and bread soaked in wine are simply examples, not prescriptions.

ment Jupiter told Mercury to escort her to the underworld: Mercury raped her, and she gave birth to twins, who are now the Roman Lares, protectors of the home and of city streets.[52] The nymph Carna, honored on June 1, was also raped, this time by Janus: but the rape produced no offspring. Instead Janus granted her power over the hinge (*cardo*) and a whitethorn branch to repel harm from house doors (6.101–131).[53] Thus when the evil *striges* (witches in the form of screech-owls) attack, Carna drives then away from the baby inside, sealing the door against them with her whitethorn, water, and the raw entrails of a newly sacrificed piglet. She conjures the evil spirits to accept the piglet's life instead of the child's, and forbids those with her to look back at the sacrificial offerings. Here we have enough information to see how Ovid has manipulated the tradition. Macrobius (*Sat.* 1.12.32–33) reports that Carna was so called because she sustained the strength of one's *vitalia* (he is thinking of *caro/carnis*, flesh) and herself received a hearty offering of pork and bean soup. Ovid has retained the offering but changed to an alternative explanation of her name and powers, probably in order to introduce the tale of witches, which closely resembles a popular story found in Petronius (*Sat.* 63).

Like the Lares, Terminus was a guardian god, and one of unknown antiquity. According to Verrius's religious glossary, the Terminalia, like the Compitalia, Parilia, and Fornacalia, were *popularia sacra*, celebrated by all the people.[54] Where the Lares protected homes and crossroads, Terminus stood for the boundaries of land, and his refusal to be moved protected peasant farmsteads. He also symbolized the end of the old year, and Ovid makes his feast day on February 23 the occasion of one of those idyllic country celebrations familiar from the *Georgics* and from earlier elegy, with neighbors bringing garlands, cakes, and a sacrificial lamb or piglet for the peasant families' barbecue (2.639–78). The poet also records a public sacrifice to Terminus at the sixth milestone on the Via Laurentina, and deftly turns his praise of the boundary god into a panegyric couplet on Rome the world city: *Romanae spatium est Vrbis et orbis idem* (2.684).

---

[52] Ovid has not celebrated the feast of the Lares Compitales, because it was movable, oscillating between the end of December and first days of January. But he honors the Lares Praestites, and the new altars which combined their cult with that of the *genius Augusti*, at 5.129–46 (May 1).

[53] On Carna's protective powers, see McDonough (1997).

[54] Verrius's explanation survives in Festus 357 L.

As we mentioned, February was given its Roman name from the *februa* or purificatory instruments; but both Ovid and Varro (*LL* 6.34) prefer derivation from the ritual of the Luperci. This alternative serves to foreshadow the second half of the month and the days devoted to the cult of the dead. Certainly Varro is quite clear: February is so called "because the people are purified (*februantur*) and the old Palatine town surrounded with human flocks (*humanis gregibus*) is scoured (*lustratur*) by the naked Luperci." Ovid too distinguishes the purging of people, removing their guilt, from the purging of the place, where the verb *lustrare* signifies both surveying and traversing an area, and ritually cleansing a body of men.[55] Noting that the Lupercalia is supervised by Rome's most archaic priest, the *flamen Dialis* (2.282), Ovid sees the festival as originating in the undatable "limbo time" preceding Romulus's foundation, like the Parilia with which we shall compare it.[56] These two festivals were clearly rooted in a pastoral world and their very different gods were gods of the flock: Faunus, honored at the Lupercalia, lived in the untilled lands, and under his other name Inuus was associated with sexual appetite and the fertility of flocks, *ab ineundo passim cum omnibus animalibus*.[57] Both the Lupercalia and Parilia were centered on unusual physical rituals, but whereas only the Luperci ran around the site of the old Palatine village clad in goatskins,[58] and lashed the childless women who exposed their backs to them with their goat thongs, the bonfire jumping of the Parilia was open to all the men of the Roman people.

Although the value of the Luperci lay in their power to confer fertility, Ovid first spends almost a hundred lines (283–380) account-

---

[55] The *lustratio* of the Roman army or its body of citizens was performed in classical times by the censors appointed every five years to review and purge the group, and can refer both to the ritual and the social aspects of the process. Note that Ovid again refers to the Luperci—or rather their lashes—as purifying (*lustrant*) at 5.102.

[56] I owe to Beard (1987) 8 this apt designation of time "before Rome was a city but when (by a mythological paradox) many of Rome's customs already existed."

[57] The quotation comes from Servius, commenting on *Aen.* 6.775. But in *Aeneid* 7 and elsewhere Faunus was identified as father of Latinus and credited with prophecy. Ovid equates him with the Arcadian god Pan, imported by Evander (*F.* 2.267–80), but will bring him into contact with Rome's second king Numa in Books 3 and 4. For a full investigation of this primitive figure, the hairy "god of the Lupercal," in poetry and early Etruscan and Roman bronze ware, see Wiseman (1995b) 1–23.

[58] They are often called *nudi*, but Ovid himself refers to them as *cinctuti* ("short-clad") in *F.* 5.101.

ing for their traditional nakedness.[59] For this he offers four explanations: first, two trivial variants on Faunus's Arcadian origin as Pan: that the god himself runs naked on the mountains, because clothes impede running, and that the Arcadians who worshipped him were too primitive to wear clothes (287–302). Next he tells a comic myth of Faunus attempting to rape a cross-dressing Hercules, which probably derives from a mime (303–58). His final explanation is both Roman and religious: that Romulus and Remus were making a sacrifice of a goat to Faunus, but while the priests were preparing the meat and the young men were exercising, they heard that robbers were rustling their cattle. The story does not spell out whether both brothers ran naked, or only Remus and his band, but it was Remus who intercepted the rustlers and returned first to consume the sacrificial meat. Romulus laughed at his own discomfiture. The problem is that the story simultaneously treats the ritual sacrifice to Faunus and running of the Luperci as preceding Romulus (compare *de more*, 361, and the two named bands of Luperci, Fabii and Quintilii, 377–78) and credits the custom of running naked to Romulus himself.

And any Roman would be tempted to relate the Lupercalian festival to the Lupercal beneath the Palatine where the she-wolf had suckled the twins—a site newly restored by Augustus himself.[60] Hence Ovid's next move is to tell the story of the twins' exposure and rescue by the she-wolf, to explain how the wolf gave the name to the place, and the place itself to the festival: it has now become part of Romulus's life history. But he knows another etymology, a Greek one from the Arcadian Mt. Lycaeus, which gave a title to Lycaean Pan. Without settling the issue he passes on to the most spectacular aspect of the festival: the exposure of the wives seeking pregnancy. Only after rejecting prayers or magic in favor of the fertilizing blows (*fecundae uerbera dextrae*, 2.427) does Ovid provide his own legend to explain the custom and foreshadow the honors paid to another equally important deity, Lucina.

In the poet's explanatory tale (*aition*) Romulus was disillusioned when the new Sabine brides (whom he will not actually kidnap until the following book) did not become pregnant: so his people, both

---

[59] This may be designed to provoke Augustus, who had disapproved of the naked Luperci and imposed a more respectable costume in his "reformed" rite. See Holleman (1973) who is otherwise rather extreme.

[60] *Res Gestae* 19.

men and wives, went to the Esquiline grove of Juno Lucina and
begged for help in conceiving. Her reply was riddling, and punned
on Inuus/Faunus. '*Italidas matres . . . sacer hircus inito*': "Let the sacred
he-goat penetrate the Italian wives" (2.441).[61] But an Etruscan augur
understood the riddle, and slaughtered a he-goat, so that the women
could offer their backs to be beaten by strips of its hide. Thus, thanks
to the advice of the goddess of childbirth, the fertilizing god was
able to make the women pregnant without sexual contact. Wiseman
has shown that Ovid transferred this episode to Romulean times
from the third century,[62] but in the calendar it usefully anticipates
the anniversary of the temple dedicated to Lucina on March 1
(3.245–58). This is recounted by Mars himself immediately after his
narrative of the rape of the Sabine women and their heroic recon-
ciliation of their husbands and fathers on the battlefield (3.173–234).
It thus provides joint *aitia* for the two celebrations that open March:
the women's festival of the Matronalia, and the dedication of the
temple of Juno Lucina.

Ovid's account of the Parilia will also celebrate two aspects of the
same day.[63] The first eighty lines appeal to the pastoral deity Pales
for a blessing on him as he sings of the shepherds' rites: with an
autobiographical touch[64] Ovid claims to have collected his ritual
purification agent, the *suffimen*, and leapt the bonfires with the best.
It is a festival for everyone (*popularia sacra*), and so he instructs the
people to fetch *februa* from Vesta's representatives and describes the
ritual ingredients before turning to instruct the shepherd (735) in his
procedure of cleansing the flock and pens, his ritual food offerings,
and the prayer addressed to Pales. This is one of three extended
prayers in *Fasti*, each of them differentiated. The poet's own prayer
to Tellus and Ceres on behalf of the arable farmers after the win-
ter sowing at 1.675–94 rapidly turns away from the goddesses' usual
powers to urge them to drive off pests, then apostrophizes the pests
themselves, and ends with third-person wishes on behalf of the crops.
It is a literary prayer deliberately evoking Virgil's list of pests in the
First *Georgic*. The shepherd's prayer is more consistently addressed

---

[61] Ovid's word *matres* is probably proleptic here ("in order to be mothers"). He
commonly uses the form as a synonym for *matronae*, married women.
[62] Cf. Livy fr. 63 and Aug. *Civ. Dei* 3.17.
[63] On the blending of these aspects see Beard (1987).
[64] Compare 3.273–74 and 6.395–416, cited above.

to Pales, begging forgiveness for any trespass by shepherd or flock on holy ground, and temporarily diverting to other more literary pastoral figures (*nymphae*, Dryades, Diana, even Faunus, 755–61) before more requests: for freedom from sickness, wolves, and hunger, and the positive fertility of ram and ewe, and high quality wool. And it ends with a Roman bargain: in return for these blessings the shepherds will offer huge honeycakes to Pales on her annual feast-day (775–76). The third poetic prayer is that of the Flamen of Robigo (mildew, but also rust), an apotropaic prayer to an unwanted natural force, begging it to attack swords and leave the crops themselves healthy (4.911–32).

His prayer to Pales complete, the shepherd must turn to the east, and repeat the prayer four times (*dic quater*, itself a ritual eccentricity), washing his hands in a running stream before he may drink the offering of milk and unfermented grape juice. Soon he joins in leaping across the bonfires (777–82). As with the naked runners of the Lupercalia so here Ovid seizes on the extraordinary bonfire-leaping to search for an explanation—actually six explanations.[65] We have learned to expect a sort of progress from short general suggestions to increasingly plausible reasons, and this is what Ovid provides. Fire purifies all, so it should be used to cleanse both shepherd and flock: as fire and water are opposed our ancestors naturally applied both elements to the body. Or is it because life depends on the two elements, which are denied to the exile and offered at marriage? This he doubts, and distances himself from a fourth version invoking the Greek myths of Deucalion's flood and Phaethon's fire. Then comes a naturalistic suggestion: was it an accident, when a spark from the shepherd's fumigation kindled the straw? Finally he produces the explanation that welds together the pastoral festival and Romulus's founding of Rome. Ordered to migrate to their new homes, the shepherds set fire to their huts and leap with their flocks across the flames to safety.

Ovid has prepared his readers for a rustic Romulus by more than one episode: I think particularly of 1.199–206, 3.113–20, and 3.179–86 filled with simple huts and straw mattresses, and a settlement where

---

[65] For this multiple causality compare Beard (1987) 3: "it is the continuing capacity to generate stories and aitiologies that is crucial for the continuance of a festival . . . as new stories take over from old, so the "meaning" of the ritual changes." See also Miller (1992), Scheid (1992).

there was even respect (*reuerentia*) for the bundles of hay that were
the first standards of the Roman maniples. But now he shifts to the
crucial taking of the omens to determine who should be the city's
founder, to Romulus's victory and the selection of the feast of Pales
as the date of foundation. Ovid follows exactly the foundation rit-
ual prescribed by Varro of plowing the circuit for the walls with a
white cow and steer; then he composes for Romulus an invocation
to Jupiter, Mars, Vesta and the proper deities (*quosque pium est adhibere
deos*, 4.829), asking their auspices for Rome's lasting domination over
all the earth from the eastern lands of the sunrise to the sunset.
Jupiter sends a thunder of approval and all the citizens turn to dig-
ging and building the wall—until the disaster of Remus's challenge,
and Celer's hasty but deadly attack. No episode of legendary his-
tory seems to have received more discussion, but the issue is essen-
tially political, not religious. The poet has chosen the version more
favorable to Romulus, but then Remus may have been a later polit-
ical invention, if we are persuaded by the arguments of Wiseman's
monograph (1995a).

Hinds, Boyle, and other recent students of *Fasti* have offered elo-
quent arguments hinging on Ovid's disrespect for Rome's first king,
but no one has disputed his respectful attention to Numa, his suc-
cessor. Numa is prominent in *Fasti*, as Hinds has shown, for his pro-
motion of a peaceful settled life, and his religious reforms.[66] There
was in fact a stable tradition of these reforms even before Varro's
writings on religion, or the surviving histories of Sallust and Livy.
Cicero's brief and too often neglected account of the monarchy in
De re publica 2.25–29 introduces Numa as a model of *uirtus* and *sapi-
entia*. Rome's second king taught the Romans to abandon their love
of war and gave them an alternative, by awarding them the lands
of conquered tribes to farm so they would love peace, justice, and
good faith. The rest of Cicero's account covers Numa's religious acts:
he instituted the public auspices, appointed five pontifices from the
leading men in charge of *sacra*, and established religious laws and
ceremonies. He also appointed *flamines*, Salii, and Vestal Virgins, and
established *mercatus, ludos, omnesque conueniundi causas et celebritates* (2.27).
Thus Cicero attributes to Numa the markets, holidays, and accom-

---

[66] Hinds (1992) 118–31; cf. Porte (1993) 148: "le héros étiologique par excel-
lence, c'est Numa." See now Gee (2000) 41–47.

panying games of the public calendar. In the second book of *De legibus*, when Cicero draws up his ideal religious laws, he credits Numa, as does Ovid, with intercalation to bring the lunar calendar into harmony with the solar cycle. Indeed, he puts a very significant comment into his brother's mouth: "this religious system of yours does not differ a great deal from the laws of Numa and our own customs" (2.23). As this shows, Romans believed the fundamentals of their continuing religious law and rites were devised six hundred years before, by King Numa.

Almost all of these religious institutions are repeated in the longer accounts of Livy (1.19–21) and Dionysius of Halicarnassus (2.63–69). Livy lists under Numa's concern for the creation of priesthoods (*sacerdotibus creandis*) the Flamines, Vestal Virgins, Salii, and a single Pontifex (Maximus?), but adds that he made all public and private rites subject to the decrees of the Pontifices. To this Livy adds Numa's rules for funeral rites and his measures to propitiate celestial prodigies through consultation of Jupiter Elicius. Dionysius, as a good Augustan, adds that Numa secured the deification of his predecessor Romulus as Quirinus, and as an antiquarian, refers to the king's creation of Curiae and Curiones.

Numa is mentioned only once in the *Aeneid*, in Anchises' parade of Roman heroes, but rather subordinated to his surroundings (6.808–12):

> Quis procul ille autem ramis insignis oliuae
> sacra ferens? Nosco crines incanaque menta
> regis Romani primam qui legibus urbem
> fundabit, Curibus paruis et paupere terra
> missus in imperium magnum.

> Who is that, far off but conspicuous with olive branches and bearing holy objects? I recognize the locks and hoary chin of the Roman king who will give the early city its foundation of laws, sent from little Cures and a poor land to a mighty command.

Hinds claims that when Ovid too celebrated Numa as a peace-loving founder of religious laws and institutions—and reformer of the calendar—he was in part using the king to discredit his predecessor Romulus.[67] Yet Hinds also admits that Augustus had clearly seen Numa as a model for his own religious reforms and revival of institutions.

---

[67] See Hinds (1992) part II.

So let us concentrate on Numa. There was a strong tradition crediting him with admirable and fundamental religious institutions; but they are not in themselves appealing material for narrative elegy. Nor do they occupy an obvious place in the calendar which was Ovid's formal framework. So what does Ovid make of this unified but sober tradition?

As Miller has noted at the end of the previous chapter, Numa was credited with reforms in both funerary rites and the "Romulean" calendar. His supposed institution of the additional months January and February in honor of Janus and the dead ancestors brings him early into Ovid's text (1.43–45), but he is given much more attention at 3.151, again for realizing the need for twelve instead of ten months. Here for the first time Ovid introduces Numa's supernatural counsellor, Egeria (treated by Cicero *De leg.* 1.4 as a fantasy, and by Livy 1.19 as a prudent fiction of the king). But the king's main presence in Ovid's poem is in the long episode at 3.275–398, where Ovid exploits the elegiac appeal of Egeria as lover and adviser, while turning the sage Numa from a wise man into a trickster. In the one episode he combines the evocation of Jupiter Elicius and the Ancile with its priests the Salii (unconnected in all other sources) and borrows three times from Virgil to color Numa's virtue with cleverness.[68] Like Cyrene advising Aristaeus in *G.* 4.387, Egeria advises him to respond to alarming portents by catching the deities Picus and Faunus so as to learn from them how to expiate the thunderbolts. Like Virgil's shepherds in *Eclogue* 6, Numa catches the deities by making them drunk, and obliges them to answer him. But Ovid goes one step beyond Virgil. Whereas Silenus in *Eclogue* 6 and Proteus in the Aristaeus narrative told their human captors what they wanted,[69] Picus and Faunus tell Numa that this information is beyond them as simple rustic gods; he must obtain it from Jupiter himself. Parading his poetic discretion, Ovid too suppresses the secret of compelling Jupiter: *nobis concessa canentur* (3.325).[70] But in some mysterious way they succeed (*eliciunt*, 327, marks Jupiter's title Elicius). Confronted

---

[68] Here and in the account of the Fordicidia I follow Porte (1984) 130–38 and (1993) 147–48.

[69] Silenus, rather than Virgil or the shepherds, voices their request at *Ecl.* 6.25, 'carmina quae uultis cognoscite,' and Proteus supposedly knows what Aristaeus needs to be told (*G.* 4.447).

[70] The epithet *concessus* inevitably recalls Ovid's self-protecting formula in *Ars Amatoria* 1.33: there he will teach only *concessa furta*.

with Jupiter himself Numa argues his way past Jupiter's riddles to escape the threat of human sacrifice. Jupiter in turn promises him a guarantee of his authority, *pignora certa* (346). The next morning Numa and the Roman people await the omens, and Jupiter sends three thunder claps and a celestial shield, the *ancile*. Numa's last proof of cleverness is traditional, the making of the counterfeit shields to protect the sacred one from theft (3.380). Ovid completes the tale conventionally with the creation of the Salii and the rewarding of the bronze worker Mamurius.[71]

Thus, although the framework of the calendar does not provide a place for the expiation of occasional prodigies, Ovid has included an example. Nor do the historians connect Numa with the Fordicidia of April 17, but Ovid creates a connection. He has some justification in view of the role played by the Vestal Virgins, whom Numa supposedly brought to Rome, in preserving the sacrificial remains of the Fordicidia for redistribution at the Parilia four days later:[72] indeed, the rites of Vesta instituted by Numa will receive extended attention in Book 6. What Ovid does for the Fordicidia is again to borrow from Virgil (this time from Latinus in *Aeneid* 7) an incubation rite which is otherwise unattested for Numa.[73] Like Latinus, Numa approaches Faunus to expiate a famine. He goes to a wood sacred to Faunus (4.649) and again seeks rites to expiate an unnatural happening. But this time he does not petition Faunus, but sacrifices two sheep and lies down in a carefully described state of ritual purity to sleep and dream. In his dream Faunus gives him a riddling prescription, to sacrifice one heifer so as to offer two lives. Once again Egeria rescues him by interpreting the offering as a pregnant cow: he makes the offering and fertility returns.

And Numa returns also, in a prominent introduction to Ovid's panel honoring the Vestalia of June 9, the central panel of the last

---

[71] Note that (cf. Porte (1984) 422–24) Ovid's story of Mamurius Veturius adopts an *aition* which might seem to contradict Varro's express denial (*LL* 6.49) that the words *Mamuri Veturi* in the song of the Salii referred to a legendary shield-maker. Varro interprets the phrase as *memoriam veterem*. But Ovid also knows this: he has his cake and eats it, when the successful shield-maker asks as his reward to be named *extremo carmine* (3.390).

[72] Cf. 4.731–32, *I pete uirginea, populus, suffimen ab ara:/ Vesta dabit, Vestae munere purus eris*, with Fantham (1998) ad loc.

[73] See Porte (1984) 160–63 and Fantham (1998) on 4.641–72, also *Aen*. 7.81–101 with Horsfall (1998) ad loc. As Horsfall notes, Virgil himself combines incompatible elements from other contexts with the incubation, itself unknown in Latium.

month celebrated. His introduction as *rex . . . placidus* (6.259) and his reverence for the divinity of Vesta, whose worship he introduces in 6.257–64, recall the prominent role of Peace in *Fasti* 1. Given the close association of Ovid's celebration of the Vestalia with Numa it will be appropriate to use the complex of ritual and *aitia* for this festival as a sample of how the poet handles a major feast day. In fact, just as Janus, who opened the Roman prayer litany and the Roman year, appears in person to Ovid, so Vesta (traditionally the final deity in the litany)[74] will also be the last deity to offer the poet an epiphany, but of a special kind not visible but perceptible by all the other senses.

I shall use as a guide a fine article with which I have some disagreements. Gareth Williams (1992) has approached Ovid's Vestalia narrative (6.249–468) in terms of its narrative dissonances, and rightly begins with Ovid's pointed and unpersuasive rejection of poetic fiction (*ualeant mendacia uatum*, 253). This is a concept of the lying *uates* previously applied (cf. *Am.* 3.12.41 and the whole argument of that elegy) to his own fictional erotic autobiography, and to mythical monsters like Scylla. But this time he uses it to deny that he has enjoyed a visual epiphany of Vesta. So did his readers believe, in Book 1, for example, that Ovid had experienced an epiphany of Janus? Of course not, but he offers a different reason for his denial: Vesta must not be seen by any man. Of course, the taboo was well-known, but this too will later, if briefly, turn out to miss the point. After praising Numa for introducing her cult, Ovid explains the circular form of her temple as an allegory: Vesta is the Earth and a constant fire burns beneath both earth and hearth. But the earth is spherical and held in equilibrium by its position at the center of the cosmos; so her temple too is spherical. A fragment of Varro's *theologia physike*? If so, Ovid rapidly glides via a practical comment on the conical roof's utility for drainage to *theologia mythike*, disguised as an *aition* for Vesta's virgin attendants. The *aition*, as Williams notes, is Hesiodic, like the reports Ovid has already offered on three previous occasions of Saturn/Cronus's expulsion by Jove (1.235–36), of

---

[74] So Cic. *De nat. deorum* 2.29. Perversely Ovid actually contradicts this tradition in 6.303–4, *inde precando/praefamur Vestam, quae loca prima tenet.* Presumably he does so in the knowledge that his readers would recognize the Greek tradition which put Hestia first. Cf. Dumézil (1970) 322.

his consumption of his children (4.197–211), and of his subsequent castration of Uranus (4.61–62).

But myth gives way again to allegory, this time identifying Vesta with fire itself (291–94) before an explicit self-correction. Ovid had foolishly thought there were images of Vesta, but now he has learned—presumably from Vesta herself in the instructions of 255–56—that there is no image beneath the round temple, only an undying fire; Vesta and fire alike have no visible form (*effigies*). And like earth, Vesta is held firm by her own force (*ui stando Vesta uocatur*, 299): an unprecedented etymology, as Williams notes, but one bringing a cluster of etymologies true and false, and the un-Roman claim that in prayers "we name Vesta first, because she occupies the first places."[75] Does Ovid care that he has mixed philosophical theories with theogony, competing and incompatible etymologies, and Greek practice with Roman? Or is this a piece of verbal prestidigitation, to dazzle the reader so that he comes with relief to antiquarian and perhaps familiar cult details? I do not believe it is haste or carelessness, nor that Ovid was deconstructing his own credibility, so much as demonstrating the very poetic fictions he has denounced.

The recall of Roman prayers leads to an evocation of ancient family worship, when men sat on long benches before the hearth and believed the gods shared their table—as did Jupiter, Neptune, and Mercury in *F.* 5.495–534. Ovid has regularly associated the gods of each festival with special foodstuffs—Liber's honey-cakes (3.735–36), Cybele's *moretum* (4.367–68), Pales' offering of milk and millet cakes and unfermented must (4.743–75, 779–80), and Carna's hearty dish of fat bacon, emmer, and beans (6.169–72). Now the poet moves from the enclosed service of the Vestals to public cult, first to the now obscure feast of Vacuna, then to an unnamed offering of bread to Vesta in a ritually pure dish (310). Ovid does not immediately call it bread, since *panis* is almost unacceptable in high poetry.[76] Nor could he call it *Ceres* in a passage honoring Vesta; so *cibos* (310) must stand in; but the allusion to bread prepares for the next narrative unit.

---

[75] On the contradictions produced by Ovid's blend of cosmological and etymological theories, and the primacy of Vesta suggested by the etymological link with *uestibulum* and her traditional role as last in the Roman liturgy, see Gee (2000) 141–42.

[76] For the pointed exception at *F.* 4.395 see Fantham (1998) ad loc.

In February Ovid had described the last day of the Fornacalia, in honor of the goddess Oven, who (or which?) had saved Rome's first clumsy farmers from scorching their emmer (*far*) as they roasted it for grinding into meal (2.515–32). Now he resumes the theme: "On Vesta's holyday the mill donkeys are garlanded and the mills themselves are covered. Once Rome's peasant farmers prepared only emmer, baking it on broken tiles beneath the ash of the hearth. That is why the baker now honors the hearth and Vesta as its mistress, and the little donkey that turns the mill." I have offered such a close paraphrase for 6.311–18 because of the abrupt intrusion of the disgraceful tale of Priapus that interrupts before the poet calmly resumes with his bakers and their cult of Jupiter Pistor at 349–50. At 351 Ovid will offer his readers an *aition* from a crisis in Roman history for a little known Roman cult. When he introduces the unprecedented tale of Priapus's failed attempt to rape Vesta, is he simply providing a Greek *aition*, and one that will offer a relaxation of tone?[77]

There are, as I see it, two difficulties about the story of Priapus's attempted rape of Vesta: the apparent duplication of the same god's earlier attempt on the nymph Lotis (1.393–440) and the incongruity of attaching this mythical fiction to Vesta. The structure and even some of the language of the two stories are parallel, and the version in Book 1 occurs à propos in a sequence on animal sacrifice added by Ovid in exile. Here too Ovid tells the story to explain a feature of worship, and one confirmed by the paintings of Pompeian domestic shrines, Vesta's patronage of the miller's donkeys.[78] In both stories the donkey is rewarded for sounding the alarm that drives off the rapist. Where I had argued that this version of the story could not stand in the same version of *Fasti* as the attempt on Lotis, because they are so close in form, Gareth Williams has argued that Ovid wanted both stories and intended the resemblances to emphasize the radical difference between a casual attempt on an available nymph, and an assault on chastity personified. I see one real literary objection to this: that Ovid has not provided a reminder of Priapus's lustful habits to recall that earlier episode. But whether Williams or I

---

[77] There is a good parallel for this in the Greek and Roman *aitia* offered for the naked Luperci at 2.305–58 and 359–80.

[78] For the depictions of Vesta with a donkey in *lararia* see Fantham (1983).

come closer to divining Ovid's intentions, the story points to the
poet's priorities. Sentiment or piety towards traditional cult comes
second to entertainment. Vesta's dignity is damaged even by being
exposed to the risk of assault, but Book 6 is in need of a lighter
episode. The story is out of keeping here, and this is one episode
which could have been expected, but surely not intended, to offend
Vesta's Pontifex Maximus.

Strangely, the Roman *aition* that follows is seen by Williams as
unstable, just because Ovid has turned a recorded failure into a
Roman success. Livy (5.48.4–9), echoed by Valerius Maximus (7.4.3),
reports that the garrison besieged on the Capitol by the Gauls tried
to deceive their besiegers by pretending to have abundant food and
throwing stale bread down onto the enemy. As Williams has shown,
Ovid's story reflects his knowledge of Livy's narrative of the Gallic
invasion, but goes on to contradict the Livian account. He uses the
siege as an excuse to compose his own council of the gods in the
fashion of Ennius and to echo the Ennian appeal of Mars to Jupiter
on behalf of his son Romulus from *F.* 2.481–90. When Rome is
besieged and Jupiter summons the council, Mars makes a powerful
speech, recalling from the Livian narrative the slaughter of the old
men and flight of Vesta's sacred objects (*Iliacae . . . pignora Vestae*, 365),
and appealing on behalf of Jupiter's own Roman citadel. He is backed
by the supporting gods, Venus, Quirinus, and Vesta herself,[79] and
Jupiter charges Vesta with imposing the deception about the garri-
son's supply of grain (6.379–82). Rhetorically this is a brilliant answer
to the need to enrich Vesta's celebration with a happy patriotic myth,
exploiting the license of epic tradition to bring on stage the gods of
Augustan cult, and crediting Vesta with the rescue of the garrison
which should have happened. If the story had existed before Ennius
it would have been a precious Roman legend. Must we blame Ovid
because he has come too late?

The Vestalia panel has two more elegiac units: the poet's personal
encounter with the old lady who describes the former flooding of
the forum,[80] and the history of the Trojan Palladium and its rescue

---

[79] With the *indigetes* these are the gods appealed to by the poets of *G.* 1.498,
Romule Vestaque mater, and *Met.* 15.862–65, *genitorque Quirine/urbis, et inuicti genitor Gradiue
Quirini,/Vestaque Caesareos inter sacrata Penates,/et cum Caesarea, tu, Phoebe domestice, Vesta.*
(Apollo was not yet prominent in 390 B.C.E.)

[80] Briefly discussed above. Note that Ovid does not digress here to tell any of

when the temple was set on fire. This is itself a continuation of a theme we have briefly noticed above: the *pignora imperii*.[81] Just as the *ancile* answers Numa's request for *imperii pignora* at 3.345 and 354, just as Augustus himself is called a *pignus* equal to Vesta's flames at 3.422, so now Apollo tells the Trojans who have just received the image of Pallas from heaven that it will preserve the city and transfer to it the empire that once was Troy's (6.427–28). Despite Greek tales to the contrary, the image was saved (by Aeneas?, 434) and brought to Vesta for safekeeping. Williams has suggested that Ovid allows for doubt as to the piety of the high priest Metellus when he rescued the *fatalia pignora* from the burning temple, but that the goddess's approval should not be questioned. As we saw above, Vesta has come into Caesar's care, and Ovid's language has no sous-entendus to prevent us from accepting it in panegyric spirit. The poet rounds off with a last allegorical *aition*, for the notorious punishment of Vestals by burial alive: the offender is buried in the element against whom she has offended, in the Earth that is Vesta.

As Williams has shown, Ovid handles this sequence with great variety of tone and a variety of modes that provoke constant readjustment of response. Judged by purely didactic standards, it falls short, and as a religious exegesis it is both openly contradictory and covertly inventive. Both Scheid (1993) and Horsfall (1993) have argued for the long-standing freedom of the exegete to offer incompatible options and of the poet to invent. This sequence would not have raised an eyebrow among Callimachus's connoisseur audience. But then, I believe we should judge Ovid's *Fasti* as a poetic enterprise, an artistic meditation on the calendar and its religious associations, which shows considerable consultation of learned sources, but as much poetic invention as religious expertise.

And this is what his readers would expect from him. They would also have expected his endorsement of the *laudes* of the new Princeps and his dynasty, and this I believe he tried to carry out with style and even wit. But clearly when he abandoned the poem on the

---

the stories associated with the Lacus Curtius. And unlike the non-visual epiphany of Vesta, the claim of personal experience is perfectly naturalistic and credible.

[81] Servius on *Aen.* 7.188 claims that there were seven *pignora imperii*, including the Palladium, Ilione's veil, and Priam's scepter (see Dumézil (1970) 323). Other Roman texts such as Plaut. *Bacch.* 953 reflect a similar tradition of the *tria fata* of Troy; one was the loss of the Palladium, hence perhaps *pignora fatalia* in 6.445.

verge of July and August, the proliferating imperial festivals would have begun to swamp the traditional religious occasions. There are signs that he worked on his last book, Book 6, to create elements of both echo and ring composition with his first book, but he went no further, perhaps from weariness of panegyric, more likely because he was overtaken by the anger of the Princeps who relegated him to the cultural wasteland of Tomi. As Peter White has shown in the introductory chapter,[82] Ovid began to remodel the poem when he returned to it on Augustus's death. He rededicated it to Germanicus, but he was able to make few changes outside the first book,[83] so that we finally have inherited his half-year of *Fasti* in a version contaminating the Augustan and post-Augustan texts.

This sampling of Ovid's treatment of politics, history, and religion in *Fasti* may in the end suggest a further dimension to religion in Roman literature. In *Fasti*, as in both *Aeneid* and the final, Roman, books of *Metamorphoses*, religion is not just a matter of Feeney's useful categories divinity, myth, and cult. We should recognize that, though cult is the preeminent ingredient in Ovid's poem of the festival calendar, it cannot be separated from history, or the contemporary rereading and reconstructing of history implicit in what we call politics. In the age of Augustus the poets, loyal or skeptical, could not avoid being Augustan in their conceptions and presentation of the world of Rome.

Appendix: A Bibliographical Note on Roman Religion

In addition to works cited in the General Bibliography, interested readers should have access to the following items:

Beard, M. (1994). "Religion." In J.A. Crook, A. Lintott, and E. Rawson (eds.), *The Cambridge Ancient History*. 2d ed. Vol. 9: *The Last Age of the Roman Republic, 146–43 B.C.*, 729–68. Cambridge.
Beard, M. and J. North (1990). *Pagan Priests*. London.
Beard, M., J. North, and S.R.F. Price (1998). *Religions of Rome*. 2 vols. Cambridge and New York.

---

[82] White accepts the arguments for both certain and merely probable changes from Fantham (1986).

[83] Fantham (1986).

Dumézil, G. (1970). *Archaic Roman Religion*. Trans. P. Krapp. Chicago.

Fauth, W. (1978). "Römische Religion im Spiegel der *Fasti* des Ovid." *Aufstieg und Niedergang der Römischen Welt* 2.16.1:104–86.

Gagé, J. (1977). *Enquêtes sur les structures sociales et religieuses de le Rome primitive*. Collection Latomus 152. Brussels.

Graf, F. (1993). "Der Mythos bei den Römern. Forschungs- und Problemgeschichte." In Graf (1993GB): 25–43.

———. (1997). *Der Lauf des rollenden Jahres: Zeit und Kalender in Rom*. Stuttgart and Leipzig.

Le Bonniec, H. (1959). *Le Culte de Cérès à Rome*. Paris.

———. (1989). *Études Ovidiennes: introduction aux "Fastes" d'Ovide*. Frankfurt-am-Main—New York.

North, J. (1989). "Religion in Republican Rome." In F.W. Walbank, A.E. Astin, M.W. Frederiksen, R.M. Ogilvie, and A. Drummond (eds.), *The Cambridge Ancient History*. 2d ed. Vol. 7.2: *The Rise of Rome to 220 B.C.*, 573–624. Cambridge.

Price, S.R.F. (1984). *Rituals and Power*. Oxford.

———. "The Place of Religion: Rome in the Early Empire." In A.K. Bowman, E. Champlin, and A. Lintott (eds.), *The Cambridge Ancient History*. 2d ed. Vol. 10: *The Augustan Empire, 43 B.C.–A.D. 69*, 812–47. Cambridge.

Schilling, R. (1954). *La Religion Romaine de Vénus*. Paris.

———. (1979). *Rites, cultes, dieux de Rome*. Paris.

Wissowa, G. (1912). *Religion und Kultus der Römer*. 2d ed. Munich.

I briefly describe here the character of these works, as well as of a few others found in the General Bibliography. Items in the latter group are indicated by the letters GB.

Until recently Roman religion was most keenly studied by German religious historians. Most important of these are Wissowa's monumental work (1912) and the differently organized history of Latte (1960/1976GB). Other important if controversial contributions include those of Gagé (1977) and Dumézil (1970). French and Belgian scholars have taken different approaches: Le Bonniec (1959) and Schilling (1954) are major monographs on cult, and Le Bonniec (1989) and Schilling (1992/93GB) offer texts and commentaries on *Fasti* itself. Scheid (1992GB), (1993GB) and Porte (1985GB), (1993GB) have contributed both books and articles on Roman cults and on *Fasti*. Fauth (1978), in spite of his title, is more concerned with recovering lost religious forms than with Ovid's own transformation of the beliefs and practices known to him, and has therefore limited value for this study.

Bömer's great two-volume edition of *Fasti* (1957–58GB) has a valuable introduction and excellent discussions preceding each section to introduce a commentary which unfortunately is crowded with cross-references to German scholarship that may not be easy of access. His articles in *Gymnasium* and elsewhere include important *Fasti*-related studies. Much of Graf's work on mythology, religion, and magic is available in English, but two works bearing on religion in *Fasti*, (1993) and (1997), are not. In the last fifteen years comprehensive new work has also appeared in English. Readers can now turn with confidence to the chapters of volumes 7, 9, and 10 in *CAH*² and the two volumes of continuous religious history and translated sources by Beard, North, and Price (1998). There is also much to be learned, despite his predominant focus on the republican period, from the essays of Wiseman (1995bGB), (1998GB). Until now his focus has been on recovering historical fact from literary, epigraphical, and archaeological evidence, rather than on literary representation, but he is currently preparing a translation and commentary on *Fasti* which can be expected to show some of the breadth and daring of Frazer's landmark five-volume edition.

CHAPTER EIGHT

SOURCES AND GENRES IN OVID'S
METAMORPHOSES 1–5[1]

Alison Keith

Two German philologists set the parameters of scholarly discussion of Ovid's *Metamorphoses* at the beginning of the twentieth century. Hugo Magnus's 1914 edition of the *Metamorphoses* at last made a "scientific" text of the poem available to scholars and inspired further research into the textual tradition of the poem,[2] while the 1919 publication of Richard Heinze's *Ovids elegische Erzählung* established the fundamental interpretive framework of the poem for the rest of the century. In an elegant study of the twin Proserpina narratives of *Metamorphoses* 5 and *Fasti* 4, Heinze argued that the version in the *Metamorphoses* constitutes an essay in the diction, style, and thematics of high epic, while the *Fasti* presents a less elevated account of the rape conforming to the stylistic principles of elegy. These findings he extended to the poems in their entirety, to conclude that the question of genre is a central preoccupation of both texts and that the *Metamorphoses* displays a consistent generic alignment with epic, the *Fasti* with elegy. Heinze's focus on the question of genre has been accepted by the majority of scholars who have since studied the *Metamorphoses*, up to and including the 1987 publication of Hinds's no less important re-examination of the Proserpina narratives.[3] So influential has Heinze's argument been that even those scholars who reject his conclusions have in the main worked within the framework of his analysis by concentrating their studies on elegiac motifs in the *Metamorphoses*.[4] Contemporary scholarly attention to issues of

---

[1] I am grateful to Barbara Weiden Boyd, Dan Curley, Ingo Gildenhard, Stephen Hinds, and Stephen Rupp for their comments on earlier versions of this chapter.
[2] On its reception, see Lenz (1967); Tarrant (1982). Anderson's Teubner edition has superseded Magnus (1914). Richard Tarrant's forthcoming *OCT* is eagerly awaited.
[3] Hinds (1987a). Heinze's formulation is accepted, e.g., by Wilkinson (1955) 149–50, 279; Bernbeck (1967); Otis (1970) 49–59.
[4] Tränkle (1963); Knox (1986a) 9–26.

genre in Ovid's *Metamorphoses* has coincided with a renewed interest in *Quellenforschung*, as critics have investigated in detail how the literary antecedents of individual episodes simultaneously engage and challenge the generic norms of epic.[5] This chapter testifies to the continuing influence of Heinze's work by taking as its subject Ovid's creative exploitation of sources and genres in the first five books of the *Metamorphoses*.

1. *Epic*

It has often been suggested that Ovid chose to write the *Metamorphoses* in dactylic hexameters, the meter in which epic poems were composed in classical antiquity, in response to "the impulse of the *Aeneid*."[6] Yet while Virgil may have been the most immediate spur to Ovid's epic production, the whole of the classical epic tradition informs his essay in hexameter poetry. Examination of the proem has confirmed the poem's general pretensions to epic status and particular debts to the *Aeneid*:

> In noua fert animus mutatas dicere formas
> corpora; di, coeptis (nam uos mutastis et illa)
> adspirate meis primaque ab origine mundi
> ad mea perpetuum deducite tempora carmen (1.1–4).

> My mind moves me to tell of shapes changed into new bodies; gods, inspire my beginnings (for you have changed even those) and spin a fine thread of continuous song from the first origin of the world to my own times.[7]

von Albrecht has demonstrated the specifically epic characteristics of the diction and tone of this passage.[8] He identifies epic antecedents for the opening words in the Homeric phrase ὅππῃ οἱ νόος ὄρνυται ("wherever his mind urges," *Od.* 1.347), with which Telemachus char-

---

[5] Knox (1986a); Hinds (1987a); Farrell (1992); Myers (1994a); Gildenhard and Zissos (1999b).

[6] Galinsky (1975) 14. The view is common: see, e.g., Wilkinson (1958); Bernbeck (1967); Otis (1970) 1–3; Due (1974) 36–41. On Ovid's debt to Virgil, see Bömer (1959); Lamacchia (1960); Bernbeck (1967); Döpp (1968) 104–40, (1991); Tissol (1993); Esposito (1994); Baldo (1997); Hinds (1998) 104–22.

[7] I cite the text of Ovid's *Metamorphoses* from Miller, except at 1.2 where I read *illa* with Anderson. Translations are my own.

[8] von Albrecht (1961).

acterizes the decision of the bard Phemius to sing "the Achaeans'
return from Troy" (*Od.* 1.326–27), and two similar formulations about
the bard Demodocus.[9] The stylistic elevation of the infinitive *dicere*
is confirmed by reference to the Virgilian vocabulary of epic pro-
gram in which it repeatedly appears (*Ecl.* 4.54; *G.* 3.46, 4.5; *bis, Aen.*
7.41–42).[10] Virgil also employs the substantive *coepta* ("beginnings,"
G. 1.40, *Aen.* 10.461; cf. *Culex* 25), and the verb which governs it,
adspirare ("inspire," *Aen.* 9.525; cf. *Ciris* 99), in programmatic passages.[11]

Despite these prominently signalled debts to Homeric and Virgilian
epic, many critics have been reluctant to accept that the *Metamorphoses*
belongs to the genre of epos, and certainly Ovid's professed subject
matter, *mutatas...formas* (1.1), is far from the heroic themes of the
Iliad, Odyssey, and *Aeneid*. Latacz, however, has drawn attention to
the parallel between Ovid's subject and the themes of didactic epic.[12]
The phrase *mutatas...formas*, by which title Ovid elsewhere refers
to his poem (*Tr.* 1.1.117, 1.7.13, 3.14.19), is especially close to that
which opens the *Theriaca* of the Hellenistic Greek poet Nicander (μορ-
φάς τε σίνη τε, "shapes and wounds," *Ther.* 1), whose *Transformations*,
no longer extant, was undoubtedly an important model for the
Metamorphoses though its loss makes it difficult for us to assess Nicandrian
influence in detail.[13] In addition, Myers has identified a linguistic
debt to didactic epos in Ovid's opening prepositional phrase (*in
noua...corpora*, 1.1–2).[14] She notes the frequency with which didac-
tic epics (and the Homeric hymns) open with such phrases, and we
may compare in particular the *incipit* of Cicero's Latin version of
Aratus's *Phaenomena* (*a Ioue Musarum primordia*, Cic. *Aratea* fr. 1; cf. the
opening of Orpheus's song at *Met.* 10.148: *ab Ioue, Musa parens*).

Ovid comments on the innovation of his poetic endeavor in his
opening words, *in noua fert animus*, which can be read autonomously

---

[9] ὅππῃ θυμὸς ἐποτρύνῃσιν ἀείδειν (*Od.* 8.45); Μοῦσ' ἄρ' ἀοιδὸν ἀνῆκεν ἀειδέμεναι
κλέα ἀνδρῶν (*Od.* 8.73, where Μοῦσα replaces θυμός). von Albrecht (1961) 274
concludes that "Ovid's *animus* enters the epic with the claim of the Homeric θυμός."

[10] von Albrecht (1961) 269–72. On the literary critical implications of the Virgilian
passages, see Conte (1992).

[11] Due (1974) 95.

[12] Latacz (1979); cf. Myers (1994a) 5–6.

[13] On Ovid and Nicander, see Lafaye (1904) 46–65; Vollgraff (1909); Kraus
(1942) 1938–40, 1943 [= (1968) 105–8, 112]. On the popularity of metamorphosis
as a theme in Hellenistic and neoteric poetry, see O'Hara (1996a) 179–80 n. 6.

[14] Myers (1994a) 6 n. 14.

to mean "my inspiration bears (me) on to new things."[15] The nov-
elty of the poem's subject-matter is complemented by the poet's new
excursion into hexameter verse, a metrical innovation underscored
in the parenthetical comment *nam uos mutastis et illa* (1.2). The medieval
variant *illa*, first adopted by Lejay in his 1894 school edition of the
Metamorphoses and defended in the following century by Hartman,
Luck, and Kenney, among others, is currently accepted as the correct
lemma.[16] On this reading, the parenthesis pointedly credits the gods
with transforming not only the changed forms which constitute the
poem's subject-matter but also Ovid's verse-form itself, since they
have metamorphosed his poetry from elegiac couplets into dactylic
hexameters. This metaliterary aside on the poet's innovation in meter
revisits and reverses the opening scene of the *Amores*, where the god
Cupid steals a foot from the second line of Ovid's projected epic
and thereby sets him on an elegiac course (*Am.* 1.1–4). The parenthesis
thus implies a rejection of elegy in favor of epic.[17] Its self-referential
commentary on the literary aims of the *Metamorphoses* is buttressed
by Ovid's use of *forma* and *corpora* (1.1–2), which in stylistic discus-
sion can refer to literary "forms" and "works" respectively:[18] the poet
undertakes to transform the diverse literary forms of his sources into
the hexameter body of his epic.

The last two lines of the proem emphasize this new commitment
to epos. The Lucretian phrase *prima . . . ab origine mundi* (1.3 = Lucret.
5.548; cf. *ab origine prima*, Lucret. 3.331, 5.678; Virg. *G.* 3.48, 4.286)
explicitly introduces the didactic tradition of cosmogonic epic (going
back to Hesiod and Empedocles, and including Lucretius's *De rerum
natura*) into the Homero-Virgilian matrix which dominates the open-
ing lines of the poem. Scholars have also noted the parallel with
Ennius's project in the *Annales*, originally conceived as a fifteen-book
historical epic treating events from the foundation of Rome down
to the poet's own day.[19] Finally, Ovid's claim to undertake a "con-

---

[15] Kenney (1976) 46.

[16] Lejay (1894); Hartman (1905) 83–84; Luck (1958); Kenney (1976) 46–50. The
reading is accepted by Anderson (1993); Tarrant (1982) 351.

[17] Wheeler (1999) 19, however, notes the paradox that "[i]n programmatic terms,
Ovid's explanation of the origin of his hexameters lends support to critics who
underscore the continuing elegiac tendencies of the *Metamorphoses*." Cf. Knox (1986a) 9.

[18] For *forma* in ancient literary critical discussion, see *TLL* 6.1.1072.19–71; for
corpora, see *TLL* 4.1020.62–1021.39. Cf. Keith (1999a).

[19] Hardie (1995); Feeney (1999).

tinuous song" (1.4) has long been recognized as an espousal of grand epic in its ironic adaptation of Callimachus's tendentious refusal in the *Aetia* prologue to produce "one continuous song" (ἓν ἄεισμα διηνεκές, *Aet.* 1, fr. 1.3 Pf.).[20]

The range and precision of Ovid's references to the classical epic tradition in articulating the program of the *Metamorphoses* establish the poem's generic alignment with epos. Quintilian provides valuable corroborative evidence in his discussion of Greek and Roman authors, for he includes Ovid's *Metamorphoses* in his discussion of Latin epic (*IO* 10.1.88) and treats under the rubric of epos, in addition to Homer and Virgil, the poets invoked by Ovid in his proem: Hesiod, Nicander, Ennius, and Lucretius. Recent discussions of genre and allusion in Latin poetry, especially Virgilian and Ovidian poetry, have distinguished between an "example model," the particular source to which an author alludes in a specific word, phrase, or scene, and the "code model," the representative of the "rules and codifications" of the genre in which an author writes.[21] This work supplies a theoretical basis for Due's observation that Homeric epic is the ultimate model for Ovid's literary project in the *Metamorphoses*.[22] Despite the essentially Hesiodic (catalogue)[23] character of the *Metamorphoses*, Homer, as the fountainhead of epic, and Virgil, his Roman heir, remain for Ovid "the representative[s] of the institution of epic poetry itself."[24] By invoking not only Homer and Virgil but also Hesiod, Ennius, and Lucretius so prominently in his proem, Ovid signals that the *Metamorphoses* will combine the traditions of heroic and didactic epos in a comprehensive culmination of the genre.[25]

Ovid implicitly confirms the generic classification of the *Metamorphoses* as epic by opening the poem proper with a cosmogony (1.5–88), a philosophical subject traditionally considered the most elevated poetic theme and therefore the subject best suited to the most elevated

---

[20] Kraus (1942) 1943 [= (1968) 113]; Herter (1948) 145; von Albrecht (1961) 278; Otis (1970) 45–46.

[21] Conte (1986) 31, discussed by Hinds (1998) 41–47; cf. Due (1974) 16. Conte (1986) and (1992) and Hinds (1998) engage the related issues of allusion and "genre blending" (*Kreuzung der Gattungen*) first discussed by Pasquali (1951) and Kroll (1924) 202–24, respectively.

[22] Due (1974) 21–23; cf. Baldo (1986).

[23] Martini (1933) 29–36; Herter (1948).

[24] Conte (1986) 31.

[25] Cf. Latacz (1979) 144; Due (1974) 16–24, 28–33, 36–41, 120; Myers (1994a) 1–26.

poetic genre, grand epic.[26] The subjects that succeed the cosmogony down to the flood narrative also seem to have been chosen by Ovid to exemplify the conventional themes of high epic,[27] and similarly extensive panels of grand epic subjects composed in the grand epic manner open books 2, 3, and 5. Constraints of space do not permit detailed examination here of the Phaethon episode in Book 2, well discussed by Brooks Otis as an instance of high epic.[28] Nor is there any need to rehearse Hardie's argument that the themes of foundation epic inform Ovid's "Thebaid" (3.1–4.603), which opens with Cadmus obeying the Delphic oracle's instructions to found Thebes and closes with his self-imposed exile from the city.[29] Analysis of Ovid's adaptation of heroic epic in the Perseus narrative of 4.610–5.251, however, will allow us to explore more fully his relationship to Homer and Virgil, the primary representatives of Greek and Latin epic.

Ovid depicts Perseus, preeminent among heroes in Homer's phrase (*Il.* 14.320; cf. Hes. *Cat.* 129.15 M–W), as the quintessential epic hero whose *uirtus* is tested in a series of trials.[30] In *Metamorphoses* 4, he is a Herculean hero, first in his visit to the garden of the Hesperides (4.628–62) and then in his conquest of the sea-monster that threatens Andromeda (*labor,* 4.739; cf. Virgil's Herculean Aeneas, *Aen.* 1.10).[31] Just as the golden apples of the Hesperides' garden will be despoiled by Hercules (4.643–45),[32] so Medusa's head is the spoil, won by heroic valor (4.770), which confers on Perseus the lasting renown of the epic hero (*spolium memorabile,* 4.615). Another prize worthy of the hero is Andromeda, both the reason for and the reward

---

[26] On cosmogony as a theme of grand epic, see Innes (1979) and Hardie (1986) 6–84. On Ovid's cosmogony, see Bömer (1969) 15–17; Maurach (1979); Helzle (1993); Myers (1994a) 5–15; Wheeler (1995).

[27] Heinze (1919) 11–13 [= (1960) 315–17]; Fränkel (1945) 75–76; Otis (1970) 91–101. Kraus (1942) 1944–45 [= (1968) 114–15] lists epicizing passages in the poem.

[28] Otis (1970) 108–16; cf. Zissos (1996).

[29] Hardie (1990). For discussion of epic themes in an episode of the "Thebaid," see Hardie (1988).

[30] Keith (1999b) 221–23; cf. Otis (1970) 145, 159–64; Due (1974) 77–79; Nischke (1982). On a possible epic source, see della Corte (1958). On the Perseus myth, see Schauenburg (1960); Nischke (1982).

[31] Cf. Hercules' rescue of Hesione from the sea-monster sent by Neptune because of Laomedon's perjury, known already to Homer (*Il.* 20.145–48) and treated by Ovid at *Met.* 11.194–217.

[32] Cf. 9.188–90, where Hercules himself mentions this labor.

of Perseus's battle with the sea-monster (*pretium et causa laboris*, 4.739; cf. 4.757, 5.25). If his Herculean deliverance of maiden from monster constitutes proof of Perseus's heroism in Book 4, his Odyssean defense of his bride against Phineus and his retainers in the following book confirms it.

The wedding banquet that closes *Metamorphoses* 4 features Perseus's account of his exploits (4.765–5.2) on the model of Odysseus at the court of the Phaeacians (*Odyssey* 9–12) and Aeneas in Carthage (*Aeneid* 2–3), though on a much reduced scale.[33] The festivities are shattered at the outset of Book 5 by the arrival of Cepheus's brother Phineus, who comes to avenge Perseus's "theft" of his fiancée, Andromeda. Accompanied by a band of armed retainers, Phineus introduces an epic battle scene (*belli temerarius auctor*, 5.8). Brandishing an ash spear like a Virgilian villain (*fraxineam quatiens . . . hastam*, 5.9; cf. Mezentius, *Aen.* 10.762; Arruns, 11.767), Phineus claims to avenge a ravished wife (*adsum* **praereptae coniugis** *ultor*, 5.10), like the Homeric Menelaus (*Il.* 9.340–41) and Virgilian Turnus (*coniuge praerepta*, *Aen.* 9.138).[34]

The ensuing battle constitutes a sustained meditation on the action of heroic epic. Bride-theft motivates Homeric battle narrative not only in the *Iliad* but also in the *Odyssey*, and the situational parallels between Ovid's "Perseid" and *Odyssey* 22 are particularly striking. Assisted by a few adherents, Perseus fights Phineus, a single challenger who comes with an armed entourage, for possession of Andromeda in her father's palace during their wedding banquet (5.3), just as Odysseus, assisted by a few adherents, fights a group of armed suitors at a banquet (*Od.* 22.12–14) for possession of his wife in his own palace and conceals their deaths by pretending to celebrate a marriage (*Od.* 23.131–40).[35] Minerva even assists her protégé Perseus (5.46–47, 250–51) as Athena aids Odysseus (*Od.* 22.205–40, 297–308).

Ovid also reworks specific details of the Odyssean battle narrative in his "Perseid." A Libyan Amphimedon fights against Perseus (5.75), while a suitor of that name opposes Odysseus (*Od.* 22.242, 277, 284). Among Perseus's victims is Aethion, wise in avian omens but deceived on this occasion (5.146–47), who is modelled on Leodes, the suitors'

---

[33] Nischke (1982) 81.

[34] A trace of the Homeric intertext lingers in Ovid's specification of the spear as ash, like Achilles' (Πηλιάδα μελίην, *Il.* 16.143, 19.390, 20.277).

[35] Nischke (1982) views Odysseus as the model for Perseus throughout Ovid's "Perseid."

soothsayer killed by Odysseus (*Od.* 22.310–29). Ovid's emphasis on Perseus as one against many (*omnibus unum*, 5.149; cf. 5.157) evokes the rhetorical question posed by Homer following the killing of Antinous, with which Odysseus inaugurates the slaughter of the suitors: "for who would think that in the company of men feasting, one man among many (μοῦνον ἐνὶ πλεόνεσσι), even if he were especially strong, would bring on himself evil death and black doom?" (*Od.* 22.12–14).[36]

In addition to the Odyssean parallels, the central figures in Ovid's "Perseid" correspond to characters in the *Aeneid*: Perseus, Phineus, Andromeda, and Cepheus reprise the roles of Aeneas, Turnus, Lavinia, and Latinus.[37] As wedding turns into war Bellona (5.155–56) replaces Hymenaeus and Amor (4.758–59), in another allusion to Virgil whose Juno invites Bellona to preside over the marriage of Lavinia and Aeneas (*Aen.* 7.318–19). Cepheus decisively rejects Phineus's claim to Andromeda (5.12–29), as Latinus tries to dissuade Turnus from maintaining his claim to Lavinia (*Aen.* 12.18–45), and he characterizes Phineus's motivation as *furor* (5.13), the emotion that animates Turnus throughout the *Aeneid*. Unable to prevent Phineus from attacking Perseus, as Latinus is unable to stop Turnus from mustering troops against Aeneas, Cepheus abandons the banquet-hall (5.43–45) on the model of Latinus overwhelmed by the rising tide of war (*Aen.* 7.591–600). In the opening simile of the book (5.5–7), Ovid reworks a Virgilian simile characterizing Latinus's futile attempt to resist Turnus (*Aen.* 7.586–90).

Drawing on the full range of battle episodes in the *Aeneid*, Ovid refines disparate episodes into a single consummate distillation of Virgilian war narrative. Thus the first episode, in which Perseus kills the lovers Athis and Lycabas (5.47–73), conflates two Virgilian episodes: specifically modelled on a celebrated episode in the Italian war of *Aeneid* 9–12, the night raid of Nisus and Euryalus (*Aen.* 9.176–449), it also alludes to the scene in which Virgil introduces the lovers (*Aen.* 5.286–361).[38] Just as the beauty of the youthful Athis (*egregius forma*, 5.49) recalls that of Euryalus (9.179–81; cf. *forma insignis, Aen.* 5.295), so the love of Lycabas for Athis (5.60–61) evokes that of Nisus for

---

[36] On the epic theme of "one versus many," see Hardie (1993) 3–11.
[37] Otis (1970) 347.
[38] Otis (1970) 347–48; Esposito (1994) 37–39.

Euryalus (*Aen.* 9.182; 5.296).[39] Lycabas's cry that Perseus's quarrel is with him (5.64) echoes Nisus's plea that the Rutulians who have overpowered Euryalus restrict their quarrel to him (*Aen.* 9.427–30). Like Nisus, Lycabas sees his beloved's beauty defiled in a brutal death (5.59–60; *Aen.* 9.431–34), and himself falls to his friend's killer, casting himself on his lover's corpse in death (5.69–73; *Aen.* 9.444–45).[40]

Ovid complicates his reworking of Virgil in this passage still further by alluding to other episodes in the Italian war. The Euryalan Athis bears a name which evokes another Trojan follower of Aeneas (Atys, *Aen.* 5.568); his outstanding beauty recalls that of the first victim of the broken truce (*egregium forma iuuenem*, *Aen.* 12.275);[41] and his rich clothing and war gear (5.49–55) are modelled on those of the Trojan Chloreus (*Aen.* 11.768–77), a priest of Cybele whose most famous worshipper also bore the name Athis (Catull. 63). The Ovidian Athis is killed by a crushing blow to the face from a burning log snatched from an altar (5.56–58) on the model of Corynaeus's attack on Ebysus in the last book of the *Aeneid* (12.298–301). Lycabas's vaunt that Perseus will not long enjoy the glory of killing Athis (5.65–66) evokes the dying words of the Trojan Orodes, who tells his killer Mezentius that he will not long glory in his death (*Aen.* 10.739–41).

Individual details of the battle in Cepheus's halls are also drawn from the night raid of Nisus and Euryalus, which takes place in the aftermath of a drinking party in the Rutulian camp (*Aen.* 9.316–19). Ovid offers a particularly concentrated example in his reworking of the death of Euryalus's last Rutulian victim, Rhoetus, run through by Euryalus's sword as he cowers behind a wine-mixing bowl (*Aen.* 9.345–50). Ovid gives the name Rhoetus to Perseus's first kill, who dies from a spear in his face (5.38–40), but he transfers the detail of the *crater* to Perseus's killing of Eurytus (5.79–84) in a death scene that annotates its debt to Virgil's Rutulian setting when Eurytus belches "red" blood: **rutilum** *uomit ille cruorem* (5.83; cf. *purpuream uomit ille animam*, *Aen.* 9.349 of Rhoetus).[42] To Eurytus's death Ovid appends a brief catalogue of Phineus's war dead, among them a Caucasian

---

[39] Esposito (1994) 39 notes Ovid's amplification of their love in his rewriting of *Aen.* 5.293–96.
[40] Cf. Esposito (1994) 40.
[41] Esposito (1994) 38.
[42] On wordplay in Ovid, see Ahl (1985); Keith (1992a); O'Hara (1996b).

Abaris (5.86) whose name is drawn from the brief catalogue of Rutulians killed by Euryalus just before Rhoetus's death (*Aen.* 9.344). Blood drenches the ground of the Ovidian battlefield (**sanguine**, *quo late* **tellus madefacta tepe***bat*, 5.76) just as Virgil's Rutulian camp runs with the blood of the slaughtered (*atra* **tepefacta cruore/terra** *torique* **madent**, *Aen.* 9.333–34).

The interior of Cepheus's palace, however, is very different from the outdoor settings of Virgil's Italian war. Here Ovid's Virgilian model is the sack of Troy in *Aeneid* 2, and specifically the famous death scenes of Polites and Priam in the Trojan king's palace (*Aen.* 2.506–53). The death of Emathion (5.99–106) recalls this Virgilian intertext especially closely. Old Emathion (*grandaeuus*, 5.99), like the aged Priam (*longaeuum*, *Aen.* 2.525), has taken refuge at an altar (*huic . . . amplexo tremulis altaria palmis*, 5.103),[43] where he curses the impiety of the battle (5.101–2) in a speech that recapitulates in abbreviated form Priam's condemnation of Pyrrhus's murder of his son Polites (*Aen.* 2.535–43). Emathion is silenced in death by the sacrilegious Chromis, who decapitates him as he clings to the altar (5.103–4) on the model of the Virgilian Pyrrhus, who stabs Priam at his altar (*Aen.* 2.550–53).[44] Again, however, Ovid complicates his model by drawing on a second Virgilian episode, for Emathion's age and respect for justice (*aequi cultor timidusque deorum*, 5.100) recall the just and aged Italian Galaesus (*seniorque Galaesus/. . . iustissimus unus*, *Aen.* 7.535–36), who is among the first to die in the Italian war.

Ovid concludes the episode with the victory of Perseus over Phineus, which revisits Aeneas's defeat of Turnus at the end of the *Aeneid*. Both Phineus (5.210–11) and Turnus (*Aen.* 12.930–38) regret their rash pursuit of war against a greater foe, and raise their hands in supplication (5.214–15; *Aen.* 12.930–31), acknowledging defeat (Phineus, '**uincis**,' *ait*, '*Perseu!*,' 5.216; Turnus, '**uicisti** *et* **uictum** *tendere palmas/Ausonii uidere*,' *Aen.* 12.936–37). Both renounce their claim to the woman for whom they have fought, assigning Andromeda and Lavinia to Perseus and Aeneas respectively (5.219–22; *Aen.* 12.937). Both beg for their lives (5.221–22; *Aen.* 12.931–38), but are nonetheless killed by their victors after a brief speech (5.224–35; *Aen.* 12.947–52).

---

[43] Cf. *hoc dicens altaria ad ipsa trementem/traxit* (*Aen.* 2.550–51); for further verbal parallels between the two passages, see Bömer (1976) 253–54; Anderson (1997) 509.

[44] Esposito (1994) 42–43 compares the death of the singer Lampetides (5.113–16) with that of Priam (*Aen.* 2.544–53).

The range of Ovid's debts to Virgilian and Homeric battle narrative in the brief compass of his "Perseid" has suggested to some scholars that the scene is a parody or burlesque of heroic epic, lacking in the high seriousness and sustained plot of Homeric and Virgilian epic.[45] Yet the very precision with which Ovid has synthesized his Greek and Roman models argues against this kind of reading. Ovid neither parodies nor burlesques high epic, but rather reinterprets the form, intensifying both the brutality of Homer and the sentimentality of Virgil by limiting his war narrative to 250 lines.[46] He offers oblique commentary on his renovation of heroic epic in a passage describing the amplification of battle in Cepheus's halls:

> ... ululatuque atria complent,
> sed sonus armorum superat gemitusque cadentum,
> pollutosque simul multo Bellona penates
> sanguine perfundit renouataque proelia miscet (5.153–56).

> The halls are full of lamentation, but it is overwhelmed by the clash of weapons and groans of the fallen, as Bellona drenches and pollutes the household gods with much bloodshed, and stirs up renewed battles.

The clash of arms and groans of the fallen exemplify Homero-Virgilian war poetry, which Ovid self-consciously renews in Perseus's battle with Phineus, both doubling and making new Odysseus's battle with the suitors in *Odyssey* 22 and Aeneas's conflict with Turnus in *Aeneid* 7–12.[47] Just as Homer reshapes traditional material, and Virgil adapts Apollonian, Ennian, and Lucretian epic with constant reference to Homer in the *Aeneid*, so Ovid renegotiates Virgilian epic with an eye to his Homeric model, looking to the preeminent masters of Greek and Latin epos to shape his own essay in the genre.

2. *Elegy*

Despite Ovid's explicit mobilization of the epic tradition in the *Metamorphoses*, the poem displays a stylistic and thematic polyphony

---

[45] Otis (1970) 350; Anderson (1997) 497–519. The charge is commonly levelled against Ovid: see, e.g., Bömer (1959); Horsfall (1979); Latacz (1979) 147–55. It is refuted by Hinds (1987b), (1998) 107–22; cf. Due (1974) 36–41; Baldo (1986); Esposito (1994).

[46] Cf. Due (1974) 76; Hinds (1987b) 13; Esposito (1994) 101.

[47] Bömer (1976) 263 notes Ovid's debt to *Aen.* 2.3 ("*infandum, regina, iubes* **renouare** *dolorem*"), where Virgil offers metaliterary comment on his renewal of Homeric epic.

that has been taken to complicate generic categorization. How, for example, can we explain the many amatory episodes in this complex text? Reconsideration of the proem will open up a second strand of generic play in the poem and introduce the erotic narratives of *Metamorphoses* 1–5 into this study.

The second imperative addressed to the gods, *deducite* (1.4), evokes a Callimachean resonance that complicates the poem's high epic pretensions. Due first observed that if the gods accomplished Ovid's request, the result would be a *carmen* at once *perpetuum* and *deductum*, "fine-spun."[48] Among Callimachus's Roman adherents, the adjective *deductum* enjoyed a certain cachet as a translation of the Greek poet's ideal of refined poetry, τὴν Μοῦσαν ... λεπταλέην ("the slender Muse," *Aet.* 1 fr.1.24 Pf.), a stylistic principle connoting delicacy and subtlety.[49] The poetics of λεπτότης are associated especially closely with elegy in Rome (whatever their relationship to the genre in Callimachean poetry),[50] perhaps because they are enunciated most explicitly in the elegiac *Aetia*. Ovid's expression of a Callimachean impulse at the end of the proem, along with the allusion to *Am.* 1.1.3–4 at 1.2, has therefore led scholars to explore his thematic and stylistic debts to elegy in the *Metamorphoses*.[51]

Much discussed in this context is the Apollo-Daphne episode (1.452–582). Fränkel noted "the programmatic character of [t]his first love tale,"[52] and Nicoll has elaborated its significance in detail.[53] The action of the episode arises out of the earth's parthenogenic birth of the monster Python (1.438–50). Ovid emphasizes his huge size (*maxime*, 1.438; *tantum spatii de monte tenebas*, 1.440) and the terror he inspires (1.439–40) in order to underline the epic heroism Apollo displays in

---

[48] Due (1974) 95.

[49] Eisenhut (1961). Gilbert (1976) collects and discusses the evidence in connection with *Met.* 1.4; cf. Kenney (1976) 51–52, and Heyworth (1994) 72–76.

[50] On this contentious issue, see most recently Cameron (1995).

[51] On Callimachus's *Aetia* as an important model for the *Metamorphoses*, see Due (1974) 19–20; Knox (1986a); Myers (1994a) 15–21, 61–132. On Ovid and Callimachus, see also Diller (1934); de Cola (1937); Herter (1948); Keith (1992a); Tissol (1997). Other scholars discuss elegiac tendencies in the *Metamorphoses* without linking them to the example of Callimachus: see, e.g., Kraus (1942) 1945 [= (1968) 115]; Pöschl (1959); Tränkle (1963), who takes issue with Heinze (1919); Sharrock (1991); Fabre-Serris (1995) 22–36, 247–96, who argues that Gallus is an important model for Ovid's program in the *Metamorphoses*.

[52] Fränkel (1945) 78.

[53] Nicoll (1980); cf. Knox (1986a) 14–19, (1990).

killing him (cf. the god's epic epithet *arcitenens*, 1.441).[54] The great
number of arrows Apollo requires to dispatch Python (*mille grauem
telis exhausta paene pharetra*, 1.443) further underscores the monster's
epic proportions (*pestifero tot iugera uentre prementem/strauimus innumeris
tumidum Pythona sagittis*, 1.459–60) and elevates the contest between
god and beast into an epic confrontation on the model of Hercules'
contest with Cacus (*Aen.* 8.184–279).[55]

In the aftermath of his feat of arms Apollo exhibits an epic arro-
gance (*Delius . . . uicta serpente superbus*, 1.454) which is deflated by
Cupid, whose arrows transform Apollo from an epic hero into an
elegiac lover. The confrontation between Apollo and Cupid, in which
the heroic archer denies the licentious demi-god's fitness to handle
arms ('*quid'que 'tibi, lasciue puer, cum fortibus armis?,*' 1.456), enacts a
literary contest between epos and elegy.[56] Apollo, the divine patron
of epic, demands that Cupid, the divine patron of Ovidian elegy
(*Am.* 1.1–4), observe a distinction between their respective spheres,
contrasting his heroic glory (*laudes*, 1.462) with Cupid's amatory
escapades (*amores*, 1.461). Cupid, however, scorns the distinction and
comprehensively bests Apollo by shooting him with one of his own
arrows and inspiring in him an unrequited love for the virginal
Daphne (1.465–74).

The Greek elegiac poet Parthenius, widely credited with intro-
ducing an earlier generation of Latin poets to Callimachus's poetry,
included the tale of Apollo's love for Daphne in the handbook of
erotic narratives he dedicated to Gallus (*Erot.* 15), but we do not
know what use, if any, Gallus made of the story in his elegiac *Amores*.[57]
Ovid, however, signals the incursion of elegiac material into the
realm of epos here with an extensive reworking of the opening poem
of his own *Amores*: *primus amor* at 1.452 self-reflexively annotates the
elegiac provenance of the episode. Apollo reprises the role of the
poet-lover in *Amores* 1.1, who disputes *Cupido*'s jurisdiction over poetry
(1.456 ~ *Am.* 1.1.5, 1.1.24) even as he falls victim to the god's erotic
arrows (1.466–74 ~ *Am.* 1.1.21–26; 1.495–96 ~ *Am.* 1.1.26; 1.519–20

---

[54] The epithet, a calque on the Homeric epithet "bow-bearing" (τοξοφόρος, *h.
Hom.* 3.13, 126), was introduced into Latin by Naevius (*Bel. Pun.* fr. 30 Büchner).
[55] Nicoll (1980) 181.
[56] Nicoll (1980) suggests that Ovid models the contest between Apollo and Cupid
on the literary form of *recusatio*. Davis (1983) 31–34 views Cupid as the *praeceptor
amoris* of Apollo.
[57] On the sources, see Knox (1990).

~ *Am.* 1.1.25–26).[58] The following narrative draws on the diction
and themes of amatory elegy, from the conventionally unyielding
disposition of the beloved (figured in Daphne's flight from Apollo,
1.469, 474–89, 502–52, 556) to the lover's unsuccessful use of ele-
giac "flattery" (*blanditiae*, 1.531; cf. 1.504–25, 557–65), vain pursuit
of the beloved (1.502–42, 553–67), obsessive fixation on her beauty
(1.490–502, 527–30), and inability to cure himself of love (1.521–24).[59]
Even the aetiological framework in which the narrative is embed-
ded, describing the foundation of the Pythian games and origin of
Apollo's association with the laurel (1.445–51, 557–67), contributes
to the elegiac tenor of the episode, since it gestures towards Calli-
machus's *Aetia* as a model.

Ovid complicates the elegiac tone of the passage, however, by set-
ting the erotic themes in an epic context.[60] In his first appearance
in the *Metamorphoses*, Cupid is inspired by the savage anger that moti-
vates Juno in the *Aeneid* (*primus amor Phoebi Daphne Peneia, quem non/fors
ignara dedit, sed* **saeua Cupidinis ira**, 1.452–53; cf. **saeuae** *memorem*
Iunonis *ob* **iram**, *Aen.* 1.4).[61] Moreover, by contesting Cupid's right
to bear epic *arma*, Apollo leaves himself open to challenge on his
own ground when his rival lays claim to epic "glory": *filius huic Veneris
'figat tuus omnia, Phoebe,/te meus arcus' ait; 'quantoque animalia cedunt/cuncta
deo, tanto minor est tua gloria nostra'* (1.463–65). The scene illustrates
the Virgilian (but perhaps originally Gallan?) maxim "love conquers
all" (*omnia uincit amor, Ecl.* 10.69), which paradoxically elevates the
god of love to the Jovian status of ruler of the universe.[62]

Ovid bolsters epic content with epic form by introducing similes
at points of heightened tension in the amatory narrative. He com-
pares Apollo falling in love with Daphne at first sight, an elegiac
topos,[63] with stubble or a hedge suddenly catching fire (1.492–95).
Epic poets from Homer on characteristically draw on material from
the natural world in their similes, a practice Ovid follows here by

---

[58] Nicoll (1980) 175–76; Knox (1986a) 14–17.
[59] Nicoll (1980) 177; cf. Due (1974) 113. On elegiac diction here, see Bömer
(1969) 146–68; Knox (1986a) 14–19, and (1990) 200–201.
[60] Cf. Due (1974) 112.
[61] Fränkel (1945) 208 n. 5.
[62] Due (1974) 112. Cf. Venus's plan to achieve dominion over the underworld
by causing the marriage of Pluto and Proserpina (5.362–84), with Otis (1970) 52–59;
Hinds (1987a) 103–13, 133–34; Johnson (1996); Barchiesi (1999).
[63] Rosati (1997) 173–74, with examples and bibliography.

evoking an image from Virgil's *Georgics* (1.84–85) where it also appears in a simile (3.99–100): Apollo's elegiac flame of love is thereby drawn into the ambit of (didactic) epic. Recognizing the futility of persuasion, Apollo resorts to the chase:

> . . . sed enim non sustinet ultra
> perdere blanditias iuuenis deus, utque monebat
> ipse Amor, admisso sequitur uestigia passu (1.530–32).

But the youthful god disdains to waste his flattery further, and as Love himself advised, follows her tracks with lengthened stride.

Ovid underscores Apollo's rejection of elegiac *blanditiae* for epic chase with a Virgilian archaism, *sed enim*,[64] and a simile likening the god's pursuit of Daphne to a Gallic hound's pursuit of a hare follows (1.533–39). This simile has a long epic pedigree: deriving ultimately from Homer (*Il.* 22.188–93), it is reworked by Apollonius, Ennius, and Virgil (*Aen.* 12.746–55).[65] Homer and Virgil apply the simile to Achilles and Aeneas in their final pursuits of Hector and Turnus. Ovid's reapplication of the simile to an erotic context likens elegiac conflict to epic duel, an interpretation perhaps not entirely incompatible in its eroticization of epic with the Homeric model, which follows shortly after Hector's internal debate recognizing that an appeal to Achilles in lovers' language is now too late (*Il.* 22.126–28).

Daphne's rejection of love, forcefully expressed in her request to her father that she be permitted to remain a virgin like Diana ('*da mihi perpetua, genitor carissime,' dixit/'uirginitate frui! dedit hoc pater ante Dianae,'* 1.486–87), assimilates her to the figure of the elegiac *puella* spurning her lover, but her specific formulation complicates this correspondence, for it closely translates Artemis' demand for perpetual virginity in Callimachus's (hexameter) hymn to Artemis ('δός μοι παρθενίην αἰώνιον, ἄππα, φυλάσσειν,' *Hymn* 3.6). Indeed, the ancient hymnic tradition, most famously represented by Homer (in the *Hymns*), Hesiod (*Erga* 1–10, *Theog.* 1–115), and Callimachus, provides another important literary context for the Ovidian episode.[66] Barchiesi has observed that Ovid here reverses the narrative sequence of the Delphic section of the Homeric *Hymn to Apollo* (207–15) by transforming the Homeric prelude (Apollo's amours) into his main theme, and the

---

[64] Knox (1986a) 29.
[65] Cf. Hom. *Il.* 10.360–64, 11.292–95; Ap. Rhod. 2.278–83; Enn. *Ann.* 332–34 Sk.
[66] Barchiesi (1999); cf. Williams (1981); Wills (1990).

Homeric theme (the killing of Python and foundation of the Delphic oracle) into his prelude.[67] Wills, moreover, has argued that "the content of Ovid's story properly constitutes a hymn to Apollo, with a listing of his attributes from his own mouth: lord of prophecy, the lyre, the arrow, medicine and even Capitoline processions" (1.515–22, 558–65).[68] Apollo himself praises Daphne, transformed into the laurel, in hymnic *du-stil* at the end of the episode, lauding her association with his hair, cithara, and bow, as well as the Roman triumph, and Augustus's palace ('*semper habebunt/* **te** *coma,* **te** *citharae,* **te** *nostrae, laure, pharetrae;/* **tu** *ducibus Latiis aderis/. . ./* **tu** *quoque perpetuos semper gere frondis honores!*,' 1.558–65). The episode ends with an image of the laurel tree shaking her foliage (*factis modo* **laurea ramis***/adnuit utque caput uisa est* **agitasse** *cacumen,* 1.566–67) which evokes the *incipit* of Callimachus's hymn to Apollo (οἶον ὁ τὠπόλλωνος ἐσείσατο δάφνινος ὄρπηξ, *Hymn* 2.1).[69] Like the epic framework which opens the episode, the hymnic intertexts elevate the stylistic pretensions of an amatory narrative, and a trace of the sacral context may still be felt in Ovid's use of the religious word *adoleo,* already naturalized in epic (Lucret. 4.1237; Virg. *Aen.* 1.704, 3.547, 7.71).[70] The generic tension generated by the juxtaposition of epic, elegiac, and hymnic conventions is congruent with the proem's announcement of a poem that aspires to both epic grandeur and Callimachean refinement.

It should be noted, however, that the epic tradition itself supplies Ovid with precedent for including amatory narrative in epos. Critics have adduced in comparison Hesiod's *Theogony* in combination with the amours of the gods in his *Catalogue of Women,* to which the *Theogony* served as preface in antiquity.[71] Recent scholarship has also related Ovid's amatory program in the *Metamorphoses* to Virgil's example in the *Eclogues,* whose song of Silenus (*Ecl.* 6.31–83) has been identified as the primary model for the *Metamorphoses* as a whole,[72] and in the

---

[67] Barchiesi (1999) 116.

[68] Wills (1990) 151–54, quote at 154; cf. Williams (1981) 251. Wills (1990) identifies Callimachus's *Hymn to Delos* as the specific source of the Ovidian narrative and implies, 155, that Apollo's epithet *Delius* (1.454) may have an arch annotative function like *primus amor* (1.452).

[69] Wills (1990) 151; Barchiesi (1999) 124.

[70] On its religious character and history, see *TLL* 1.794.8–30; Lewis and Short (1879) s.v.

[71] Lafaye (1904) 4–7; Ludwig (1965) 83–86; Otis (1970) 48–49, 318; Due (1974) 23–24.

[72] Knox (1986a) 10–19, (1990); Helzle (1993); Myers (1994a) 7–9; cf. Due (1974) 27–28.

fourth *Georgic*, where Clymene sings to her spinning companions a song that recapitulates the narrative trajectory of Hesiod's *Theogony* and *Catalogue of Women* from chaos to the amours of the gods (*aque Chao densos diuom numerabat amores*, G. 4.347).[73] In the *Metamorphoses*, the tale of Apollo and Daphne follows a reprise of the cosmogonic motif and announces *amor* as a pervasive theme of the poem.[74]

This is not to diminish the importance of work on elegiac style and content in the *Metamorphoses*, but rather to emphasize that Ovid's use of elegiac themes and sources is itself consonant with his demonstrable engagement with the generic conventions of epic: in addition to the amatory tales contained in Hesiod's *Theogony* and especially the *Catalogue*, we may note Homer's interest in Helen and Penelope; Empedocles' emphasis on Love in opposition to Strife; Apollonius's romance between Jason and Medea; Lucretius's hymn to Venus; and Virgil's Dido narrative. If the extensive engagement of epic with amatory themes is not new in the *Metamorphoses*, what does seem novel is Ovid's self-conscious commentary on his contamination of epic with elegy, "his continual awareness of the system of genres," whether observed, transgressed, or problematized.[75]

The conclusion of the Phaethon episode in Book 2 offers a particularly concentrated set of elegiac reflections on epic action as Phaethon's death transforms the tone and content of the episode from epic to elegiac. The Italian Naiads bury the youth and commemorate him with an epitaph: *hic situs est Phaethon currus auriga paterni/ quem si non tenuit magnis tamen excidit ausis* ("Here Phaëthon lies: in Phoebus' car he fared,/and though he greatly failed, more greatly dared," 2.327–28).[76] Ovid thus incorporates funerary epigram,[77] a literary form most frequently composed in elegiac couplets, into his polyphonic epic. Although by Ovid's day elegy was most closely associated with amatory themes, its genesis was presumed to lie in funerary lament.[78] Phaethon's epitaph thus introduces an elegiac inflection

---

[73] Knox (1986a) 12–13; Rosati (1999) 241–43.

[74] For the preeminence of love in the *Metamorphoses*, see Fränkel (1945) 78; Otis (1970); Galinsky (1975) 31–40, 97; Davis (1983).

[75] Conte (1994) 124.

[76] Translation from Miller (1977) 83.

[77] On the funerary formula *hic situs est*, see Bömer (1969) 325; Moore-Blunt (1977) 71.

[78] See Hinds (1987a) 103–4, 160 nn. 13–14, with examples and bibliography. The Roman elegists frequently include funerary epigrams in their verse: Tib.

which Ovid amplifies in the following lines as the dead youth's father, mother, and sisters abandon themselves to grief (2.329–43). The elegiac tone is intensified by Ovid's use of vocabulary drawn from the *sermo amatorius* (*miserabilis, amens, lacrimae, fouit, fletus, querellas*). An elegiac continuity even links the Heliades' lamentation for Phaethon (*querellas,* 2.342; *plangorem dederant,* 2.346) with their plaintive wonder at their transformation into poplar trees (*questa est,* 2.347; *dolet,* 2.352), and underwrites the parallel between the tears the Heliades weep for their brother (*fletus,* 2.340; *lacrimas,* 2.341) and the "tears" of amber that flow from the poplars (*inde fluunt lacrimae, stillataque sole rigescunt/de ramis electra nouis,* 2.364–65).[79]

Almost every episode in the *Metamorphoses* repays analysis in elegiac terms. Teiresias's arbitration of the dispute between Jupiter and Juno at 3.316–38, for example, combines a (pseudo)-Hesiodic and Nicandrian subject, the double sex-change of Teiresias (Hes. *Melampodia,* fr. 275 M–W; Nic. *apud* Ant. Lib. *Met.* 17), with the divine comedy of Homeric epic, the whole couched in the legal rhetoric of Ovid's day;[80] but in our poet's hands this epic material takes on a distinctly elegiac cast.[81] Having laid aside his (epic) cares, the ruler of the cosmos indulges in frivolous discussion with his consort over which gender enjoys greater sexual pleasure:

> forte Iouem memorant diffusum nectare curas
> seposuisse graues uacuaque agitasse remissos
> cum Iunone iocos et 'maior uestra profecto est,
> quam quae contingit maribus' dixisse 'uoluptas' (3.318–21).

> Once, they say, Jove, relaxed by nectar, laid aside his weighty cares and teased Juno, at her leisure, with casual jokes; he said, "Your sexual pleasure is, indeed, greater than that which comes to males."

An elegiac theme *par excellence, uoluptas* holds programmatic sway over Ovid's *Amores* (Epigr. 3).[82] The trivial subject of the jocular dispute

1.3.55–56, 3.2.29–30; Prop. 2.13.35–36, 4.7.85–86; Ov. *Am.* 2.6.61–62, *Her.* 2.147–48, 7.195–96, 14.129–30, *F.* 3.549–50, *Tr.* 3.3.73–76.

[79] Ovid extends the play with elegiac convention in the final pendant to the Phaethon episode, the transformation of his relative Cycnus into a swan, by combining the themes of erotic love and funerary lament: see Keith (1992a) 140–45, with bibliography.

[80] See Coleman (1990). On legal terminology in Ovid, see Kenney (1969).

[81] O'Hara (1996a) discusses an elegiac poem of uncertain date on Teiresias's (six) sex-changes.

[82] Ov. *Am.* 1.4.47, 1.10.35, 2.10.25, 3.4.31: see McKeown 2:5–6.

(*lite iocosa*, 3.332), moreover, suggests the frivolous tone of Ovid's wanton elegiac Muse.[83] Juno, however, takes Teiresias's adverse verdict more seriously than the joke warrants, and punishes the judge with blindness (3.333–35). Her overreaction can be read on one level as a grand epic disavowal of elegiac levity, in accordance with the relentless anger the goddess displays in the *Aeneid*. Jupiter, however, lightens the punishment, thereby restoring the playful (elegiac) tone of the narrative (*poenam . . . leuauit honore*, 3.338).

Teiresias connects the divine dispute with the following tale of Narcissus (3.339–510), a locus classicus for analysis of erotic themes in the *Metamorphoses*.[84] The tale is ostensibly introduced to illustrate the seer's acquisition of prophetic power, a mise-en-scène that allows Ovid to accommodate oracular discourse to his hexameters: *de quo consultus, an esset/tempora maturae uisurus longa senectae,/fatidicus uates 'si se non nouerit' inquit* ("consulted about Narcissus, whether he would see a long period of ripe old age, the destiny-dealing seer said, 'if he should not know himself'," 3.346–48). The participle *consultus* recalls Teiresias's adjudication of the dispute between Jupiter and Juno,[85] while the seer's response is couched in the enigmatic language of the Delphic oracle whose motto (γνῶθι σεαυτόν) he echoes and eroticizes by playing on the sexual connotations of *nosco* and *cognosco*.[86]

In the course of his erotic career, Narcissus assumes the characteristics of both beloved and lover. His beauty makes him sought after by both sexes, but he spurns all advances with the conventional *duritia* of the elegiac beloved:

> multi illum iuuenes, multae cupiere puellae;
> sed fuit in tenera tam dura superbia forma,
> nulli illum iuuenes, nullae tetigere puellae (3.353–55).

> Many youths and maidens desired him; but there was such unyielding pride in his slender form, no youths nor maids touched him.

Ovid here adapts a floral image from Catullan (hexameter) epithalamium (62.42–44), itself modelled on Callimachean elegy (*Aet.* 3, fr.

---

[83] *Musa proterua*, *Rem.* 362; cf. *Tr.* 2.354, 3.2.6.

[84] Kenney (1972) 41; Davis (1983) 84–97; Knox (1986a) 19–23, 32–33; Fabre-Serris (1995) 182–89; Rosati (1997), with bibliography. *Contra*, Heinze (1919) 126 [= (1960) 400]; Bömer (1969) 538.

[85] Coleman (1990) 573–75 discusses Ovid's characterization of Teiresias as a jurisconsult.

[86] Fränkel (1945) 213 n. 30; Knox (1986a) 20–21.

67.9–10 Pf.; fr. 69 Pf.), in subtle anticipation of Narcissus's trans-
formation into a flower.[87] The responsion of 3.353 and 3.355 her-
alds the interrelated themes of echo and reflection explored in the
episode,[88] and may also evoke the regular alternation of hexameter
and pentameter lines in the elegiac couplet.[89] The central line com-
ments self-consciously on the elegiac provenance of the theme:
Narcissus's delicate beauty (*tenera forma*) is the very embodiment of
Ovidian elegiac form.[90]

The scene with Echo, in which she assumes the lineaments of the
elegiac lover, illustrates Narcissus's cruelty in the role of the beloved.
Echo rehearses the elegiac career of Apollo in Book 1 as she falls
in love with Narcissus at first sight (3.370–71), fans the flame of love
by tracking his movements (3.371–74), and longs to court him with
blandishments (3.375–76). When the opportunity she desires presents
itself, their dialogue takes the form of fragments of elegiac discourse
embedded in the hexameter texture of the *Metamorphoses*. The ele-
giac lover longs for the beloved's infrequent invitation to come (*'ueni!,'*
3.382);[91] protests her flight (*'quid' inquit/'me fugis?,'* 3.383–84);[92] desires,
but only rarely achieves, admission to her presence (*'adest,'* 3.380;
'huc coeamus,' 3.386),[93] let alone sexual congress (*'coeamus,'* 3.387);[94]
but repeatedly hopes for the opportunity (*'sit tibi copia nostri!,'* 3.391).[95]
Echo's final transformation from body into voice, moreover, literal-
izes the elegiac metaphor of wasting away from love (*extenuant uigiles
corpus miserabile curae/adducitque cutem macies*, 3.396–97) in a passage
that employs the diction of the *sermo amatorius* to sketch the refined
poetics of Callimachean program.[96]

Narcissus's habitual arrogance towards his admirers prompts a
spurned lover to ask that he too experience frustration in love, a

---

[87] Fränkel (1945) 213 n. 31; Davis (1983) 88; Knox (1986a) 21; Rosati (1983) 28
n. 63, (1997) 167–69. On the seductive associations of the narcissus flower, see
Rosati (1983) 14–15.
[88] Hardie (1988).
[89] Cf. Sharrock (1990); differently, Hinds (1998) 6–8.
[90] Ov. *Am.* 3.15.1, *Ars* 1.7, *Tr.* 3.3.73, 4.10.1.
[91] Prop. 2.25.2, 3.23.15; Ov. *Am.* 1.11.24, *Her.* 1.2, 19.1.
[92] Prop. 1.8.38, 1.17.1, 2.30.1–2; Tib. 1.8.61–62, 1.9.74; Ov. *Am.* 2.19.36.
[93] Prop. 1.14.23, Ov. *Am.* 2.16.12.
[94] Ov. *Her.* 19.67, *Ars* 2.615, *Rem.* 33.
[95] Prop. 2.20.24, 2.33.44, 3.8.39; Tib. 2.3.77: see Bömer (1969) 547.
[96] Cf. Ov. *Am.* 1.6.5–6, with McKeown 2:126–27. See also Knox (1986a) 22–23,
and 26–27 nn. 64–66, on Narcissus's final transformation.

prayer answered by the elegiac goddess Nemesis.[97] His strange passion for his own reflection results in his simultaneous assumption of the roles of lover and beloved. Like Echo and Apollo, he falls in love at first sight (3.416) and dwells admiringly on his beloved's wonderful beauty (3.418–24). Ovid emphasizes his dual role in the erotic contract through a series of active-passive verbal pairs (*qui* **probat,** *ipse* **probatur,**/*dumque* **petit, petitur,** *pariterque* **accendit** *et* **ardet,** 3.425–26). Narcissus's monologue rehearses a series of elegiac conceits: the cruelty of the beloved (3.442, 477) who rejects his lover's advances (3.454–56); the lover's recourse to the woods (3.443–45) where he wastes away from love (3.445), his unwanted separation from his beloved (3.446–53), the flame of love (3.464), and the madness of his passion (3.350, 479); lovers' secret signals (3.460), and the death of two in one (3.473).[98] Knox has shown that Ovid's lexical choices in the episode are consistent with elegiac practice,[99] and we may note in addition the pervasive deployment of the *topoi* of Callimachean poetics, from the isolation and purity of the pool's setting (3.407–12),[100] to the youth's posture (*paulum* . . . *leuatus,* 3.440), the barrier separating him from his beloved (*exigua prohibemur aqua,* 3.450), his ripping of his clothing (*deduxit,* 3.480), and his final wasting away from love (*attenuatus amore,* 3.489).

The amatory themes and elegiac style of the episode emphasize Ovid's debt to erotic elegy in shaping a tale for which we cannot identify his specific source(s).[101] Particularly vexed is the question of the relationship of Echo's story to Narcissus's, for nowhere in earlier classical literature is the connection between the two extant, although a Callimachean epigram (in elegiac couplets) links a much admired youth with Echo in a subtle articulation of poetic program (*Epigr.* 28 Pf.). Hardie, however, has suggested that the myth of Hylas, a popular subject of Hellenistic and neoteric epic, "helped to shape the Ovidian narrative," for Hylas is another "beautiful boy who wanders until he stops at a fatal pool."[102] Of particular significance for

---

[97] On Nemesis, see Murgatroyd (1994) xvii–xviii.

[98] On the two-in-one motif see Kenney (1972) 42; Knox (1986a) 21–22.

[99] Knox (1986a) 19–23, 32–33.

[100] Cf. *Aet.* 1 fr. 1.25–34; Call. *Hymn* 2.105–12, with Williams (1978) 85–97. Segal (1969) 45–48 discusses the sexual symbolism of the setting of Narcissus's metamorphosis.

[101] Bömer (1969) 537–38; Rosati (1983) 1–20, with bibliography.

[102] Hardie (1988) 77. For the myth, see Ap. Rhod. 1.1207–72; Theocr. 13; Nic.

Ovid's Narcissus is Nicander's version of the Hylas myth in his *Transformations* (not discussed by Hardie), which describes the nymphs' transformation of Hylas into an echo out of fear that Hercules will discover him among them (Nic. *apud* Ant. Lib. 26.4). Nicander thereby makes explicit the connection between Hylas and Echo which remains implicit but audible in other treatments of the myth.[103]

The *locus amoenus* setting of Narcissus's erotic encounter is unusual in Roman elegy, however, and especially in Ovidian elegy, which celebrates the genre's cosmopolitan outlook (*Ars* 3.121–28).[104] More typical in this regard is the urban context in which Pyramus and Thisbe pursue their love affair (4.55–166). Ovid's internal narrator, a daughter of Minyas, opens the tale by emphasizing its metropolitan setting:

> Pyramus et Thisbe, iuuenum pulcherrimus alter,
> altera, quas Oriens habuit, praelata puellis,
> contiguas tenuere domos, ubi dicitur altam
> coctilibus muris cinxisse Semiramis urbem (4.55–58).

> Pyramus and Thisbe—the one the most handsome of youths, the other the most beautiful of the maidens whom the Orient contained—dwelt in neighboring houses, where Semiramis is said to have girt a lofty city with brick walls.

The reference to Semiramis's foundation of Babylon gestures towards the narrative context of the tale in Ovid's "Thebaid," briefly recapitulating the episode's frame in ktistic epic, but the Minyeid highlights elegiac conventions against this urban backdrop.[105] Although the youngsters' love is mutual, their parents' refusal to sanction marriage allows Ovid to sketch their love as an illicit affair prosecuted in the secret signals and clandestine meetings of elegiac lovers (4.61–64, 69–70, 83–88, 93–96). Ovid even includes a miniature paraclausithyron in the speech the young lovers address to the wall that separates them (4.73–77). When, however, the young lovers abandon the conventional urban setting of elegy for the world of untamed nature beyond the city walls, their love takes a tragic turn.

---

apud Ant. Lib. *Met.* 26; Virg. *Ecl.* 6.43–44; Prop. 1.20; cf. Ov. *Ars* 2.110, *Naiadumque* **tener** *crimine raptus* **Hylas**.

[103] Ap. Rhod. 1.1248–49; Theocr. *Id.* 13.58–60; Virg. *Ecl.* 6.43–44; Prop. 1.20.48–50. For visual similarities, see *LIMC* s.v. "Hylas."

[104] Due (1974) 59–61.

[105] Perraud (1983–84); Knox (1986a) 35–37; cf. Due (1974) 126–27.

"Pyramus and Thisbe" is the first of the tales narrated by the daughters of Minyas, who scorn participation in the new rites of Bacchus to stay home and ply their woolwork. Despite their ostensible devotion to the chaste Minerva, the three sisters narrate tales whose keynote is *amor.* "Pyramus and Thisbe";[106] the "loves of the Sun," prefaced by the adulterous affair of Venus and Mars;[107] and "Salmacis and Hermaphroditus."[108] Knox has demonstrated Ovid's pervasive use of the diction, style, and themes of erotic elegy in the sisters' tales,[109] while Myers, noting their aetiological motivation, has related them to Callimachus's *Aetia.*[110] The delicate artistry of their textile work, emphasized by the poet (4.34–36, 54, 275, 389–90, 394–98), also reflects their Callimachean subtlety.[111]

Again, however, Ovid complicates the elegiac associations of his themes by setting the tales in the context of Dionysiac ritual and by reworking prominent passages of Homeric epic. Leuconoe's tale of Venus and Mars is the theme of a song performed by the bard Demodocus in *Odyssey* 8 (266–369). Ovid had already exploited the story for elegiac *color* in *Ars* 2.561–88, and here offers a refined Callimachean version of the Homeric tale, abbreviating it and recasting it as a preface to the obscure amatory and aetiological tales that follow.[112] Alcithoe too adapts Homer in "Salmacis and Hermaphroditus," for her characterization of Hermaphroditus exhibits points of contact with Odysseus, even before she recasts Odysseus's supplication of Nausicaa (*Od.* 6.149–59) in Salmacis's lewd proposition of Hermaphroditus (4.320–28).[113] Ovid exploits and extends the erotic content of his Homeric models by grafting the codes of Roman elegiac discourse onto them.

Rosati has recently argued that the Minyeid episode as a whole elaborates the themes of Clymene's song in Virgil's Fourth *Georgic,* which we have already considered as a model for Ovid's *Metamorphoses*

---

[106] On the sources, see Bömer (1976) 33–36; Duke (1971); Knox (1989).

[107] On the sources, see Bömer (1976) 67–69, 75–77, and 95; Castellani (1980); Baldo (1986) 124–28.

[108] On the sources, see Bömer (1976) 100–105; Baldo (1986) 128–29; Labate (1993); Robinson (1999).

[109] Knox (1986a) 35–37, 41; cf. Labate (1993) on Alcithoe's tale.

[110] Myers (1994a) 34, 79–80, 152.

[111] Rosati (1999) 243–48.

[112] On the Callimachean stylistic vocabulary in the episode, see Janan (1994) 435.

[113] Keith (1999b) 216–17; cf. Labate (1993) 53–54.

in its entirety.[114] This attractive suggestion identifies a Virgilio-Hesiodic model for the Homeric amatory tales narrated by the sisters, and may also account for the novelistic features of the first sister's tale. Drawing attention to the activity of Clymene's audience in the Virgilian passage, nymphs spinning richly-dyed Milesian wool and listening to tales of love, Rosati suggests that "[w]e may also think of 'Milesian tales' to go with Milesian wool, risqué erotic stories."[115] The romance *color* of "Pyramus and Thisbe" lends support to this hypothesis, for Ovid exploits conventional features of the ancient novel throughout the episode, from the opening conjunction of the names of the young lovers, their superlative beauty, the fabulous Eastern setting, and the reference to Semiramis (legendary queen of Babylon and heroine of the Ninus-romance), through the initial sketch of the innocence of the love-struck teenagers and the obstacles to their love, to their determination to marry one another, their inadvertent separation, and the apparent death of the heroine.[116]

3. *Tragedy*

The Dionysiac context in which the Minyeides spin and tell stories complicates the generic interplay in this section of the poem still further, and introduces the final thread of my discussion. The impious daughters of Minyas are otherwise known only from three Greek writers of imperial date,[117] although we know that the story was treated by Nicander in his *Transformations* (Nic. *apud* Ant. Lib. 10). The Greek mythographers relate that the three daughters of Minyas were excessively devoted to woolworking and its patroness, Minerva, and reviled the other women of Orchomenus for abandoning the city and going off to the mountains to celebrate the rites of Dionysus; the spurned god grew angry and caused them to go mad, appearing to them successively as maiden, bull, lion, and leopard; at the same time their looms began to drip with milk and wine. In their madness the sisters drew lots to contribute a sacrifice to the god, and when the lot fell to Leucippe, they tore her son Hippasus to

---

[114] Rosati (1999) 242.
[115] Rosati (1999) 242 n. 6.
[116] Due (1974) 123–27; Newlands (1986); Holzberg (1988).
[117] Plut. *Quaest. Gr.* 38; Ant. Lib. *Met.* 10; Ael. *VH* 3.42.

pieces, then rushed off to join the maenads in the mountains, where
Mercury finally transformed the sisters into birds. Tales of divinity
spurned are frequent in Greek literature, of course, but are partic-
ularly characteristic of the mythic material associated with Dionysus
and purveyed to the audiences of Greek tragedy; it has therefore
been suggested that Aeschylus's lost Dionysiac tragedy *Xantriai* ("Wool-
carders") dealt with the daughters of Minyas.[118] Since Ovid's only
other foray out of elegiac composition was in tragedy, it will prove
worthwhile to examine his debt to tragedy in the final section of this
inquiry.[119]

Ovid contrasts the Minyeides' impious rejection of Bacchus at the
outset of Book 4 with the piety of the Theban women, who invoke
the god in lengthy recitation of his titles:

> turaque dant Bacchumque uocant Bromiumque Lyaeumque
> ignigenamque satumque iterum solumque bimatrem;
> additur his Nyseus indetonsusque Thyoneus
> et cum Lenaeo genialis consitor uuae
> Nycteliusque Eleleusque parens et Iacchus et Euhan,
> et quae praeterea per Graias plurima gentes
> nomina, Liber, habes . . . (4.11–17).

> They bring incense and invoke Bacchus as Bromius and Lyaeus, fire-
> born, twice-born, who alone has two mothers; to these titles are added
> Nyseus and unshorn Thyoneus, along with Lenaeus, sower of the festive
> grape, Nyctelius, father Eleleus, Iacchus, and Euhan, and the very many
> names besides which you have, Liber, among the Greek peoples . . .

Ovid here assimilates the Theban women worshipping the new god
Bacchus to tragic choruses of Bacchantes hymning the god of drama
(αἰεὶ Διόνυσον ὑμνήσω, Eur. *Ba.* 71), for they invoke the god in the
hymnic style and ritual language familiar from tragedy.[120] A fragment
of Ennian tragedy furnishes a model for the passage: *his erat in ore*
Bromius, his Bacchus pater; / illis Lyaeus uitis inuentor sacrae. / tum pariter Euhan
<euhoe euhoe>[121] *Euhium / ignotus iuuenum coetus alterna uice / inibat alacris*

---

[118] Seaford (1996) 26 nn. 6, 8, 9, and 37 n. 49.

[119] On tragedy in the *Met.*, see Lafaye (1904) 141–66; D'Anna (1959); Due (1974)
24–25; Currie (1981); Barchiesi (1993) 340–53; Gildenhard and Zissos (1999b);
Curley (1999).

[120] D. Curley notes (*per litteras*) that "Ovid's catalogue of Dionysiac epithets here
recalls the *parodos* of Euripides' *Bacchae*, which is itself an annotated history of the
god."

[121] On the text, see Jocelyn (1967) 269.

Bacchico insultans modo (*trag.* LII 120–24 Jocelyn). Ovid employs all four Ennian titles of the god in his hymn, and signals his debt by preserving their initial and final positions in his own catalogue. The shape of the Ennian phrase *Lyaeus uitis inuentor sacrae*, though without overlap in diction, serves as a model (perhaps mediated through elegy; cf. Tib. 2.3.63, Ov. *Am.* 1.3.11) for the construction of Ovid's half-line *Lenaeo genialis consitor uuae* (4.14). Even the context of the Ennian lines is relevant, for they are attributed to the tragedy *Athamas*, whose hero is the subject of the episode immediately following the Minyeides' transformation.

Ovid nonetheless drastically curtails the Dionysian elements of the tale: although the sisters' transformation into bats remains the god's punishment for their impiety, they neither go mad nor indulge in Bacchic rending of flesh. Moreover, both their tales and the quiet domestic setting in which they tell them contrast strikingly with the frenzied rites of Bacchus celebrated by the rest of the Theban women. Yet the first of the sisters, at least, deploys Bacchic themes and imagery in her tale as Ovid weaves an intricate web of connections between the inset narrative and its frame.

I have already discussed "Pyramus and Thisbe" in relation to the generic conventions of elegy and novel, but the tale also displays considerable thematic and imagistic overlap with the sphere of Dionysus.[122] An early example is the superlative beauty of the adolescent lovers (4.55–56, quoted above). Outstanding beauty is a conventional feature of the heroes and heroines of ancient romance, but at the beginning of the book it is Bacchus whose superlative beauty the Theban women hymn, in terms applicable to both sexes (*tu puer aeternus . . . tibi . . . uirgineum caput est*, 4.18–20; cf. 3.607). The first Minyeid rejects the adolescent beauty of the dangerous god of the theater in favor of a beautiful pair of adolescent lovers drawn from elegy and romance, but the ominous presence of Dionysus constrains her narrative increasingly forcefully as it proceeds.

Pyramus and Thisbe decide to elude their parents and meet by night under a mulberry tree near the tomb of Ninus outside the city (4.84–95, 99, 111).[123] Nocturnal action is another staple of the romance genre, but the night setting is also a prominent feature of Dionysiac worship, to which Ovid alludes in the god's epithet Nyctelius (4.15).

---

[122] Curley (1999) 217–20 shows "how fundamental tragic coding is to the episode."
[123] On the setting, and its sexual symbolism, see Segal (1969) 50–51.

Outside the comparative safety of the city and their parents' guardian-ship, the youngsters encounter the terrors of untamed nature, a more obviously Dionysiac theme, in the form of a lioness which comes from the kill to slake her thirst at a nearby spring (4.96–98). Bacchus is associated with wild cats both in the preceding book (3.668–69) and in the hymn that opens the fourth (4.25), and as early as the Homeric *Hymn to Dionysus* the god himself is represented as taking the form of a lion to threaten the sailors who have kidnapped him (*h. Hom.* 7.44–48).[124] Moreover, the "sure traces of a wild beast" (*ues-tigia . . . certa ferae*, 4.105–6) Pyramus sees when he arrives at the ren-dezvous anticipate the "phantoms of savage beasts" (*saeuarum simulacra . . . ferarum*, 4.404; cf. 3.668) whose howling terrorizes the Minyeides just before the god transforms them into bats.

More Dionysiac still is the suggestion of dismemberment (σπαραγμός) and eating of raw flesh (ὠμοφαγία) in Thisbe's torn and bloodied cloak (4.103–4, 107–8), and Pyramus's despairing invitation to the lions to rend and devour his body (*'nostrum diuellite corpus / et scelerata fero consumite uiscera morsu / . . . leones!*,' 4.112–14). Gruesome descrip-tions of blood and intimations of mangled flesh recur throughout the episode, from the bloody mouth of the lioness to the blood-spattered tree under which Pyramus kills himself (4.125–27, 160–61), and Thisbe's death by a sword still warm from Pyramus's blood (4.163). The most spectacularly bloody scene is the graphic description of Pyramus's self-inflicted death:

'accipe nunc' inquit 'nostri quoque sanguinis haustus!'
quoque erat accinctus, demisit in ilia ferrum,
nec mora, feruenti moriens e uulnere traxit.
ut iacuit resupinus humo, cruor emicat alte,
non aliter quam cum uitiato fistula plumbo
scinditur et tenui stridente foramine longas
eiaculatur aquas atque ictibus aera rumpit (4.118–24).

"Now," he said, "drink my blood too!" And he plunged the sword which he wore into his groin, and without delay, dying, drew it from the warm wound. As he lay on his back on the ground, his blood spurts high, just as when a pipe with a crack in the lead is split, and spurts long streams of water through the slender hissing opening, and strikes the air with its jets.[125]

---

[124] For Dionysus's association with the lion, see Dodds (1960) xviii.
[125] On the Lucretian overtones of this simile, see Newlands (1986).

His twitching limbs are still writhing on the bloody ground when Thisbe arrives moments later (*tremebunda uidet pulsare cruentum/ membra solum*, 4.133–34).

If Thisbe's apparent death lies fully within the generic parameters of the ancient novel, Pyramus's real death breaks sharply with novelistic conventions to introduce a familiar motif of tragedy, the suicide of a protagonist.[126] Beyond Dionysus's traditional patronage of the tragic drama, we may relate the manner of Pyramus's death here to two specifically Bacchic contexts. What is generally taken to be a characteristically Ovidian excess in the simile has an intriguing parallel in Ennius's description of the suicide of Ajax in his tragedy of the same name: *misso sanguine tepido tullii efflantes uolant* ("with gushing warm blood the spouting jets fly," Enn. *trag.* XII Jocelyn).[127] The Minyeid's use of the unpoetic *foramine* (4.123), moreover, recalls the poet's description of the boxwood flute among the paraphernalia of Dionysiac worship (*concauaque aera sonant longoque* **foramine buxus**, 4.30), as does her remark that Thisbe grows "paler than boxwood" at the sight of her mortally wounded lover (*oraque* **buxo**/*pallidiora gerens*, 4.134–35). Verbal details evocative of the rites of Bacchic worship and the larger themes of Dionysiac myth repeatedly intrude into the tale and suggest the god's diffuse penetration of the Minyeides' household long before the decisive revelation of his godhead.

The episode has traditionally been held to constitute a digression from the overarching narrative of the foundation and precipitate decline of Thebes which spans *Met.* 3.1–4.603, because it is set at some distance from Thebes in Boeotian Orchomenus and concerns a family unrelated to the House of Cadmus. But Ovid's play with tragic intertexts relates the episode closely to its context, for the "Thebaid" in which it is embedded comprises a series of narratives drawn from the tragic repertoire: Cadmus, Actaeon, Semele, Pentheus, Athamas, and Ino.[128] Although Ovid's Theban sequence is framed as a mini-foundation epic, the tales which constitute it exemplify the

---

[126] Katsouris (1976); Seidensticker (1982); Zeitlin (1996) 350–52.

[127] D. Curley adds (*per litteras*), "the spurting blood, in its vivid and fertile richness, evokes the gushing liquids of many kinds found in Dionysiac myths."

[128] Hardie (1990); Gildenhard and Zissos (1999b) 170–76. For plays on Dionysiac themes, see Dodds (1960) xxviii–xxxiii; Seaford (1996) 26 nn. 8–9; Flower (2000) n. 27. I note in addition Aeschylus's *Toxotides* (on Actaeon), *Athamas*; Sophocles' *Athamas A* and *B*; Euripides' *Ino*.

themes not of epic but of tragedy, while oracles and prophecies, two kinds of riddling utterance characteristic not only of epic but especially of tragic narrative, articulate the action.

Ovid reworks the opening of the *Aeneid* in his portrait of the exiled Cadmus wandering the Mediterranean before consulting the oracle at Delphi to learn where to settle (3.6–9), on the model of the exiled Aeneas consulting the oracle of Apollo at Delos (*Aen.* 3.84–89).[129] But he follows even more closely Euripides' account of Cadmus's foundation of Thebes (*Phoen.* 638–75),[130] and explicitly signals his engagement with tragedy soon after when Cadmus, having killed the snake that attacked his men, hears a disembodied voice prophesy his own transformation into a snake ('*quid, Agenore nate, peremptum/serpentem spectas? et tu spectabere serpens,*' 3.97–98). Spoken by Minerva, this prophecy echoes that given to Cadmus by Dionysus as *deus ex machina* at the conclusion of Euripides' *Bacchae* (δράκων γενήσῃ μεταβαλών, *Ba.* 1330). A famous simile in the following scene confirms the generic significance of the allusion. Like Virgil, who marks an important debt to tragedy in the Dido episode by comparing her to characters from the tragic stage (*Aen.* 4.469–73), Ovid signals the central importance of tragic conventions in his "Thebaid" with a simile, comparing the birth of the Spartoi, the Sown Men who emerge from the earth after Cadmus sows the slain serpent's teeth, to the figures represented on the stage curtain which rise from the ground when the stage curtain is raised (3.111–14).[131] The poet thereby "glosses" his literary "operations outside the epic code."[132]

The tales that follow engage tragic themes and intertexts with increasing intensity. The first of the disasters to come upon the House of Cadmus, Actaeon's fatal fascination with the hunt, recalls the hunts and hunters of the Athenian stage, both literal (Hippolytus, the Eumenides) and metaphorical (Oedipus).[133] A series of fatal encounters with the divine—Actaeon with Diana; Semele, Athamas, and Ino with Juno; Pentheus and the Minyeides with Dionysus—dramatizes

---

[129] Cf. Ovid's reprise of the motif in Pentheus's speech, *profugos posuistis . . . penates* (3.539), with Hardie (1990) 226–27.

[130] Accius adapted Euripides' play for the Roman stage.

[131] Hardie (1990) 226 n. 14.

[132] Barchiesi (1993) 353.

[133] Euripides alludes to Actaeon throughout the *Bacchae*: see Dodds (1960) 113–14; Seaford (1996) 179. On Ovid's Actaeon episode and its relation to tragedy, see Gildenhard and Zissos (1999b) 172–74.

the conflict between man and god that pervades Athenian tragedy. The quintessential tragic theme of blindness and insight informs every tale in the sequence, including even the otherwise anomalous Narcissus episode.[134] Finally, the Aristotelian pattern of recognition and reversal structures each episode starting with the framing tale of Cadmus himself, who kills a serpent to found the city of Thebes but ends by going into exile and becoming a serpent.

Ovid's focus on the Dionysian themes and primal subjects of Greek tragedy in this section of his poem emerges still more clearly from comparison with the conventional treatment of Thebes in ancient epic. Theban epos seems traditionally to have avoided material associated with the arch anti-Apollonian Dionysus in favor of the more martial themes of the Seven against Thebes and the Epigoni, and Propertius's allusions to the *Thebaid* of Ponticus (1.7.1–2, 17–18) suggest that contemporary Augustan epic shared this bias.[135] Ovid, by contrast, saturates his Theban narrative with tales drawn from the tragic repertoire and specifically associated with Dionysus, while avoiding the martial subjects of Theban epic.[136]

Ovid's treatment of Pentheus is particularly rich in tragic intertexts.[137] A popular tragic theme, Pentheus's story was most famously told in Euripides' *Bacchae* which Ovid imitates in a number of places.[138] Teiresias's warning that Pentheus will regret his contempt for the prophet (3.517–25) functions as a prologue to the episode like that spoken by Dionysus himself in the *Bacchae* (1–63), while Ovid announces the arrival of the god (*Liber adest*, 3.528) with a brusqueness and an economy of phrasing reminiscent of the opening words of Euripides' tragedy ("Ηκω Διὸς παῖς, *Ba.* 1). The emphases on Dionysus as a new god (3.520 ~ *Ba.* 219–20, 256–57, 272) and on Actaeon as a standard of comparison for Pentheus (3.720–22 ~ *Ba.* 337–40) are also derived from Euripides.[139] Indeed, the Ovidian episode as a

---

[134] On Narcissus as a figure for Oedipus, see Gildenhard and Zissos (2000).

[135] Cf. Statius's *Thebaid*. The archaic Greek Theban cycle consisted of an *Oedipodea*, *Thebaid* (apparently treating the Seven against Thebes), and *Epigoni*: see Lesky (1966) 80–81. In the classical period, Antimachus narrated the story of Oedipus and the Seven against Thebes in Homeric style: see Wyss (1936) and Lombardi (1993).

[136] On Dionysiac myth as the original subject of tragedy, see Dodds (1960) xxviii–xxxiii; Seaford (1996) 26–52.

[137] D'Anna (1959); Otis (1970) 371–72; Currie (1981).

[138] See Bömer (1969) 570–624.

[139] Bömer (1969) 573–74.

whole is modelled generally on Euripides' play, beginning with Pentheus's hostility to the new god (3.531–61 ~ *Ba.* 215–370), his order that the imposter be apprehended (3.562–63 ~ *Ba.* 352–57), and the opposition of Cadmus and the rest of the Thebans to his actions (3.564–65 ~ *Ba.* 330–469). In addition, formal features testify to the influence of tragedy on the shape of the narrative in Ovid's use of diction and metrical effects drawn from the dramatic register,[140] high proportion of direct speech (167 of 223 lines), and temporal abridgement characteristic of tragedy (3.528, 572).[141]

The centerpiece of the Ovidian narrative, however, Pentheus's interview of Bacchus's adherent Acoetes (3.572–695), replaces the three Euripidean scenes in which Pentheus spars with the Stranger, the disguised Dionysus. Acoetes explains the origins of his devotion to the god: originally a helmsman (3.593–94), he had opposed his shipmates' capture of a divine youth and so was the only member of the crew not transformed into a dolphin by the outraged god. Ovid here rehearses the subject of the Homeric *Hymn to Dionysus*, signalling the allusion by setting the tale in the mouth of the hymn's "rightminded helmsman" (*h. Hom.* 7.49). Like the pirates of the hymn (Τυρσηνοί, *h. Hom.* 7.8), Acoetes is a Tyrrhenian (3.576) from "the Maeonian land" (*patria Maeonia est*, 3.583), a provenance that annotates Ovid's literary debt to Homer, "the son of Maeon" (*Maeonides*, *Am.* 1.15.9).[142] Ovid thus incorporates a hexameter model, the Homeric hymn, into an episode that owes its overall shape to tragedy.

The Homeric hymn, however, does not name the helmsman. Ovid takes Acoetes' name from another tragedy, Pacuvius's *Pentheus*, for which Euripides' play also provided the model. An augmentor of Servius summarizes the plot of Pacuvius's play, which corresponds closely to the action of Ovid's "Pentheus":

> Pentheus . . . sent servants to bring [Bacchus] back to him in chains; since they could not find him, they captured one of his followers, Acoetes, and brought him to Pentheus. . . . He ordered him bound

---

[140] Diction: *actutum* (3.557), with Kenney (1973) 120, Kenney, chapter 2 above, and Barchiesi (1993) 343 n. 13; *lanigeros* (3.585), an Accian coinage (*praetext.* 20); *repandus* (3.680), reminiscent of Pacuvius's celebrated description of dolphins (*Nerei repandirostrum incuruiceruicum pecus*, *trag.* 352). Unusual scansion: *quem quidem ego actutum* (3.557), with Currie (1981) 2717.

[141] Bömer (1969) 586.

[142] On the epithet, see McKeown 2:395–96.

and imprisoned, but when the doors of the prison sprang open by
themselves and Acoetes' chains fell off, Pentheus was amazed and went
to Cithaeron to watch the rites of Father Liber, and the Bacchants
dismembered him when they saw him; his mother Agave is said to
have cut off his head first, thinking him a wild animal. (Serv. *auct.* ad
Aen. 4.469)

In addition to the name of his helmsman, Ovid has taken over the
structure of the Pacuvian play for his "Pentheus."[143] He thus indulges
in two of his favorite compositional strategies, alluding to his Euripidean
model both directly and indirectly through the Pacuvian intermediary,
and epicizing material drawn from another literary genre, here tragedy.

In the confrontation between Pentheus and Dionysus Ovid implic-
itly inscribes a literary contest between the genres of epic and tragedy.
Pentheus overvalues his descent from Echion (3.513, 531, 701), one
of the Spartoi sprung from the teeth of the serpent of Mars, and
repeatedly contrasts his martial ancestry and morals with Dionysus's
softness and effeminacy (3.531–37, 540, 553–56). When Pentheus
goes to Cithaeron, Ovid compares him to a horse fired to battle by
the war trumpet:

> ut fremit acer equus, cum bellicus aere canoro
> signa dedit tubicen pugnaeque adsumit amorem,
> Penthea sic ictus longis ululatibus aether
> mouit, et audito clamore recanduit ira (3.704–7).

> As a keen horse rages, when the war-trumpet of sonorous bronze
> sounds the signal, and he is fired by love of battle, so was Pentheus
> stirred by the long-drawn cries ringing in the ether, and his anger kin-
> dled at the sound of the clash.

The simile, drawn from martial epic (Hom. *Il.* 6.506–11, 15.263–68;
Ap. Rhod. 3.1259–62; Enn. *Ann.* 535–39 Sk.; Virg. *Aen.* 11.492–97),
stamps Pentheus as a heroic figure, especially in conjunction with
the anger that traditionally motivates epic action (3.577, 693). Pentheus,
however, is unable to sustain the role of epic hero to which he
aspires, for on Mount Cithaeron he finds himself in the theater not
of war but of Dionysus: *monte fere medio est, cingentibus ultima siluis,/
purus ab arboribus,* **spectabilis** *undique, campus* (3.708–9). Ovid's empha-
sis on the visibility of the setting of Pentheus's demise, continued in
the following lines where the watching Pentheus is himself the object

---

[143] D'Anna (1959); Currie (1981) 2716–18.

of others' gaze (*hic* **oculis** *illum* **cernentem** *sacra profanis/prima* **uidet**, 3.710–11; cf. 3.725), cannot fail to evoke the Greek θέατρον, literally "place for seeing," the setting in which tragedy was staged.[144]

The episode culminates in Pentheus's dismemberment at the hands of his mother and aunts, in a mythical enactment of Dionysiac *sparagmos* punningly anticipated in Teiresias's prophecy:

> quem nisi templorum fueris dignatus honore,
> mille lacer *spargere*[145] locis et sanguine siluas
> foedabis matremque tuam matrisque sorores (3.521–23).

> Unless you deign to honor him with temples, you will be torn apart and scattered in a thousand places, and you will befoul the woods, your mother, and your mother's sisters, with your blood.

At the end of the episode the poet restores Pentheus to the fold of epic with the application of a famous Homeric simile (*Il.* 6.146–49, 21.464–66) to the scene:

> non citius frondes autumni frigore tactas
> iamque male haerentes alta rapit arbore uentus,
> quam sunt membra uiri manibus direpta nefandis (3.729–31).

> The wind does not snatch from a lofty tree its leaves, touched by autumn's chill and now scarcely attached, more swiftly than the man's limbs were torn apart by their impious hands.

Ovid illustrates the close relationship between the genres, attested by Aeschylus's comparison of tragedy to "slices from the banquet of Homer" (Ath. *Deipn.* 8.347c), in an epic "embrace" of the tragic hero's dismembered limbs.

Although Ovid's "Thebaid" is constructed throughout by reference to the genre of tragedy, the intensity of his engagement with the tragic code increases as the narrative moves towards and decreases as it moves away from the death and dismemberment of Pentheus, the central panel of the "Thebaid" and the primal scene that stages the "dramatic basis of Greek tragedy."[146] Moreover, this tragic program is framed by an epic, indeed Virgilian, narrative of city foundation, in Cadmus's foundation of and exile from Thebes. Ovid underscores

---

[144] For a different analysis of spectacle in the episode, see Feldherr (1997).

[145] I am grateful to Sarah Sheehan for drawing my attention to the pun. Ovid's implied etymology is proposed by Frisk (1970) 757, s.v. σπαράσσω.

[146] Zeitlin (1996).

the continuing relevance of epic norms by characterizing Pentheus as a would-be epic hero (cf. the recurrence of the "one against many" theme, 3.513, 715) and by adapting a Homeric hymn at the center of the episode. The ease with which the primal hero of Greek tragedy is assimilated to the epic code suggests Ovid's recognition of thematic overlap between epic and drama.[147]

Burrow has observed that Ovid annotates his debt to Virgilian epic in the final episode of the "Thebaid" with a description of the underworld and its inhabitants:

> errant exsangues sine corpore et ossibus umbrae,
> parsque forum celebrant, pars imi tecta tyranni,
> pars aliquas artes, antiquae imitamina uitae (4.443–45).

> Bloodless shades wander, without body and bones; some throng the forum, others the halls of the underworld tyrant, others pursue their erstwhile occupations, imitations of the old life.

The dead who imitate their former life evoke on a metaliterary level the Virgilian traces in Ovid's poem, literary imitations of their former (Virgilian) life.[148] This stimulating suggestion nicely captures Ovid's self-confident play with sources and genres in the *Metamorphoses*, as he thematizes a poetics of transformation in self-reflexive commentary on his models. Ovid adapts a wide array of literary sources from many different genres in the hexameter fabric of the *Metamorphoses*, from the formal alignment of the poem with the thematic and stylistic codes of grand epic through the sustained use of elegiac and tragic codes down to the highly localized use of philosophical, religious, hymnic, funerary, legal, oracular, and novelistic modes. As universal history, the *Metamorphoses* is also a universal literary history.[149] In this we see the subtlety and sophistication of Ovid's foray into epic. By the Hellenistic period Homer was regarded as the fountainhead of all literary genres, a view which enjoyed wide circulation in Roman literary circles long before its canonization in Quintilian (*IO* 10.1.46).[150] A writer of elegy and tragedy, Ovid had already had

---

[147] Cf. Curley (1999) *passim*.
[148] Burrow (1999) 276.
[149] Lafaye (1904) 89–90; Wilkinson (1955) 450 n. 31; Kenney (1986) xviii; Solodow (1988) 18–19.
[150] Williams (1978) 85–89.

occasion to explore those genres' debts to epic. This process of generic exploration culminates in his comprehensive summation of epos with the return of all literary streams to their generic origin in the *Metamorphoses*.[151]

---

[151] Cf. Galinsky (1998) 326–27.

CHAPTER NINE

NARRATIVE TECHNIQUES AND NARRATIVE STRUCTURES IN THE *METAMORPHOSES*

Gianpiero Rosati

1. *A Text That Mirrors Itself*

Among all the narrative works of classical antiquity, there is probably no other that, like Ovid's *Metamorphoses*, is so clearly concerned with reflecting upon itself, considering its own nature and the context which produced it, and exhibiting the mechanisms of its own functioning. The Ovidian poem narrates the story of a world in which many of the characters in their turn participate in offering narratives to a particular audience. Indeed, storytelling is one of the most frequent actions in the world of the poem, involving many characters in the most varied situations.[1]

The action which gives birth to the poem is continually replicated internally through the mediation of *mise en abyme*, a narration within a narration, which, by substituting for the voice of the external narrator that of a character internal to the diegetic world, reproduces the situation from which the text has originated. It has been estimated[2] that about a third of the length of the poem, including about 60 of the episodes (and in increasing proportion from the beginning to the end of the poem), is narrated not by the external narrator, but by about 40 internal narrators. Instead of giving us the impression that we are present at the happenings in the poem, the text continually maintains our awareness that we are hearing *narratives of events*, and insists on the function of mediation, on the filter that

---

[1] Although I shall here emphasize above all a few important episodes found in the central section of the poem (Books 5, 6, and 10), the techniques under consideration of course extend to the entire poem.

[2] Cf. Wheeler (1999), the fullest and most recent narratological study of the *Metamorphoses*, 49, 162–63, 207–10. Nagle (1989) provides a catalogue of embedded narratives.

selects those events and reconstructs them, giving them a form and a significance.

But Ovidian narratives are frequently constructed with an uncommon complexity: the internal narrator, to whom the narrator-author (let's call him "Ovid") has yielded the floor, gives it instead to a character-narrator internal to the story who himself narrates and thus periodically reproduces the narrative situation (with a new narrator who speaks to his own audience), to the point of multiplying the narrative levels as in a game of Chinese Boxes. The most complicated example (three narrative levels embedded one inside another) occurs in the fifth book, where the story of Minerva's journey to Helicon (250–678) contains the narrative delivered by one of the Muses to the goddess concerning the song-contest between the Muses themselves (represented by Calliope) and the Pierides.

Within her narrative (the rape of Proserpina and other stories: 5.341–661), Calliope in turn encloses the story of the nymph Arethusa, who narrates to the goddess Ceres her own metamorphosis into a fountain (577–641). Every change of speaker, then, introduces a new voice, which, however, is controlled by each of the voices that precede it, beginning with the primary narrator, the external narrator; and it is certainly not always easy either to preserve one's awareness of the precise narrative situation in which each story is located, or to perceive the subjective intentions or effects of distortion produced by the play among narrative voices.

In other words, the text reproduces itself in miniature, repeatedly mirroring within itself the act of its own enunciation, and the interest that this metanarrative procedure holds for an analysis of the Ovidian text is obvious. The attention given by scholars to narrative techniques and the reflexive attitude of the *Metamorphoses*, progressing from the narratological studies developed in the wake of structuralism between the beginning of the 1970s and the first half of the 80s,[3] has opened up new perspectives on the interpretation of both individual episodes and the entire poem. The poem is no longer read as a collection of mythological stories which can, if need be, be removed from their contexts and analyzed individually;[4] rather, attention to the figure of the narrator as well as to his audience and

---

[3] Cf. esp. Genette (1980); Prince (1982); Bal (1985).
[4] Wheeler (2000) vigorously emphasizes the continuity of the Ovidian poem.

consideration of the rhetorical strategy which governs their relationship allow us to reconstruct the entire narrative situation.

Besides revealing a greater semantic complexity, this diverse approach to the text often allows the modifications introduced by some narrators into the facts of the mythological tradition to be explained as intentional alterations (rather than as less well-known versions of the story), and invites us to consider the individual myth, the story narrated by a narrator, as the truth of a given character.

The many narrators (Todorov's "narrative-men")[5] are clearly surrogates for the author, and thus the awareness with which they construct their tales and the meaning that they attribute to them give us valuable information about how the primary, extradiegetic narrator ("Ovid") organizes the structure and the meaning of the entire poem. In the same way, the repeated creation of a listener (the recipient of the narrative, or the narratee) produces interpreting characters, i.e., surrogates for the reader, and thus introduces several (possible) models of interpretation.

The external, or primary, narrator of the poem, who renounces epic anonymity and who has an omniscient view, speaks freely (much more so than the narrator of the *Aeneid*) of his own era, identifying it with the Augustan age (1.1–4; 200–206). He hopes for immortal fame (15.871–79), sets up a dialogue with his Roman contemporaries, and includes among his addressees Augustus himself (1.201). The evident status of the narrator as protagonist (and in general the extraordinary profile that the narrative function has throughout the poem)[6] leads some scholars to dismiss every distinction between narrator and author and to identify the external narrator, i.e., the one who speaks by himself in the first person in the prooemium and in the epilogue of the poem, with the historic author, i.e., Ovid himself.[7] On the other hand, it is difficult to attribute directly to the poet certain features that the narrator reveals or even intentionally exhibits (a sometimes naïve psychological attitude, religious propriety, or "political correctness"), and it is therefore necessary to provide for the intervention of an "implicit author." The implicit author permits us to perceive a distancing of the real author from the *persona* of his narrator, to whom the author looks with detachment and

---

[5] Todorov (1977) 66.
[6] Cf., e.g., Galinsky (1975) 99; Solodow (1988) 37–73.
[7] The position taken most decisively by Solodow (1988) 41.

irony, and from whom he thus manages to distinguish himself.[8] The general communicative situation can be looked at in the following way: inside the frame that connects the historic author, Ovid, to his reader, is inscribed a second frame that connects the fictitious narrator of the poem (i.e., "Ovid") with his audience: this can be thought of as consisting of contemporary Romans, rhetorically educated and knowledgeable in Greek and Latin literature, to whom the narrator repeatedly turns, involving them through various dialogic signals (like the generic "we,"[9] or the frequent phrase *nunc quoque*, a marker of aetiological poetry,[10] or other similar markers).[11] Inside this second frame are inscribed in turn further narrative levels (with new narrators and narratees) that the technique of *mise en abyme* sometimes creates.

The importance of storytelling in the economy of the poem is expressly (and programmatically) declared from the very first book. The first embedded narrative is entrusted to the voice of Jupiter (1.209–43), the very embodiment of power, and the effects of distortion produced by the narration of the story of Lycaon through the mouth of the god immediately thematize the problem of the authority of political power (and its concomitant association with the authority of the word) and of the truth constructed by power. Storytelling is also the instrument which Mercury uses to lull to sleep—and so to decapitate—Argus, the hundred-eyed watchman of Io (1.671–721), in an episode frequently noted for its obvious metanarrative character.[12] When Mercury, telling the story of the pursuit of Syrinx by Pan, ends up repeating the narrative pattern of the erotic pursuit of Daphne by Apollo (the story narrated just before, at 1.452–567, and which, as the *primus amor Phoebi*, is in some sense a prototype of the many erotic stories which will follow in successive books), his listener, Argus, falls asleep. The effect produced by the narrator, Mercury, on his audience, Argus, is that which the narrator-author, Ovid, unintentionally runs the risk of producing in

---

[8] Graf (1988) 67; Wheeler (1999) 73–74.

[9] Wheeler (1999) 103–5.

[10] Cf. Myers (1994a) 66–67; Wheeler (1999) 238 n. 14. Wheeler (esp. 34–65) interprets the role of the primary narrator as that of an epic poet who entertains his audience for the duration of the *carmen perpetuum* as if with an uninterrupted "viva-voce" performance.

[11] Full analysis in Wheeler (1999) 94–116.

[12] Fränkel (1945) 85; Galinsky (1975) 174; Ahl (1985) 202; Wheeler (1999) 1 and 80–81; and see esp. Konstan (1991).

his audience, and he takes precautions by means of *mise en abyme* to declare himself aware of the problem caused by such repetition (i.e., the problem of how, without causing boredom, to narrate the "doublets" which such a long poem inevitably contains). But the range of programmatic discourse is much greater than this. At 1.700, the marking of a transition to direct discourse is unexpectedly employed to introduce a transition to indirect discourse ('*talia uerba refert*'—*restabat uerba referre*) and to a reduction of narrative levels with the return to the voice of the external narrator, who carries the story to completion in 701–12. This story, which Mercury would have narrated if he had continued the narration (*talia dicturus . . .*, at 713, terminates the part omitted by the god and resumes the narrative of his action with the killing of Argus), is suppressed as now useless to the character-narrator (Mercury, for whom it was important only that Argus fall asleep), but is nonetheless completed for the benefit of the other audience, the audience external to the diegetic world (let us call this, to be brief, that of "Ovid"), which is very interested in learning the outcome of the plot and the *aition* of the Pan pipe (*syrinx*). The logic which controls the narrative transaction between the external narrator and his audience takes the place of the logic internal to the diegetic world, in which Mercury's narration originated. Through the marked change of narrative modalities, i.e., the transition from direct discourse to indirect discourse, the text invites us to consider the plurality of narrative levels and the different involvement and interests of the actors who participate in the narrative transaction. At the same time, by avoiding the replication of an all-too-similar story of frustrated erotic pursuit and of the metamorphosis of the pursued woman into a plant, the text also shows us how the same story can be narrated in completely different ways (for example, by changes in the times and rhythms of the narration, narrating voice, and point of view).

Other episodes also play an important role in creating the reflexive attitude of Ovid's poem. First and foremost are the two great narrative complexes of the fifth and tenth books (entrusted respectively to the voices of two "professional" narrators: Calliope, the muse of epic, and her son Orpheus), that have been considered "miniatures" of the entire poem, marking its division into three pentads.[13] I should

---

[13] Cf. esp. Rieks (1980) and Nagle (1988d). Holzberg (1997a) 134–36 sees a poetological epilogue at the end of each of the three pentads (including, i.e., the discourse of Pythagoras).

also mention, for example, the tales of the Minyeids, the three sisters devoted to Minerva, who spin and weave while taking turns telling stories of love, and of Arachne, the boastful weaver transformed into a spider by Minerva.[14] While this last seems to constitute or to provide the foundation myth for the semantic field in which the Callimachean poetics of λεπτότης is based (as in the metaphor of *deducere*, recalled in 1.4, or the image of the poet-spider, known above all from *Culex* 1–4), the episode of the narrating spinners, with its insistence on the parallelism of the two processes, on the simultaneous "running" of the thread and of the narration (*talibus orsa modis lana sua fila sequente*, 4.54), represents an *aition* for storytelling, and the three "Callimachean" narrators of erotic stories appear to be obvious substitutes for the narrator-author who had declared in the prooemium his intention to spin (*deducere*) a *perpetuum carmen*.[15]

2. *Chronology and Analogy: An Order Without End*

The Homeric-Virgilian epic tradition included a narrative flashback on the part of the protagonist (cf. Books 8–12 of the *Odyssey* and 2–3 of the *Aeneid*), who, through homodiegetic analepsis, narrated events anterior to the chronological arc traced by the poem, but relevant to it and to its narrative continuity.[16] Nonetheless, repeated and widespread recourse to storytelling in the *Metamorphoses* recalls instead to Ovid's reader the narrative technique of the *Fasti*, which entrusts the explanation of the *aitia* of the most varied antiquarian subjects to a great number of informants, both divine and human. Recourse to internal narrators as sources of aetiological knowledge has been traced back to the model offered by Callimachus,[17] who in the first two books of the *Aetia* questioned the Muses regarding various antiquarian matters and received their responses.[18] The storytelling procedure in the larger poem has therefore been associated

---

[14] Rosati (1999).

[15] A full analysis of various aspects of the prooemium in Wheeler (1999) 8–30.

[16] Cf. Barchiesi (1997a) esp. 138–39 and n. 18; Barchiesi also shows (126–36) how Homer and Virgil had already confronted questions of poetic metadiegesis similar to those posed by Ovid.

[17] Cf. Myers (1994a) 67–73.

[18] Of course, Callimachus did not limit the use of internal narrators to this work alone.

with this model, rather than with the widespread predilection of Alexandrian poetry for complex narrative structures. This is not only because many internal narratives in the *Metamorphoses* originate in aetiological questions put by one character to another, who thus becomes a narrator, but also because in both Ovidian poems the introduction of multiple voices has something to do with the problem (as previously articulated in Alexandrian poetry) of "truth," in particular the pretense of "truth" claimed by works of fiction.

While this flexible narrative technique seems particularly useful to a poem like the *Fasti*, much more problematic is its use in a poem that declares itself to be epic, and that preserves the continuity of epic; the phrase *carmen perpetuum* of 1.4 cannot *not* recall the famous Callimachean polemic found in the prologue of the *Aetia* against ἓν ἄεισμα διηνεκές (*Aet.* 1, fr. 1.3 Pf.), and so suggests a reconciliation of Callimachean and anti-Callimachean approaches.[19] In fact, the establishment of a vast chronological horizon, from the origin of the world to the time of the narrator, accentuates the problem. An "impure" epic, scarcely epic in its chronological arrangement (and typical instead of the *Weltgeschichte* beloved by Hellenistic historiography), it incorporates stories of metamorphosis, a subject typical of catalogue poetry, dating all the way back to Hesiod's *Catalogue of Women* and in vogue in Hellenistic poetry (Nicander, Aratus, Hermesianax, and Phanocles). The result is a poem which follows a double structural principle, combining chronological order (from chaos to the present) with analogic order (stories linked by connected themes, characters, or places).

Storytelling is useful to the catalogue aspect of the poem, because by relying on internal narrators, it allows material which would otherwise be difficult to insert into a rigidly chronological framework[20] to be brought together (the chronological relationship of the embedded story to its framing narrative, meanwhile, can remain rather vague: it is necessary only that it has taken place before the point in time at which the "history of the world" has arrived). Yet the repeated regressions and digressions of the narrators, who pile up stories of indeterminate chronology, tend to nullify our awareness of the framework established at the beginning of the poem (especially in the great

---

[19] Cf. Wheeler (1999) 25–30.
[20] Coleman (1971) 471.

central section of the "period of heroes"; the phenomenon is less
noticeable in the final "historical" section of the poem). The per-
ception of linear sequence is disturbed by the repeated *analepseis*
(flashbacks) generally entrusted to the voices of characters who some-
times introduce homodiegetic stories, i.e., stories experienced in the
first person, but who more often introduce heterodiegetic stories, i.e.,
stories heard from others, and having taken place in an uncertain
past; and the various *prolepseis* (anticipations), i.e., allusions to the
future (in the poem's "history of the world"), which ought to recall
the poem's complex structure and contribute to its cohesion (e.g.,
6.415; 7.233; 10.207–8), do not in fact manage to compensate for
a sense of fluctuating chronological indefiniteness. The sense of a
vague and indefinite chronology, in which many stories are located,
contributes further still to the complexity of the problem (to which
we shall turn below) of the nature of the contents of the poem and
of the sources from which they derive: the problem, in short, of the
guarantee of truth which they claim to provide.

The fact is that a poem of such vast ambitions, that ruptures and
overwhelms the boundaries of genre, and at the same time mixes
them with each other, contains in itself the potential to destabilize
the order that governs it. Between chronological order and analog-
ical order, there is an intrinsic incompatibility, which forces the
author-narrator to assume a very flexible attitude towards the arrange-
ment to be followed (flexibility that is made evident by the need
always to invent new transitions from one story to another).[21] Indeed,
if the narrator privileges the first of these, he runs the risk of leav-
ing aside similar stories that took place in a distant past, in the "his-
tory of the world," because that would entail a departure from
chronological order; but if he uses analogical order to draw together
all the stories related by their contents, he runs the risk of under-
mining the delicate chronological foundation on which the poem is
based. Along the path that, broadly speaking, runs from elemental
chaos to the time of the narrator-author, are located three major
"moments": the age of gods, the age of heroes, and finally, with the
arrival of the Trojan War (a frequent threshold delimiting this bound-

---

[21] As is well known, Quintilian had already been struck by this virtuosity: *illa
uero frigida et puerilis est in scholis adfectatio, ut ipse transitus efficiat aliquam utique sententiam
et huius uelut praestigiae plausum petat, ut Ouidius lasciuire in Metamorphosesin solet, quem
tamen excusare necessitas potest, res diuersissimas in speciem unius corporis colligentem (IO 4.1.77).*
On diverse transitional techniques cf. Solodow (1988) 41–46.

ary in ancient chronologies), the age of history. But within this broad framework, the collocation of individual events is rather fluid, and the sense of chronological succession is frequently entirely lost; thus, stories seem to follow upon each other in a vague achrony, as if in a world without time, in which, bit by bit, another order in the collocation of events is established. The listener-reader of the poem progressively loses the sense of a sequential ordering of events (as it is assumed that they happened in the history of the world) and begins instead to perceive, as a sort of guiding thread, a *narrative* order of the same events (as the narrator arranges them in the story of the world that he narrates). It is in respect to this "history of the world" that the chronological links take on meaning, the "before" and the "after" of events.

When, for example, the chariot of Juno pulled by colorful peacocks is described at 2.531–33, the narrator recalls the origin of the peacock as he himself, "a little earlier" (*nuper*, i.e., in the chronology of the narrative, at 1.722–23), had narrated in relation to the killing of Argus (*habili Saturnia curru/ingreditur liquidum pauonibus aethera pictis,/tam nuper pictis caeso pauonibus Argo*). The chronological relationship perceived here is not so much that between two moments in the "history of the world" but rather that which falls between "now" and "before" in the narrative, based on the time of the narrative transaction.

An even more evident example of this occurs at 2.748–49, where, in reference to the meeting of Mercury with Aglauros, the narrator refers back to an event narrated just before: *adspicit hunc oculis isdem, quibus abdita nuper/uiderat Aglauros flauae secreta Mineruae*. This reference (even more explicit at 755–57) looks back to the bothersome curiosity of Aglauros, who in an earlier episode (*nuper*) had opened the basket entrusted to her by Minerva and containing the infant Erichthonius (2.552–61). In reality, this event had been *narrated* a little earlier (by the crow, the narrator of 2.549–95), but just because it had been narrated by a character, it has happened in a past certainly far distant from the "present" of Mercury, i.e., from his meeting with Aglauros. Furthermore, the crow locates it *tempore quodam* (2.552), far indeed in time even in respect to its present; and we know that the longevity of this bird was proverbial.[22] Thus, the word

---

[22] Cf. Keith (1992a) 13 n. 17.

nuper reveals here, too, a concept of the internal chronology of the poem which is not so much that of a "real" unfolding of events, of their occurrence corresponding to the sequence of their realization in the "time of the world," but deriving from their arrangement in the narrative sequence, in the "time of the narration."[23]

The problem of time in the *Metamorphoses* is nowadays seen to be among the most complex and interesting aspects of the poem. While for a long time scholars approached it with the assumption of a difficulty on Ovid's part in controlling this dimension of the poem, today the poem's temporal shifts tend rather to be seen as strategic, and as a device that the poet manipulates with great skill and awareness. The numerous discrepancies that emerge from the temporal organization of the poem are no longer attributed to the poet's inability to control and organize his vast and erratic narrative subject-matter,[24] but tend rather to be considered deliberate and indeed frequently highlighted as a way to show that "reality," the organization internal to the text constructed by the poet-narrator, is in fact an artificial construct, depending on subjective choices rather than on an objective and absolute truth.[25]

Likewise, the numerous anachronisms,[26] so often deplored by critics in the name of objectivity and impersonal epic narration, can from this perspective be understood as serving to rupture the fictitious and artificial continuity of the narrated story-world, and to affirm instead the real continuity of the narration, and of the rapport which the narrator has with his audience.[27] But an interpretation that has recently been gaining in popularity among critics has more specifically political implications: through the deliberate and at times explicit recourse to anachronism (as in the well-known but impossible meeting between Numa and Pythagoras), Ovid may intend to subvert the chronographically official order, the order of power, introducing uncertainty and disorder instead into the teleological structure of the "Age of Augustus."[28] In short, it is as if the deliberate fragmenta-

---

[23] Cf. Rosati (1994) 14–15; Feeney (1999) 24; and esp. Wheeler (1999) 117: "The ostensible linearity of a world history of metamorphosis thus furnishes a pretext for a second narrative, or metanarrative, which is that of the poem's own performance."

[24] Cf., e.g., Fränkel (1945) 74.

[25] Wheeler (1999) 134.

[26] Cf., e.g., Galinsky (1975) 85; Solodow (1988) 29.

[27] Wheeler (1999) 117.

[28] A firm push in this direction is now given by Feeney (1999); Zissos-Gildenhard (1999); Hinds (1999).

tion of time that controls the "fictitious world" of the poem is aimed at unmasking the arbitrary, indeed even fictitious character of the supposed cosmic order established by the power of Augustus.

A further, and fundamental, "political" feature that is connected with the hybrid character of the poem as an impure epic, is that the *Metamorphoses* contravenes a peculiar characteristic of the epic genre, its intrinsically teleological nature;[29] the contamination that epic undergoes when mingling with other genres implies in some sense the abandonment of its totalizing pretenses, and of the character of absolute "truth" that epic innately possesses. The vast chronological arc—all of time, mythical and historical—that frames this story of the world ends with Augustan Rome, and the geographical horizon, no less vast, that provides a background for the poem (Europe, Asia, and even Africa, i.e., the entire world) entails a spatial movement from east to west (as in the *Aeneid*), i.e., from Greece to Rome (where many of the stories in the final books take place). It is nevertheless not possible to say that, like the Virgilian poem, the *Metamorphoses* is sustained by a "sense of history" that makes Rome the zenith of *Weltgeschichte*, the summit of its earthly destiny. This is an epic in which there is no *telos*; unlike the *Aeneid*, there is no opposition here between the forces that promote action and those that prevent it, between "Jupiter" and "Juno": the world does not have its limit, its summit, in Augustus. It has been rightly observed[30] that the *terminus* fixed in the prooemium (*ad mea tempora*) clearly excludes Augustus. The forward movement of events does not permit us to glimpse any plot, meaning, or conclusion that might be suggested to the reader by the story.[31] The exclusion of Augustus is further accentuated by the fact that the words *coeptis . . ./adspirate meis* (1.2–3) recall clearly the invocation with which Virgil, in an analogous prooemial context, had requested his protection: *G.* 3.6, *da facilem cursum atque audacibus adnue coeptis.* Yet Ovid now requests this protection not from him but from the gods of heaven. The exile Ovid betrays an awareness of this absence (seeking belatedly, and

---

[29] Quint (1993) 45–46.

[30] Cf. esp. Due (1974) 95; later, Barchiesi (1989) 91.

[31] Barchiesi (1999) 113–14 remarks, "the Ovidian narrator has as much *authority* as the Virgilian narrator—that is, a lot of it—but much less *responsibility* . . . the author reaps the benefit of controlling and editing the multitude of voices in his enormous narrative world, but Ovid's responsibility for the overall plot is not as clear as in Virgil, where the author, the plot, and Fate tend to be perceived as co-operative forces. There is no masterplot in Ovid."

opportunistically, to fill it: cf. *Tr.* 2.559–60, *quibus prima surgens ab origine mundi/in* **tua** *deduxi tempora, Caesar, opus*). In a world in which everything is transformed, there is no place for any permanence, neither *imperium sine fine* (*Aen.* 1.279) nor *Capitoli immobile saxum* (*Aen.* 9.448).[32]

3. *Narrative Voices*

The importance of metadiegesis (i.e., the replication of narrative levels) in the *Metamorphoses* cannot be overestimated: in the analysis of a single episode we are nowadays generally attentive to a reconstruction of the entire narrative situation, i.e., the identities of the narrator and his interlocutor, the motivations for the inclusion of a particular story, the manner of the narration and the circumstances in which it occurs, and the reactions of the audience and the interpretation that they give to the story they have heard, in addition to resulting interactions between the framework and the embedded story. The necessity, or even the usefulness, of distinguishing the voice of the primary narrator from those of the internal narrators is not fully agreed upon: some scholars limit the function of a proliferation of narrative voices to a few practical aims, like enabling interactions between and among characters and varying the techniques of transition from one story to another, but they deny that the procedure can have other significant functions. Perhaps the most determined proponent of the unified identity of the narrating voice is Solodow, whose view has been frequently noted: "I believe there is basically a single narrator throughout, who is Ovid himself. The introduction of other speakers is more formal than consequential; the words are heard as those of the poet."[33] According to Solodow, it is not possible to isolate an individual characterization of the narrating voice on the level of language and style, nor does the role of the narrator play a part in the characterization of characters: "other figures in the poem are characterized by their speech—Deucalion is shown by his words to be pious, Niobe arrogant, Ulysses clever—but no narrator is."[34] In reality, while it is true that it is not always easy to

---

[32] Cf. Hardie (1992) 60–61.
[33] Solodow (1988) 38.
[34] Solodow (1988) 39.

single out the personal stylistic stamp of the narrator on the narration, which seems in effect to maintain a certain uniformity of tone,[35] and that of the external narrator who controls the gathering and managing of narrative material with a firm grasp, to ignore the poem's framework and change of voices[36] obliterates shades of meaning important for the comprehension of the poem. Indeed, as we shall see, the recognition of a character is often precisely the function of the narrator.

The socio-cultural characterization of numerous narrators (including, in addition to humans, gods, and demi-gods, even animals, like the crow of Book 2) is very varied (and often neglected with apparent indifference: e.g., *nescioquis*, 6.382; *proximus aut idem*, 11.751), just as the occasions that provide a context for the narrative situations are extremely diverse: stories seem to occur independent of their context, and often without precise motivation, as if from some instinct or primary necessity.[37]

Aside from the situation that provides a basis for the narration, however, the various narrators are generally attentive to their role and aware of their authorial responsibility. The signs of this awareness are numerous. Within the story of Proserpina, for example, when Arethusa is about to reveal to Ceres where her stolen daughter can be found, she postpones to a more peaceful moment the story of her own transfer from Greece to Sicily (5.498–501):

> mota loco cur sim tantique per aequoris undas
> aduehar Ortygiam, ueniet narratibus hora
> tempestiua meis, cum tu curaque leuata
> et uultus melioris eris.

> An opportune time will come for my telling why I was moved from my place and am come to Ortygia through the waves of so great a sea, when you have been relieved of care and are of more cheerful countenance.

Arethusa recognizes that the dramatic tension of the situation cannot be interrupted and that the postponement of this story to an

---

[35] Cf., e.g., also Leach (1974) 106; Barchiesi (1989) 55–56.

[36] For an attempt to differentiate the style of the narrating voices ("Ovid" and Orpheus respectively) see Nagle (1983). A fully developed (albeit also *sui generis*) voice is that of Pythagoras: cf. Barchiesi (1989) 73–83.

[37] On this indifference to the problems of motivation, see Barchiesi (1989) 56 and (1997a) 136–41 (also noting the ineffectiveness of many internal narratives).

emotionally more relaxed occasion enables the narrative economy of
the entire complex of stories to be effective: Arethusa's courteous
gesture towards Ceres gives the external narrator a way of intro-
ducing a comment on his own choices of narrative strategy.[38]

Apart from the arrangement of the narrative, the narrators are
concerned as well with other features connected to their role, for
example, with the relationship between narrated time and the time
of the narration. Jupiter himself, the first internal narrator in the
poem, shows himself attentive to the narrative economy of his story
('*longa mora est, quantum noxae sit ubique repertum,/enumerare,*' 1.214–15);
and after him other narrators will do the same thing, concerned to
save their audiences from annoying delays, e.g., Diomedes at 14.473
('*neue morer referens tristes ex ordine casus*'), or Aeacus at 7.520 ('*ordine
nunc repetam, neu longa ambage morer uos*').[39] More interesting is the case
of the herdsman Onetor, who hastens to announce a great calamity
('*magnae tibi nuntius adsum/cladis,*' 11.349–50) and to ask for help, but
rather than immediately reporting what has occurred, he begins a
long *rhesis* typical of the messengers of tragedy (352–78), lingering
over otiose descriptive details before getting to the substance of the
facts (366). Finally, realizing at last the incongruity of his behavior,
he expresses self-criticism of his own verbosity, which clashes with
the urgency to act: '*sed mora damnosa est, nec res dubitare remittit:/dum
superest aliquid, cuncti coeamus et arma,/arma capessamus . . .*' (376–78). In
addition to making an ironic comment on the typical verbosity of
tragic messengers,[40] Onetor also voices an awareness of another prob-
lem: viz., that narration, an important component in the *rheseis* of
messengers, is more appropriate to a narrative work than to a tragedy,
where the constraints of dramatic verisimilitude render incongruous
the inevitably slow tempo of the narration that habitually charac-
terizes these *rheseis*.

Arethusa is also concerned with the time that narration takes.
When Ceres, by now calm (*nata secura recepta*, 5.572), asks her for the
promised story, Arethusa tells of her pursuit by Alpheus (5.599–641):

---

[38] Rosati (1981) 307–8.

[39] Cf. also Pythagoras, 15.418–20 and 453. The (external) narrator of the Actaeon-
story makes fun of this convention, concluding a catalogue of 33 dogs' names,
extending for approximately 20 verses, with an analogous comment: *quosque referre
mora est*, 3.225.

[40] Due (1974) 144.

a long and stressful flight, retold from the point of view of the victim, but interrupted when the nymph, about to be overtaken, asks Diana for help and dissolves into water (5.632–36):

> occupat obsessos sudor mihi frigidus artus,
> caeruleaeque cadunt toto de corpore guttae,
> quaque pedem moui, manat lacus, eque capillis
> ros cadit, et citius, quam nunc tibi facta renarro,
> in latices mutor.

> A cold sweat takes hold of my possessed limbs, and sea-blue drops fall from my whole body; where I move my foot, a lake pools, and from my hair dew falls; I was turned to liquid more quickly than I now can narrate the events to you.

The narrator sets up a confrontation between the time of the narration, inevitably slow, and the swift passing of the metamorphosis itself. It is not always possible to find a correspondence or a balanced relationship between these two times. This problem is also considered by Venus, the narrator of the racing contest between Atalanta and Hippomenes, who is aware of the danger that the narration of a race may end up lasting longer than the race itself, and that the time of the narration can overwhelm the extent of the narrated time: 'neue meus sermo cursu sit tardior ipso,/praeterita est uirgo: duxit sua praemia uictor' (10.679–80). This gently self-critical comment insists on the necessity of a balanced relationship between the flow of time used by the contestants and the flow of the text that narrates it.[41] Thus, the sudden final acceleration, which in a single verse relates both the factual outcome of the contest and its consequences, also seems intended to bring out all the conventionality that such a scene entails, and that can be omitted in order to pass directly to the conclusion.[42]

These narrators' preoccupation with the relative slowness of narration also reflects a more general problem that faces the primary narrator: the proliferation of embedded stories (especially in narratologically complex blocks like those in the fifth and the tenth books, where narrative levels are multiplied) slows the progress of the main story. Through the mouths of his surrogate characters, "Ovid" shows

---

[41] Nagle (1988b) 37.

[42] Also see 5.395–96, 'paene simul uisa est dilectaque raptaque Diti:/usque adeo est properatus amor' (spoken by Calliope, narrating the rape of Proserpina): these words seem like a comment on the extreme contraction of narrative time, suddenly accelerated after the peaceful description of the setting in which the rape occurs (5.385–91).

his concern to control the regular development of a *carmen perpetuum*, and to avoid a situation in which the repeated use of metadiegesis compromises the epic continuity of the poem.

Confronted with this danger, however, a good narrator also knows how to suggest a solution. This is exactly what Orpheus does, when the narration of the story of Venus and Adonis is entrusted to him; this same story also provides a link with the preceding story of Myrrha, mother of Adonis. The transition between the two stories comprises the time between the birth of Adonis and his adulthood (*uir*, 10.522), and the narrator formulates a commentary on the subject of the swiftness of narrated time, demonstrating authorially how, if need be, the time of the narration too can be accelerated to advantage (10.519–24):

> Labitur occulte fallitque uolatilis aetas,
> et nihil est annis uelocius: ille sorore
> natus auoque suo, qui conditus arbore nuper,
> nuper erat genitus, modo formosissimus infans,
> iam iuuenis, iam uir, iam se formosior ipso est,
> iam placet et Veneri matrisque ulciscitur ignes.

> Fleet time moves secretly and deceptively, and nothing is swifter than the passage of years. That boy, son of his sister and grandfather, just now hidden in a tree, just now born, just now the fairest infant, now a youth, and even now a man, is now more beautiful than himself. Now he pleases even Venus, and avenges his mother's passion.

In short, metadiegesis constitutes an ideal space to make room for effects that "double" the voice of the external narrator, and that reveal an awareness of the complex problems of narrative technique that the creation of an anomalous epic poem like the *Metamorphoses* entails.

4. *The Story and Its Double*

Metadiegesis is thus a powerful instrument of literary self-concious-ness: the serial reproduction of narratives in miniature within the main narrative provides us with a method for the analysis and inter-pretation of the main narrative. It is not appropriate, however, to take this or that embedded story as a model in miniature of the entire poem (as has been done many times, especially with the sec-tions featuring Calliope or Orpheus): rather, in some of the stories we can see examples, or paradigms, "stamped" with the registers of genre that are inscribed in a complex and polyphonic text like the *Metamorphoses*[43] (e.g., the hyper-epic narrative of Nestor [12.169–576], or the hyper-didactic narrative of Pythagoras [15.75–478]). "Ovid uses internal narratives self-referentially to highlight and comment upon the generic and interpretive tensions of the epic as a whole."[44]

Analogous effects of generic and interpretive tension can also be found from time to time in the interaction between frameworks and embedded narratives, and we should therefore pay due attention to the specific narrative situation that produces them.[45] We know, for example, that the emotion with which Theseus listens to the narrative of the story of Philemon and Baucis is not casual (*Desierat, cunctosque et res et mouerat auctor,/ Thesea praecipue . . .*, 8.725–26). This Ovidian story is in fact modeled on Callimachus's *Hecale*, of which Theseus himself had been the protagonist;[46] and Theseus himself hears the memory of his own past and of his own literary existence recalled in this story.[47]

Another case in which metadiegesis serves to underline the intertextual relationship with the *Hecale* is in the famous episode of the crow in Book 2.[48] In Callimachus's poem, a crow tells another bird about the punishment that has transformed its feathers from white to black, and *prophesies* that one day the raven too, now white, will become black, likewise as a result of having wanted to become a messenger of bad news, and in particular for having told Apollo about the infidelity of Coronis (260.56–61 Pf. = 74.15–20 Hollis (1990)). The future announced by Callimachus becomes the present in Ovid: as the raven hastens to bring Apollo the unwelcome news of Coronis's betrayal, the crow attempts to dissuade it, reporting that, in the *past*,[49] the same thing happened to it as the result of a similar excess of zeal (2.549–52). Of course, the raven does not listen to this warning and is punished precisely as had been foretold (2.631–32). Exploiting a traditional belief in the prophetic gifts of

---

[43] Myers (1994a) 73–94, 162–63.
[44] Myers (1994a) 162.
[45] Cf., e.g., Keith (1992a) 39–61, 119–24.
[46] Cf. Kenney (1986) xxviii; Barchiesi (1989) 57–58.
[47] On Ovid's sensitivity to this narrative device, cf. Barchiesi (1986) esp. 102ff.
[48] On which see in general Keith (1992a).
[49] I.e., in the text of Callimachus (cf., e.g., '*nota loquor,*' 2.570; '*ne sperne mea praesagia linguae./ quid fuerim quid simque uide,*' 2.550–51).

crows, Ovid upsets the chronological perspective by making Calli-
machus's future become his own present, and the event prophecized
in the *Hecale* is realized *now* in the *Metamorphoses*.[50] The Ovidian text
thus presents itself as the future foretold in the Callimachean text:
the Latin poet "forces" the Greek poet to allude to him, constructing
a precursor-prophet for himself and presenting himself as the outcome
of a prophecy, the fortunate realization of destiny. In other words, he
constructs for himself a past and appropriates for himself a tradition
which has its *telos*, foreseen and anticipated, in the Ovidian text.[51]

The entire complex of stories with Callimachean roots in the eighth
book (of which the tale of Philemon and Baucis is a part) invites us
to look at the interference between frame and embedded narrative:
it is no coincidence that these stories develop around Achelous, a
swollen and torrential river-god, i.e., the symbol used by Callimachus
to define the "grand" epic poetry he rejected. Especially when Achelous
begins to narrate the story of Erysichthon, the Callimachean narra-
tive material is intoned in a swollen, redundant, and markedly epic
style. While recalling Callimachus, the river-narrator "epicizes" him,[52]
adapting Callimachus to the style with which Callimachus himself
had branded the symbol of the river in flood.

Again in an episode involving Achilles, a particular effect (in this
case not of genre but of gender) can be associated with the narra-
tee. When Nestor mentions the unusual story of Caeneus and his
sex change, Achilles shows great interest in the change, and asks the
old man to narrate it (12.175–79):

> monstri nouitate mouentur
> quisquis adest, narretque rogant: quos inter Achilles:
> 'dic age! nam cunctis eadem est audire uoluntas,
> o facunde senex, aeui prudentia nostri,
> quis fuerit Caeneus, cur in contraria uersus . . .'

> Those present are moved by the novelty of the creature, and ask that
> he tell them the story; among them is Achilles: "Well, then, speak! For
> it pleases all of us to hear the same story, o elequent old man, wis-
> dom's embodiment for our age. Who was Caeneus? why did he turn
> into the opposite? . . ."

---

[50] Rosati (1994) 15–17.
[51] For Ovid's attitude (seen in connection with Virgil) cf. Hinds (1998) 104–22.
[52] Hinds (1987b) 19 ("he is de-Callimachising Callimachus"); Barchiesi (1989)
58–61.

His concern with this particular story, together with the fact that, as if to divert malignant suspicion from himself, Achilles attributes curiosity to all present, authorizes us to suspect that this has something to do with the hero's youthful sojourn on Scyrus, and his embarrassing concealment in women's clothes while there.[53] This suspicion is reinforced by Nestor's (malicious?) reference to the "familiarity" of Achilles with Caenis/Caeneus (*'tibi enim popularis, Achille,'* 191; cf. also 193–95).

At the same time (and as we might expect), once Ovid has accustomed his reader to paying attention to these interactions between framework and embedded narrative, he also enjoys frustrating our expectation of them.[54] There is, furthermore, a frequent tendency in the poem to frustrate expectations previously aroused, as for example in the case of Acrisius, unwilling to recognize the divine descent of Bacchus and of his grandson Perseus and therefore condemned to a punishing defeat (4.607–14), modelled on that already suffered by Pentheus—but this punishment is then omitted. This movement helps to sustain the sense of arbitrariness that the principal narrator claims for himself in the performance of his *carmen perpetuum*. References to narrative conventions are frequent, often indeed in order to contradict them: as when Perseus, at his wedding banquet with Andromeda, rather than narrating his own story (and so replicating the epic model of Odysseus and Aeneas, i.e., of the narrating hero as banquet-guest), is the one to ask for information regarding the local people (4.767–68). Then, when asked to tell of his victory over Medusa, he limits himself to a few verses (772–86; furthermore, his words are reported not in direct discourse, but summarized indirectly by the narrator), breaking off his narrative before his audience expects him to (*ante exspectatum tacuit*, 4.790)—an audience accustomed to the familiar conventions which are now ignored.[55]

There are many means through which the arbitrariness of the narrative can be made evident: but a revelation of this sort obviously also has as a consequence the abandonment of any pretense to truth that might otherwise be attributed to the narrative. Sometimes we have only the admission that the narrator's report is not full, as

---

[53] The transvestism of Caeneus is one of the precedents mentioned by Thetis in the *Achilleid* of Statius to convince Achilles to don feminine garb (1.264).

[54] Cf. Barchiesi (1997a) 139–40.

[55] Cf. Nagle (1988b) 45–46; Nagle (1998c) 24–25; Wheeler (1999) 115.

in the introduction of Hecuba's words at 13.493, *plura quidem, sed et haec laniato pectore dixit*, or in the recurrent concluding formula, without parallel in classical epic, *talibus atque aliis* (7.661; 13.228; 13.675; 15.479). In cases like these, we are made aware that the narrative is the product of a selection, and we are therefore invited to consider the hypothesis that this process may not be objective, but is the result of personal choices on the part of the narrator. But sometimes our suspicions are aroused even further when there is an explicit confession that the report is a reconstruction by the narrator, as at 6.702, *haec Boreas aut his non inferiora locutus*, where we are allowed to understand that the narrator is not concerned so much with rendering the precise words pronounced by Boreas, but only with reproducing the general tone of his speech. The same nonchalance is exhibited elsewhere in the generic identification of the narrator to whom a speech is entrusted, for example, the narrator who tells the story of Latona and the Lycian farmers, introduced as *unus* (6.317) and at the end of the narrative referred to as *nescio quis* (382), and thereby confirmed in his anonymity.[56] The discourse of an unidentified character is not unusual in epic (so-called τις-speech),[57] but Ovid uses this device in combination with an Alexandrian/Callimachean scrupulousness about indicating one's source. The result is not a guarantee of veracity but a marked show of uncertainty, a contradictory combination of imprecision and specificity. At 11.751, likewise, the narrator's responsibility to identify characters is directly entrusted to chance (*proximus, aut idem, si fors tulit, 'hic quoque' dixit*): this accuracy in "identifying" an anonymous character is surely humorous,[58] but it also has the effect of turning inside out the Alexandrian veracity formula, by insisting on the arbitrary character of the narration (independent of the narrating voice), and on its fundamental unreliability.

This arbitrariness is also revealed through comments on conventionality (and on a limited pretense to truthfulness) in certain parts of the story: an example is the description of the manifestations of grief on the part of Iphis's mother at 14.744–45 (*membra sui postquam miserarum uerba parentum/edidit et matrum miserarum facta peregit*), where the almost formular repetition of the adjective *miser* emphasizes the

---

[56] Other similar instances in Nagle (1988b) 49 n. 20.

[57] Cf. de Jong (1987).

[58] "Ovid gently mocks the learned poet's obsession with sources": Kenney (1986) ad loc.; Myers (1994a) 82.

"manneredness" of the situation and of the words and gestures that accompany it. These words and gestures are so conventional that the narrator supresses their description, inviting his audience to fill the gap by recourse to their own literary competence. The demands of the "typical" lead the narrator to imagine events and situations that *can* have happened (as, e.g., when Cephalus tells of his ambiguous summoning of *aura*/Aura: *'forsitan addiderim/. . ./dicere sim solitus,'* 7.816–18), even when he is not in fact sure that they *have* happened. Conversely, if they are depicted as having in fact happened, they contribute to the pathos or to the paradoxical nature of the situation, as when Meleager, seized by the torments of death, calls upon his wife and "perhaps" his mother Althea, too (*forsitan et matrem,* 8.522), who, without his knowledge, has brought about his death. The same effects are operating in the case of Cinyras, during his embrace with the young woman who, unbeknownst to him, is his daughter Myrrha: *forsitan aetatis quoque nomine 'filia' dixit:/dixit et illa 'pater,' sceleri ne nomina desint* (10.467–68). The final remark, *ne nomina desint,* contains an admission on the part of the narrator that the narrative of the events is a construct, and that he is concerned not so much to claim for it the character of objective truth as to give it all the details necessary for full dramatic effectiveness.

This insistence on the arbitrariness of the narrative leads us to the decisive role of storytelling in the interpretation of the *Metamorphoses*. The multiplication of narrative voices sheds light, at the level of narrative structure, on a problem central to Ovid's poem (as it had been central to Alexandrian poetry): that of tracing the contents (of a poem that, as we know, does not invoke the inspiration of the Muses) back to precise sources of knowledge, and of anchoring it to secure foundations that can act as a guarantee of truth. Through the technique of storytelling, Ovid teaches us to recognize that doubt regarding the pretense of the truth of every story is legitimate, and that the truth is not an absolute fact but is negotiable, the creation of a particular narrator under particular circumstances.

Positive statements like that expressed by the narrator Lelex to affirm the reliability of his source (*'haec mihi non uani (neque erat, cur fallere uellent)/narravere senes,'* 8.721–22) provoke the suspicion that a narrative may not always be true, and that sometimes there may be a reason for a person telling a story to lie. And the way in which the external narrator will sometimes guarantee the veracity of the internal narrator (e.g., of Perseus, describing his overpowering of

Medusa: *addidit et longi non falsa pericula cursus*, 4.787), legitimizes the
suspicion at least that, in cases like this, the narrator may exaggerate
the importance of his own actions. A good example of this is Achelous,
when he distances himself from a suspect simile: '*siqua fides—neque
enim ficta mihi gloria uoce/quaeritur*,' 9.55–56).

In short, Ovid reflects on the problem of producing truth through
storytelling and on the relationship between the intention of a nar-
rator and the reception of the narrator's story by its audience. A
person who tells a story affirms, in every case, his own truthfulness,
but the listener is not required to accept this truth passively; in fact,
he can resist (like, e.g., Pentheus, who rejects the threatening mes-
sage contained in the narrative of Acoetes: 3.582–691).[59] Between
the narrator and the narratee, in other words, a dialogue is estab-
lished, a negotiation that has as its object the meaning of the story.

5. *Narration and Interpretation*

The *Metamorphoses* is rich in episodes that explore ways of reading
and the interpretation of stories. On various occasions Ovid examines
the related acts of narration and interpretation, i.e., the problem of
controlling the meaning of a text. Especially significant are the stories
of artistic competition, foremost among them the song-contest between
the Muses and the Pierides (an episode privileged, on account of the
complexity of its structure, in narratological analyses)[60] and the weav-
ing-contest between Minerva and Arachne. The two contests are for-
mally different: in the first case speech is entrusted to the characters,
while in the second we are dealing with an *ecphrasis*, i.e., a pair of
"figured narratives" on tapestries that the external narrator illustrates
and translates into the narrative fabric. Translating the figured text
into the form of a story, "Ovid" thus performs the opposite opera-
tion from that performed by the two artists, who had translated their
"stories" to the web. Nonetheless, to the extent that they concern
us here, we can consider the two contests in similar terms: while not
actually having the responsibility for the narrative voice, Minerva

---

[59] On this aspect cf. Wheeler (1999) chapter 7, esp. 181–93.
[60] Leach (1974) 113–15; Rosati (1981), (1994) 29ff.; Hofmann (1986); Hinds
(1987a) 126–34; Nagle (1988d); Johnson and Malamud (1988); Cahoon (1996); Zissos
(1999); Wheeler (1999) 81–83.

and Arachne act as narrators, selecting the precise content, affirming its truth, and asserting their points of view in the *textus* that each of them creates.

A frequent scholarly approach to the opponents in these two artistic competitions has been to interpret them as opposing paradigms of "good" art and of "bad" art, and to seek in the text for evidence to identify the positive paradigm with the Ovidian poem itself, i.e., to read the internal narratives that are presumed to be "good" as models in miniature of the *Metamorphoses*. Nevertheless, the very disagreement among scholars regarding the paradigmatic relationship of these narratives to the *Metamorphoses* is proof that the function served by these episodes is more complex than that suggested by any rigid oppositional scheme. Rather, they aim to explore the many responsibilities that come into play in the creation and interpretation of a work of art, the tensions that permeate the process of its production and reception.

Let us consider this more carefully. At the center of her tapestry Minerva depicts the competition she won against Neptune for supremacy over Attica (6.70–82), and at the sides four smaller scenes with stories of arrogant mortals punished by the gods (6.83–100). The structure is dominated by order and symmetry, and has as its subject two themes that clearly mirror the frame situation, and prefigure its outcome (6.70–102):

Cecropia Pallas scopulum Mauortis in arce	70
pingit et antiquam de terrae nomine litem.	
bis sex caelestes medio Ioue sedibus altis	
augusta grauitate sedent; sua quemque deorum	
inscribit facies: Iouis est regalis imago;	
stare deum pelagi longoque ferire tridente	
aspera saxa facit, medioque e uulnere saxi	
exsiluisse fretum, quo pignore uindicet urbem;	
at sibi dat clipeum, dat acutae cuspidis hastam,	
dat galeam capiti, defenditur aegide pectus,	
percussamque sua simulat de cuspide terram	80
edere cum bacis fetum canentis oliuae;	
mirarique deos: operis Victoria finis.	
ut tamen exemplis intellegat aemula laudis,	
quod pretium speret pro tam furialibus ausis	
quattuor in partes certamina quattuor addit,	
clara colore suo, breuibus distincta sigillis:	
Threiciam Rhodopen habet angulus unus et Haemum,	
nunc gelidos montes, mortalia corpora quondam,	

nomina summorum sibi qui tribuere deorum;
altera Pygmaeae fatum miserabile matris   90
pars habet: hanc Iuno uictam certamine iussit
esse gruem populisque suis indicere bellum;
pinxit et Antigonen, ausam contendere quondam
cum magni consorte Iouis, quam regia Iuno
in uolucrem uertit, nec profuit Ilion illi
Laomedonue pater, sumptis quin candida pennis
ipsa sibi plaudat crepitante ciconia rostro;
qui superest solus, Cinyran habet angulus orbum;
isque gradus templi, natarum membra suarum,
amplectens saxoque iacens lacrimare uidetur.   100
circuit extremas oleis pacalibus oras
(is modus est) operisque sua facit arbore finem.

Pallas depicts the rock of Mars on the Cecropian citadel and the ancient contest about the name of the land. Twice six divinities with Jupiter in the middle sit in august solemnity on their lofty seats. Each of the gods is distinguished by his particular features: the image of Jupiter is kingly; she makes the god of the sea stand and strike the rough rock with his long trident; a sea-wave has leaped forth from the middle of the broken rock, with which token Neptune would claim the city. But she gives herself a shield, and a sharp-bladed spear, she puts a helmet on her head, her breast is protected by the aegis; and she depicts the earth shaken by her blade giving forth the grey-green olive's offspring, with berries; and she shows the gods marvelling: Victory is the end of her work. So that her competitor may nonetheless learn from example what reward she may expect for her insane daring, the goddess adds four contests in four places, each noteworthy because of its color and distinguished by small symbols: one corner has Thracian Rhodope and Haemon, now cold mountains but once mortal bodies, who assigned the names of the greatest gods to themselves. A second corner has the sad fate of the Pygmy mother: Juno ordered her, when defeated in competition, to be a crane and to declare war on her people. And she depicted Antigone, who once dared to compete with the wife of great Jupiter, and was turned into a bird by queen Juno; Ilium did not profit her, nor her father Laomedon; now a stork, white with assumed feathers, she applauds herself with clapping beak. The one corner which remains has Cinyras, bereft; embracing the steps of a temple, the limbs of his former daughters, and lying on the stone, he seems to cry. She binds the outer edges with peaceful olive (this is her way) and makes an end of the work with her tree.

Minerva asserts her truth: a world governed by the justice of the gods, who are represented in their *augusta grauitas* as vouching for order and hierarchy in the face of the insubordination of mortals.

Hers is an example of authoritarian art,[61] celebrating divine power, and a self-representation drawing attention to the threatening power of her military attributes (78–79).

The truth of Minerva is opposed to that of Arachne, who depicts a gallery of gods in shocking forms full of erotic menace, who assume the most varied animal shapes to deceive and rape innocent mortal women (103–28):

> Maeonis elusam designat imagine tauri
> Europam: uerum taurum, freta uera putares;
> ipsa uidebatur terras spectare relictas
> et comites clamare suas tactumque uereri
> adsilientis aquae timidasque reducere plantas.
> fecit et Asterien aquila luctante teneri,
> fecit olorinis Ledam recubare sub alis;
> addidit, ut satyri celatus imagine pulchram   110
> Iuppiter inplerit gemino Nycteida fetu,
> Amphitryon fuerit, cum te, Tirynthia, cepit,
> aureus ut Danaen, Asopida luserit ignis,
> Mnemosynen pastor, uarius Deoida serpens.
> te quoque mutatum toruo, Neptune, iuuenco
> uirgine in Aeolia posuit; tu uisus Enipeus
> gignis Aloidas, aries Bisaltida fallis,
> et te flaua comas frugum mitissima mater
> sensit equum, sensit uolucrem crinita colubris
> mater equi uolucris, sensit delphina Melantho: 120
> omnibus his faciemque suam faciemque locorum
> reddidit. est illic agrestis imagine Phoebus,
> utque modo accipitris pennas, modo terga leonis
> gesserit, ut pastor Macareida luserit Issen,
> Liber ut Erigonen falsa deceperit uua,
> ut Saturnus equo geminum Chirona crearit.
> ultima pars telae, tenui circumdata limbo,
> nexilibus flores hederis habet intertextos.

The Maeonian girl depicts Europa, deceived by the appearance of a bull; you would have thought the bull and the waves were real. She herself seemed to be looking at the land left behind and shouting for her companions, fearing the touch of the water as it jumped up and pulling back her timid feet. And she showed Asterie, being held by a struggling eagle, and Leda reclining beneath a swan's wings; and she added how Jupiter, disguised by the appearance of a satyr,

---

[61] On the problem of the relationship between artistic creativity and power in the *Metamorphoses*, cf. esp. Leach (1974).

impregnated the fair daughter of Nycteus with twin children; how he
was Amphitryon when he captured you, Tirynthian woman, how as
gold he deceived Danae and as fire the daughter of Asopus, how as
shepherd he tricked Mnemosyne and as snake, mother Deo's girl. You,
too, Neptune, she depicted, changed to a tawny bull on account of
the Aeolian girl; looking like Enipeus you produce the Aloidae, as a
ram you deceive the daughter of Bisaltes, and the blond-tressed, gen-
tle mother of grain felt you as a horse; the mother of the winged
horse, her hair snaky, knew you as a bird; and Melantho knew you
as a dolphin. To all of these the weaver gave the appropriate appear-
ance and setting. Phoebus is there, too, rustic in appearance, and how
sometimes he wore the feathers of a hawk, sometimes, the hide of a
lion, how as a shepherd he deceived Macareus's daughter Isse; how
Liber deceived Erigone with false grapes, and how Saturn created the
two-natured Chiron from a horse. The outer edge of the web, sur-
rounded by a narrow border, has flowers interwoven with twisting ivy.

Both of the two "tales" are directed "against" their audience, assert-
ing two opposing visions of the world and of divine power (as well
as opposing aesthetic ideals),[62] and they aim to appear threatening
and unpleasant to the eyes of their opponent. The external narra-
tor makes explicit the obvious intentions of the goddess in depicting
exempla that prefigure the destiny of Arachne (83, *ut . . . intellegat*), but
an analogous malignant intention in the tapestry of Arachne does
not escape the attentive reader, constructed as it is around a theme
unpleasant to a goddess (like Minerva) allergic to sex, and specifically
recalling an episode (Neptune's assault on Medusa: 119–20) hateful
to her because it occurred in her temple (4.798–801).

In showing how a story is constructed vis-à-vis its narratee, and
how this person negotiates its interpretation, Ovid invites us to con-
sider the complexity of the construction of meaning. The two artistic
contests, both that under consideration here and that between the
Pierides and Muses, thematize this crucial problem. The earlier story
is narrated from the point of view of the winners, the Muses, who
justify their victory (attributing the verdict to the nymphs of Helicon)
with predominantly artistic reasons (even though it cannot escape our
notice that their reasons result from sheer authority).[63] The later story
is narrated by the external narrator, and the defeat of Arachne is
attributed not to artistic inferiority but, uniquely here, to reasons of
power: Minerva punishes her for her pride and the insubordination

---

[62] Anderson (1968) 103; Lausberg (1982); Harries (1990).
[63] Cf. Johnson and Malamud (1988) 30–33.

shown to a divine power. The differing motivations for the outcomes of the two contests, not coincidentally juxtaposed, raise questions about justice, and the criteria used to evaluate a work of art—aesthetic criteria, but also ethical ones (the Muses are the ones to condemn the arrogance of the Pierides, but "Ovid" too blames the behavior of Arachne), and about basic power relations. The external narrator does not assume a position openly in favor of a just interpretation or against a mistaken interpretation: he limits himself to taking account of the multiplicity and inevitable partiality of every interpretation.

It is almost superfluous to add that, by an analogy that is repeated among the various narrative levels, readers are also invited to assume the role of judges and interpreters. The first interpreters of the Ovidian poem are inside it, where we see that the reception of a text, like its production, can be biased, tendentious, partial; the audience itself can even be divided (e.g., 4.272–73, *pars fieri potuisse negant, pars omnia ueros/posse deos memorant*). In other words, through metadiegesis the Ovidian text depicts within itself possible models of reception and of the creation/construction of a text.

Indeed, the multiplication of narrative voices serves to give a narration of events that is varied, direct, and personalized on the part of the very characters who have experienced them (as seen in Homer and in Virgil, too). This narration is, in other words, "truer"—whether on the emotional level or on that of "historic" reliability—because it has been traced back to the sources of evidence that guarantee its provenance. This form of narration is also more "mimetic," in accordance with Aristotle's estimation of Homer, who speaks as little as possible in the first person and "dramatizes" the dialogues of his characters.[64] At the same time, the disintegration of the authorial voice also entails the loss of the narration's unity, and of the authoritative control that assures the truth of the epic text. The result is a shattered truth, a multiplicity of autonomous, relative, and conflicting voices: the poet evokes this multiplicity in his description of the house of Fama, a place at the center of the world, crowded with voices that are drawn together, intertwined, and confused ceaselessly. These voices and words are in eternal movement, as if they too were subject to metamorphosis, changeable mixtures of true and false (12.39–63):

---

[64] Wheeler (1999) 186.

Orbe locus medio est inter terrasque fretumque
caelestesque plagas, triplicis confinia mundi;   40
unde quod est usquam, quamuis regionibus absit,
inspicitur, penetratque cauas uox omnis ad aures:
Fama tenet summaque domum sibi legit in arce,
innumerosque aditus ac mille foramina tectis
addidit et nullis inclusit limina portis;
nocte dieque patet: tota est ex aere sonanti,
tota fremit uocesque refert iteratque quod audit;
nulla quies intus nullaque silentia parte,
nec tamen est clamor, sed paruae murmura uocis,
qualia de pelagi, siquis procul audiat, undis   50
esse solent, qualemue sonum, cum Iuppiter atras
increpuit nubes, extrema tonitrua reddunt.
atria turba tenet: ueniunt, leue uulgus, euntque
mixtaque cum ueris passim commenta uagantur
milia rumorum confusaque uerba uolutant;
e quibus hi uacuas inplent sermonibus aures,
hi narrata ferunt alio, mensuraque ficti
crescit, et auditis aliquid nouus adicit auctor.
illic Credulitas, illic temerarius Error
uanaque Laetitia est consternatique Timores   60
Seditioque repens dubioque auctore Susurri;
ipsa, quid in caelo rerum pelagoque geratur
et tellure, uidet totumque inquirit in orbem.

There is a place in the middle of the world, between the earth and
the sea and the heavenly regions, the end of the threefold universe:
from here, whatever is anywhere can be seen, however distant it may
be, and every sound reaches its empty ears. Fame possesses this place,
and chooses a home for herself on the highest citadel, and added
countless entrances and a thousand openings in the roof, and has shut
the threshold with no doors. Night and day the house lies open; it is
made entirely of echoing bronze; the whole house roars and carries
sounds and repeats what it hears. There is no quiet within and silence
nowhere, but nor is there shouting, but only the murmurs of a small
voice, such as are accustomed to come from the waves of the sea, if
anyone were to listen from afar; or like the sound when Jupiter rum-
bles the black clouds, and distant thundering echoes. A crowd fills the
halls; a flimsy folk, they come and go, and thousands of lying rumors
mixed with truth roam here and there, and confused words flit about.
Some of these fill empty ears with talk, others carry the talk elsewhere,
and the measure of invented talk grows, and the new inventor adds
something to what he has heard. There is Gullibility, there rash Error;
hollow Happiness is there, and troubled Fears, surreptitious Sedition
and Whispers with no known source. And Fame herself sees and seeks
out through the whole world whatever transpires in heaven, at sea,
and on land.

All voices converge on the house of Fama, and in this process of confusion and diffusion, the distortion of truth into fiction, *mensura ficti*, increases (and in re-writing an essay in Homeric epic as spoken by Nestor, Ovid shows how report and tradition can be censored and distorted).[65] The frequent invocation in the poem of *fama* and of the *uestustas* of a tradition has an ambiguous outcome: while it is sometimes intended as a guarantee of credibility, at other times it emphasizes the *in*credibility of what has been narrated.[66] The text of the *Metamorphoses* too is a place in which a polyphony of autonomous, biased, and distorted voices resounds, and in which the external narrator—in his omniscience—refuses to make distinctions and impose order. Fama herself does this, too:[67] she too repeats what she hears, gathering and diffusing a proliferation of stories that mix truth and invention, voices that assert constructed, manipulated, and self-interested truths.

Let us consider some examples of this, again in the contest between the Pierides and the Muses. The narration of the contest is entrusted to the voice of a Muse (unidentified) who has as her listener the goddess Minerva: the Pierides, impious and blasphemous in their arrogance, sing an episode of the Gigantomachy (i.e., the flight into Egypt by the terrified gods, shamefully disguised through animal metamorphoses, in the face of Typhoeus's assault), that is partly retold in indirect discourse by the Muse (319–26) and partly reproduced in the exact words of one of the Pierides (327–31). In the section narrated indirectly, the Muse both judges the narrated events and directs the judgement of Minerva (obviously, narrator and listener share the same ideology and the same desire to condemn the Pierides), giving the impression of a narrative that is anything but objective and impartial. This impression is reinforced by the disproportionate number of verses allotted to the two competitors: about a dozen to the Pierid, more than 300 to Calliope.[68] Let us look first at the section reported indirectly (5.319–26):

> bella canit superum falsoque in honore gigantas
> ponit et extenuat magnorum facta deorum;
> emissumque ima de sede Typhoea terrae

---

[65] Well illustrated by Zumwalt (1977).
[66] Zumwalt (1977) 212.
[67] Feeney (1991) 248.
[68] Leach (1974) 114–15; Hinds (1987a) 128.

caelitibus fecisse metum cunctosque dedisse
terga fugae, donec fessos Aegyptia tellus
ceperit et septem discretus in ostia Nilus.
huc quoque terrigenam venisse Typhoea narrat
et se mentitis superos celasse figuris;

> She sings of the wars of the gods, setting the Giants in false honor
> and diminishing the deeds of the great gods: that Typhoeus, sent forth
> from the deepest place in earth, brought fear to the gods and put all
> of them to flight, until the land of Egypt and the Nile, split into seven
> mouths, received them in their exhaustion. She tells how earth-born
> Typhoeus came here, too, and how the gods concealed themselves
> with false shapes . . .

The following verses delivered in direct speech—as if the narrating
Muse wished to distinguish her own voice, not contaminating it with
that of her impious enemy—contain the most blasphemous slander-
ing of the gods, with a description of their less-than-honorable meta-
morphoses (5.327–31):

'duxque gregis' dixit 'fit Iuppiter: unde recuruis
nunc quoque formatus Libys est cum cornibus Ammon;
Delius in coruo, proles Semeleia capro,
fele soror Phoebi, niuea Saturnia uacca,
pisce Venus latuit, Cyllenius ibidis alis.'

> "And Jupiter becomes the leader of the herd," she said; "and so even
> today Libyan Ammon is modelled with his curved horns. The Delian
> hid in a crow, Semele's son in a goat, the sister of Phoebus in a cat,
> the Saturnian goddess in a white cow, Venus in a fish, the Cyllenian
> in the wings of an ibis."

With the gods in flight,[69] the story as told by the Pierides—who
make it appear a victory for the Giants—closes (at least according
to the hurried report of the Muse); meanwhile, the "official" truth,
the cosmology asserted by the victorious gods, foresees the defeat
and punishment of the rebel Giants. It is this very truth that, as
soon as she begins her song, Calliope strives to reassert ('*Vasta Giganteis
ingesta est insula membris/ Trinacris et magnis subiectum molibus urget/ aethe-
rias ausum sperare Typhoea sedes,*' 346–48), and in so doing she exposes
the tendentious distortion of the truth on the part of her rival. The

---

[69] The absence of Minerva from this catalogue of principal Olympian divinities
may be the result of benevolent reticence on the part of the narrating Muse (Rosati
(1994) 33). On the importance of the audience (the presiding nymphs) in the episode,
cf. Zissos (1999).

characterization of the Pierides is thus produced not only directly through their speech, which qualifies as blasphemous, but also indirectly through their use of narrators, which exposes them as falsifiers of the truth responsible for a partial and tendentious selection of contents.[70]

Just as evident as the tendentiousness of the Pierides' narration is the partiality of the summary that the Muse offers to Minerva. The demonization of the enemy-rival effected by the Muse is the same as that of Jupiter with regard to Lycaon, and of other narrators who through the "power of the word" are able to direct and affect the interpretation of their narration. (It is no coincidence that the judgement expressed by the external narrator regarding Arachne in her confrontation with Minerva is somewhat more toned down.) Through metadiegesis and the reproduction of the entire narrative process, Ovid raises the issues of the reliability of various narrators, the authority that the narrative function confers, and the truth that it asserts.

Thanks to the *mise en abyme* of the entire narrative situation, a few examples will show even more clearly this fundamental aspect of the function of storytelling in the poem. During his stay at the home of Achelous, Theseus notices that the river-god has been disfigured by the breaking of one of his horns, and asks him how this happened. Achelous balks at the suggestion that he recall his defeat by telling of the cause of this mutilation (brought about by an encounter with Hercules), and openly acknowledges his reluctance to do so (9.4–5): '*Triste petis munus. quis enim sua proelia uictus/ commemorare uelit?*' In his reluctant granting of the request, Achelous declares himself a reticent narrator, implicitly admitting that every narration is the product of a selection, and that besides the story which is told, there is also that which is omitted, or even consciously suppressed: that every story, in short, entails censoring.[71]

---

[70] Hofmann (1986), seeing an opposition between the *carmen perpetuum* of the Pierid and the *carmen deductum* of Calliope, attempts to explain the result of the contest in stylistic terms. Meanwhile, Hinds (1987a) 166–67 n. 40 finds a positive connotation, in Callimachean terms, in the Pierid's use of the word *extenuat* (320). Cf. Rosati (1994) 31 n. 38.

[71] I use the term in a sense different from that used by Nagle (1988c), who includes among "reticent" narrators characters who, like Perseus, arouse expectations of "heroic" narratives through their epic stature (in the manner of Ulysses and Aeneas)—expectations that Ovid frustrates, limiting the function of these characters to that of simple "occasions" for stories told by others (on "untold stories" see Mack (1988) 135–42).

We hear an analogous assertion from Nestor,[72] by antonomasia
the epic narrator, when Tlepolemus notes an odd censoring in the
narrative of the old man, in particular, a silence regarding the deeds
of his father Hercules. Tlepolemus asks Nestor the reason (12.542–48):

> tristis ad haec Pylius: 'quid me meminisse malorum
> cogis et obductos annis rescindere luctus
> inque tuum genitorem odium offensasque fateri?
> ille quidem maiora fide, di! gessit et orbem
> inpleuit meritis, quod mallem posse negare;
> sed neque Deiphobum nec Pulydamanta nec ipsum
> Hectora laudamus: quis enim laudauerit hostem?'

> Sadly the Pelian replied: "Why do you compel me to remember trou-
> bles and to call back grief overlaid with age, and to confess my hatred
> toward your father and his offenses? To be sure, he did things greater
> than can be believed—o gods!—and filled the world with his fame,
> which I would prefer to deny; but we praise neither Deiphobus nor
> Polydamas nor Hector himself; who has ever praised the enemy?"

A little later, Nestor confirms his intention not to include the accom-
plishments of his enemies in his story (573–76):

> nunc uideor debere tui praeconia rebus
> Herculis, o Rhodiae ductor pulcherrime classis?
> nec tamen ulterius, quam fortia facta silendo
> ulciscor fratres: solida est mihi gratia tecum.

> Do I now seem to owe to the deeds of your Hercules an announce-
> ment, o most excellent captain of the Rhodian fleet? No further do I
> take vengeance for my brothers than by being silent about brave deeds;
> my pleasure with you is firm.

The narrator's desire for revenge is expressed here through silence,
and through the power that speech confers: a story is never neutral,
but is an instrument of power, always disposed to assert a certain
truth. Through the use of *mise en abyme*, the external narrator, "Ovid,"
demonstrates the unreliability of his internal narrators and puts his
audience on guard against taking literally their assertions and the
stories that they tell, recommending instead that attention be paid
to what they do *not* say, to their silences. In other words, Ovid puts
us on guard against overlooking the dynamics of narrative levels and
of voices internal to the poem, while advising us that every narrator

---

[72] Zumwalt (1977) 216–17; Mack (1988) 128–31; Nagle (1989) 116–17.

constructs a personal, particular truth, containing silences, omissions, and evasions, as well as the story told—Nestor himself says that he has forgotten much ('*quamuis obstet mihi tarda uetustas/multaque me fugiant primis spectata sub annis,*' 12.182–83).[73] The narrating voice confers on every "narrative-man" the authority to orient the story to please himself: it is a useful instrument for manipulating the meaning of a story that in some way involves him or in which his self-interest is evident.

Through metadiegesis Ovid emphasizes the often tendentious biases and the evasions of his narrators: making them speak tendentiously also serves to show the subjectivity of the story, of every story, and to provoke doubt about narrative authority (obviously, including that of the author of the *Metamorphoses*). The manipulation of personal stories is, in turn, an indication of the manipulation of the Story, of the past (and of epic as a genre), which is also the product of things forgotten, omitted, evaded, and wilfully falsified. Ovid problematizes the appeal to tradition by altering, or rather by overturning, the meaning of an attribution to the so-called "Alexandrian footnote," i.e., the "bibliographical" references with which Alexandrian poets documented the source of their knowledge and so authenticated its truths. In Ovid these annotations assume forms of the type *fama est, fertur, dicitur*, and so forth, and also occur rather frequently in the mouths of the internal narrators.[74] Rather than certifying the truth, however, they lead to the opposite conclusion: to declare "it is said" or "rumor reports" is equivalent to saying "I have not seen it myself," and so equivalent to insisting on the distance that separates the narrator from the events and to rejecting the eye-witness guarantee of the truth of that which is narrated.

The multiplication of narrative voices works in powerful cooperation with this destabilization of the text, and with the truth that the distortion of this marker of reliability communicates. The primary narrator not only does not, according to convention, call on the wisdom of the Muses, but also renounces control of narration in the first person and the opportunity to impose a point of view

---

[73] An obvious case of evasion occurs with Cephalus (cf. Otis (1970) 179–82; Ahl (1985) 208–11), and perhaps "Ovid" himself, though 7.687–88 are suspected of being interpolated: see Tarrant (1995b).

[74] Cf. Wheeler (1999) 114 and 227–28 n. 44.

that is unified, secure, and authoritative. He refuses his own centrality as well as authorial control of voice and of meaning, and incorporates instead within himself individual truths and relative points of view: by delegating the narration to characters and so distancing it from himself (i.e., by transforming reality into a "reality of stories"), he registers their voices and their personal, partial truths. The result is a world of fluid truths, protean and prone to change, a world upon which only the narrator's role as protagonist manages to confer the unity of a *carmen perpetuum*.[75]

---

[75] The author extends his thanks to the editor for her assistance with the translation of this chapter.

CHAPTER TEN

THE HOUSE OF FAME: ROMAN HISTORY AND AUGUSTAN POLITICS IN *METAMORPHOSES* 11–15

Garth Tissol

1. *History Ovidianized*

For readers of Ovid's *Metamorphoses* who have made their way through the labyrinth of mythological tales that comprise Books 1–10, Book 11 is in some ways a fresh start. It begins the third and last pentad; and, as he marks this formal boundary, Ovid introduces a new historical emphasis. Troy is founded, and from Troy's story that of Rome soon arises: Roman subject matter, settings, and themes occupy ever more of our attention as the work approaches its end. Ovid includes some of the same tales that appear also in the *Fasti*, his most Roman work in terms of its proclaimed subject matter, the Roman calendar: *tempora cum causis Latium digesta per annum* (*F.* 1.1).[1] As we read of Hippolytus deified as Virbius, for instance, or encounter the list of Alban kings, the last pentad of the *Metamorphoses* may sometimes begin to resemble the *Fasti*, most of which Ovid composed during the same period of his life.[2] And yet Books 11–15 of the *Metamorphoses* are fully continuous with the first ten books—simultaneously a fresh start and a seamless continuation. Even the historical emphasis is a development of long-established patterns. First Trojan, then Roman subjects signal the work's conclusion, wherein the large-scale historical progression promised in the work's opening lines will be fulfilled: having set out "from the first beginnings of the world," *primaque ab origine mundi* (1.3), Ovid's narrative will now reach "my own times," *mea tempora* (1.4)—the present for both author and

---

[1] In fact, the *Fasti* blends Greek and Roman tales, "*res Romana* served up *à la grecque*," as Kenney (1982) 430 remarks; for its aetiological mode, see Miller, chapter 6 above.
[2] Virbius, *Met.* 14.497–546; *F.* 6.737–56; Alban kings, *Met.* 14.609–22; *F.* 4.41–52.

readers. Thus, if we, after reading of so many nymphs and maidens transformed into trees or waterfowl, are surprised to find Romulus turning up in Book 14 of the *Metamorphoses* and Julius Caesar in Book 15, Ovid's development and fulfillment of narrative patterns also remind us that from the start we had reason to expect such figures to appear. His vast work of transformative myth embraces even them.

Whereas Troy and Rome contribute something new to the last pentad of the *Metamorphoses*, they also function in a fashion that Ovid has made throughly familiar. Already in Book 1, the council of the gods, called by Jupiter to discuss Lycaon's crime, offers striking Romanization of heaven's architecture and social distinctions, with mention of *atria nobilium* (1.172), *plebs* (1.173), and the like.[3] When Ovid represents Jupiter summoning the gods to the *palatia caeli* (1.176), Jupiter becomes not only Romanized but a reflection of Augustus, whose house stood on the earthly Palatine Hill. Shortly thereafter, Ovid explicitly addresses Augustus in a context that links Lycaon's assassination attempt on Jupiter to contemporary attempts on Augustus's life (1.200–205). Both crises cause astonishment throughout the world: *nec tibi grata minus pietas, Auguste, tuorum est,/quam fuit illa Ioui* (1.204–5). Thus, in returning to current events at the end of the work, Ovid recalls to our minds their heralded arrival near the beginning.

Also familiar is the narrative use Ovid makes of his Trojan and Roman subject matter: it functions largely as a frame for other tales, which are often only tenuously related to the newly-prominent national themes. We are well aware, when we arrive at this point, that traditionally important and familiar cycles of myth, such as those concerning Theseus and Hercules in Books 8 and 9, function mainly as framing devices that connect tales; many of these are only tangentially related to the framing narrative, or are even altogether remote from it. No sooner does Ovid introduce Troy than he begins to employ it in this now-familiar narrative mode: the traditional story appears to establish a structural pattern for the progress of the narrative, but it is soon displaced, as tales succeed tales. Troy may be familiar ground, but its familiarity does not enable us to predict our convoluted path through Ovid's work with any confidence. Who could guess, when Laomedon founds Troy at 11.194, that Ceyx and

---

[3] On Romanization see Wheeler (1999) 172–77, 197–205; Solodow (1988) 82–86.

Alcyone would occupy much of our attention in Book 11? As we read their tragic tale, we may observe thematic links to other tales in the *Metamorphoses*, as in the personification of Somnus (11.592–649), which formally recalls those of Inuidia in Book 2 (760–832) and of Fames in Book 8 (799–822); yet the topic of Troy has disappeared, at least for now, from view. So has the new historical emphasis; for the tale of Ceyx and Alcyone is as mythical, as fabulous, as anything in the preceding ten books.

Indirection and unpredictability remain characteristic of the narrative even as Ovid draws historical and Roman material within his scope. One might expect history and Roman themes to alter the *Metamorphoses*; instead, as this chapter aims to show, the *Metamorphoses* alters them. An especially powerful symbol of Ovid's transformative language is his last and most ambitious personification, the House of Fame near the beginning of Book 12. After Ceyx and Alcyone, Ovid abruptly returns to Trojan subjects with Aesacus, as we will see below, then recounts the sacrifice of Iphigenia and the arrival of the Greek fleet at Troy. But before proceeding with the Trojan War, he introduces a remarkable descriptive passage on Fama, beginning with these lines:

> orbe locus medio est inter terrasque fretumque
> caelestesque plagas, triplicis confinia mundi;
> unde, quod est usquam, quamuis regionibus absit,
> inspicitur, penetratque cauas uox omnis ad aures.
> Fama tenet summaque domum sibi legit in arce. (12.39–43)

> There is a place at the middle of the world, between land, sea, and the heavenly region, at the boundary of the threefold universe. From here one can see anything anywhere, however distant its place; and every voice comes to one's hollow ears. Rumor holds it, and selected its topmost summit for her house.

This is the last and the most ambitious, though not the longest, of the large-scale personifications in the *Metamorphoses*—ambitious because, whereas with Inuidia (2.760–832) and Fames (8.799–822) Ovid achieves a rich and grimly detailed impression of corporality through his descriptive language, here indistinctness is paradoxically the goal of precise description.[4] The lines just quoted appear to establish the

---

[4] For a longer treatment of Fama in the context of Ovidian wit, see Tissol (1997) 85–88, and Rosati, chapter 9 above.

place of Fama's house, but in a way that defeats definition; for the house occupies a liminal site, hovering at the boundaries between earth, sea, and sky. The structure itself—if it can be called a structure—scarcely separates inside from outside, for its porous nature defeats such distinctions:

> innumerosque aditus ac mille foramina tectis
> addidit et nullis inclusit limina portis:
> nocte dieque patet; tota est ex aere sonanti,
> tota fremit uocesque refert iteratque, quod audit.
> nulla quies intus nullaque silentia parte. (12.44–48)

> She added innumerable approaches to the building, and a thousand openings. With no doors did she shut its threshold: it lies open night and day. The whole house is of resounding brass, produces a roar, echoes and repeats what it hears. There is no quiet within, silence in no quarter.

In and out of the house issue personified rumors:

> atria turba tenet: ueniunt, leue uulgus, euntque
> mixtaque cum ueris passim commenta uagantur
> milia rumorum confusaque uerba uolutant. (12.53–55)

> A throng occupies its halls; they come and go, a light crowd; lies mixed with truth wander here and there by the thousands; and the confused words of rumor roll about.

Only when this expansive description is finished do we learn its relevance to its surroundings: rumors of the Greek expedition have reached Troy (12.63–66). This house of Fama and her attendant rumors, "lies mixed with truth," creates a remarkable preface to the beginning of the Trojan War, inviting us readers to consider it as an interpretive comment on all that follows. Feeney connects the passage to themes of poetic authority in the *Metamorphoses*;[5] indeed, the authority of Ovid's epic predecessors, especially Homer's *Iliad* and *Odyssey* and Virgil's *Aeneid*, is at issue in the later books of the *Metamorphoses*, where extensively adapted—sometimes severely distorted—versions of their tales are woven into a new fabric. For much of the rest of Book 12, for instance, Nestor narrates the battle of Lapiths and Centaurs (12.210–535), as he did in Book 1 of the *Iliad* (1.263–68): but Homer's version is a brief summary, meant to illus-

---

[5] Feeney (1991) 247–49; see also Zumwalt (1977).

trate a point in its context, Ovid's a vast expansion that engulfs its context, displacing the Trojan War in our attention for hundreds of lines.

Fama dominates the rest of Ovid's poem, from Book 12 to the end, not only because of the formal introductory description of the house of Fama, but also because of the increasing role of internal narration in the later books: as the poem proceeds, the epic narrator recedes, and more and more tales are reported by an internal narrator to an internal audience.[6] Fama also forms a boundary for Books 12–15, prominently recurring at the very end of the *Metamorphoses*, where *fama* provides the means of the poet's continued survival: *perque omnia saecula fama,/siquid habent ueri uatum praesagia, uiuam* (15.878–79).

The recurring presence of Fama serves as a reminder of the fundamental lack of definition and stability characteristic of narrative style throughout the work. Flux remains Ovid's theme to the end, and Fama provides both a symbol and an embodiment of flux within the narrative. Fama resists the tendency toward interpretive simplicity and transparency that the introduction of historical and political topics might lead us to expect. As we proceed through the last pentad, historical and historico-political modes of understanding events, however pervasive their presence, ultimately never reduce Ovidian flux to order. Fate, for instance, a cosmic principle beloved of some Greek and Roman historians, whose workings they trace in the unfolding of events,[7] duly turns up from time to time in Ovid's *Metamorphoses*, and does so as a theme of historicized myth that is likely to remind us of Virgil's *Aeneid*. Yet, whereas the *Aeneid* is deeply imbued with a sense of fate, guiding the reader to a teleological understanding of myth and history, fate is an historical prop in the *Metamorphoses*—part of the furniture of historicized myth. Far from dominating its context, the context dominates it, as in the summaries of the *Aeneid* that Ovid employs as framing devices in Books 13 and 14: *non tamen euersam Troiae cum moenibus esse/spem quoque fata sinunt* (*Met.* 13.623–24). These lines introduce Aeneas's departure from Troy with unmistakable reference to Virgil's plot and theme. Whereas

---

[6] See Wheeler (1999) 162–65 and Rosati, chapter 9 above.
[7] See Walbank (1957) 1:16–26 on Tyche in Polybius; Fornara (1983) 81–82 on fate in Livy.

Virgil integrates fate into the structure and architecture of his poem, however, Ovid reduces fate and its impact on events to barest summary. He acknowledges Virgil's historical vision without permitting that vision to structure his narrative or his readers' experience of it. Instead, he appropriates Virgilian language for a characteristic Ovidian witticism, playing simultaneously on the literal and figurative senses of *euersam*. Troy's walls are physically overturned, but her hopes— conceptually and metaphorically—are not overturned. "Sylleptic wit" of this kind, as I have maintained elsewhere,[8] saturates the *Metamorphoses* and embodies its themes of transformation on the narrative surface: the loss of human identity in metamorphosis, the shifting of boundary between human and natural, indeed the obscuring of any such boundary—are events typical of the *Metamorphoses*; and Ovid now sets the plot of Virgil's *Aeneid* among them, exploiting Virgilian language for his own transformative wit. Although in the last pentad there is a shift to historical and national themes, and with them a more direct engagement with Ovid's epic predecessors, the *Metamorphoses* remains the same poem it was. The porous, echoing, boundary-less, and visually indistinct house of Fame incorporates all within it.

Ovid's epic predecessors are a conspicuous presence in the last pentad, and readers familiar with them may try to understand Ovid's material in similar terms. Yet Ovidian slipperiness remains: Ovid refuses to be pinned down, to yield to interpretive stability, although his readers may crave it. In fact, by introducing interpretive frameworks familiar from his predecessors—Virgilian fate, for instance, in the lines quoted above—Ovid takes advantage of his readers' desire for clarity: he invites us to reach conclusions, then fails to sustain them. Virgilian fate is one interpretive possibility that turns up in the *Metamorphoses*, yet without the structured development that Virgil gave it; Augustan historical vision is another.

By introducing historical and political subjects into his work, Ovid invites readers to consider the relationship of the *Metamorphoses* to the world outside it—not only to the *Aeneid* and earlier Roman epic on historical themes, but also to Augustan ideology and its expression outside poetry—in the architectural projects, for instance, by which Augustus transformed the Romans' physical environment. When Ovid introduces the voyage of Aeneas—alluding to the plot and even

---

[8] Tissol (1997) 18–26.

the vocabulary of Virgil's epic—he acknowledges his contemporary readers' awareness that the *Aeneid* has overwhelmed other versions of this story: Ovid could not retell this story with directing readers' awareness from his own text to Virgil's. When Ovid incorporates the apotheosis of Romulus into the narrative of Book 14, readers are likely to find that their thoughts turn unavoidably to Augustus's identification of himself as the new Romulus, and to accompanying images and slogans concerning the re-foundation and renewal of Rome. Because Augustus eventually gains, like Romulus, a place among the *diui*, Ovid's apotheosis of Romulus invites his readers at least provisionally to define the relationship between this figure from the remote past and his contemporary embodiment.

Ovid presents a parade of heroes in the later books of the *Metamorphoses*. Hercules leads the way in Book 9; then Aeneas, Romulus, Julius Caesar, and Augustus form a sequence of apotheosized mortals. These figures are already iconic when they turn up in Ovid's poem—iconic in the sense that they resemble images that are powerfully identified with meanings, like the statues of these very heroes that stood in Augustus's forum. Because Ovid's parade of heroes arrives accompanied by preexisting interpretive baggage, it will be worthwhile to contrast these two fundamentally different sites of meaning, each with its own ways of associating ancient with contemporary heroes: the Forum of Augustus, an architectural space well designed and equipped to promote a unified and coherent set of messages about the relationship of past to present; and Ovid's *Metamorphoses*, a fluid narrative on the prevalence of change, whose author enacts his theme by mischievous artistry, establishing patterns of meaning, then disrupting and fracturing them. Historical patterns are among those that Ovid deliberately reduces to incoherence. Each of these sites of meaning is powerfully manipulative, and each achieves its impact by means well suited to the message. Meeting a Roman hero in the Forum Augusti, the observer's upward gaze would encounter not only an impressive image, but also a *titulus*, identifying him, and an *elogium*, recording his achievements.[9] Furthermore, this experience takes place within an architectural complex, the Forum Augusti, erected by Augustus in payment of a vow made while

---

[9] On the Forum Augusti and its sculptural program, see Zanker (1968); Kockel in Steinby (1993–2000) 2:289–95.

fighting his adoptive father's assassins at the Battle of Philippi. Within so structured an experience, the observer of its visual images and inscriptional texts is unlikely to go far astray in interpreting them.

Although the battle occurred in 42 B.C.E., the Forum itself, dedicated in 2 B.C.E., was a recent reminder of that event for the readers of Ovid's *Metamorphoses*. In the parallel exedras along its longer sides stood statues of Aeneas on one side and Romulus on the other.[10] For Ovid to set the parallel apotheoses of these same heroes near each other in Book 14 is to make inevitable the reader's recognition of Augustan meanings attached to these deified heroes. At the same time, in the *Metamorphoses* these figures are iconic in a far less tightly regulated context of meanings than they are in the forum. Though now purely verbal, they resemble ideological statements less than do the forum's statues; for Ovid presents his portraits, so to speak, without *titulus* and *elogium* to regulate their interpretation. Thus exposed, the portraits lose their interpretive transparency and become vulnerable to incorporation into Ovidian flux.

Consistent with the organization and coherence of the Forum Augusti is the fact that its symbolism is easy to interpret. Within the temple of Mars Ultor, for instance, stood cult statues of Mars, the father of Romulus, parent and protector of the Romans, and Venus, the ancestress of the Julian *gens*. Everything about these images directs the viewer's attention away from the adultery of Mars and Venus so prominent in their mythological tradition. Only the irreverent and satirical perspective that Ovid offers in *Tristia* 2 resists the ennobling abstraction of such figures and drags adultery back into view. There, Ovid describes the cult statues of Mars and Venus, who stood next to each other in the temple's cella, as *Venus Vltori iuncta* (*Tr.* 2.296), "Venus joined to the Avenger"—an expression that invites reflection on the sexual significance of *iungere*.[11] Venus's husband stands outside the door, *uir ante fores*.[12]

A myth of political origin, its official representation in art, and resistance to it are prominent also in the *Metamorphoses* in the tale of

---

[10] See Zanker (1988) 201–3. On juxtaposed portraits of Aeneas and Romulus in a Pompeian wall-painting, taken to reflect the appearance of the statues in the Forum Augusti, see Zanker (1988) 202.

[11] See Adams (1982) 179–80.

[12] For the sense and topographical significance of Ovid's expression, see Owen (1924) 174–76 on *Tr.* 2.296.

Arachne (Book 6), which Rosati has discussed in the preceding chapter. Here it is enough to emphasize that the tale offers rich reflections on official interpretation of art. When Minerva chooses to depict her victory over Neptune in the two divinities' dispute over the naming of Athens, her tapestry, decorously ordered and balanced, promotes its didactic message with unavoidable clarity, while offering an aesthetic correlate to the power of enforcement that lies behind that message. Readers often side with the Arachne and her irreverent depiction of divine misbehavior; yet Minerva does not ask for our approval, nor need she take much thought for the judges of the contest. Her views of the story are enforceable and will determine the outcome of the plot. Her power allows her to impose her perspective on events.

Because the historical subjects of the later books of the *Metamorphoses* so often bring official interpretations within view, it is worth noting that, according to one political approach to literature currently in favor, only official interpretations are possible. On this view, all activity of writing and reading takes place within a fixed political system, often unrecognized by the participants, that "advances the interests" of "elites."[13] Proponents of this approach offer a powerfully reductive historicism: nothing is important about literature except the historically determined power-relationships that govern its production and reception; all attention to literary qualities of a text is sentimental and self-indulgent aestheticism.

Whereas this view contracts all understanding of literature to the narrowly political, some recent writers on history in Roman literature expand the historical to a larger field that embraces Varro's *theologia tripertita* and the universal history of Cornelius Nepos, Diodorus Siculus, and others.[14] In the shift, for instance, from mythological to historical subjects in the *Metamorphoses*, we can see a broad similarity to Varro's *De gente populi Romani*.[15] Wheeler's work on elements of universal history in the *Metamorphoses* shows that Ovid's awareness of historical principles is far deeper and more intimate than has been recognized before: for instance, the poem's "alternation between diachrony and synchrony is a narrative technique characteristic of

---

[13] Habinek (1998) 3; see also Kennedy (1992) 26–58.
[14] On Varro see Lieberg (1973); on universal history Wheeler (1999) 125–28, and (2002).
[15] Wheeler (1999) 126.

universal history."[16] The poem's chronological framework from first origins to the present also reflects the aims of universal history; yet Wheeler, like most critics today, does not view the poem "as a natural process of evolution from chaos to cosmos, culminating in the peace and properity of the Augustan age."[17] Arguing for a subtler and less overtly political patterning of events, he traces historical principles behind the increasingly historical subject matter of the last pentad. The movement from myth to history represents "a shift," in Wheeler's view, "from a *theologia fabulosa* to a *theologia civilis*."[18] The terms are Varronian, and invite us to contemplate the *Metamorphoses* alongside Varro's *Antiquitates rerum humanarum et divinarum* (47 B.C.E.), a massive and comprehensive work, among whose aims was to organize conceptions of divinity into mythical, natural, and civic (Aug., *Civ. Dei* 6.5). Ovid is known to have used the *Antiquitates* as a source in the later books of the *Metamorphoses* as well as in the *Fasti*, and it is surely right to call attention to the presence of Varronian principles in Ovid's work. Yet Varro's conceptual organization does not structure Ovid's work, and Varro's religio-historical vision only partly informs Ovid's. Ovid brings Varro into the mix just as he does Augustan mythologizing and the historical mythologizing undertaken by his epic predecessors, especially Homer, Ennius, and Virgil. P. Hardie has recently argued for the presence of Livy in the *Metamorphoses*, arguing that Ovid's vision is fundamentally historical: "Ovid writes the long historical epic that Virgil self-consciously had abjured."[19] Recent emphasis on history in Ovid has much to teach us about the poet's intellectual depth and awareness of contemporary thought; yet it also runs the risk of presupposing a conceptual tidiness and order that Ovid's work in fact thwarts and defies. The historical vision of the *Metamorphoses* remains deeply fractured, stubbornly resistant to schematizing, and intentionally incoherent. Ovid acknowledges historical conceptions, but his work escapes their power to shape his material and to govern our responses to his text. Ovid's "historical" books are as strange, perverse, unpredictable, and provocative as the "fabulous" books that precede them.

---

[16] Wheeler (2002).
[17] Wheeler (2000) 109.
[18] Wheeler (2000) 139–40.
[19] Hardie (2002).

2. *From Trojan History to Natural History*

In Book 11, the *Metamorphoses* suddenly becomes historical: "the 'historical' section actually begins at 11.194 with Laomedon's founding of Troy."[20] To be sure, the poem has pursued the course of history from the opening lines of Book 1, while, I have suggested, Romanization on both a large and small scale has kept contemporary reference, analogies, and allegorical interpretive options before our eyes throughout the progress of the work. Yet the foundation of Troy, which turns up as a narrative topic just after King Midas has received ass's ears, abruptly brings the poem's subject-matter within the boundaries of history. As Kenney notes, "For the ancients, in so far as a distinction was made between history and myth, the Trojan War tended to mark the dividing line. This, with its aftermath, occupies the next three books [11–13]."[21] Because, however, Rome's origins are in Troy, Book 11 also begins a narrative sequence that continues to the end of the poem, and indeed to the moment of reading for Ovid's Roman audience. In the last pentad, Books 11–15, "mythical" tales continue unabated, but now jostle with tales from Roman history and even "current events," all brought within the narrative sweep. Among "current events" we may locate the transformation of Julius Caesar's soul into a star near the end of Book 15. Yet this transformation is thoroughly mythologized, for it occurs among the activities of the goddess Venus.

With Troy's foundation, history arrives well integrated into the poem's patterns of mythological narrative. We might expect that linearity and clarity of narrative progress would arrive along with historical subjects, and indeed the last pentad is sometimes described as if this were the case. Wilkinson writes, "When we reach Laomedon's Troy (11, 194) the principle of chronological sequence takes charge again: it is 'after that' rather than 'meanwhile' that sustains the illusion of reality."[22] But Wilkinson's impression is in fact illusory. The amount of material recounted by internal narrators steadily increases in the later books,[23] so that chronological movement is constantly interrupted and postponed by tales of the past, recent or remote.

---

[20] Coleman (1971) 472 n. 1.
[21] Kenney (1986) 439.
[22] Wilkinson (1978) 238.
[23] See Wheeler (1999) 162–63, and Rosati, chapter 9 above.

Even more remarkable is the fact that history arrives together with manifest anachronism. It is often noted that the participation of Hercules in the foundation of Troy—his rescue of Hesione and his capture of the city after Laomedon refuses him the promised horses (11.212–15)—occurs some 1400 lines after the hero's death and apotheosis in Book 9 (134–272): "Ovid makes no attempt to reconcile the chronology."[24] Wheeler has explored Ovid's anachronisms in revealing detail, showing that at Hercules' death in Book 9, "Troy is assumed to exist already in the world of the poem," and that "Ovid could have avoided the anachronism by placing stories about the dead and deified Hercules in the mouths of characters who report retrospective events in inset narratives that temporarily suspend the main chronological thread."[25] Instead, Ovid flaunts his disruption of chronology, first recounting Hercules' death and apotheosis, then introducing a narrator, Alcmene, mother of Hercules, to recount his birth (9.273–323). In Book 9, chronology appears to reverse direction, but at Book 11 chronological dislocation turns out to be more complex than simple reversal. Wheeler's conclusions refute the common notion that Ovid's shift to historical topics results in a more linear narrative explication and greater chronological regularity:

> The reintroduction of Hercules in Book 11 is therefore part and parcel of a larger web of anachronism involving the foundation of Troy and the marriage of Peleus and Thetis, both of which should have occurred already in the poem's historical continuum. It should be clear, furthermore, that Ovid's transpositions of the foundation of Troy and the marriage of Peleus and Thetis are a deliberate structural strategy to furnish new points of origin for the narrative of the final books of the poem. That is, Ovid deliberately violates his earlier chronological scheme to provide new beginning points for the final pentad (i.e., from the foundation of Troy and the birth of Achilles to the present).[26]

As a result, the formality and regularity of the pentadic structure produces a paradoxical result: on the one hand, it divides the work symmetrically into thirds and hence to some extent structures the experience of the reader: we may compare the division of Virgil's *Aeneid* into halves, in allusive reference to the *Odyssey* (1–6) and *Iliad* (7–12).[27] On the other hand, in effecting a new beginning for the

---

[24] Kenney (1986) 439.
[25] Wheeler (1999) 137, 136.
[26] Wheeler (1999) 138.
[27] See Servius on *Aen.* 7.1.

last pentad, Ovid reinforces the narrative indirection and unpredictability that have characterized the *Metamorphoses* from its beginning.

The tales that follow the foundation of Troy both illuminate and obscure the newly initiated narrative patterns of the last pentad. At this point, Ovid's readers may expect him to expand upon the origins of the Trojan conflict. He does so in his account of Peleus and Thetis, the parents of Achilles, but hastily summarizes the elements of the story that are traditionally the most important: Thetis receives a prophecy that she will bear a son who will surpass his father; Jupiter, despite his passion, avoids mating with Thetis "lest the universe contain anything greater than Jupiter" (*ne quicquam mundus Ioue maius haberet*, 11.224). Ovid alters the authority for the prophecy, substituting the shape-shifting divinity Proteus for Themis as its source.[28] He then develops the story in his own way, dwelling upon a description of the bay frequented by Thetis, Peleus's attempt to assault her (which she thwarts by shape-shifting), Proteus's advice to Peleus that he tie her up as she sleeps, and the successful results. Some of this account will remind us of epic predecessors, for Proteus is familiar from the *Odyssey* (4.384–470) as well as from a brief appearance earlier in the *Metamorphoses* (8.732–37), and from Virgil's *Georgics* (4.387–453). Yet in emphasizing shape-shifting and sexual assault, Ovid flaunts the unedifying nature of his account and its lack of relevance to any of the large-scale themes, providential, historical, and originary, that one might expect at the threshhold of events that lead to the foundation of Rome. An account of origins this may be, with reference to historical subjects, and formally analogous to Virgil's reworking of Homeric material in the *Aeneid*; yet Ovid offers it manifestly without the interpretive guidance that would associate it with Virgilian themes. As an account of origins, it explores causes of the Trojan War still more remote than those developed by Ovid's predecessors, suggesting a line of interpretation that traces events back to lust, violence, and deception at least as much as to beneficent destiny.

In the rest of Book 11, Ovid on the one hand traces Trojan subject matter from its origins, and on the other characteristically takes his narrative into unforeseen directions. The tales of Daedalion and his daughter Chione and of Ceyx and Alcyone are intricately linked to the matter of Troy; yet in them Ovid pursues free-wheeling digressive

---

[28] Themis: Pindar, *Isthm.* 8.32.

variety that is entirely consistent with the earlier books of the *Meta-morphoses*, in no way more linear, predictable, or goal-directed than formerly.

At the end of Book 11, Troy, chronology, and fate turn up in another tale of amorous pursuit. Ovid attaches his tale of Aesacus, a son of Priam first known from Ovid's version, to that of Ceyx and Alcyone, whose unhappy tale of fidelity and loss has long occupied our attention. Observing the royal couple, now transformed to kingfishers, near the shore, an old man and his neighbor shift their conversation to another sea-bird, the diver, who likewise turns out to have a human history and even royal lineage. In a send-up of learned claims to poetic authority,[29] Ovid's narrator cannot tell us which of the two interlocutors is the source for the story: *proximus, aut idem, si fors tulit . . . dixit* (11.751). The irony of this crisis of authority is especially marked by the genealogical king-list that follows, which approaches annalistic, even inscriptional style:

> et si descendere ad ipsum
> ordine perpetuo quaeris, sunt huius origo
> Ilus et Assaracus raptusque Ioui Ganymedes
> Laomedonue senex Priamusque nouissima Troiae
> tempora sortitus. frater fuit Hectoris iste:
> qui nisi sensisset prima noua fata iuuenta
> forsitan inferius non Hectore nomen haberet (11.754–60).

> And if you wish to follow his lineage down to him in continuous sequence, his ancestors were Ilus, Assaracus, Ganymede, seized by Jupiter, and Priam, allotted Troy's last days. That bird there was Hector's brother. If he had not experienced a strange fate in early youth, perhaps he would have no less a name than Hector's.

Ovid appears simultaneously to claim and to obscure authority for the tale. To complete the paradox, he refers to the king-list as *ordo perpetuus* (755), "a continuous list": thus the pretensions of his *carmen perpetuum* to be a universal history, conducted in unbroken sequence from first beginnings to the present, serve to introduce a tale of admittedly indeterminate origin.

The tale that follows is primarily a natural aetiology, incorporating both historical and epic subjects into an account of how Hector's brother became the origin of a species of sea-bird. Aesacus chases

---

[29] See Rosati, chapter 9, above.

Hesperie, who in her hasty flight steps on a snake, Eurydice-like, and dies of its bite. Her pursuer is introduced as hating cities and devoted to rural life, yet unrustic in his susceptibility to love: *non agreste tamen nec inexpugnabile amori/pectus habens* (11.767–68). *Amor agrestis* is not uncommon in the *Metamorphoses* and will soon be fully developed in the tale of Polyphemus (13.750–897). What is unusual in Aesacus are his guilt and remorse at Hesperie's death:

> uulnus ab angue
> a me causa data est. ego sum sceleratior illo,
> qui tibi morte mea mortis solacia mittam. (11.780–82)

> The wound was given by the snake, the cause by me. I committed a greater crime than the snake, and will send you consolation for your death by my own.

When he throws himself from a cliff, the sea-goddess Tethys pities him and transforms him into the diver: the verb *mergitur* (795) at the end of the story echoes the noun *mergus* (753) at its beginning. Thus, the whole story is framed as an aetiology of the bird's name, and so establishes a link between the history of Troy and the origins of the natural world. Trojan history, along with all notions of historical progress to the glorious present, becomes naturalized and incorporated into aetiological explication; natural phenomena, meanwhile, receive a history, and suggest that an historicized understanding of nature is possible.[30]

3. *Aeneas, Romulus, and Hersilia*

Natural aetiologies are prominent in Ovid's integration of Trojan subjects into the *Metamorphoses*. As he introduces more Roman subjects and Roman heroes into his narrative, his aetiological focus turns from the earth to the heavens. The poem's first apotheosis is that of Hercules in Book 9; a sequence of apotheoses and catasterisms follows. Near the end of Book 15, after Jupiter has promised Venus to make the soul of her descendant, Julius Caesar, into a star, she, although unable to prevent Caesar's murder, snatches the soul from

---

[30] On aetiological explication in the *Metamorphoses*, see the comprehensive work of Myers (1994a).

his limbs and carries it to the heavens. There, having become a star, it rejoices to see its own deeds outdone by those of Augustus (15.840–51). When Augustus forbids his own deeds to be preferred to his father's, personified Fama reappears to thwart him:

> hic sua praeferri quamquam uetat acta paternis,
> libera fama tamen nullisque obnoxia iussis
> inuitum praefert unaque in parte repugnat. (15.852–54)

> Although he forbids his own deeds to be preferred to his father's, nevertheless Fame, free and not yielding to any commands, prefers him against his will, defying him in this matter only.

To attribute *modestia* to a ruler is standard in panegyric, and equally standard are the *exempla* that follow;[31] but because these lines appear in the *Metamorphoses*, they invite multiple perspectives on the events described. Readers are already familiar with Fama as the source of "lies mixed with truth," which issue from her echoing house, and have met her also as "the herald of truth," offering an accurate prophecy about the royal succession among Rome's early kings: *destinat imperio clarum praenuntia ueri/fama Numam* (15.3–4). Later in Book 15, Pythagoras claims Fama as his authority for predicting the rise of Rome: *'nunc quoque Dardaniam fama est consurgere Romam'* (15.431).

To be sure, any claims of truth for Fama are problematic in the *Metamorphoses*. The identification of Fama as *praenuntia ueri* occurs in a context of manifest anachronism, the irony of which would have been obvious to Ovid's Roman readers. The succession of Numa, the second king of Rome, was an accepted part of the historical record; but Ovid's readers knew well that the tradition of his visit to Croton as a student of Pythagoras was chronologically impossible. As Wheeler observes, "Cicero (*Rep.* 2.28–29; *Tusc.* 4.2) and Livy (1.18.2–5) point out that Pythagoras did not come to Italy until the fourth year of the reign of Tarquinius Superbus (c.530 B.C.), 140 years after Numa's death. The Ovidian narrator, however, exploits the audience's awareness of the anachronism to launch one of the greatest non-events of the poem."[32]

After Fama's appearance in the tale of Numa, her recurrence as an agent in the tale of Caesar's soul exemplifies the ambiguous nature

---

[31] See Bömer *Met.* 7:482–83 on 15.852.
[32] Wheeler (1999) 127. On the problematic nature of Fama, see also Hardie (1997) 193–95.

of the politically charged episodes at the end of the *Metamorphoses*. Few passages in the work provoke such widely divergent views as the apotheosis of Caesar's soul, and all of them, I would maintain, can find support in Ovid's text and are in fact generated by it: that Ovid introduces the apotheosis and Augustan panegyric "in all seriousness," and "employs the official terminology in an entirely loyal fashion";[33] that this material is ridiculous, satirical, even subversive. My own view is that it is intentionally incoherent, presenting the reader with irreconcilable interpretive options. Certainly there is a striking dichotomy in modern critical positions taken on whether the apotheosis is integral to the larger work or loosely added as extraneous matter. According to Galinsky, "The eulogy of Augustus and the account of Julius Caesar's apotheosis are not the organic end of a persistent thematic development." Wheeler maintains the opposite position: "It should be evident from the numerous examples of apotheosis in the *Metamorphoses* that Julius Caesar's catasterism is the repetition of a common tale-type, which is associated with the end of narrative sequences, books, and pentads, and the poem as a whole."[34]

When we turn to consider the apotheoses of Aeneas and Romulus in Book 14, we find that they prepare for and introduce not only the apotheosis itself of Caesar's soul, but also the interpretive questions it raises. At 14.441 Ovid resumes the engagement with Virgil's *Aeneid* that he had begun, and intermittently pursued, in the preceding book.[35] Ovid takes over from Virgil the burial of Aeneas's nurse Caieta as an initiatory gesture: in the *Aeneid* it begins Book 7, and Ovid's version of *Aeneid* 7–12 begins here, too. Ovid adds an epitaph for Caieta: *hic me Caietam notae pietatis alumnus/ereptam Argolico quo debuit igne cremauit* (14.443–44). By emphasizing Caieta's rescue from one fire and cremation by another, Ovid calls attention to an etymological explanation of her name from καίειν, glossed by *cremare*. Thereby Ovid alludes "to the derivation that Virgil omitted," as O'Hara notes.[36] Ovid is in a sense commenting on Virgil's text,

---

[33] Bömer *Met.* 7:453–54 on 15.745; 7:250 on 15.1.
[34] Galinsky (1975) 253; Wheeler (2000) 139, and similarly 143: "the Caesar episode . . . participates in the poem's dynamics of repetition and continuity as much as any other episode."
[35] On Ovid's little *Aeneid* see Tissol (1993), (1997) 177–91; Hinds (1998) 107–19.
[36] O'Hara (1996) 268. Hinds (1998) 108, on another Ovidian rewriting, notes "the air of editorial comment."

noting an etymology that would later find a place also in Servius's commentary on the *Aeneid*.[37] Another effect of Ovid's revision is to fill out the earlier account, suggesting that there is more to the story than what Virgil provides.

There follows a severely abridged summary of Books 7–11 of the *Aeneid*. After Aeneas's arrival, the subsequent war in Latium up to Venulus's embassy to Diomedes requires only nine lines (14.450–58). Ovid here resumes his earlier procedure in retelling the *Aeneid*: most of Virgil's work he reduces to brief, sometimes comically abbreviated, summary; he also adds many tales not in Virgil. In parallel fashion, Ovid had earlier refashioned the *Iliad*, expanding the inset tale of the Lapiths and Centaurs to great length, and adding two tales not in Homer's account: a nearly inconclusive struggle between Achilles and the invulnerable Cygnus (12.63–167), and a verbal battle, the debate over the arms of Achilles (13.1–398); in both of them, Homeric heroism becomes attenuated until it is barely noticeable. Ovid now reworks two tales from the *Aeneid* that had offered accounts of transformation: the companions of Diomedes, transformed to seabirds (*Aen.* 11.271–74; *Met.* 14.494–509), and Aeneas's ships, transformed to nymphs (*Aen.* 9.77–122; *Met.* 14.546–65).[38] In Ovid's account, the first of these becomes a tale of unequal justice typical of the *Metamorphoses*, though thematically remote from the *Aeneid*: Acmon, recounting the miseries that Diomedes' crew has endured at the hands of Venus, impiously provokes her (*Met.* 14.486–95). *Dicta placent paucis* (*Met.* 14.496), "his words please few" of his comrades; but Venus punishes both Acmon and those who opposed him with arbitrary transformation. Her power is amply demonstrated; yet the lesson of the tale remains at best ambiguous, and its conclusion seems to transfer its uncertainties into the visual sphere. These are *uolucres dubiae*, and any attempt to identify them must remain frustrated: '*si, uolucrum quae sit dubiarum forma, requiris,/ut non cygnorum, sic albis proxima cygnis*' (*Met.* 14.508–9).

The alternating pattern of severe abbreviation and vast expansion of Virgilian material provides a context for the apotheosis of Aeneas, an event foretold but not narrated in the *Aeneid*. Jupiter begins his consolatory prophecy to Venus in *Aeneid* 1 by mentioning the foun-

---

[37] Servius on *Aen.* 7.1: *unde Caieta dicta est*, ἀπὸ τοῦ καίειν.
[38] On the ships transformed to nymphs see Fantham (1990).

dation of Lavinium and Aeneas's apotheosis. Both are assurances that fate and Jupiter's established plans have not changed:

> parce metu, Cytherea, manent immota tuorum
> fata tibi; cernes urbem et promissa Lauini
> moenia, sublimemque feres ad sidera caeli
> magnanimum Aenean; neque me sententia uertit. (*Aen.* 1.257–60)

> Cease from fear, Cytherea: your fates remain for you unmoved. You will see the city and promised walls of Lavinium, and you will carry aloft great-souled Aeneas to the constellations of heaven; my decision has not changed.

Jupiter's prophecy, which at this point already has passed well beyond the plot of the *Aeneid*, embraces all Rome's fortunes within a reassuring teleological vision. Among the events prophesied is the reconciliation of Juno with the Romans, which is to prove important both for the *Aeneid* and for Ovid's recontextualization of Virgilian topics:

> quin aspera Iuno,
> quae mare nunc terrasque metu caelumque fatigat,
> consilia in melius referet, mecumque fouebit
> Romanos, rerum dominos gentemque togatam. (*Aen.* 1.279–82)

> Furthermore, harsh Juno, who now wears out sea, earth, and heaven with fear, will turn her plans to a better course: along with me she will cherish the Romans, lords of all, the people of the toga.

We ought better to call this not *the* but *a* reconciliation, for, introduced after Jupiter's mention of Romulus and the foundation of Rome, it appears not to refer to the reconciliation that actually occurs in *Aeneid* 12. There, shortly before the final encounter of Aeneas and Turnus, Jupiter appeals to Juno to give up her wrath; she does so, stipulating that the Latins not be required to give up their language and dress, and that Troy remain fallen (*Aen.* 12.791–842). In *Aeneid* 1, however, Virgil follows Ennius's *Annales* in dating Juno's reconciliation to the time of the second Punic War, Ennius's own subject, as Servius notes on the words *consilia in melius referet: quia bello Punico secundo, ut ait Ennius, placata Iuno coepit fauere Romanis (Ann.* 8.16 Skutsch).[39] Virgil mentions the chronologically later reconciliation long before describing the former. In Book 1 Jupiter takes a longer view of destiny, showing that a conflict introduced but unresolved in the *Aeneid*,

---

[39] Cf. also Servius on *Aen.* 12.841: *constat bello Punico secundo exoratam Iunonem.*

the future hostility of Carthage, will eventually be resolved happily. Whether we take Juno's reconciliation in *Aeneid* 12 to be incomplete, impermanent, or, as Feeney concludes, limited to only some of Juno's grudges,[40] it contributes only a partial sense of closure to the end of Virgil's poem.

Ovid's transformation of Aeneas into the divine Indiges more specifically recalls *Aeneid* 12 than *Aeneid* 1, especially the beginning of Jupiter's address to Juno at *Aen.* 12.794–95: '*indigetem Aenean scis ipsa et scire fateris/deberi caelo fatisque ad sidera tolli.*' Ovid does not closely follow the chronology of Juno's reconciliation in *Aeneid* 12, however, shifting it instead to a time beyond Vergil's plot, and just preceding the apotheosis of Aeneas, which indeed it serves to introduce:

> iamque deos omnes ipsamque Aeneia uirtus
> Iunonem ueteres finire coegerat iras,
> cum bene fundatis opibus crescentis Iuli
> tempestiuus erat caelo Cythereius heros. (14.581–84)

> And now Aeneas's virtue had compelled all the gods, even Juno herself, to put an end to old anger, when the resources of rising Iulus were well established, and the hero, Venus's son, was ripe for heaven.

The thoughts and language strongly recall the *Aeneid*, but Ovid introduces these lines into bizarre, surreal surroundings of his own making. Their immediate context is one of the strangest transformations in the poem—the tale of Turnus's hometown, Ardea, changed into the heron. Turnus and the town Ardea may be Virgilian in their associations, but Ovid's treatment is remote from Virgil, and takes his own aetiological procedure to new extremes. It is typical of Ovid's natural aetiologies that they account for the first animal of a species, *tum primum cognita praepes* (14.576), and that they stress the continuity of traits and features in the change from the old to the new shape. This case goes beyond the typical in the sheer imaginative effort required to make the shift from a ruined city, with all its attributes, to a heron. Cities, as human social organizations, are characteristically distinct from the natural; this is not just any city, but one embedded in the human history of Rome and Rome's enemies, and familiar in Rome's national epic. Yet Ardea retains even its name in its migration into the avian realm as the first heron:

---

[40] Feeney (1984) 184.

et sonus et macies et pallor et omnia, captam
quae deceant urbem, nomen quoque mansit in illa
urbis et ipsa suis deplangitur Ardea pennis. (14.578–80)

> It had the sound, the wasted condition, the pallor—everything that
> befits a conquered city; even the city's name remained in the bird,
> and Ardea beats her breast, in mourning for herself, with her own
> wings.

These remarkable lines, which immediately precede the apotheosis
of Aeneas, provide no contextual introduction to the apotheosis, no
invitation to form a close approximation of Ovid's and Virgil's Aeneas.
Aeneas and his *uirtus* abruptly arrive at 582; yet no sooner do the
gods and Juno give up their wrath, introducing a new and impres-
sive array of literary, historical, and political associations, than the
tone of Ovid's version of the apotheosis becomes intrusively comic.
Venus canvasses the gods like a Roman politician: *ambieratque Venus
superos* (14.585).[41] She appeals to Jupiter's grandfatherly pride, and
seems to treat *numen* as a rare and valuable commodity in begging
some of it for her son, '*quamuis paruum des, optime, numen,/dummodo des
aliquod*' (14.589–90). All these details are at least potentially comic,
as is the argument—wholly successful in the event—with which Venus
concludes her speech. One trip to hell is enough: '*satis est inamabile
regnum/adspexisse semel, Stygios semel isse per amnes*' (14.590–91). These
lines are a comic correction of Virgil.[42] Later readers were to be dis-
tressed that Virgil's Sibyl, otherwise a knowledgeable prophetess, was
unaware of Aeneas's apotheosis, which Jupiter had explicitly proph-
esied in Book 1 and was to prophesy again in Book 12. Otherwise
she would not have assumed a second trip for Aeneas to the infer-
nal regions after his death:

quod si tantus amor menti, si tanta cupido
bis Stygios innare lacus, *bis* nigra uidere
Tartara, et insano iuuat indulgere labori,
accipe quae peragenda prius. (*Aen.* 6.133–36)

---

[41] Feeney (1991) 207: "Yet Venus 'canvasses' the gods, as does Hercules in the
Apocolocyntosis: the author of that skit knew exactly what he was about when he
inserted his splendid joke on Claudius's apotheosis being added as a footnote to
the *Metamorphoses*, for he thereby declares the basis of his and Ovid's procedure to
be the same parody of senatorial procedure (*Apoc.* 9)."
[42] On "correction" of Virgil see Thomas (1986), Zetzel (1989), Finkelpearl (1990)
340, Martindale (1993) 45, Feldherr (1999).

But if your mind has so great a longing, so great a desire to swim the Stygian pools twice, twice to look upon dark Tartarus, and it pleases you to indulge in an insane effort, learn what must be accomplished first.

Servius tries to reconcile the death of Aeneas, implied here, with Ovid's apotheosis of him, though he could have mentioned Jupiter's two prophecies in the *Aeneid* itself; Servius proposes that *simulacra* of apotheosized heroes, no less than of ordinary folk, are to be found in the underworld.[43] We do not know whether readers and critics in Ovid's time were already vexed about the Sibyl's evident lack of knowledge,[44] but Ovid's Venus, correcting *bis* with *semel*, sets the record straight.

Once Venus has asked the help of the river Numicius in washing away all that is mortal in Aeneas, she completes the process of making him into a divinity "whom Quirinus's crowd calls Indiges, and has received with altars and a temple" (*quem turba Quirini / nuncupat Indigetem temploque arisque recepit*, 14.607–8). This information is profoundly historical, for how Romans understand the altars and temples of their gods, how they connect the remote to the recent past, depends on the symbolic narrative or narratives that their minds associate with monuments in their city. Ovid's revision of Vergil is the revision of a well known and compelling historical vision. Ovid's concluding lines on Aeneas also, as editors note, offer a parallel to the language of an inscription for a statue of Aeneas found at Pompeii: *appel[latus]q.est Indigens [pa]ter et in deo[rum n]umero relatus* (*CIL* 1².189.1 = Dessau 63).[45]

Mention of the *turba Quirini* looks forward to the apotheosis of Romulus later in Book 14, but first there intervenes a king-list—an annalistic structuring of the past remarkable in finding a place in the *Metamorphoses*. Like the renaming of Aeneas, the list of Latin kings (14.609–22) also recalls to Roman readers their reading of inscriptions.[46] This king-list also recalls earlier lists in the *Metamorphoses*, such as the genealogy of Aesacus. His transformation is a natural aetiology,

---

[43] Servius on *bis Stygios innare lacus: modo et post mortem. quod autem dicit Ouidius, Aeneam inter deos relatum, non mirum est. nam ut supra etiam diximus, necesse est etiam relatorum inter deos apud inferos esse simulacra: ut Herculis, Liberi patris, Castoris et Pollucis.*

[44] On prophetic unawareness in general, see O'Hara (1990); on inconsistencies in prophecy esp. 27–33, 123–27, 141–47.

[45] See Bömer *Met.* 7:154–55 on 14.445; Degrassi (1937) #85.

[46] Haupt-Ehwald on *Met.* 14.609 cite the *elogia* in the Forum Augusti in connection with this king-list.

and likewise Aeneas's shift to divine status as Indiges can be viewed as just another transformation, an addition to the tale of Ardea transformed into a heron. We might almost think of it as an undifferentiated item in a vast accumulation of transformation-tales that could be arbitrarily lengthened by further addition. The reason, however, that we cannot quite do so is the fact that it is not isolated, but participates in a pattern of apotheoses. The apotheosis of Hercules in Book 9 establishes a pattern that is reinforced strongly by the apotheoses of Romulus and of Julius Caesar's soul. Their greater number toward the end of the poem appears to signal both their own importance and their closural impact.[47]

Ovid's list of Latin kings does not lead directly to the apotheosis of Romulus, but to the tale of Pomona and Vertumnus, which he dates to the reign of Proca (14.623). Myers argues that the tale is rich in closural features,[48] cut from the same cloth as the apotheoses that frame it. Viewed as an incident of deceptive seduction and barely-suppressed violence, the tale of Vertumnus can also appear a distraction, leading the reader's attention away from the transformation of historically important heroes into gods. Johnson views the tale positively as a "romantic comedy," yet regards it as compromising its context: "It is no secret that it disrupts what might be called the Aeneadization of what is otherwise far from being a Roman epic just when it begins to show promise (or make fraudulent promises) of turning a new leaf and beginning to be such an epic, and one in the Augustan mode to boot." Johnson concludes that, coming as it does between Aeneas and Romulus, the tale of Vertumnus defeats closure and "deflates any last hope of the poem's imagining Roman Historical Destiny (or imagining the World's destiny as Rome's) because an ample and effective representation of the myth of Romulus would be crucial to a celebration of Rome's place at the end of history as the end of history."[49]

When Ovid abruptly returns to his long-interrupted king-list at 14.772, he remarkably fails to mention Romulus: Rome's walls are founded in the passive voice, and only Romulus's enemy, the Sabine king Tatius, receives mention by name:

---

[47] Wheeler (2000) 152 describes the concentration of apotheoses toward the end of the poem as a closural gesture.
[48] Myers (1994b).
[49] Johnson (1997) 373–74.

proximus Ausonias iniusti miles Amuli
rexit opes, Numitorque senex amissa nepotis
munere regna capit, festisque Palilibus urbis
moenia conduntur. Tatiusque patresque Sabini
bella gerunt. (14.772–76)

Next the military might of unjust Amulius ruled rich Ausonia; old
Numitor received, by his grandson's gift, the kingdom that he had lost;
on the festival of Pales the city's walls are founded. Tatius and the
Sabine fathers wage war.

Scholars have attempted to explain by various means "Ovid's dras-
tic compression of Rome's origins," as Wheeler remarks. Bömer sug-
gests that Ovid wants to avoid repeating what he writes in the *Fasti*;
Granobs, that the foundation of Rome offers no opportunity for
metamorphosis, although Helenus is to represent Rome's foundation
exactly in such terms later, in another context, in Book 15 (434–35);
Wheeler's own suggestion is that Ovid wishes to avoid competing
with Ennius's account in the *Annales*.[50] These explanations themselves
are speculative, but the text seems to call for explanation because
Ovid has so strikingly omitted an obvious opportunity to serve up
an account of Rome's origins. Ovid's critics easily fall into the poet's
hermeneutic trap: his text demands interpretation without providing
the resources to arrive at one. Romulus and his apotheosis are an
especially impressive instance of the self-consciously missed opportu-
nity, the Ovidian narrative tease. Because Romulus was so well-
known to Ovid's Roman readers as a mythico-historical parallel to
Augustus, few topics are richer in potential for allegorical exploita-
tion and panegyric symbolism; and this potential goes almost totally
unrealized here.

Ovid's approach to Romulus is no approach at all: he omits the
founder's exploits and shifts all attention to the divine sphere. The
apotheosis of Romulus and, as it turns out, that of his wife Hersilia
result from divine actions, whose description is the province of myth.
Historians who record their exploits give them standing as histori-
cal figures; deprived of exploits, they re-enter myth. By remytholo-
gizing history Ovid incorporates it into the world of the *Metamorphoses*,
in which divinities are active and humans largely are acted upon.
He also opposes euhemeristic modes of interpreting the shift from
mortal to divinity, in accordance with which a human's heroic actions
approach and approximate the divine, resulting in the hero's ven-

---

[50] Bömer *Met.* 7:231 on 14.772–74; Granobs (1997) 108–9; Wheeler (2000) 113.

eration as divine by other humans, and his reception among the divinities as one of them. Book 1 of Ennius's historical epic, the *Annales*, reports that at Romulus's death he now has a life among the gods: *Romulus in caelo cum dis genitalibus aeuom/degit* (1.62 Skutsch). Ennius probably took a euhemeristic interpretation of Romulus's deification, one aptly summarized by Skutsch: "virtue and political merit open the gates of heaven."[51] "It is highly likely," as Feeney writes, "that the deification of Romulus, who performed the mighty benefaction of founding the city, was the innovation of Ennius. Ennius here will have been placing Romulus in the tradition of the great Hellenistic monarchs who won immortality by emulating Hercules."[52] Although the details of Ennius's account are far from clear, Ovid's non-euhemeristic approach is apparently the reverse of his principal source, the original and canonical version of Romulus's deification.[53]

History appears to be going backwards as the divine agents in the Romans' war with Tatius take action. Juno unlocks the gate to the invading Sabines despite having so recently (only two hundred lines earlier, 581–84) given up her wrath against the Romans:

> inde sati Curibus tacitorum more luporum
> ore premunt uoces et corpora uicta sopore
> inuadunt portasque petunt, quas obice firmo
> clauserat Iliades; unam tamen ipsa reclusit
> nec strepitum uerso Saturnia cardine fecit. (14.778–82)

> Then the Sabines, born at Cures, keep their voices muffled like silent wolves; they assault the Romans, whose bodies are sunk in slumber; they seek the gates, which Ilia's son [Romulus] had barred; yet one of them Saturnian Juno unlocked. She made no noise as she turned it on its hinge.

After all the emphasis on Juno's reconciliation earlier, in the apotheosis of Aeneas, her behavior here is glaringly inconsistent. We may try to rationalize Juno's actions by appealing to Ennius's historical framework, by which Juno gives up her wrath at the second Punic War. But Ovid makes no attempt to clarify and so rescue historical consistency; indeed, he appears to mock the tradition of multiple

---

[51] Skutsch (1985) 260 ad loc.

[52] Feeney (1991) 122–23.

[53] Schmitzer (1990) views Ovid's presentation of several gods and heroes in the *Metamorphoses* as euhemeristic allegory. He draws parallels, for instance, between Cadmus and Augustus, Bacchus and Augustus, and Hercules and Augustus. The running head for this section is "Heroes as Prototypes of Rulers." Ovid's Aeneas and Romulus allow Schmitzer little scope for this approach; see 250–51.

reconciliations of Juno, exploiting it for its comic absurdity. There are serious consequences as well: the equation of history with destiny breaks down.

Soon Juno will be favorable to the Romans once again at the apotheosis of Hersilia, but meanwhile two other divinities intervene: first Venus, unable to undo Juno's hostile act in unbarring the gate, entreats the Naiads living next to Janus's shrine in the Forum Romanum to come to her assistance. Their spring, normally cold, they bring to a hasty boil, thus blocking the way to the Sabines and allowing the Romans time to arm themselves. Next, Mars addresses Jupiter, requesting deification for Romulus as the fulfillment, now due, of a long-standing promise. Mars cites Jupiter's original words, representing them as an exact quotation:

> tu mihi concilio quondam praesente deorum
> (nam memoro memorique animo pia uerba notaui)
> "unus erit, quem tu tolles in caerula caeli"
> dixisti: rata sit uerborum summa tuorum! (14.812–15)

> Once, at an assembled council of the gods, you told me (for I remember, and marked the pious words in my retentive mind), 'there will be one whom you will carry to the blue of heaven.' Let the content of your words be fulfilled!

The words Mars quotes appear to gain even more authority by referential confirmation from outside the text of the *Metamorphoses*—doubly cited, as it were: for while Mars cites Jupiter, Ovid cites Ennius's *Annales* (1.33 Skutsch). Readers of Ovid's contemporary *Fasti* will remember the recurrence of Ennius's line in a third context, for Mars cites it there as part of a parallel appeal for Romulus's deification (*F.* 2.487). Although Mars describes his son to Jupiter as the latter's "worthy grandson" (*Met.* 14.810), Romulus's exploits have no part in the appeal. Deification results directly from Jupiter's promise, so strongly emphasized, and at the beginning of the speech Mars needs only to establish that now is the time for its fulfillment:

> tempus adest, genitor, quoniam fundamine magno
> res Romana ualet nec praeside pendet ab uno,
> praemia (sunt promissa mihi dignoque nepoti)
> soluere et ablatum terris inponere caelo. (14.808–11)[54]

---

[54] In *Met.* 14.809 Anderson reads *et* for *nec*, following most mss.; most other editors, following N. Heinsius, prefer *nec*. See the parallel speech of Mars to Jupiter at *F.* 2.483–84.

> Since, father, Roman affairs are well established on great foundations, and do not depend on a single protector, it is time to pay the reward— it was promised to me and to my worthy grandson—to remove him from the earth and to place him in heaven.

In all this there is no mention of Romulus's great benefactions, such as might sustain a euhemeristic interpretation of the hero's advancement to divine status. Far from avoiding comparison to Ennius, Ovid ostentatiously quotes his predecessor's work, as if to flaunt the fact that in stripping the hero of exploits he has eliminated Ennius's interpretation of them. Ennius's words, transferred to so un-Ennian a context, may appear well suited to a familiar allegorical parallel, reminding Roman readers once again of their second Romulus, likewise destined for the skies.[55] Yet Ovid's apotheosis of Romulus functions but feebly as an Augustan icon precisely because of its lack of historical specificity: lacking *res gestae*, Ovid's Romulus offers readers little to go on in drawing conceptual parallels to the achievements of Augustus.

There are many similarities between the apotheosis of Romulus in the *Metamorphoses* and that in the *Fasti*: in both works Ovid makes an emphatic identification of deified Romulus with Quirinus, reinforcing relatively recent developments in the story;[56] in both he quotes the line from Ennius and repeats the apostrophe *Romule, iura dabas* (*Met.* 14.806, *F.* 2.492) at the moment when the apotheosis occurs. Yet in their larger contexts the two passages are remarkably dissimilar: while in the *Metamorphoses* Romulus's apotheosis is his whole story—simply one in a series of apotheoses extending from Hercules to the end of the work—in the *Fasti* his apotheosis has a context in the life and exploits of the hero. Romulus appears so often in the *Fasti* that, as Barchiesi notes, the episodes concerning him "are numerous enough to trace out a biography of him, even if by installments"; Ovid's "version of the Roman year gives Romulus an unprecedented amount of space, far beyond the "natural" occasions offered by tradition (such as, for example, Romulus's involvement in the foundation myths or in the actual rituals of the Parilia or the Lupercalia)."[57]

---

[55] On political exploitation of Romulus-Quirinus during the republic see Classen (1962), Burkert (1962); in the Augustan period Alföldi (1951), Jocelyn (1989).
[56] On Romulus and Quirinus see Barchiesi (1994) 102–4 = (1997b) 113–14.
[57] Barchiesi (1994) 132 = (1997b) 144, 143.

In an allegorical discussion of Aeneas and Augustus, Binder writes, "The identification of Augustus with Romulus even to the point of his apotheosis demanded a 'positive' picture of Romulus."[58] If, as Barchiesi suggests, the violence and ruthlessness of Romulus's exploits in the *Fasti* make him a problematic parallel to Augustus,[59] we may suppose that Ovid gives himself an easier task in the *Metamorphoses* by keeping Romulus's deeds out of his narrative. In the *Fasti*, for instance, Mars mentions Romulus's dead brother Remus—always a difficulty in positive portrayals of the founder—whereas in the *Metamorphoses* Mars prudently omits any mention of Remus. Yet even the attenuated Romulus of the *Metamorphoses* presents difficulties to allegorical interpretation. As we saw earlier, Mars explains that it is now time for apotheosis because Rome's condition, now well-established, "does not depend on a single protector" (*nec praeside pendet ab uno*, *Met.* 14.809); hence, Romulus can be safely removed from the earth. Applied to Augustus, this remark makes a poor allegorical fit: it calls attention to problems of succession that afflicted the *princeps*, on whom alone the *res Romana* manifestly did depend.

The apotheosis of Hersilia is even more remarkable, and Ovid's de-euhemerizing revision of Roman history enters upon fresh territory with her. With Hersilia there was probably no euhemeristic tradition for Ovid to work against, so he could invent an apotheosis for her, representing it as a purely divine initiative.[60] Tradition granted her notable exploits without apotheosis; Ovid grants her apotheosis without notable exploits. She was well known to Roman readers for being the Sabine wife of Romulus and for her active role in reconciling her own people to the Romans. In several accounts, after the abduction of the Sabine women and subsequent conflict between Romulus's men and the angry parents, Hersilia sues for peace with Tatius and the Sabine fathers (Gellius 13.23.13; Dio Cass. 1.6). Her other signal achievement takes place shortly thereafter. According to Livy, Romulus blames the Sabine parents for the conflict, which resulted from their pride in not allowing intermarriage in the first place (1.9.14). Hersilia, importuned by the entreaties of her sister

---

[58] Binder (1971) 163 n. 68.
[59] On Romulus and Augustus in the *Fasti*, see Barchiesi (1994) 101–12, 143–53, 155–65 = (1997b) 112–23, 154–64, 166–77.
[60] Wissowa (1904) 142 regards Hersilia's apotheosis as Ovid's invention; see Skutsch (1985) 246, Domenicucci (1991) 223–24.

Sabines, intervenes with Romulus to argue that their parents ought
to be pardoned and allowed to live in Rome: *ita rem coalescere con-
cordia posse* (1.11.2). Harmonious union of Romans and Sabines is,
according to Livy's patriotic interpretation, the whole point of the
rape of the Sabine women; and this view was widespread: "it was
not in wanton violence or injustice that they resorted to rape, but
with the intention of bringing the two peoples together and uniting
them with the strongest ties." So writes Plutarch in introducing
Hersilia (*Romulus* 14.7); Dionysius of Halicarnassus also accepts this
pro-Roman motive for the rape (2.30.6).[61]

Hersilia's achievements, like those of her husband, disappear entirely
from Ovid's account of her apotheosis, as does the whole story of
the rape of the Sabines, in which she traditionally plays so impor-
tant a part. After Romulus's transformation into the deified Quirinus,
Juno sends Iris to bring instructions to the grieving widow, address-
ing Hersilia as "chief glory of both the Latin and Sabine peoples":
'*o et de Latia, o et de gente Sabina/praecipuum, matrona, decus*' (14.831–32).
Has Juno become reconciled to the Romans this time because of
their union with the Sabines, a people known for exemplary piety?
We might suppose so, especially now that Romulus is identified with
the Sabine divinity Quirinus.[62] For whatever reason, Juno offers
Hersilia a chance to see her husband again if she will go, under
Iris's guidance, to the Quirinal, "Quirinus's hill," a place associated
with the Sabines' presence in Rome:[63]

> siste tuos fletus et, si tibi cura uidendi
> coniugis est, duce me lucum pete, colle Quirini
> qui uiret et templum Romani regis obumbrat. (14.835–37)

> Stop your tears and, if you care to see your husband, under my guid-
> ance seek the grove that grows green on Quirinus's hill, and shades
> the temple of Rome's king.

Hersilia follows Iris's instructions and proceeds to Romulus's hill; a
star descends, causing Hersilia's hair to catch fire—a divine portent—

---

[61] See Wiseman (1983) 445–46.

[62] See Salmon (1967) 145: "No doubt Varro has exaggerated the number of gods
supplied to the Romans by his ancestors. Even so, the Sabines' reputation for *pietas*
shows that their influence on Roman religious development could hardly have been
negligible."

[63] As Salmon (1967) 145 n. 3 remarks, "Varro automatically regarded any cult
that was fostered on the Quirinal (the hill with Sabine associations) as Sabine."

and she passes into the air; Rome's founder receives her, changes
her name and body, calling her Hora, '*quae nunc dea iuncta Quirino
est*' (*Met.* 14.851).[64]

Of course, Hersilia's apotheosis, like Romulus's, can be allegorized
as panegyric: Domenicucci draws the expected parallel to Livia, so
reinforcing the connection of Romulus to Augustus.[65] Yet if Ovid's
goal in this double apotheosis is to promote panegyrical identifications,
he has lost an impressive opportunity. Especially after his irreverent,
even scandalous, version of the rape in *Ars amatoria* 1, Ovid could
now have made amends with Augustus and with history by serving
up a traditionally patriotic rape of the Sabines, including the achieve-
ments of Romulus and Hersilia, both available for euhemeristic treat-
ment. Ovid's version is once again conspicuously remote from Ennius's.
It is unlikely that Hersilia's transformation into the divine Hora
occurred in the *Annales*, and Ovid probably originated Hersilia's apo-
theosis.[66] In doing so, Ovid remythologizes history, reducing human
agency and minimizing the potential of his Roman characters to
serve as flattering parallels.

In evaluating the historical character of the *Metamorphoses*, we can
view apotheosis as part of historical progress in the work. As we saw
above, Wheeler regards the movement from fable to history, from
the heavens to the city of Rome, as "a shift from a *theologia fabulosa*
to a *theologia civilis*."[67] Another view is, however, possible, in accord-
ance with which the fabulous incorporates all else into its domain—
including history, politics, and current events. Terms like "fabulous"
and "mythological," of course, are not simply descriptive of the sub-
ject matter that Ovid has taken up; he has entirely transformed the
nature of the fabulous, mythological, and the historical alike. He
Ovidianizes them all, Hersilia no less completely than the rest. When
Iris reports Juno's words to the bereaved Hersilia, she eagerly asks
to see once again the face of her husband, concluding her request
with these words: '*quem si modo posse uidere/fata semel dederint, caelum
accepisse fatebor*' (*Met.* 14.843–44). Hersilia is using *caelum* as a metaphor-
ical equivalent for the summit of happiness, as Bömer aptly notes,

---

[64] On the name Hora, see Bömer *Met.* 7:244–45.
[65] Domenicucci (1991) 228.
[66] On Hora in Ennius see Skutsch (1985) 247–49; he does not regard Ovid as
following Ennius in the deification of Hersilia.
[67] Wheeler (2000) 139–40.

citing Cicero's letters to Atticus: *in caelo sum* (*Att.* 2.9.1); *Bibulus in caelo est* (*Att.* 2.19.2). Hersilia supposes Romulus "lost" (*amissum, Met.* 14.829) and evidently knows nothing yet of his apotheosis—certainly nothing about her own. She simply uses a conventional, proverbial form of speech to express her anticipated happiness.[68] But events make her expression literally true, as the star descends and Hersilia rises to the heavens. Ovid's transformative wordplay often operates in just this way: words that initially appear figurative become literal, the conceptual shifts to the physical, and a transformation described in terms of plot is enacted first on the level of style.[69] Hersilia's apotheosis is a fine instance of Ovidian wit, yet is also a typical instance, similar to many others that readers have enjoyed by this stage in the work's progress. As they enjoy another of Ovid's transformative witticisms, they also may reflect on the power of his transformative vision, which now incorporates even their own history. As he exploits Hersilia's apotheosis for so fine a joke, Ovid grants us an ironic perspective on Roman origins, compromising their fatedness and bringing out their contingent character.

Throughout the last pentad, historical events lose their connection to *fata* and pass under the sway of Fama in its full range of ambiguity and contradiction: "lies mixed with truth" (*mixtaque cum ueris . . . commenta*, 12.54) issue from the house of Fama, while "Fame, the herald of truth" (*praenuntia ueri/fama*, 15.3–4), announces Numa's impossible visit to Pythagoras. Fama is a touchstone for the fractured historical vision of the *Metamorphoses.*

---

[68] See Otto (1890) 62.9.
[69] On witticisms of this sort, see Tissol (1997) 20–26.

CHAPTER ELEVEN

OVID'S EXILIC POETRY: WORLDS APART

Gareth Williams

Of the two reasons which Ovid himself gives for his banishment from Rome in A.D. 8, *carmen et error* (*Tr.* 2.207), the second was by his own account not a wilful crime but an innocent misdemeanor (cf., e.g., *Tr.* 2.103–4, 3.1.51–52, 3.5.45–52) which nevertheless directly offended Augustus (cf., e.g., *Tr.* 2.133–34, 3.8.39–40, *Pont.* 1.6.26). Its real nature is never revealed in the exilic poetry and remains mysterious despite "the attentions of the erudite, the ingenious, the frivolous."[1] One of the more plausible conjectures is that Ovid was implicated in a political scandal, and possibly in a dynastic plot to thwart the Claudian succession (via Tiberius) upon Augustus's death;[2] but there is room for further speculation.[3] Whatever the truth of the matter, Ovid had already flirted with danger by the publication in c. 1 B.C.–A.D. 1 of the risqué *Ars amatoria*,[4] in his judgement harmless enough on the kind of 'proper' reading which he urges in his own defense in *Tristia* 2, addressed directly to Augustus, but from an official standpoint hardly helpful to Augustus's program of moral reform, spearheaded by legislation in 18 B.C. to curb adultery (the *Lex Iulia de adulteriis coercendis*) and to promote marriage (the *Lex Iulia de maritandis ordinibus*).[5] But if the *Ars* was instantly notorious, why did Augustus wait eight or so years before punishing its author? If it was no simple matter to take action against Rome's greatest living poet, Ovid's *error* may have supplied a long-awaited pretext for harsh retaliation against the *Ars*: relegation to Tomis (modern Constanza) on what is now the Romanian coast of the Black Sea, according to

---

[1] Syme (1978) 216; Verdière (1992) updates the survey of conjectures in Thibault (1964).
[2] For judicious remarks see Syme (1978) 216–22; for the political line updated see Green (1982a) 49–59, (1982b) and (1989) 210–22.
[3] See White, chapter 1 and Watson, chapter 5 above.
[4] See Watson, chapter 5 above.
[5] On the legislation see Treggiari (1996) 886–93.

Ovid a remote and culturally barren wasteland from which he was never to return and where he died, probably in A.D. 17.[6]

The last four decades have witnessed a resurgence of scholarly interest in Ovid's two collections of exilic elegies—five books of the *Tristia* (A.D. 8–12; fifty poems in all) and four of the *Epistulae ex Ponto* (1–3 published together in A.D. 12–13, Book 4 perhaps posthumously; forty-six poems in all)[7]—as well as in the elegiac *Ibis* (not later than A.D. 12),[8] in which he elaborately curses an unnamed enemy at Rome who is pseudonymously called Ibis. In reaction to the harsh opinion of earlier times, when few scholars saw much reason to dispute Ovid's own assessment of his exilic works as the monotonous and artistically deficient outpourings of a poet broken by his banishment from Rome,[9] the *Tristia* and *Epistulae ex Ponto* (to say nothing as yet of the *Ibis*) have been rehabilitated as typically innovative Ovidian productions, elusive and dissimulating, in which he returns elegy to its alleged origins as a song of lament[10] in fitting penance for the *Ars amatoria*, and gives new direction to the epistolary experiment already conducted in the *Heroides*;[11] so that in launching his "myth of exile"[12] he (again) creates "an invention without parallel," albeit with "some extant 'earlier traditions' as points of departure."[13]

If in his letters from exile in 58–57 B.C. Cicero was "the unconscious creator of the autobiographical genre 'complaints from exile',"[14] Ovid's exilic poetry is without parallel in classical Roman literature as a meditation on the state of exile itself, and of the psychological pressures which divide the self between 'here' and 'there' with little or no mediation between them. Cicero's letters lack this introspec-

---

[6] So Jerome *Chron.* 171 g Helm; *relegatio* as opposed to *exilium*, which would have deprived him of his Roman citizenship and property (cf., e.g., *Tr.* 2.137–38, 5.2.55–62, 5.11.21–22; Evans (1983) 4, 27).

[7] For the chronology see Syme (1978) 37–47.

[8] For the date see Williams (1996) 132 n. 52.

[9] Wilkinson (1955) 347, 359–61 is representative.

[10] See Harvey (1955) 170–72 with Brink (1971) 165 on Hor. *Ars* 75–78, and cf. Ov. *Am.* 3.9.3–4; hence the correlation between form and content at *Tr.* 3.1.9–10, 5.1.5–6, *flebilis ut noster status est, ita flebile carmen,/materiae scripto conveniente suae.*

[11] See further Rahn (1958) and now Rosenmeyer (1997).

[12] Claassen (1999) 10, announcing a major emphasis in her treatment of the exilic poetry.

[13] Claassen (1999) 32.

[14] Claassen (1999) 27 (cf. again 108).

tive depth, not least because of the relative brevity of his exile;[15] the gradual evolution of Ovid's estrangement from Rome and of his secondary exile among his new cohabitants in Tomis is pictured on a broader canvas spanning eight and more years of self-observation. True, Ovid's declared motives for persevering with poetry in Tomis are practical enough: destroyed by the Muses (via the *Ars amatoria*), he nevertheless turns to them as a source of distraction from his exilic grief (cf., e.g., *Tr.* 4.1.19–52, 4.10.115–22); by communicating with his friends at Rome he performs an act of *utilitas officiumque* (*Pont.* 3.9.56), of duty according to the code of *amicitia* and of utilitarian appeal for help in securing his removal from Tomis;[16] and while he doubtless communicated in prose as well, his commitment to verse allows him to reward his loyal friends through poetic celebration of them in Tomis (cf. *Tr.* 5.9.1–6, *Pont.* 3.6.51–54, 4.1.1–22; *named* celebration at least in the *Epistulae ex Ponto*, as Ovid preserves the anonymity of his addressees in the less certain times of the *Tristia*).[17] But these utilitarian motives are only one aspect of the greater emotional drama which Ovid's persona plays out in the exilic poetry, and which is dominated by his uncertain sense of Roman identity and 'belonging' in Tomis. This vulnerability also distinguishes Ovid's exilic writings from Seneca's response to his Corsican exile (A.D. 41–49) in the *Consolatio ad Helviam*, where he takes comfort in the Stoic doctrine of 'citizenship of the universe' and in the familiar consolatory topos that the exile makes his home in any land (cf. *Helv.* 8.5–6).[18]

---

[15] For his letters surveyed see Edwards (1996) 114 and Claassen (1999) 27–28, 105–10 with Hutchinson (1998) 25–48 for a more positive assessment. For suggestive thematic coincidences between Cicero's and Ovid's exilic writings see Nagle (1980) 33–35, but cf. Kenney in Melville (1992) xvii n. 5 (that Ovid had read Cicero's letters "is on balance unlikely, but the possibility that they were accessible in Ovid's lifetime cannot be entirely ruled out").

[16] For definition and discussion of *officium* and *utilitas* see Evans (1983) 149–50 with Nagle (1980) 71–82. Cf. Millar (1993) 10 on the *Epistulae ex Ponto* in particular as "remarkably vivid representations of the central role which the arrival of monarchic power had conferred on petitioning" and on appealing through influential intermediaries to "the real holders of power."

[17] *Tristia* 2 (to Augustus) and 3.7 (to Perilla) are exceptions to the rule, as are *Ex Ponto* 3.6 and 4.3 (unnamed addressees). But for the veil of anonymity in the *Tristia* as strategic for reasons other than protecting Ovid's friends from named association with him see Evans (1983) 58 (his elegies "gain a generality of appeal which they would lack if addressed to particular individuals") and below, sections 4 and 5.

[18] See further Claassen (1999) 92–94 with Davisson (1983) 174. But Seneca offers a very different account of his exilic hardships at *Pol.* 18.9, Ovidian in color (see Griffin (1976) 62 and Degl' Innocenti Pierini (1980) 114–22) and clearly strategic; see also Dewar's discussion below, pp. 388–93.

Ovid's lack of philosophical fortification in Tomis[19] lends greater
human interest to the exilic poetry as a study of raw psychological
struggle—of melancholic struggle in the *Tristia* and the *Epistulae ex
Ponto* counterbalanced (as we shall see) by a contrived display of
manic rage in the *Ibis*. Our journey into exile begins with Ovid's
exaggerated portrayal of his Tomitan landscape; the inner turmoil
which he projects on to his physical environment will in turn be
connected with his disorientation on so many other fronts in Tomis,
chief among them his complex relationships with his fellow but for-
eign Tomitans, with his familiar but alien Roman past, with his wife
and close but so distant friends, and of course with Augustus himself.

1. *Peoples and Places*

Despite Ovid's insistence on the sincerity of his exilic persona (cf.
Tr. 3.1.5–10, 5.1.5–6, *Pont.* 3.9.49–50), the Tomis he describes bears
little or no relation to its historical counterpart. Originally a Milesian
foundation, Tomis appears to have retained its Greek language and
culture down to and beyond the spread of Roman influence in
Moesia, its surrounding region which was finally brought under firm
Roman control only late in the first century B.C.[20] Ovid's Tomis is
populated by the crude and unlettered Getae, but "Tomitan archae-
ological finds show a fine indigenous culture, use of Roman arte-
facts, even coins, also locally made fine Thracian metalwork, and
inscriptions in Greek and Latin;"[21] one would indeed "never imag-
ine from Ovid's account that Tomis boasted a gymnasium and richly
decorated civic buildings, that its epitaphs give evidence of its inhab-
itants' familiarity with Euripides, Theocritus, and other Greek authors,
or that it served as religious and civic center of the five Greek city-
states in the immediate Danube delta."[22] Inscriptional evidence sup-
ports Ovid's claims that the town is vulnerable to outside attack, not
least because of the poor state of its defensive wall (cf. *Tr.* 5.10.17–18).[23]
But it defies geographical logic to suppose that peoples as diverse as

---

[19] Green (1994) xlvi–xlvii.
[20] Williams (1994) 5–7 with further bibliography.
[21] Claassen (1999) 196.
[22] Habinek (1998) 158 (with 219 n. 15 for further bibliography).
[23] Williams (1994) 6.

the Bastarnae, Bessi, Bistonii, Sarmatae, and Sauromatae were *all* simultaneously present as menacing threats in the Tomitan region; if "the exotic names of remote peoples conquered by Rome caught the imagination of Augustan poets,"[24] Ovid aims to impress (and disconcert) his audience with the exotic names of peoples not yet fully subdued by Rome. The list of Ovid's distortions extends much further, leading some scholars to speculate that he never in fact set foot in Tomis and may even have invented his exile;[25] an intriguing possibility, but (i) while it is striking that Tacitus, say, or Cassius Dio makes no allusion to his exile, the meager external evidence that *does* exist cannot be ignored;[26] and (ii) if entirely fictional, his nine books of exilic elegy, supplemented by the *Ibis*, would surely carry any such venture to very improbable lengths. Ovid's distortions are better viewed as tactical in a different way, and not simply designed to elicit the sympathies of his distant Roman readers, few of whom presumably had direct experience of Moesia and whose ignorance he might therefore seek to exploit for strategic advantage.

Ovid's distortions can also be viewed as the 'sincere' outpourings of a persona whose inner crisis, lacking all proportion and balance, is inevitably expressed in terms of hyperbolical excess. Already in *Tristia* 1 his descriptions in 1.2, 1.4, and 1.11 of his turbulent voyage into exile symbolize his inner trauma (cf. 1.11.9–10, *tantis animique marisque/ fluctibus*),[27] the epic dimension of the raging storms en route (1.2.13–40, 1.4.5–28, and 1.11.13–24) conveying through their generic resonances the 'epic' scale of his disaster and its aftershocks.[28] The lingering effects of this inner disturbance continue to be felt throughout the exilic poetry without respite as the years pass. In the relatively late *Ex Ponto* 2.7 (to Atticus), for example, the restlessness

---

[24] Gransden (1976) 183 on Virg. *Aen.* 8.722–25.

[25] See especially Fitton Brown (1985) with Claassen (1999) 34 on the history of the theory, which she rejects (Little (1990) and Green (1994) xvii still more firmly); but cf. Habinek (1998) 218 n. 9: "the ideological force of his depiction of the Tomitans and of himself would not be categorically different if the whole project were fictitious."

[26] Stat. *Silu.* 1.2.254–55 (cf. Plin. *HNat.* 32.152); then silence until Jerome (n. 6 above), [Aur. Vic.] *Epit.* 1.24 and Sidon. *Carm.* 23.158–61. The elaborations of at least Sidonius warrant much suspicion (cf. Syme (1978) 215–16). Hollis (1996) 26 draws attention to the interesting case of a graffito from Herculaneum which includes the words MORIERIS TOMI—a suggestive allusion to Ovid's fate.

[27] Cf. Dickinson (1973) 162–63, 167–68.

[28] See Videau-Delibes (1991) 73–82, relating 1.2 and 1.4 to *Met.* 11.479–572 and *Aen.* 1.81–156.

of "the scarcely pacified Getae" (2, *male pacatis ... Getis*) is sugges-
tively paralleled by the disquiet within Ovid's persona, leading to
the kind of insecurity glimpsed in lines 5–7:

> me timor ipse malorum
>   saepe superuacuos cogit habere metus.
> da ueniam, quaeso, nimioque ignosce timori.

> My very dread of misfortunes often drives me to feel unnecessary fears.
> Pardon me, I beg you, and forgive this excessive fear.

The paranoid excesses of *superuacuos ... metus* and *nimio ... timori* are
precipitated by the same loss of balanced perspective which resur-
faces when Ovid pictures himself as persecuted simultaneously by
fate and the gods as well as by fortune (17–20), the latter's prover-
bial fickleness now giving way in his over-dramatized, victim-like
imaginings to a fixed determination to harm him (21–22, 41–42).
Couplet after couplet sustains this hyperbolical pitch, so that even
the Getae, allegedly the most fierce race on earth (31), are appar-
ently moved to pity by his plight (32); for his epic hardships to be
properly memorialized in literature, nothing less that "a long *Iliad*
of his fate" (cf. 34) would have to be attempted; and so countless
are they that their number defies description by all but *adynata*:

> Cinyphiae segetis citius numerabis aristas,
>   altaque quam multis floreat Hybla thymis,
> et quot aues motis nitantur in aere pinnis,
>   quotque natent pisces aequore, certus eris,
> quam tibi nostrorum statuatur summa laborum,
>   quos ego sum terra, quos ego passus aqua. (25–30)

> You'll sooner count the ears in a Libyan cornfield and the sprigs of
> thyme which lofty Hybla brings to blossom, and you'll sooner know
> the number of birds winging their way in the air, the number of fish
> swimming in the sea, than reckon the true amount of my sufferings
> which I've undergone on land and at sea.

Ovid's familiar exempla of countlessness here[29] also reinforce the des-
olation of Tomis by alluding to a very different natural and literary
environment which, through the Libyan associations of the river
Cinyps (25), stands at a southern global extreme in contrast to Ovid's
Scythia (cf. *Tr.* 1.3.61, *Scythia est quo mittimur*). In contrast to the fer-

---

[29] Discussed with *Tr.* 4.1.55–60, 5.1.31–34, and 5.2.23–28 by Bernhardt (1986)
217–21.

tile corn-producing region by the Cinyps (cf. Herod. 4.175, 198), and in contrast to Sicilian Hybla (26), famous for its honey and here evoking its idyllic Virgilian character in the *Eclogues* (cf. 1.54, 7.37), Ovid's Tomis is a frozen wasteland (*Pont.* 2.7.72) in which the soil, even if not infertile, is left uncultivated because of the constant threat of war (69–70; cf. *Tr.* 3.10.67–70). The number of birds in the sky and fish in the sea (27–28) also serves to illustrate Ovid's countless sufferings at *Tr.* 5.2.25–27; but a closer analogy for lines 25–28 as a whole is supplied by *AA* 1.57–59:

> Gargara quot *segetes*, quot habet Methymna racemos,
>   aequore quot *pisces*, fronde teguntur *aues*,
> quot caelum stellas, tot habet tua Roma puellas.

> The number of Gargara's cornfields, of Methymna's grape-clusters, of fish concealed in the sea and birds in the trees, of stars in the sky; so many girls your own Rome contains.

The striking parallels between the two passages raise the specter of the *Ars amatoria* in a suitably chastened exilic form: Ovid's emphasis on Rome as an exciting social playground in the *Ars* is gently evoked and disowned when he steers his similar exempla of countlessness in a very different direction in drab Tomis. A similar effect is achieved in 2.7.43–45:

> nec magis assiduo uomer tenuatur ab usu,
>   nec magis est curuis Appia trita rotis,
> pectora quam mea sunt serie calcata malorum . . .

> The ploughshare is no more worn from constant use, the Appian Way worn down by curved wheels, than my heart has been trampled by a succession of misfortunes.

The triteness of the topoi in lines 43–44[30] is offset first by the contrast between the agricultural world evoked in 43 and Ovid's own Tomitan 'reality' (cf. 70, *non patitur uerti barbarus hostis humum*), and then by his remoteness from Italy, reinforced by his familiar but distant vision of the Appian Way in 44. These contrasts between the irreconcilable worlds of 'here' and 'there' are symptomatic of the polarizing mentality which, as often in the exilic corpus, Ovid's persona reveals in lines 47–74, where each pentameter exacerbates the excesses of his unique exilic plight (e.g., 66, *ultima me tellus, ultimus*

---

[30] See Galasso (1995) 330 on 39–44.

orbis habet) by overthrowing the more ordinary and measured expe-
rience of life/exile portrayed in each hexameter (e.g., 65, *est aliquid
patriis uicinum finibus esse*).[31]

This technique of constructing a hyperbolical picture of exile which
is believable only at an emotional level, and hence a 'realistic' rep-
resentation of the loss of balanced focus in his traumatized persona,
is predicated on Ovid's portrayal of Rome as the stabilizing center
of his entire existence. Excluded from Rome, he suddenly loses the
familiar balance of life amid his family, his friends, and the city's
cherished landmarks and involvements (cf. *Pont.* 1.8.35–38), a loss
symbolized when he loses the delicate balance of his health through
constant illness in Tomis (cf. *Tr.* 3.3.3–14, 3.8.23–34, 4.6.39–44,
Pont. 1.10.3–14). At the environmental level Ovid's Scythia is itself
'unbalanced' in relation to Italy. In Virgil's third *Georgic* Italy rep-
resents the temperate center between the climatic extremes of Libya
to the south (339–48) and Scythia to the north (349–83); the Scythian
section in particular reveals extensive and explicit contrasts with the
laudes Italiae at *G.* 2.136–76.[32] Virgil's picture of Scythia, itself tradi-
tional and "virtually a paradigm for the wintry north,"[33] is in turn
the dominant model for Ovid's account of the Tomitan winter in
Tristia 3.10.[34] But whereas the Virgilian contrast arguably "does not
work entirely to the credit of Italy, nor to the total detriment of the
Scythian landscape,"[35] Ovid's contrast is simpler: whereas Virgil views
the Libyan and Scythian extremes from the balanced Roman cen-
ter, Ovid views Scythia from his own *dislocated* perspective on the
margins of empire; and by 'confirming' through direct experience of
the region the accuracy of Virgil's account, he also creates the illu-
sion that his own version commands special trust. From this remote
vantage-point the extremity of Ovid's sufferings in exile (*Tr.* 3.2.11,
ultima nunc patior) is in direct proportion to his distance from Rome
(cf. *Tr.* 3.4b.51, *ulterius nihil est nisi non habitabile frigus*, 3.13.27, 4.4.83),
the medial center by which the remoteness of that *ultimus orbis* is
always defined in the exilic poetry.

---

[31] Cf. Davisson (1983) 173: "Many of the advantages which Ovid methodically
eliminates [in his own case in 47–74] resemble the consolations traditionally used
of exile" (illustration follows).

[32] See Thomas *G.* on 3.349–83.

[33] Thomas (1982) 51.

[34] See Evans (1975).

[35] Thomas (1982) 52.

That Tomis was located in Moesia is irrelevant to Ovid's creative vision of the region as a reincarnation of the literary Scythia which extends back at least to Herodotus.[36] In winter this Scythia is Stygian in its frozen sterility (e.g., *Tr.* 3.10.71–76, *Pont.* 1.3.51–52; cf. of the underworld Tib. 1.10.35, *non seges est infra, non uinea culta*), long inviting the comparison drawn explicitly at *Pont.* 4.14.11–12:

> Styx quoque, si quid ea est, bene commutabitur Histro,
>   si quid et inferius quam Styga mundus habet.

> Even the Styx, if such a thing exists, will be a good exchange for the Hister; and anything that the world has even lower than the Styx.

In the deathly stillness evoked in *Tristia* 3.10 the seemingly endless winter (cf. 13–16) holds the landscape in the grip of a frozen present (e.g., 25, *uincti concrescant frigore riui*, 29–30, *Hister/congelat*).[37] The timeless 'now' held in suspension by Ovid's use of the present tense in 11–46 stretches into the indefinite future in 47, *inclusaeque gelu stabunt in*[38] *marmore puppes*, where the familiar poetic use of *marmor* of the whitened sea in churning motion[39] gives way to *marmor* denoting the whiteness of the frozen (even tomb-like) waters; the sea thus becomes indistinguishible from the land (29–34; cf. 10, *terra . . . marmoreo est candida facta gelu*), Ovid's environment as monotonous and unremitting as his inner mood. The lifeless environment suitably reflects (and is a projection of) his frequent equation of exile with death (e.g., *Tr.* 5.9.19, *Pont.* 1.8.27, 4.9.74);[40] in describing himself as *Nasonis adempti* (1), his apparently novel use of *adimo* in the sense of "remove by exile" (*OLD* s.v. 8b; cf. *Tr.* 1.1.27, *Pont.* 4.6.49) barely disguises the verb's more familiar nuance, here foreshadowing the funeral atmosphere of *Tristia* 3.10 generally, of "remove by death" (*OLD* s.v. 8a; cf. *Tr.* 4.10.79, *Pont.* 1.9.41).[41]

Ovid's Tomis is not only Stygian in its lifeless sterility; war-torn and abundant only in the dismal growth of wormwood (*absinthium*; cf. *Tr.* 5.13.21, *Pont.* 3.1.23, 3.8.15), the region also reverses the familiar characteristics of the idealized literary Golden/Saturnian

---

[36] See Williams (1994) 9–10.
[37] See further Videau-Delibes (1991) 117–19.
[38] *in* with most modern editors, but *ut* Hall (both with MS support).
[39] Cf. *OLD* s.v. 5a.
[40] See for further examples and discussion Nagle (1980) 23–32 with Claassen (1996) 576–85 and (1999) 239–40.
[41] Cf. on the wordplay Helzle (1989) 155 on *Pont.* 4.6.49 and Dehon (1993) 212.

Age.[42] Rugged Tomis has more in common with the Iron Age,[43] when war first raged (*Met.* 1.141–43) and "men lived by plunder" (144, *uiuitur ex rapto*; cf. *Tr.* 5.10.16, *quae [sc. gentes] sibi non rapto uiuere turpe putant*); the proverbial hardness of the Iron Age (cf. Hor. *Epod.* 16.65 *aere, dehinc ferro durauit [sc. Iuppiter] saecula*) is perhaps implicated in Ovid's portrayal of his own *ferrea sors uitae* (*Tr.* 5.3.28) and *tempora dura* (*Tr.* 5.10.12) among the hard (*duros*) Getae (*Pont.* 1.5.12, 3.2.102). Further traces of Ovid's *durum exilium* as an inversion of the Golden Age may be detected in his (by now) standard description of the Tomitan environment at the opening of *Ex Ponto* 3.1, to his wife:

> Aequor Iasonio pulsatum remige primum,
>   quaeque nec hoste fero nec niue terra cares,
> ecquod erit tempus, quo uos ego Naso relinquam
>   in minus hostili iussus abesse loco? . . .
>
> pace tua (si pax ulla est tua, Pontica tellus,
>   finitimus rapido quam terit hostis equo),
> pace tua dixisse uelim: 'tu pessima duro
>   pars es in exilio, tu mala nostra grauas.'
> tu neque uer sentis cinctum florente corona,
>   tu neque messorum corpora nuda uides,
> nec tibi pampineas autumnus porrigit uuas,
>   cuncta sed immodicum tempora frigus habent . . .
>
> non igitur mirum, finem quaerentibus horum
>   altera si nobis usque rogatur humus. (1–4, 7–14, 29–30)

Sea first struck by the oars of Jason, land never free of cruel enemies and snow, will there ever be a time when I, Ovid, shall leave you, ordered to exile in a less hostile place?

Without disturbing your peace (if you have any peace, land of Pontus, ever trodden by the swift horses of your neighboring enemies), and with your leave I would say: 'You are the worst element in my hard exile; you increase the weight of my hardships.' You neither feel the spring bedecked with wreaths of flowers, nor do you see the bare bodies of the harvesters; to you autumn extends no clusters of grapes, but all the seasons possess the same extreme cold.

No wonder, then, if I seek an end to these hardships and plead constantly for a different place of exile.

Ovid's allusion to the Argo in line 1 revives the Pontic associations of the Medea and Jason myth which have already been drawn ear-

---

[42] See Williams (1994) 14–16.
[43] Katz (1992) 127–32.

lier in the *Tristia* and *Epistulae ex Ponto*, most obviously in *Tristia* 3.9, where Ovid's "fanciful and aptly cruel etymology for Tomis"[44] derives the name from the Greek τέμνω ("cut") and from Medea's murder and dismemberment of Absyrtus, her brother; and also in *Ex Ponto* 1.4, where Ovid predictably defeats Jason in a point-by-point comparison (*syncrisis*) of their respective sufferings (23–46). But in Tomis the peaceful bountifulness of the Golden Age in eternal spring (cf. *Met.* 1.107, *uer erat aeternum*) gives way to the permanent winter (*Pont.* 3.1.11, *tu neque uer sentis...*) of Ovid's war-torn (7–8, 25–26) and sterile (11–13, 19–20) landscape; in this context his opening allusion also resurrects the Argo as a familiar literary symbol of decline from the Golden Age[45] and orientates the ensuing picture of his 'Iron Age' sufferings.

By returning to such well-trodden ground in the first lines of this new book, Ovid revisits exilic topoi which, by this stage in the corpus, are textually as inescapable and confining as the physical environment which he yearns to leave (cf. 3–4, 29–30); hence in part the charge of monotony allegedly brought against the exilic poetry (cf. *Pont.* 3.9.1–4). Directly addressing *Pontica tellus* (7), Ovid (re)constructs her familiar exilic persona in lines 7–28 in order to impress upon his wife the exilic hardships from which he seeks removal through her help, in this case through her intercession before Livia on his behalf (95–166). To be well intentioned is not enough, he asserts; his wife must be passionate about attaining her goal (cf. 35). The difference thus drawn between inclination and firmer will is restated later:

> magna tibi imposita est nostris persona libellis:
>   coniugis exemplum diceris esse bonae.
> hanc caue degeneres... (43–45)

> Great is the role that my writings have imposed on you: you are called the model of a good wife. Take care not to fall short of that...

If by approaching Livia Ovid's wife lives up to the idealized persona envisaged in these lines, which Livia awaits to receive her? The Livia who lives up to her own august image as *femina... princeps*

---

[44] Claassen (1999) 192; cf. Oliensis (1997) 186–90 on the possible Augustan implications of 3.9 (Caesar as "the cutter").

[45] See Smith (1913) 245–47 on Tib. 1.3.37–40.

(125)?[46] Or one not so easily separated from the monstrous types
(e.g., Medea, Clytemnestra) from whom she is (all *too*) emphatically
distinguished in lines 119–24?[47] When shades of Ovid's didacticism
in the *Ars amatoria* are detected in the advice which he gives to his
wife about how best to approach Livia (129–66),[48] how to interpret
the reappearance of the *Ars* here in exilic guise? As a sign of penance
for the incriminating work, or as a defiant resurrection of it? Such
questions ultimately complicate Ovid's opening description of *Pontica
tellus* (7): how in retrospect to reconcile the 'truth' of her persona in
Ex Ponto 3.1 with (i) the *real* environmental picture which the extra-
poetical evidence reveals about Pontus, and (ii) with Ovid's gentle
probing later in the poem into the potential differences between one's
projected persona and 'real' self? The further question left open-
ended by this complex poem is whether Livia will be any more
receptive to the pleas of Ovid's wife than the cold and unrespon-
sive *aequor* and *terra* (1–4) and the *Pontica tellus* addressed in 7–18.[49]

Beyond representing Italy as the global median point in contrast
to extreme Scythia, Ovid exploits in a conventional way the famil-
iar ancient theory that a people's character is directly related to its
physical environment and climate.[50] In keeping with this theory Ovid's
Getae are predictably dull (cf. *Tr.* 5.10.38, *stolidi*) and as hard (*duri:
Pont.* 1.5.12, 3.2.102), wild (*feri: Pont.* 3.9.32, 4.15.40), and savage
(*saeui: Pont.* 1.7.2, 4.8.84) as their surroundings. Their *feritas* is reflected
in their "harsh voices and grim countenances" (cf. *Tr.* 5.7.17, *uox
fera, trux uultus*), and partly also in their unkempt appearance. Unshorn
and unshaven (*Tr.* 5.7.18, *non coma, non ulla barba resecta manu, Pont.*
4.2.2), they represent the opposite of Roman neatness (cf. *AA* 1.518,
sit coma, sit trita barba resecta manu); the foreign breeches they wear
(*braca(e)*, itself a word of Celtic origin:[51] cf. *Tr.* 3.10.19, 4.6.47, 5.7.49)
symbolize their general isolation from Greco-Roman culture and
mores (cf. *Tr.* 5.10.33–34); and in their rough hides (*Tr.* 3.10.19, *pel-*

---

[46] See Johnson (1997b).

[47] Cf. for the approach Davisson (1984) 331–32 (similar comparisons at *Pont.*
1.2.119–20, 2.2.113–14; cf. *Pont.* 3.6.41–42) and (1993) 231 (the catalogue in 119–24
"is unlikely to reassure").

[48] Cf. Davisson (1984) 324–25 (with emphasis on "Livia characterized as resem-
bling a capricious *domina*").

[49] Cf. Davisson (1984) 325: "Even Pontus itself resembles certain amatory ele-
giac addressees in that it is indifferent to the poet's pleas."

[50] See Williams (1994) 16–18.

[51] See Palmer (1954) 53.

libus, 5.7.49, 5.10.32) and shaggy dishevelment (*Pont.* 1.5.74, *hirsu-tos . . . Getas*, 3.5.6; cf. *Tr.* 5.7.50) they approach the bestial in appearance as well as in manner.[52] The language they share is but a basic social expedient (cf. *Tr.* 5.10.35, *exercent illi sociae commercia linguae*), their system of justice regulated more by the sword than by rational argument (hence the barbaric significance of "wounds often inflicted in the middle of the forum" at *Tr.* 5.10.44, *dantur . . . in medio uulnera saepe foro*). In this Tomis Ovid's Roman cultural identity is under siege and, in its different way, as vulnerable to barbaric infiltration as the town itself at, e.g., *Tr.* 5.10.17–18: *nil extra tutum est; tumulus defenditur aegre/moenibus exiguis ingenioque loci.* The arrows which are shot into the town (21–22) are a deadly sign of how thin the dividing-line is between the safety within and the barbarian threat outside; so thin that in lines 23–26 the literary worlds of pastoral and martial epic symbolically collide (or collude) in Ovid's vision of the helmeted shepherd (25, *sub galea pastor iunctis pice cantat auenis*) and the ploughman carrying arms as he works the soil (24). This lack of any firm boundary between the Tomitans and the external enemy is matched inside the town by the blurring of Greek and barbarian origins and identities (27–28, *et tamen intus/mixta facit Grais barbara turba metum*) in a form of cultural hybridization which ultimately threatens Ovid himself: living under the same roof as local tribesmen, with no dividing wall to separate him from them (29–30), he has no defense against the cultural corruption which, he insists, reveals itself in his failing grasp of Latin and in the *barbara uerba* that allegedly creep into his diction (cf. *Tr.* 3.1.17–18, 3.14.45–50, 5.7.55–60) and culminate in his writing of a Getic poem in Latin meter (*Pont.* 4.13.19–20). His resulting crisis of cultural identity threatens to alienate him on two fronts: on the Roman side, his waning linguistic powers transform him into a *barbarus* of sorts who is exiled ever further from his cultural origins by each progressive stage of his Latin failure; and on the Tomitan side he ironically portrays himself as a *barbarus* (*Tr.* 5.10.37, "here *I*'m the barbarian") for whom a secondary form of exile beckons because he cannot communicate in the local language with the Getae, who openly mock his *uerba Latina* (38).

---

[52] See further Videau-Delibes (1991) 139–41.

2. *Epic in Elegy*

In war-torn Tomis Ovid's menacing Getae are suitably described in language reminiscent of martial epic. So, e.g., *Tr.* 5.7.13–20:

> Sarmaticae maior Geticaeque frequentia gentis
> per medias in equis itque reditque uias.
> in quibus est nemo qui non coryton et arcum
> telaque uipereo lurida felle gerat.
> uox fera, trux uultus, uerissima Martis imago;
> non coma, non ulla barba resecta manu,
> dextera non segnis fixo dare uulnera cultro,
> quem uinctum lateri barbarus omnis habet.

A larger number of Sarmatae and Getae comes and goes on horseback along the middle of the roads, every one of them carrying a quiver and bow and poisoned arrows, yellow with snake-venom. Their voices are harsh, their countenances grim, the very image of Mars; neither their hair nor beard is trimmed by any hand; their hand is not slow to stab and wound with the knife which every barbarian wears fastened to his side.

The Homeric γωρυτός (a combination of bow-case and quiver) first appears in Latin verse at *Aen.* 10.168–69 (of the followers of the Etruscan chief Massicus): *quis tela sagittae/gorytique leues umeris et letifer arcus*, where *goryti . . . et . . . arcus* surely supply Ovid's *coryton et arcum* (15). The Scythian associations of the *gorytus*[53] here characterize a distinctly non-Roman force; so also Ovid's allusion to the Getic use of poisoned arrows in line 16 (cf. *Tr.* 3.10.64, *Pont.* 1.2.16, 3.1.26), another "standard motif of epic"[54] (e.g., *Aen.* 9.773, 10.140, 12.857–58) denoting a practice considered "barbarous and unnatural" by the Romans.[55] The Virgilian presence in 15–16 is completed by *uipereo . . . felle*: the noun is first used of (snake-)venom at *Aen.* 12.857 (of the poisoned arrows of the Parthians and Cydonians), while the adjective is apparently a Virgilian coinage, its ending in *-eus* "characteristic of the grand style."[56] And if *uerissima Martis imago* is read in line 17,[57] Ovid echoes *Aen.* 8.557, *maior Martis iam apparet imago*, where

---

[53] Southern and Dixon (1996) 118.
[54] Helzle (1989) 170 on *Pont.* 4.7.36.
[55] Harrison (1991) 99 on *Aen.* 10.140.
[56] Helzle (1989) 166 on *Pont.* 4.7.20.
[57] *Martis* (attested in the second hand of a single MS) is read by most modern editors. Hall *mentis* after Housman (1890) 342 = (1972) 134–35 to avoid the incon-

"the specter of war" against Turnus looms larger for the Etruscans; at *Tr.* 5.7.17 Ovid modifies the Virgilian sense of *imago* to create the still more ominous (and hyperbolical) effect of directly encountering a living likeness of the god of war. Despite these dominant epic resonances, however, Ovid's allusion in line 18 to *AA* 1.518 (*sit coma, sit trita barba resecta manu*) evokes the contrasting world of erotic elegy and of Roman cultural finesse, if only in a nostalgic and futile way (*non . . . non*) in distant exile—an effect reinforced when he has the Getae use the *culter* (19) as a weapon, its familiar Roman use as a tool for trimming the beard or hair[58] apparently unheard of in Tomis.

One of the more obvious techniques which Ovid uses in Tomis to distance himself from his erotic elegiac past is to reverse staple amatory topoi in the exilic poetry. One way of demonstrating that "he is not what he was" (*Tr.* 3.11.25, *non sum ego quod fueram*) and that he now renounces his once cherished place (*Tr.* 4.10.53–54) as the elegiac successor to Gallus, Tibullus, and Propertius (cf. *Tr.* 5.1.19, *atque utinam numero non nos essemus in isto!*) is to convert the symptoms of elegiac love-sickness into his harsher exilic ailments, to expose the *exclusus poeta* (himself a shadow of the *exclusus amator*) to the venom of Getic arrows (e.g., *Tr.* 5.7.16) rather than that of Cupid's figurative shafts (cf. *AA* 2.520, *quae patimur, multo spicula felle madent*), and to replace the erotodidaxis of the *Ars* with instruction in how to win over Augustus (*Pont.* 1.2.67–128, 2.2.39–90) and Livia (*Pont.* 3.1.129–66).[59] But while these traces of his erotic past may also signal a certain (even reassuring) continuity amid exilic change, they also contribute to the generic complexity of the exilic poetry in relation to its Roman elegiac precursors. In generic terms the *Tristia* and *Epistulae ex Ponto* match Ovid's exilic experience in that he is detached from the Roman center to which he still belongs in all but body, they from the elegiac tradition to which *they* still belong; and their generic identity is further complicated by the epic scale of Ovid's sufferings in Tomis. The tension between his elegiac medium and epic content, or between his programmatically limited powers of song (cf. *Tr.* 2.327, *tenuis mihi campus aratur*) and the epic task of

---

gruity of calling "an unkempt savage" the image of *Roman* Mars; but for Mars's presence in Ovid's barbaric surroundings cf. *Tr.* 5.2.69.

[58] See Courtney (1980) 580 on Juv. 14.216–17; the *culter* was also in common Roman use as a sacrificial and hunting knife (*OLD* s.v. 1b, c).

[59] See further Nagle (1980) 43–70.

describing his hardships, leads to a form of generic dislocation which may contribute to his alleged decline as a poet in Tomis; after all, his delicate abilities had apparently already broken under the strain of an epic Gigantomachy which he claims to have undertaken and soon discarded in his pre-exilic days (cf. *Tr.* 2.331–38).[60] From this perspective the crude Getae portrayed at *Tr.* 5.7.13–20 not only invert the Roman cultural norms which Ovid poignantly evokes through negative reminiscence (18, *non coma, non ulla barba resecta manu*); the epic credentials of these Getae also make them an intrusive generic presence here, as alien to the traditional world of Roman elegy as arms are to Ovid himself at *Tr.* 4.1.71–74:

> aspera militiae iuuenis certamina fugi,
>   nec nisi lusura mouimus arma manu;
> nunc senior gladioque latus scutoque sinistram,
>   canitiem galeae subicioque meam.

> As a youth I avoided the fierce conflicts of military service and I handled arms only in play. But now in my old age I arm my side with a sword, my left hand with a shield, and I put my grey hair under the helmet.

Ovid's youthful aversion to a military career (*Am.* 1.15.3–4), matched by his natural proclivity towards writing love-elegy, not epic (cf. *Am.* 2.18.1–4), gives way in exile to 'real' military service, and so to his writing of a curious generic hybrid in Tomis, a form of "elegiac epic."[61]

This technique of conveying the extremity of his exilic sufferings by straining to recount his epic hardships in 'mere' elegy is a pervasive feature of the *Tristia* and *Epistulae ex Ponto* and already evident in the distinctly epic storms which rage on his voyage to Tomis in *Tristia* 1.2, 1.4, and 1.11. So also when he launches in *Tristia* 1.5 the point-by-point comparison of sufferings (*syncrisis*) in which he triumphs over Ulysses on every count:

> si uox infragilis, pectus mihi firmius aere,
>   pluraque cum linguis pluribus ora forent:
> non tamen idcirco conplecterer omnia uerbis,
>   materia uires exuperante meas. (53–56)

---

[60] But for possible mischief in Ovid's adaptation of a familiar *recusatio* motif here see Williams (1994) 189–93.

[61] Claassen (1999) 69.

If I had a tireless voice and lungs stronger than brass, and if I had many mouths with many tongues, not even then would I encompass everything in my words; for the theme surpasses my powers.

Introducing the catalogue of ships at *Il.* 2.488–90, Homer appeals to the Muses for their support: without them, "I could not tell over the multitude of them [sc. the Greeks] nor name them,/not if I had ten tongues and ten mouths, not if I had/a voice never to be broken [φωνὴ . . . ἄρρηκτος] and a heart of bronze within me . . ." (trans. Lattimore). Although the many-mouthed poet was a familiar Roman literary topos by Ovid's time,[62] line 53 is virtually a translation of *Il.* 2.490, Ovid's *infragilis* possibly a new coinage to render Homer's ἄρρηκτος. In both this introduction and in the *syncrisis* itself (cf. also Jason defeated in similar circumstances at *Pont.* 1.4.23–46 and Ulysses again at *Pont.* 4.10.9–30), Ovid devises an elegiac method of writing his own epic story;[63] and underlying these explicit points of epic reference is an extensive subtext of more general epic allusion:

> The topic of wandering over land and sea, driven by an angry god, shows the exiled poet as a lonely Odysseus-Aeneas, *fato profugus* (driven forth by his fate), as in *Tristia* 1.5.64: *me profugum comites deseruere mei* (my companions deserted me as I was driven forth). The tie with Troy is subtly spelt out in the evocation of the exile's last night at Rome, *Tristia* 1.3.26: *haec facies Troiae, cum caperetur, erat* (just so was the appearance of Troy when it was taken).[64]

This epic dimension obtrudes upon even the physical act of writing in exile, as Ovid claims that he composes his verse while on active service (cf. *Pont.* 1.8.10, *in procinctu*) and even in the midst of war (cf. *Pont.* 2.5.19, *hic structos inter fera proelia uersus*).[65] In such a context the elegist is generically dislocated like the armed ploughman and the helmeted shepherd at *Tr.* 5.10.23–26, the peaceful gardens in which he composed in happier times now but a distant memory (*Tr.* 1.11.37).

---

[62] See Skutsch (1985) 627–29.
[63] See Williams (1994) 108–13.
[64] Claassen (1999) 70.
[65] Cf. his claim that he writes amid the raging seas en route to Tomis: *Tr.* 1.11.7–8, *quod facerem uersus inter fera murmura ponti,/Cycladas Aegaeas obstipuisse puto.*

3. Changing Times: The Poet in Decline

One of the more poignant ways in which Ovid pictures the deracinating effects of exile is through his transformed perception of time in Tomis. In *Tristia* 4.6, for example, his exilic isolation is compounded by his isolation from the assuaging effects of time:

> tempore ruricolae patiens fit taurus aratri,
> praebet et incuruo colla premenda iugo;
> tempore paret equus lentis animosus habenis,
> et placido duros accipit ore lupos . . .
>
> hoc tenuat dentem terram renouantis aratri,
> hoc rigidas silices, hoc adamanta terit;
> hoc etiam saeuas paulatim mitigat iras,
> hoc minuit luctus, aegraque corda leuat.
> cuncta potest igitur tacito pede lapsa uetustas
> praeterquam curas attenuare meas. (1–4, 13–18)

In time the bull becomes accustomed to the tiller's plough and offers its neck to the pressure of the curved yoke; in time the spirited horse learns to obey the pliant bridle and with quiet mouth receives the hard bit.

Time wears down the edge of the ploughshare that renews the land, it wears away hard flint and adamant; it gradually softens even fierce anger, it lessens grief and relieves pained hearts. The long lapse of silent-footed time can diminish everything, then, except for my distress.

Ovid's exempla here are as well-worn[66] as the proverbial theme ('time cures all') which is inverted in 17–18: time has only intensified, not eased or reconciled Ovid to, his exilic hardships (cf. 25–28, 37–44). His "comparative platitudes of conventional life and literature" in 1–16 thus underscore "the appalling singularity of his own position,"[67] partly by evoking a fertile agricultural world (1–2, 13) of regular seasonal time (cf. 9–12 for harvests of grape and corn) far separated from barren Tomis. The taming of horses over time (3–4; cf. lions and elephants in 5–8) offers a suggestive point of contrast with Ovid's experience among the wild and untamed Getae (cf. *Pont.* 2.2.3–4, *indomitis . . . Getis*), while the theme of anger assuaged by time (15–16) has significant implications for Augustus himself: if Ovid's hardships and grief are so disproportionate that they defy the

---

[66] See Luck (1977) 256.
[67] Green (1994) 265.

regular ameliorating effects of time, then Augustus's anger (cf. *Tr.* 1.5.84, 2.21, 2:28, 3.6.23) is equally 'unnatural' in its hard intransigence.[68] This sense of isolation from the easing effects of time recurs throughout the exilic poetry and is still felt in *Ex Ponto* 4.11, where Ovid offers his addressee, Junius Gallio,[69] consolation for the death of his wife (7–8). A year will have passed, Ovid supposes (15–16), before this poem, his reply to Gallio's original letter, reaches its addressee; the consolation Ovid offers may thus be untimely, opening old wounds (17–20) when Gallio may already have remarried (21–22). The poem is indeed "a statement on his exile," but not just to the effect that, because letters travel so slowly between Rome and Tomis, "the contacts normally maintained between friends are impossible"[70] for Ovid. Gallio is twice bereaved, having lost his wife after losing Ovid to exile (cf. 5–6, *atque utinam rapti iactura laesus amici/sensisses ultra, quod quererere, nihil*). But if time has eased Gallio's grief at his wife's death, how deeply does he still feel the loss of Ovid? Is the poet's memory still cherished? The poem gently revives Ovid's familiar anxiety in Tomis as to whether his Roman friends still feel his absence long after his relegation; but in alluding to the familiar alleviating effects of time (cf. 19, *longa dies sedauit uulnera mentis*), he also touches indirectly (and therefore with a degree of ironic pathos) on the very *opposite* of his own exilic experience: after six years or so in Tomis (cf. *Pont.* 4.10.1–2, 4.13.39–40) Pontus is as hateful (*Pont.* 4.12.34, *inuisus*) to him as it ever was.[71]

Already when Ovid recalls his last night at Rome in *Tristia* 1.3 the indifferent workings of universal time (cf. 27–28, *iamque quiescebant uoces hominumque canumque,/Lunaque nocturnos alta regebat equos*) are set in contrast to his last precious hours at home. As morning approaches (5) and night "now hurrying to her close refuses him time to linger" (47, *iam ... morae spatium nox praecipitata negabat*), his awareness of time becomes ever more solipsistic and separate from his 'official' time-table (cf. 51, *a! quotiens aliquo dixi properante 'quid urges? ...'*), so that his departure is held in suspension by his anguished

---

[68] See further on 4.6 and "its adroit manipulation of a topos" Davisson (1983) 179–80.

[69] For whom see Syme (1978) 80.

[70] Evans (1983) 163.

[71] For different emphases (including possibly "a joking reference to the Augustan marriage laws compelling quick remarriage") see Claassen (1999) 23–24 and 121.

oscillations between the threshold and back and by his always penul-
timate words of farewell (cf. 55, *ter limen tetigi, ter sum reuocatus*; 57,
saepe 'uale' dicto rursus sum multa locutus).[72] The poem's funereal atmos-
phere (cf. 22, *forma . . . non taciti funeris intus erat*) characterizes Ovid's
last hours at Rome as those of a dying man who urgently clings to
life in his last, elongated moments before passing away into exile,
where the timelessness of his living death is itself reflected in the
frozen immobility of his Stygian landscape and in the monotone of
his emotionally frozen persona. The steady pulse of life and of (his
structured existence in) Roman time thus ceases to apply in Pontus,
where three years of exile seem like ten because time moves so slowly
(*Tr.* 5.10.1–6), and where Ovid's nostalgic vision of the returning
Italian spring in *Tristia* 3.12 (5–24) is but a distant memory in com-
parison with only the relative thaw in Tomis (cf. 27–32); his evoca-
tions of the familiar topos of spring's return merely emphasize his
remoteness from the workings of seasonal (Italian) time.[73] Similarly,
in *Tristia* 3.13 Ovid rejects his birthday (or 2, *Natalis* 'his birthday
god'/*genius*)[74] and its customary rituals before the altar (with the usual
white robe, flowers, incense, and cake in lines 13–18) as redundant
in Tomis, where funeral preparations in the form of "an altar of
death girdled with funereal cypress" (21, *funeris ara . . . , ferali cincta
cupressu*) are better suited to his exilic mood. In this "inverse geneth-
liakon"[75] it is not just the Roman conventions of (literary) birthday
celebration which are out of place in Tomis; the Roman birthday
as a marker of time and progress in life is also redundant in exile,
where his existence lacks all positive development and the years
merge into each other without meaningful distinction.

If time loses shape and structure for the poet in exile, and if he
is isolated from 'Roman' time and annual ceremony (as in the case
of his birthday), his linguistic identity is also compromised in Tomis

---

[72] See further on the textual strategies of delay in 1.3 the excellent analysis of
Videau-Delibes (1991) 24–49.

[73] On the topos and Ovid's variation on it see Evans (1983) 64–65 with Kenney
(1965) 42–44. Only in line 14 does it become clear (Green (1994) 249) that in 5–13
Ovid visualizes the Italian, not the Tomitan, spring; *pace* Videau-Delibes (1991) 121
(the *Tomitan* spring described in 1–12), a poignant ambiguity down to 14.

[74] See *OLD* s.v. *natalis* 3.

[75] Cairns (1972) 137; also in *Tristia* 5.5 Ovid's celebration of his wife's birthday
"subverts usually joyful celebration into a subjective narration of the distant hus-
band's vicarious and lonely birthday ritual, comprising just another aspect of his
sadness" (Claassen (1999) 214).

as he wavers between being Roman and becoming "almost a Getic poet" (*Pont.* 4.13.18, *paene poeta Getes*) and communicates first by gesture (*Tr.* 5.10.36) and then in local dialect(s) because he cannot make himself understood in Latin. The penalty he pays for his *Ars amatoria* (his *uerba Latina* have been 'misunderstood' at Rome as well . . .) is a form of solitary linguistic confinement in which his Latin (again?) makes no impact on a barbarian audience; the sudden verbal rupture when Ovid leaves for Tomis in *Tristia* 1.3 (69, *nec mora, sermonis uerba inperfecta relinquo*) offers a suggestive metaphor for the silence suddenly imposed by Augustus on the suppressed *Ars* (cf. *Tr.* 3.1.65–66, 3.14.5–6) and on his literary life at Rome.[76] Although Greek and Latin were used in historical Tomis, Ovid portrays a different cultural fusion of Sarmatic and Getic language there: *ipse mihi uideor iam dedidicisse Latine,/iam didici Getice Sarmaticeque loqui* (*Tr.* 5.12.57–58). Alienated from his fellow Tomitans who laugh at his *Latina uerba* (*Tr.* 5.10.38) and are no more impressed by Roman language and culture than they are intimidated by Roman arms (cf. *Pont.* 1.2.81–82), Ovid also faces linguistic alienation from Rome as he claims to forget his Latin and to have no books or Latin-speaking companions (cf. *Tr.* 3.14.37–40, 43–44, 4.1.89–94) to help him slow its deterioration. The hallowed name of *Romanus uates* (cf. *Tr.* 5.7.55–56, *ille ego Romanus uates—ignoscite, Musae!—/ Sarmatico cogor plurima more loqui*) thus loses all meaning in this cultural wasteland, where the wild environment is reflected in the *uox ferina* of the Getae and in the barbarian words which allegedly infiltrate Ovid's Latin (cf. *Tr.* 3.1.17–18, 3.14.49–50), consequently contaminating the verse which he struggles to compose in Tomis.

The artistic failure which results from his linguistic crisis in Tomis is aggravated by the alleged decline of his poetic talent in exile, where his *ingenium* pays for its excesses in the *Ars amatoria* by succumbing to the weight of his Pontic hardships (*Tr.* 3.14.33, 5.12.31). Its exilic deterioration runs parallel to Ovid's physical illness in Tomis (cf. *Tr.* 3.3.3–14, 3.8.23–34), while its sterility (cf. *Tr.* 3.14.33–34, 5.12.21–22, 29–32, *Pont.* 4.2.15–20) matches the barren environment in which it is produced. The wintry cold of Tomis is reflected both in the "cold comfort" (cf. *Pont.* 4.2.45, *solacia frigida*) which Ovid

---

[76] For this approach see further Forbis (1997) 246–49, 252–54; cf. Feeney (1992) 14–15 on the unfinished state of the *Fasti* (cf. *Tr.* 2.549–50) delivering (Feeney (1992) 19) "a mute reproach to the constraints set upon the poet's speech."

claims to derive from his exilic Muses and in the torpor which freezes
his creativity (*Pont.* 3.4.33–34, *pectora sint nobis . . . licebit/. . . hoc, quem
patior, frigidiora loco . . .*). If for Horace the combination of natural tal-
ent (*ingenium*) and technical skill (*ars*) is a prerequisite for poetic suc-
cess (cf. *Ars* 408–11), Ovid lacks both equally and so becomes the
pioneer of his own negative poetics (cf. *Tr.* 5.1.27, *non haec ingenio,
non haec componimus arte*), the failure of his *ingenium* removing any incen-
tive for him to emend and polish his defective verse in Horatian
fashion (cf. *Tr.* 5.1.71–72, *Pont.* 1.5.17–18, 3.9.13–32).[77] Apparently
unembellished and unrevised, his exilic poetry thus becomes char-
acterized as the sincere and unadorned expression of his all too 'real'
misery (cf. *Pont.* 3.9.49–50), so that his defective exilic voice pro-
duces its own form of inarticulate cry to rival (in a moment of hyper-
bolical self-dramatization) the irrepressible screams of (*inter alios*)
Phalaris's victims in the brazen bull or Philoctetes in agony on lonely
Lemnos (cf. *Tr.* 5.1.49–62, perhaps with shades of Augustus in
Phalaris, of Ovid's Tomis in Lemnos). The alleged monotony of the
corpus contributes to its imperfection, Ovid himself anticipating at
Tr. 5.1.35 ('*quis tibi, Naso, modus lacrimosi carminis?*' *inquis*) the criticism
reported at *Pont.* 3.9.1–2: *quod sit in his eadem sententia, Brute, libellis,/
carmina nescioquem carpere nostra refers.* The charge of monotony char-
acterizes the exilic poetry as a *carmen perpetuum* of sorts (cf. *Met.* 1.4),
in which Ovid's consistent tone ironically fulfils the Horatian man-
date that a work be coherent and unified in all of its parts (cf., e.g.,
Ars 24–37). Already in *Tristia* 1.1 and 3.1 the physical appearance
of the book which Ovid dispatches to Rome reflects the many imper-
fections of its contents: without ornament (1.1.5–10) "and neither
golden with cedar-oil nor smooth with pumice" (3.1.13, *neque . . . cedro
flauus nec pumice leuis*; cf. 1.1.7, 11), unshaven (1.1.12, *hirsutus*), and
blotted (13; cf. 3.1.15–16), it limps and stammers (3.1.11–12, 21) its
way around Rome, a physical reflection of Ovid's own miserable
circumstances in Tomis (cf. 1.1.4, *infelix, habitum temporis huius habe*),
of the defective verse which it contains, and of the unkempt Getae
(*hirsuti: Pont.* 1.5.74, 3.5.6) among whom it was written;[78] "a sorry
figure in the heart of fashionable Rome, it shockingly advertizes its

---

[77] For the Horatian dimension see Nagle (1980) 128–30 with Williams (1994)
83–91.
[78] See further Williams (1992b) 181–88.

difference from the sophisticated narrative personae of the *Amores* and *Ars amatoria*."[79]

Even though Ovid's insistence on his poetic decline in Tomis has long confirmed the judgement of his harsher modern critics, the fact remains that on a technical level his verse shows no real signs of departure from its pre-exilic standard.[80] The pose is strategic, and designed in part to arouse in his Roman audience "a desire that Ovid's circumstances might improve so that his poetry could, too."[81] From an Augustan perspective the pose is double-edged, confirming the extent to which Ovid has paid heavily for the *Ars amatoria* while also gently challenging the emperor: indirectly responsible for the poor quality of Ovid's 'deficient' exilic verse, Augustus has it in his power (and owes it as a matter of national duty?) to transform the fortunes and therefore the writing of Rome's greatest living poet (cf. *Tr.* 5.1.41–42, *lenior inuicti si sit mihi Caesaris ira,/carmina laetitiae iam tibi plena dabo*), apparently thus ensuring Ovid's future cooperation (cf. 45, *quod probet ille [sc. Caesar], canam*) while also making amends for what Ovid portrays in *Tristia* 2 as the emperor's drastic misjudgement of the *Ars*; the fact that Ovid produces even 'second-rate' poetry in such adverse exilic conditions could even be interpreted as an act of defiance against imperial efforts to silence him.[82] Beyond these strategic possibilities, however, Ovid also "represents the impact of the colonized on the colonizer as anxiety about the linguistic and literary corruption of the latter," so that "he concentrates in a concern about language . . . the anxieties about intercultural contact that absorb the attention of colonizers everywhere."[83] By repeatedly insisting on his poetic decline Ovid creates and reinforces the illusion that his failure is real enough. Whether or not we accept "the important—if unprovable—truth, discernible more between the lines of Ovid's exile poetry than in the never-faltering decorum of decline *in* the lines, that as the long years wear on Ovid *does* fall away from his peak as a poet," Hinds rightly observes that "his exile books grow into their trope: 'decline' becomes decline,"[84] at least in the

---

[79] Newlands (1997) 62.
[80] Luck (1961) offers important analysis.
[81] Nagle (1980) 171.
[82] Cf. Helzle (1989) 16: "One might argue that this very difficulty of writing Latin poetry among the Getae enhances the value of the exile-poetry."
[83] Habinek (1998) 162.
[84] Hinds (1998) 90.

sense that Ovid's persona gradually succumbs to its own (misguided) belief in its poetic failure. Ovid relies on the tension between his pose of decline and the 'real' quality of his verse (still *undeniable* quality even if "Ovid *does* fall away from his peak as a poet") in order to play out the anxiety of his cultural estrangement from Rome; the 'reality' or otherwise of his decline is of less interest than the neurosis symbolized by his pose.

4. *Keeping Faith: Friendship in Exile*

Ovid's mixed cultural identity as the hallowed Roman bard (*Tr.* 5.7.55, *Romanus uates*) who struggles in exile to cling to his Latin while evolving into "almost a Getic poet" (*Pont.* 4.13.18, *paene poeta Getes*) is complicated by many other tensions in the exilic poetry between 'here' and 'there,' Rome and Tomis, past and present. In his mental travels back to Rome, for example, he still visits the urban landmarks, the friends and the family from whom he is separated.[85] He still takes part in Roman civic life by 'attending' the consular inaugurations of Sextus Pompeius in A.D. 14 and C. Pomponius Graecinus in 16,[86] events graphically pictured at *Pont.* 4.4.27–46 and 4.9.9–56. Barred from Rome in all but visual memory and imagination (cf. *Tr.* 4.2.58, *erepti nobis ius habet illa [sc. mens] loci; Pont.* 4.9.41), he revisits Rome to witness in vivid ecphrastic detail (*Tr.* 4.2.19–56) the triumphal procession which he predicts for Tiberius in anticipation of the latter's success against the Germans in A.D. 10–12.[87] In *Ex Ponto* 3.5 he is free still to enter the city and to 'converse' with Cotta Maximus (45–52), while Ovid's friends and family also accompany him in Tomis as constant mental presences there (e.g. *Pont.* 2.4.7, *ante oculos nostros posita est tua semper imago*, of Atticus; cf. of his wife *Tr.* 3.4b.59–62). But while Ovid is 'there' at the very heart of empire to witness in *Tristia* 4.2 the humbling of Germany (43–44) and the endless procession of captured kings and subjugated peoples, *his* Tomis in *his* distant outpost of the empire is constantly

---

[85] Nagle (1980) 91–99 collects examples.

[86] For both of whom see Syme (1978) 74–75, 156–68.

[87] Tiberius eventually celebrated this (his *Pannonian*) triumph on October 23 A.D. 12 (commemorated in *Pont.* 2.1); in fact awarded in 9, the triumph was postponed because of the *clades Variana*, whence Tiberius's avenging campaign in 10–12.

threatened by attack from peoples yet to be broken by Rome; *this* is the grim reality which reduces his mental travels to the escapist projections of an exile still striving to belong in the lost world. In 'attending' Sextus Pompeius's inauguration as consul in *Pont.* 4.4, Ovid first "seems to see" (27, *cernere iam uideor...*) the crowds and then really *does* witness the proceedings as his presence hardens into direct vision (31, *colla boues uideo certae praebere securi*),[88] only for the illusion finally to be dispelled by his harsh return to reality (43, *me miserum, turba quod non ego cernar in illa*); his mental vision ultimately offers meager compensation for his real loss. So also in *Ex Ponto* 3.5 Ovid's imaginary conversations at Rome with Cotta Maximus merely harshen his return to hellish Pontus: *rursus ubi huc redii, caelum superosque relinquo,/a Styge nec longe Pontica distat humus* (55–56). For all his defiance in asserting his freedom of mind (cf. *Tr.* 3.7.48, *Caesar in hoc [sc. ingenium] potuit iuris habere nihil*) and its ability to travel where it will (*Tr.* 4.2.57–62), his Tomitan reality inevitably awaits to shatter his fragile escapist efforts.

Ovid's yearning still to 'belong' in the lost world places special value on his communication with his friends, family, and fellow countrymen. With the return of spring in *Tristia* 3.12 the ice melts sufficiently to allow the arrival of the occasional ship on the Pontic coast (29–32); Ovid hastens to the shore in the hope of encountering a sailor who speaks Greek or Latin (33–44) and who might have news of the latest imperial conquests (45–48, in fact written in hopeful anticipation of Tiberius's success against the Germans in A.D. 10–12 after the *clades Variana* of 9).[89] In his yearning for linguistic contact with a fellow Italian and to hear news of Roman successes abroad (ironic given his own situation on the untamed margins of empire), so loyal a Roman no more 'belongs' in Tomis than his soft evocations of the Italian spring (5–24)[90] are reconcilable with hard Pontus. Beyond the practical claims of *utilitas officiumque* (*Pont.* 3.9.56), or writing as a duty of friendship and as a way of appealing for help in securing his removal from Tomis, Ovid also relies on the written word as a form of personal and cultural lifeline in exile: *exulis haec uox est; praebet mihi littera linguam,/et, si non liceat scribere, mutus ero*

---

[88] Reading (*pace* Richmond *niueos*) *uideo* with Helzle (1989) 115 ad loc. and Green (1994) xlvi and 356.

[89] Green (1994) 251 ad loc.

[90] See above, p. 356.

(*Pont.* 2.6.3–4). In Tomis Ovid has no one with whom to communicate in Latin (cf. *Tr.* 3.14.39–40, 4.1.89–90, 5.12.53–54); if he lacked written contact with Rome his linguistic isolation would be complete (cf. *mutus*).[91] But beyond exercising his Latin and finding linguistic escape by writing to his friends at Rome, he still 'converses' with the likes of Graecinus in *Ex Ponto* 2.6 or Atticus in *Ex Ponto* 2.4 (cf. 1, *accipe conloquium . . . Nasonis*), thus keeping alive the precious exchanges of his pre-exilic relationships:

> utque solebamus consumere longa loquendo
>   tempora, sermonem deficiente die,
> sic ferat ac referat tacitas nunc littera uoces,
>   et peragat linguae charta manusque uices (*Tr.* 5.13.27–30).

> Just as we used to spend long hours in conversation, the day not lasting long enough for our talk, so now may our letters carry our voiceless words to and fro, and paper and hand perform the duty of our tongues.

The literary aspect of Ovid's relationship with his unnamed addressee here is underscored by the Callimachean associations of lines 27–28, where poetic reminiscence is combined with personal reminiscence: the couplet echoes Callimachus's own fond recollection of the conversations which he too used to share until well after sunset with the now deceased Heraclitus of Halicarnassus (*A.P.* 7.80.2–3 = *Epig.* 2.2–3 Pf.).[92] By continuing to communicate in his allusive poetic voice Ovid actively sustains his former literary friendships, so that in, e.g., *Ex Ponto* 2.4 the same Callimachean echo (11–12) characterizes the poem as itself an offering of the sort described in lines 13–14: *saepe tuas uenit factum modo carmen ad auris,/ et noua iudicio subdita Musa tuo est*. By continuing to write to (/for), e.g., Salanus (Germanicus's coach in oratory) in *Ex Ponto* 2.5 or the epic poet Macer in *Ex Ponto* 2.10, to Severus in *Ex Ponto* 1.8 or to Albinovanus Pedo in *Ex Ponto* 4.10,[93] Ovid still belongs to a literary fellowship of sorts at Rome, thus compensating for his absence from the 'official' circle of his fellow-poets (cf. *Tr.* 5.3.47) among whom he still hopes to be remembered (58). Any breakdown in his channels of commu-

---

[91] And yet for Ovid's dissatisfaction with the written word as scant compensation for the spoken word see Forbis (1997) 255–59.

[92] See Williams (1991a) and (1994) 115–16.

[93] For all four see Syme (1978) 73, 80–81 (presumably a different Severus from the epic poet Cornelius Severus, addressed in *Pont.* 4.2 and 16), 88.

nication with Rome threatens to isolate him culturally as well as personally; hence the praise and the blame, the anxieties and the exhortations, the mild rebukes and the insistent pleadings, which complicate Ovid's construction in the exilic poetry of an informal *De amicitia*.

One consequence of Ovid's reluctance to name his addressees in the *Tristia* is that they are identified by moral type,[94] so that the model friend addressed in, e.g., *Tristia* 1.5 is defined by his actions—the haste with which he approached Ovid to console him after his fall (3–4), the encouragement he offered (5–6), and his ceaseless commitment to the poet (8). These actions are the *signa* which identify him in line 7: *scis bene quem dicam, positis pro nomine signis*. If at the beginning of the *Tristia* Rome (*urbem* at 1.1.1) is represented as Ovid's emotional center and as the idealized metropolis against which all the subsequent imperfections of Tomis are ultimately to be measured,[95] then his model *amicus* in *Tristia* 1.5 sets an ethical standard, reinforced by the poet's informal lecture on the responsibilities of friendship in lines 17–44, by which to measure the conduct of his addressees in, e.g., *Tristia* 1.8 (a faithless friend), *Tristia* 3.5 (a mere acquaintance who showed the devotion of an old friend), *Tristia* 3.6 (an old friend and true), and *Tristia* 4.7 (a close companion who is slow to write to Ovid); and so on throughout the exilic corpus, which amounts to a typological case-book of sorts documenting manifold kinds and qualities of behavior in friendship. Given that only a few *amici* stood by him after his fall (cf. *Tr.* 1.3.16, 1.5.33–34, 3.5.10, *Pont.* 2.3.29–30), the poet in exile gains an external perspective (as it were) on the 'true' nature of so many of his fair-weather friends at Rome and on the unpalatable reality underlying "that sacred and revered name of Roman friendship" (*Tr.* 1.8.15, *illud amicitiae sanctum et uenerabile nomen*; cf. *Pont.* 2.3.19–20). In one ironic reversal the Getae, themselves apparently recognizing the meaning and value of (Roman) friendship (cf. *Pont.* 3.2.43, *nos quoque amicitiae nomen bene nouimus, hospes*), set a salutary example for the 'civilized' Romans ("if the Getae honor friendship, [Ovid] expects at least as much from fellow Romans");[96] while in another reversal Ovid's cynical view of friendship in the *Ars amatoria*—*nomen amicitia est, nomen inane fides*

---

[94] Williams (1994) 105–6.
[95] On the significance of 1.1.1 *urbem*, cf. Edwards (1996) 117.
[96] Evans (1983) 118.

(1.740)—is ultimately confirmed by his own experience of still harsher betrayal upon his banishment.

The isolating effects of exile from Rome, compounded by Ovid's secondary form of social and linguistic exile in Tomis, are further intensified by the instability which characterizes so many of his relationships even with his loyal Roman friends. The "poet between two worlds"[97] is inevitably invaded by uncertainty about his standing in either, so that in Tomis he naturally suspects that the Getae insult him when they speak within his earshot in their own language, which he cannot understand (*Tr.* 5.10.40). On the Roman front the betrayal of so many false friends increases his reliance on, and generates his constant appeals to (e.g., *Tr.* 1.9.65–66, 3.6.19–24, 4.5.17–24, 5.3.47–58), the few friends who do remain loyal, while his heightened sensivity to any possible rupture in his emotional linkage with Rome leads to the mixture of confidence and doubt glimpsed in, e.g., *Tristia* 4.3, to his wife:

> ei mihi! cur nimium quae sunt manifesta requiro?
>   cur labat ambiguo spes mihi mixta metu?
> crede quod est et uis, ac desine tuta uereri,
>   deque fide certa sit tibi certa fides . . . (11–14)

> Alas, why do I seek answers to what is only too apparent? Why does my hope falter, mingled with fear and doubt? Believe that which is exactly as you wish, and stop fearing what is secure; and have firm faith about [her] firm faith.

Ovid's opening appeal to the stars (the Greater and Lesser Bears) to turn their gaze upon his wife and to report whether she still thinks of him (1–10) merely emphasizes the vast distance which separates him from her and which leads to his anxious efforts at self-persuasion in lines 11–14. Further reassurance (16–17, *non mentitura tu tibi uoce refer,/esse tui memorem*) is blended with direct interrogation of his wife (21–30) which again builds his confidence (27, *non equidem dubito, quin haec et cetera fiant*) before he proceeds to an informal lecture on how she should behave as the wife of an exile (31–74)—advice which is obsessive in tone, as if Ovid (over)compensates for their separation by striving all the harder directly to influence his wife's conduct from afar.[98] These different emotional reflexes characterize *Tristia*

---

[97] Fränkel (1945).
[98] On the (under)currents of uncertainty see Green (1994) 259 with Nisbet (1982)

4.3 as a complex, one-sided (even paranoid) study of the psychological tensions bearing upon lives intimately connected but lived apart, a condition paralleled in numerous addresses to loyal friends in the exilic poetry; but Ovid also glimpses the emotional chaos which threatens to erupt if his confidence in his closest associates should ever prove to be misplaced. In *Tristia* 4.7, for example, Ovid mildly rebukes his anonymous addressee for failing to write to him in his two years of exile (1–10); and yet he would sooner believe in the impossible than accept that his friend is disloyal:

> credam prius ora Medusae
> Gorgonis anguinis cincta fuisse comis,
> esse canes utero sub uirginis, esse Chimaeram,
> a truce quae flammis separet angue leam,
> quadrupedesque hominum cum pectore pectora iunctos,
> tergeminumque uirum tergeminumque canem,
> Sphingaque et Harpyias serpentipedesque Gigantas,
> centimanumque Gygen semiuirumque bouem—
> haec ego cuncta prius, quam te, carissime, credam
> mutatum curam deposuisse mei (*Tr.* 4.7.11–20).

I'll sooner believe that the face of the Gorgon Medusa was surrounded by locks of snakes, and that there are dogs below the virgin's [sc. Scylla's] belly, that there is a Chimaera, formed of a lioness and a cruel serpent kept apart by fire; and that quadrupeds joined at the breast with human breast [sc. Centaurs] exist, and a three-bodied man [sc. Geryon] and a three-headed dog [sc. Cerberus], and that the Sphinx exists and the Harpies and the snake-footed Giants, and Gyges with his hundred hands and a bull who's half-man [sc. the Minotaur]; all these things shall I believe, my dearest friend, before accepting that you have changed and given up your concern for me.

The dramatic effect of the *adynata* here and elsewhere in the exilic poetry[99] is to picture the emotional chaos precipitated by unthinkable betrayal: Ovid unleashes an unnatural fantasy to show the irrational imagination running riot, his grotesque piling of polysyllables in lines 15–18 itself contributing to the monstrous effect. The alternative to ordered friendship and the 'proper' meeting of souls (cf. *OLD* s.v. *pectus* 4a) is represented by the grotesque union of horse and human in line 15 (breast to breast, *cum pectore pectora . . .*), of snake and lioness in 13–14, and of man and bull in 18; to be disloyal

---

50–55, also observing (56) that in exile Ovid ironically "professes an Augustan ideal of marriage."

[99] See Williams (1994) 118–21 and 119 n. 35 for bibliography.

is itself to be transformed (cf. 20, *mutatum*) into an unnatural monstrosity. When the unthinkable has already once happened, as in the case of Ovid's exile (cf. *Tr.* 4.8.43–44, *Pont.* 4.3.51–53, '*litus ad Euxinum*' *si quis mihi diceret* '*ibis . . .*'/ '*i, bibe*' *dixissem* '*purgantes pectora sucos*'), the limits of the impossible become less stable and definite; in this respect his *adynata* in *Tristia* 4.7 and at, e.g., *Tr.* 5.13.21–23, *Pont.* 2.4.25–29, and 4.12.33–37 act as an uneasy defense-mechanism against the very eventuality—his friends' betrayal—which they so confidently exclude, so that his reassurance device *itself* shows signs of exilic insecurity.

5. *Augustus in Tomis*

Another effect of Ovid's reluctance to name his addressees in the *Tristia* is to underscore "the tragic metamorphosis that defines life in Tomis."[100] Whereas in the *Epistulae ex Ponto* "the naming of names does in fact suggest some degree of 'normalisation' of life in Tomis and some degree of continuity between the exiled poet and the community he has left behind," the silence which prevails in the *Tristia* enables Ovid "to dramatize how exile has jammed the works of *amicitia*."[101] The further inference, of course, is that *Augustus* has jammed those works, and that the veil of anonymity is designed to protect Ovid's friends from the dangers of association with him (cf. *Tr.* 3.4b.63–72, 4.5.15–16). Even though Ovid's rule of silence in the *Tristia* presumably offered no real protection at least to those friends who were his well known associates before his fall, the device contributes to "the strategic centrality of doubt"[102] in the work and to the "oppressive, anxiety-ridden atmosphere"[103] thus projected on to (the tyranny of) Augustus's Rome. This aura of uncertainty and fear takes programmatic shape in the instructions which Ovid gives in *Tristia* 1.1 to the poetic book which he dispatches to Rome: careful in what it says to whom (21–22; cf. *Tr.* 3.1.21–22), the *liber* is to exercise the greatest caution in approaching the imperial palace (69–92) and possibly, just possibly, gaining access to Augustus him-

---

[100] Oliensis (1997) 178.
[101] Oliensis (1997) 178.
[102] Oliensis (1997) 176.
[103] Casali (1997) 84.

self (93–96); as for the book's reception and Ovid's own fate, so much hangs on the luck of the day (97–98), on the timing of the approach (cf. 92), and on the emperor's disposition (93–94). The complicating effects of this elusive characterization of Augustus in *Tristia* 1.1 (approachable or hostile, clement or unforgiving, fickle or reliable?) are felt throughout the exilic poetry, not least in Ovid's attempt to persuade his friends that they have no reason to fear being named in his verse:

> cur tamen hoc aliis tutum credentibus unus,
>   appellent ne te carmina nostra, rogas?

> non uetat ille sui quemquam meminisse sodalis,
>   nec prohibet tibi me scribere teque mihi.

> at tu, cum tali populus sub principe simus,
>   alloquio profugi credis inesse metum?
> forsitan haec domino Busiride iure timeres
>   aut solito clausos urere in aere uiros.
> desine mitem animum uano infamare timore (*Pont.* 3.6.5–6, 11–12, 39–43).

But why, when others think it safe, do you alone ask that my poems not name you?

He does not forbid anyone to remember a close companion, nor does he prevent me from writing to you or you to me.

But you, given that we live as a people under such an emperor, do you believe that there is any fear in communicating with an exile? Perhaps under a master like Busiris you would rightly fear as much, or under him [sc. Phalaris] who used to shut and burn men inside the brazen bull. Cease to defame a gentle heart with your idle fears.

The more Ovid insists that Augustus poses no threat, the clearer it becomes that his friends suspect otherwise, that they might be slower to agree that the emperor is no Busiris or Phalaris (41–42),[104] and that in seeking to ease their paranoia (cf. 43, *uano . . . timore*) Ovid's encomia "function simultaneously as praise and as blame:"[105] by rejecting the harsh image of Augustus which he simultaneously constructs (and even promotes), this loyal subject can always disclaim responsibility for his indirect assault on the emperor.

This emphasis on the ambivalence of Ovid's treatment of Augustus

---

[104] Cf. above, p. 348 and n. 47.
[105] Oliensis (1997) 179.

in the *Tristia* and *Epistulae ex Ponto* offers a compromise between the
more traditional scholarly view of the exilic poetry as an extended
exercise in imperial flattery and its revisionist ('anti-Augustan') alter-
native, which stresses the many hints of defiance beneath Ovid's sur-
face posturings.[106] On this more flexible approach Augustus emerges
as an ambiguous figure whose reputation for mildness (e.g., *Tr.* 1.9.25,
2.27, *mitissime Caesar*, 41–42, 4.8.38, 5.8.25–26) and clemency (e.g.,
Tr. 2.43–50, 4.4.53–54, 4.8.39, *Pont.* 1.2.121–23) is tested by each
of Ovid's repeated requests for his removal at least to a more com-
fortable place of exile (e.g., *Tr.* 2.185–86, 4.4.51–52, *Pont.* 1.2.128,
1.8.73–74);[107] despite Ovid's tactful assertions that Augustus imposed
a fair and even lenient punishment on him (e.g., *Tr.* 2.125–38, *Pont.*
1.7.45–46, 3.6.9–10), we can indeed learn from his experience "the
extent of Caesar's clemency in mid-anger, if you don't know it" (*Pont.*
3.6.7–8, *quanta sit in media clementia Caesaris ira,/ si nescis*)—if you don't
yet know it after so many direct and indirect appeals to the emperor
have come to nothing and Ovid's confidence in the imperial image
(*Pont.* 1.2.59–60, *cum subit, Augusti quae sit clementia, credo/ mollia naufragiis
litora posse dari*) has brought only disappointment (cf. 61, *cum uideo
quam sint mea fata tenacia, frangor*).[108] The extremes of his exilic suffering
are (we infer) in proportion to the extreme anger that banished him
to Tomis and to the obdurate inclemency which keeps him there;
and yet until his death in A.D. 14 Augustus remains Ovid's only
possible savior. The tension which results from Ovid's reliance on
Augustus and yet his perception of the grim 'reality' behind the
Augustan myth makes the exilic corpus one of the more interesting
political documents of its age, especially as an oblique form of com-
mentary on the nature of Augustan rule as witnessed not from the
center of the empire but from its margins.

One of the preliminary arguments which Ovid makes in defense
of the *Ars amatoria* in *Tristia* 2 is that the offending work hardly

---

[106] For basic bibliography on the applicability of the terms pro- and anti-Augustan
in relation to Ovid see Gibson (1999) 19 n. 2 and Myers (1999) 196–98. For sta-
ple items emphasizing criticism of Augustus in the exilic poetry see Evans (1983)
181 n. 4; Evans himself plays down the subversive element (10–30; cf., e.g., Williams
(1978) 97 and Millar (1993) 6: "Far from being expressions of spiritual resistance,
the poems of exile should be read as the protests of a rejected loyalist").

[107] See Videau-Delibes (1991) 243–57 for the Augustan image of clemency (243–50)
complicated (cf. 254, "Un personnage en oxymore").

[108] For this approach to *Pont.* 3.6.7–8 extended further into the poem see Casali
(1997) 85–88.

deserves Augustus's attention when he is so burdened by responsibilities both abroad (225–32) and at home (233–34). The obsequious tone in which Ovid portrays Augustus as essential to the preservation of Rome's universal supremacy (cf. 217, *de te pendentem . . . orbem*) may itself appear suspiciously excessive in comparison with Horace's more controlled approach to the emperor at the opening of *Epistulae* 2.1, where the poet is tactfully aware that by taking up Augustus's time he interferes with the Roman public interest at home and abroad (cf. 1–3, *cum . . ./res Italas armis tuteris, moribus ornes,/legibus emendes . . .*). But whereas Horace surveys Augustus's responsibilities from the secure vantage-point of Rome and far from the clash of frontier arms, Ovid is closer to the hostilities which he describes at *Tr.* 2.225–30 (trouble in Pannonia, Illyria, Germany, and elsewhere).[109] Contrary to official appearances in the *Res Gestae* (cf. 12.2–13 on the Augustan peace and 31.2 for the pacification of the Bastarnae and Scythians),[110] Ovid knows a very different 'reality' on the Pontic margins: *uix hac inuenies totum, mihi crede, per orbem,/quae minus Augusta pace fruatur humus* (*Pont.* 2.5.17–18). Had Augustus known what conditions are really like in Tomis, he would never have exiled Ovid to such a place:

> nescit . . . Caesar, quamuis deus omnia norit,
>   ultimus hic qua sit condicione locus.
> magna tenent illud numen molimina rerum,
>   haec est caelesti pectore cura minor,
> nec uacat, in qua sint positi regione Tomitae,
>   quaerere (finitimo uix loca nota Getae) . . .
>
> maxima pars hominum nec te, pulcherrima, curat,
>   Roma, nec Ausonii militis arma timet (*Pont.* 1.2.71–76, 81–82).

Although a god knows everything, Caesar has no notion of what life is like in this remote place. The weight of great affairs preoccupies his godhead: this is a matter too slight for his heavenly mind. Nor does he have leisure to inquire where the Tomitans are situated (the region is scarcely known to the neighboring Getae).

The bulk of these peoples cares nothing for you, most beautiful Rome, and doesn't fear the arms of Roman soldiers.

Ovid loyally upholds and yet undermines another aspect of the imperial legend by attempting to explain (73–74) why Augustus, although

---

[109] See Habinek (1998) 156–57.

[110] For Ovid's possible allusions to Augustan autobiography see Claassen (1999) 221–22 with Fairweather (1987) 193–95.

a god,[111] is not all-knowing (71): he is evidently too busy (with other troublespots of the 'peaceful' empire?) to give thought to Tomis (75–76), a region which reciprocates by apparently giving no thought to Rome (81–82).

A Rome-based and (as it were) centripetal explanation for Ovid's exilic interest in this tension between the center and the periphery is that he involves the reader "in the project of Roman imperialism,"[112] inviting "the metropolitan subject of Roman imperialism to condition himself or herself to the laborious process of pacification of the unruly forces the empire has taken under its control."[113] From this perspective Ovid's account in *Ex Ponto* 4.13 of the Getic poem set to Latin meter on the apotheosis of Augustus (25–32) which he allegedly performed before an enthusiastic local audience again has imperialist overtones; for "Ovid's poetry thus embodies in its implied personal narrative a political narrative as well, one that must have been familiar in many communities as Rome sought not merely to conquer but also to tame the far reaches of her empire."[114] From a Tomis-based perspective, however, Ovid's Getic poem projects a rather different image of Augustus and the imperial family, one that loses its awesome metropolitan *auctoritas* as Rome reaches an accommodation with, rather than simply subdues, the now compliant but still armed (cf. 35) Getae. Whether or not Ovid ever did actually write this hybrid poem (there is no surviving evidence of it, and good reason to doubt its existence),[115] his feat of cross-cultural invention marks an extreme stage not only in his gradual "gétisation"[116] in Tomis, but also in the compromising of 'pure' Roman authority/identity on the margins. If the reader responds with disbelief to Ovid's portrayal of the crude Getae (22, *inhumanos*) attending a poetic recitation in the first place and then showing their appreciation for Ovid's performance by politely shaking their quivers (35) and murmuring (36) their support, the (Ovidian) myth of Augustus's imperial success in the Tomitan region is undermined; and yet if Ovid is believed, how appropriate is it for the imperial family to be lauded

---

[111] Identified with Jupiter, cf., e.g., *Tr.* 1.1.20, 1.2.3–4, 12, 1.3.37–40, 1.5.77–78, 2.37–40.
[112] Habinek (1998) 152.
[113] Habinek (1998) 14.
[114] Habinek (1998) 161.
[115] Williams (1994) 91–92.
[116] Lozovan (1958) 402.

in "barbarian words" (20, *barbara uerba*) and in a Geto-Latin medium as unique (or monstrous?) as the Augustan phenomenon which it celebrates? When Ovid has a local tribesman assert that so loyal a supporter of Augustus should have been recalled by the emperor (37–38), does he imply that the Getae have a sympathetic sensibility which Augustus himself lacks?

These and other unsettling implications of Ovid's treatment of Augustus in *Ex Ponto* 4.13[117] result from the tension in exile between the poet's 'loyal' Roman persona and his external perspective on the 'reality' at the imperial periphery—on the fact that Roman *imperium* is not the clinical instrument of subjection envisaged at the Roman center and pictured at, e.g., *Tr.* 3.7.51–52 (*dum . . . suis uictrix omnem de montibus orbem/prospiciet domitum Martia Roma, legar*), but a fluid process of confrontation, negotiation, and uneasy compromise between Rome and her neighbors. In this respect the exilic poetry pursues from a different angle Ovid's longstanding exploration (especially in the *Metamorphoses* and *Fasti*) of the nature of Augustan rule, or of "the manipulations of culture, power, and identity"[118] which so complicated Augustus's identity as "an anomaly, a novelty, a challenge to Roman powers of definition, occupying novel, uncategorisable conceptual areas."[119] If in general "Ovid's challenge to Augustus is embodied precisely in his profound engagement with the regime's whole programme, his insistent probings of the very underpinnings of its authority,"[120] then Augustus's decision to banish Ovid actually privileges the exile with a potentially embarrassing vantage-point on the fragile underpinnings of his imperial authority and on the limits of his divine reach. Ovid is ironically empowered by his exilic insight into the pretensions of Augustan rule, or by the opportunity to promote in Tomis one myth (the Getae still untamed by Rome) in opposition to the 'authorized' Roman version of Pontic supremacy.

There are hints of sharper defiance and protest, not least in Ovid's assertion that Augustus is powerless to control his freedom of mind and creative talent (*ingenium*) and his lasting fame as a poet (*Tr.* 3.7.47–52);[121] Augustus's authority over the poet appears relatively

---

[117] See Casali (1997) 92–96.

[118] Myers (1999) 197.

[119] Feeney (1992) 2.

[120] Myers (1999) 197.

[121] Much cited as Ovid's most defiant statement of spiritual freedom in exile; see Evans (1983) 17–19 and 182 n. 20 for bibliography.

limited by comparison, his divinity overshadowed by Ovid's confidence
in his own immortality. But if in the exilic poetry Ovid "asserts and
justifies himself in the face of his smothering catastrophe, vindicat-
ing his right to speak, maintaining his voice,"[122] his most direct chal-
lenge to Augustus is found in his defense of the *Ars amatoria* against
the charge of immorality in *Tristia* 2.[123] Indeed, it may well be
doubted that *Tristia* 2 was ever in fact meant for Augustus's own
eyes,[124] unless Ovid calculated that the emperor would read the work
with the same lack of sophistication with which (the poet alleges) he
judged the *Ars amatoria*. Given the weight of his responsibilities at
home and abroad (213–36), is it surprising that Augustus never read
the work (237–38)? But how can he then have condemned it? Augustus
can no more control and fix the interpretation of *Tristia* 2 than he
can of the *Ars*: in asserting that his character differs from his verse
(354, *uita uerecunda est, Musa iocosa mihi*) and that "the larger part of
[his] writings is unreal and fictitious" (355, *magna . . . pars operum men-
dax et ficta meorum*), or that "a book is no index of character" (357,
nec liber indicium est animi), Ovid is left with no way of proving (and
Augustus with no firm grounds for believing) that the poet's imper-
ial praises of the emperor in, e.g., the *Metamorphoses* (cf. *Tr.* 2.65–66)
are truly sincere; not even his considerable flattery of Augustus in
Tristia 2 is immune to the suspicion that it belongs to the 'insincere'
portion of his oeuvre.

Surely his boldest and most controversial argument, however, is
that although he is far from the only poet to have written on 'ten-
der' love, he alone has been punished for it (361–62). At stake here
is not only his vindication of the *Ars* as a work misjudged by Augustus;
in constructing what amounts to an informal history of Greco-Roman
literature (363–470),[125] he confronts the emperor with the weight of
a cultural tradition which is so well established and wide-ranging
both chronologically and geographically that it merely emphasizes
the relative insignificance of Augustus's efforts to regulate literary
morality at a particular moment in Roman political time. By attach-
ing himself to this tradition (cf. 467, *his ego successi*), Ovid sides with

---

[122] Feeney (1992) 18.
[123] See now Gibson (1999), stressing the open-endedness of the work at its point
of (reader-)reception, and with rich bibliography.
[124] See Wiedemann (1975) 271.
[125] See now the stimulating treatment of Gibson (1999) 27–34.

writers whose immortality serves both as an example to the legacy-conscious Augustus and as an implicit warning: Augustus depends partly on poets (even on Ovid), and on the immortality of poets, for his own *fama* in life and after-life. But in surveying the Greco-Roman literary tradition Ovid gradually moves to his more overt point: if Augustus will incriminate the *Ars amatoria*, then why not take action against any other salacious work ever written? What is the *Iliad* if not a poem both based on adultery (Helen: 371–72) and actually featuring it in the approximate form of Briseis's abduction (373–74)? What is the *Odyssey* if not a poem about Penelope's temptation (375–76) and featuring in Book 8 an explicit act of adultery (Venus and Mars: 377–78)? And yet who would dream of incriminating such 'offensive' works? Ovid's reading of literary history in lines 363–470 is of course deliberately one-sided, but in a way which subtly entraps Augustus: if the latter were to object that Ovid offers a perverse assessment of, e.g., Homer, emphasizing the sexual angle to the exclusion of so much else in the *Iliad* or the *Odyssey*, then the emperor is left open to the charge of being an equally perverse reader of the *Ars amatoria*. In its very different way *Tristia* 2 is no less provocative than the *Ars*, for in this *reductio ad absurdum*[126] Ovid confronts Augustus with the consequences of (mis-)reading literature in the 'Augustan' way.

6. *The* Ibis *in Context*

Through provocative arguments of this sort Ovid's Muse survives the transforming effects of exile still to work mischief in *Tristia* 2, and the tactlessness, even defiance, which (s)he shows suggests that Ovid's anxiety in lines 3–4 is fully justified: *cur modo damnatas repeto, mea crimina, Musas?/ an semel est poenam commeruisse parum?* In striving to appease Augustus in *Tristia* 2 his Muse takes risks which continue to characterize her as both friend and foe to Ovid, beneficial but *still* potentially baneful. If in the exilic poetry his wife supplants the erotic elegiac *puella*, the elegiac tension between love and hate, *odi et amo* (Catul. 85.1; cf. *Am.* 3.11b.1–2, *luctantur pectusque leue in contraria tendunt/ hac amor, hac odium; sed, puto, uincit amor*), resurfaces in Ovid's exilic relationship with the Muse.[127] *Carmen demens carmine laesus amo*

---

[126] Wilkinson (1955) 311.
[127] See Williams (1994) 150–53.

(*Tr.* 4.1.30): his faithful companion (*Tr.* 4.1.20), she "brings him comfort" (*Tr.* 4.10.117, *tu solacia praebes*) in the manner of a devoted friend (cf. *Pont.* 2.7.81, *nec uos parua datis pauci solacia nobis*), distracting him from his exilic grief (*Tr.* 4.1.49–50). But this mood of grateful reliance is punctuated by fits of rage in which he burns his exilic verses (cf. *Tr.* 4.1.99–102), partly out of frustration at their 'poor' quality, partly in anger at the disastrous consequences of his *ars*(/*Ars*). So also *Tr.* 5.7.31–33:

> quamuis interdum, quae me laesisse recordor,
>   carmina deuoueo Pieridasque meas,
> cum bene deuoui, nequeo tamen esse sine illis . . .

> Although I sometimes curse my poems when I remember the harm they have done me, and although I curse my Muses, when I've duly cursed them I still cannot be without them . . .

Ovid's exilic persona *needs* the emotional outlet which cursing provides here, as if he discharges his pent-up frustrations in outbursts which are as necessary as they are futile (*nequeo tamen* . . .). For "sorrow that is suppressed chokes us and seethes within and under that pressure inevitably redoubles its strength" (*strangulat inclusus dolor atque exaestuat*[128] *intus,/cogitur et uires multiplicare suas*, *Tr.* 5.1.63–64). Ovid's love-hate relationship with the Muses is only one source of the seething tensions which build up within his exilic persona and lead to the occasional explosions of the sort pictured in *Tristia* 5.7. His oscillating attitude towards the Muses is also symptomatic of the instability which characterizes so many of his exilic relationships. His words to his wife in, e.g., *Tristia* 4.3 are infected with signs of paranoid insecurity, while his frequent recourse to *adynata* to persuade himself of the impossibility of his friends' betrayal itself betrays his own endless need for reassurance. Has Augustus begun to forgive him? Is his name cherished by the literary circle to which he once belonged (cf. *Tr.* 5.3.49–56), his downfall lamented by rank and file Romans (cf. *Tr.* 2.569–70)? Who and how many are the Roman detractors who apparently still act against him after his fall? How effective are the warning shots that he delivers to his unnamed enemy (or enemies?) in *Tristia* 1.8, 3.11, 4.9 and 5.8? While Ovid's prose correspondence with his friends and family at Rome presumably sup-

---

[128] Most editors read *atque exaestuat* with MS support; but *at mens aestuat* Hall (his own conjecture after (1990) 94).

plied practical answers to these and other such questions, his exilic
persona is only too vulnerable to the self-doubt generated by his
many insecurities in Tomis. In this climate of uncertainty the noto-
rious and little read *Ibis* is open to reassessment as an artistically
controlled explosion, a curse which satisfies an emotional need sim-
ilar to that expressed in Ovid's outbursts against the Muses at *Tr.*
5.7.31–32.

A long introductory section (1–250) in which Ovid formally curses
Ibis, his pseudonymous enemy, gives way to a vast catalogue of
imprecations drawn from the obscure byways of history, mythology,
and legend (251–638); the pseudonym is drawn from the lost
Callimachean curse-poem on which Ovid models his own:

> nunc, quo Battiades inimicum deuouet Ibin,
>   hoc ego deuoueo teque tuosque modo,
> utque ille, historiis inuoluam carmina caecis,
>   non soleam quamuis hoc genus ipse sequi.
> illius ambages imitatus in Ibide dicar
>   oblitus moris iudiciique mei.
> et, quoniam qui sis nondum quaerentibus edo,
>   Ibidis interea tu quoque nomen habe (55–62).

For the present I curse you and yours in the manner[129] in which
Callimachus, Battus's son, curses his enemy Ibis; and just as he does,
I'll envelope my verses in dark researches, even though I'm hardly
accustomed to this kind of writing. By emulating his obscurities in the
Ibis, I'll be said to have forgotten my usual custom and judgement.
And since I've yet to disclose who you are to anyone who asks, for
the present you too take the name of Ibis.

As much a stranger to bellicose poetics (cf. *Ibis* 9–10, *quisquis is
est . . ./ cogit inadsuetas sumere tela manus*) as he is to real arms in Tomis
(cf. *Tr.* 1.5.73–74, 4.1.71–74), Ovid projects an innocent and injured
persona as one *compelled* to retaliate to his enemy's vicious provoca-
tion; but this apprentice to cursing also shows signs of personal and
poetic strain in looking to Callimachus for guidance and departing
from the habits of a lifetime in the process (58, 60; cf. 1–10). As he
gradually warms to his task, this uneasy combination of diffidence
and resolve gives way to a series of increasingly bizarre maneuvers,
many based on standard literary curse-techniques,[130] which distance

---

[129] Or *modo* "meter," the Callimachean *Ibis* elegiac? Controversial: Watson (1991)
79 and n. 92.
[130] Well documented by Watson (1991).

his persona ever further from 'ordinary' reality. Already in 67–88
his appeal for support to every god who ever existed goes far beyond
the more restrained invocations found in popular curses and curse-
tablets (*defixiones*) and offers an early sign of his insecurity not just as
a newcomer to curse-magic (experienced practitioners of magic such
as Medea are far more selective in the deities they invoke at, e.g.,
Met. 7.192–98); his excessive prayer also hints at the hopelessness of
his situation as an exile powerless to exact any kind of revenge at
Rome except through words, threats, and the magical intervention
of whatever divine forces he can miraculously summon on his behalf.
As his curse unfolds, this hint of lonely despair suggests that all his
persona can really achieve by the punishments which he heaps on
Ibis is the satisfaction of uselessly indulging his anger. Hence his
meticulous preparations for the human sacrifice of Ibis in lines 97–106,
where Ovid appears so insulated from reality ("The poet is, after
all, in Tomi; 'Ibis' is in Rome (13ff.) . . .")[131] that he is capable of
the extraordinary scene-changes and impossible transitions which fol-
low in, e.g., 106–7: *da iugulum cultris hostia dira meis./terra tibi fruges,
amnis tibi deneget undas.* A sacrificial victim in line 106 who survives
to become a global and social outcast in a sequence of maledictions
(107–26) apparently endorsed by a sign from Apollo himself (127–28),
Ibis is later characterized as (*inter alia*) a betrayer persecuted by Ovid's
Dido-like shade (141–44), as a reviled corpse (163–72), as a worthy
companion of the proverbial sinners of the underworld (e.g., Sisyphus
and Ixion; 173–94) and, in the horoscope which Ovid constructs for
him in lines 209–44, as a child born at a moment of planetary ill-
omen on the ill-starred *dies Alliensis* (217–20) in a part of Libya (222,
Cinyphiam . . . humum) which regularly produces monsters. As Housman
saw clearly enough, this Ibis "is much too good to be true."[132]

After Clotho is made to predict that "there will be a poet who
will sing your destiny" (246, *'fata canet uates qui tua' dixit 'erit'*), Ovid
masquerades as her appointed harbinger of vatic truth (247, *ille ego
sum uates*) before spinning his own Clotho-like yarn in the vast cat-
alogue of imprecations which dominates the second half of the *Ibis*.
The Hellenistic curse-tradition had already inflicted on its targets
exotic punishments delivered in verse of intimidating obscurity and

---

[131] Watson (1991) 211.
[132] Housman (1920) 316 = (1972) 1040.

learning;[133] but Ovid's collection is no slavish replica of those prototypes, even though his deference to Callimachus (55–62) has encouraged modern critics to dismiss the catalogue as a self-indulgent *tour de force*, very possibly unprecedented in length but still a display-piece of Hellenistic *aemulatio*, an impotent weapon whose only utility lay in diverting Ovid from his exilic grief.[134] After being mauled to death by a lioness as was Phalaecus, the tyrant of Ambracia (501–2), and then being gored by a wild boar as were Ancaeus, Adonis, and Idmon, all of them contained in a single couplet (503–4), Ibis is destined to suffer the fate of the hunter who once killed a boar and hung it from a tree without first dedicating it to Artemis, only to pay for his oversight when the boar's head fell on him, killing him as he slept (505–6).[135] After encountering these and countless other bizarre fates in this mysterious playground of the imagination, with one horrendous fate always inspiring or surpassing another in a sadistic torture-sport, Ibis finds himself still living at the end of this *carmen perpetuum* of sorts and faced with still worse to come if he still persecutes the poet; the *Ibis* is after all but a preamble (!) to the real onslaught threatened by its iambic sequel (639–44). The disproportionate length of the catalogue is itself a gauge of the irrational dynamic that drives it, while time loses all shape and meaning in Ovid's anachronistic revival of so many mythical and historical horrors in a frozen 'present' of simultaneous and unending torture; the tears which the Furies destine for the infant Ibis *tempus in immensum* (239) give way in the catalogue to *measureless* time, or to "just a big plot (or unplot) of suffering, unstructured, open-ended and incalculable, *tempus in immensum*."[136]

Housman's firm dismissal of Ibis as a fiction has not altogether killed him off in modern scholarship. Even if he did exist, his true identity remains elusive despite the extensive efforts of modern theorists.[137] But the fact remains that this enemy, whether real or imagined, has nothing to fear from the curse as soon as (if not before)

---

[133] See in general Watson (1991) 79–193.
[134] See Williams (1996) 22 and 29 n. 72.
[135] See further Williams (1996) 98–99.
[136] Hinds (1999) 65.
[137] For candidates see La Penna (1957) xvi–xix with Watson (1991) 130 n. 344 for newer developments. *Not* Augustus, whose praises are sung in lines 23–28; or possibly Augustus by the method of Freudian substitution explored by Casali (1997) 107–8?

Ovid himself effectively admits that Ibis will survive the onslaught
(cf. 53, *postmodo, si perges* . . .). Why, then, should Ovid persevere with
such a bizarre and futile project? For Housman, Ovid attacks a
purely notional enemy for the sake of thematic *uariatio* within the
exilic corpus;[138] André, holding that Ibis did indeed exist, has to
assume that Ovid sets out to curse a real enemy in real earnest but
loses his way in a cloud of *doctrina* in the catalogue, which André
(like Housman) rules a mere *jeu d'esprit*.[139] A third approach, how-
ever, contests the view that a curse with an imaginary target
(Housman's *Ibis*) loses all claim to being taken seriously, and also
the argument that Ovid somehow lost his way in a curse which he
undertook in full seriousness (André's *Ibis*), as if his *real* hatred, deep
and true, could so easily transform itself into another display of his
literary virtuosity. Already in *Tristia* 5.7 cursing features prominently
in the self-expression of the poet in exile, whose persona *needs* the
emotional outlet which his occasional (and ultimately futile) outbursts
against the Muses provide (31–34). Viewed from this perspective, the
Ibis offers a spectacular example of this manic phase in Tomis, where
Ovid portrays the isolated self receding ever further into a dream-
like fantasy of revenge, as if the frustration of not being able directly
to confront his Roman enemy or enemies, real or perceived, builds
up in his warning poems (*Tristia* 1.8, 3.11, 4.9, and 5.8) until it
finally erupts into violence in his volcanic curse—only to give way
(one suspects on the analogy of Ovid's reconciliation with the Muses
after cursing them at *Tr.* 5.7.31–34) to another phase of resignation
and renewed frustration. On this approach[140] the *Ibis* is no awkward
appendage to the rest of the exilic corpus, and no *jeu d'esprit* which
Ovid undertook merely to fill his time in Tomis; as a manic alter-
native to the melancholy which pervades the *Tristia* and *Epistulae ex
Ponto*, the curse makes a significant (even required) contribution to
the psychological 'wholeness' of the corpus.

7. *Before Exile and After: Ovidian Continuity*

The obsessive tendencies which characterize Ovid's persona in the
Ibis find striking parallels in various episodes of the *Metamorphoses*.

---

[138] Housman (1920) 317–18 = (1972) 1041–42.
[139] André (1963) xxxviii.
[140] Williams (1996).

Aglauros, for example, once bitten by jealousy (2.798–805), can only feed her obsession until she is devoured by it (805–13); even when turned to stone (819–32) she still shows her jealousy in her livid discoloration. So also Byblis: spurned by her brother Caunus, who flees the country to escape her incestuous advances, she follows in hot but futile pursuit (9.633–48) until she collapses in a flood of tears which eventually consume her (663), transforming her into a fountain whose gushing endlessly perpetuates her grief (664–65). The sheer length and density of Ovid's curse-catalogue in the *Ibis* suggest that his persona, like Aglauros and Byblis, is emotionally imprisoned by its obsessive behavior; and Niobe's endless tears after being turned to stone (*Met.* 6.310–12) offer another suggestive analogy for Ovid's post-transformation grief, still keenly felt in the *Tristia* and *Epistulae ex Ponto* even after his exilic 'death.'[141] Moreover, Actaeon's fate (cf. *Met.* 3.138–252) is invoked at *Tr.* 2.105–6 as a paradigm for Ovid's own unintentional but still disastrous *error* (105, *inscius Actaeon uidit sine ueste Dianam . . .*); beyond the implication that Ovid too has been unfairly persecuted in a fit of divine pique, his alienation as a poet between two worlds and as a foreigner linguistically isolated in Tomis finds a loose but suggestive parallel[142] in Actaeon's agonizing alienation after he is transformed into a stag and yet still retains human feeling (201–3). In this in-between state he too belongs neither 'here' nor 'there,' in neither the woods nor the palace (204–5); he tries to cry out to his fellow huntsmen and to establish his true identity (230) but words fail him (231; cf. 201–2), just as Ovid allegedly struggles in exile to express himself in Latin (cf., e.g., *Tr.* 3.14.45–50, 5.7.55–64, 5.12.57–58) and to retain his identity as *Romanus uates* (cf. *Tr.* 5.7.55). Actaeon's death at the jaws of his own hounds is also tangentially related to the recurrent theme in the *Metamorphoses* of artists directly or indirectly harmed or destroyed by their own supreme talent (so, e.g., Arachne, 6.1–145, Marsyas, 6.383–400, Daedalus-Icarus, 8.183–235, Perdix, 8.236–59). In the cases of Arachne and Marsyas as well as of the daughters of Pierus, transformed into loquacious *picae* (magpies) after losing their poetic contest with the Muses (5.294–678), the theme of the artist victimized by divine persecution suggests that Ovid "saw the real-world potential for an analogous silencing of artists by the Olympians' mortal counterparts in Rome

---

[141] Cf. for the approach Williams (1996) 86–89.
[142] Cf. Forbis (1997) 262.

long before A.D. 8"[143] and passes oblique comment in the *Metamorphoses*
on the limits and dangers of free artistic expression under Augustus.[144]
The theme of self-destruction implicit in the stories of Actaeon and
Arachne is also developed in a different way in those episodes fea-
turing the disastrous effects of personal obsession (so Phaethon,
1.747–2.332, Aglauros, 2.708–832, Narcissus, 3.339–510, Erysichthon,
8.738–878). Destroyed by the excesses of his own *ars/Ars* (cf. *Tr.*
2.313, *cur in nostra nimia est lasciuia Musa . . .?*), Ovid lives out a form
of experience which he had already visited in the *Metamorphoses*, itself
portrayed in *Tristia* 1.7 as his *maior imago* (11).

   In its apparently incomplete and unpolished state the *Metamorphoses*
is said to offer a greater and truer reflection of the transformed poet
in exile than does the image of him which is engraved on his
addressee's ring (*Tr.* 1.7.5–8). In *Tr.* 1.7.35–40 Ovid offers a six-line
epigraph for addition to the *Metamorphoses*, a preface which transforms
the poem of change by making "pointed reference, like the begin-
ning of *Tristia* 1 itself, to its author's exile; and which, again like the
beginning of *Tristia* 1, will claim a reflection of the author's woes in
the poem's own rough and unfinished state."[145] Through the the-
matic coincidences reviewed above, however, the *Metamorphoses* also
anticipates and illustrates significant aspects of Ovid's psychological
self-portrayal as an alienated exile ruined by his own wayward genius;
but the coincidences with his pre-exilic oeuvre are not confined only
to the *Metamorphoses*. The many structural and thematic overlaps
between the exilic poetry and the *Heroides*,[146] for example, are accom-
panied by the need for "psychic gratification"[147] which Ovid shares
with many of his authoresses, or for the reassurance which both he
and they derive from their necessary but potentially futile outpour-
ings to their distant addressees. The classic symptoms of elegiac love-
sickness (pallor, loss of appetite, insomnia) resurface in Ovid's ailments
in Tomis,[148] where the 'shut out lover' (*exclusus amator*) gives way to
the *exclusus poeta* and Ovid begins to test (as throughout his career)
the conventional limits of genre and topos. Already as a youthful

---

[143] Johnson (1997a) 243.
[144] See further Johnson (1997a) 243–44 and cf. Harries (1990) 76–77 on "Arachne
and Ovid: the poet's fate."
[145] Hinds (1985) 26.
[146] See opening discussion above and n. 11.
[147] Jacobson (1974) 372.
[148] See above, p. 351 and n. 59.

love-elegist he portrays himself as alienated from the usual *cursus honorum* (cf. *Am.* 1.15.1–8) and following the Muses against the advice of his father (cf. *Tr.* 4.10.15–40); and given the ruinous consequences of his *Ars amatoria*, his early claim that he is vulnerable to his own teachings in the *Ars* being used against him (*Am.* 1.4.46, 2.18.20, 2.19.34) appears oddly prophetic. In so many ways the exilic corpus represents the latest stage in Ovid's open-ended and career-long metamorphosis as a poet who never fully leaves his past behind. His journey into exile may thus be viewed as a voyage of return to strangely familiar psychological territory, a coincidence which does much to reconcile the exilic poetry with the rest of an oeuvre from which it is too often, and too rigidly, segregated by modern critics.

CHAPTER TWELVE

SIQUID HABENT VERI VATUM PRAESAGIA: OVID IN THE 1ST–5TH CENTURIES A.D.

Michael Dewar

For Roman moralists, refinement and effeminacy were pretty much two sides of the same coin. Writing in the reign of Nero, the satirist Persius denounced the vices of contemporary poetry and society alike in violent terms. To make his point clear, he imagined his interlocutor, a defender of the avant garde, producing specimens of the kind of dissolute verse that so offended him:

'sed numeris decor est et iunctura addita crudis.
cludere sic uersum didicit "Berecyntius Attis"
et "qui caeruleum dirimebat Nerea delphin,"
sic "costam longo subduximus Appennino."
"Arma uirum," nonne hoc spumosum et cortice pingui
ut ramale uetus uegrandi subere coctum?'
quidnam igitur tenerum et laxa ceruice legendum?
'torua Mimalloneis inplerunt cornua bombis,
et raptum uitulo caput ablatura superbo   100
Bassaris et lyncem Maenas flexura corymbis
euhion ingeminat, reparabilis adsonat echo.'
haec fierent si testiculi uena ulla paterni
uiueret in nobis? (*Sat.* 1.92–104)

'But to rough old verses grace and smoothness have been added. "Berecynthius Attis" has learned how to round off a line, and so has "The dolphin that was parting sea-blue Nereus," and "a rib we stole from Appennine's long flank." "Arms and the Man!" What a lot of froth, just swollen bark, like a branch, of old cork, all dried up and with its bark stunted.' Well, what about something delicate, the kind of stuff you have to recite with your neck drooping to one side? "They filled their fierce horns with Mimallonean boomings. And the Bassarid poised to tear the head from the exulting calf, and the Maenad ready to guide the lynx with her ivy-rein cry out 'Euhion!' and again 'Euhion!,' and the restoring Echo sounds back in turn." Would such things be if we still had an ounce of our fathers' balls?

One of several considerations that underlie the interest modern scholars have shown in this fascinating passage is the fact that the scholiast identifies a specific target, the poet-emperor Nero himself.[1] More than that, he asserts firmly that lines 99–102 are actually a quotation from Nero's own infamous verse. Even the scholiast, however, has enough scruples to record the alternative opinion, that the lines are Persius's own, composed solely to serve as extreme examples of the kind of modish rubbish that is, as he puts it, "full of sound and fury, signifying nothing" (*sonum grandem habent, sensum nullum*), and therefore, we might add, is nothing more than "a tale told by an idiot." The most cogent defense of the case for Neronian authorship is made by Sullivan.[2] To Griffin, however, the sceptical view is so obviously the only sensible one that an opinion on the matter is thought to be worth presenting only in a firmly phrased footnote.[3] For us, there is no need to worry too much about this precise issue, because one thing is clear: whoever is being attacked is a poet, real or fictional, who writes in a style that might loosely be characterized as Ovidian. The features that distinguish the lines held up to scorn include a general mellifluousness of sound, the avoidance of elision, the use of Greek words to give color and an exotic feel, rhyming patterns, strained word play, and a generally overwrought stylization that aims at elegance of sound rather than originality of content. All that is missing to make this a description of the artistic effect of the *Metamorphoses*, the hostile critic might say, is Ovid's frivolity. Indeed, many of the individual phrases and metrical or grammatical features of these lines have counterparts in Ovid. *Berecyntius Attis*, for example, could be said to conflate the line-endings *Cybeleius Attis* (*Met.* 10.104) and *Berecyntius heros* (*Met.* 11.106, of Midas).[4] The mannered metonym *Nerea* for the sea is on old one, in that even Homer can be found using a god's name for something closely associated with him,[5] but we should note in particular *Her.* 9.14, *qua latam Nereus caerulus ambit humum*. The use of the polysyllabic *Appennino* to occupy both of the last two feet of the line and to create a spon-

---

[1] See Sullivan (1985) 101.

[2] Sullivan (1985) 100–108.

[3] Griffin (1984) 275 n. 58: "No credence can be given to the scholiasts . . . they seem to see Nero everywhere, spotting allusions in 1.4; 1.29; 1.28 and 1.121."

[4] Harvey (1981) 44.

[5] See Nisbet and Hubbard (1970) 104 (on Hor. *C.* 1.7.22, *Lyaeo*) and Harrison (1991) 256 (on Virg. *Aen.* 10.764–65). Cf. also, e.g., [Tib.] 3.7.58, Luc. 2.713.

deiazon along the way is an affectation singled out for criticism by Quintilian (*IO* 9.4.65) as *praemolle*. It is found in a hexameter as early as Hor. *Epod.* 16.29, but its first appearance in epic seems to be at *Met.* 2.226 (thereafter in, e.g., Cornelius Severus 10 Courtney, Luc. 2.396, Sil. 4.742). The highly recherché adjective *Mimalloneus* cannot be paralleled in classical Latin verse, but it is Ovid who calls Bacchants *Mimallonides* at *Ars* 1.541. The attributive use of the future participle to indicate purpose, as seen here in *ablatura* and *flexura*, is common in such authors as Lucan and Statius, but its frequency in these poets seems to have been influenced by Ovid, who clearly found the economy it offered him metrically useful.[6] The lines quoted by Persius's interlocutor are also notable for their abundance of Graecisms and the prominence given to upsilon, a sound singled out by Quintilian for its euphonious quality (12.10.7–28). Although it is true that Virgil chose to signal the Greek quality of his *Eclogues* by making his first sentence in that work begin *Tityre* and end *Amaryllida siluas* (*Ecl.* 1.1–5), and true, also, that he scatters all through it such lines as *nec tantum Rhodope miratur et Ismara Orphea* (*Ecl.* 6.30), there is nothing that quite compares to Ovid's catalogue of the flowers picked by the innocent Proserpina and her companions at Henna: *has, hyacinthe, tenes; illas, amarante, moraris:/pars thyma, pars rhoean et melitonon amat* (*F.* 4.439–40).[7]

Many of these features, then, can be paralleled in authors other than Ovid. And Ovid himself cannot be Persius's target, because the satirist is concerned with attacking the degeneracy of poets in his own day, not with the poems of a man who had been dust and shadow for nearly half a century. But it would seem that Persius is enraged by the influence of Ovid, in that the poets who over-use the refinements that he and the more skilful of his admirers had made the common currency of Latin poetry thereby produce hexameters that, far from being in keeping with the sonorous majesty of heroic poetry, are in fact jejune, enfeebled, and effeminate. What Seneca the Elder said of Ovid and his abuse of his *ingenium*—*nescit quod bene cessit relinquere* (*Contr.* 9.5.17)—might equally be said of the abuse his imitators made of his *ars*.

Making it look as easy as it was polished is perhaps Ovid's greatest contribution to the development of the sound and aesthetics of

---

[6] See for example Knox (1995) 130 (on *Her.* 2.99).
[7] Cited by Wilkinson (1963) 12.

Latin poetry. In part this was because he stood at the end of a long process of experimentation and refinement. Most famously, his elegiacs mark the point at which it became effectively compulsory to end a pentameter with a disyllable. According to Wilkinson's statistics,[8] only two in five of Catullus's pentameters end this way, but disyllables dominate as early as the Monobiblos of Propertius (61%), and this practice has effectively become a rule for Tibullus (93% in Book 1) and an absolute rule for Ovid (100% in the *Heroides*). Similarly, in the dactylic hexameter, he built on the work of Cicero and Virgil to fashion something distiguished for its fluidity and smoothness, a rolling, little-varied line marked by dactyls, predictable caesurae, and the absence of elision. Roman poets adapted the alien meters of Greek to their own language through a long but accelerating process of trial and error. It would be a gross overstatement to say that Ovid created the rules, but in a sense he gave them the *summa manus* that he claimed he had not been able to give his great epic. At any rate, significant experimentation thereafter practically comes to an end.

What was the effect of this final setting down of the rules? The answer is not only that Ovid etablished a new benchmark for mellifluousness, but that he provided, in his vast corpus, a pattern book for all his successors. For Alan Cameron, there is no real difference, in this activity at least, between a fourth-century native speaker of Greek and an English schoolboy of the mid-twentieth century:

> Writing, like the schoolboy composer today, in a language he had learned from books according to strict rules, [Claudian] had only to follow those rules. Anyone who has written Latin verses himself knows that it is, paradoxically, easier to write Ovidian than Vergilian hexameters, precisely because Ovid is stricter. This is why Silver poets follow Ovid rather than Vergil in their metrical practice—a tendency carried even further by Claudian.[9]

What a difference a generation makes! Few schoolboys, and presumably just as few schoolgirls, learn to write Latin verses in school nowadays, and most professional scholars fight shy of the hierarchy implied in the phrase 'Silver poets.' More important, however, Cameron is in essence right. It is easier in technical matters to imitate Ovid passably than to imitate Virgil, and the fact that most

---

[8] Wilkinson (1963) 119.
[9] Cameron (1970) 320.

subsequent classical Latin poets writing in hexameters rarely sound like Virgil but often sound more or less like Ovid without the jokes is testament to the fact. Modern critics are inclined to value the expressiveness of Virgil's meter or the power of Lucretius's over the relentless smoothness of post-Ovidian poets, but the disdain Roman critics felt toward the 'harshness' of the pre-Augustans should serve to remind us how much they valued the gains that had been made in this area. Nonetheless, Cameron himself acknowledges that Claudian's verse departs from the Ovidian 'norm' in two important ways. It is "not at all dactylic," given that the proportion of spondees in the first four feet is about 55%—roughly the same as Virgil, and heavier than Statius (50%) as well as Ovid (45%).[10] He also avoids elision with a thoroughness that far outstrips even Ovid.[11] We must be on guard here against the seductions of aggregates and generalizations. Roughly speaking, Claudian tries to sound more like Virgil when he is writing serious panegyrical epic, but often sounds more like Juvenal when he is engaging in quasi-satirical diatribe in the invectives against Rufinus and Eutropius. It is in the *De Raptu Proserpinae*, a mythological narrative that had featured prominently in *Metamorphoses* (6.346–571), that he is at his most Ovidian. In other words, the Ovidian mode is one of several that post-Augustan authors could find in the canon, and what needs more careful consideration in future literary criticism of these poets than it usually receives even today is the question why a given poet with a given subject might opt for the full-blooded Ovidian style, and hence the question what later poets thought that style was best equipped to achieve. Sounding like Ovid is a choice, not the inevitable end point of some determinist history of the development of the Latin hexameter.

If diction and meter belong to the realm of *ars*, Ovid's influence on later Latin poets in the field of *ingenium* was almost as great. It is, however, harder to pin down, and harder still to talk about meaningfully. The Elder Seneca tells a famous anecdote that helps mark the boundaries of taste in the early empire. Ovid, the story goes, was asked by his friends to remove three lines from his works. He agreed, on the condition that he be allowed to exempt three lines of his own choosing. Each party wrote down their choices in private, and when all revealed what they had written, it was discovered that they

---

[10] Cameron (1970) 291. See in general Duckworth (1967) 77–150.
[11] Cameron (1970) 289.

had chosen the same set of three lines. *ex quo adparet,* says Seneca regretfully, *summi ingenii uiro non iudicium defuisse ad compescendam licentiam carminum suorum, sed animum (Contr.* 2.2.12).[12]

Perhaps the achievement and influence of Ovid's *ingenium* can be best gauged by seeing a post-Ovidian poet outdoing Ovid in the Ovidian style, and in Ovidian circumstances to boot. That Seneca the Younger should respond to Ovid is no surprise if we listen to Quintilian's characterization of him as one who possessed, among many other qualities, abundant ingenuity. Indeed, what the Elder Seneca said of Ovid, Quintilian says of his son: he would have won the approval of all if he had not himself been so attached to every word he wrote (10.1.128, 130), but unfortunately he had a perverse attraction to epigram that undermined everything in his writings that had any weight (*si rerum pondera minutissimis sententiis non fregisset,* 10.1.130).

Seneca could be said to have exercised an influence over the development of Latin prose style that matched that of Ovid over verse, and Quintilian for one feels much the same way about this influence as Persius seems to feel about Ovid's, even if he does phrase things more temperately. But the two innovators had more in common than that. As Ovid suffered *relegatio* to Tomis as a result, it seems, of some kind of involvement in the sexual scandal surrounding the disgrace of the younger Julia,[13] so also Seneca suffered *relegatio* from 41 to 49 to the almost equally uncivilized Corsica on a charge of adultery with a niece of Claudius. Given the similarity between both their natural gifts and their situations, it is hardly surprising in principle that Seneca should write about his plight in terms that recall Ovid, and attempt to outdo him. Ovid had made some play in the *Tristia* with the idea that, as a ruined and disgraced man banished from his native city and the presence of his loved ones, he was in a sense dead already. The idea appears early in the collection, ingeniously presented as a conclusive argument why the gods of the sea should not drown him in the storm that assails the ship taking him to Tomis:

> parcite, caerulei, uos parcite numina ponti,
>   infestumque mihi sit satis esse Iouem.
> uos animam saeuae fessam subducite morti,
>   si modo, qui periit, non periisse potest. (*Tr.* 1.4.25–28)

---

[12] Cf. Quint. *IO* 10.1.88, *nimium amator ingenii sui.*
[13] See White, chapter 1 and Watson, chapter 5 above.

Spare me, blue spirits, spare me, you powers of the sea, and let it suffice that Jove is my enemy. Rescue my weary soul from a cruel death, supposing only that a man who is dead can indeed avoid dying.

These lines close the poem and end its description of the epic-style storm. The effect is consequently that of an epigram. A later poem finds the poet imagining his literal death, and seems to conflate it with the social death he experienced because of his *ingenium* in the *Ars Amatoria*:

> hic ego qui iaceo tenerorum lusor amorum[14]
>   ingenio perii Naso poeta meo.
> at tibi qui transis ne sit graue quisquis amasti
>   dicere Nasonis molliter ossa cubent. (*Tr.* 3.3.73–76)

> I who lie here, Naso the poet, who played the games of tender love, of my own talent died. But you who pass by and have loved, whoever you may be, do not begrudge saying "softly let the bones of Naso lie."

This is the epitaph he instructs his wife to carve in large letters on his tombstone. The traditional request to the passer-by that he pray that the dead man's bones will rest easily[15] is given a new spin. The address is to *quisquis amasti*—not just those who have loved the poet personally, but all those who have experienced love. Or perhaps, more than that, all those who have learned the art of loving from that same work of *ingenium* that has brought the *tenerorum lusor amorum* to this sad pass. The *ingenium* lives on after death, and the poet is still playing.[16]

An epigram of Seneca on his place of exile seems to play with, and to seek to cap, both ideas:

> Corsica terribilis, cum primum incanduit aestas,
>   saeuior, ostendit cum ferus ora Canis:
> parce relegatis; hoc est, iam parce solutis!
>   uiuorum cineri sit tua terra leuis! (*Anth.* 236.5–8)

> Corsica, you are fearsome when the summer has blazed into its first heat, but more savage still, when the fierce Dog-star shows his jaws. Spare the exiled; that is, spare those who are now set free! Let your land be not heavy on the ashes of the living!

---

[14] Cf. *Tr.* 4.10.1.

[15] The association of the topos with love elegy may go back as far as Gallus. See Clausen (1994) 302 (on Virg. *Ecl.* 10.3, *ossa molliter quiescant*).

[16] Cf. also *Tr.* 3.3.51–54.

Ovid complained of the terrible winters in his place of exile, but in Corsica it is the fierce summers that cause the torment. Here too, although we have the plea for mercy (*parce religatis*), various other aspects of Ovid's situation and his reaction to it are cleverly reversed. Now it is the land, not the sea, that is asked for mercy; now the poet has arrived, rather than being on his way; the *terra* itself is asked not to lie heavily, rather than being asked through an intermediary, the passerby; and though the confusion between death and life is continued, the punch comes in the word *uiuorum*, and it has a different thrust. The *terra* here is not the small amount of soil that covers an ordinary grave. Instead, the whole land (*terra*) of Corsica itself is asked to lie lightly upon the living, because all Corsica is a tomb imprisoning the living dead, the exiles.

This experimenting with Ovidian ideas and Ovidian techniques of *ingenium* is not confined to the poetry that Seneca wrote in his exile. These are the closing words of the letter of consolation that Seneca wrote to Claudius's freedman secretary Polybius in 42:

> haec, utcumque potui, longo iam situ obsoleto et hebetato animo composui. quae si aut parum respondere ingenio tuo aut parum mederi dolori uidebuntur, cogita quam non possit is alienae uacare consolationi quem sua mala occupatum tenent, et *quam non facile latina ei homini uerba succurrant quem barbarorum inconditus et barbaris quoque humanioribus grauis fremitus circumsonat.*
>
> (*Dial.* 11.18.9)

> These thoughts, as best I could, I have put together though my mind is now weakened and dulled by long neglect. If they seem too little suited to your intelligence, or to offer too little healing for your sorrow, consider how one who is kept preoccupied by his own woes cannot be at leisure to console another, *and consider too with what difficulty Latin words will come to a man around whose ears there sounds the disordered jabbering of barbarians, at which even the more civilized barbarians flinch.*

Seneca, we presume, hoped that the letter would help secure his recall. Once again, we think of Ovid, not solely because so many of his own *Tristia* and *Epistulae ex Ponto* make it clear that recall is their aim, but because so often in the exile poetry he, like Seneca here, complains pitifully that he is losing his familiarity with Latin and that this is what explains the faults of his verse. For example, consider

> non liber hic ullus, non qui mihi commodet aurem,
>   uerbaque significent quid mea, norit, adest.

omnia barbariae loca sunt uocisque ferinae,
    omniaque hostilis plena timore soni.
ipse mihi uideor iam dedidicisse Latine:
    nam didici Getice Sarmaticeque loqui.
nec tamen, ut uerum fatear tibi, nostra teneri
    a conponendo carmine Musa potest. (*Tr.* 5.12.53–60)

I have no book here, nor anyone to listen to me or to understand the meaning of my words. Everywhere is full of barbarism and animal noises, and everything is full of the fear that hostile sounds inspire. I even seem to have unlearned my Latin: for I have begun to speak Getic and Sarmatic. But all the same, if I am to admit the truth to you, my Muse cannot be restrained from composing verse.

or

unus in hoc nemo est populo, qui forte Latine
    quaelibet e medio reddere uerba queat.
ille ego Romanus uates (ignoscite, Musae)
    Sarmatico cogor plurima more loqui.
en pudet et fateor, iam desuetudine longa
    uix subeunt ipsi uerba Latina mihi.
nec dubito quin sint et in hoc non pauca libello
    barbara: non hominis culpa, sed ista loci. (*Tr.* 5.7.53–60)[17]

There's not one single man in all this nation who might reply to me in even the most ordinary Latin. I, that famous bard of Rome—forgive me, O you Muses—am compelled to make most of my utterances in Sarmatic. I confess it, and I am ashamed, from long disuse I myself can hardly think of the Latin words. And I do not doubt that in this book there are not a few barbarisms: the fault lies not with the man, but with the place.

But Seneca is surely recalling a particular passage from the *Tristia*, the closing lines of the last poem of Book 3:

saepe aliquod quaero uerbum nomenque locumque,
    nec quisquam est a quo certior esse queam.
dicere saepe aliquid conanti (turpe fateri)
    verba mihi desunt dedidicique loqui.
Threicio Scythicoque fere circumsonor ore,
    et uideor Geticis scribere posse modis.
crede mihi, timeo, ne sint *inmixta Latinis*
    inque meis scriptis *Pontica uerba* legas.
qualemcumque igitur uenia dignare libellum
    sortis et excusa condicione meae. (*Tr.* 3.14.43–52)

---

[17] Cf. also *Tr.* 4.1.89–90, 5.2.67–68, and Williams's discussion in the preceding chapter.

Often there's some word or name or place that I cannot bring to mind, and there is no one who can put me straight. Often as I try to say something—I'm ashamed to admit it—the words fail me and I've forgotten how to speak. *I am all but surrounded by the noise of Thracian and Scythian tongues*, and I feel I could write poetry in Getic. Believe me, I am afraid that *mixed in with my Latin* and in with what I write you may read *Pontic words*. And so, such as my book is, grace it with your pardon, and excuse it for the condition of my lot.

This poem is addressed to an unnamed *cultor et antistes doctorum . . . uirorum* (3.14.1) who has usually been identified as Julius Hyginus, freedman of Augustus and keeper of the Palatine Library.[18] As Ovid wrote to the freedman of the emperor who had sent him into exile in the hope, no doubt, that he would put a word in for him, so Seneca wrote to the freedman of his tormentor in his turn. And both excuse themselves, at the end of the work, for any deficiencies in the elegance and correctness of their Latinity in terms that are designed to arouse pity. There are, of course, no such deficiencies, and the effect is to draw more strongly the contrast between the refinement of the writer's literary culture and the barbarism of the only audiences he can normally count on in his dismal exile. Hyginus and Polybius, we are left to infer, are men who would appreciate both the works presented and the presence in Rome of those who created them. But Seneca cannot resist a small Ovidian touch that the master did not include. Corsica, it seems, has some barbarians who have at least enough refinement to share Seneca's distaste for the truly horrendous dialect of the least civilized: here, it seems, there are *barbari* and *barbari humaniores*. Perhaps Seneca was thinking of the gods who assemble in heaven in the first book of the *Metamorphoses*, some of whom are mere *plebs* who live scattered in other outlying districts (*diuersa locis*, 1.173), as it were, while others are *nobiles* living in fine houses along the Milky Way, a place, says Ovid, which he would not be afraid to call *magni . . . Palatia caeli* (1.176).[19] Polybius and Seneca are kindred spirits, but Polybius, we

---

[18] Above on p. 18 n. 51, White follows Kaster (1995) 212 in identifying Ovid's Hyginus not with the famous freedman and keeper of the Palatine Library, but with a bookseller. This may very well be correct, but the general parallels between Ovid's situation and Seneca's seem to me to suggest strongly that, rightly or wrongly, Seneca at least was thinking of Augustus's freedman.

[19] See also Claud. *Rapt.* 3.8–17 for a more fully developed late-antique style hierarchy among the gods on Olympus.

might say, lives on the Palatine, with a better class of 'gods,' and Seneca on Corsica with no grander company than a better class of barbarians. How could that be just and right?

Ovid was the first major poet to fall foul of the new political realities of life under an autocrat, and the first to adapt to them by creating the elaborate mix of the personal and the panegyrical that we find in the exile poetry. It is therefore hardly surprising that later writers found the range of techniques and ideas developed in those poems a fruitful source of material when writing under, and sometimes for, later emperors and imperial officials. But the most influential of his works, both in its *ars* and in its *ingenium*, was beyond a doubt the *Metamorphoses*. Quint has recently argued the case for seeing later Latin epic as being characterized by two ideological streams, a "Virgilian tradition of imperial dominance" and "the second tradition of Lucan that arose to contest it."[20] But as soon as we create any firm dichotomy to aid our interpretation of a complex genre with a long history we will see that other texts may be given a comparable canonical status that undermines or even replaces it. In discussing Roman epic poets of the imperial period it might make more sense to speak of a Virgilio-Lucanian tradition of broadly explicit engagement with politics and a more resolutely narrative tradition, led by Ovid, that concerns itself primarily with the aesthetics of the neo-Callimachean project that dominated Roman literature from the time of Catullus.[21] Ovid, famously, does in the *Metamorphoses* what Callimachus scorned to do:[22] that is, he writes a *carmen perpetuum*, but by ostentiously doing so in the Callimachean style, he also pulls off a *tour de force* unmatched in classical literature for its marriage of *ars* and *ingenium*. Here, though, we come up against other, older dichotomies. One is the distinction made between Ovid's supposedly trivial, frivolous 'entertainment' of the reader and the 'serious' epic of Virgil and Lucan. This has a long history: Quintilian famously complained that Ovid was facetious even in epic, and much too fond of his own cleverness (*lasciuus quidem in herois quoque Ouidius et nimium amator ingenii sui, IO* 10.1.88). The matter of Ovid's 'excessive' ingenuity and his supposed self-indulgence, however, has been noted repeatedly in this book; more relevant to our present purposes is the

---

[20] Quint (1993) 8.
[21] Sullivan (1985) 74–114.
[22] But see now Cameron (1995) 339–61.

division made between Ovid and his imitators. So deep-seated is the
prejudice against post-Augustan poetry even today, after four decades
of revisionism, that we can still find those who see Ovid as a kind
of forerunner of Pope, a master of wit and grace which his would-
be followers could only succeed in imitating in the palest fashion.
This position omits due consideration of the fundamental fact that,
as part of the canon, Ovid was not there merely to be imitated: he
was there to be used. It may indeed be true that the Ovidian mytho-
logical narrative provided one way for poets to take on aesthetically
ambitious projects with little or no political risk, as is perhaps implied
by Juvenal's sardonic observation that no one ever got into trouble
with the authorities for writing on hackneyed themes like the death
of Achilles or the abduction of Hylas (*nulli grauis est percussus Achilles/
aut multum quaesitus Hylas urnamque secutus*, 1.163–64).[23] It does not fol-
low that such poets were content to produce pastiche. The most
obviously Ovidian epic surviving from the century after Ovid's death
is surely the *Achilleid*, as the following passage will suggest:

> ille aderat multo sudore et puluere maior,
> et tamen arma inter festinatosque labores   160
> dulcis adhuc uisu: niueo natat ignis in ore
> purpureus fuluoque nitet coma gratior auro.
> necdum prima noua lanugine uertitur aetas,
> tranquillaeque faces oculis et plurima uultu
> mater inest: qualis Lycia uenator Apollo
> cum redit et saeuis permutat plectra pharetris.
> forte et laetus adest—o quantum gaudia formae
> adiciunt!—: fetam Pholoes sub rupe leaenam
> perculerat ferro uacuisque reliquerat antris
> ipsam, sed catulos adportat et incitat ungues.   170
> quos tamen, ut fido genetrix in limine uisa est,
> abicit exceptamque auidis circumligat ulnis,
> iam grauis amplexu iamque aequus uertice matri. (*Ach.* 1.159–73)

And there he is, made to look older under so much sweat and dust,
and yet amid his weapons and his hurried labors he was still sweet to
look upon: over his snow-white face there floats a crimson fire and
his hair shines lovelier than tawny gold. Not yet is his early youth
changed by the new-grown down, and in his eyes fire calmly blazes,
and his mother is there to be seen in all his features: just as when the
hunter Apollo returns from Lycia and changes his savage quiver for

---

[23] A dig not just at Statius and his *Achilleid*, perhaps, but also at Valerius Flaccus,
who gives a version of the Hylas story at 3.481–4.57.

the quill. And as it happens he arrives in happiness—O how much his joy contributes to his beauty!—: beneath the cliff of Pholoe he had struck with steel a lioness that had lately given birth, and had left her in the empty cave, but he brings the cubs with him and teases them to make them show their claws. But when his mother appeared upon the familiar threshold, he cast them aside and seized her in welcome, binding her with his eager arms, his embrace already crushing, and almost as tall as the crown of his mother's head.

The young Achilles, who has been left in the care of the centaur Chiron, returns from the hunt to find that his mother has just arrived on a visit. There is much here to remind us of the *Metamorphoses*. The predominance of dactyls and the decorative Greek words that color the line and set up subtle patterns of alliteration (*qualis Lycia, permutat plectra pharetris, fetam Pholoes*) are already familiar from Persius's denunciation of the *Ovidiani poetae*. The oxymoron in *natat ignis* is a good example of Ovidian-style wit. The play between the innocence of the boy who teases the lion cubs into showing their claws and the obvious strength of the growing hero who can abduct them by force from the proverbially fierce lioness[24] is also fully in the Ovidian spirit of taking the *données du mythe* literally. But it would be a mistake simply to label a passage like this as 'whimsical,' or, to use a fashionable word, 'ludic.' Quite how the *Achilleid* would have developed if Statius had finished it we cannot know, but he announces in the proem his intention to "lead the young man down through all the tale of Troy" (*tota iuuenem deducere Troia*, 1.7). His choice of the verb *deducere* hints at an Ovidian *carmen deductum*, an exhaustive working of the myth done in the Callimachean manner, and hence a *tour de force* to rival Ovid's great poem just as the *Thebaid* clearly rivals Virgil's. But as Statius became embroiled in later books with the tragic subject-matter of the *Iliad* it might have proved impossible to maintain the lightness of tone. That, however, merely leaves us with the question whether he would have wanted to. The passage goes on in terms that foreshadow that narrative future and also that other intertext, so much more solemn and so much more prestigious than the *Metamorphoses*:

insequitur magno iam tunc conexus amore
Patroclus tantisque extenditur aemulus actis,

---

[24] E.g., Hor. *C.* 3.20.1–2.

par studiis aeuique modis, sed robore longe,
et tamen aequali uisurus Pergama fato. (*Ach.* 1.174–77)

> Following behind, and already bound to him by a mighty love, comes Patroclus. He strains to rival such valiant deeds, Achilles' match in passions and in the ways of youth, but far behind in strength. And yet was he destined to look on Pergamum with an equal fate.

This is beautifully understated, with the pathos kept on the right side of sentimentality. Patroclus here is not the older, more mature friend of the Homeric Achilles, but one who matches him in age and youthful passions, though he cannot match him in heroic strength. And it is precisely because of that one deficiency that he will also match him in destiny. Behind Statius's lines we feel the presence of Virgil, and Aeneas's pitying question to Lausus, '*quo moriture ruis maioraque uiribus audes?*' (*Aen.* 10.11). The Hellenistic fantasy in which goddess, hero, and centaur are all domesticated into a trio of anxious mother, exuberant teenager, and gruff but affectionate schoolmaster is restored to the world of epic, of death and loss, as the passage ends with the grim juxtaposition of *Pergama fato*. And if we had not noticed it before, perhaps we now reflect that it is not just a desire for neoteric coloring that leads Statius to remark that the boy is now as tall as his mother (*iamque aequus uertice matri*, 1.173). This is what marks him out as ready for the transition from the Ovidian world he now inhabits into the Homeric-Virgilian one that is his intertextually ordained destiny. The cubs, too, are more than an example of Ovidian whimsicality or of bucolic prettiness. The lioness deprived of her young prefigures Thetis's knowledge of her own impending bereavement in the *Iliad*.

Much the same can be said of, for example, Statius's description of the house of Sleep at *Theb.* 10.84–117. It is too easy to label this an imitation of Ovid's description of the *penetralia Somni* at *Met.* 11.592–615, to count off the topoi and the verbal reminiscences, and to think that criticism has done its job. The dominant tone of the Ceyx and Alcyone episode into which Ovid's description has been set is one of pathos, and its narrative function is to provide Alcyone with a dream vision of her drowned husband that will at least give her the consolation of knowing his fate. The purpose in Statius is quite different, and its effect on the narrative far grimmer. In the *Thebaid*, Juno sends Iris to fetch Somnus from his rest so that he can come to Thebes and lull the Theban troops, camped before the walls of their city, into a double oblivion. The result of Somnus's appearance in the poem is not the emotional release and narrative closure given by yet another highly stylized metamorphosis, but is rather sheer horrific carnage as Juno's beloved Argive warriors massacre their sleeping enemies. The rivers of blood are so copious and so forceful that the very tent pegs of the Thebans' camp are all but washed out of their post-holes:

> stagnant nigrantia tabo
> gramina, sanguineis nutant tentoria riuis;
> fumat humus, somnique et mortis anhelitus una
> uoluitur; haud quisquam uisus aut ora iacentum
> erexit: tali miseris deus aliger umbra
> incubat et tantum morientia lumina soluit. (*Theb.* 10.298–303)

> The grass grows black, a standing pool of gore, and the tents totter in the streams of blood. The earth steams, and the breath of sleep and death roll on together; not one of those that lay there raised his eyes or head: such was the shadow within which the winged god brooded over the wretched creatures, and when he opened up their eyes, it was in death alone.

Here, we might say, Ovid's aesthetics are appropriated and made to serve those of Lucan. At any rate, the dichotomy with which we replaced Quint's appears only to have existed for Statius as something for him to negotiate or, if you like, to mediate. Ovid's canonical status was not something inert. It was something that extended the range of that canon, and poets as gifted as Statius were not shy of exploiting the openings offered by the gap between Ovid and more traditional epic. The same can be said even for Silius, who may have revered Virgil to the extent of treating his tomb like a temple and celebrating his birthday more solemnly than he celebrated his own (Plin. *Ep.* 3.7.8), but who was perfectly willing to insert into his determinedly patriotic account of the war against Hannibal such Ovidian narratives as his account of the role played by Anna Perenna in, of all things, the battle of Cannae (8.25–241). Similarly, Claudian generally aims to sound like Virgil or Lucan when writing imperial military panegyric, and like Ovid and Statius's *Achilleid* when he turns his hand to the mythological (and doubly Ovidian) subject matter of the *De Raptu Proserpinae*. But the panegyrics benefit from the groundwork done in the *Fasti* and the exile poetry in establishing the correct vocabulary for consular and imperial encomium,[25] while the *De*

---

[25] See, e.g., Dewar (1996) 417. Statius, especially in *Silu.* 4.1, provides an impor-

Raptu Proserpinae, in the view of some modern scholars at least, conceals not too far beneath its surface of Ovidian fantasy serious dialogue with the religious and cultural politics of Claudian's day.[26]

There is, however, one form of poetry in which what we might call a relatively naive version of the Ovidian mode proved to be especially attractive and useful. That was occasional poetry, an essentially disposable form of writing that was intended for immediate consumption, was usually presented in circumstances that did not permit the depth and sublety of epic, and often had to be composed at considerable speed.[27] Here the Ovidian hexameter was all the more useful, in that it was both easier to improvise and ideally suited for the kind of swift narrative that was not intended to bear too much analysis, and where the story was what counted. The *Siluae* of Statius are among our most varied and informative collections of occasional poetry from the early empire, and the best example of Ovidian narrative in the *Siluae* must be the fanciful little poem written to provide an aetiology for the "Tree of Atedius Melior" (2.3). Melior, the dedicatee of the second book of the *Siluae*, happened to have a plane tree of unusual shape in the grounds of his house. It grew beside a pool, with its trunk at first bending down towards the surface of the water and then shooting straight up once more. After a few lines spent describing this minor oddity of nature, Statius rolls up his sleeves and gets on, straight-faced, with the narrative:

> nympharum tenerae fugiebant Pana cateruae;
> ille quidem it cunctas tamquam uelit, it tamen unam
> in Pholoen.
>
> *(Silu. 2.3.8–10)*

The tender troops of nymphs fled from Pan; he, to be sure, came on as if he wanted them all, but to Pholoe alone he made his way.

We are immediately taken from Flavian Rome to some unspecified time in the past. This is the world of the first book of the *Metamorphoses*, in which Pan was found chasing Syrinx. If we think of that scene, we already have our cue to expect a number of things—that the nymph will seek to evade Pan's embraces, that a metamorphosis will

---

tant intermediary between Ovid's *Fasti* and exile poetry and the panegyrical poets of late antiquity, however: see Coleman (1988) 64–66, 69, 76, 81.

[26] See Duc (1994) and Kellner (1997) passim. Contrast Gruzelier (1993) xxi.

[27] See the preface to *Silu.* 1, e.g., *epithalamium tuum quod mihi iniunxeras scis biduo scriptum (audacter mehercules, sed ter centum tamen hexametros habet)*.

occur, that the defeated Pan will be moved to make some graceful compromise—and we will not be disappointed.[28] Back to the chase:

> insequitur uelox pecorum deus et sua credit
> conubia; ardenti iamiam suspiria librat
> pectore, iam praedae leuis imminet.
>
> *(Silu.* 2.3.18–20)

Swiftly the god of flocks comes after her and thinks that union now is his; and now, and now, with burning heart he holds his panting breath, and now swoops lightly on his prey.

But the word *imminet* leaves Pan freeze-framed while the poet changes scene. *ecce*, he says, a knowing little word that signals what we surely ought to have expected. This is a nymph, and she must belong to Diana: after all, nymphs tend to. This is Rome; Diana has a famous temple on the Aventine; so, in a move that asserts the same literalness of myth that characterizes the humor of the *Metamorphoses*, enter Diana stage left:

> *ecce citatos*
> *aduertit Diana gradus*, dum per iuga septem
> errat Auentinaeque legit uestigia ceruae.
> paenituit uidisse deam, conuersaque fidas
> ad comites: 'numquamne auidis arcebo rapinis
> hoc petulans foedumque pecus, semperque pudici
> decrescet mihi *turba chori?*'
>
> *(Silu.* 2.3.20–26)

Behold, Diana turns her hastening steps, while over the seven hills she roams and tracks the prints left by an Aventine hind. The goddess was aggrieved by the sight, and turning to her loyal companions she said: 'Shall I never keep from greedy rape this foul and insolent herd, and will the chaste *band of my followers* forever grow smaller?'

Of course this happened while she was hunting, because hunting is how Diana spends her time. There is more humor in the idea that anyone could go hunting at all on the built-up hills of Domitian's Rome, but once again, Statius's fudging of the temporal distance between his day and the time of Ovidian myth contributes to the sense of pleasurable unreality. This, though, is not just a goddess who lives in an Ovidian world. She is also one who knows her Ovid, it seems, and she remembers not only the lucky escape of Syrinx but also the disgrace of Callisto:

---

[28] See in general Van Dam (1984) 284.

ecce, suo comitata choro Dictynna per altum
Maenalon ingrediens et caede superba ferarum
aspicit hanc uisamque uocat

(*Met.* 2.441–43)

Behold, accompanied by her band, Dictynna stepped over lofty Maenalus
and exulting in her slaughter of the beasts, sees this girl, and seeing
her, summons her.

Callisto was revealed to be pregnant by Jupiter, and was therefore
banished by the virgin goddess from her company (*'i procul hinc' dixit
'nec sacros pollue fontis!'/ Cynthia deque suo iussit decedere coetu, Met.* 2.464–65).
Better that Pholoe should meet the fate of Syrinx than endure that.
Syrinx had hidden in the stream of the Ladon, begging her sisters
to change her form, and so when Pan tried to seize her, he found
himself holding nothing but marsh reeds. Statius's Diana finds Pholoe,
asleep in exhaustion from her chase, by the side of Melior's pool,
with Pan poised to snatch her. The goddess wakes her by touching
her with a reversed arrow, and, like Syrinx before her, she plunges
to safety in the water. It only adds to the Ovidian tone when Statius
patiently forestalls the objections of even the most literal-minded
readers by observing that Pan was thus foiled because he had never
learned to swim: *a tenero nandi rudis* (2.3.37). Ovid's Pan, of course,
was charmed by the gentle sound of the wind in the reeds and so
sentimentally invented the pipes: *'hoc mihi colloquium tecum' dixit 'manebit'*
(*Met.* 1.710). Statius's Pan shows a similar ingenuity with the local
fauna and a similar sentimentality, as he begs the young plane tree
he sees there to cease straining upwards to the sky and instead to
stretch out across the pool, to shade from the fierce sun and the
hail the waters that are now her home, and so to serve also as a
memorial to their love:

'uiue diu nostri pignus memorabile uoti,
arbor, et haec durae latebrosa cubilia nymphae
tu saltem declinis ama, preme frondibus undam.
illa quidem meruit, sed ne, precor, igne superno
aestuet aut dura feriatur grandine; tantum
spargere tu laticem et foliis turbare memento.
tunc ego teque diu recolam dominamque benignae
sedis et inlaesa tutabor utramque senecta,
ut Iouis, ut Phoebi frondes, ut discolor umbra
populus et nostrae stupeant tua germina pinus.'

(*Silu.* 2.3.43–52)

'Live long, O tree, as a fit memorial of my vow, and do you at least, stooping down, caress the secret chamber of my hard-hearted nymph, and cover with your leaves her waters. She, it is true, has deserved it, but even so, I beg of you, let her be not scorched by heaven's heat or lashed by the hard-hearted hail. Only remember to scatter and trouble the pool with your leaves. Then shall I long remember you and the mistress of this kindly home, and keep you both safe and unharmed till old age comes, so that the trees of Jove and Phoebus, and the poplar with its parti-colored leaves, and my own pines will stand in awe of these your buds.'

The tree agrees, and even the nymph—now a Naiad (2.3.60)—is moved to accept the compliment, graciously inviting the tree's branches (so much less threatening than Pan's arms) into her waters.

It is only when the narrative is concluded that the poem reveals that its motivation is not merely, not even principally, to invent the *aition* for Melior's peculiar tree. Rather, it functions as a birthday gift: *haec tibi parua quidem genitali luce paramus/dona* (2.3.62–63). Up to this point the "Tree of Atedius Melior" might be said to be a perfect example of those essentially substanceless compositions that many scholars say typify the uninspired and characterless imitators of Ovid. Compositions, that is, which can be written off as "graceful" and "charming," which in technical matters are modelled on Ovid's "comfortable, well-sprung, well-oiled vehicle for his story," and in which, as in the *Metamorphoses* itself, "everything depends on whether the story itself can retain the reader's attention,"[29] but which are essentially lightweight and with nothing much to say. And such a reading is effectively invited by Statius himself when, in the preface to Book 2 of the *Siluae*, he refers to this and the following poem on Melior's pet parrot as *leues libellos quasi epigrammatis loco scriptos*. Statius's poem goes on a little longer, however, praising the honorand in terms that present him as an ideal Epicurean who lives a life of serenity far from the dirty world of politics. The intention, as Vessey has argued, is to reassure a suspicious-minded Domitian that Melior, for all his wealth and potential influence, has opted out of politics and presents no threat to his rule.[30] Whether we accept Vessey's argument or not, it is clear that Ovid has served as model for a poem that aims to compliment a sophisticated, well-read patron in a style that eschews solemnity and pompousness. But there is still something more

[29] Wilkinson (1963) 202.
[30] Vessey (1981) 47–48, 51–52.

to say. Pan is not the only god who goes chasing nymphs in the
first book of the *Metamorphoses*, and no doubt Melior was expected
to recall Apollo's unsuccessful pursuit of Daphne, and indeed the
reference to the *Phoebi frondes* at the end of Pan's prayer to the tree
(2.3.51) will have served as a prompt. In Ovid's account, the nymph
is actually turned into a tree, of course, rather than merely into a
Naiad who lives in its shadow. Apollo continues to love her, and to
honor her, promises that her leaves will decorate his hair and his
lyre—but also the triumphs of the Romans and the doors of the yet-
to-be-born Augustus:

> hanc quoque Phoebus amat positaque in stipite dextra
> sentit adhuc trepidare nouo sub cortice pectus
> conplexusque suis ramos, ut membra, lacertis
> oscula dat ligno: refugit tamen oscula lignum.
> cui deus 'at quoniam coniunx mea non potes esse,
> arbor eris certe' dixit 'mea. semper habebunt
> te coma, te citharae, te nostrae, laure, pharetrae;
> tu ducibus Latiis aderis, cum laeta triumphum   560
> uox canet et uisent longas Capitolia pompas;
> postibus Augustis eadem fidissima custos
> ante fores stabis mediamque tuebere quercum,
> utque meum intonsis caput est iuuenale capillis,
> tu quoque perpetuos semper gere frondis honores.'
> finierat Paean: factis modo laurea ramis
> adnuit utque caput uisa est agitasse cacumen.
>   (*Met.* 1.553–67)

Her too does Phoebus love, and placing his right hand upon her trunk,
he feels her heart still trembling beneath the new-formed bark, and
embracing in his arms her branches as if they were human limbs he
presses kisses on her wood; but even from his kisses the wood shrank
back. And to this the god cried out, 'And yet, since you cannot be
my bride, my tree you shall surely be! My hair, my lyre, my quivers,
O laurel, will always possess you; you will accompany the generals of
the Latins when the joyful voice calls out the song of triumph and the
Capitol looks down on long processions. Upon the posts of Augustus's
door you too shall stand as his most loyal guardian and keep safe the
oak that lies between. And as my head is ever youthful and my hair
unshorn, do you also keep the glory of your leaves forever green!'
Paean had spoken: with her newly fashioned branches the laurel gave
her assent and seemed to set her tree-top nodding like a head.

The parallels with Statius are very close. Both Pan and Apollo address
the tree, and seek to honor the nymph associated with it. And as
Ovid honors Augustus through his narrative, so Statius's narrative

is keyed to honor Melior. The Ovidian passage is one of the first
major elements of panegyric of Augustus in the *Metamorphoses*, and
as such it has attracted the attentions of scholars who variously see
it as seriously intended as compliment to the emperor or as covert
ridicule.[31] There is no visible reason why Statius should be thought
to want to mock Atedius Melior, and that perhaps implies that he
detected no mockery of Augustus in his Ovidian model. The issue
is a live one in contemporary criticism of almost every poet who
lived under the growing autocracies of the Julio-Claudians and the
Flavians. Gordon Williams, in what is perhaps still the single most
influential discussion of the use to which Ovid and his experiments
in extending the range of Roman poetry were put, argues that he
showed his successors how to cope with the new political reality by
providing them with three escape routes, into antiquarianism, mythol-
ogy, and ingenious panegyric of the emperor.[32] That set of propo-
sitions has been much challenged and greatly nuanced by recent
scholarship,[33] but we still need a much more subtle investigation of
how individual poets use Ovid in their own mythological and pan-
egyrical writings. Whatever ironies we detect either in a given pas-
sage of Ovid, or in the works of a poet who imitates it, they must
be viewed in their own context. To argue that Ovid's Daphne and
Apollo is ironic is one thing; to argue that in using it as a model
for his own panegyric Statius *must* have been mocking Domitian, let
alone Atedius Melior, would be quite another. Not the least strik-
ing thing about Ovid's achievement in both mythological narrative
and encomiastic writing is the flexibility of approach his works seem
to have offered his more thoughtful successors.

Examples of that flexibility are abundant, but two in particular
may serve to show the advantages offered by the less solemn approach
to encomium pioneered by Ovid. The mythopoeic fantasy-world of
the *Metamorphoses* was called into service again by Statius when he
was asked by Domitian's freedman Flavius Earinus to compose a
poem celebrating the occasion on which he cut his long hair in
fulfilment of a vow and sent it in a golden box to be dedicated in
the temple of Asclepius in his home town, Pergamum. It was a tricky
commission, because Earinus was that very un-epic character, a

---

[31] Williams (1978) 89–91, attacking Coleman (1971).
[32] Williams (1978) 100.
[33] Hinds (1987b), especially 24–29.

eunuch. The difficulty lay partly in the simple frivolity and lack of *grauitas* that a traditionalist like Persius would have thought marred the subject matter and hence any debased composition that attempted, in whatever manner, to treat it seriously. But in addition to that generic consideration there was also the delicacy required to treat Domitian's fondness for the young eunuch in a way that did not impair his dignity, or infringe the rights of his wife Domitia. And as if that was not difficult enough, the relationship between the emperor and the eunuch had to be set against the inconvenient fact that Domitian himself had issued an edict, albeit long after Earinus had been subjected to the grim operation in question, that outlawed castration.[34] Plain solemnity no doubt risked looking absurd, but the same literalness in the treatment of myth that showed us Pan pursuing a nymph into the grounds of Melior's house provided Statius with a mode that could accommodate fantasy with fact. The narrative begins:

> dicitur Idalios Erycis de uertice lucos
> dum petit et molles agitat Venus aurea cycnos
> Pergameas intrasse domos, ubi maximus aegris
> auxiliator adest et festinantia sistens
> fata salutifero mitis deus incubat angui.
> hic puerum egregiae praeclarum sidere formae
> ipsius ante dei ludentem conspicit aras.
> ac primum subita paulum decepta figura
> natorum de plebe putat; sed non erat illi
> arcus et ex umeris nullae fulgentibus umbrae.
>
> (*Silu.* 3.4.21–30)

As she made her way from Eryx's summit to the groves of Idalium and drove her soft swans onwards, golden Venus is said to have entered the halls of Pergamum, where their most-mighty helper is present to aid the sick, and the gentle god, staying the hurrying fates, lies in the lair of the healing serpent. Here she saw, playing before the god's own altars, a boy who shone with the star-light of wonderful beauty. And at first deceived for a moment by the sudden appearance of his form, she thought him one of her own mob of sons; but he had no bow, and no wings shaded his brilliant shoulders.

The "Alexandrian footnote" in *dicitur*[35] is a joke worthy of Ovid: there is no poetic model for this particular *aition* and the ceremony

---

[34] For Domitian's edict forbidding castration see Suet. *Dom.* 7, Mart. 2.60, 6.2.
[35] For the "Alexandrian footnote" see Ross (1975) 78.

whereby a eunuch dedicates his hair to Asclepius which the poem goes on to account for. The style and, for want of a better word, the 'take' are also Ovidian. As usual, this is most easily quantified by reference to the technicalities of meter, so let it be noted that these ten lines, in addition to their being overwhelmingly dactylic, contain only a single elision, and that of the easiest kind (*puerum egregiae*). The use of Greek words and of sound effects that build upon them (*Erycis . . . lucos*) is familiar too. But the truly Ovidian element is the matter-of-factness in the face of the nominally supernatural. Venus is headed for the Idalian groves, so Pergamum is on her way; it is natural enough that she should stop off for a brief visit at the great temple dedicated to Asclepius, wholly unsurprising that the young Earinus should happen to be playing in front of the altar at just that moment, and entirely predictable that she should for a moment be so confused by his beauty that she mistakes him for one of her own children, the Amores. The impudent realism of *natorum de plebe* is also something we have seen before. Being a rational, Ovidian kind of goddess, however, she is not taken in for long, and, spotting that he has no wings on those gleaming shoulders, she quickly shifts ground and takes sensible action. This boy is destined to servitude and to what might normally be considered even worse than that, but in this fantasy world consolation is easily arranged. She will personally take him to Rome in that nicely convenient swan-drawn chariot, as a treat for the ruler of the earth (*donum immane duci*, 3.4.37). So, she tells him, his destiny will not be a plebeian one, for, though he will be a slave, his master will be love and he will serve in the imperial Palace (*nec te plebeia manebunt/iura: Palatino famulus deberis amori*, 3.4.37–38). The boy and his beauty must, however, be more firmly established in the world of myth, so she continues:

> nil ego, nil, fateor, toto tam dulce sub orbe
> aut uidi aut genui. cedet tibi Latmius ultro
> Sangariusque puer, quemque inrita fontis imago
> et sterilis consumpsit amor. te caerula Nais
> mallet et adprensa traxisset fortius urna.
> tu, puer, ante omnes; solus formosior ille
> cui daberis.
>
> (*Silu.* 3.4.39–45)

Nothing, I confess it, nothing have I ever seen or given life in all the world that is so sweet. The Latmian boy and the Sangarian will yield you their place without complaint, along with him whom the spring's useless reflection and barren love consumed. The blue-green water-nymph would have chosen you, and, grasping your urn, would have dragged you down with greater force. You, my boy, surpass them all: only he to whom you shall be given is lovelier.

The hero of this Ovidian-style tale outdoes all the standard beautiful boys of myth, all of whom are also in one sense or another Ovidian: Endymion (*Latmius Endymion, Ars* 3.83), Attis (*Met.* 10.104), Narcissus (*Met.* 3.341–510), and Hylas (*Naiadumque tener crimine raptus Hylas, Ars* 2.110). But the constraints of the real world can be sensed in the goddess's final hierarchical ploy: Earinus surpasses all the beautiful boys of Ovidian myth, but even he must yield in beauty to the emperor. It is precisely such details, of course, that arouse suspicion of irony in those who cannot take such panegyric at face value. Any suggestion that Domitian is in some sense to be compared to, of all people, Attis, they will feel, can only be mocking. But the poem can easily be read in such a way that any such suggestion is limited to the essential point of the comparison: it is beauty and beauty alone that links Domitian with these mythical characters. This integration of the real world into the Ovidian fantasy can be seen again when Statius presents Venus as overcome by anxiety as Earinus goes under the knife. Statius does not hide from the fact that Domitian had subsequently banned castration. Rather, he boldly uses her humane emotion as a peg on which to hang a few lines of praise for the *clementia* of the emperor and the superiority of these times to those (3.4.73–82), thus formally subordinating the aims of panegyric to the demands of a unified aesthetic. Perhaps it will be felt that it does not quite come off, but it is, once again, the Ovidian conflation of myth and reality—myth taken literally and reality turned into myth— that makes the attempt feasible.

Statius was not the only poet who wrote on the subject, and we possess the following epigram of Martial:

> consilium formae speculum dulcisque capillos
>   Pergameo posuit dona sacrata deo
> ille puer tota domino gratissimus aula,
>   nomine qui signat tempora uerna suo.
> felix quae tali censetur munere tellus!
>   nec Ganymedeas mallet habere comas.
>   (Mart. 9.16)

The counselor of his beauty, his mirror, and his sweet locks, as gifts consecrated to the god of Pergamum: these have been offered by the boy who, in all the palace, wins most favor in his master's eyes, and

who with his own name puts his mark upon the spring. Happy the
land thought worthy of such a gift as this! Nor would it prefer to pos-
sess the locks of Ganymede.

Martial chose to write in a different genre, and he copes with the
inherent delicacy of the subject matter by a combination of brevity,
selectivity, and wit. We might argue that there is a trace of Ovidian
technique in the way he alludes to Earinus's metrically intractable
name through a pun that also functions as a compliment: the boy
is imagined not as being named for the spring, but the spring as
being in some sense named for him. But this is of quite a different
order from Statius's poem, which is a daring *tour de force* and a splen-
did response on a much larger scale to a whole subject far more
intractable than the patron's name. "The emperor who can accept
flattery of such a kind," wrote Butler with the trenchant morality of
the Edwardians,[36] "has certainly qualified for assassination." The
emperor who could appreciate the nature of the exercise, at any
rate, possessed a literary sophistication Ovid would have welcomed
in the autocrat who exiled him to Tomis.

Lastly, an example of the use made of a famous passage from the
Ars Amatoria by a much later panegyrist may perhaps help to make
clear not only the extent and range of Ovid's influence, but also the
manner in which, by blurring the boundaries between genres, he
enriched the whole corpus of encomiastic Latin poetry. The first
extended encomium of Augustus and his family in Ovid is to be
found not in the exile poetry, but in that very poem whose com-
position provided one half of the charge sheet against him. His dis-
cussion of the best places to pick up girls leads him to talk at length
of the circus, and from there he moves on to the other public spec-
tacles given to the city by the emperor to commemorate political
and military events. Before long he has begun a lengthy digression
on the expedition of the emperor's adopted son Gaius Caesar against
the Parthians in 1 B.C. He imagines the young prince's return to
the city and the great triumph he will celebrate on that day:

> ergo erit illa dies, qua tu, pulcherrime rerum,
>   quattuor in niueis aureus ibis equis;
> ibunt ante duces onerati colla catenis,
>   ne possint tuti, qua prius, esse fuga.

---

[36] Butler (1909) 229, cited by Vessey (1973) 28.

spectabunt laeti iuuenes mixtaeque puellae,
    diffundetque animos omnibus ista dies.
                                        (*Ars* 1.213–18)

And so that day will come, when you, fairest of beings, shall ride in
gold behind four snow-white steeds; chieftains shall march before you,
their necks weighed down with chains, so that they cannot take refuge
in the flight that made them safe before. Youths, happily mingling
with girls, will watch, and that day will spread joy through every heart.

It is necessary for the pseudo-didactic poet to steer his way back
from where his digression has led him to the work in hand, and
Ovid achieves this by presenting the triumph as another opportu-
nity to strike up conversation with a likely lass. When a girl asks
you to identify the captives and to explain the floats representing
conquered nations and territories, he instructs his pupils, be sure not
to miss your chance. And if you happen not to know the answers
to any of her questions, freely invent:

atque aliqua ex illis cum regum nomina quaeret,
    quae loca, qui montes quaeue ferantur aquae,
omnia responde, nec tantum si qua rogabit;
    et quae nescieris, ut bene nota refer:
hic est Euphrates, praecinctus harundine frontem;
    cui coma dependet caerula, Tigris erit;
hos facito Armenios, haec est Danaeia Persis;
    urbs in Achaemeniis uallibus ista fuit;
ille uel ille duces, et erunt quae nomina dicas,
    si poteris, uere, si minus, apta tamen.
                                        (*Ars* 1.219–28)

And when some girl among them asks you the names of the kings,
and what the places and the mountains and the rivers are that are
shown on the floats, give her an answer every time—and not just if
she asks you anything. And if there is anything you don't know, reply
as if you knew perfectly well: this is Euphrates, with his forehead bound
with reeds, and the one with the blue-green hair hanging down, that's
Tigris; tell her this lot are Armenians, and this is Persia, descended
from Danae: that was a city in the Achaemenid hill-country; this chap
and that one are chieftains—and you'll find names to give them, cor-
rectly, if you can, and if you can't, ones that suit them anyway.

Inevitably, this passage is one of those that most divides scholars of
Ovid. Is it ironic, undercutting all the pomp and majesty of Augustan
military patriotism by presenting it as no more than a chance for a
little erotic campaigning of one's own? Or is it a serious compliment,
with a neat transition effected by a poet of great *ingenium* between

the intrusive encomium he wanted to make room for and the erotic-
comic subject matter that was his main concern? Gordon Williams
at any rate is sure of the answer, feeling as he does that, "The tone
of panegyric throughout is unmistakable."[37] And, as he sees things,
"The problem that Ovid has solved was not how to make fun of
Augustus, but how to accommodate panegyric artistically to the con-
text of his poem without painful disruption."[38] We can leave this
argument aside for the moment, merely noting in passing the good
sense of Hinds's claim that "[t]he real error, into which critics on
both sides tend to fall, is to imagine that the matter is susceptible
to final proof either way."[39] Let us instead concern ourselves with
the question how the apparent dissonance between the two forms of
writing—encomium and love poetry—was used by Claudian to enrich
his own poetry.

In January 404, the Emperor Honorius celebrated his sixth con-
sulship, not in Milan, the city where he usually resided, but in old
Rome itself. This marked the occasion as one of particular symbolic
significance, as indeed it was. In 402 the Visigothic invaders led by
Alaric had been turned away from Italy by the western armies under
the command of Honorius's father-in-law Stilicho. The visit to Rome,
at least in the description provided by Claudian, combined elements
of the traditional consular procession, of the *aduentus* (or ceremonial
entry of the emperor into the city), and of a triumph. As Honorius
makes his way through the city, the crowds come out in force to
watch the procession go by, and the women of Rome look on in
awe at the magnificent figure of their handsome young prince:

> conspicuas tum flore genas, diademate crinem   560
> membraque gemmato trabeae uiridantia cinctu
> et fortes umeros et certatura Lyaeo
> inter Erythraeas surgentia colla smaragdos,
> mirari sine fine nurus; ignaraque uirgo,
> cui simplex calet ore pudor, per singula cernens
> nutricem consultat anum, quid fixa draconum
> ora uelint, uentis fluitent an uera minentur
> sibila suspensum rapturi faucibus hostem.
> ut chalybe indutos equites et in aere latentes
> uidit cornipedes, 'quanam de gente' rogabat   570

[37] Williams (1978) 77.
[38] Williams (1978) 79.
[39] Hinds (1987b) 25.

'ferrati uenere uiri? quae terra metallo
nascentes informat equos? num Lemnius auctor
indidit hinnitum ferro simulacraque belli
uiua dedit?'

(VI Cons. 560–74)

And then the women gazed in endless wonder at the matchless bloom
upon his cheeks, at his hair crowned with the diadem, at limbs that
reflected the green light from his jewel-studded consular robe, at his
broad shoulders and at his neck, which, soaring through oriental emer-
alds, could rival that of Lyaeus; and the innocent maiden, the blush
of simple modesty burning on her cheek, lets her gaze rove over every
detail, plying her aged nurse with questions: What do the dragons
attached to their standards signify? Are they only fluttering in the
winds, or is their menacing hissing real, ready as they are to seize
some enemy in their jaws and brandish him aloft? When she saw the
horsemen clad in steel and the stallions hidden beneath their coverings
of bronze, she would ask, 'From what nation have these men of iron
come? What land forms horses born of metal? Surely it cannot be that
the Smith of Lemnos has implanted in iron the power to neigh and
given us living images of battle?'

As the young emperor marches through the city towards the Capitol,
the married women (<i>nurus</i>) of Rome knowingly admire both his per-
sonal appearance and the splendor of his dress. Their understated
worldly wisdom is contrasted with that of a naive young girl (<i>ignara
uirgo</i>) in the same crowd. She is accompanied by an old woman, her
nurse, whom she plies with questions about what she sees, thereby
revealing an innocence that is meant to charm us. Those dragons
floating in the air with their jaws wide open—could it be that they
are real? They are so lifelike, you could swear they were ready to
snatch up some Goth and brandish him above everybody's heads!
And what about those strange steel-clad creatures sitting astride their
metal steeds? What race are they? What land, stranger than any
known to Herodotus, made them? Or are they in fact automatons
fashioned by none other than Vulcan himself? These are not ques-
tions the <i>nurus</i> have to ask, because they know the imperial army's
regulation dragon standards when they see them, and they are no
strangers to the idea of cataphracts, those heavy-armored horsemen
that formed the shock troops of late antique Roman armies and can
be said to be the forerunners of the stereotypical medieval knight.
But there is more to <i>ignara</i> than the suggestion that this girl needs
some basic instruction in the current state of military equipment.
Though Claudian does not spell it out, we sense that the married

ladies are connoisseurs of more than one form of beauty: they admire
"without end" Honorius's ornate robe with its jewel-studded belt,
but also his broad shoulders, and they admire the strong, muscled
(*surgentia*) neck as well as the collar of emeralds that encircles it. This
innocent young girl, however, truly is a *uirgo*, and what she is think-
ing but not daring to voice can be deduced from her tell-tale blush
(*cui simplex calet ore pudor*). We might recall here the blush of Lavinia:

> accepit uocem lacrimis Lauinia matris
> flagrantis perfusa genas, cui plurimus ignem
> subiecit rubor et calefacta per ora cucurrit.
> > (Virg. *Aen.* 12.64–66)

> Lavinia heard her mother's words with tears spreading over her burn-
> ing cheeks, as the deep red blush kindled fire beneath and sped over
> her glowing face.

She does not dare to ask questions directly about the handsome
young prince who so excites her. But we are not fooled by the ques-
tions she asks instead, and neither, we imagine, is her aged chap-
erone. That the emphasis is moved smartly to the cataphracts, with
their subtle suggestion of that same invincible strength that has so
recently kept Rome safe from the barbarian invaders, reinforces the
principal theme of Claudian's panegyric. But this brief cameo of
erotic desire in the midst of epic grandeur helps bring the emperor's
victory down to a more everyday level, while also reminding the
audience of that whole subtle and learned culture that Alaric had
put at risk, a culture of luxury and peace.

Claudian's audience no doubt knew from Ovid's story of Scylla
in the *Metamorphoses* just what dangers a girl could get into as a result
of eyeing military men in full armor from the heights of a palace
tower. The rooftops of Rome tantalizingly present the same risks,
but only for a fleeting moment—Megara was betrayed for love of
an enemy attacker, but Rome is safe, and the object of desire is not
the city's attacker, but its successful defender. Those who knew their
Statius might also sense here the presence of *rudis Antigone* (*Theb.*
7.253), the virgin daughter of Oedipus who, from a distant tower
on the walls, questions Laius's old squire Phorbas about the iden-
tity of all the Theban troops gathered on the plain before the city.
Like the echo of Lavinia's blush, any such intertextual reference helps
integrate the erotic content into the world of lofty epic, and it should
also be noted that innocent young maidens falling for handsome

strangers just arrived in their city go back in Latin epic at least to
Catullus's Ariadne. But here the elements of the triumph, of the
understated sexual interest, and of the many innocent questions asked
by the *ignara uirgo* surely recall Ovid. As the seduction scene at the
triumph of Gaius has been re-epicized, so also here it is stripped of
any real hint of danger. Whatever Ovid's imagined lovers may have
got up to, this girl's passion will remain an unfulfilled crush, for the
object of her half-hidden desire is far beyond her reach, and is in
any case safely married to Stilicho's daughter Maria. The allusion,
though, serves to humanize the experience of the triumph, to under-
cut the encomium of victory in battle with a hint of the arts of
peace. We shall never know for sure quite what Augustus made of
the *Ars Amatoria*. Williams's argument that the indignity of seeing his
adoptive son's imagined triumph over the Parthians frivolously intro-
duced almost as a prelude to the lover chatting up the gullible tal-
ent in the crowd will probably have given offense seems perfectly
reasonable.[40] It is quite possible that Augustus understood the inge-
nuity of the technique, that he even understood that the compliment
was sincere in intention, but that he was nonetheless outraged by
what he saw as an affront to his dignity. But we can surmise that
he might have been still more annoyed if he had been made to deal
with a poem presenting young Gaius Caesar as inspiring unclean
thoughts in the daughters of the good burghers of Rome. That
Claudian seems to have no such fears may indicate that the autoc-
racy of late imperial Rome was perhaps not so oppressive, or so
intolerant of literary fantasy, as is sometimes assumed. At any rate,
the echoes of Ovid and the intrusion of elegiac concerns into the
solemn world of epic contribute to a gentle dilution, if not quite a
deflation, of all the grandeur of Honorius's big day. We may end
by saying that if Latin verse panegyrics are on balance more varied
and inventive than prose ones, we probably have Ovid to thank
for that. The prose writers had as their primary model Pliny the
Younger's panegyric to Trajan. And without meaning any disrespect
to that honest consul and administrator, he never came up to Ovid's
standards.

---

[40] Williams (1978) 80.

CHAPTER THIRTEEN

OVID IN THE MIDDLE AGES: EXILE, MYTHOGRAPHER, AND LOVER

Ralph Hexter

1. *Introduction*

"Ovid in the Middle Ages" is a perennial topic, and rightly so, since the medieval centuries were crucial for the transmission of Ovid.[1] Not only was the great bulk of his oeuvre passed on, so that the manuscript witnesses to all his extant works are the products of medieval scriptoria,[2] but the Middle Ages elevated Ovid to the point that he has enjoyed ever since as one of the three great Augustan poets, alongside Virgil and Horace. So seriously was he studied in the Middle Ages that he could join his older contemporaries as stylistic master and model in Traube's schema for the history of medieval Latin poetry, where an *aetas Virgiliana* of the eighth and ninth centuries is succeeded by an *aetas Horatiana* in the tenth and eleventh centuries, which itself gives way to an *aetas Ovidiana* of the twelfth and thirteenth centuries.[3] Among the most tangible signs of the enterprise of studying Ovid are the commentaries devoted to his works, a tradition of scholarship in large measure created by medieval masters for medieval students, in this regard in contrast to the traditions of Virgilian and Horatian commentary that have their roots in the Late Antique.[4]

Ovid foresaw a posterity, most famously for his greatest work, the *Metamorphoses*.

---

[1] A shortlist of bibliographical items would include Battaglia (1959), Munari (1960), Rand (1963), and a host of more focussed recent studies.

[2] Munk Olsen (1982–89).

[3] Traube (1911) 113; cf. Hexter (1986) 2–3 and, most recently, Holsinger and Townsend (2000) 242–43; at its fullest extent, Gallo and Nicastri (1995).

[4] The Ovidian exception might be scholia on the *Ibis*. See Hexter (1986) 84–85 n. 12.

Iamque opus exegi, quod nec Iouis ira nec ignes
nec poterit ferrum nec edax abolere uetustas.
cum uolet, illa dies, quae nil nisi corpus huius
ius habet, incerti spatium mihi finiat aeui:
parte tamen meliore mei super alta perennis
astra ferar, nomenque erit indelibile nostrum,
quaque patet domitis Romana potentia terris,
ore legar populi, perque omnia saecula fama,
siquid habent ueri uatum praesagia, uiuam. (15.871–79)

Now I have completed this work, which neither Jove's wrath nor fire
nor iron nor rapacious old age can destroy. When it will, let that day,
which has no power save over this body, finish off the term of my
mortal life. With my better part I'll be borne, everlasting, beyond the
stars and my name will be unexpungeable, and wherever Roman power
extends over conquered lands, I will be read by the people and, if the
prophesies of poets are indeed true, through all ages with renown I
shall live.

Ovid could not, to be sure, foresee the particularities of his after-
life (*Nachleben*), for no Roman poet could envision the changed social,
political, and religious contexts that would provide the conditions for
his reception in distant times and places. Horace, when he wrote the
passage that was surely the one most keenly on Ovid's mind when
the younger poet concluded his *Metamorphoses*, had made his survival
dependent on the continuance of specific Roman rites.

Exegi monumentum aere perennius
regalique situ pyramidum altius,
quod non imber edax, non aquilo impotens
possit diruere aut innumerabilis
annorum series et fuga temporum.
non omnis moriar multaque pars mei
uitabit Libitinam; usque ego postera
crescam laude recens, dum Capitolium
scandet cum tacita uirgine pontifex . . . (*C.* 3.30.1–9)

I have raised a monument longer-lasting than brass and loftier than
the pyramids of kings, which neither voracious rains nor angry wind
can destroy, nor the run of years or lapse of time. Not utterly will I
die: the great part of me will avoid the curse of death, and I will be
continuously renewed with the praise of posterity so long as priests
accompanied by silent virgins climb the Capitoline hill . . .

Horace was, of course, not only closer to the powers that were but
more directly aligned with the cultural agenda—however articulated—

of Augustus and Maecenas.[5] It was his sense of the Romanness of his world that led him to assume that the survival of his verse was inextricably linked with Roman institutions.

A sound historical sense, but in the event, not accurate. Ovid's bolder, more universal claim proved closer to the truth for both poets. His metamorphic imagination would, one imagines, take delight in the very misprisions that often constituted the particulars of his reception, though we would be doing a disservice to the supremely ironic Horace not to credit him with the capacity to appreciate comprehension that includes miscomprehension. Indeed, at one particular moment, in the final poem of the first book of his *Epistles*, Horace invoked one Roman institution that was continued, if altered, through the Middle Ages, and thus presciently described the context of the preservation and reading of all Roman poets: the school. Addressing that first volume of letters as both book and liberated slave (*liber*) now free to prostitute it-/himself to the public, "Horace" foretells rough times for the product of his study. After all other indignities have come upon him, particularly after he is aged and sullied, what will be his fate?

> Hoc quoque te manet, ut pueros elementa docentem
> occupet extremis in uicis balba senectus. (*Epist.* 1.20.17–18)

> This too awaits you, that stammering old-age find you in far-flung townships teaching the boys their abc's.

All this is to suggest that the "Ovid," "Horace," or "Virgil" who— that?—finds himself 'in the Middle Ages' is of course not Ovid, Horace, or Virgil at all. It is a vision, a new understanding, of the ancient poet, so that, in fact, the real object of a study of 'Ovid in the Middle Ages' is 'the Middle Ages in Ovid.' In other words: it is a study of what individuals of the subsequent period find in Ovid that speaks to them. The Middle Ages are themselves a congeries of many times and places, and in this brief survey, I will exemplify medieval response to Ovid from only a few of these. I will limit my survey to the early and high Middle Ages, and almost exclusively to response to Ovid that left its precipitates in Latin texts. Those two

---

[5] On Ovid's position in the face of political reality, see Fantham and Tissol, chapters 7 and 10, respectively, above.

limitations are closely related, for while Latin response to Ovid continues through the late medieval period and into the Renaissance, no account of Ovid in the late Middle Ages, the fourteenth and fifteenth centuries, would be possible without close attention to the vernacular cultures of medieval Europe. Ovid's output is itself rich and varied, and different works seem to have appealed more at one time than another. Any brief survey of this sort will tend to exaggerate this effect, so even as the framework I have devised may seem to suggest a linear narrative, it is important to note that the reality is much more complex. With that caveat registered, permit me to organize this review of medieval response around three highly productive facets of Ovid's poetic persona—exile, mythographer, and lover—and to do so in that order, which, though it may seem backwards for Ovid's career, paradoxically better fits the centuries covered here.

2. The Exile as Poet

Ovid could not foresee his posterity, but in an uncanny way, he was thrust into it in 8 C.E., when he was relegated to Tomis on the Black Sea by the emperor Augustus. Ovid himself tells us that the causes were two: a poem and a mistake (*carmen et error*, *Tr.* 2.207). The poem was the *Ars amatoria*; we never learn what the mistake was, which itself only fanned speculation over the centuries.[6] I will refer to some of the more popular medieval explanations in section 4, but here I wish to present a sort of historical paradox and claim that in a way neither of the two players could have anticipated, by sending Ovid to the very fringes of the empire, Augustus virtually placed him in a time machine and set the dial to 650 C.E.—I suppose this imaginary dial would have read "MCCCC a.u.c."—plus or minus a century or so.

In a matter of months, Ovid traveled from the center of the empire to the marches, from a capital city dense with a personal network and literary contacts to a barbaric outpost on the periphery. There

---

[6] For an overview of explanations, see Thibault (1964). For Ovid's biography, see White, chapter 1 above. The image of Ovid on the shores of the Black Sea continues to inspire and intrigue; for two late-twentieth-century novels, consider Malouf (1978) and Ransmayr (1988), (1990).

Latin was a foreign language, virtually the only link to a now distant otherworld of culture and learning. Contact with Rome was only to be had by post. Via a transformation hardly less strange than the ones he had sung of in his *Metamorphoses*, Ovid had become a stranger in a strange land.

It took several centuries for the forays of northern tribes—along with a good number of other forces—to break down the patterns of communication and association throughout most of the Roman world and bring about conditions along the shores of the Mediterranean comparable to those in Tomis that Ovid describes, but Ovid experienced in the time of Augustus many of the circumstances later litterateurs would. Ovid, of course, knew well what he was missing—the glittering life of Rome of which he had once been a part. That was the cruelest aspect of his punishment. One could say that to the extent later writers knew what they were missing by being separated from Rome at its height, they had Ovid to thank.

Ovid's *Tristia* and *Epistulae ex Ponto* were unique in their day, born of unique circumstances. Generally overlooked, when not disparaged, from the Renaissance through most of the twentieth century—apart from writers who found themselves exiles—they are now coming back into favor as scholars appreciate and explore their extraordinary modernity.[7] It may well only be an accident of transmission that the oldest extant manuscript of Ovid's works is a now fragmentary sixth-century text of the *Epistulae ex Ponto*,[8] but if it is mere happenstance, as we shall see, these late works of Ovid spoke early to medieval poets.

The particular nostalgia for Rome that Ovid's exile elegies bespeak is echoed already in Late Antiquity in Rutilius Namatianus's 'itinerary' (the so-called *de reditu suo*), without notable Ovidian overtones to be sure. I mention it, nonetheless, because from its early fifth-century perspective, it suggests that geographical distance can figure temporal and cultural distance as well. Rutilius breathed Mediterranean air, and the Rome he visited was still a fairly bustling city, however diminished its imperial significance. Two and three centuries later, would-be poets found themselves in a different world altogether. That

---

[7] Well exemplified by Williams (1994) and his contribution to this volume, chapter 11 above.

[8] Wolfenbüttel 3036; see Hexter (1986) 86–87 and n. 20. On the transmission of Ovid's works, see Richmond, chapter 14 below.

they studied, read, and strove to write in Ovid's language was itself
a miracle of sorts, an act of linguistic nostalgia. Nostalgia in, of
course, a figurative sense, for this was a return to an imagined home-
land. The value of this home was, above all, that it could be home
to many. It was a center, a common place. I mean not only that
Latin could serve, as it did, as a lingua franca by which individu-
als with diverse vernaculars came together, though of course this is
no little thing. Even more: to individuals gathered in small groups
in monasteries now being established across ever wider expanses of
northern and central Europe, Latin served as a 'chat room' for the
clerical elite. Given the resources and resonances of the Latin on
which they modelled their own communications, it would not be too
much to say that this was a virtual urban space, for through it a
simulacrum of the *urbs* itself came into being. And given the all too
evident disconnect between reality and that imaginary city, what
came nearest to this evocation was the phantom Rome of Ovid's
exile poetry, a city already invisible to him that he treasured in mem-
ory and longingly evoked. At a distance, the network of contacts and
communications that are the hallmarks of city life can only be recre-
ated in letters. The epistle, prose or verse, becomes then the means
par excellence of connecting. The poetic letters of Ovid, not only
the exile elegies but the *Heroides* as well, model the writer reaching
out across a void to an absent other. The *Heroides*, the zenith of
whose popularity will fall later,[9] present, singly or in pairs, unique
situations from the world of Greek and Roman poetic legend; the
Tristia and *Epistulae ex Ponto*, in contrast, weave a text of achievable
connectedness, in particular, connectedness with Rome. Hence their
particular popularity for writers participating in what scholars gen-
erally term the Carolingian Renaissance, when recall of imperial
Rome was conscious and calculated.[10] Einhard modeled his *Vita Caroli
Magni* (c. 833) on Suetonius's *Vitae Caesarum*, and a generation earlier
court poets adopted classical sobriquets. For example, Alcuin (d. 804)
styled himself and was referred to as Horace ("Flaccus"), his student

---

[9] See Hexter (1986) 136–209 (= part III). For a survey of the vast culture of
responding (in multiple senses) to the *Heroides*, Dörrie (1968) remains indispensable.
    [10] For example, *Prospicit alta novae Romae meus arce Palemon,/Cuncta suo imperio con-
sistere regna triumpho,/Rursus in antiquos mutataque secula mores/aurea Roma iterum renovata
renascitur orbi*, Modoin, *Egloga* 1.24–27, in Korzeniewski (1976) 76–87, here 78; in
part anthologized and translated in Godman (1985a) 190–97, who highlights just
these verses as a motto for the renaissance (1).

Angilbert (d. 814) was "Homer," and the longer-lived Modoin (d. c. 840) was Ovid ("Naso").[11]

In his poetic catalogue, their contemporary Theodulf (d. 821) lists Ovid among the authors he once had read,[12] and while it is true that Ovid was at this time not so widely read and studied as Virgil or Horace, still, the top literary talents of the age had at least a selective knowledge of him and his works. While their texts now and then echo and thus pay homage to the *Ars amatoria* or the *Metamorphoses*, it would seem that the imaginations of these Carolingian poets were haunted by the image of Ovid as exile, an image that could have been based on familiarity with Ovid's own exile elegies but whose evocative power did not depend on it. In 820, Modoin, writing to Theodulf, confined in the monastery of St. Aubin in Angers on suspicion of involvement in a plot against Charlemagne's son and successor Louis the Pious, draws heavily on Ovidian phraseology as he invokes the specter of the exiled Ovid:

> Livor edax petit alta fremens, consternere temptans
> id quod ovans simplex pectore turba colit.
> pertulit an nescis quod longos Naso labores?
> insons est factus exul ob invidiam.[13]

> Voracious greed seeks the heights and, growling, attempts to bring low that which the simple-hearted crowd, applauding, approves. Or do you not know that Ovid endured long years of suffering? Innocent, he was exiled on account of envy.

Modoin consoles Theodulf with the names of notable predecessors, placing him in a procession beginning with Ovid and continuing (without concern for strict chronology) with Boethius, Virgil, Seneca, St. John on Patmos, Hilarius, Peter, and Paul.[14]

So popular was the image of the exiled poet that some Carolingians adopted the Ovidian pose even when their place of 'exile' was hardly so cruel as Scythia. Louis, having decided to exclude Ermoldus

---

[11] On the practice, see Garrison (1997).

[12] *Et modo Pompeium, modo te, Donate, legebam,/et modo Virgilium, te modo, Naso loquax* (*De libris quos legere solebam* 17–18), *PLAC* 1.543.

[13] *PLAC* 1.571. *Livor edax* obviously echoes *Am.* 1.15.1 and *Rem.* 389. Further on the Carolingian Naso's Ovidianism, see Whitta (forthcoming, 2002). I have benefited from a presentation by Dr. Whitta based on his forthcoming article as well as from the generous and careful reading he gave the penultimate draft of this chapter and the many suggestions he made.

[14] *Modoinus Indignus Episcopo Theodulfo Suo* 47–62, *PLAC* 1.571. Modoin has the *senex* refer to Ovid's exile in the eclogue quoted above, at 60–66.

Nigellus (d. c. 835) from son Pippin's entourage, packed him off to
Strasbourg.[15] Even as he begged to be recalled, Ermoldus had to
admit that his exile was not so severe as Ovid's; indeed, Ermoldus
admires the beauty of Strasbourg and its surroundings and diplo-
matically lauds the city's bishop. In 841, Walahfrid Strabo (d. 849),
taking refuge in Speyer, sends a poem to Lothar in which he, too,
styles himself an exile. Though he praises Speyer, the troop of exiled
poets, philosophers, and prophets he evokes is, in defiance of chro-
nology, headed by Ovid, freezing in Scythia.[16] More interestingly,
he refers to Ovid's own exile poetry and suggests that as poetry it
is superior to Ovid's Roman works.

> Est veluti proprium et cunctis civile poetis
> extera regna pati tormentaque mentis amarae
> carmine solari vario: sub frigore Naso
> congemuit Scythiae, Musarum ubi munere tantum
> excoluit, quantum Romanae moenibus urbis
> non faceret, patriae praedulci nomine captus.[17]

> It is as it were the appropriate and civil right of all poets to suffer
> distant lands and to console the torments of a bitter mind with vari-
> ous song: Ovid lamented beneath the frosts of Scythia, where by the
> gift of the muses he perfected [sc. his poetry] as much as he had not
> [sc. done so] within the walls of the Roman city, captivated as he was
> [there] by the sublimely sweet name of his homeland.

We can only regret the fact that Walahfrid did not expound his
higher valuation of Ovid's exile poetry at greater length. We can-
not know whether he actually preferred the themes of these later
works to either the erotic or mythological poetry of Ovid's Roman
period, whether he was drawing on the spiritual topos that idealized
exile as a figure for monastic withdrawal from earthly cares, a com-
monplace itself susceptible to broad interpretation,[18] or whether he

---

[15] On Ermoldus and Walahfrid Strabo, i.a., see Godman (1985b).

[16] To Modoin's list, Walahfrid adds Porphyry, Anaxagoras, Socrates, and the
man not a prophet in his own country (Matthew 13:57); see Hexter (1986) 91 n. 37.

[17] Carmen 76.60–67; I follow the punctuation of Stroh (1969) 15, rather than that
of Duemmler at *PLAC* 2.415.

[18] According to this commonplace, the ideal monastic life was an exile from the
world and from the joys and pleasures in which lay persons are enmeshed. The
monk's exile is exemplary of a larger human truth, for man's whole earthly life is
a *peregrinatio* and exile from his true homeland (*patria*) in heaven. As Hugh of St.
Victor (d. 1141) wrote, "He is soft, to whom his fatherland is sweet; he is already
strong, to whom every land is a fatherland; but he is perfect, for whom the whole

was responding to some other element, perhaps a formal one. While Walahfrid's reference to the muses seems to point to an aesthetic or rhetorical distinction, one should not underestimate the visceral appeal of Ovid's fate for medieval Latin authors. The spiritual commonplace of 'earthly sojourn as exile,' surely at play here, had the resonance it did because exile is a trope for more keenly felt human separation and isolation. The separation of intimate friends is a universal phenomenon, but there are reasons to imagine it may have been experienced more keenly in literate circles of the ninth and following centuries. In a world where international diplomatic and cultural links were being reestablished, when the relatively few clerics who were, along with very few exceptions, the readers and writers of Latin in the period and had shared in their youth with others of their cadre the intense joys of learning at one of a limited number of cultural centers and then were often posted for the rest of their lives to a distant monastery, perhaps one of recent foundation and geographically remote—in such a world, I maintain, friends might well have felt that they were not just separated but exiled from one another. If so, Ovid's sense of separation from Rome and from his friends would have spoken directly to them.

It is in this sense that I suggested initially that when he was transported to Tomis, Ovid was figuratively transported to a situation more akin to the one experienced by medieval monks than by his contemporaries in Rome or in other Roman cities. Many of the poems we have from monastic authors are addressed to absent friends, separation itself providing an occasion for the writing and sending of a letter. These participate in (as they provide much of the evidence for) what seems to us a cult of sensitive friendship, itself another means of cementing and preserving relationships among a clerical network stretched thin. In Gottschalk (d. c. 868) of Orbais's *Ut quid iubes, pusiole*, to take one famous example, the speaker/poet laments a separation that seems the result of an actual exile. While his lyric is utterly un-Ovidian in style (as it is likewise unclassical in meter), it speaks nonetheless to the larger cultural meaning exile could have.[19]

---

world is a place of exile" (*Delicatus ille est adhuc, cui patria dulcis est; fortis autem iam, cui omne solum patria est; perfectus vero, cui mundus totus exilium est*), *Didascalion* 3.20 (Buttimer (1939) 69), with a distant echo of *Pont.* 1.3.35–36; see Hexter (1986) 92–93. Throughout this section I retrace portions of the chapter on the *Epistulae ex Ponto* in Hexter (1986), esp. 89–97; 83–99 have also been reprinted as Hexter (1995).

[19] For the poem, *PLAC* 4.731–2; with English translation, Godman (1985a) 228–33.

As Ovid's works were adopted ever more frequently in school cur-
ricula, medieval Latin poets took inspiration for their own creations
from Ovidian genres, characters, and poses, and as they read him
ever more intensively, they developed the skill of writing with increas-
ing fidelity to the Ovidian style with which their schooling had made
them familiar.[20] Hence the *aetas Ovidiana* as Traube originally con-
ceived the term. A school can teach you to admire and imitate
Ovid's metrics and to appreciate and even emulate his wit, but these
are but tools and techniques. It is doubtful to me that more Ovid-
ian, or Ovid-like, means of expression guarantees more heart-felt
Ovidian inspiration. From my perspective, even if the Latin verse
the Carolingian poets composed does not move as fleetly as Ovid's
elegiacs, these poets were capable of being moved by Ovid's plight,
and Modoin in particular, who bore the nickname "Naso" after all,
seems to have experimented with a deeper identification.

When we look to the high Middle Ages, when Ovidianism was
widely popular, one poet stands out as combining a sensitive read-
ing of Ovid's exile poetry with a well-nigh Ovidian sophistication. I
refer to Baudri of Bourgueil (1046–1130), whose poetic corpus, known
from one manuscript in the Vatican, is replete with Ovidian echoes
and references.[21] Many are epistles to friends and other correspon-
dents. The impress of the newly popular *Heroides* is quite strong. In
poems 7 and 8, Baudri actually rewrites *Heroides* 16 and 17, invent-
ing new letters from Paris to Helen and Helen to Paris as he alters
the meter from Ovid's elegiacs to hexameters. In these he plays a
fascinating game of intentional anachronism. Baudri's Paris tells Helen
of the fine wines of a city called Orléans under a certain King Henry
(7.193–98), and the remarks both correspondents express over the
sexual preferences of Greeks (7.111–38 and 185–86, 8.107–10) bespeak

---

On the symbolism of exile, see Godman (1985a) 40–41 as well as Hexter (1986)
91–93.

[20] On the *auctores* in school curricula, Glauche (1970) remains essential. For an
example of Ovidian school compositions, see Glendinning (1986).

[21] Hilbert (1979). One, *Ad eum qui Ovidium ab eo extorsit* (Hilbert no. 111), is an
amusing poem of abuse against someone who has borrowed his copy of Ovid but
has not returned it. The long (if imperfectly transmitted) mythological poem no.
154 can not be read without constant reference to Ovid. On Ovid, Baudri, and
subjectivity, see especially Bond (1985), who builds on and largely subsumes two of
his own earlier important studies. Still valuable on Ovid's impact on the style of
Baudri as well as other medieval Latin erotic poets is Offermanns (1970). Godman
(1990) offers a broader perspective.

medieval anxieties about sodomy. Baudri is playing a yet more com-
plex historical game when he has his Helen vaunt Greece's conquest
of "the language Greek calls Latin" (8.42). The learning and wit of
Baudri's Helen has nothing over that of one of Baudri's real corre-
spondents, Constance, with whom one epistolary exchange is pre-
served (200–201). From the second of these two poems, it is clear
that the otherwise unknown nun Constance was an attentive reader
of the *Heroides*, and no mean Ovidian stylist herself.[22]

It is a third pair of letters among Baudri's poems that most appro-
priately concludes this section on the poet as exile. Here, in a maneu-
ver that the genre-bending and -blending Ovid himself might well
have applauded, Baudri grafts the *Epistulae ex Ponto* onto the *Heroides*,
creating a pair of letters—like *Heroides* 16–17, 18–19, or 20–21—that
arise from Ovid's own situation.[23] In his poem 97, "Florus"—a cre-
ation of Baudri—writes from Rome to the exiled Ovid. "Florus"
touches on the rumor of "Ovid"'s adultery with Livia (97.31–32),
but more tellingly he seeks to share in Ovid's exile. He will come
to Pontus:

> Sim Nasonis ego, Naso sit Cesaris exul;
>   Naso potestatis, exul amoris ego.
> Debeat inscribi nostro res ista sepulchro
>   'Exul Nasonis sponte sua iacet hic.' (97.83–86)

> Let me be Ovid's exile, Ovid Caesar's; Ovid is the exile of tyranny,
> I of love. My tomb would then needs be engraved thus: 'Here lies the
> man who chose to be Ovid's exile.'

In 98, "Ovid" writes back, opening with phraseology that calls the
Heroides to mind.[24] His somewhat lengthier response bids Florus not

---

[22] Constance is discussed by Dronke (1984) 84–91 and Bond (1995), who offers
English translations of Baudri and Constance's epistolary exchange (in Appendix II
and III, 170–93). On the identification of this Constance with the Constance of
the convent of Sancta Maria Caritatis/Le Ronceray in Angers to whom Baudri
addresses three other poems and an epitaph, see Dronke (1984) 298 n. 18 and
Bond (1995) 229 n. 71.

[23] This is very Ovidian. Transferring the idea of paired letters from *Her.* 16–21
to Ovid's own situation recalls the response to *Her.* 1–15 of Ovid's friend Sabinus,
who penned responses to (some of) these single letters. Ovid seemed to take delight
in this twist on his own letter game, penning pairs of letters himself. On the *cor-
pus* and *corpora* of *Heroides*, and questions of authenticity, see Knox, chapter 4 above;
on the tendency of Ovid's poetic *corpus* to invite prostheses, see Hexter (1999). For
a specific study of Baudri 97–98, see Schuelper (1979).

[24] Male-male *Heroides* are rare, but not unknown. Published for the first time are
two poetic epistles of the musician Leonin in Holsinger and Townsend (2000);

to risk the journey. He is to stay at Rome and seek to obtain Ovid's
return. Ovid longs passionately for Rome, to refresh himself at her
breasts (98.154), and should he ever see Rome again, he would cover
Florus with kisses (158; comically, it seems to me, in 157 he says he
would kiss the senators as well). He breaks off his verse, offering
Florus a final adieu (174). Underlying this unsatisfied longing there
lies, one feels, an anachronism more fundamental than the obvious
intrusions of eleventh-century France into Helen's Sparta. Nothing
of the sort breaks the historical fiction here, yet it is hard not to
read "Florus" as a persona for Baudri himself and his longing for
an exiled Ovid as the desire to bridge not the physical distance
between Rome and Tomis but rather the gap between the high
Middle Ages and the first century. Baudri's "Ovid" has his own rea-
sons to wish that his Florus remain in Rome, but as the *auctor* in
Baudri's world, he can no more step out of his *auctoritas* and into
"Florus"'s arms than he can, like the Phyllis to whom he alludes
(98.167), change into a tree.

3. *The Poet as Mythographer*

In the thirteenth century, Alfonso X el Sabio of Spain wrote the
following in his *General Estoria*:

> Los auctores delos gentiles fueron muy sabios omnes e fablaron de
> grandes cosas . . . ; et sobre todos los otros auctores, Ouidio en el su
> Libro mayor, e esto tira ala su theologia delos gentiles mas que otras
> razones que ellos ayan, e el Ouidio mayor non es al entrellos si non
> la theologia e la Biblia dello entre los gentiles.

> The pagan authors were all very wise and spoke about great things . . . ;
> and above all other authors, Ovid in his "Liber maior," which treats
> the theology of the pagans more than other matters pertaining to them,
> and "Ovidius Maior" is among them nothing other than the theology
> and Bible of the pagans.[25]

"Ovidius Maior" was the name commonly used in the Middle Ages
to describe the poet's fifteen-book *Metamorphoses*. If there was any

---

dating to the 1150s and 1160s, both are to men, and both may well have homo-
erotic overtones. The one gestures to *Amores* 2.15, the other has a *Heroides*-style
opening comparable to that of Baudri 98.

[25] Solalinde (1930–61) 1.162–63. Cited also in Stroh (1969) 23–24. I thank Prof.
John Geary for help in translating this passage.

global compilation of the stories and legends of the ancient Greeks and Romans of Biblical scale and authority that circulated widely in the Latin Middle Ages, it was indeed, as Alfonso observed, Ovid's *Metamorphoses*.[26] Ovid intended the *Metamorphoses* as (among other things) an essay in the genre of learned Hellenistic epic,[27] but as much as 'learning' and lore were a part of that tradition, neither Ovid nor anyone of his contemporaries would have mistaken the *Metamorphoses* for an encyclopedia. For serious scholarship, one would have turned to the works of Varro in Latin, or other authors in Greek and Latin many of whose works are known to us today merely as titles. A bit later on, Romans might have had recourse to Pliny's *Natural History*, which did survive, for many subjects; to give for the present purpose a somewhat simplified genealogy of medieval encyclopedias, Varro (much of whom was lost at some point) and Pliny begat Isidore of Seville (d. 636), and Isidore begat Hrabanus Maurus (d. 856) and high medieval encyclopedists such as Vincent of Beauvais (d. c. 1264).

Isidore exhibits what one might term 'knowledge deflation.' (Not for nothing has he recently been proposed, quite seriously by the Vatican, as the official patron saint of the internet.) What was once common knowledge is now rare and precious; what 'every [educated] person' knew is now the purview of the erudite and assigned to ever more precious and rare books. Of course, later scholars knew about things the learned among Ovid's contemporaries need not have bothered with, such as Jewish history, Christian theology, or how to compute the date of Easter. But given the extraordinary fact that schooling in grammar and rhetoric largely on the basis of canonical Roman authors continued, there was still a premium on the learning needed to explicate these texts. As a pedagogic canon formed, and the range of reading narrowed—I am speaking here of the later Roman empire, not yet the Middle Ages—knowledge was increasingly organized around certain key texts. Scholarship on Virgil's poetry began early, but it experienced a remarkable, and remarkably long-lived, efflorescence at the end of the fourth century and the beginning of the

---

[26] The *Fasti* formed another important such assemblage among Ovid's works, but while not entirely unknown in the Middle Ages, it was not prominent. The acme of its 'popularity' came in the sixteenth and seventeenth centuries, well after the endpoint of our survey, and even then that popularity was largely scholarly. See Fritsen (1995).

[27] See Keith, chapter 8 above.

fifth, when Servius wrote his commentary, destined to be massively influential, and Macrobius his *Saturnalia*. The latter, which describes a social gathering of epic length at which Virgil's learning is the prime topic of conversation, well shows a corollary which followed quickly on the organization of learning around texts, namely, that the author of said text was himself thought to possess all human knowledge. If much of this sounds like the reverence due sacred scripture, this may be no accident. It was at virtually the same time that the Christian Bible was given its classical redaction in Latin by Jerome, a text later to be called the Vulgate. Through his intensive scholarly involvement with the Bible, Jerome contributed to the establishment of the Biblical canon and not a little to the traditions of Biblical commentary.

In *De civitate Dei*, the equally influential Augustine expressed in classic form the opposition between pagan and Christian learning, yet in such a way that the former remained virtually indispensable to Christian education. Just as one needed to read the best Latin authors—and here Virgil and Lucan, Cicero and Sallust were unavoidable—in order to become an eloquent and persuasive Christian preacher, so one had to have mastery of pagan learning for multiple purposes, from apologetics to universal history.

The specific, typological arrangement of *De civitate Dei* inspired a very special set of relations between pagan legend and Biblical truth. Augustine's master book is also a book of mastery in which all elements of the city of man—Rome as the summation of all gentile history—are troped and trumped by the city of God, Jerusalem.[28] The (canonical) Biblical narratives report the verities of the one true God, and pagan myths and legends are either rank falsifications, misrepresentations or misunderstandings of true events, or true accounts of the activities of the demons and devils who were worshipped as pagan gods. This conceptualization undergirds a long-lasting tradition of Christian exegesis and treatment of the myths of the pagans. The fascinating conundrum is that, by and large, poetry itself remained, thanks to the conservatism of the educational system and the prestige accorded ancient Greece and Rome, the world of pagan mythology. As late a text as Milton's *Paradise Lost* is rich with references to

---

[28] There is of course a further stage: the terrestrial Jerusalem itself points to and toward the celestial Jerusalem.

the pagan pantheon and the landscape of Greek and Roman mythology, but they are introduced only to be dismissed. As the narrator's classic formulation has it, "thus they relate,/erring."[29]

This tactic was, when Milton deployed it in English, at least a thousand years old. In the Latin hexameter poem *De Sodoma*, likely the product of the mid-sixth century, the anonymous poet also evokes Ovidian subtexts only to dismiss them.[30] While the longer, canonical Latin Biblical epics gesture above all to Virgil (obsessively if programmatically in the cento of Proba, who represents, admittedly, an extreme case), it is clear that the author of *De Sodoma* has Ovid uppermost in mind as he presents this narrative segment drawn from Genesis. The poet describes the fiery destruction of the cities of the plain in terms of a virtually global conflagration.

> fumantes coeunt nubes, nouus inruit imber,
> sulpura cum flammis flagrat chaos, aestuat aether:
> exustus crepitat liquidis ardoribus aer. (104–6)

> Smoking, the clouds gather, a new rain falls, a sulphurous chaos bursts into flames, the ether blazes: the air, consumed, crackles with waves of heat.

Ovid, too, told of a nearly global conflagration in the *Metamorphoses*, the fire that wreaked destruction on a large swath of earth as a result of Phaethon's daring but failed attempt to control the steeds of his father Sol's chariot (2.209–303). The author of *De Sodoma* does not seek to imitate Ovid's account; his avoidance of verbal echo may well be calculated. Instead, he challenges the Ovidian account directly, claiming that his own story has priority.

> Hinc habet in falso de uero fabula fama
> Solis progeniem currus optasse paternos
> nec ualuisse leuem puerum frenare superbos
> ignis equos, arsisse orbem, tunc fulmine raptum
> aurigam inclitum, planctum mutasse sorores. (107–11)

> From this the story—a false from a true one—arose that the Sun's son wished [to drive] his father's chariot and the tender boy, unable to rein in the high-spirited horses, set the world in flames; then the

---

[29] 1.746–47. Cf. 1.197, "As whom the Fables name. . . ."

[30] For a fuller treatment, see Hexter (1988b). The text is best consulted in Peiper's edition at *CSEL* 23.212–20.

famous charioteer was taken off by a lightening bolt and mourned; his sisters changed shape.[31]

The poet rejects Ovid's account and its constituent metamorphoses as fable, but the *Metamorphoses* is not mere foil to the true (insofar as Biblically attested) transformations the Christian poet relates. Inspired by Ovid's *Metamorphoses*, the poet provides a new narrative studded with metamorphoses, elaborating on the story in Genesis with landscape changes and natural wonders that are hyper-Ovidian in their strangeness. Significantly, to do so the poet follows one of Ovid's characteristic structural patterns, setting the metamorphosis (or a series of metamorphoses) as a coda to a longer narrative. Ovid's lengthy Phaethon complex (1.747–2.400) is a classic example. The narrative emphasis is on Phaethon's search for his father, and while Phaethon is destroyed, he is himself not strictly metamorphosed. Instead, the metamorphoses occur along the way and in a series following the thunderbolt that literally grounds Phaethon.[32]

The author of *De Sodoma* understood Ovid's organizing principle well. He presents a veritable catalogue of the changes brought about throughout the region by the fire and brimstone which destroy Sodom. While the first, the metamorphosis of Lot's wife into a pillar of salt, is Biblical, the subsequent wonders are not. As he catalogues them, he adds geographical lore that, whether true or false, is understood to represent scientific reality. The shift from narrative to geographic and 'scientific' lore is, of course, quite Ovidian. Such 'just so' stories correspond to the aetiologies (*aitia*) with which Ovid peppers— Why is the Nile's source hidden?—or concludes—Where did amber come from?—an episode such as the Phaethon narrative.

However fascinating *De Sodoma* is as a poem, it seems to have had limited impact on medieval Latin letters. Not so a tenth-century poem that had impressively wide circulation in subsequent centuries

---

[31] It is interesting that here the poet follows, whether wittingly or not I cannot say, in the footsteps of one of Ovid's precursors, Lucretius, who narrated the story of Phaethon only to dismiss it as so much fabling of the Greek poets: *scilicet ut ueteres Graium cecinere poetae,/ quod procul a uera nimis est ratione repulsum* (5.380–415, here 405–6). Of course, Christian rejection of poetic fabling is itself a prolongation of the longer argument philosophers had with poetry.

[32] Along the way: the darkening of the Ethiopians' skin (2.235–36), the creation of the Libyan desert (237–28), the hiding of the Nile's head or source (255). After Phaethon's destruction: the boy's mourning sisters, the Heliades, are transformed into poplars (346–56) and their tears turn to amber (364–66); Phaethon's kinsman, Cygnus, also mourning the boy he loved, is transformed into a swan (377).

and was part of many a school curriculum: the *Ecloga Theoduli* (or *Theodoli*).[33] While it is much less 'Ovidian' than the *De Sodoma* in form—as an 'eclogue' it gestures to Virgil first and foremost (not to mention others who, like Modoin named above, worked in the genre after Virgil)—it rehearses and recycles vastly more Ovidian material. Like *De Sodoma*, it seeks to suppress and surpass Ovid, and indeed repeated dismissal of Ovidian fable becomes its central structural principle. But as in the case of *De Sodoma*, Ovid is not thereby erased.

The structure of the *Ecloga Theoduli* is simple. All but fifty of its 344 hexameters (lines 37–332) are devoted to a debate between Pseustis ("Falsehood"), proponent of the pagan gods, and Alithia ("Truth"), defender of the Christian faith. Debates or contests are often the subject of eclogues; the tradition runs back to Theocritus, but in the Latin tradition, the six dialogues among Virgil's ten *Eclogues* (1, 5, 8, and 9 have two speakers, 3 and 7 three) served as the models of the 'amoebaeic eclogues' for, among poets before the *Ecloga Theoduli*, Modoin, and, among later poets, Petrarch. At the end of Virgil's *Eclogue* 3, Palaemon says he is not able to resolve the quarrel between Menalcas and Damoetas, but in the *Ecloga Theoduli*, the judge, Fronesis ("Thought" or "Reason"), has no such difficulty. At the poem's conclusion she consoles Pseustis for his inevitable loss with, of all things, pagan mythological learning (341–44), showing that the learned Ovid still has a place in a rational Christian comity.

A detailed analysis of the specific Ovidian tales Pseustis relates and the Christian 'antidotes' Alithia offers would spring the mold of this survey.[34] It would be worth pausing, though, to reflect a moment longer on the fact that the *Ecloga Theoduli*, however much it draws on the *Metamorphoses* for *materia* (to use a term from medieval literary theory), does not use it as a formal model (or what that theory might call *ordo*). To be sure, its debating personifications and final judgment are perfectly apt for its didactic and religious *intentio*, and follow a tradition that goes back to the early church (e.g., the *Octavius* of Minucius Felix) and even beyond, to philosophical dialogues. But the *Ecloga Theoduli* shares this eschewal of Ovidian form with much more ambitious and experimental twelfth-century mythographies.[35]

---

[33] For detailed analysis, see Green (1982), supplemented by Vredeveld (1987); more briefly, Hexter (1987) 78–80. On 'Carolingian pastoral' generally, cf. Green (1980).

[34] A condensed conspectus may be found at Hexter (1987) 79 and 89–90 n. 50.

[35] For example, those of Bernardus Sylvestris and Alain de Lille (d. 1203). In

Ovid himself was, of course, perhaps the greatest of all Latin mythographers, but medieval authors seemed by and large disinclined even to attempt to recreate the *Metamorphoses* on a structural level. Why? While the *Metamorphoses* does not lack structure or system, its structure is by no means obvious or unambiguous. What systematization scholars agree upon says very little of interest about the poem, and, conversely, everything that makes the *Metamorphoses* truly Ovidian lies beyond any possible systematization. In a sense, of course, this fits Ovid's theme: flux. But no other poet known to me has had the strength so thoroughly to resist the temptation to impose a more simple-minded order on the welter of creation. Medieval mythographers were nowhere near so 'strong.' Moreover, their view of the universe was itself a bounded and structured one, bounded and structured by God, who created and ordered all. The degree to which Ovid's mythological masterwork could not serve them as a master model is telling.

Of course, where the *Metamorphoses* was encountered head on, and where one engaged its narrative complexity directly, was in the school, and this survey would be incomplete if it did not include the very stratum that made Ovidian poetry the stuff of learning, and endlessly reinforced its status as learning. Schooling often falls beneath the horizon of accounts of literary reception, but the role of the schools is hard to overestimate in the case of a Latin author in the Middle Ages, since students were not merely set the task of reading specific literary texts but were reading the *auctores* in part to learn Latin itself. It is the rare medieval manuscript of a school author such as Ovid that does not bear traces of the teaching functions to which the texts were put. Interlinear and marginal glosses, sparse or dense, as well as those glosses and explanatory notes on a given text transmitted separately as a more or less continuous commentary, show how these texts were used to teach Latin grammar, figures of speech, and above all the body of reference and lore that anyone who sets out to read Latin poetry needs to have. Who was Thetis? What was the Calydonian boar? Why is Ariadne called "the Cretan"

---

prose mixed with verse (a form called Menippean satire), these natural scientific allegories *cum* moralizing have strong elements of contemporary Chartrian Platonizing, but for their structured hypertrophy take their inspiration from works such as Martianus Capella's late antique *Marriage of Mercury and Philology*. On the twelfth-century mythographers, see Wetherbee (1972), and on the entire tradition, Chance (1994–2000).

(*Cressa*)? Here, when confusion looms, systematization is imported. The glosses seem to say: "Don't be confused: there are two distinct figures named Scylla, each with different stories."[36] Ovid, like virtually every Roman poet, refers to the names of places and persons throughout his oeuvre, not just in the *Metamorphoses* and *Fasti*. Whenever any of Ovid's texts were read, schoolmasters instructed students in Greek and Roman mythology. The *Heroides* were particularly well suited to offer students a manageable set of stories, many of which conveniently revolve around travels to or from the Trojan War, although the poetic letters themselves bristle with references to a broader mythological universe. But even the *Ars amatoria* or *Remedia amoris* could be turned into a lesson in Greek mythography.[37] One receives, after all, an unforgettable impression of Pasiphae. And as for the narrative complexity of the *Metamorphoses*, each book of that large poem was conceived as consisting of so many narrative chunks (*fabulae*) each centered on a different shape change.[38]

Wisely, then, did Alfonso describe Ovid as the "Bible of the pagans," but as so often, such analysis sheds at least as much light on the period of its formulation, for Ovid could equally well have been described as the "pagan Bible of the Middle Ages," the ultimate source of mythological facts just as all the *auctores* were authoritative models for language and poetry. In vain did the Carolingian Smaragdus attempt to turn Donatus into a purely Christian grammar. In the schools of the high medieval period, at least to judge from extant sources, there was astonishingly little anxiety about the non-Christian source of these stylistic models and an apparently sophisticated appreciation of the fact that Ovid represented the beliefs of his time, which quite understandably diverged from those of

---

[36] As Arnulf of Orléans does in his note on *Rem.* 737: "Due fuerunt Scille . . .," Roy and Shooner (1996) 173.

[37] Hexter (1986). For the much larger bibliography on scholarship on the *Metamorphoses*, consult the work of Coulson; among his many publications, Coulson (1991) is particularly important. Coulson and Roy (2000) now offers the most complete listing of medieval *glosule* and other parerga on all Ovid's works, with generous reference to secondary bibliography. To instance one poem from several thousands, consider Walter of Châtillon's *Propter Sion non tacebo* (also transmitted as CB 41); while not Ovidian in any real sense, it shares with Ovid such figures as Scylla, Charybdis, the Sirens, and Thetis. Knowledge of these may have come from multiple sources, but Ovid's texts, especially as augmented by school glosses and commentary, were part of the mix.

[38] There were different ways of effecting the segmentation. See Hexter (1988) and Hexter (1989).

Christian Europe. Nor should we be surprised by this, since the
Gospels, Acts of the Apostles, and Pauline and other letters, not to
mention the lives of early martyrs and saints, all frequently refer to
the different beliefs of non-Christian Romans. We might imagine
medieval schoolmasters reasoning somewhat as follows: "If we want
to read Roman poetry—and we do—then we need to understand as
much of it as we can, so let's get on with it."

When broader interpretation was attempted, and especially when
tales from Ovid became popular outside of the schools, not only in
Latin but in vernacular form, matters were seen to grow more fraught,
and a range of prophylactic measures were taken including whole-
sale and thoroughgoing allegorization and moralization. One example
of the latter might be Pierre Bersuire's fourteenth-century moraliza-
tions of Ovid's *Metamorphoses*. Like "Lactantius" and Arnulf of Orléans
before him, Bersuire divided the Ovidian narrative into segments,
but since his aim was to provide ready material for preachers, it was
the moralization that drove both segmentation and interpretation.[39]
In this survey, this one example will have to suffice. If it teases, then
it will serve also to exemplify the virtually unbounded, and in that
sense nicely Ovidian, nature of the medieval Ovid himself.

4. *Ovid as Lover and Poet*

It is 'Ovid the lover' who, in the popular imagination of virtually
every age, comes first to mind, an image based of course on his
Amores, which invite, as love elegy always does, an autobiographical
reading. Ovid himself suggests that it was his experience as a lover
which gives him the wisdom and authority to speak as a veritable
'doctor of love' and write as the *praeceptor Amoris* in the *Ars amato-
ria*,[40] so that we can hardly fault the medieval biographers who trace
precisely this progression. So full is Ovid's experience that eventu-
ally, older and wiser, he can teach youth how to fall out of love, as
the sequel to the *Ars amatoria*, the *Remedia amoris*, was in all serious-
ness expected to be able to do.

---

[39] This aspect of Bersuire's method is explored in Hexter (1989). For example,
in *Metamorphoses* 1, Phoebus pursuing Daphne may be interpreted as the devil pur-
suing a Christian soul: Hexter (1989) 58.

[40] Experience: *usus opus mouet hoc: uati parete perito* (*Ars* 1.29). The phrase *praeceptor
Amoris* appears at 1.17; cf. *praeceptor amandi*, 2.161.

So deep were expectations of a link between Ovid and love that medieval explanations for the 'real story' behind Ovid's exile almost inevitably engaged the erotic register. Ovid's own references to the *error* that, along with the song (*carmen*, taken to be the *Ars amatoria*), he says provoked Augustus to send him from Rome are intentionally imprecise. This seems to have inspired fantasies about things that might have outraged Augustus, and as examples of what medieval authors think would have enraged a Roman emperor, they are telling. One obvious theory was that Ovid slept with Livia, cuckolding Augustus. The purported adultery of Ovid and the empress made its way as historical fact into the German *Kaiserchronik*: Ovid, here a chancellor to Augustus, is "put on a ship and abandoned to the waves,"[41] although the adultery itself is alleged in not a few earlier accounts, as we shall see shortly. Livia was the central figure in another popular scenario. Since Ovid more than once indicates that his crime involved his having seen something (*Tr.* 2.103–6 and 3.5.49–50), and since in the first of the two passages, Ovid likens himself to Actaeon, who was punished when he unwittingly caught sight of the goddess Diana in her bath, it is no surprise that some medieval biographers claimed that Ovid saw Livia bathing.[42]

Commentaries by definition, and often design, agglomerate materials, and in many *accessus* or introductions three charges are listed together. I cite here the *accessus* to the *Tristia* in clm 19475 (twelfth century), which involves both the *carmen et error* of *Tr.* 2.207 and which gives as options for the latter both Ovid's adultery with the empress and a perhaps surprising elaboration of the idea that Ovid saw something the emperor did not want him to see:

> It is asked why he was sent into exile. Three causes are given in response: first, because he slept with Caesar's wife, Livia; second, because, as a member of the household, crossing the portico he saw Augustus having sex with his [i.e., Augustus's] boyfriend [*amasius*], and Augustus, fearing that he might be betrayed by him, sent him into exile; and third, because he had written the *Art of Love*, in which he instructed young men to deceive married women and ally them to

---

[41] Ghisalberti (1946), here 33 note, col. 1. For a variant with a twist that shows the impress of the motif of Potiphar's wife and Joseph (or, for that matter, Phaedra and Hippolytus), cf. Hexter (1999) 334–35.

[42] Ghisalberti (1946) 33 note, col. 2 (Giovanni del Vergilio) and 59 (Cod. Laur. 36.2). Cf. also Williams's discussion of the Actaeon story above, pp. 379–80.

them, and having so offended the Romans it is said that he was sent into exile.

In typical school commentary fashion, the compiler or master gives no indication that he prefers one explanation over another. In contrast, an *accessus* to the *Epistulae ex Ponto* found in at least two manuscripts lists the same three explanations but singles out the boyfriend story as the "best," concluding that "this was the principal cause of his expulsion."[43] Perhaps the prominence of this unlikely scenario is indicative of what may have been on the minds of many monks and schoolmasters.

In another Munich manuscript (clm 631), an even more fabulous (and fabliaux-like) story appears in an *accessus* on the *Tristia* before the standard three explanations. In this story Ovid's rival for the affections of Augustus's wife is none other than Virgil![44] That same *accessus* offers yet more solid evidence for the rounding out and consolidation of an erotic biography of Ovid that mixes life and poetry, for it claims not only that "Ovid loved Augustus's wife" but that it was she "whom he celebrated in his 'book without a title' under the name of Corinna"—in other words, in the *Amores*, which indeed often circulated in the Middle Ages as the *de sine titulo* or *de sine nomine*.

Speculations about the 'real story' behind Ovid's mysterious exile that, one way or another, implicate Ovid in amorous intrigues or sexual scandals of the imperial household—a book about 'his' love affairs that dares not speak its name—suggest that love under the sign of Ovid inevitably involved guilty pleasures. But we would err if we emphasized only sin and scandal, for on a much broader scale Ovid's celebration of the sheer joy of love inspired a corresponding medieval celebration, even cult of love.[45] Much of this efflorescence appears in vernacular romances and lyric, but it also appears in

---

[43] *uel quod melius est, quia uidit Cesarem cum amasio suo concumbere . . . Hec causa principalis erat sue expulsionis*, clm 14753, folio 40v; cf. Hexter (1986) 220; for Bibl. Nat. 8207, see Ghisalberti (1946) 33, note (col. 2) and 50 (*Hanc autem causam esse principalem innuit ipse . . .*). In a version of this anecdote in a manuscript in the Bancroft Library at the University of California, Berkeley, UCB 95, here folio 60ra, the emperor whose boyfriend Ovid sees him abusing is Nero; cf. Hexter (1999) 342. The manuscript was described, and the headnote first published, in Jeauneau (1988). The most important work of gathering, editing, and printing Ovidian biographies since Ghisalberti is Coulson (1987).

[44] Hexter (1986) 221 and (1999) 335–36.

[45] That Ovid's was but one of the many 'voices' in the discourse constituting medieval attitudes to love is the valuable perspective of Baldwin (1994).

medieval Latin. It is often difficult to determine the precise role which specific medieval Latin texts played in mediating Ovid's impact on vernacular literature,[46] but we can confidently assert that medieval Latin culture played such a mediating role if we understand all medieval reading of Ovid in Latin to be an element of that culture. Certainly, the impact of the Latin Ovid can be more direct on Latin texts, and more directly gauged. I select not one author or group of authors to illustrate medieval Latin lyric, but a medieval verse collection, perhaps the most famous one of all: the *Carmina burana* (henceforth "CB"). These "songs from Beuron" are so called because the manuscript containing the collection was found in the Bavarian monastery at Benediktbeuron, whence it was brought to Munich, where it now resides (as clm 4660 and 4660a). The value of using the *Carmina burana* as our sample is that, whatever questions still remain about its provenance and precise date,[47] it represents authentic early thirteenth-century tastes in collecting and compiling Latin and German verse. Though the manuscript is no longer entirely complete, in what remains we have over two hundred items, clearly sorted into groups: moral and satiric songs, love poetry, tavern songs, and religious dramas. Ovid appears in many places. For example, four verses from the *Tristia* (5.8.15–18) are simply cited, without attribution, as part of CB 18 among the moral-satirical poetry. Above all, Ovid is the force, usually invisible, sometimes visible, behind the love poetry, which constitutes over half the entire extant collection.[48]

The section begins—"incipiunt jubili"—with rhythmic strophes celebrating love and spring. *Janus annum circinat,/ver estatem nuntiat,/calcat Phebus ungula . . .*: "Janus rounds out the year, spring heralds summer, and Phoebus's steeds stamp their hooves . . ." (CB 56.1–3). The first word is a classical name, familiar from multiple sources, but a figure in Ovid; the very first verb is a fairly rare one, but one that appears in Ovid's *Metamorphoses* (2.721). But the following strophes are yet more Ovidian still. Take, for example, the second stanza:

---

[46] On the vexed question of 'priority,' see Dronke (1968).

[47] Provenance: Steer (1983), analyzing the dialectal features of the German verses, makes a strong case for Tirol/Südtirol, indeed the Augustiner-Chorherrenstift near Brixen. Date: "after 1220, before 1250, perhaps even before 1230," Bernt (1979) 839.

[48] Walsh (1993) offers convenient access to the love lyrics in CB, with English translations.

Procul sint omnia
tristia!
dulcia
gaudia
sollemnizent Veneris gymnasia!
decet iocundari,
quos militare contigit
Dioneo lari.
(Refrain) Amor cuncta superat,
    Amor dura terebrat.

Banish all sorrows! Let sweetness and joy be practiced in Venus's schools! Those who serve in the military should rejoice in the goddess's service. Love rules over one and all, Love pierces all that is hard.

With Ovid in mind, the word for sorrows—*tristia*—takes on special significance. "Venus's schools" is clearly the place where a *praeceptor Amoris* such as Ovid would be in charge. And the reference to *militare* brings Ovid's own *militat omnis amans* to mind.[49]

Make no mistake about it: these poems speak a language that is very different from Ovid's. Ovid's world, especially his erotic hunting grounds and trysting places, are not the flower-strewn fields of spring. His is an urban poetry, his conquests 'ladies' in grand houses and their slaves, not shepherdesses. But neither would this poetry be what it is without Ovid. However non-Classical the Latin often is (as are, in most of the poems in this section, the meters), the medium is nonetheless Latin, often directly echoing Ovid and other classical authors from the medieval curriculum. A classical and often specifically Ovidian pantheon presides over this contemporary Latin world: Hymeneus (57.2.3), Aquilo (57.3.1), Thetis, Ceres, and Proserpina (57.5.1, 5, and 8) hold sway. Hercules (63.1ª.1) and Hippolytus (178.4.2) are but a few of hundreds of figures who populate these poems and whose names would mean nothing to the authors, or to

---

[49] *Am.* 1.9.1. The motif of *militia amoris* or *militia Veneris* occurs frequently in the CB. *Dum Diane vitrea* ends with the phrase *sic Veneris militia* (62.8.6), as if to say "see Ovid." Other references include *dudum militaveram* in a poem by Peter of Blois giving thanks to Venus (72.1b.1) and *Iam dudum Amoris militem/devotum me exhibui* (166.1–2); cf. also 19.17.1, 94.2, and 167.5.1–4. Ovidian touches are frequent in the CB. For example, Bernt (1979) highlights the Ovidian overtones of the words *tener* and *ludere*, which occur frequently in the poems. In his elegant formulation, "An Ovids Dichtungen wird der Ausdruck, aber auch der Blick für Regungen und Situationen geschult" (848). His convenient edition offers the complete text of the critical edition of the CB, Hilka et al. (1930–70).

their readers and listeners, without learning derived from study of Ovid and the other school authors. Sometimes a nightingale is just a nightingale, singing in the woods (173.2.1). But the Latin word (*philomena*) always stands ready for these poets and readers to invoke Ovid's horrifying tale of Procne, Tereus, and Philomela from *Metamorphoses* 6. Such is the nightingale of CB 58, who sings, to be sure (58.1.8), but sings her complaint of old (*antiquatum*, 58.1.10), in which Tereus and the hapless Itys also figure (58.1.9 and 14, respectively).

Such explicitly Ovidian learning seems rather gratuitous in a spring song, and yet that very observation may lead us to the insight that what seems gratuitous to us likely fulfilled other functions for those who created, copied, and treasured such poetry. It may have been the element that made it most valuable in the eyes of some readers and anthologizers. Other poets were more successful at integrating classical and specifically Ovidian figures into their creations. Such was the author of *Dum Diane vitrea* (CB 62), among the most remarkable and sublime of medieval lyrics.[50] For all its distinctly unclassical, indeed uniquely mysterious atmosphere, it cannot even be understood at the most basic level if one does not know that Diana is the moon, that her brother is Apollo, or who Morpheus is.

Ovid's *Amores* are directly called to mind when "Corinna" appears as the name for a girl (CB 103.2.7 and 164.2.4). Ovid's own poetry appears also as citations in this section of the CB as well as among the 'moral and satiric' verses. A couplet from Deianira's letter to Hercules is copied into this portion of the manuscript (CB 104a = *Her.* 9.31–32) as is a distich from one of Ovid's own letters from exile (CB 123a = *Pont.* 4.3.49–50). Both of these provide the sort of general observation that lends itself to decontextualization and subsequent collection in florilegia.[51] A more specific sentiment, whose context is, I should have thought, unforgettable, appears as CB 99b; these two verses comprise the inscription Ovid's Dido imagines carved on her tomb and with which she concludes her letter to Aeneas (*Her.* 7.195–96). Ovid's poetic voice enters even more dynamically into CB 105. The appearance of the god of love (*En Cupido pharetratus*,

---

[50] Dronke (1968) 306–13.

[51] One should not forget the circulation of bits of Ovid in this fashion, often, as here, without explicit identification of the Roman poet. A convenient way to gain a sense of this is from Dörrie (1971), where the editor's sigla indicate which verses are preserved in one of several florilegia.

105.2.1, *Amor*, 105.5.1) to a dreaming poet is already Ovidian. When Love speaks to the poet, he speaks six goliardic stanzas *cum auctoritate*, where three lines of the typical goliardic rapping verse are followed by a regular hexameter. Four of the six "authorities"—these metrically distinct final lines—are direct citations or partial reworkings of verses from either the *Ars amatoria* or the *Remedia amoris*.[52]

Ovid's impact at its most powerful and productive may be seen in a poem such as CB 83, which is one of at least ten[53] of Peter of Blois's compositions collected here. Peter opens with the winds of winter (*sevit aure spiritus*), but this is but foil against which to contrast the warmth of spring and the heat of love. Peter, too, plays with the topos of the service of love: the refrain begins *quam dulcia/ stipendia*, and if *stipendia* itself could have a range of other meanings ("tributes" or "taxes"), in the second strophe it becomes clear that he means his pay as a soldier in love's army (*nobili remuneror stipendio*, CB 83.2.3–4). This is thus a reference to *militia amoris*, but somewhat more subtle than many others.[54] He rejoices in the beauty of Flora, naked on the bed (*nudam fovet Floram lectus:/ caro candet tenera*), which would recall for any reader Ovid *Amores* 1.5.[55] The exploration of Flora's body lifts him above mortal heights: *Hominem transgredior/ et superum/ sublimari glorior/ ad numerum,/ sinum tractans tenerum* . . . (CB 83.4.1–5).

The last stanza of Peter's luscious song, indeed the climax of the poem, takes place in a thoroughly Ovidian space, a world that can only exist in the imagination of one who has read the *Metamorphoses*:

> O si forte Iupiter
> hanc videat,
> timeo, ne pariter
> incaleat

---

[52] 105.6.4b = *Rem.* 139b; 8.4 ~ *Ars* 2.501; 9.4 = *Ars* 2.607; 10.4 ~ *Ars* 2.625. The fourth verses of quatrains 7 and 11 also play with other verses from *Ars* 2 (435 and 624, respectively), but only directly cite one word in each case. For a study of this practice, see Schmidt (1990).

[53] Bernt (1979) 860.

[54] Peter plays with the topos more directly in another poem included in the CB: *Dudum militaveram/ nec poteram/ hoc frui stipendio* (72.1b.1–3).

[55] So beloved was *Am.* 1.5 that it inspired an imitation, *de somnio*, that circulated as one of Ovid's poems; see Lenz (1968). This poem begins *Nox erat, et placido capiebam pectore sompnum* and is to be distinguished from *Am.* 3.5, *Nox erat et somnus* . . .; on the latter, see Richmond, chapter 14 below. Both *Am.* 1.5 and 3.5 are copied separately in some medieval manuscripts, the first sometimes with the title *de meridie* (Walther (1969) no. 632), the latter as *de somno*.

et ad fraudes redeat:
si vel Danes pluens aurum
imbre dulci mulceat,
vel Europes intret taurum,
vel Ledeo candeat
rursus in olore. (83.7.1–10)

> If Jupiter should chance to see her, I fear that he would grow equally heated and return to his deceptions: either raining Danaë's gold he would suborn her with sweet shower, or enter Europa's bull, or appear once more as Leda's swan.

The return of the refrain may remind readers that this is a medieval song, but Peter's sovereign command of the Ovidian world, which he deploys not only artfully but as a virtual way of thinking, foreshadows some of the great *canzoni* of Petrarch, for instance *Rime sparse* 23, with its rich Ovidian mythography. The wind that blows here—the *aura* of the opening line—will under sunnier skies easily modulate into *l'aura*/Laura.

5. *Conclusion*

Exile, lover, poet of wisdom—the medieval Ovid was a conglomeration. As many of the examples above suggest, the various and multiple aspects of his persona combine playfully in medieval Latin texts. Peter of Blois's *Sevit aure spiritus* blends both love and mythological learning. The biographical speculations that circulated in many manuscripts link Ovid's exile to the poet's imagined involvement in a word of sexual mischief. As a work that combines all these elements, the thirteenth-century poem *De Vetula* can serve as a fitting conclusion to this partial survey of Ovid in the Middle Ages.[56] *De Vetula* purports to be Ovid's poetic autobiography, his last will and testament, as it were, rescued literally from his grave. Or so the literary fiction would have us believe. One of the *accessus* (known from its incipit as *Capta Troia*) which accompany the poem in the manuscripts explains it thus:

> When he fully learned from the letters of his friends that so long as Augustus was alive, he would never be recalled [from Tomis], he

---

[56] Best consulted in Klopsch (1967); the next year saw the publication of another edition, Robathan (1968). Its composition must fall between 1222 and 1268.

composed this tenth and last book, in which, despairing and seeking consolation from every quarter, he commemorated the mode of living he had when he gave himself over to love . . .[57]

Upon Ovid's death, this book was placed in his tomb; over a thousand years later it was discovered and made its way to a Latin-speaker in Byzantium, through whom it supposedly became available to readers in the Latin West.[58]

Despite the fact that it was a blatant literary fiction, *De Vetula* was often listed among Ovid's works, along with other pseudo-Ovidiana. Given its contents, not to mention the style of the nearly 2400 hexameters of its three books, no well-schooled reader of Ovid could have been deceived for very long. The actual author remains unknown, although its likely date (first half of the thirteenth century) sorts well with one name that has been suggested: Richard de Fournival.[59] Interest in Ovid was not limited to one individual, of course, and the poem had the popularity it did not only because of its racy content but because it touched on themes familiar, and of interest, to readers of Latin, by definition products of the contemporary education system in which Ovid played so large a part.

The frame of the literary fiction, including its various *accessus*, its *introit*, and other prefatory material refer to Ovid's exile.[60] The body of the poem offers us "Ovid"'s erotic autobiography, which moves (on its own terms) from an *ars amatoria* to a *remedium amoris*. The first book begins with Ovid's confession that at the beginning of his erotic life, he was obsessed with women:

> O quam carus erat michi quamque optabilis ille
> femineus sexus, sine quo nec vivere posse
> credebam quemcumque virum . . . (1.1–3)

> O how dear and how desirable was to me that feminine sex, without which I believed no man able to live . . .

---

[57] *Cumque per litteras amicorum suorum didicisset ad plenum, quod vivente Augusto revocari non posset, decimo et ultimo composuit librum istum, in quo iam desperatus et undecumque solaci sibi querens reducit ad memoriam modum suum vivendi, quem habuerat dum vacaret amori . . .*, Klopsch (1967) 280–81.

[58] For an excellent review of the topos, see Klopsch (1967) 22–34.

[59] On the question of authorship, see Klopsch (1967) 78–99. In the end, Klopsch thinks the attribution to Richard "unlikely" (*unwahrscheinlich*), but admits that it is not possible to exclude it unconditionally (99).

[60] The second preface smacks of the schoolroom: it raises the question why, since there are no descriptions of heroes, "Ovid" should have written hexameters instead of pentameters.

By the third book, this belief will be radically altered, but not before the author of *De Vetula* presents "Ovid" as both an everyman and a superman of heterosexuality.[61]

De Vetula was also popular because it touches on a vast range of fields and disciplines of interest to a thirteenth-century audience. It thus updates Ovid's learning and makes him a contemporary expert. "Ovid" details not just love but a whole gamut of popular leisure-time activities, including hunting, fishing, and even swimming. He then describes an astonishing range of indoor pastimes, including dice, chess, and other contemporary board games. These accounts involve the real poet in a tour-de-force of mathematical descriptions. Along the way, "Ovid" laments the decline of philosophical learning and lampoons lawyers.

The second book resumes his erotic autobiography. Opening with a denunciation of *semiviri*—eunuchs, but hitting quite likely all those whose sexual proclivities are 'unnatural'—"Ovid" goes on to give the actual history of the central love affair of his life, which has little to do with Corinna and the *Amores*. To be sure, we meet figures with analogues in the world of Roman love elegy: a beautiful girl and her older female companion, the *lena* in love elegy, here the old lady (*vetula*) who gives the poem its name. The old lady pretends to be a go-between, but the two women conspire in tricking "Ovid" out of his longed-for intercourse with the young beauty by substituting the "hag" herself—the 'bed-trick' of fabliaux.[62] "Ovid" meets her some twenty years later, after the beautiful young girl has married and born children. Now widowed and of course older, she consents to intercourse, which our 'hero' enjoys moderately, but clearly, the joys of the flesh are not the same at this more mature age.

In the third book, "Ovid" moves to put these earthly joys and vanities behind him. As "Ovid" turns successively to scholarly disciplines—philosophy, mathematics, geometry, music, and astronomy—Ovid the

---

[61] I use the term "heterosexuality" advisedly; for a somewhat fuller, but by no means exhaustive, discussion of these issues, see Hexter (1999) 340–44. The author of the *De Vetula* drew on discourses of sexuality rooted in the "nature" of Alan Lille's *Plaint of Nature* and *Anticlaudianus* (1182/3) and John of Hautville's *Architrenius* (1184).

[62] Not unwittily "Ovid'" describes this substitution in language drawing on "his own" *Metamorphoses*: ... *In nova formas/corpora mutatas cecini, mirabiliorque non reperitur ibi mutatio quam fuit ista,/scilicet, ut fuerit tam parvo tempore talis/taliter in talem vetulam mutata puella* (2.495–99). Bedtricks are not unknown to Ovid; the story of Myrrha in *Metamorphoses* 10 turns on one, but that is a very different motif.

poet of learning moves from worldly expertise to more sublime topics. As the characteristically lengthy glosses to the opening verses of the first book of the *Metamorphoses* testify, Ovid himself was read as a cosmologist, and "Ovid"'s speculations here fit with that tradition. His reasoning leads him to reflect on the first causes of the world. Ultimately, "Ovid" arrives at a prophesy of Christ's birth based on astrological lore. Indeed, learned in the tradition of prophesy in the Hebrew Bible, his prophesy includes a virgin birth, even if it—as well as the other Christian mysteries, such as the incarnation and the trinity—explicitly escapes his capacity to understand. He ends his book with hopes for salvation and a prayer to the virgin mother of god (*optima virgo*, 3.805).

De Vetula is by no means typical of the medieval Ovid, not even of the bulk of other pseudo-Ovidiana,[63] and yet it is a piece of the authentically medieval Ovid and for that reason it, too, along with the other medieval poems attributed to Ovid, provides another perspective on the adaptations Ovid—or "Ovid"—underwent in medieval Latin culture. *De Vetula* is, in another sense, perfectly representative, because it embodies and embroiders three of the more persistent aspects of Ovidian personae: the exile, the lover, and the poet of learning. No doubt what the shape-changing Ovid experiences in *De Vetula* is not up to the Roman poet's own standards of wit and elegance, but as he himself showed us, the metamorphic universe holds many surprises, and one thing is forever becoming another.

---

[63] Most of these build directly on or imitate canonical poems by Ovid. I provide a list of many of these poems in Hexter (1999) 339–40 (with bibliography in the attendant notes, 349–50).

CHAPTER FOURTEEN

MANUSCRIPT TRADITIONS AND THE TRANSMISSION OF OVID'S WORKS

John Richmond

Introduction[1]

All study of Ovid ultimately is based on our imperfect knowledge of what he actually wrote. That knowledge depends almost entirely on some hundreds of manuscripts preserved in a multitude of libraries, situated for the most part in Western Europe. The versions of the text that they give all differ to a greater or lesser degree, and scholars must try to divine the errors that obscure the truth. In places where the manuscripts disagree none of them may be right,[2] and even where they are unanimous there is no guarantee that what they show is what Ovid wrote.[3] This chapter will give a sketch of the complex process by which the poems came down to us, first looking generally at the common factors in the process, and then examining in more detail the different traditions of the various works or groups of works. It will not be possible to discuss all the special problems that occur in the extensive ramifications of the tradition.

---

[1] Unless otherwise stated, all *sigla*, collations, and line numbers are taken from the standard text-editions listed in the General Bibliography. The dating of manuscripts occasions differences of opinions among scholars: the dates I give have often been influenced by Munk Olsen (1982–89). In indicating the contents of manuscripts I have usually ignored minor omissions. Unless otherwise indicated manuscripts from Antwerp are in the Museum Plantin-Moretus, from Berlin are in the Staatsbibliothek zu Berlin (Preussischer Kulturbesitz), from Brussels are in the Bibliothèque Royale, from Florence are in the Bibliotheca Medicea Laurenziana, from London are in the British Library, from Milan are in the Biblioteca Ambrosiana, from Oxford are in the Bodleian Library, from Paris are in the Bibliothèque Nationale, from St. Gall are in the Stiftsbibliothek. In the Bibliography to save space I have not included particulars of editions of works by Ovid and other ancient authors referred to in this chapter by the editor's name with place and date of publication.

[2] Thus at *Ars* 1.620 the manuscripts give *subetur, subitur, sudetur, cauatur, salitur*—all are wrong.

[3] E.g., *Met.* 1.580: the *eridanus* of all the manuscripts is wrong.

General

1. *Before the Carolingian Renaissance*

Scholia; inscriptions; quotations in ancient books; late antique codices

The history of the transmission of Ovid's works in the centuries after
their publication is wrapped in obscurity. In the prefatory epigram,
he tells us that his *Amores* appeared in a first edition in five books,
and that the present edition in three books omitted some poems con-
tained in the earlier edition. Nothing can be identified as belonging
to the first edition.[4] The 'single' *Heroides* (1–14—if they are all Ovid's)
inspired replies written by Sabinus (*Am.* 2.18.27); Ovid, it seems, then
wrote three sets of double epistles (16–21), so publication was in at
least two stages.[5] He claims he burned his unrevised *Metamorphoses*
in disgust as he went into exile, but that copies survived at Rome
(*Tr.* 1.7.13–30). He asked that six verses extenuating faults (*Tr.*
1.7.35–40) be prefixed to those copies, and Luck[6] believes that they
were prefixed to the first edition. They are found written in some
manuscripts before (or occasionally after) the *Metamorphoses*, though
editors usually (and rightly, I believe), omit them as additions by
scribes.[7] Some scholars think this lack of formal 'publication' may
explain the existence of differing versions of a few passages in the
long poem. There is a brief discussion later in this chapter. The
Fasti, as they have been transmitted, show (almost exclusively in Book
1) signs of revision after the death of Augustus (A.D. 14) to permit
a new dedication to Germanicus.[8] The poems of *Tristia* 1, 3–5 and
Ex Ponto 1–3 may have been sent individually to their recipients: in

---

[4] See Boyd, chapter 3 above; for further speculation on the first edition and the
complex question of the chronology of the *Amores*, see Oliver (1945) and McKeown
1:74–89 (with references to other discussions).

[5] See Knox, chapter 4 above.

[6] Luck 2:67.

[7] Munari (1957) indicates the manuscripts containing them; thus of his 40 Vatican
manuscripts they are contained in Vat. lat. 2781 (s. XIV–XV), Vat. lat. 5179 (s.
XIII¹), Vat. lat. 5859 (a. 1275), Chis. H.VI.203 (s. XV), Chis. H.VII.230 (s. XIV),
Ottob. lat. 3313 (s. XI), Pal. lat. 1663 (s. XIII–XIV), Pal. lat. 1664 (s. XIII).

[8] At *Tr.* 2.549 Ovid states that the *Fasti* were dedicated to Augustus, but incom-
plete at the time of his exile (cf. Bömer, *F.* 1:17–19); it seems to be a fair infer-
ence that they had not yet been published. We cannot decide on the evidence we
possess how far Ovid progressed in writing the planned twelve books, how much
was published, and when (see Miller, chapter 6 above).

the form in which we have them they evidently were collected in books by the author and then published.[9] He was famous from his youth, and his works were widely known and very popular for the first few centuries of their existence. Readers of the *Metamorphoses*, of the *Fasti*, and especially of the *Ibis* needed explanatory comment. Some material from late antique commentary survives in the 'Lactantian' summaries[10] found in manuscripts of the *Metamorphoses* and in the farrago of medieval scholia on the *Ibis*: we cannot say when these comments were compiled.

Ovid's influence on poetry is to be seen in the works of later poets and in the very many verse inscriptions gathered in the epigraphic collections.[11] Later prose-writers also quote him, especially Seneca. As it was not easy to find passages quickly in ancient books (especially in papyrus rolls), it is probable that quotations were nearly always made from fallible memory, unless Ovid was appealed to in a case where the *ipsissima uerba* were of importance. When poets used Ovid, they naturally took a free hand in making any variations that they wished. Consequently, it is not easy to decide in all cases whether such **indirect transmission** has value for establishing exactly what Ovid wrote. The grammarians were a special case, and they made use of Ovid's poetry, and especially of the *Metamorphoses*, as an authority.[12]

As examples we may note (i) *Am.* 3.4.4, a verse quoted by Seneca (*Ben.* 4.14.1) with *licuit . . . dedit . . . dedit* for the *liceat . . . facit . . . facit* of the manuscript tradition—editors prefer the latter; (ii) *Ars* 2.300, where two grammarians (Charisius p. 104K, and Priscian in *GLK* 2.333.16) give *sumpsit*, preferred by editors to the *sumit/sumat* of the surviving manuscript tradition; (iii) *Tr.* 1.11.11–12, where a lost inscription from Padua,[13] though it wrongly inserted an unmetrical *est* into v. 11, preserved in v. 12 the correct *cura cura leuata* for the *cura mens releuata* given in the manuscripts (which evidently resulted from the loss of *cura* by haplography and a subsequent attempt to restore meter and sense).

---

[9] Each book of the *Tristia* was published separately; *Ex Ponto* 1–3 were published as one work, but the fourth book appears to have been published posthumously; see Froesch (1968).

[10] Cf. Otis (1936), Tarrant (1995a), and p. 31, below.

[11] On verse inscriptions see Lissberger (1934).

[12] A useful index to the passages of Ovid quoted in grammatical works is to be found in *GLK* vol. 7 (but cf. Housman (1922)).

[13] *CIL* 6.2.9632.

The **direct transmission** consists of surviving manuscripts that have descended from lines of successive copies of Ovid's originals. (These can occasionally be supplemented by information recorded by earlier scholars from manuscripts now lost.) The different works were transmitted to us by different channels. Modern scholars sometimes attempt to discern features of the format of the most recent common ancestor (or 'archetype')[14] of all surviving manuscripts of any particular work, but in Ovid the clues are insufficient to give significant results.[15] The poet worked on writing tablets,[16] and fair copies were prepared by him or by another on papyrus rolls. Further copies were made for friends or for commercial circulation. In the centuries after Ovid's death the *codex* (a book made of 'gatherings' of leaves folded in pages and bound in the modern fashion) gradually supplanted the roll form, and parchment, being more durable, was preferred to papyrus for preserving documents. This was an important change, as the new material could last for centuries, and gave books a much greater chance of surviving the Dark Ages, when Ovid was little read and seldom copied. No papyrus of Ovid survives, and the only remnant of an early *codex* is that of the *Ex Ponto* known as **G**:[17] a badly damaged and barely legible pair of small fragments (parts of 4.9.101–8; 127–33 and 4.12.15–19; 41–44) written in uncial script of the second half of the fifth century. If it correctly reads *sit* at 4.9.103 for the *est* of all other manuscripts, as other editors believe,[18] then **G** represents a lost branch of the tradition, because that reading is nowhere else to be found. The other unique errors it contains probably arose when it was last copied, as they are of a kind that would inevitably be noticed and soon subjected to attempts at correction (e.g., 4.9.108 *fato* for *facto*; 4.9.132 *miss* for *misi*). As there are no signs of corrections, it seems the *codex* was

---

[14] In the lines of descent from an archetype we may often infer the existence of one or more 'hyparchetypes'—the latest common ancestors of groups of manuscripts that share distinguishing characteristics, e.g., Γ, the ancestor of **A V G H L4 P** of the *Tristia*, cf. p. 476, below.

[15] Most recently, Luck (1969).

[16] So Ovid asserts, but *tabulae* and δέλτοι were secure in the poetic tradition; Horace (Brink (1971) on Hor. *Ars* 388–89) is the earliest writer clearly to mention using parchment for drafts.

[17] Wolfenbüttel, Aug 4° 13.11. Lowe gives a description at *CLA* IX 1376, 1377, and decides "presumably Italian"; Bischoff (1966–81) 2:325 suspects it came from Bobbio.

[18] I dissent for reasons given in Richmond vi.

very little read. The leaves were cleaned and re-used at the beginning of the eighth century to write a text in the script of Luxeuil. In the fourth and fifth centuries efforts were made in aristocratic circles at Rome to prepare corrected editions of the classical Latin authors; little is known of the effects of these efforts.[19] Nothing else survives of the direct transmission of Ovid before the Carolingian Renaissance. With the triumph of Christianity, the establishment of a new morality, the collapse of the Western Roman Empire and its book trade, and the decline of literacy and learning in the Latin-speaking West, it was natural that the popularity of Ovid should fade, and that copies of his works should become scarce. Some verses ascribed to Isidore of Seville (*ob.* 636) appear to imply that his library contained "Naso" but one cannot be sure how many of the works were in question.[20] Aldhelm of Malmesbury (c. 639–709) apparently had some access to Ovid.[21] No doubt there were some works of Ovid copied in the 'national' scripts that developed in different regions in the centuries after the collapse of the Western Empire, but nothing of Ovid survives in such manuscripts. Those early manuscripts, like all others, were exposed to accidents of transmission, but liability to error was increased by the frequent lack of word division in the exemplar (as in *codex* **G**, already mentioned), by the misreading of unfamiliar script or older systems of abbreviation, and by the substitution (either deliberate or accidental) in an ancient text of what was familiar to the later scribe for what had become with the passage of time strange or unintelligible in form or meaning. The commencement of a new poem within a book was often indicated by a marginal diacritical mark, a larger initial letter, or one or more blank lines, and it seems that these indications were sometimes overlooked or misunderstood by later scribes.[22] In short, the decline of learning and literacy, the new scripts, the profound social and intellectual changes, and the accelerating alterations in the forms and pronunciation of words made the transmission of texts very precarious.

---

[19] Cf. Zetzel (1981) 206–54 and Jocelyn's review (1983).

[20] Migne *PL* 83:1109 (No. IX); his quotations, listed in Manitius (1900) 729, may often have been taken indirectly through intermediaries.

[21] Despite the parallels between his *aen.* 95 and Ovid *Met.* 14 (details in Ehwald (1919) 142), he may not have had access to more than quotations or excerpts.

[22] Cf. Heyworth (1995a) for a good discussion.

2. *The Carolingian Renaissance; Eighth to Tenth Centuries*

Texts copied and revised: glosses and variants

The great impetus given to learning in the monastic and cathedral schools under Charlemagne in the second half of the eighth century saw the serious organization of the copying of classical texts in a number of centers. Religious foundations in Northern and Central France were to play a significant part in the transmission of the Ovidian works. Theodulf(us) (c. 760–821), who was of Visigothic origin, abbot of Fleury, and later Bishop of Orleans, already showed acquaintance with the works of Ovid.[23] It was necessary to seek out the texts that were becoming ever scarcer. Old luxury copies might be expected to have a good text, and they certainly would be easier to read than any in the 'national' scripts that became prevalent from the sixth century. When old parchments written in uncial script came to the end of their life, they were frequently washed and reused (as in the case of the fragments from the *Ex Ponto* mentioned above) in order to make 'palimpsest'[24] copies of other works in the newer scripts.

By the eighth century the vernacular Latin language had changed considerably from the classical form. From the ninth century we have a *codex* of *Ars* 1 (**O**, see below) with glosses of an elementary nature, explaining in Latin or in Welsh even quite simple words, and features of life in the classical period that were no longer familiar. Explanatory glosses were often indicated with '.i.' for *id est* or 's' for *scilicet*, and variant readings by the use of an abbreviation for *uel*, but glosses could be either accidentally understood as variants, or deliberately introduced to the text as easier readings. Texts used for teaching Latin needed editorial work to purge the old exemplars of errors arising from simple mis-copying, and of orthographic and grammatical errors. With more or less success the texts were corrected by the application of the grammarians' rules for orthography,

---

[23] The parallels indicated in the *apparatus* of Duemmler – Traube (1881–96) 1:437–581 imply Theodulph's knowledge of *Am., Ars, Rem., Met., Fast., Tr.,* and *Pont.* It was suggested (Tafel (1910) 35–39, 53–57) that the *codex* (**α**, cf. p. 461, below) from which the older texts of the amatory works derive may have had a Spanish origin, but Kenney (1962) 24 is rightly skeptical. The poetry of the Carolingian period shows considerable Ovidian influence, cf. Manitius (1899) 730.

[24] On palimpsests see Lowe (1972) 2:480–519.

accidence, syntax, and meter.[25] Attempts at orthographic correction both removed later corruptions and tended to eliminate older spelling that may have survived, and even to introduce errors.[26] Typical orthographic changes included restoring lost *h*, distinguishing *ae* from *e*, and substituting unassimilated for assimilated forms of compound words. The more unusual Greek words presented a serious difficulty, as any knowledge of Greek was rare and the temptation to change the unknown to the known was strong. Thus, names like *Atlas* with genitive *Atlantis* are often given a nominative in *-ans* on the analogy of words like *dans, dantis*.[27] In addition, accusatives like *Argon* (from *Argo* (*Her.* 6.65)) and *Didon* (*Her.* 7.7, 135) show rare terminations replaced by those more familiar. For Ovid Carolingian copies are the earliest continuous sources of information about the text. However, the study of Ovid was apparently not very widespread in the ninth century, despite the literary echoes in poets of the period: few Ovidian manuscripts from the ninth century survive or are attested in library catalogues.[28] The evidence from catalogues and from the collections of excerpts known as *libri manuales* also indicates that Ovid's works were slow to gain popularity even in the tenth century.[29] In general Carolingian scribes appear to have copied their exemplars carefully, often leaving illegible passages blank, to have had recourse to other manuscripts if available, and to have noted variants, but to have been sparing in attempts to correct unintelligible texts.

For most Ovidian works much depends on what survives from the ninth and tenth centuries. One may take an instance from the *Metamorphoses* (a work preserved wholly or partially in over 450 *codices*). At *Met.* 6.58 the transmission gives *feriunt* with the exception of **M** (= Florence, San Marco 225 (s. XI)), which has *feriu* substituted for the original script by the second hand followed by *nt* written by the

---

[25] Traube (1911) 101 cites a *capitulare* of Charlemagne *anno* 789, c. 71 (correctly 72; Boretius (1883) 60) claiming it directed that attention be given to correcting orthography and punctuation in manuscripts; in fact it simply directs that copies of religious and various non-literary texts be emended, without specifying how. No doubt the precautions to remove scribal errors from literary works (*emendatio*) continued from antiquity.

[26] Goold (1965) 9–14.

[27] *Atlans* was already common in late antiquity as may be seen from the early Virgilian *codices*, and the difference in pronunciation between *-as* and *-ans* was little or nothing.

[28] For catalogues consult Munk Olsen (1995) 73 n. 1 (= (1987) 89 n. 4).

[29] McGregor (1978), Munk Olsen (1995) 29–30 (= (1984–85) 177).

first hand. However, a tenth-century fragment (β = London Addit. 11967) reads *pauent* which enables the restoration of the correct *pauiunt*.[30]

The earliest Ovidian manuscripts

The importance for Ovid's works of the copies made in the Carolingian period and their immediate successors of the tenth and eleventh centuries makes it convenient here to take a general view of their varying fortunes.

The fragment of the *Halieutica* (mistakenly) ascribed to Ovid survives in a French manuscript dating from the late eighth or early ninth century; a second French manuscript of the ninth century may be an independent witness and has been ascribed to the abbey of Fleury.[31] The *Amores* are transmitted by two ninth-century French *codices* that do not overlap, but give almost the whole work, and by one eleventh-century Italian manuscript. The *Ars Amatoria* is transmitted in one French *codex* of the ninth century, and there is also a ninth-century Insular *codex* for Book 1 only; there are two *codices* of the eleventh century (one Italian, one (fragmentary) German or Swiss). The text of *Remedia Amoris* primarily depends on one ninth-century French and two eleventh-century Italian *codices*. The *Ex Ponto* is transmitted in one ninth-century *codex* (French) that unfortunately ceases after 3.2.67; two German manuscripts of the twelfth century are the next best for the whole work. Substantial fragments of one ninth-century French copy of a Carolingian *codex* survive for the *Heroides*, but unfortunately it seems to have been copied from a exemplar that was in very poor condition, and the rest of the tradition (which includes one incomplete eleventh-century South Italian manuscript) is more corrupt, and gives little help. The *Metamorphoses* have some substantial fragments from the ninth and tenth centuries (one in Insular script, three French, one German, one Italian) containing between them most of the poem to 8.104 but nothing after; complete (or nearly complete) texts date from the eleventh century. The *Fasti* are found in three eleventh-century manuscripts (one from France ceases at 5.24, one from Mon-

---

[30] N. Heinsius independently thought of *pauiunt*, but rejected it, deciding *feriunt* was defended by Varro *LL* 5.113, and by Seneca's loose quotation of this passage at *Epist.* 90.20, where a minority of the witnesses gives *feriunt*, as opposed to the *pariunt* of the older manuscripts from which Gruter had conjectured *pauiunt*.

[31] Cf. Richmond (1998) for details.

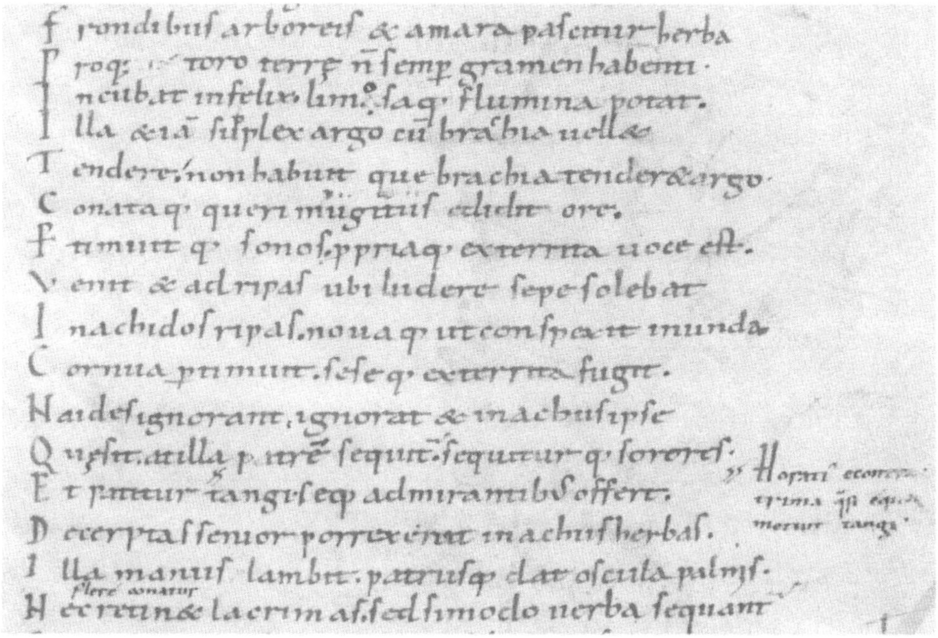

Pl. I. *Caroline minuscule*: London Harl. 2610 (= ε) (s. X), fol. 11r., Ovid *Met.* 1.632-47. There is a marginal reference to Horace *carm.* 3.11.9-10.

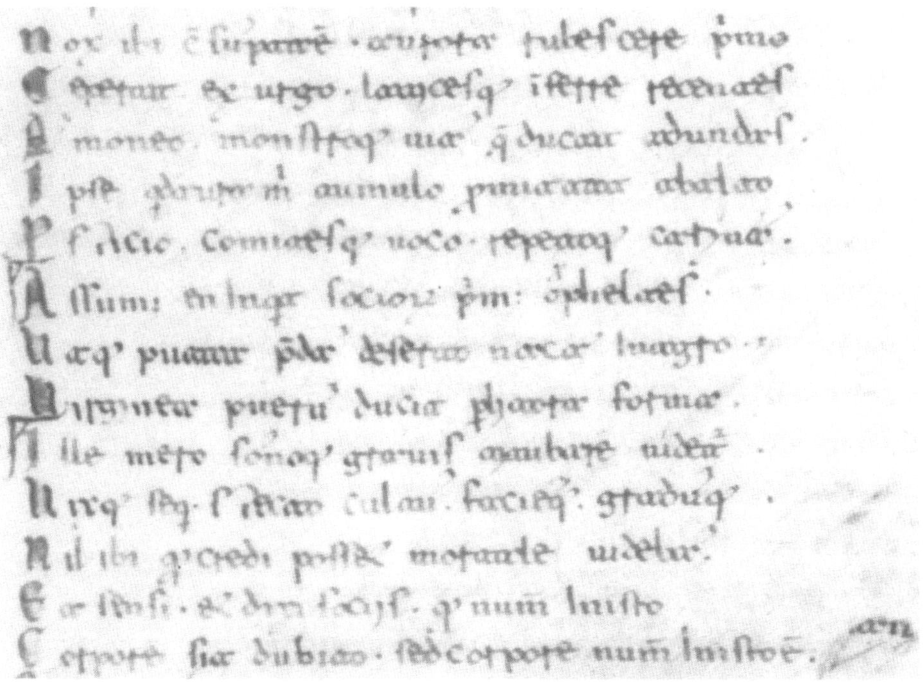

Pl. II. *Beneventan script*: Vatican City Urbin. lat. 341 (= U) (s. XI^ex.), fol. 36r., Ovid *Met.* 3.600-612.

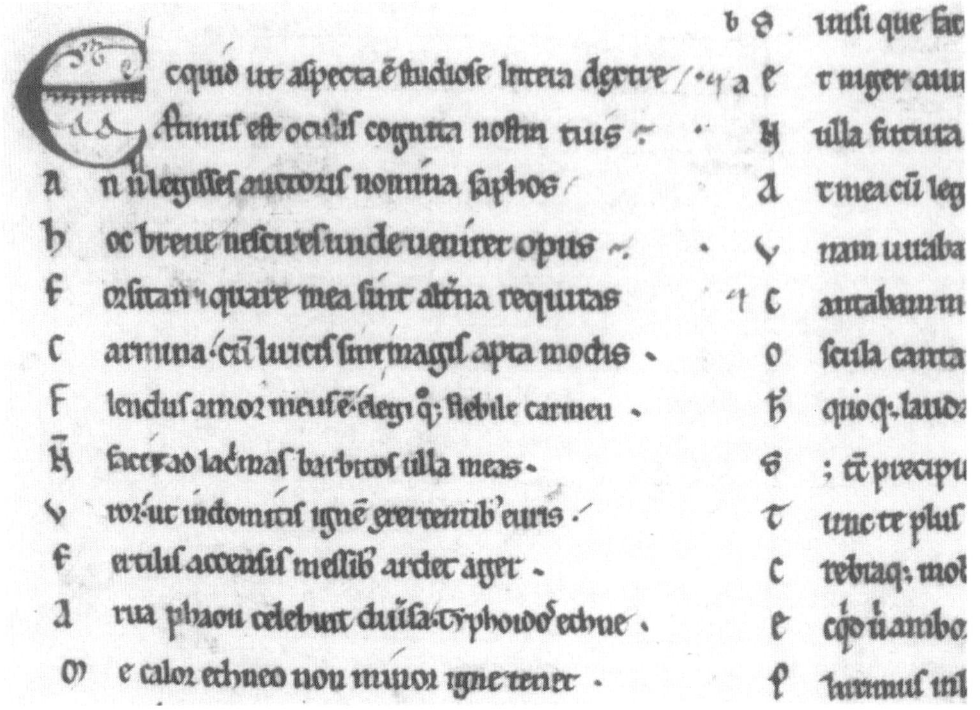

Pl. III. *Gothic script*: Frankfurt-am-Main S. Barthol. 110 (= **F**) (s. XII^{ex.}), fol. 133v., Ovid [?] *Ep.* 15.1-12 and parts of 39,38,40-50. Note 'b' 'a' in margin to restore order of misplaced verses.

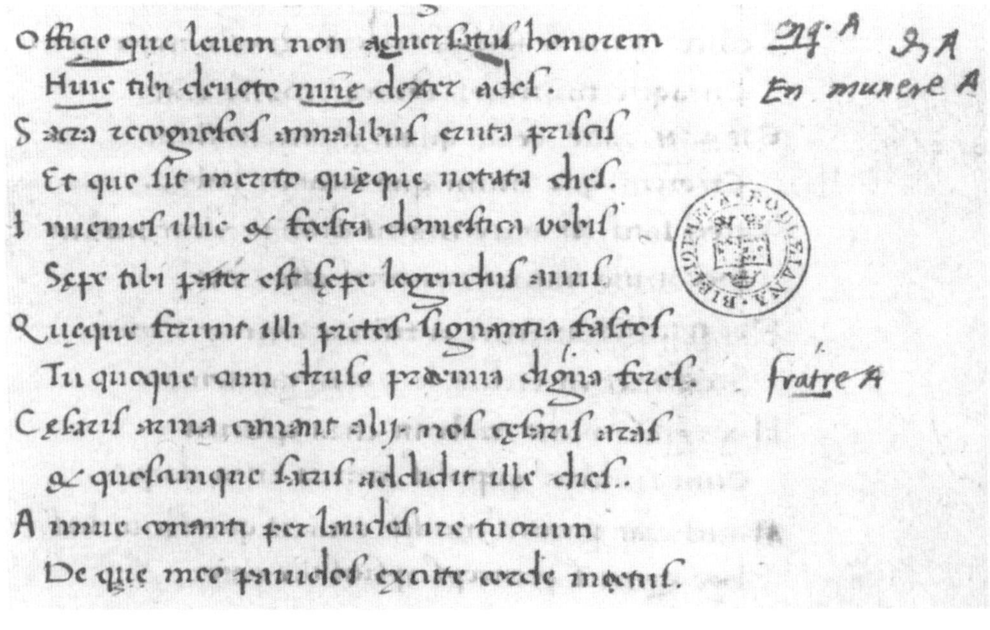

Pl. IV. *Humanist script*: Oxford Auct. F. 4. 25 (= **M**) (s. XV^{in.}), fol. 3r., Ovid *Fast.* 1.5-16. In the right margin are collations in the hand of N. Heinsius.

tecassino is complete, one from Belgium has lost most of Book 1 and some of Book 6). The *Tristia* have a poor tradition, and the earliest witness consists of two almost illegible leaves (?German) dating from the tenth century. The editor's next resources are a lacunose manuscript of the eleventh century that contains 1.5.11–3.7.1 and 4.1.12–7.5, and an Italian *codex* of the late eleventh century. The best witness (?Italian) for the *Medicamina Faciei Femineae* dates from the eleventh century. (The tradition of the probably spurious *Nux*, as will be seen, is closely connected with that of the *Medicamina*.) The tradition of the *Ibis* begins only in the late twelfth century.

The Caroline minuscule script (see **Plate I**)

The reform of script[32] that took place in the Carolingian *scriptoria* forced the monks to alter the writing conventions in their exemplars. In particular the use of changing systems of abbreviation had a fertile potential for error.[33] It was easier for subsequent scribes to copy from a manuscript in the new script than to transcribe an older exemplar. Frequently, as in the case of the *Heroides*, we find that the tradition of a work seems to have passed, so to say, though a bottleneck about the year A.D. 800. The new script became quickly diffused. Though additional texts written in older scripts might be compared with recent copies, and some of the older readings noted in the newer copies, inevitably this was a hit-and-miss process, and much was lost. However, it did mean that stray readings could, so to say, slip through the bottleneck.

The Beneventan script (see **plate II**)

This script,[34] which was independently developed at Montecassino in Southern Italy, an area well removed from the imperial center of gravity in Northern France and Western Germany, was used from the eighth, and survived even after the fifteenth century. That remoteness and the individuality of the script meant that less influence was exerted by South Italian centers on the tradition of Ovid than might otherwise have happened. Thus, the two *codices* Naples IV F 3 (s. XI^ex.–XII^in. = **N**) and Vatican City Urbin. lat. 341 (s. XI^ex. = **U**)

---

[32] Traube (1911) 25–30 gives a summary account of the complex origins of the script.

[33] Lindsay (1963) provides a guide through the maze.

[34] Full description and history in Loew (1980).

written in Beneventan script have a special place in the tradition of the *Metamorphoses*.

Florilegia

Here one may remark the making of anthologies of short excerpts, the *florilegia*. Our earliest surviving examples were made for proso-diacal and grammatical purposes from the early ninth century;[35] and from the twelfth century[36] we find Ovidian passages that were selected to teach literature and morality. There was no very strong desire to give the *ipsissima uerba* of the author quoted. Nevertheless one must reckon with the possibility that a *florilegium* was copied from a manu-script of Ovid with readings better than those that now survive. Unfortunately, the *florilegia* have little to contribute for the criticism of Ovid's works. The most significant of these compendia is the *Florilegium Gallicum*, a vast anthology from the Latin poets.[37]

3. Eleventh to Thirteenth Centuries; The Aetas Ovidiana

In the troubled years immediately after the death of Charlemagne there was rather a lull, but the study of Ovid began slowly to regain impetus in the eleventh century,[38] a period of political and intellec-tual recovery. Ovid's popularity soon became so great that Traube styled the following two hundred years the *Aetas Ovidiana*. Yet even in the twelfth century Ovid was less read than Virgil, Horace, Terence, Lucan, Statius, and Juvenal, if one is to judge by the number of manuscripts now extant.[39] However, all the surviving works of Ovid were sought out, copied, and studied. Some *scriptoria* gathered into a single volume all the Ovidian works that could be found and often

---

[35] Duemmler – Traube (1881–96) 3:265–74.
[36] Paris lat. 8069 (cf. p. 459, below) is a rare example from the eleventh cen-tury: Munk Olsen (1995) 80 n. 1 (= (1987) 91 n. 20).
[37] Burton (1983) has an introductory discussion (1–45), and a text of some of the Ovidian excerpts (200–225, 248–73).
[38] Munk Olsen (1995) 80–82 (= (1987) 76–77) makes the interesting observation that several manuscripts recorded in the medieval library catalogues of this century were texts of Ovid that had belonged to monks who were teachers.
[39] Details in Munk Olsen (1995) 29–30 (= (1984–85) 177). The figures may be distorted because copies in private hands were less likely to survive than those held in institutional libraries (cf. Munk Olsen (1995) 93–94 (= (1987) 88)).

included spurious works with the genuine. An important example is
Frankfurt-am-Main, S. Barthol. 110 written in different hands at
different dates. It includes the *Epistula Sapphus* (= *Heroides* 15), which
(save for excerpts in the *Florilegium Gallicum*) is not found in any other
codex earlier than the fifteenth century. It is worth setting out the
contents of this Frankfurt *codex*, as they show a determination to
gather everything written by Ovid, and include many spurious works:
Nux, Philomela, Cuculus, De Med. Aurium, De Somnio,[40] **Metamorphoses,
De Vino, Ars Amatoria, Remedia Amoris, Amores, Ibis, De
Somnio,**[41] **Epistula Sapphus**, *De Humoribus, De Nemore, Pulex*,
Heroides (1–14; 16–21), **Fasti, Ex Ponto, Tristia**. (The works indi-
cated in bold type were transcribed towards the end of the twelfth
century; the others not earlier than the late thirteenth.) The only
genuine work missing is the fragmentary *Medicamina Faciei Femineae*.
Similarly Tours 879 (s. XII–XIII) collected all the genuine works
with the exception of the *Medicamina*, and added the spurious *Pulex*
and *de Pediculo*.

At this time, when familiarity with Ovid was growing and facil-
ity in imitating his style increasing, it was natural that many spuri-
ous works should be written and attributed to Ovid,[42] and then
gathered in collections and included in excerpts. Scribes who saw,
detected, or fancied they perceived lacunae in their exemplars did
not scruple to fill them out with phrases and verses of their own
composition. Later scribes or readers finding different supplements
in different *codices* conflated or altered what they found, and these
parasitic growths flourished from a laudable desire to lose nothing
of what was believed to be, or possibly to be, ancient. (A glance at
Dörrie's *apparatus* to *Her.* 9.81–84 will show the process beginning
with a marginal addition in the ninth-century *codex* Paris lat. 8242
(= **P**) and quickly proliferating in later manuscripts.) From the ninth
century onwards, if not earlier, fugitive pieces from antiquity were
included with or within the genuine works: the *De Somn(i)o* (= *Am.*
3.5), the *Epistula Sapphus* (= *Heroides* 15), and the *Nux*.

From the beginning of the twelfth century, though the monastic
system was expanding, cathedral schools begin to rival and outstrip

---

[40] A medieval poem: text in Lehmann (1927) 63–65.

[41] I.e., [Ov.] *Am.* 3.5.

[42] Summary accounts of the medieval Ovidian *spuria* will be found in Lenz (1959)
and Lehmann (1927) 2–15.

the monastic schools, and education to spread outside clerical circles.[43] During the eleventh century a new script, Gothic, was gradually developing from the Caroline minuscule and later displaced it. (**See Plate III.**) Whatever its aesthetic merits, it lost some of the legibility of the earlier script.

Educational change

The University of Paris was formally recognized about A.D. 1200 and became a dominant intellectual institution. The introduction of Aristotle to the curriculum and the development of scholasticism resulted in a concentration on logic and the introduction of a new type of grammar largely divorced from the study of the classical authors.[44] Despite the new approach in grammatical and literary studies some centers, such as Orleans, maintained the traditional study of classical literature. Municipal elementary schools continued to proliferate and stimulated a demand for texts of Ovidian poetry.

The multiplication of texts and the classroom use of them led to a constant process of 'contamination': texts were compared, glosses were added, variants were noted or substituted for the original text, conjectures were made, and they were then diffused through the tradition. Teachers had an interest in easy variants that could be understood by them and their pupils, but also tended to cling to what they had learned. For most Ovidian works a comparatively large number of *codices* survives from the twelfth or thirteenth century showing a state of text distinct from that precariously preserved in earlier periods. For them it is impossible to construct any useful *stemma codicum*, because the relationships were so intricate, and because so much of the tradition has been lost irretrievably.

4. The Renaissance[45]

The fourteenth and fifteenth centuries were to see in Italy the growth of a new spirit, which fostered a fresh approach to the classical authors. Petrarch at the beginning of the period urged the creation

---

[43] In Italy some secular tradition of education had always persisted.

[44] Minnis and Scott (1991) provide orientation.

[45] Sabbadini (1967a and b) gives a good general account of the results of the searches in the libraries. With the exception of the *Ibis* the genuine works of Ovid were already known to the humanists.

of public libraries that would store in security the manuscripts that had to be rescued from the monastic libraries, where the classical works were often housed negligently at a time of decline in the monasteries. States and individuals in Italy devoted themselves to the task of rescue, preservation, and propagation. This work was in the hands of the humanist scholars, men whose great talents were not always matched by integrity of character. The competitive situation in which they found themselves, their entire devotion to rescuing the classics from the monasteries, and their obsession with fame inclined them to actions and claims sometimes unscrupulous. A great part of the manuscripts of this period was written by Italian copyists. They used the new 'humanist' script devised by a few influential scholars about the beginning of the fifteenth century, who looked back to the Caroline minuscule. (**See Plate IV.**) The new script combined elegance, simplicity, and fluency and suited the new paper books that began slowly to supplant the durable but expensive parchment. The humanists had a confidence in their knowledge and taste that led them boldly to alter texts. When they were working on Ovidian exemplars of the twelfth or thirteenth centuries that had already been subjected to contemporary conjecture and enriched with the variants of earlier ages, the result is often a copy where the tradition may be seriously obscured. Nevertheless the conjectures may be acute, and stray items of tradition not found elsewhere may be preserved. The humanists traveled and corresponded widely, and many older *codices* now lost were then still available. Most *codices* of this period, often conveniently named '*Itali*' in the *apparatus critici*, are principally valuable only for the conjectures they may contain; but occasionally, when important tradition survives in them, they merit special mention.[46] The contacts between Venice and Constantinople in the thirteenth and fourteenth centuries had a curious result in the production of Greek translations of the Amatory Works, the *Heroides*, and the *Metamorphoses* by the Byzantine monk Maximus Planudes (c. 1255–1305), who served as ambassador to Venice. These literal translations usually enable one to reconstruct the readings of the Latin manuscripts translated. Those manuscripts were not of high quality, but sometimes

---

[46] Cf. Pasquali (1962) 43–108. Two cases in the transmission of Ovid are the Gudianus (= **Gu**) of the *Heroides* (see p. 463, below), and the Mazarinianus (= **M**) of the *Fasti* (see n. 88, below).

are useful,[47] and the translator's knowledge of Greek and of Greek myths often enabled him to restore Greek proper names that had been seriously corrupted by Western scribes.

5. *The invention of printing*[48]

A decisive change in the process of transmission came with the invention of printing from moveable type, and (from c.1470) with the printing of classical texts. All the genuine and some of the spurious works of Ovid were printed in 1471 in the *editiones principes* of Sweynheym and Pannartz at Rome, and of F. Puteolanus at Bologna. The Roman edition, though it drew on Florence San Marco 225 (s. XI) and other good manuscripts, and was superior to the Bolognese edition, was to have little influence until it was used by Naugerius for the second Aldine edition (Venice 1515–16). This neglect may have resulted from the fact that most of the incunabula of Ovid were published at Venice and other north Italian cities adjacent to Bologna. Bad marketing of the Roman edition may also have played a part in its eclipse.[49] Jacobus Rubeus used the Bolognese edition for his edition (Venice 1474), and he drew on other manuscripts adding from them the passage *Her.* 21.15–146. Stephanus Corallus at Parma in 1477 made an important contribution in adding from a "*uetustissimus codex*," which is now lost, two passages of the *Heroides* (16.39–144 and 21.147–250) missing from the rest of the tradition. Unfortunately, Corallus seems to have made no use of his *uetustissimus codex* for the rest of the *Heroides*, but merely to have copied the Bolognese *editio princeps* of 1471 and the additions to it of Rubeus.[50] Almost all the many early editions that followed (mostly published at Venice), including the first of Aldus (Venice 1503), depended on these editions of Rubeus and Corallus. The printers of the fifteenth century took a recent printed edition, corrected some evident errors, whether of the press or of the tradition, and had recourse to such manuscripts (if any) as were readily available to seek help in passages where they suspected corruption. The consequent multiplica-

---

[47] E.g., Planudes is the only source for *forma* (*Her.* 17.167) conjectured by Bentley and accepted in Kenney (1996).

[48] Kenney (1995b) and Steiner (1952) give useful accounts.

[49] Kenney (1995b) 18.

[50] Dörrie (1960) 369–70.

tion of cheaper copies provided a fixity of tradition that could not be secured by manuscripts. The early printers, like the contemporary copyists whom they were gradually supplanting, worked from the materials to hand and permitted themselves freedom in arriving at a readable text. Unfortunately, having printed their books they often had no interest in preserving the manuscripts from which they worked. When once a text was in print, even manuscript copies were often made by scribes from a printed text: printed copies were very much more readily available than manuscripts, and were often more legible. If printed editions have had recourse to manuscripts now lost, their readings may bear independent witness to the tradition just as well as do manuscripts. No complete work of Ovid, however, depends solely on an *editio princeps* or other early printing.

6. *The rise of critical editing*

Early publishers of Ovid had commercial motives, and economic pressure forced hasty publication. Naturally an intelligible and accurately printed text had a greater appeal than one that lacked those qualities, but most readers hardly worried greatly about corruption that did not obtrude on them. However, efforts were made to satisfy an immediate demand for explanatory commentary. Some scholars had realized both the importance of establishing an authentic text and the laborious work necessary to do so, especially A. Politianus (1454–94), who died before he could make the impact that his insight promised. At Venice the scholar-publisher Aldus Manutius (1449–1515) had higher ambitions than had inspired other publishers, and he made more effort to restore the authentic texts of the ancient world. The critical work of A. Naugerius, who edited the second Aldine edition of Ovid's works (Venice 1515–16), included the consultation of the Roman and Bolognese first editions in addition to the *textus receptus* represented by the first Aldine, and he used some manuscripts now lost. Naugerius made significant improvements to the text and set a standard for subsequent editors. The conditions under which they worked were difficult, and, because they were feeling their way, their work tended to be haphazard and vague. G. Bersmannus (Leipzig 1582) attempted an advance on Naugerius. The work on Ovid of Nicolaus Heinsius (1620–81), "*sospitator poetarum Latinorum,*" marked an epoch. It was not all incorporated in his own edition

(Amsterdam 1659–61). From the abundant and meticulously accurate marginal collations made by him in several printed editions of Ovid we get some access to the many manuscripts he examined.[51] Some of the manuscripts he consulted are now lost. Unfortunately, it was P. Burmannus the elder to whom fell the task of editing Heinsius's materials after his death. Despite Burmannus's unparalleled industry and occasional insights the task was beyond his capacity, whether from defects of intellect or of character. Heinsius's own contribution was immense: it depended on his exquisite feeling for Ovid's style, his deep learning, methodical work, scrupulous attention to detail, percipience, abundant common sense, intimate knowledge of the ways of scribes, and the opportunities afforded by his diplomatic career to travel so that he could collate a vast number of manuscripts and meet foreign scholars.[52]

After Burmannus's edition Ovidian criticism languished: the aristocratic book purchasers in the age of Baskerville, Bodoni, the Didots, and the brothers Foulis cared more for fine printing and elegant production of their Latin classics than for critical advances. The development of the science of paleography in the eighteenth century and the further concentration of manuscripts in large public libraries after the French Revolution provided the opportunity for the gradual development of a new critical approach based on German method and science. The incomplete edition of J.C. Jahn (2 vols., Leipzig 1828–32) represented a first advance, and the critical editions of R. Merkel marked a new epoch (Leipzig 1837–75). Much work was done on aspects of Ovid towards the end of the nineteenth century, but the progress in editing Ovid was not remarkable at a time when immense advances were made in classical studies. The labor of H. Magnus (1914) and D.A. Slater (1927) in the earlier part of the twentieth century on the text of the *Metamorphoses* showed the magnitude of the task of editing that masterwork. The improvement of photography and the development of international cooperation greatly facilitated the survey of the tradition. Very considerable progress was

---

[51] The identification of many of Heinsius's manuscripts was a task left to the scholars of the twentieth century: details in Reeve (1974, 1976) with full references to earlier work. The important conjectures of Richard Bentley are best found by use of Hedickius (1905).

[52] P. Burmannus (1727) in his compilation of scholarly epistles gives interesting correspondence to and from Heinsius. His edition of Ovid (4 vols., Amsterdam 1727) is still an invaluable compendium of earlier work, especially that of Heinsius.

made during the second half of the same century in examining the transmission and providing good critical texts with reliable and convenient *apparatus critici*.

A great and probably largely unrewarding task remains to be done in investigating the hundreds of later manuscripts that at most have had only a cursory examination.

The Individual Transmissions

The Amatory Works: Amores, Ars Amatoria, *and* Remedia Amoris

The manuscripts of the Amatory Works of Ovid fall into two groups: an earlier and a later. The older manuscripts show common errors that distinguish them from the more recent *codices*. The later manuscripts in this group, **E, K**, and especially **A**, are less clearly members of it, showing many readings of the vulgate tradition of the remaining manuscripts. The *Heroides* are also found in two of these older manuscripts (**P** and **E**). The *sigla*, identifications, and approximate dates of the older manuscripts follow:

$$\begin{aligned}
\textbf{R} &= \text{Paris lat. 7311 (s. IX}^1\text{) (France)} \\
\textbf{P} &= \text{Paris lat. 8242 (s. IX}^{2/3}\text{) (France, Corbie)} \\
\textbf{b} &= \text{Bamberg, Class. 30 (s. IX}^2\text{) (France, Reims)} \\
\textbf{O} &= \text{Oxford Auct. F. 4. 32 (s. IX}^{\text{ex.}}\text{) (Wales)} \\
\textbf{Y} &= \text{Berlin Ms. Hamilton 471 (s. XI}^1\text{) (?Italy)} \\
\textbf{p}_6 &= \text{Paris lat. 8069 (s. XI) (France)} \\
\textbf{S}_a &= \text{St. Gall 821 (s. XI) (Germany or Switzerland)} \\
\textbf{E} &= \text{Eton 150 (s. XI}^{\text{ex.}}\text{) (Beneventan script)} \\
\textbf{S} &= \text{St. Gall 864 (s. XI–XII) (Germany or Switzerland)} \\
\textbf{A} &= \text{London Addit. 14086 (s. XII}^1\text{)} \\
\textbf{K} &= \text{Paris lat. 8460 (s. XII}^2\text{) (Italy or Germany).}
\end{aligned}$$

The portions of each work contained by these manuscripts may be indicated as follows (the order *Ars—Rem.—Am.* is given in **R** and **Y**):[53]

---

[53] I neglect short omissions of text, in particular *Am.* 1.13.11–14, 2.2.18–27, *Ars* 1.466–71 discussed below.

Codex	Ars Amatoria	Remedia Amoris	Amores	Heroides
R	(all)	(all)	1.1.3–2.19	
			1.2.25–50	
P			1.2.51–3.12.26	2.14–4.47
			3.14.3–15.8	4.104–5.96
				6.50–14.132
				16.1–38
				16.145–20.177
b	(excerpts, mostly from Book 1; six verses from Book 2)			
O	Book 1			
Y	1.1–2.112	(all)	(all)	
	2.259–3.812			
p₆	3.65–66	(excerpts)	3.11.35–36	
	3.73–74			
Sₐ	1.1–230			
E		(all)		1.1–7.161
S			1.1.1–6.45	
			1.8.75–3.9.10	
A	(all)			
K		(all)		

S. Tafel[54] at a time when the importance of **Y** was unknown observed that **R** and **P** showed many errors of the same type and had many characteristics in common. As **P** began just where **R** ceased, he suggested that **P** was probably copied from the lost portion of **R** and that both derived from a manuscript that contained *Ars—Remedia—Amores—Heroides* in that order. He thought that such a manuscript was the source of all the older manuscripts then known. At present **P** shows the order *Heroides—Amores*, but Tafel pointed out that, as no gathering preserved portions of both works, it was possible that the original order could have been reversed in the binding. Yet an examination[55] of the number of missing verses has shown that an order *Amores—Heroides* in **P** is impossible without the insertion of some other work between them. Moreover, despite the neat fit of the contents of **R** and **P**, it appears that **P** originally contained more of the text of the *Amores* before 1.2.51 and that hence it cannot be

---

[54] (1910) 26–32.
[55] Ably executed by McKie (1986).

argued that it was copied from a manuscript that began with that verse. The other works (*Ars—Rem.—Am.*) may have survived in one hyparchetype, but there is no significant evidence to show that such a work contained the *Heroides* too. Apart from many distinguishing readings the *codices* **R P O Y S** show short omissions (*Am.* 1.13.11–14, 2.2.18–27, *Ars* 1.466–71) that distinguish them from the later manuscripts; this indicates that they (with **b**, **p₆**, and **Sₐ**, as their variants indicate), collectively shared a hyparchetype (the symbol **α** is commonly used) for all of the works, or a set of separate hyparchetypes (**α** (*Am.*), **α′** (*Ars*), **α″** (*Rem.*), for the individual works. It seems probable that **α** (or its equivalents) may have been the product of a Carolingian *scriptorium* about A.D. 800.

In *Am.* the readings show that **R/P** and **Y** tend to side against **S**, e.g., 1.2.6 *secta* **R Y**: *tacita* **S** ς; 2.6.34 *miluus et* **P Y**: *miluus et est* **S N Vₐ**; 2.11.22 *credenti* **S y** ω: *quaerenti* **P Y**. In *Ars* the division **R O** (**Sₐ**) against **Y A** may be found, e.g., at 1.2 *hoc* **R O Sₐ** ς: *me* **Y A** ω; 1.518 *tuta* **R O**: *docta* **Y A** ω; 1.620 *subetur* **R O**: *subitur* **Y A** ω, but seldom **R A** against **O Y**, as 1.592 *uerba* **R A**: *bella* **O Y** ω. In *Rem.* the omission of 9–10 in **R Y** and errors like 611 *decidit* **E K** ω (for *reccidit* **R Y** London Addit. **49368** (s. XIII)) establish the grouping of **R Y** against **E K**, but this pattern is often obscured.

A common hyparchetype (**β**) may be postulated for the more recent manuscripts of the Amatory Works,[56] but they sometimes show variants that suggest contamination from sources other than **α** or the hypothetical **β**. As remarked above, **E K** and especially **A** show many readings of the **β** group.[57] Despite the general superiority of the older **α** manuscripts, the **β** manuscripts preserve in the *Ars* and *Amores* verses wrongly omitted in the **α** branch, and in all three works give correct readings that the **α** branch of the tradition has lost, e.g., *Am.* 1.2.6 *tecta* ω, *Am.* 1.13.4 *parentet auis* ω, *Ars* 1.715 *accedere* ω, *Ars* 2.426 *terenda* ω. In the case of readings transmitted by one, or by a small number, of the *codices* of the **β** tradition it can be difficult to say whether these were transmitted in **β** itself, entered the transmission from an independent source, or are conjectures, e.g., *Am.* 1.9.14

---

[56] Discussed by McKie (1986) 231–36.

[57] Goold (1965) 8 argued that **E** and **K** are members of the **β** group contaminated with **α** readings; Kenney (1962) 16–17 discusses the intermediate position **A** holds between **α** and **β**.

uerrendis ς; *Ars* 2.718 *prolicienda* ς; *Ars* 3.217 *formam* ς; *Rem.* 409 *rarae sibi* **Paris lat. 7993** (s. XIII); *Rem.* 804 *expediere* ς.

De Somn(i)o

The poem *Amores* 3.5 is transmitted in that place only by the **α** branch and a few manuscripts of the **β** branch. Other manuscripts have inserted it elsewhere in the *Amores* or transmit it separately under the title *De Somn(i)o* (or the like). E.J. Kenney makes a convincing case for believing it is an ancient imitation of Ovid's style that first entered the Ovidian tradition in early medieval times.[58]

The Amatory Works: Heroides[59]

Of the older manuscripts of the amatory works listed above only **P** and **E** transmit (in part, as shown above) the *Heroides*. There is no ninth-century or tenth-century *codex* other than **P**. As **P** apparently was copied from a damaged exemplar and has suffered considerable later alteration, the tradition of the *Heroides* is especially precarious. About 200 later manuscripts exist. They were derived from a source similar to **P**, but have been subjected to extensive conjecture and arbitrary alteration. The *Heroides* became popular from the twelfth century, and scribes provoked by many textual difficulties so constantly had recourse to conjectures and adopted readings from sources other than their exemplar in attempts to improve the text, that the tradition is thoroughly contaminated. Among the oldest and best of the later *codices* are:

V = Vatican City Vat. lat. 3254(II) (s. XI–XII) (Italy, contains 1.1–14.132; 16.1–38; 16.145–17.238)

W = Vienna series nova 107 (s. XI–XII) (Germany or Austria, contains 10.14–11.68; 12.21–102; 12.184–14.132; 16.1–38; 16.145–319; 16.368–17.69; 17.114–50; 17.155–91; 17.196–18.4; 18.169–20.226)

G = Wolfenbüttel 260 Extrav. (s. XII) (?Germany, contains 1.1–14.132; 16.1–38; 16.145–21.14)

---

[58] Kenney (1969a).
[59] I have had to use Dörrie's flawed edition, since no other has so much information. Dörrie (1960–72) did very usefully clarify the complicated tradition. I borrow the symbols **a** and **ξ** from the latter work.

L = Louvain 411 (s. XII) (contained 1.1–9.133; destroyed 1940, but microfilms survive)

F = Frankfurt-am-Main S. Barthol. 110 (s. XII[ex.]) (France, contains 1.1–14.132; 16.1–38; 16.145–21.14) [**see Plate III**].

Of these **L** and **F** are somewhat less interpolated and closer to **P**; and surprisingly

Gu = Wolfenbüttel Gud. lat. 297 (s. XV) (contains 1.1–14.132; 16.1–38; 16.145–21.146) was carefully transcribed from an early copy in Caroline script very like the exemplar of **P**, but tends to leave lacunae in corrupt passages. Its greatest service is to transmit 21.15–146 (see below). The remaining manuscripts give less help, but occasionally appear to preserve good readings or to have stray fragments of a different tradition, as will be indicated below. The corruption of the archetype is indicated by the paradosis at 2.122 *litora*, which has strayed in from the previous verse, or 3.58 *lintea uela*, or 7.171 *frangentia*, or 12.167 *repuli* **F G P² V**, **plurimi**: *repudi* **P**. (Upon the detection of these faults various attempts were made in some *codices* at emendation, of which 2.122 *aequora* **Ab Go′ Mz Q** and 12.167 *pepuli*, found by Heinsius in two Medicean *codices*, may be taken as correct.) That the archetype had passed through a stage in minuscule may be inferred from errors like *cerno* or *cerna* (for *terna*) in all manuscripts at 9.38, and *aliae* for *asiae* in almost all at 17.212. The excellence of **P** may be inferred from such readings as 3.57 *eos* **P**: *(h)ora* **P² E F G L V, rell.**: *aura* **Ab Bx C² F² H K^v**; 10.71 *uictor* **P**: *uictus* **F G V W, rell.**

When **P** is in error, the truth may be found in the other manuscripts, as at 6.137 *refert* **E D Dp**: *referat* **P**: *referam* **P^{corr}, rell.**; 6.162 *exspes* **G**: *expers* **P L V, rell.**: *mentis* **E F Bx C Ea Ep Go′ K Mi N² Ob R Ri T Z**; 7.68 *Et frigia* (= *Phrygia*) **F¹ Gu Go′ K Mz R Sp Vb Y^v, Planudes**: *Et tiria* (= *Tyria*) **P G V, rell.**: *et troica* **E L**: *et tua sic* **Ep**: *atque tua* **Q Y^v**; 7.105 *debita* **E** (but Knox (1995) reports *dedita*) **F G +**: *dedita* **P L V Gu +**; 8.117 *iuro* **G L +, Planudes**: *iuno* **Gi**: *oro* **P F V +**. How far these correct readings represent tradition is hard to say.[60] When **P** is lacking, the editor's task is even

---

[60] Dörrie, with the agreement of Kenney (1961) 480, argues that it is very improbable that a medieval scribe could have corrected the text at 7.68. I do not feel so confident: as the variation *et troica* seems to show (for it hardly arose from a gloss on *Phrygia*, as the word seems not to have occasioned variants elsewhere in the

more difficult. Readings like 8.45 *regebat* **rell.**: *petebat* **P**: *petebant* **Gu**; 8.77 *ph/febique* **P F Ea**: *phebiti* **Gu**: *flebatque* uel sim. **G L V, rell.**; 18.169 *caes* **P Gu**: *caelis* **W Pb T**: *caelo* **F G, cett.** show how closely the late *codex* **Gu** can transmit an early tradition like that of **P**.

Special Problems

Some difficult special problems vex the tradition of the *Heroides*:

21.15–146

This passage is transmitted in **Gu**.[61] It was first printed in the *editio princeps* at Rome in 1471, then independently in the Venetian edition of Jacobus Rubeus in 1474, and was copied thence to the edition at Parma by Stephanus Corallus in 1477. Since **Gu**, as explained above, has a close affinity with **P**, it is reasonably believed that lines 15–146 derive from an earlier stage of the tradition before the loss of some leaves at the end of a *codex* that then became the hyparchetype of most of the tradition.

21.147–250

The edition by Stephanus Corallus (Parma 1477) is the sole independent source for these lines, which it credits to a *uetustissimus codex*. The Ovidian origin of this passage and of that next discussed, though often impugned, is accepted by Kenney after a convincing discussion.[62]

16.39–144

The Parmesan edition of 1477, again the sole independent source for these lines, ascribes them too to the *uetustissimus codex*. Verses 101–2 appear to have been imitated in *anth.* 702.1–2 (transmitted in a lost ninth-century manuscript): this supports the belief that the *uetustissimus codex* was not a fraud of some humanist.

Heroides), someone could see that *ti/yria* was wrong, and looked for another epithet, but made a metrical blunder. A luckier scribe may have remembered *Phrygius* from other passages in the *Heroides*.

[61] Though Dörrie (1960) 379–84 argues for the independence of two other fifteenth-century *codices*, each is very closely related to one of the two editions that issued at Rome in 1471 and at Venice in 1474, and Kenney (1996) 26 n. 102 believes they have no independent authority.

[62] Kenney (1979).

Stray distichs

As well as the above three passages there are found in a small number of witnesses (often including **E**) additional distichs at the beginnings of several *Heroides* and additional short passages of one or more distichs within the text. It is impossible to be sure that any one explanation will cover all the cases. Some idea of the transmission may be gained from a sample:

> *Her.* 5.0a–b: **Bx C E Ea Ep K** (*post v. 2*) **Pa R²** (**mg**) **Vb Z** (10
>   *codices* ex 37 reported)
> *Her.* 6.0a–b: **E** (1 ex 36)
> *Her.* 7.1–2: **Bx** (*post v. 4*) **E Ep Z** (*post 6.164*) (4 ex 36)
> *Her.* 7.25a–b: **Ab²** (**mg**) **Bx C D Ea Ep F Gi K M²** (**mg**) **Mi Y** (**mg**)
>   (12 ex 36)
> *Her.* 7.25b (only): **Q¹** (**mg**) **R²** (**mg**)
> *Her.* 7.98: **Bx C Of Pa T Y** (**mg**) (*cum 97*) **Z** (7 ex 38)
> *Her.* 7.99: **Bx C Of Pa T Z** (6 ex 38).

Some of the additional passages are evidently interpolations, and all have been suspected as non-Ovidian by some scholars. Those who accept some as Ovidian follow Dörrie in referring to an "apocryphal" tradition (**a**) independent of the main stream, which possibly was drawn on solely for additional verses.

It appears that at some early stage of the tradition there was a more complete *codex* in minuscule, very probably Caroline, which included 16.39–144, 21.15–146, 21.147–250: we may call it $\mathfrak{s}^1$. It, or a subsequent copy, lost the leaves containing 16.39–144 and 21.147–250, a stage we may denote as $\mathfrak{s}^2$. It seems $\mathfrak{s}^2$ or an early descendant in Caroline script was transcribed by **Gu** in the fifteenth century with uncommon fidelity. Later $\mathfrak{s}^2$ or a descendant lost 21.15–146, and from the resulting state ($\mathfrak{s}^3$) is descended the vast bulk of surviving *codices*, which stop at 21.14. The Bolognese *editio princeps* (1471) drew on the $\mathfrak{s}^3$ stage of the tradition The $\mathfrak{s}^2$ state is contained in the Roman *editio princeps* (1471); the Venetian edition of Jacobus Rubeus (1474) also added the passage 21.15–146 to supplement the Bolognese edition of 1471. It is remarkable that Rubeus seems to have used for these verses a manuscript source rather than the Roman *editio princeps*:[63] only a few surviving *codices* transmit

---

[63] Elsewhere Rubeus sometimes agrees with the readings of the Roman edition; he drew the initial "stray distichs" for *Heroides* 8–12 from one or more manuscripts.

21.15–146. The edition at Parma in 1477 apparently used a descendant of ϛ¹ (not ϛ¹ itself, which before then had arrived at the ϛ³ state), to supplement the text of Rubeus. As the oldest extant *codex*, **P**, ends at 20.177, and as **E V W** and **L** also cease well before 21.14, one cannot know whether they were copied at the ϛ² or the ϛ³ stage of the transmission, but the character of **P**'s readings suggests an exemplar earlier than those of the others. The *florilegia* have no trace of the verses transmitted only in stages earlier than ϛ³; yet, if the puzzling presentation by the *Florilegium Gallicum* of the *Epistula Sapphus* as *Heroides* 15 is derived from tradition, it draws on a source otherwise unknown.[64]

These relationships may be illustrated in rough outline as follows:

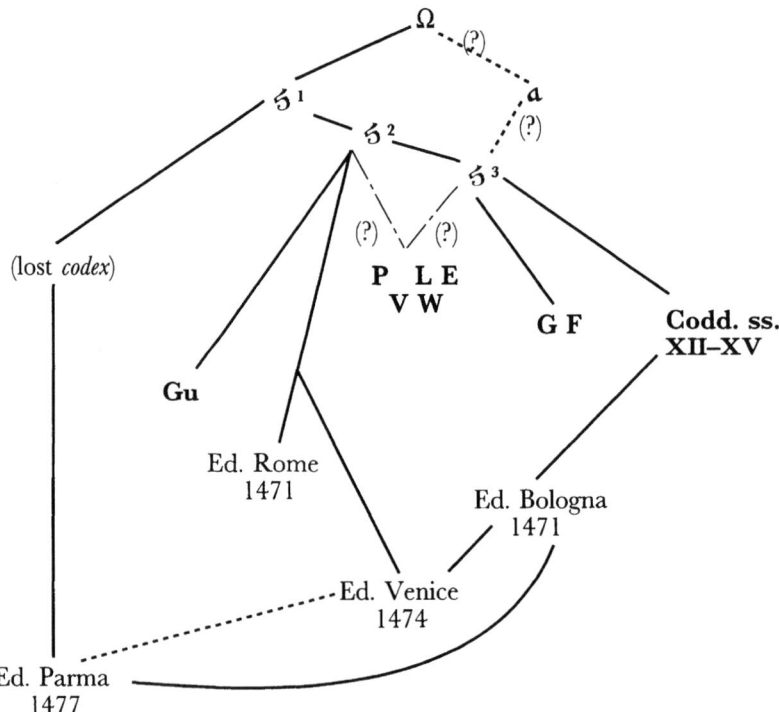

The single epistles (1–14) and the double (16–21) are transmitted together, but since Lachmann (1848) serious objections have been

---

[64] Kenney (1961) conveniently and critically summarizes the first two parts of Dörrie's exhaustive discussion (1960–72).

raised against the Ovidian authorship of some of the former and all of the latter.[65] The tradition of the *Heroides* came near to extinction. The poor materials that we have apparently bring us back no farther than a damaged archetype of the Carolingian period.

Heroides 15: Epistula Sapphus

This poem is transmitted apart from the *Heroides* only in **F** (s. XII[cx.]): in the other manuscripts (none earlier than the 15th century) it is found with them, sometimes placed in the first and sometimes in the last place. D. Heinsius[66] placed it at the end of the single epistles as number 15. If the single epistles ever circulated as a group separately from the double, a poem at the end would be more easily lost, and the order given at *Am.* 2.18.26 may suggest a letter from Sappho once closed the series. The *Florilegium Gallicum* quotes some verses from the *Epistula Sapphus*, placing them between excerpts from *Heroides* 14 and 16.[67] It has been argued that this may be the result of rearrangement by a compiler who followed the order indicated at *Am.* 2.18.26.[68] *A priori* this seems to me to be implausible; it appears more probable that the *florilegium* drew on a manuscript with an order that is found nowhere else in the tradition; it is possible that that order was the result of an intrusion of *Heroides* 15 by some ancient or medieval editor. The original order of the leaves in **F** has been disturbed, but it is clear that the *Epistula Sapphus* did not come from the same source as the other *Heroides*. Apart from **F** and the few verses in the *Florilegium Gallicum* (s. XII?) the tradition consists of some 150-odd manuscripts of the fifteenth century and later, which derive from a common source other than **F**. The *Epistula Sapphus* evidently was a rare text. However, when once re-discovered c. 1420, it was rapidly diffused by the humanists, and was included in both the editions of 1471 at Rome and Bologna. The case for and against authenticity has been much discussed.[69]

---

[65] Courtney (1965) summarizes the very real difficulties, cf. Knox, chapter 4 above.

[66] Edition, Leiden 1629.

[67] Text in Burton (1983) 214–16.

[68] Tarrant (1981) 151 argues that *Am.* 2.18.26 and 34 are interpolated.

[69] For: Dörrie (1975) 203–7; 216–26; Rosati (1996b)—against: Tarrant (1981); cf. Knox, chapter 4 above.

Medicamina Faciei Femineae *and* Nux

As the tradition of these two works is so similar, it is convenient to treat them together. I list the principal manuscripts used by editors, giving Kenney's *sigla* for the *Medicamina*, and (in square brackets) those of Lenz (1956) for the *Nux*:

M [F] = Florence S. Marco 223(I) (s. XI²) (?Italy)
[O₁] = Oxford Auct. F. 2. 14 (s. XI²) (England; *Med.* not included)
N [N] = Naples IV F 13 (s. XII–XIII)
Q [A] = Antwerp lat. 68 (s. XIII)
Pᵦ [P₁] = Paris lat. 7994 (s. XIII)
U [R₁] = Florence *Biblioteca Riccardiana* 489 (s. XIII)
Cₑ = Phillips 6912 (now in anonymous ownership) (s. XIII) (*Nux* not included)
Nᵦ = Naples IV F 12 (1385–86) (Italy; *Nux* not included)
Bₑ [B₁] = Berlin Ms. Phill. 1796 (s. XIV–XV) (Italy)
Lₐ [L₁] = Leiden Periz. Q. 7 (s. XV) (Italy).

Lenz (1965) in his edition of the *Medicamina* used two additional manuscripts of the thirteenth century, one of the fourteenth, and twelve of the fifteenth;[70] Lenz (1956) used 40 *codices* in all for his edition of the *Nux*, Pulbrook (1985) collated 67 and regularly gives the readings of 15 (including only **F**, **P₁**, and **A** of the selection above).

M [F] stands apart from the other manuscripts. Sometimes it has correct or nearly correct readings that have almost vanished from the other *codices* (e.g., *Med.* 69 *torrere* (**M** and two fifteenth-century *codices*); *Nux* 173 *pandens* (for *candens*) (**F** and **Göttingen Ms. Philol. 127** (s. XIII)). At *Nux* 31–32 it is free from interpolations that the scribes introduced in the rest of the tradition (even in **O₁**, possibly older[71] than **F**). It has some unique errors (e.g., *bulli*, *Med.* 65; *petat*, *Nux* 74). The remaining manuscripts appear to be contaminated to some extent with readings from the tradition surviving in **M[F]**.

At some stage of the tradition antecedent to all surviving manuscripts the *Med.* lost everything after v. 100: it may be that the *Nux* and these first hundred verses occupied one bifolium surviving from a late antique or Carolingian *codex*, as suggested by Tarrant.[72] Despite some suspect features it is hard to demonstrate that Ovid could not

---

[70] A. Kunz in his edition (Vienna 1881) had already used nearly all these.
[71] So Tarrant (1983) 285; but Pulbrook ((1985) 109 n. 19) dissents, and Baehrens (*PLM* 1 (Leipzig 1879) 89) gave his view of it as "*nulla est fides.*"
[72] Tarrant (1983) 275.

have written the *Nux*.[73] However, it seems to lack the stamp of Ovid's personality and his sure artistic touch, and I find it hard to accept it as his work.

Metamorphoses[74]

In several manuscripts the texts of the individual stories are preceded by headings (*tituli*) and brief summaries (*narrationes*).[75] Some of this material has a late antique origin, and was ascribed in the fifteenth century to 'Lactantius,' a name that may have been a humanist guess inspired by the commentator on Statius. In my discussion below I have indicated with an asterisk the manuscripts that transmit (or transmitted) the 'Lactantian' *tituli* or *narrationes* in whole or part.[76]

A valuable source for the text of the *Metamorphoses* is given by fragments of six early manuscripts:

π* = Paris lat. 12246 (s. IX) (France, contains 1.81–193; 2.67–254)
λ* = Leipzig Rep. I. 74 (s. IX) (France, contains 3.131–252)
α* = Bern 363 (s. IX²) (Insular script; contains 1.1–199, 1.304–9, 1.773–79; 2.1–22; 3.1–56)
ε* = London Harley 2610 (s. X) (Germany, contains 1.1–3.622) [**see Plate I**]
β* = London Addit. 11967 (s. X–XI) (Italy, contains 2.833–3.510; 4.292–5.389; 5.588–6.411)
υ = Vatican City Urbin. lat. 342 (s. XI) (France, Fleury, contains 5.483–6.45; 7.731–8.104).

To the extent that the same portions of text are presented in these fragments, we can see that many variants found in the later tradition were already current. At 3.39 α correctly gives *urnae* for the *undae* found in β, ε, and in the rest of the tradition with the exception of a correction by the third hand in **N** (listed in next section). At 1.70 α shares with **N** *fuerant caligine caeca* (*multa* **N**) against the

---

[73] Lee (1958) assembles evidence against Ovid's authorship; Pulbrook (1985) 29–35 argues for the defense.

[74] Details of manuscripts will be found in Munari (1957) as supplemented by himself and others (especially Coulson (1995)); some *sigla* are added to Anderson's from Tarrant (1995a) 102–3.

[75] Text in Slater (1927). In addition to π α ε β **M N S κ Y** listed in the text below, he makes use of London Burney 311 (a. 1462) and Copenhagen Gl. kgl. S. 2008 (s. XII–XIII).

[76] Tarrant (1995a) discusses the *narrationes* (83–100) and their implications for the history of the transmission (100–115).

massa latuere sub ipsa/illa of **ε** and of all the rest of the tradition. At the date when these manuscripts were written the *Metamorphoses* was the most popular of Ovid's works, and it had a long history of scholarly interest behind it, with the result that the tradition was already too contaminated to admit the construction by modern editors of a *stemma* from which archetypal readings could be inferred.

The next stage of the tradition is represented by early *codices* that preserve the bulk of the poem, firstly:

> **M*** = Florence San Marco 225 (s. XI) (Italy, contains 1.1–14.830)
> **N*** = Naples IV F 3 (s. XI^ex.–XII^in.) (Beneventan script, contains 1.1–14.838)
> **U*** = Vatican City Urbin. lat. 341 (s. XI^ex.) (Beneventan script, contains all text, but 1.1–76, 15.494–879, and some other folios have been replaced in s. XIII–XV) **[see Plate II]**.

M, **N**, and **U** are closely related: they (and their common ancestor) are often referred to with the *siglum* **O**. **M** was written in Northern or Central Italy, **N** and **U** are both written in the variation of the Beneventan script current at Bari, and the **O** branch of the tradition is sometimes referred to as the 'Lactantian' or 'Italian' branch. **U** shares singular readings with **N**, but shows signs of some relationship with manuscripts of the so-called 'French' branch. That 'French' influence is stronger in an intermediate group that also shows the influence of **O**:

> **S*** = a lost *codex* from Speyer, which contained 3.506–4.786 and 6.439–12.278, and was collated for Heinsius; a portion (9.324–10.707, known to some editors as **κ**) survives as Copenhagen, Ny. kgl. S. 56 2° (s. XI²) (Germany)
> **R*** = Naples IV F 2 (s. XII^ex.) (Italy, contains 1.1–15.863)
> **W*** = Vatican City Vat. lat. 5859 (a. 1275) (contains whole text)
> **Z*** = Vienna series nova 12746 (c. 1470) (contains whole text)
> **J*** = a lost *codex* of Padua, inspected by Heinsius.

The loss of **M N** after *Met.* 14.830(838), and of the first hand of **U** after 15.493, gravely injures the textual state of the end of the poem.

The 'French' branch (Magnus's **X**) is represented by the following early manuscripts:

> **T** = Munich Clm 29208 + Cgm 4286 (s. XI²/⁴) (South Germany, Tegernsee, extensive fragments from Books 1 & 2 (apparently copied from **ε**), and 4, 6, 8–15 (independent))
> **E** = Vatican City Pal. lat. 1669 (s. XI²) (France (?Southern), contains whole text except lacunae in 2–6)

F* = Florence San Marco 223(I) (s. XI²) (?Italy, contains whole text, but seven lost folios (including 1.1–1.445) have been replaced by a hand of s. XIV–XV)

L* = Florence Plut. 36.12 (s. XI–XII) (Germany, contains 1.1–12.298)

P = Paris lat. 8001 (s. XII^med.) (Germany, contains whole text)

G = St. Gall 866 (s. XII²) (Swiss, St. Gall, contains 1.1–8.547; 10.429–15.879).

From more than 450 other known *codices* Anderson makes a selection of ten that he dates to s. XI, XII, XIII, which he uses especially for the verses at the end of the poem where **M, N, U, L**, and others are wanting. Occasional use is made of a further sixteen.

A simplified version of the *stemma* suggested by Tarrant[77] may clarify the relationships:

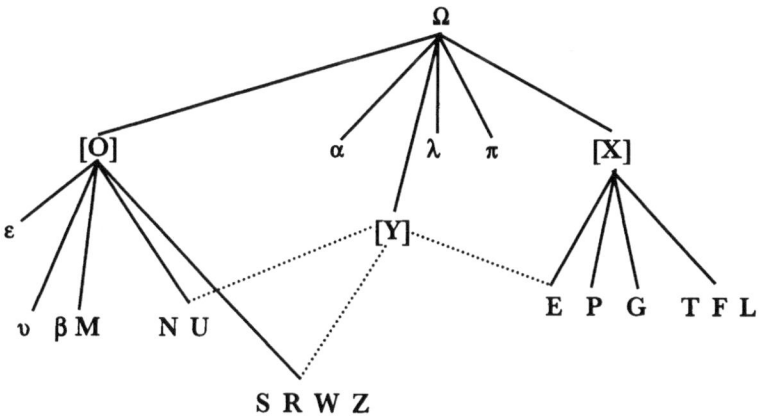

The following readings sketch the relationship of **M N U** and the remaining *codices*: 9.503 *ante* **M N U²**: *ipsa* **U¹ S W E P F L**; 9.350 *adoratis* **M N S**: *et oratis* **N² U W E P F L**; 9.718 *formaque* **M N**: *par forma* **cett.**; 13.724 *pennis* **M N¹**: *linguis* **N² U W E P F**; this pattern is often disturbed, as at 5.390 *tyrios* **M N W F**: *uarios* **N³ U E P L**; 7.710 *referam quoque* **M N W F L**: *referebam* **M² N² U W² E P F²**.

In the case of a text so widely read, no doubt there was already contamination in antiquity; some is shown in the *stemma* above, and the plentiful later manuscripts of the **X** branch abound in it. Despite

---

[77] Tarrant (1983); cf. Tarrant (1995a): **Y** is an hypothetical manuscript or group of manuscripts he postulates to account for certain correspondences between the descendants of **O** and **X**.

the many *codices* that survive, correct readings may be found in iso-
lated places: (a) only hinted at in the indirect transmission, as *pauiunt*[78]
(6.58), of which the only traces in the direct transmission are *pauent*
in β and ****nt (with *feriu* written in the erasure by the second hand)
in **M**; (b) only in a Caroline fragment as *fulgora* (1.56) in α; (c) in a
single early medieval *codex* as *siccaque* (2.278) in **U**, and *ictus* (5.389)
in **N**, or somewhat later as *minyae subit* (7.115) in Oxford Auct. F.
4. 30 (s. XII[med.]);[79] or (d) from lost or unidentified *codices* as *cultus* (8.
854) reported by Naugerius and *fuco* (6.222) reported by Heinsius.
A remarkable case occurs at *Met.* 8.237, where all Anderson's manu-
scripts give *ramosa . . . ilice*. However, the second hand of Copenhagen
Gl. kgl. S. 2008 (s. XII–XIII) shows *elice*.[80] If this reading is tradi-
tional it shows an interesting link with the quotation in the Auctor
de dubiis nominibus (?s. VII) (*GLK* 5.587.1) which has the superior
limoso . . . elice.

Double Recension?

In several passages the **O** branch has, or originally had, a text quite
different from that in the rest of the tradition, and the **O** text is
usually shorter. The view has been advanced that the discrepant ver-
sions represent (i) the text that survived in Rome when Ovid went
into exile, and (ii) a text that Ovid revised in Tomis.[81] If this view
is correct, then **O** and **X** have no common origin other than what-
ever copy may have been the basis of Ovid's two versions. The pas-
sages are (1) 1.544–47, (2) 6.281–82, (3) 7.145–46, (4) 8.285–86, (5)
8.597–610, (6) 8.651–56, (7) 8.693a–b, (8) 8.697–98, (9) 11.57a–b,
(10) 12.192.[82] Inevitably, the following brief discussion cannot do jus-
tice to a very complex problem that has been the subject of a long
and vigorous debate not yet concluded.

It may be best to begin by considering passage (6): here the context
(8.639–65) shows evidence of imitation of a passage in Callimachus's

---

[78] See details pp. 449–50, above.
[79] Naugerius, however, ascribes it to *"veteres."*
[80] According to Slater (1927).
[81] See p. 444, above.
[82] I do not consider 8.186 merits mention. It is remarkable that most of these
doublets come from Book 8: some see this as evidence of the activity of a tinker-
ing scribe; one might also speculate that Book 8, if it formed the end of the first
codex of a set of the *Metamorphoses* divided into two *codices*, would be (like Book 15)
especially liable to damage. Slater (1927) 23–24 in discussing the cause of the lacu-
nae in **M** and **N** at 8.340–402 attempts to discover the history of the damage.

Hecale (Pfeiffer gives the details in his note on fr. 240 Pf.). The three extra verses in the version of **X** show evidence of reminiscence of two fragments of the *Hecale* (frr. 246, 247 Pf.), and hence are very unlikely to result from interpolation:[83] their omission in **M N** may result from confusion of the initial letters of 651 (*inter-*) and of 654 (*istep-*), which in minuscule would be very similar. I agree with the view that the versions of 655, 656 in **M N S W** mark an attempt[84] to mend a faulty text which resulted from the accidental omission of 652–54. In passage (3) 7.146 appears before 7.145 in **F L P²** and has the appearance of an intrusive parallel. Though it occurs in all the manuscripts, it seems Heinsius was correct in deleting it. Verse 11.57a (9), present in **N U S** only and in the margin of **W**, is inappropriate to the context: it can hardly have any Ovidian origin. The variant of 12.192 (10) found in **M N S** and partly in **W** probably has arisen from unease with the long appositional phrase in 190–92 and has been borrowed from *Met.* 4.795 (= 9.10) by scribal intervention. At 6.281–82 (2) it is significant that the phrase *corque ferum satia dixit* is substituted by the third hand in **N** for the erased original text, and *corque ferum satia* is also found at 9.178. The repetition of the initial *pascere* in 280 and 281 suggests that some kind of dittography has caused textual corruption, and that *corque ferum satia* was imported to remedy the damage. In passage (8) the version in **W P F** is corrupt and looks like an attempt to patch up a partly illegible text. In passage (4) 8.285 is transmitted by all the manuscripts, but it contains a clumsy repetition of words from 284. Yet 8.286, though it avoids that repetition, is transmitted in the text only by **F L P** and is a marginal addition in **W** by the first hand, and in **M N U E** by later hands. Neither version seems to me to achieve Ovidian elegance.

The remaining passages are harder to explain on an assumption of scribal repair work. The longer version of (7), 8.693 a–b, originally lacking in **M N S**, could have been the original, and the shorter text have been reconstructed from an exemplar so damaged that only *ambo* and *leuant baculis* were legible. An alternative hypothesis is that the longer version is an expansion. In passage (5) although the

---

[83] One must guard against the danger of a circular argument here: these fragments (frr. 246, 247 Pf.) are ascribed to the *Hecale* because they are paralleled in this episode of the *Metamorphoses*.

[84] Perhaps with a reminiscence of *fluminis ulua torum*, *F.* 1.200.

longer version (**W**, **P**, and some *recentiores*) has been criticized as un-Ovidian, no serious fault has been detected. If it is the work of a forger, he was an uncommonly skilled one. If, however, the longer version is Ovidian, it is very difficult to explain how the shorter version became current. I find the theory of double recension more attractive here than elsewhere. Finally on passage (1): Murgia[85] has written a very thorough and closely-argued paper to prove that we should read 544, 547, 546, 545, and that Ovid made Daphne appeal both to Tellus and to Peneus. Space precludes my discussion here of his thorough and ingenious treatment of this question, save to indicate that I find intolerable his admission of both 545 and 547 to the text.[86]

To sum up: many alleged cases of double recension are untenable: we know so little of the early history of the text that we must consider all doubtful.[87]

Fasti

The tradition of the *Fasti* depends in the main on five *codices*:

A = Vatican City Reg. lat. 1709 (s. XI) (France, Fleury; contains 1.1–5.24)

U = Vatican City Vat. lat. 3262 (s. XI[ex.]) (Beneventan script, Montecassino)

G = Brussels 5369–5373 (s. XI[1]) (Belgium; contains 1.505–6.812)

I = Cologny (Geneva) *Bibliotheca Bodmeriana* lat. 123 (s. XII[in.]) (?Germany; contains small fragments at the end of Book 1 and at the beginning of Book 2; 2.568–3.204; 4.317–814)

M = Oxford Auct. F. 4. 25 (s. XV[in.]) (Italy) [**see Plate IV**].

A, **U**, and **G I M**[88] represent three strands of the tradition, but their relationship is not clear. **A** and **U** on one hand (e.g., 3.146 *repe*nte* **A**: *repente* **U**: *perenna* **G I M**; 3.659 *Alanida* **A U**: *Azam(n)ida* **G M**),

---

[85] Murgia (1984).

[86] Note that the earliest witness (ε) gives the unmetrical *quae fecit ut laedar* (545), which looks like a gloss on *qua nimium placui* (547) in the same tense.

[87] The passages are conveniently set out in Enk (1958); there are full discussions in Bömer's commentary with abundant reference to the voluminous writings of earlier scholars.

[88] Courtney achieves a neat *apparatus* by using the *siglum* **Z** for the agreement of **G I M**, and **ζ** for **G M**. **M**, once known as the Mazarinianus (see further Alton – Wormell – Courtney (1977) 53), despite its late date, is especially important for the passage 1.1–504 because **G** and **I** lack it.

and **U** and **G I M** on the other (e.g., 2.585 *indomito* **U G M**: *immo-dico* **A I²**; 2.772 *neglectae* **U G I M**: *inlectae* **A**; 3.107 *uocatur* **U I M**: *uocetur* **G**: *petatur* **A**) will often be found to agree in error, and occasionally **U** shows a correct reading where **A** and **G I M** both err, e.g., 2.568 *pedes* **U**: *dies* **A G I M**; 4.295 *nurusque* **U**: *uirique* **A G M**. The scribe of **U** appears to have devoted much effort to making his text intelligible, sometimes having recourse to conjecture and interpolation. The balance of probability suggests that **U** was closer to the tradition of **G I M**, but had access to another source connected to the **A** branch of the tradition. The true reading may be found in **A** alone, **U** alone, or **G I M** alone, or in one[89] (e.g., 5.626 *iouis* **Göttingen Ms. Philol. 127** (s. XII–XIII)) or more (e.g. 4.745 *mul-tramque* **h B²**—see below—and others, and 5.161 *Argestes* **Modena, Bibl. Estense, α H. 6. 11** (s. XV), **Chicago, University Library, MS 494** (s. XV)) of the *recentiores* alone.

There are about 160 other manuscripts. Courtney considers that the following are the most useful:

F = Cambridge *Pembroke College* 280 (s. XII) (England; contains 1.1–6.791)

L = Florence Plut. 36.24 (s. XII–XIII) (Italy)

Δ = Paris lat. 7993 (s. XIII) (France)

Y = Berlin Ms. lat. oct. 134 (s. XII¹) (?Venice)

h = London Harley 2564 (s. XV) (Italy)

θ = Milan N 265 sup. (s. XII) (contains 1.195–394; 2.467–664; 3.1–6.640)

d = Oxford D'Orville 172 (s. XV) (contains 1.1–4.313; 4.877–6.812)

σ = Berlin Ms. Diez. B. Sant. 29 (s. XV)

B = Leiden Voss. lat. O 27 (s. XII^med.) (Italy)

C = Oxford Auct. F. 4. 29 (s. XII–XIII)

D = Munich Clm 8122 (s. XII²) (Germany; contains 1.71–6.812).

Of these the consensus of **F L Δ** goes some slight way to fill the gaps in the related *codex* **A**; similarly **θ d σ** give some assistance when **I** and **G** are wanting; and **Y** is a copy of **U** that helps editors to discern late alterations made to the original text of **U**.

Tristia

The older tradition for the *Tristia* consists of three incomplete manuscripts:

---

[89] Further investigation may always yield more witnesses.

Tr = Trier (no pressmark) (s. X) (contains 1.11.1–31; 1.11.33–2.21; 4.4.35–65; 4.4.67–5.9)
M = Florence San Marco 223(II) (s. XI) (Germany or Italy, contains 1.5.11–3.7.1; 4.1.12–7.5)
V2 = Vatican City Ottob. lat. 1469 (s. XI^{ex.}) (Italy, contains 1.1.1–4.8.17).

M is a carelessly written manuscript, abounding in errors, but free from many interpolations that have invaded the more recent manuscripts. Thus the reading of **M** at 1.5b.9, *haeret*, points to the *aere* convincingly conjectured by Daniel Heinsius (and reported from two manuscripts by his son); the interpolated *esset* reported from the rest of the tradition is evidently an accommodation to *forent* in the following line. **Tr** almost alone[90] transmits the correct *axenus* at 4.4b.2. At 5.4.14 **V2** alone has the *docenda* conjectured by Burmannus for the *dolenda* of the rest. These three *codices* do not agree with each other very closely: one may note, e.g., at 2.8 *demi iussa* **Tr M**: *pridem iussa* **V2**: *demum uisa* **A V G H L4 P**: *pridem (in)uisa* **cett.**;[91] at 3.5.40 *darei* **M**: *darii* **V2**: *praeclari* **cett.**[92] (*pharii* **Q**); in the welter of readings at 1.11.31 **M** has *auidae ad aethera pennae*, **Tr M^v V2** with several of the *recentiores* show *auidae substrata rapinae*; at 4.1.102 **V2** and several of the *recentiores* have *focos*, **M** with **A V G H L4 P** and some others *rogos*. Already **Tr M** and **V2** show variant readings added by the scribe or contemporary hands, and quite possibly variants were shown in their exemplars. The missing portions at the beginning and at the end (but not in the middle) of **M** and at the end of **V2** have been supplemented by hands of the fifteenth century.

One group of manuscripts among the *recentiores* merits special attention:

A = A collation entered by Politianus in the margins of a printed edition (Oxford Auct. P. 2. 2) of a lost *codex* once in the Marcian Library at Florence
V = Vatican City Vat. lat. 1606 (s. XII) (Italy; contains 1.1.1–5.7(8).14)
G = Wolfenbüttel Gud. lat. 192 (s. XIII)
H = London Addit. 49368 (s. XIII)
L4 = Florence 91 sup. 25 (s. XV)
P = Vatican City Pal. lat. 910 (s. XV).

---

[90] Owen (1889) reports it from Paris lat. 7993 (s. XIII).
[91] The variants may be explained as expansions of *dem iussa*.
[92] Expanding a misread *clari* (< *dari* < *darii*) to give three syllables.

Of these **L4** is a copy of the lost Marcian *codex* reported in **A**. The *siglum* **Γ** is convenient to report the consensus of this group. Individual members show contamination from readings of the rest of the *recentiores*. At 5.1.18, where **Tr, M**, and **V2** are wanting, **Γ** has *aptior, ingenium come, Tibullus erit*, and the rest of the tradition has interpolated *et plures quorum nomina magna uigent*. The remaining *recentiores* show more extensive interpolation and contamination, but also some possible evidence of independence of **Tr, M, V2** and **Γ**, e.g., 4.1.81 *saepe* **London Addit. 18384** (s. XIII), **Paris. lat. 15143** (s. XIII), and a few others.

Since **Tr** is of slight extent, since **M** has many errors and is lacunose, and since **V2** is often infected with the vices of the *recentiores*, the establishment of the true text of the *Tristia* is (as in the roughly parallel case of the *Heroides*) a difficult and frustrating task.

The relationship of the *codices* may be outlined thus:

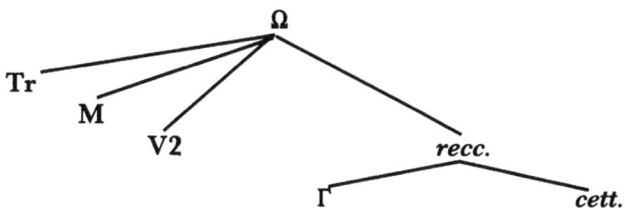

G. Luck[93] attempts a fuller but more hazardous reconstruction.

Ibis

I list the main *codices*, none earlier than the late twelfth century:

G = Cambridge *Trinity College*, 1335 (s. XII^ex.)
P = Berlin Ms. Phillips 1796 (s. XIII–XIV)
P₁ = Paris lat. 7994 (s. XIII)
E = Berlin Ms. lat. oct. 167 (s. XIII)

T = Tours 879 (XII–XIII) (French)

F = Frankfurt-am-Main S. Barthol. 110 (s. XII^ex.) (France)
V = Vienna 885 (s. XII–XIII) (Austria)
H = London Addit. 49368 (s. XIII)
A = Antwerp lat. 68 (s. XIII)
Z = Paris *Bibliothèque Sainte Geneviève* 1210 (s. XII^ex.–XIII).

---

[93] Luck 1:18.

That all the surviving manuscripts come from a common archetype
is clear from the errors they almost all share, e.g., 84 *chori* for *chao*;
178 *egisti* for *aegypti*; 412 *gery/ionea* for *cercyonea*. Because the *Ibis* in
large part consists of a catalogue of imprecations, expressed in sepa-
rate elegiac couplets and showing no very obvious pattern of arrange-
ment, it was easy for the order of the couplets to become confused,
and no manuscript shows the original order. An examination of the
dislocations enabled editors to discern that the older *codices* fall into
three main groups: (i) **G P P₁ E** (ii) **T** (iii) **F V H A Z**. I insert a
table constructed from data in La Penna's edition.[94] In this table
verses added in the margin are marked [+]; repeated verses are
marked [!]; **XXX** denotes an interpolated medieval couplet; under
E the bracketed entry [461–62] represents an interpolated couplet
based on those verses; and misplaced verses are underlined.

From the data in this table La Penna indicates the following rela-
tionships:

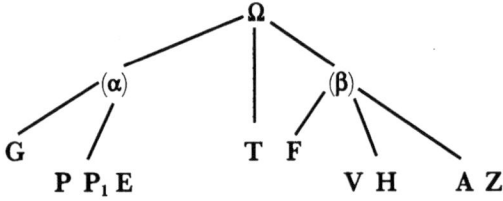

Fairly exact instances of the basic divisions may be seen at, e.g., 30
heu **G P₁**: *et* **P E**: *hei* **T** + **F V H A Z**; 76 *netis* **T**: *nestis* **E**: *nectis/t*
G P P₁ + **F V H A Z**; 193 *erit et* **G P P₁ E**: *et erit* **T** + **F V H A**
Z; 404 *Temporibus* **G P P₁ E** + **T** + **Z**: *Vulneribus* **F V H A**; but
already contamination between the groups is rife: e.g., 415 *(a)et(h)na*
T + **F A Z**: *(h)ora* **G P P₁ E** + **V H**; 539 *Conditor* **E** + **T** + **H Z**:
Cognitor **G P P₁** + **F V A**; 557 *gnosia* **P E** + **T** + **F H A**: *noxia* **GP₁**
+ **VZ**; 617 *di/yane* **G** + **F A Z**: *deorum* **P₁**: *minerue* **P E** + **T** + **V**
H. La Penna lists about 80 more *codices*, dating from the thirteenth
to the sixteenth century, which show texts that have further conta-
minated the lines of descent indicated above.

Scholia to Ibis

Several *codices* of the *Ibis* including **G P E F H Z** already listed
above are furnished with scholia, which are written sometimes by

---

[94] P. lxxvii.

G	P	P₁	E	T	F	V	H	A	Z
1–40	1–40	1–40	1–40	1–40	1–40	1–40	1–40	1–40	1–40
								43	43–44
				133–34[!]	133–34 [+!]	133–34	133–34[!]	134, 133[!]	133–34[!]
43–130	43–130	43–130	43–130	43–130	43–130	43–130	43–130	44–130	45–130
					131–32	131–32		131–32	
XXX	XXX	XXX	XXX	XXX	XXX	XXX	XXX	XXX	XXX
131–338	131–338	131–338	131–338	131–338	133–338	135–338	131–288	133–338	131–262
							291–92		
							289–90		
133–338							293–338		265–338
637–38[!]	637–38 [!]		637–38 [+]	439–40	637–38	637–38	637–38	637–38	637–38
			461–62 [+!]	461–62	439–40	439–40	439–40	439–40	439–40[!]
			[461–62] [!]		461–62	461–62	461–62	461–62	461–62[!]
339–644	339–644	339–571	339–636	339–438	339–438	339–438	339–438	339–438	339–438
				441–60	441–60	441–60	441–60	441–60	439–60
									461–62
				463–644	463–636	463–636	463–636	463–506	463–506
								509–10	509–10
								507–8	507–8
								511–636	511–636
		574–644	639–44		639–44	639–44	639–44	639–44	639–44

the first hand, sometimes by a later. The scholia were written in the period c. 1200–c. 1500. Some other manuscripts also are important:

C₁ = Pisa *Conv. S. Caterina* 37 (s. XV) (scholia perhaps by another hand)
B = Bern 711 (s. XII²) (France) (lemmas and scholia only)
C = Oxford *Corpus Christi College* 66 (s. XV) (lemmas and scholia only)
D = Berlin Ms. Diez. B. Sant. 21 (s. XV).

The version in **P** contains some material from the scholarly tradition of late antiquity and lacks the medieval additions abundant in the other branch of the transmission: guesswork, inferences from the text, and forged quotations from a range of Greek and Latin authors. A *stemma* is given in La Penna (1959).

Ex Ponto

If one may neglect the very small fragments from the fifth century, which may show a tradition differing from all the other witnesses,[95] and use the *siglum* Γ to indicate the more recent manuscripts, the transmission of the poems may be represented by a simple *stemma*:

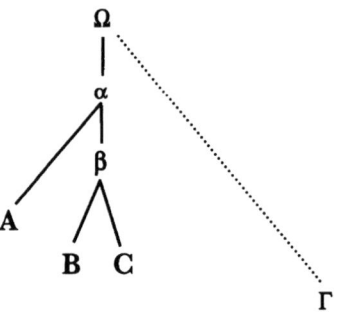

However, this merely reflects the fact that the *recentiores* in some way have some few readings that apparently come from a common source earlier than α: much else in Γ may come from **α, β**, or an intermediate source.

A = Hamburg scrin. 52 (s. IX^med.) (France; contains 1.1.1–2.150; 1.4.1–3.2.67)
B = Munich Clm 384 (s. XII²) (Germany)
C = Munich Clm 19476 (s. XII²) (Germany, Tegernsee).

---

[95] Cf. p. 446, above.

More than 150 *codices* from the vulgate tradition are not yet fully explored. Among those most used by editors are:

s	=	Strasbourg *Séminaire Évangélique* C.V.27 (?s. XII–XIII) (lacked 3.5.34–4.16.52; destroyed in 1870)[96]
d	=	Gotha membr. II 121 (s. XII–XIII)
le	=	Linz 329 (s. XII²) (Austria)
t	=	Tours 879 (s. XII–XIII) (France)
p	=	Paris lat. 7993 (s. XIII)
e	=	Eton 91 (s. XIII)
l	=	Leipzig Rep. I. 7 (s. XIII)
pp	=	Paris lat. 8239 (s. XIII)
v	=	Vatican City Barb. lat. 26 (s. XIII).

Full and accurate collations of these (except **v**) and some 8 others of the *recentiores* are given for Book 2 in Galasso's edition: as indicated below, no clear pattern of relationships emerges.

Though **A** has many errors of its own, its text is free from various interpolations inserted in the other *codices* to repair omissions in the tradition, and its corrupt readings often show an earlier stage of depravation than the progressive corruptions in the other *codices*. There are in **A** several places where the scribe has left a blank. Some of these lacunae have been filled with interpolations in **B** and **C**; all show interpolations in the *recentiores*. **B** and **C** are closely related, and both show an abundance of variant readings. The text of **B** has been altered frequently by the second hand from another source or sources, and the readings of the first hand are sometimes completely erased. The script and condition of **C** make it an especially hard manuscript to read. Later hands in **B** often show the influence of the tradition of the *recentiores*, and **B²** contributes some interesting unique readings. **C** is difficult to evaluate: it is the only manuscript other than **A** that is free from interpolation at 1.2.10. **C** seldom preserves the truth when **B** is in error,[97] but sometimes keeps a superior reading where the original text of **B** was altered by the first or a subsequent hand.[98] **A** omits 1.3, but we cannot say whether it may not have been inserted in the portion of the *codex* now lost. It is found after 3.1 in **le**, after 1.7 in Munich Clm 14753 (**mo**

---

[96] Our knowledge of it is derived from readings recorded by N. Heinsius and a description and readings reported in Korn (1868). It seems that the text had some affinity with **A**, e.g., they share the error *tenens* at 3.1.15.

[97] E.g., *finxerit* 3.9.47.

[98] E.g., *agarius* 3.9.9; *Dignam* 4.12.27.

(s. XII–XIII)), and after 1.8 in Vatican City Vat. lat. 3254(III) (**vf** (s. XII[1], Germany)); **s** had it after 1.4. These puzzling displacements indicate the complexities of the lost portion of the tradition.

The *recentiores* can never be neglected, for the true reading may lurk in one or more of them, and they become especially important for the later part of the work (from and including 3.2.68) missing from **A**. It is often difficult to know whether good readings derive from tradition, error, or conjecture, and there are few grains of truth to separate from a vast accumulation of chaff. Thus, *uideris* (corrected by Heinsius at 1.2.9) so far has been reported only from **a** (Milan G 37 sup. (s. XIV)), and *fulcra* (corrected by Scaliger at 3.3.14) only from **vh** (Vatican City, Vat. lat. 3292 (s. XIII)). Though defaced by many rash conjectures, **e** and some few others of the *recentiores* preserve *decens* at 2.5.52, where the rest of the tradition has the corrupt *docens*, in a context that rules out conjecture (because all the tradition has the misleading *amicus* for the *amictus* restored by Heinsius), but, since we are considering a variation of a mere two similar letters only, random accident cannot be completely excluded from our reckoning. It is remarkable that the title *Ex Ponto*, preserved in **A** only as the subscription of Book 2, has so far been reported from Oxford Douce 146 (s. XV) and Dresden Dc 147 (s. XV–XVI) only: the rest of the tradition gives the title *De Ponto*.

One may illustrate the lack of clear lines of descent in the *recentiores* by taking three sets of readings from Book 2 of the *Ex Ponto*: 2.7.4, *si quid* (1) **A**: *si quidquid* (2) **B C le m**: *iam/nunc/modo quidquid* (3) **b f o pp vf**: *bene/iam/modo si quid* (4) **s d e fr l mo p pk t**; 2.7.24, *planis* (1) **A**: *planus* (2) **B C**: *fraus in* (3) **s² d e m o mo³ᵛˡ pk t vf**: *numerus/numeris*: (4) **s b f fr l le mo pp**; 2.10.43, *ipsam* (1) **A**: *absim/absimus* (2) **B C b e mo t**: *absens* (3) **d fr**: *hic sim* (4) **s f l le m o p pk pp**.[99] The following table will show the lack of a pattern in the distribution of the readings, for, of the 14 *deteriores* legible and extant, only **s** and **l**, **e** and **t**, **f** and **pp** show matching patterns of readings:

A	B	C	s	b	d	e	f	fr	l	le	m	mo	o	p	pk	pp	t	vf
1	2	2	4	3	4	4	3	4	4	2	2	4	3	4	4	3	4	3
1	2	2	4	4	3	3	4	4	4	4	3	4	3	—	3	4	3	3
1	2	2	4	2	3	2	4	3	4	4	4	2	4	4	4	4	2	—

---

[99] I have used the readings in Galasso (1995) adapted to the *sigla* in Richmond, and in the table I have neglected readings other than those of the first hand.

Halieutica

There are two early manuscripts, that transmit—interspersed with a few minor items—(1) extracts from Martial, (2) *Halieutica* (under the title *Versus Ouidi de piscibus et feris*), and (3) Grattius (a few later manuscripts have no independence):

A = Vienna 277 (s. VIII–IX) (France; quires i and xvii of a lost *codex*)
B = Paris lat. 8071 (s. IX) (France).

A has lost many leaves believed to have contained the poems transmitted in the corresponding portion of B; B lacks the verses of Grattius after 159. There is an independent transmission of the extracts from Martial contained in B.

Although there is evidence to suggest that B may have been copied from A (perhaps through an intermediary), there is some reason to believe that B (or a recent ancestor) had access to an ancestor of A. Perhaps an ancestor of B was copied from A, and then readings were imported from a copy that derived from an ancestor of A. When the great corpora of Ovid's works were put together in the twelfth and thirteenth centuries the *Halieutica* was not included, nor did any of the anthologists take verses from it.

The Ovidian authorship, though attested in the manuscripts and by Pliny the Elder, is untenable.[100]

---

[100] See Richmond (1962), (1976); the case for authenticity is argued at length in Capponi (1972) 1:3–162.

GENERAL BIBLIOGRAPHY

1a. The standard editions of the text of Ovid cited throughout this book are, except where noted, as follows. Editors' names are cited in the notes without date:

Amatory works   KENNEY, E.J. (ed.) (1994; with corrections, 1995). *P. Ovidi Nasonis Amores, Medicamina Faciei Femineae, Ars Amatoria, Remedia Amoris.* 2d ed. Oxford.
MUNARI, F. (ed.) (1964). *P. Ovidi Nasonis Amores.* 4th ed. Florence.
SHOWERMAN, G. (ed., trans.) (1914; 1977). *Ovid, Heroides and Amores.* 2d rev. ed. G.P. GOOLD. Cambridge, Mass. and London.
Heroides   DÖRRIE, H. (ed.) (1971). *Ovid. Epistulae Heroidum.* Berlin and New York.
SHOWERMAN, G. (ed., trans.) (1914; 1977). *Ovid, Heroides and Amores.* 2d rev. ed. G.P. GOOLD. Cambridge, Mass.
Fasti   ALTON, E.H., D.E.W. WORMELL, and E. COURTNEY (eds.) (1978). *P. Ovidii Nasonis Fastorum Libri Sex.* Leipzig.
FRAZER, J.G. (ed., trans.) (1931; 1989). *Ovid, Fasti.* 2d rev. ed. G.P. GOOLD. Cambridge, Mass. and London.
Metamorphoses   ANDERSON, W.S. (ed.) (1993). *P. Ovidii Nasonis Metamorphoses.* 6th ed. Stuttgart.
HAUPT, M., R. EHWALD, O. KORN, and H.J. MÜLLER (eds.) (1966). *P. Ovidius Naso: Metamorphosen.* Corrected and with bibliographical supplement by M. VON ALBRECHT. 2 vols. I: Books I–VII, 10th ed.; II: Books VIII–XV, 5th ed. Zurich and Dublin.
MAGNUS, H. (ed.) (1914). *P. Ovidi Nasonis Metamorphoseon libri xv. Lactanti Placidi qui dicitur Narrationes Fabularum Ovidianarum.* Berlin.
MILLER, F.J. (ed., trans.) (1916; 1977 and 1984). *Ovid, Metamorphoses.* 2 vols. 2d rev. ed. G.P. GOOLD. Cambridge, Mass. and London.
Exile poetry etc.   OWEN, S.G. (ed.) (1922). *P. Ovidi Nasonis Tristium Libri Quinque, Ibis, Ex Ponto Libri Quattuor, Halieutica, Fragmenta.* Oxford.
WHEELER, A.L. (ed., trans.) (1924; 1988). *Ovid, Tristia and Ex Ponto.* 2d rev. ed. G.P. GOOLD. Cambridge, Mass. and London.
Tristia   HALL, J.B. (ed.) (1995). *P. Ovidi Nasonis Tristia.* Stuttgart and Leipzig.
LUCK, G. (ed.) (1967–77). *P. Ovidius Naso. Tristia.* Heidelberg.
Epistulae ex Ponto   RICHMOND, J.A. (ed.) (1990). *P. Ovidi Nasonis Ex Ponto libri quattuor.* Leipzig.
Ibis   LA PENNA, A. (ed.) (1957). *Publi Ovidi Nasonis Ibis.* Florence.

1b. Several standard commentaries cited repeatedly throughout this volume are abbreviated as follows:

Bömer, *F.*   Bömer, F. (ed.) (1957–58). *P. Ovidius Naso. Die Fasten.* 2 vols. Heidelberg.
Bömer, *Met.*   Bömer, F. (ed.) (1969, 1976a, 1976b, 1977, 1980, 1982, 1986). *P. Ovidius Naso Metamorphosen.* 7 vols. Heidelberg.
McKeown   McKeown, J.C. (ed.) (1987, 1989, 1998, –). *Ovid: Amores. Text, Prolegomena and Commentary.* 4 vols. Liverpool – Wolfeboro, N.H. – Leeds.
Thomas, *G.*   Thomas, R.F. (ed.) (1988). *Vergil's Georgics.* 2 vols. Cambridge.

2. Collections and editions of ancient texts and reference works such as lexica are referred to where appropriate by standard acronyms or other abbreviations, as found in *L'Année Philologique*, the *Oxford Latin Dictionary*, and the *Oxford Classical Dictionary* (3d ed.). Among the most frequently used are:

CA	Powell, J.U. (ed.). *Collectanea Alexandrina*. Oxford, 1925.
CIL	*Corpus Inscriptionum Latinarum*. Berlin, 1863–.
CLA	Lowe, E.A. (ed.). *Codices Latini Antiquiores: A Palaeographical Guide to Latin Manuscripts Prior to the Ninth Century*. 11 parts and supplement. Oxford, 1934–81.
Courtney	Courtney, E. (ed.). *The Fragmentary Latin Poets*. Oxford, 1993.
CSEL	Multiple editors. *Corpus Scriptorum Ecclesiasticorum Latinorum*. Multiple vols. Vienna etc. 1866–.
GLK	Keil, H. (ed.). *Grammatici Latini*. 8 vols. Leipzig, 1857–70. [Repr. Hildesheim, 1961.]
HE	Gow, A.S.F. and D.L. Page (eds.). *The Greek Anthology. Hellenistic Epigrams*. 2 vols. Cambridge, 1965.
H–S	Hofmann, J.B. and A. Szantyr. *Lateinische Syntax und Stilistik*. Munich, 1965.
LIMC	*Lexicon Iconographicum Mythologiae Classicae*. Multiple vols. Zurich, 1981–97.
N–W	Neue, F. and C. Wagener. *Formenlehre der lateinischen Sprache*. 3rd ed. 4 vols. Leipzig and Berlin, 1892–1905.
OLD	Glare, P.G.W. (ed.). *Oxford Latin Dictionary*. Oxford, 1982.
Pf.	Pfeiffer, R. (ed.). *Callimachus*. 2 vols. Cambridge, 1949 and 1953.
PL	Migne, J.P. (ed.). *Patrologiae Cursus Completus, series Latina*. Paris, 1844–65.
PLAC	Duemmler, E. (ed.). *Poetae Latini Aevi Carolini*. Monumenta Germaniae Historica: Poetarum Latinorum Medii Aevi. 4 vols. Munich, 1978. [Cf. in section 4 of the General Bibliography below Duemmler and Traube (1881–96), of which *PLAC* is a partial reissue.]
Servius	Thilo, G. and H. Hagen (eds.). *Servii Grammatici qui feruntur in Vergilii Carmina Comentarii*. 3 vols. Leipzig, 1881–1902.
SH	Lloyd-Jones, H. and P.J. Parsons (eds.). *Supplementum Hellenisticum*. Berlin and New York, 1983.
TLL	*Thesaurus Linguae Latinae*. Munich, 1900–.

3. In the General Bibliography, individual entries from the following works, containing articles or chapters by multiple authors, are referred to in abbreviated form by the name(s) of editor(s) or short title and page numbers:

Atti	Istituto di Studi Romani (1959). *Atti del Convegno Internazionale Ovidiano Sulmona Maggio 1958*. 2 vols. Rome.
von Albrecht and Zinn	Albrecht, M. von and Zinn, E. (eds.) (1968). *Ovid*. Wege der Forschung 92. Darmstadt.
Binns	Binns, J.W. (ed.) (1973). *Ovid*. London and Boston.
CHCL	Easterling, P.E. and E.J. Kenney (eds.) (1982). *The Cambridge History of Classical Literature*. Vol. II: *Latin Literature*. Cambridge.
Gallo and Nicastri	Gallo, I. and L. Nicastri (eds.) (1991). *Cultura poesia ideologia nell'opera di Ovidio*. Naples.
Godman and Murray	Godman, P. and O. Murray (eds.) (1990). *Latin Poetry and the Classical Tradition: Essays in Medieval and Renaissance Literature*. Oxford.
Graf	Graf, F. (ed.) (1993). *Mythos in Mythenloser Gesellschaft: Das Paradigma Roms*. Colloquium Rauricum 3. Stuttgart and Leipzig.

Harder et al.	Harder, M.A., R.F. Regtuit, and G.C. Wakker (eds.) (1993). *Callimachus.* Groningen.
Hardie et al.	Hardie, P., A. Barchiesi, and S. Hinds (eds.) (1999). *Ovidian Transformations. Essays on Ovid's Metamorphoses and Its Reception.* Cambridge.
Herescu	Herescu, N.I. (ed.) (1958). *Ovidiana. Recherches sur Ovide. Publiées a l'occasion du bimillénaire de la naissance du poète.* Paris.
Levene and Nelis	Levene, D.S. and D.P. Nelis (eds.) (2002). *Clio and the Poets: Augustan Poetry and the Traditions of Ancient Historiography.* Leiden.
Papponetti	Papponetti, G. (ed.) (1997). *Metamorfosi: Atti del Convegno Internazionale di Studi (Sulmona, 20–22 Novembre 1994).* Sulmona.
Pecere and Reeve	Pecere, O. and M.D. Reeve (eds.) (1995). *Formative Stages of Classical Traditions: Latin Texts from Antiquity to the Renaissance, Proceedings of a Conference Held at Erice, 16–22 October 1993, as the 6ᵗʰ Course of International School for the Study of Written Records.* Biblioteca del "Centro Collegamento degli Studi Medievali Umanistici in Umbria" 15. Spoleto.
Powell	Powell, A. (ed.) (1992). *Roman Poetry and Propaganda in the Age of Augustus.* Bristol.
Richlin	Richlin, A. (ed.) (1992). *Pornography and Representation in Greece and Rome.* Oxford.
Schubert	Schubert, W. (ed.) (1999). *Ovid, Werk und Wirkung: Festgabe für Michael von Albrecht zum 65. Geburtstag.* 2 vols. Frankfurt-am-Main.
Zinn	Zinn, E. (ed.) (1970). *Ovids Ars amatoria und Remedia amoris. Untersuchungen zum Aufbau.* Der altsprachliche Unterricht, Reihe XIII Beiheft 2. Stuttgart.

4. In the notes, the following works are referred to by author/editor, date of publication, and page numbers:

Adams, J.N. (1982). *The Latin Sexual Vocabulary.* Baltimore.

Ahl, F. (1985). *Metaformations: Soundplay and Wordplay in Ovid and Other Classical Poets.* Ithaca and London.

Albrecht, M. von (1961). "Zum Metamorphosenproem Ovids." *Rheinisches Museum* 104:269–78.

——. (1963). *Die Parenthese in Ovids Metamorphosen und ihre dichterische Funktion.* Spudasmata 7. Würzburg.

——. (1968). "Zur Funktion der Tempora in Ovids elegischer Erzählung (*Fast.* V, 379–414)." In von Albrecht and Zinn: 451–67.

——. (1977). *Römische Poesie: Texte und Interpretationen.* Heidelberg.

——. (1992). "Ovidian Scholarship: Some Trends and Perspectives." In K. Galinsky (ed.), *The Interpretation of Roman Poetry: Empiricism or Hermeneutics?*, 176–90. Studien zur klassischen Philologie 67. Frankfurt-am-Main – Bonn – New York – Paris.

——. (1997). *A History of Latin Literature from Livius Andronicus to Boethius with Special Reference to Its Influence on World Literature.* 2 vols. Mnemosyne Supplement 165. Leiden – New York – Cologne.

d'Alessio, G.B. (1996). *Callimaco: Inni, Epigrammi, Frammenti.* Milan.

Alföldi, A. (1951). "Der neue Romulus." *Museum Helveticum* 8:190–215.

Allen, W.S. (1973). *Accent and Rhythm. Prosodic Features of Latin and Greek: A Study in Theory and Reconstruction.* Cambridge.

Alton, E.H., D.E.W. Wormell, and E. Courtney (1977). "A Catalogue of the Manuscripts of Ovid's *Fasti.*" *Bulletin of the Institute of Classical Studies (London)* 24:37–63.

Anderson, W.S. (1968). Review of Otis (1966). *American Journal of Philology* 89:93–104.
——. (1989). Review of Hinds (1987). *Gnomon* 61:356–58.
——. (1997). *Ovid's Metamorphoses Books 1–5*. Norman and London.
André, J. (ed.) (1963). *Ovide: Contre Ibis*. Paris.
Arena, A. (1995). "Ovidio e l' ideologia augustea: I motivi delle *Heroides* ed il loro significato." *Latomus* 54:822–41.
Austin, R.G. (ed.) (1964). *P. Vergili Maronis Aeneidos Liber secundus*. Oxford.
——. (ed.) (1971). *P. Vergili Maronis Aeneidos Liber primus*. Oxford.
Axelson, B. (1945). *Unpoetische Wörter. Ein Beitrag zur Kenntnis der lateinischen Dichtersprache*. Skrifter utgivna av Vetenskaps-Societeten i Lund 29. Lund.
——. (1958). "Der Mechanismus des ovidischen Pentameterschlusses. Eine mikrophilologische Causerie." In Herescu: 121–35. [Repr. in A. Önnefors and C. Schaar (eds.), *Bertil Axelson. Kleine Schriften zur lateinischen Philologie*, Acta Regiae Societatis Humanarum Litterarum Lundinensis 78 (Stockholm, 1987): 262–73.]
Badian, E. (1997 [1988]). "Which Metellus?" *American Journal of Ancient History* 13:106–12.
Bailey, C. (ed.) (1947). *Titi Lucreti Cari De Rerum Natura Libri sex*. 3 vols. Oxford.
Bal, M. (1985). *Narratology. Introduction to the Theory of Narrative*. Trans. C. van Boheemen. Toronto.
Baldo, G. (1986). "Il codice epico nelle Metamorfosi di Ovidio." *Materiali e discussioni per l'analisi dei testi classici* 16:109–31.
——. (1997). *Dall' Eneide alle Metamorfosi: il codice epico di Ovidio*. Padua.
Baldwin, J. (1994). *The Language of Sex: Five Voices from Northern France around 1200*. Chicago.
Barchiesi, A. (1984). *La traccia del modello*. Pisa.
——. (1986). "Problemi d'interpretazione in Ovidio: continuità delle storie, continuazione dei testi." *Materiali e discussioni per l'analisi dei testi classici* 16:77–107.
——. (1987). "Narratività e convenzione nelle Heroides." *Materiali e discussioni per l'analisi dei testi classici* 19:63–90. [= Barchiesi (1992): 15–41.]
——. (1989). "Voci e istanze narrative nelle Metamorfosi di Ovidio." *Materiali e discussioni per l'analisi dei testi classici* 23:55–97.
——. (1991). "Discordant Muses." *Proceedings of the Cambridge Philological Society* 37:1–21.
——. (ed.) (1992). *P. Ovidii Nasonis Heroidum Epistulae 1–3*. Florence.
——. (1993). "Future Reflexive: Two Modes of Allusion and Ovid's *Heroides*." *Harvard Studies in Classical Philology* 95:333–65.
——. (1994). *Il poeta e il principe: Ovidio e il discorso Augusteo*. Rome and Bari. [= Barchiesi (1997b).]
——. (1997a). "Poeti epici e narratori." In Papponetti: 121–41.
——. (1997b). *The Poet and the Prince: Ovid and Augustan Discourse*. Berkeley – Los Angeles – London.
——. (1997c [1988]). "Ovid the Censor." *American Journal of Ancient History* 13:96–105.
——. (1999). "Venus' Masterplot: Ovid and the Homeric Hymns." In Hardie et al.: 112–26.
Barrett, W.S. (ed.) (1964). *Euripides: Hippolytus*. Oxford.
Barsby, J.A. (ed.) (1973). *Ovid's Amores Book One*. Oxford.
——. (1978). *Ovid*. Greece & Rome New Surveys in the Classics 12. Oxford.
Battaglia, S. (1959). "La tradizione di Ovidio nel medievo." *Filologia Romanza* 6:185–224.
Beard, M. (1987). "A Complex of Times: No More Sheep on Romulus' Birthday." *Proceedings of the Cambridge Philological Society* 33:1–15.
Beck, M. (1996). *Die Epistulae Heroidum XVIII and XIX des Corpus Ovidianum: echtheitskritische Untersuchungen*. Studien zur Geschichte und Kultur des Altertums, N.F. 1, Monographien 11. Paderborn.
Becker, C. (1971). "Die späten Elegien des Properz." *Hermes* 99:469–70.

Bednara, E. (1906). "De sermone dactylicorum Latinorum quaestiones." *Archiv für lateinische Lexicographie* 14:317–604. [Issued separately by B.G. Teubner, Leipzig, paginated 1–120.]

Bell, A.J. (1923). *The Latin Dual & Poetic Diction. Studies in Numbers and Figures*. London and Toronto.

Bentley, R. ([1699] 1971). *Dissertations upon the Epistles of Phalaris*. Ed. A. Dyce. Hildesheim.

Bernbeck, E.J. (1967). *Beobachtungen zur Darstellungsart in Ovids Metamorphosen*. Zetemata 43. Munich.

Bernhardt, U. (1986). *Die Funktion der Kataloge in Ovids Exilpoesie*. Hildesheim.

Bernt, G. (ed.) (1979). *Carmina Burana. Die Lieder der Benediktbeurer Handschrift. Zweisprachige Ausgabe*. Munich.

Bertini, P. (ed.) (1983). *Publio Ovidio Nasone Amori*. Milan.

Bessone, F. (ed.) (1997). *P. Ovidii Nasonis Heroidum Epistula XII: Medea Iasoni*. Florence.

Binder, G. (1971). *Aeneas und Augustus: Interpretationen zum 8. Buch der Aeneis*. Meisenheim-am-Glan.

Birley, E. (1954). "Senators in the Emperors' Service." *Proceedings of the British Academy* 39:197–214. [= *The Roman Army: Papers 1928–1986* (Amsterdam, 1988): 75–92.]

Birt, T. (1877). "Animadversiones ad Ovidi Heroidum epistulas." *Rheinisches Museum* 32:388–432.

Bischoff, B. (1966–81). *Mittelalterliche Studien: Ausgewählte Aufsätze zur Schriftkunde und Literaturgeschichte*. 3 vols. Stuttgart.

——. (1990). *Latin Palaeography: Antiquity and the Middle Ages*. Trans. from 2d rev. ed. (1986) by D.Ó. Cróinín and D. Ganz. Cambridge.

Bleicken, J. (1962). *Senatsgericht und Kaisergericht: Eine Studie zur Entwicklung des Prozessrechtes im frühen Prinzipat*. Abhandlungen der Akademie der Wissenschaften in Göttingen, Philologisch-historische Klasse, 3 Folge, Nr. 53. Göttingen.

Bleisch, P. (1996). "On Choosing a Spouse: *Aeneid* 7.378–84 and Callimachus' *Epigram* 1." *American Journal of Philology* 117:453–72.

Boissonade, J.F. (ed.) (1822). Ὀβιδίου Μεταμορφώσεις. *Publii Ovidii Nasonis Metamorphoseon libri xv Graece versi a Maximo Planude et nunc primum editi a Jo. Fr. Boissonade*. (N.-E. Lemaire, J.A. Amar, and G.F. Gierig (eds.), *Publius Ovidius Naso*, 5; Bibliotheca Classicorum Latinorum 46.) Paris.

Bömer, F. (1959). "Ovid und die Sprache Vergils." *Gymnasium* 66:268–88. [= von Albrecht and Zinn: 173–202.]

——. (1967). "Ov. met. I 39 *fluminaque obliquis cinxit declivia ripis*." *Gymnasium* 74:223–26.

——. (1987). "Wie ist Augustus mit Vesta verwandt?" *Gymnasium* 94:525–28.

Bond, G. (1995). *The Loving Subject: Desire, Eloquence, and Power in Romanesque France*. Philadelphia.

Bonner, S.F. (1949). *Roman Declamation in the Late Republic and Early Empire*. Liverpool.

——. (1977). *Education in Ancient Rome*. Berkeley.

Booth, J. (ed.) (1991). *Ovid. The Second Book of Amores*. Warminster.

Boretius, A. (ed.) (1883). *Capitularia regum Francorum*. Monumenta Germaniae Historica: Legum Sectio II. Tom. 1. Hannover.

Boyancé, P. (1963). *Lucrèce et l'Épicurisme*. Paris.

Boyd, B.W. (1997). *Ovid's Literary Loves: Influence and Innovation in the Amores*. Ann Arbor.

——. (2000). "'*Celabitur auctor*': The Crisis of Authority and Narrative Patterning in Ovid *Fasti* 5." *Phoenix* 54:64–98.

Boyle, A.J. (1997). "Postscripts from the Edge: Exilic *Fasti* and Imperialised Rome." *Ramus* 26:7–28.

Boyle, A.J. and R.D. Woodard (trans.) (2000). *Ovid: Fasti*. Harmondsworth.

Bramble, J.C. (1982). "Lucan." In *CHCL* 2:533–57.

Brandt, P. (ed.) (1902). *Ovid: De Arte Amatoria Libri Tres*. Leipzig.

Braun, L. (1981). "Kompositionskunst in Ovids *Fasti.*" *Aufstieg und Niedergang der römischen Welt* 2.31.4:2344–83.

Braund, S.H. (trans.) (1992). *Lucan. Civil War.* Oxford.

Bretzigheimer, G. (1993). "Jupiter Tonans in Ovids Metamorphosen." *Gymnasium* 100:19–74.

Brink, C.O. (ed.) (1971). *Horace on Poetry 2. The Ars Poetica.* Cambridge.

Bruère, R.T. (1939). "The Manuscript Tradition of Ovid's *Metamorphoses.*" *Harvard Studies in Classical Philology* 50:95–122.

Brugnoli, G. (1959). "Ovidio e gli esiliati carolingi." In *Atti* 2:209–16.

Brunner, T.F. (1966). "The Function of the Simile in Ovid's *Metamorphoses.*" *Classical Journal* 61:354–63.

Buchheit, V. (1966). "Mythos und Geschichte in Ovids Metamorphosen I." *Hermes* 94:80–108.

Bürger, R. (1901). *De Ovidi carminum amatoriorum inventione et arte.* Wolfenbüttel.

Burkert, W. (1962). "Caesar und Romulus-Quirinus." *Historia* 11:356–76.

Burmannus, P. (ed.) (1727). *Sylloge epistolarum a viris illustribus scriptarum.* 5 vols. Leiden.

Burrow, C. (1999). "'Full of the Maker's Guile': Ovid on Imitating and on the Imitation of Ovid." In Hardie et al.: 271–87.

Burton, R. (ed.) (1983). *Classical Poets in the "Florilegium Gallicum."* Lateinische Sprache und Literatur des Mittelalters 14. Frankfurt-am-Main.

Butler, H.E. (1909). *Post-Augustan Poetry from Seneca to Juvenal.* Oxford.

Buttimer, C. (ed.) (1939). *Hugh of St. Victor. Didascalion.* Studies in Medieval and Renaissance Latin, 10. Washington.

Cahoon, L. (1996). "Calliope's Song: Shifting Narrators in Ovid, Metamorphoses 5." *Helios* 23:43–66.

Cairns, F. (1972). *Generic Composition in Greek and Roman Poetry.* Edinburgh.

———. (1979a). *Tibullus: A Hellenistic Poet at Rome.* Cambridge.

———. (1979b). "Self-imitation within a Generic Framework: Ovid, *Amores* 2.9 and 3.11 and the *renuntiatio amoris.*" In D. West and T. Woodman (eds.), *Creative Imitation and Latin Literature,* 121–41 (notes, 229–31). Cambridge and New York.

Calderini, D. (1476). *Commentarius in Sylvas Statii, in Ovidii Sappho, in Propertii loca.* Brescia.

Cameron, A. (1968). "The First Edition of Ovid's *Amores.*" *Classical Quarterly* 18:320–33.

———. (1970). *Claudian: Poetry and Propaganda at the Court of Honorius.* Oxford.

———. (1995). *Callimachus and His Critics.* Princeton.

Camps, W.A. (1969). *An Introduction to Virgil's Aeneid.* Oxford.

Capponi, F. (1972). *P. Ovidii Nasonis Halieuticon.* 2 vols. Roma Aeterna 2. Leiden.

Casali, S. (1992). "Enone, Apollo pastore e l'amore immedicabile: giochi ovidiani su di un topos elegiaco." *Materiali e discussioni per l'analisi dei testi classici* 28:85–100.

———. (ed.) (1995). *P. Ovidii Nasonis Heroidum Epistula IX: Deianira Herculi.* Florence.

———. (1996–97). Review of Knox (1995). *Classical Journal* 92:305–14.

———. (1997). "*Quaerenti plura legendum:* On the Necessity of 'Reading More' in Ovid's Exile Poetry." *Ramus* 26:80–112.

Castellani, V. (1980). "Two Divine Scandals: Ovid *Met.* 2.680ff. and 4.171ff. and His Sources." *Transactions of the American Philological Association* 110:37–50.

Chance, J. (1994–2000). *Medieval Mythography.* 2 vols. Gainesville.

Chatelain, E. (1894–1900). *Paléographie des classiques latins.* Paris.

Citroni, M. (1995). *Poesia e lettori in Roma antica.* Bari.

Claassen, J.-M. (1996). "Exile, Death and Immortality: Voices from the Grave." *Latomus* 55:571–90.

———. (1999). *Displaced Persons: The Literature of Exile from Cicero to Boethius.* Madison, Wisconsin.

Clark, S.B. (1908). "The Authorship and Date of the Double Letters in Ovid's *Heroides.*" *Harvard Studies in Classical Philology* 19:121–55.

Classen, C.J. (1962). "Romulus in der römischen Republik." *Philologus* 106:174–204.
Clausen, W.V. (1982). "The New Direction in Poetry." In *CHCL* 2:178–206.
——. (1987). *Virgil's* Aeneid *and the Tradition of Hellenistic Poetry.* Berkeley – Los Angeles – London.
——. (ed.) (1994). *Virgil, Eclogues.* Oxford and New York.
Coffey, M. and R. Mayer (eds.) (1990). *Seneca: Phaedra.* Cambridge.
Coleman, K.M. (ed., trans.) (1988). *Statius. Silvae IV.* Oxford.
——. (1990). "Tiresias the Judge: Ovid *Metamorphoses* 3.322–38." *Classical Quarterly* 40:571–77.
Coleman, R.G.G. (1971). "Structure and Intention in the *Metamorphoses.*" *Classical Quarterly* 21:461–77.
Comparetti, D. (1876). *Sull'autenticità della epistola ovidiana di Saffo a Faone.* Florence.
Conte, G.B. (1986). *The Rhetoric of Imitation: Genre and Poetic Memory in Virgil and Other Latin Poets.* Trans., ed. C. Segal. Ithaca.
——. (1991). *Generi e lettori.* Milan. [= Conte (1994).]
——. (1992). "Proems in the Middle." *Yale Classical Studies* 29:147–59.
——. (1994). *Genres and Readers: Lucretius, Love Elegy, Pliny's Encyclopedia.* Trans. G. Most. Baltimore and London.
Conway, R.S. (1900). "On the Interweaving of Words with Pairs of Parallel Phrases." *Classical Review* 14:357–60.
Cordier, A. (1939). *Études sur le vocabulaire épique dans l'Énéide.* Paris.
Coulson, F. (1987). "Hitherto Unedited Medieval and Renaissance Lives of Ovid (I)." *Mediaeval Studies* 49:152–207.
——. (ed.) (1991). *The "Vulgate" Commentary on Ovid's Metamorphoses: The Creation Myth and the Story of Orpheus.* Toronto Medieval Latin Texts, 20. Toronto.
——. (1995). "Addenda to Munari's Catalogues of the Manuscripts of Ovid's *Metamorphoses.*" *Revue d'Histoire des Textes* 25:91–127.
Coulson, F. and B. Roy (2000). *Incipitarium Ovidianum: A Finding Guide for Texts in Latin Related to the Study of Ovid in the Middle Ages and Renaissance.* Publications of the Journal of Medieval Latin, 3. Turnhout.
Courtney, E. (1965). "Ovidian and non-Ovidian Heroides." *Bulletin of the Institute of Classical Studies (London)* 12:63–66.
——. (ed.) (1980). *A Commentary on the Satires of Juvenal.* London.
——. (1990). "Ovid and an Epigram of Philodemus." *Liverpool Classical Monthly* 15:117–18.
——. (1997–98). "Echtheitskritik: Ovidian and non-Ovidian Heroides Again." *Classical Journal* 93:157–66.
Crook, J.A. (1967). *Law and Life of Rome, 90 B.C.–A.D. 212.* London.
Curley, D.E. (1999). *Metatheater: Heroines and Ephebes in Ovid's Metamorphoses.* Diss. Seattle.
Currie, H. MacL. (1981). "Ovid and the Roman Stage." *Aufstieg und Niedergang der römischen Welt* 2.31.4:2701–42.
Dalzell, A. (1996). *The Criticism of Didactic Poetry.* Toronto.
Damon, C. (1990). "Poem Division, Paired Poems and *Amores* ii.9 and iii.11." *Transactions of the American Philological Association* 120:269–90.
D'Anna, G. (1959). "La tragedia latina arcaica nelle 'Metamorfosi.'" In *Atti* 2:217–34.
Davis, G. (1980). "The Problem of Closure in a Carmen Perpetuum: Aspects of a Thematic Recapitulation in Ovid Met. 15." *Grazer Beiträge* 9:123–32.
——. (1983). *The Death of Procris: 'Amor' and the Hunt in Ovid's Metamorphoses.* Instrumentum Litterarum 2. Rome.
Davis, J.T. (1977). *Dramatic Pairings in the Elegies of Propertius and Ovid.* Noctes Romanae 15. Bern and Stuttgart.
Davisson, M.H.T. (1983). "*Sed sum quam medico notior ipse mihi*: Ovid's Use of Some Conventions in the Exile Epistles." *Classical Antiquity* 2:171–82.

———. (1984). "*Magna tibi imposita est nostris persona libellis*: Playwright and Actor in Ovid's *Epistulae ex Ponto* 3.1." *Classical Journal* 79:324–39.

———. (1993). "*Quid moror exemplis?*: Mythological *Exempla* in Ovid's Pre-exilic Poems and the Elegies from Exile." *Phoenix* 47:213–37.

———. (1996). "The Search for an *alter orbis* in Ovid's *Remedia amoris*." *Phoenix* 50:240–61.

DeBrohun, J.B. (1999). "Ariadne and the Whirlwind of Fate: Figures of Confusion in Catullus 64.149–57." *Classical Philology* 94:419–30.

De Cola, M. (1937). *Callimaco e Ovidio*. Palermo.

Degl' Innocenti Pierini, R. (1980). "Echi delle elegie ovidiane dall' esilio nelle *Consolationes ad Heluiam* e *ad Polybium* di Seneca." *Studi Italiani di Filologia Classica* 52:109–43.

Degrassi, A. (1937). *Inscriptiones Italiae. 13.3: Fasti et Elogia*. Rome.

———. (1963). *Inscriptiones Italiae. 13.2: Fasti Anni Numani et Iuliani*. Rome.

Dehon, P.-J. (1993). *Hiems Latina: Études sur l'Hiver dans la Poèsie Latine, des Origines à l'Époque de Néron*. Collection Latomus 219. Brussels.

Della Corte, F. (1958). "Il Perseo ovidiano." In Herescu: 258–64.

Dewar, M. (ed.) (1996). *Claudian, Panegyricus de Sexto Consulatu Honorii Augusti*. Oxford.

Dickinson, R.J. (1973). "The *Tristia*: Poetry in Exile." In Binns: 154–90.

Diller, H. (1934). "Die dichterische Eigenart von Ovids Metamorphosen." *Humanistisches Gymnasium* 45:25–37. [= von Albrecht and Zinn: 322–37.]

Dodds, E.R. (ed.) (1960). *Euripides, Bacchae*. 2d ed. Oxford.

Domenicucci, P. (1991). "La caratterizzazione astrale delle apoteosi di Romolo ed Ersilia nelle *Metamorfosi* di Ovidio." In Gallo and Nicastri: 221–28.

Döpp, S. (1968). *Virgilischer Einfluß im Werk Ovids*. Munich.

———. (1991). "Vergilrezeption in der Ovidischen 'Aeneas.'" *Rheinisches Museum* 134:327–45.

Dörrie, H. (1960–72). "Untersuchungen zur Überlieferungsgeschichte von Ovids Epistulae Heroidum Teil I [–III]." *Nachrichten der Akademie der Wissenschaften in Göttingen: I Philologisch-historische Klasse* (1960): 113–230, 359–423; (1972): 297–386.

———. (1967). "Die dichterische Absicht in den Epistulae Heroidum." *Antike und Abendland* 13:45–46.

———. (1968). *Der heroische Brief. Bestandsaufnahme, Geschichte, Kritik einer humanistisch-barocken Literaturgattung*. Berlin.

———. (ed.) (1975). *P. Ovidius Naso, Der Brief der Sappho an Phaon mit literarischem und kritischem Kommentar im Rahmen einer motivgeschichtlichen Studie*. Zetemata 58. Munich.

Downing, E. (1993). *Artificial I's*. Tübingen.

Draeger, A. (1888). *Ovid als Sprachbildner*. Progr. Aurich.

Dronke, P. (1968). *Medieval Latin and the Rise of European Love-Lyric*. 2d ed. Oxford.

———. (1984). *Women Writers of the Middle Ages: A Critical Study of Texts from Perpetua (†203) to Marguerite Porete (†1310)*. Cambridge.

Drossard, P. (1972). "Structure et signification du Livre II des *Fastes* d'Ovide." *L'Information littéraire* 24:67–76.

Duc, T. (1994). *Le "De raptu Proserpinae" de Claudien. Réflexions sur une actualisation de la mythologie*. Berne – Berlin – Frankfurt-am-Main – New York – Paris – Vienna.

Duckworth, G.E. (1967). "Five Centuries of Latin Hexameter Poetry: Silver Age and Late Empire." *Transactions of the American Philological Association* 98:77–150.

———. (1969). *Vergil and Classical Hexameter Poetry. A Study in Metrical Variety*. Ann Arbor.

Due, O.S. (1974). *Changing Forms. Studies in the Metamorphoses of Ovid*. Copenhagen.

Duemmler, E. and L. Traube (eds.) (1881–96). *Poetae Latini Aevi Carolini*. Monumenta Germaniae Historica: Poetarum Latinorum Medii Aevi 1–3. Tom. 1–3. Berlin.

Duke, T.T. (1971). "Ovid's Pyramus and Thisbe." *Classical Journal* 66:320–27.

Du Quesnay, I.M.Le M. (1973). "The 'Amores.'" In Binns: 1–48.

Duret, L. (1983). "Dans l'ombre des plus grands, I: Poètes et prosateurs mal connus de l'époque augustéenne." *Aufstieg und Niedergang der römischen Welt* 2.30.3:1447–1560.

Easterling, P. and E.J. Kenney (eds.) (1965). *Ovidiana Graeca: Fragments of a Byzantine Version of Ovid's Amatory Works*. Proceedings of the Cambridge Philological Society Supplementary Volume 1. Cambridge.

Edwards, C. (1996). *Writing Rome: Textual Approaches to the City*. Cambridge.

Ehwald, R. (ed.) (1919). *Aldhelmi Opera*. Monumenta Germaniae Historica: Auctores Antiquissimi 15. Berlin.

Eisenhut, W. (1961). "Deducere carmen: ein Beitrag zum Problem der literarischen Beziehungen zwischen Horaz und Properz." In G. Radke (ed.), *Gedenkschrift für G. Rohde*, 91–104. Tübingen. [Repr. in W. Eisenhut (ed.), *Properz* (Darmstadt, 1975): 247–63.]

Eller, H.M. (1938). *Studies in ἀπὸ κοινοῦ in Ovid*. Diss. Chicago.

Enk, P.J. (1958). "Metamorphoses Ouidii duplici recensione seruatae sint necne quaeritur." In Herescu: 324–46.

Esposito, P. (1994). *La narrazione inverosimile: aspetti dell'epica ovidiana*. Naples.

Evans, H.B. (1975). "Winter and Warfare in Ovid's Tomis (*Tristia* 3.10)." *Classical Journal* 70:1–9.

——. (1983). *Publica Carmina: Ovid's Books from Exile*. Lincoln and London.

Fabre-Serris, J. (1995). *Mythe et poésie dans les Métamorphoses d'Ovide*. Études et Commentaires 104. Paris.

Fairweather, J. (1987). "Ovid's Autobiographical Poem, *Tristia* 4.10." *Classical Quarterly* 37:181–96.

Fantham, E. (1986). "Ovid, Germanicus, and the Composition of the *Fasti*." *Papers of the Liverpool Latin Seminar* 5:243–81.

——. (1990). "*Nymphas . . . e navibus esse*: Decorum and Poetic Fiction in *Aen*. 9.77–122 and 10.215–59." *Classical Philology* 85:102–19.

——. (1992a). "Ceres, Liber, and Flora: Georgic and Anti-Georgic Elements in Ovid's *Fasti*." *Proceedings of the Cambridge Philological Society* 38:39–56.

——. (1992b). "The Role of Evander in Ovid's *Fasti*." *Arethusa* 25:155–71.

——. (1995a). "Recent Readings of Ovid's *Fasti*." *Classical Philology* 90:367–78.

——. (1995b). "Rewriting and Rereading the *Fasti*: Augustus, Ovid and Recent Scholarship." *Antichthon* 29:42–59.

——. (ed.) (1998). *Ovid Fasti Book IV*. Cambridge.

Farrell, J. (1991). *Vergil's Georgics and the Traditions of Ancient Epic*. Oxford and New York.

——. (1992). "Dialogue of Genres in Ovid's 'Lovesong of Polyphemus' (*Metamorphoses* 13.719–897)." *American Journal of Philology* 113:235–68.

——. (1998). "Reading and Writing the *Heroides*." *Harvard Studies in Classical Philology* 98:307–38.

Fedeli, P. (ed.) (1985). *Properzio. Il libro terzo delle Elegie*. Bari.

Feeney, D.C. (1984). "The Reconciliations of Juno." *Classical Quarterly* 34:179–94.

——. (1991). *The Gods in Epic. Poets and Critics of the Classical Tradition*. Oxford.

——. (1992). "*Si licet et fas est*: Ovid's *Fasti* and the Problem of Free Speech under the Principate." In Powell: 1–25.

——. (1998). *Literature and Religion at Rome*. Cambridge.

——. (1999). "*Mea tempora*: Patterning of Time in the *Metamorphoses*." In Hardie et al.: 13–30.

Feldherr, A. (1997). "Metamorphosis and Sacrifice in Ovid's Theban Narrative." *Materiali e discussioni per l'analisi dei testi classici* 38:25–55.

——. (1999). "Putting Dido on the Map: Genre and Geography in Vergil's Underworld." *Arethusa* 32:85–122.

Finkelpearl, E. (1990). "Psyche, Aeneas, and an Ass: Apuleius *Metamorphoses* 6.10–21." *Transactions of the American Philological Association* 120:333–47.

Fitton Brown, A.D. (1985). "The Unreality of Ovid's Tomitan Exile." *Liverpool Classical Monthly* 10.2:18–22.

Fliedner, H. (1975). "Ohne Liebe ein Gott: Überlegungen zu Ovid *am*. 2,9,25f." In

E. Lefèvre (ed.), *Monumentum Chiloniense: Studien zur augusteischen Zeit. Kieler Festschrift für Erich Burck zum 70. Geburtstag*, 432–35. Amsterdam.

Floratos, C. (1960). "Veneralia." *Hermes* 88:197–216.

Flower, H.I. (2000). "*Fabula de Bacchanalibus*: The Bacchanalian Cult of the Second Century BC and Roman Drama." In G. Manuwald (ed.), *Identität und Alterität in der frührömischen Tragödie*, 23–35. Würzburg.

Forbis, E.P. (1997). "Voice and Voicelessness in Ovid's Exile Poetry." In C. Deroux (ed.), *Studies in Latin Literature and Roman History VIII*, 245–67. Collection Latomus 239. Brussels.

Fordyce, C.J. (ed.) (1961). *Catullus. A Commentary*. Oxford.

Fornara, C.W. (1983). *The Nature of History in Ancient Greece and Rome*. Berkeley and Los Angeles.

Fox, M. (1996). *Roman Historical Myths. The Regal Period in Augustan Literature*. Oxford.

Fraenkel, E. (1957). *Horace*. Oxford.

Franke, C. (1809). *De Ovidii Fastorum fontibus capita tria*. Halle.

Fränkel, H. (1945). *Ovid: A Poet Between Two Worlds*. Berkeley and Los Angeles.

——. (ed.) (1961). *Apollonii Rhodii Argonautica*. Oxford.

Fraschetti, A. (1995). "Sulla datazione della *Consolatio ad Liviam*." *Rivista di Filologia e d'Istruzione Classica* 123:409–27.

Frazer, J.G. (1929). *Publii Ovidii Nasonis Fastorum Libri Sex*. London.

Frécaut, J.-M. (1968). "Les transitions dans les Métamorphoses d'Ovide." *Revue des Études Latines* 47:247–63.

——. (1969). "Une figure de style chère à Ovide: le zeugma ou attelage." *Latomus* 28:28–41.

——. (1972). *L'esprit et l'humour chez Ovide*. Grenoble.

Frisk, H. (1970). *Griechisches etymologisches Wörterbuch*. 3 vols. in 4. Heidelberg.

Fritsen, A. (1995). "Renaissance Commentaries on Ovid's *Fasti*." Diss. New Haven.

Froesch, H.H. (1968). *Ovids Epistulae Ex Ponto I–III als Gedichtsammlung*. Diss. Bonn.

Galasso, L. (ed.) (1995). *P. Ovidii Nasonis Epistularum Ex Ponto Liber II*. Florence.

Galinsky, G.K. (1975). *Ovid's Metamorphoses. An Introduction to the Basic Aspects*. Berkeley – Los Angeles – Oxford.

——. (1988). "The Anger of Aeneas." *American Journal of Philology* 109:321–48.

——. (1989). "Was Ovid a Silver Latin Poet?" *Illinois Classical Studies* 14:69–88.

——. (1998). "The Speech of Pythagoras at Ovid *Metamorphoses* 15.75–478." *Papers of the Leeds International Latin Seminar* 10:313–36.

Gallo, I. and L. Nicastri (eds.) (1995). *Aetates Ovidianae: Lettori di Ovidio dall'antichità al Rinascimento*. Pubblicazioni dell'Università degli studi di Salerno: Sezione Atti, convegni, miscellanee, 43. Naples.

Gamel, M.-K. (1989). "*Non sine caede*: Abortion Politics and Poetics in Ovid's *Amores*." *Helios* 16:183–206.

Garrison, M. (1997). "The Social World of Alcuin: Nicknames at York and at the Carolingian Court." In L.A.J.R. Houwen and A.A. MacDonald (eds.), *Alcuin of York, Proceedings of the Third Germania Latina Conference Held at the University of Groningen in May 1995, 11*, 59–79. Groningen.

Gee, E. (2000). *Ovid, Aratus and Augustus. Astronomy in Ovid's Fasti*. Cambridge.

Geisler, H.J. (1969). *P. Ovidius Naso, Remedia Amoris mit Kommentar zu Vers 1–396*. Berlin.

Genette, G. (1980). *Narrative Discourse. An Essay on Method*. Trans. J.E. Lewin. Ithaca.

Ghisalberti, F. (1946). "Medieval Biographies of Ovid." *Journal of the Warburg and Courtauld Institute* 9:10–59.

Gibson, B. (1999). "Ovid on Reading: Reading Ovid. Reception in Ovid *Tristia* II." *Journal of Roman Studies* 89:19–37.

Gilbert, C.D. (1976). "Ovid *Met.* 1.4." *Classical Quarterly* 26:111–12.

Gildenhard, I. and A. Zissos (1999). "'Somatic Economies': Tragic Bodies and Poetic Design in Ovid's *Metamorphoses*." In Hardie et al.: 162–81.

——. (2000). "Ovid's Narcissus (*Met.* 3.339–510): Echoes of Oedipus." *American Journal of Philology* 121:129–47.

Gill, C.J. (1997). "Passion as Madness in Roman Poetry." In S.M. Braund and C. Gill (eds.), *The Passions in Roman Thought and Literature*, 213–41. Cambridge.

Glauche, G. (1970) *Schullektüre im Mittelalter: Entstehung und Wandlungen des Lekturekanons bis 1200 nach den Quellen dargestellt.* Münchener Beiträge zur Mediävistik und Renaissance-Forschung, 5. Munich.

Glendinning, R. (1986). "Pyramus and Thisbe in the Medieval Classroom." *Speculum* 61:51–78.

Glover, T.R. (1932). *Greek Byways.* Cambridge.

Godman, P. (1985a). *Poetry of the Carolingian Renaissance.* Norman.

——. (1985b). "Louis 'the Pious' and His Poets." *Frühmittelalterliche-Studien* 19:239–89.

——. (1990). "Literary Classicism and Latin Erotic Poetry of the Twelfth Century and the Renaissance." In Godman and Murray: 149–82.

Goold, G.P. (1965). "Amatoria Critica." *Harvard Studies in Classical Philology* 69:1–107.

——. (1974). Review of Dörrie (1971). *Gnomon* 46:475–84.

——. (1983). "The Cause of Ovid's Exile." *Illinois Classical Studies* 8:94–107.

Graf, F. (1988). "Ovide, les Métamorphoses et la véracité du mythe." In C. Calame (ed.), *Métamorphoses du mythe en Grèce ancienne*, 57–70. Geneva.

Granobs, R. (1997). *Studien zur Darstellung römischer Geschichte in Ovids 'Metamorphosen.'* Frankfurt-am-Main.

Gransden, K.W. (ed.) (1976). *Virgil: Aeneid Book VIII.* Cambridge.

Green, P. (1960). *Essays in Antiquity.* London.

——. (1979). "Ars Gratia Cultus: Ovid as Beautician." *American Journal of Philology* 100:381–92.

——. (trans.) (1982a). *Ovid: The Erotic Poems.* Harmondsworth.

——. (1982b). "*Carmen et Error*: πρόφασις and αἰτία in the Matter of Ovid's *Exile.*" *Classical Antiquity* 1:202–20.

——. (1989). *Classical Bearings: Interpreting Ancient History and Culture.* London and New York.

——. (trans.) (1994). *Ovid: The Poems of Exile.* Harmondsworth.

Green, R. (ed.) (1980). *Seven Versions of Carolingian Pastoral.* Reading.

——. (1982). "The Genesis of a Medieval Textbook: The Models and Sources of the Ecloga Theoduli." *Viator* 13:49–106.

Griffin, M.T. (1976). *Seneca: A Philosopher in Politics.* Oxford.

——. (1984). *Nero. The End of a Dynasty.* New Haven and London.

Gruppe, O. (1838). *Die römische Elegie.* Leipzig.

Gruzelier, C. (ed., trans.) (1993). *Claudian, De Raptu Proserpinae.* Oxford.

Guttmann, K. (1890). *Sogenanntes instrumentales ab bei Ovid.* Progr. Dortmund.

Habinek, T.N. (1998). *The Politics of Latin Literature: Writing, Identity, and Empire in Ancient Rome.* Princeton.

Hall, J.B. (1990). "More Notes on Ovid's *Tristia.*" *Euphrosyne* 18:85–98.

Halleran, M.R. (ed., trans.) (1995). *Euripides: Hippolytus.* Warminster.

Harder, M.A. (1988). "Callimachus and the Muses: Some Aspects of Narrative Technique in *Aetia* 1–2." *Prometheus* 14:1–14.

——. (1990). "Untrodden Paths: Where Do They Lead?" *Harvard Studies in Classical Philology* 93:287–309.

——. (1993). "Aspects of the Structure of Callimachus' *Aetia.*" In Harder et al.: 99–110.

Hardie, P.R. (1986). *Virgil's Aeneid: Cosmos and Imperium.* Oxford.

——. (1988). "Lucretius and the Delusions of Narcissus." *Materiali e discussioni per l'analisi dei testi classici* 20/21:71–89.

——. (1990). "Ovid's Theban History: The First 'Anti-*Aeneid*'?" *Classical Quarterly* 40:224–35.

——. (1991). "The Janus Episode in Ovid's *Fasti*." *Materiali e discussioni per l'analisi dei testi classici* 26:47–64.

——. (1992). "Augustan Poets and the Mutability of Rome." In Powell: 59–82.

——. (1993). *The Epic Successors of Virgil: A Study in the Dynamics of a Tradition.* Cambridge.

——. (1995). "The Speech of Pythagoras in Ovid's *Metamorphoses* 15: Empedoclean *Epos*." *Classical Quarterly* 45:204–14.

——. (1997). "Questions of Authority: The Invention of Tradition in Ovid's *Metamorphoses*." In T. Habinek and A. Schiesaro (eds.), *The Roman Cultural Revolution*, 182–98. Cambridge and New York.

——. (1998). *Virgil.* Greece & Rome New Surveys in the Classics 28. Oxford.

——. (2002). "The Historian in Ovid: The 'Roman History' of *Met.* 14–15." In Levene and Nelis: 191–210.

Harries, B. (1989). "Causation and the Authority of the Poet in Ovid's *Fasti*." *Classical Quarterly* 38:164–85.

——. (1990). "The Spinner and the Poet: Arachne in Ovid's *Metamorphoses*." *Proceedings of the Cambridge Philological Society* 36:64–82.

——. (1991). "Ovid and the Fabii: *Fasti* 2.193–474." *Classical Quarterly* 41:150–68.

Harrison, E. (1943). "Latin Verse Composition and the Nasonian Code." *Classical Review* 57:97–101.

Harrison, S.J. (ed.) (1991). *Vergil: Aeneid X.* Oxford

——. (1993). "A Roman Hecale: Ovid *Fasti* 3.661–74." *Classical Quarterly* 43:455–57.

Hartman, J.J. (1905). *De Ovidio Poeta Commentatio.* Leiden.

Harvey, A.E. (1955). "The Classification of Greek Lyric Poetry." *Classical Quarterly* 5:157–75.

Harvey, R.A. (1981). *A Commentary on Persius.* Leiden.

Haskins, G.E. (ed.) (1887). *M. Annaei Lucani Pharsalia.* Introduction by W.E. Heitland. London and Cambridge.

Hau, P. (1884). *De casuum usu Ovidiano.* Diss. Münster.

Haupt, M. (1875–76). *Mauricii Hauptii Opuscula.* 3 vols. Leipzig.

Hedickius, E. (1905). *Studia Bentleiana V: Ovidius Bentleianus.* Prog. Freienwalde.

Heinsius, N. (ed.) (1661). *P. Ovidii Nasonis opera.* Amsterdam.

Heinze, R. (1919). *Ovids elegische Erzählung.* Berichte der Sächsischen Akademie der Wissenschaften zu Leipzig, Philologisch-historische Klasse, 71.7. Leipzig. [Repr. in E. Burck (ed.), *Vom Geist des Römertums*, 3d ed. (Stuttgart, 1960): 308–403.]

Heinze, T. (1991–93). "The Authenticity of Ovid, *Heroides* 12 Reconsidered." *Bulletin of the Institute of Classical Studies (London)* 38:94–97.

——. (ed.) (1997). *P. Ovidius Naso. Der XII. Heroidenbrief: Medea an Jason.* Mnemosyne Supplement 170. Leiden.

Heldmann, K. (1981). "Schönheitspflege und Charakterstärke in Ovids Liebeslehre." *Würzburger Jahrbücher für die Altertumswissenschaft* 7:153–76.

Helzle, M. (ed.) (1989). *Publii Ovidii Nasonis Epistularum ex Ponto Liber IV: A Commentary on Poems 1 to 7 and 16.* Spudasmata 43. Hildesheim.

——. (1993). "Ovid's Cosmogony: *Metamorphoses* 1.5–88 and the Traditions of Ancient Poetry." *Papers of the Leeds International Latin Seminar* 7:123–34.

Henderson, A.A.R. (ed.) (1979). *P. Ovidi Nasonis Remedia Amoris.* Edinburgh.

Henry, J. (1873–89). *Aeneidea, or Critical, Exegetical and Aesthetical Remarks on the Aeneis.* 4 vols. London – Edinburgh – Dublin.

Herbert-Brown, G. (1994). *Ovid and the Fasti: An Historical Study.* Oxford.

Herr, M.W. (1937). *The Additional Short Syllables in Ovid.* Philadelphia.

Herter, H. (1948). "Ovids Kunstprinzip in den Metamorphosen." *American Journal of Philology* 69:129–48. [= von Albrecht and Zinn: 340–61.]

Herz, P. (1978). "Kaiserfeste der Prinzipatszeit." *Aufstieg und Niedergang der römischen Welt* 2.16.2:1135–1200.

Heyworth, S.J. (1994). "Some Allusions to Callimachus in Latin Poetry." *Materiali e discussioni per l'analisi dei testi classici* 33:51–79.

———. (1995a). "Dividing Poems." In Pecere and Reeve: 117–48.

———. (1995b). "Propertius: Division, Transmission, and the Editor's Task." *Proceedings of the Leeds International Latin Seminar* 8:165–85.

Hexter, R.J. (1986). *Ovid and Medieval Schooling. Studies in Medieval School Commentaries on Ovid's Ars Amatoria, Epistulae Ex Ponto, and Epistulae Heroidum.* Münchener Beiträge zur Mediävistik und Renaissance-Forschung 38. Munich.

———. (1987). "Medieval Latin: Horizons and Perspectives." *Helios* 14:69–92.

———. (1988a). "Medieval Articulations of Ovid's *Metamorphoses*: From Lactantian Segmentation to Arnulfian Allegory." In M.R. Desmond (ed.), *Ovid in Medieval Culture*, 63–82. Binghamton. [= *Mediaevalia. A Journal of Medieval Studies* 13:63–82.]

———. (1988b). "The Metamorphosis of Sodom: The Ps-Cyprian *De Sodoma* as an Ovidian Episode." *Traditio* 44:1–35.

———. (1989). "The *Allegari* of Pierre Bersuire: Interpretation and the *Reductorium morale*." *Allegorica* 10:49–82.

———. (1995). "The Poetry of Ovid's Exile and the Medieval Popularity of the Exile Elegies." In W.S. Anderson (ed.), *Ovid*, 37–60. New York.

———. (1999). "Ovid's Body." In J.J. Porter (ed.), *The Construction of the Classical Body*, 327–54. Ann Arbor.

Hilberg, I. (1894). *Die Gesetze der Wortstellung im Pentameter des Ovid.* Leipzig.

Hilbert, K. (ed.) (1979). *Baldricus Burgulianus Carmina.* Editiones Heidelbergenses, 19. Heidelberg.

Hilka, A., O. Schumann, and B. Bischoff (eds.) (1930–1970). *Carmina Burana, mit Benutzung der Vorarbeiten Wilhelm Meyers.* Heidelberg.

Hinds, S.E. (1985). "Booking the Return Trip: Ovid and *Tristia* 1." *Proceedings of the Cambridge Philological Society* 31:13–32.

———. (1987a). *The Metamorphosis of Persephone. Ovid and the Self-conscious Muse.* Cambridge.

———. (1987b). "Generalising about Ovid." *Ramus* 16:4–31. [= A.J. Boyle (ed.), *The Imperial Muse: Ramus Essays on Roman Literature of the Empire*, 4–31. Victoria, Australia.]

———. (1992). "*Arma* in Ovid's *Fasti*." *Arethusa* 25:81–153.

———. (1993). "Medea in Ovid: Scenes from the Life of an Intertextual Heroine." *Materiali e discussioni per l'analisi dei testi classici* 30:9–47.

———. (1998). *Allusion and Intertext. Dynamics of Appropriation in Roman Poetry.* Cambridge.

———. (1999). "After Exile: Time and Teleology from Metamorphoses to Ibis." In Hardie et al.: 48–67.

Hintermeier, C.M. (1993). *Die Briefpaare in Ovids Heroides.* Palingenesia 41. Stuttgart.

Hofmann, H. (1986). "Ovid's Metamorphoses: carmen perpetuum, carmen deductum." *Papers of the Liverpool Latin Seminar* 5:223–41.

Holleman, A.W.J. (1973). "Ovid and the Lupercalia." *Historia* 22:260–68.

Hollis, A.S. (ed.) (1970). *Ovid Metamorphoses Book VIII.* Oxford.

———. (1973). "The *Ars Amatoria* and *Remedia Amoris*." In Binns: 84–115.

———. (ed.) (1977). *Ovid: Ars Amatoria, Book I.* Oxford.

———. (ed.) (1990). *Callimachus: Hecale.* Oxford.

———. (1996). Review of Williams (1994). *Classical Review* 46:26–27.

Holsinger, B. and D. Townsend (2000). "The Ovidian Verse Epistles of Master Leoninus (1135–1201)." *Journal of Medieval Latin* 10:239–54.

Holzberg, N. (1981). "Ovids erotische Lehrgedichte und die römische Liebeselegie." *Wiener Studien* 15:185–204.

———. (1988). "Ovids Babyloniaka." *Wiener Studien* 101:265–77.

———. (1995). *Ovid, Festkalendar.* Zurich.

———. (1997a). *Ovid. Dichter und Werk.* Munich.

——. (1997b). "Playing with His Life: Ovid's 'Autobiographical' References." *Lampas* 30:4–19.

Hopkinson, N. (1982). "Juxtaposed Prosodic Variants in Greek and Latin Poetry." *Glotta* 60:162–77.

——. (ed.) (1988). *A Hellenistic Anthology*. Cambridge.

Horsfall, N.M. (1972). "Varro and Caesar: Three Chronological Problems." *Bulletin of the Institute of Classical Studies (London)* 27:120–28.

——. (1974). "The Ides of March." *Greece and Rome* 21:191–98.

——. (1979). "Epic and Burlesque in Ovid, *Met.* viii.260ff." *Classical Journal* 74:319–32.

——. (1981). "Some Problems of Titulature in Roman Literary History." *Bulletin of the Institute of Classical Studies (London)* 28:103–14.

——. (1993). "Mythological Invention and Poetica Licentia." In Graf: 131–41.

——. (ed.) (2000). *Virgil*, Aeneid 7. Leiden – Boston – Cologne.

Housman, A.E. (1890). "Notes on Latin Poets [II]." *Classical Review* 4:340–42.

——. (1920). "The *Ibis* of Ovid." *Journal of Philology* 34:222–38.

——. (1922). "*Attamen* and Ovid *Her.* I 2." *Classical Quarterly* 16:88–91.

——. (1972). *The Classical Papers of A.E. Housman.* 3 vols. Ed. J. Diggle and F.R.D. Goodyear. Cambridge.

How, F.D. (1904). *Six Great Schoolmasters*. London.

Hughes, T. (1997). *Tales from Ovid. Twenty-four Passages from the Metamorphoses*. London.

Hutchinson, G.O. (1998). *Cicero's Correspondence: A Literary Study*. Oxford.

Hutton, J. (1935). *The Greek Anthology in Italy to the Year 1800*. Ithaca – New York – London.

Innes, D.C. (1979). "Gigantomachy and Natural Philosophy." *Classical Quarterly* 29:165–71.

Jacobson, H. (1968). "Ennian Influence in *Heroides* 16 and 17." *Phoenix* 22:299–303.

——. (1974). *Ovid's Heroides*. Princeton.

Jäger, K. (1970). "Crambe repetita? Ovid, Amores 3.2 und Ars 1.135–162." In Zinn: 51–60.

Janan, M. (1994). "'There Beneath the Roman Ruin Where the Purple Flowers Grow': Ovid's Minyeides and the Feminine Imagination." *American Journal of Philology* 115:427–48.

Janka, M. (ed.) (1997). *Ovid Ars Amatoria Buch 2 Kommentar*. Heidelberg.

Janssen, H.H. (1941). *De kenmerken der Romeinsche dichtertaal*. Nijmegen and Utrecht. [= "Le caratteristiche della lingua poetica romana." In A. Lunelli (ed.), *La lingua poetica Latina*, 2d ed. (Bologna, 1980): 67–130.]

Jeauneau, É. (1988). "Berkeley, University of California, Bancroft Library ms. 2 (Notes de Lecture)." *Mediaeval Studies* 50:438–56.

Jocelyn, H.D. (ed.) (1967). *The Tragedies of Ennius*. Cambridge.

——. (1983). Review of Zetzel (1981). *Gnomon* 55:307–11.

——. (1989). "Romulus and the *di genitales*." In J. Diggle, J.B. Hall, and H.D. Jocelyn (eds.), *Studies in Latin Literature and Its Tradition: In Honour of C.O. Brink*, 39–65. Proceedings of the Cambridge Philological Society Supplementary Volume 15. Cambridge.

Johnson, P.J. (1996). "Constructions of Venus in Ovid's *Metamorphoses* V." *Arethusa* 29:125–49.

——. (1997a). "Ovid and Poetic *Facundia*." In C. Deroux (ed.), *Studies in Latin Literature and Roman History VIII*, 231–44. Collection Latomus 239. Brussels.

——. (1997b). "Ovid's Livia in Exile." *Classical World* 90:403–20.

Johnson, P.J. and M. Malamud (1988). "Ovid's Musomachia." *Pacific Coast Philology* 23:30–38.

Johnson, W.R. (1978). "The Desolation of the *Fasti*." *Classical Journal* 74:7–18.

——. (1997). "Vertumnus in Love." *Classical Philology* 92:367–75.

Jones, D. (1997). *Enjoinder and Argument in Ovid's* Remedia Amoris. Stuttgart.

Jong, I.J.F. de (1987). "The Voice of Anonymity: τις-speeches in the *Iliad*." *Eranos* 85:69–84.

Kaster, R.A. (ed.) (1995). *C. Suetonius Tranquillus De Grammaticis et Rhetoribus*. Oxford.

Katsouris, A.G. (1976). "The Suicide Motif in Ancient Drama." *Dionysio* 47:5–36.

Katz, P.B. (1992). "Ovid's Last World: An Age of Iron." *Classical and Modern Literature* 12.2:127–37.

Keith, A.M. (1992a). *The Play of Fictions. Studies in Ovid's Metamorphoses Book 2*. Ann Arbor.

——. (1992b). "*Amores* 1.1: Propertius and the Ovidian Programme." In C. Deroux (ed.), *Studies in Latin Literature and Roman History VI*, 327–44. Collection Latomus 217. Brussels.

——. (1998). Review of Boyd (1997). *Vergilius* 44:146–51.

——. (1999a). "Slender Verse." *Mnemosyne* 52:41–62.

——. (1999b). "Versions of Epic Masculinity in Ovid's *Metamorphoses*." In Hardie et al.: 214–39.

Kellner, T. (1997). *Die Göttergestalten in Claudians De Raptu Proserpinae. Polarität und Koinzidenz als anthropozentrische Dialektik mythologisch formulierter Weltvergewisserung*. Stuttgart and Leipzig.

Kelly, J.M. (1957). *Princeps Judex: Untersuchung zur Entwicklung und zu den Grundlagen der kaiserlichen Gerichtsbarkeit*. Weimar.

Kennedy, D.F. (1984). "The Epistolary Mode and the First of Ovid's *Heroides*." *Classical Quarterly* 34:413–22.

——. (1992). "'Augustan' and 'Anti-Augustan': Reflections on Terms of Reference." In Powell: 26–58.

Kenney, E.J. (1958a). "Notes on Ovid." *Classical Quarterly* 8:54–66.

——. (1958b). "Nequitiae poeta." In Herescu: 201–9.

——. (1961). Review of Dörrie (1966) I & II. *Gnomon* 33:478–87.

——. (1962). "The Manuscript Tradition of Ovid's *Amores, Ars Amatoria* and *Remedia Amoris*." *Classical Quarterly* 12:1–31.

——. (1964). Review of von Albrecht (1963). *Gnomon* 36:374–77.

——. (1965). "The Poetry of Ovid's Exile." *Proceedings of the Cambridge Philological Society* 11:37–49.

——. (1967). Review of Viarre (1964). *Classical Review* 17:51–53.

——. (1968). Review of Bernbeck (1967). *Classical Review* 18:57–59.

——. (1969a). "On the *Somnium* Attributed to Ovid." *ΑΓΩΝ* 3:1–14.

——. (1969b). "Ovid and the Law." *Yale Classical Studies* 21:241–63.

——. (1970a). "Love and Legalism: Ovid, *Heroides* 20 and 21." *Arion* 9:388–414.

——. (1970b). "Ovid." In *Oxford Classical Dictionary*, 2d ed., 763–65. Oxford.

——. (ed.) (1971). *Lucretius De Rerum Natura Book III*. Cambridge.

——. (1972–88). Reviews of Bömer (1969–86). *Classical Review* 22 (1972): 38–42; 28 (1978): 251–53; 29 (1979): 223–26; 32 (1982): 165–67; 34 (1984): 33–36; 38 (1988): 247–49.

——. (1973). "The Style of the *Metamorphoses*." In Binns: 116–53. [See also Chapter 2, above.]

——. (1976). "Ovidius Prooemians." *Proceedings of the Cambridge Philological Society* 22:46–53.

——. (1979). "Two Disputed Passages in the *Heroides*." *Classical Quarterly* 29:394–431.

——. (1982). "Ovid." In *CHCL* 2:420–57.

——. (ed.) (1984). *The Ploughman's Lunch. Moretum, a Poem Ascribed to Virgil*. Bristol.

——. (1986). Introduction to A.D. Melville (trans.), *Ovid. Metamorphoses*, xiii–xxix. Oxford and New York.

——. (1992a). Introduction to A.D. Melville (trans.), *Ovid. Sorrows of an Exile: Tristia*, xiii–xxix. Oxford and New York.

——. (1992b). "The Right Words in the Right Order." *Ad familiares. The Journal of Friends of Classics* 2:viii–ix.

——. (1995a). "'Dear Helen . . .': The *Pithanotate Prophasis?*" *Papers of the Leeds International Latin Seminar* 8:187–207.

——. (1995b). *Testo e Metodo: Aspetti dell'edizione dei classici latini e greci nell'età del libro a stampa. Edizione italiana riveduta* [of (1974) *The Classical Text: Aspects of Editing in the Age of the Printed Book*, Berkeley] *a cura di Aldo Lunelli*. Rome.

——. (ed.) (1996). *Ovid Heroides XVI–XXI.* Cambridge.

——. (1998). Review of Beck (1996). *Classical Review* 48:311–13.

——. (1999a). "*Vt erat novator.* Anomaly, Innovation and Genre in Ovid, *Heroides* 16–21." In J.N. Adams and R.G. Mayer (eds.), *Aspects of the Language of Latin Poetry*, 401–14. Proceedings of the British Academy 93. Oxford.

——. (1999b). "Greek Feminines in *-ias*: An Ovidian Predilection." *Classical Quarterly* 49:330–32.

Kirfel, E.-A. (1969). *Untersuchungen zur Briefform der Heroides Ovids.* Noctes Romanae 11. Bern and Stuttgart.

Klopsch, P. (ed.) (1967). *Pseudo-Ovidius De Vetula, Untersuchungen und Text.* Mittellateinische Studien und Texte 2. Leiden and Cologne.

Knox, P.E. (1985). "The Old Gallus." *Hermes* 113:497.

——. (1986a). *Ovid's* Metamorphoses *and the Traditions of Augustan Poetry.* Proceedings of the Cambridge Philological Society Supplementary Volume 11. Cambridge.

——. (1986b). "Adjectives in *-osus* and Latin Poetic Diction." *Glotta* 64:90–101.

——. (1986c). "Ovid's *Medea* and the Authenticity of *Heroides* 12." *Harvard Studies in Classical Philology* 90:207–23.

——. (1989). "Pyramus and Thisbe in Cyprus." *Harvard Studies in Classical Philology* 92:315–28.

——. (1990). "In Pursuit of Daphne." *Transactions of the American Philological Association* 120:183–203.

——. (ed.) (1995). *Ovid Heroides. Select Epistles.* Cambridge.

——. (1998). "Ariadne on the Rocks." In P. Knox and C. Foss (eds.), *Style and Tradition: Studies in Honor of Wendell Clausen*, 72–83. Beiträge zur Altertumskunde 92. Stuttgart and Leipzig.

——. (2000). Review of Beck (1996). *Gnomon* 72:405–8.

Konstan, D. (1991). "The Death of Argus, or What Stories Do: Audience Response in Ancient Fiction and Theory." *Helios* 18:15–30.

Korn, O. (ed.) (1868). *P. Ovidii Nasonis Ex Ponto Libri Quattuor.* Leipzig.

Korzeniewski, D. (ed.) (1976). *Hirtengedichte aus spätrömischer und karolingischer Zeit.* Darmstadt.

Kost, K. (ed.) (1971). *Musaios: Hero und Leander. Einleitung, Text, Übersetzung und Kommentar.* Bonn.

Kraus, W. (1942). "Ovidius Naso." *Real-Encyklopädie für die Klassische Altertumswissenschaft* XVIII.2, 1910–86. Stuttgart. [= von Albrecht and Zinn: 67–166.]

——. (1950–51). "Die Briefpaare in Ovids Heroiden." *Wiener Studien* 65:54–77.

Kroll, W. (1924). *Studien zum Verständnis der römischen Literatur.* Stuttgart.

Krókowski, J. (1963). "Ars Amatoria – Poème didactique." *Eos* 53:143–56.

Kühlmann, W. (1973). *Katalog und Erzählung: Studien zu Konstanz und Wandel einer literarischen Form in der antiken Epik.* Freiburg.

Labate, M. (1984). *L'arte di farsi amare.* Pisa.

——. (1991). "La memoria impertinente e altra intertestualità Ovidiana." In Gallo and Nicastri: 41–59.

——. (1993). "Storie di instabilità: l'episodio di Ermafrodito nelle Metamorfosi di Ovidio." *Materiali e discussioni per l'analisi dei testi classici* 30:49–62.

Lachmann, K. (1848). "De Ovidi epistulis." Progr. Univ. Berolinense. [= *Kleinere Schriften* (Berlin, 1876) 2:56–61.]

Lafaye, G. (1904, 1971). *Les métamorphoses d'Ovide et leurs modèles grecs.* Ed. M. von Albrecht with Additions and Introduction. Bibliothèque de la Faculté des Lettres de l'Université de Paris 19. Hildesheim and New York.

Lamacchia, R. (1960). "Ovidio interprete di Virgilio." *Maia* 12:310–30.
La Penna, A. (1951). "Properzio e i poeti latini dell' età aurea." *Maia* 4:62–67.
——. (ed.) (1959). *Scholia in P. Ovidi Nasonis Ibin.* Biblioteca di studi superiori 35. Florence.
Latacz, J. (1979). "Ovids 'Metamorphosen' als Spiel mit der Tradition." *Würzburger Jahrbücher für die Altertumswissenschaft* 5:133–55.
Latte, K. (1960). *Römische Religionsgeschichte.* Munich.
Lattimore, R. (trans.) (1951). *The Iliad of Homer.* Chicago and London.
Lausberg, M. (1982). "'Αρχέτυπον τῆς ἰδίας ποιήσεως: Zur Bildbeschreibung bei Ovid." *Boreas* 5:112–23.
Lazzeri, E. (1971). *Angelo Poliziano: Commento inedito all'epistola ovidiana.* Florence.
Leach, E.W. (1964). "Georgic Imagery in the *Ars Amatoria.*" *Transactions of the American Philological Association* 95:142–54.
——. (1974). "Ekphrasis and the Theme of Artistic Failure in Ovid's *Metamorphoses.*" *Ramus* 3:102–42.
Le Bonniec, H. (ed.) (1961). *P. Ovidius Naso Fastorum Liber Primus.* Paris.
——. (ed.) (1969). *P. Ovidius Naso Fastorum Liber Secundus.* Paris.
——. (ed.) (1969–70). *Ovide Les Fastes.* 2 vols. Catania and Bologna.
Lee, A.G. (ed.) (1953). *P. Ovidi Nasonis Metamorphoseon Liber I.* Cambridge.
——. (1958). "The Authorship of the *Nux.*" In Herescu: 457–71.
Lefèvre, E. (1976). "Die Lehre von der Entstehung der Tieropfer in Ovid's *Fasten* 1,335–456." *Rheinisches Museum* 119:39–64.
——. (1980). "Die Schlacht am Cremera in Ovids *Fasten* 2,195–242." *Rheinisches Museum* 123:152–62.
Lehmann, P. (1927). *Pseudo-antike Literatur des Mittelalters.* Studien der Bibliotheken Warburg, 13. Leipzig.
Lejay, P. (1984). *Morceaux choisis des Métamorphoses d'Ovide.* Paris.
Lennep, D.J. van (ed.) (1812). *P. Ovidii Nasonis Heroides et A. Sabini Epistolae.* Amsterdam.
Lenz, F.W. (ed.) (1956). *P. Ovidii Nasonis Halieutica—Fragmenta—Nux.* Incerti Consolatio ad Liviam. 2d ed. Corpus Scriptorum Latinorum Paravianum. Turin.
——. (1959). "Einführende Bemerkungen zu den mittelalterlichen Pseudo-Ovidiana." *Das Altertum* 5:171–82.
——. (ed.) (1965). *P. Ovidi Nasonis Remedia Amoris, Medicamina Faciei.* Corpus Scriptorum Latinorum Paravianum. Turin.
——. (1967). *Ovid's Metamorphoses: Prolegomena to a Revision of Hugo Magnus' Edition.* Dublin and Zurich.
——. (1968). "Das pseudo-ovidische Gedicht *De sompnio.*" *Mittellateinisches Jahrbuch* 5:101–14.
Lesky, A. (1966). *A History of Greek Literature.* Trans. J. Willis and C. de Heer. New York.
Leo, F. (1960). *Ausgewählte Kleine Schriften.* 2 vols. Ed. E. Fraenkel. Rome.
Lewis, C.T. and C. Short (1879). *A Latin Dictionary.* Oxford.
Levick, B. (1991). "A Note on the Latus Clavus." *Athenaeum* 79:239–44.
Lieberg, G. (1973). "Die 'theologia tripertita' in Forschung und Bezeugung." *Aufstieg und Niedergang der römischen Welt* 1.4:63–115.
Lightfoot, J.L. (ed.) (1999). *Parthenius of Nicaea.* Oxford.
Lindsay, W.M. (1963). *Notae Latinae: An Account of Abbreviation in Latin MSS. of the Early Minuscule Period (c. 700–850) [1915, reissued] with a Supplement (Abbreviation in Latin MSS. of 850 to 1050 by D. Bains, [1936]).* Hildesheim.
Linse, E. (1891). *De P. Ovidio Nasone vocabulorum inventore.* Progr. Dortmund.
Lissberger, E. (1934). *Das Fortleben der römischen Elegiker in den Carmina Epigraphica.* Diss. Tübingen.
Little, D.A. (1970). "Richard Heinze: Ovids elegische Erzählung." In Zinn: 64–105.
——. (1990). "Ovid's Last Poems: Cry of Pain from Exile or Literary Frolic in Rome?" *Prudentia* 22:23–39.

Littlewood, R.J. (1975). "Ovid's Lupercalia (*Fasti* 2.267–452): A Study in the Artistry of the *Fasti*." *Latomus* 34:1060–72.

——. (1981). "Poetic Artistry and Dynastic Politics: Ovid at the Ludi Megalenses (*Fasti* 4.179–372)." *Classical Quarterly* 31:381–95.

Loehr, J. (1996). *Ovids Mehrfacherklärungen in der Tradition aitiologischen Dichtens*. Stuttgart and Leipzig.

Loers, V. (ed.) (1829). *P. Ovidii Nasonis Heroides et A. Sabini Epistolae*. Cologne.

Loew, E.A. (1980). *The Beneventan Script: A History of the South Italian Minuscule*. 2 vols. 2d ed. V. Brown. Sussidi eruditi, 33–34. Rome.

Löfstedt, E. (1942). *Syntactica: Studien und Beiträge zur historischen Syntax des Lateins. I Über einige Grundfragen der lateinischen Nominalsyntax*. 2d ed. Acta Regiae Societatis humanorum litterarum Lundensis 10:1. Lund – London – Leipzig.

Lombardi, M. (1993). *Antimaco di Colofone: la poesia epica*. Rome.

Lörcher, G. (1975). *Der Aufbau der drei Bücher von Ovids Amores*. Amsterdam.

Lowe, E.A. (1972). "Codices rescripti." In L. Bieler (ed.), *Palaeographical Papers 1907–1965*, 2 vols., 2:480–519. Oxford.

Lozovan, E. (1958). "Ovide et le Bilinguisme." In Herescu: 396–403.

Luck, G. (1958). "Zum Prooemium von Ovids Metamorphosen." *Hermes* 86:499–500.

——. (1961). "Notes on the Language and Text of Ovid's *Tristia*." *Harvard Studies in Classical Philology* 65:243–61.

——. (1969). *Untersuchungen zur Textgeschichte Ovids*. Bibliothek der klassischen Altertumswissenschaften, Neue Folge, 2 Reihe, Band 29. Heidelberg.

Lucke, C. (ed.) (1982). *P. Ovidius Naso, Remedia Amoris. Kommentar zu Vers 397–814*. Diss. Bonn.

Ludwig, W. (1965). *Struktur und Einheit der Metamorphosen Ovids*. Berlin.

Lyne, R.O.A.M. (1987). *Further Voices in Virgil's Aeneid*. Oxford and New York.

McAlindon, D. (1957). "Entry to the Senate in the Early Empire." *Journal of Roman Studies* 47:191–95.

McDonough, C.M. (1997). "Carna, Proca and the Strix on the Kalends of June." *Transactions of the American Philological Association* 127:315–44.

McGinn, T.A.J. (1998). *Prostitution, Sexuality and the Law in Ancient Rome*. Oxford.

McGregor, J.H. (1978). "Ovid at School: From the Ninth to the Fifteenth Century." *Classical Folia* 32:29–51.

Mack, S. (1988). *Ovid*. New Haven and London.

Mackail, J.W. (ed.) (1930). *The Aeneid Edited with Introduction and Commentary*. Oxford.

McKeown, J.C. (1984). "*Fabula proposito nulla tegenda meo*: Ovid's *Fasti* and Augustan Politics." In T. Woodman and D. West (eds.), *Poetry and Politics in the Age of Augustus*, 169–87. Cambridge.

McKie, D.S. (1986). "Ovid's *Amores*: The Prime Sources for the Text." *Classical Quarterly* 36:219–38.

Maehler, H. (1982). "Ein fragment eines hellenistisches Epos." *Museum Philologum Londiniense* 1:109–18.

Malouf, D. (1978). *An Imaginary Life: A Novel*. New York.

Maltby, R. (1991). *A Lexicon of Ancient Latin Etymologies*. Leeds.

Manitius, M. (1900). "Beiträge zur Geschichte des Ovidius und anderer römischer Schriftsteller im Mittelalter." *Philologus*, Supplement-Band 7:723–68.

Marmorale, E.V. (1956). *Persio*. 2d ed. Biblioteca di Cultura 18. Florence.

Marouzeau, J. (1946). *Traité de stylistique latine*. 2d ed. Collection d'Études latines, Série scientifique 12. Paris.

——. (1949). *L'ordre des mots dans la phrase latine. III: Les articulations de l'énoncé*. Paris.

——. (1958). "Un procédé ovidien." In Herescu: 101–5.

Martin, C. (1985). "A Reconsideration of Ovid's *Fasti*." *Illinois Classical Studies* 10:261–74.

Martin, R. (1999). "Sensualité, sentiment et intelligence dans l'Ars Amatoria." In Schubert 1:197–204.

Martindale, C. (1993). *Redeeming the Text: Latin Poetry and the Hermeneutics of Reception.* Cambridge.

Martini, E. (1933). *Einleitung zu Ovid.* Schriften der Philosophischen Fakultät der Deutschen Universität in Prag. 12. Band. Brunn and Prague. [Repr. Darmstadt, 1970.]

Martinon, P. (ed.) (1897). *Les Amours d'Ovide.* Paris.

Maurach, G. (1979). "Ovids Kosmogonie: Quellenbenutzung und Traditionsstiftung." *Gymnasium* 86:131–48.

Maurer, J. (1990). *Untersuchungen zur poetischen Technik und den Vorbildern der Ariadne-Epistel Ovids.* Frankfurt-am-Main.

——. (1995). *Lateinische Dichtersprache.* Darmstadt.

Mayer, R. (ed.) (1994). *Horace Epistles Book I.* Cambridge.

Melville, A.D. (trans.) (1992). *Ovid: Sorrows of an Exile.* Oxford.

Merkel, R. (ed.) (1841). *P. Ovidii Nasonis Fastorum Libri Sex.* Berlin.

Mersmann, H. (1931). *Quaestiones Propertianae.* Diss. Münster.

Millar, F. (1977). *The Emperor in the Roman World (31 B.C.–A.D. 337).* Ithaca.

——. (1993). "Ovid and the *Domus Augusta*: Rome Seen from Tomoi." *Journal of Roman Studies* 83:1–17.

Miller, C.W.E. (ed.) (1930). *Selections from the Brief Mention of Basil Lanneau Gildersleeve.* Baltimore and London.

Miller, J.F. (1980). "Ritual Directions in Ovid's *Fasti*: Dramatic Hymns and Didactic Poetry." *Classical Journal* 75:204–14.

——. (1982). "Callimachus and the Augustan Aetiological Elegy." *Aufstieg und Niedergang der römischen Welt* 2.30.1:371–417.

——. (1983). "Ovid's Divine Interlocutors in the *Fasti*." In C. Deroux (ed.), *Studies in Latin Literature and Roman History III*, 156–92. Collection Latomus 180.

——. (1991). *Ovid's Elegiac Festivals. Studies in the Fasti.* Frankfurt-am-Main.

——. (1992a). "Research on Ovid's *Fasti*." *Arethusa* 25:1–10.

——. (1992b). "The *Fasti* and Hellenistic Didactic: Ovid's Variant Aetiologies." *Arethusa* 25:11–31.

——. (1993). "Ovidian Allusion and the Vocabulary of Memory." *Materiali e discussioni per l'analisi dei testi classici* 30:153–64.

——. (1997). "Meter, Matter, and Manner in Ovid, *Ars amatoria* 1.89–100." *Classical World* 90:333–39.

Minnis, A.J. and A.B. Scott (1991). *Medieval Literary Theory and Criticism, c. 1100–c. 1375: The Commentary-Tradition.* Rev. ed. Oxford.

Mitten, D.G. and S.F. Doeringer (1968). *Master Bronzes from the Classical World.* Cambridge, Mass.

Moles, J. (1991). "The Dramatic Coherence of Ovid, *Amores* 1.1 and 1.2." *Classical Quarterly* 41:551–54.

Mommsen, T. (1887). *Römisches Staatsrecht.* 3d ed. Leipzig.

Moore-Blunt, J.J. (ed.) (1977). *A Commentary on Ovid Metamorphoses II.* Uithoorn.

Munari, F. (1957). *Catalogue of the Mss of Ovid's Metamorphoses.* Bulletin of the Institute of Classical Studies (London), Supplement 4. London.

——. (1960). *Ovid im Mittelalter.* Zürich and Stuttgart.

——. (1965). *Il Codice Hamilton 471 di Ovidio (Ars Amatoria—Remedia Amoris—Amores)* in Appendice *Pontano's Marginalia in Berlin. Hamilton 471* by B.L. Ullman. Note e Discussioni Erudite 9. Rome.

——. (ed.) (1977–88). *Mathei Vindocinensis Opera.* 3 vols. Storia e Letteratura: Raccolta di Studi e Testi 144, 152, 171. Rome.

Munk Olsen, B. (1982–89). *L'étude des auteurs classiques latins aux XIᵉ et XIIᵉ siècles.* Documents, Études et Répertoires publiés par l'Institut de Recherche et d'Histoire des Textes. 3 vols. in 4. Paris.

——. (1984–85). "La popularité des textes classiques entre le IXe et le XIIe siècle." *Revue d'Histoire des Textes* 14–15:169–81. [= Munk Olsen (1995): 21–34.]

——. (1987). "Ovide au Moyen Age (du IXe au XIIe siècle)." In G. Cavallo (ed.), *Le Strade del Testo*, 65–96. Studi e Commenti, 5. Bari. [= Munk Olsen (1995): 71–94.]

——. (1995). *La réception de la littérature classique au Moyen Age (IXe–XIIe siècle): choix d'articles publié par des collègues à l'occasion de son soixantième anniversaire.* Copenhagen.

Murray, G. (1921). *Essays & Addresses.* London.

Murgatroyd, P. (ed.) (1980; repr. 1991). *Tibullus I.* Bristol.

——. (1994). *Tibullus, Elegies Book II.* Oxford.

Murgia, C.E. (1984). "Ovid *Met.* 1.544–547 and the Theory of Double Recension." *Classical Antiquity* 3:207–35.

——. (1985). "Imitation and Authenticity in Ovid's *Metamorphoses* 1.477 and *Heroides* 15." *American Journal of Philology* 106:456–74.

——. (1986a). "The Date of Ovid's *Ars Amatoria* 3." *American Journal of Philology* 107:74–94.

——. (1986b). "The Influence of Ovid's *Remedia Amoris* on *Ars Amatoria* 3 and *Amores* 3." *Classical Philology* 81:203–20.

Myerowitz, M. (1985). *Ovid's Games of Love.* Detroit, Michigan.

——. (1992). "The Domestication of Desire: Ovid's *Parva Tabella* and the Theater of Love." In Richlin: 131–57.

Myers, K.S. (1994a). *Ovid's Causes. Cosmogony and Aetiology in the Metamorphoses.* Ann Arbor.

——. (1994b). "*Ultimus Ardor*: Pomona and Vertumnus in Ovid's *Met.* 14. 623–771." *Classical Journal* 89:225–50.

——. (1999). "The Metamorphosis of a Poet: Recent Work on Ovid." *Journal of Roman Studies* 89:190–204.

Mynors, R.A.B. (ed.) (1990). *Virgil. Georgics.* Oxford.

Nagle, B.R. (1980). *The Poetics of Exile: Program and Polemic in the* Tristia *and* Epistulae ex Ponto *of Ovid.* Collection Latomus 170. Brussels.

——. (1983). "Byblis and Myrrha: Two Incest Narratives in the 'Metamorphoses.'" *Classical Journal* 78:301–15.

——. (1987). "Ovid, 'Facile' or 'Formulaic'? A Metrical Mannerism and Its Implications." *Quaderni Urbinati di Cultura Classica* 25:73–90.

——. (1988a). "A Trio of Love-Triangles in Ovid's 'Metamorphoses.'" *Arethusa* 21:75–98.

——. (1988b). "Erotic Pursuit and Narrative Seduction in Ovid's *Metamorphoses*." *Ramus* 17:32–51.

——. (1988c). "Ovid's 'Reticent' Heroes." *Helios* 15:23–39.

——. (1988d). "Two Miniature *Carmina Perpetua* in the *Metamorphoses*: Calliope and Orpheus." *Grazer Beiträge* 15:99–125.

——. (1989). "Ovid's *Metamorphoses*: A Narratological Catalogue." *Syllecta Classica* 1:97–125.

Newlands, C.E. (1986). "The Simile of the Fractured Pipe in Ovid's *Metamorphoses* 4." *Ramus* 15:143–53.

——. (1992). "Ovid's Narrator in the *Fasti*." *Arethusa* 25:33–54.

——. (1995). *Playing with Time. Ovid and the Fasti.* Ithaca and London.

——. (1996). "Transgressive Acts: Ovid's Treatment of the Ides of March." *Classical Philology* 91:320–38.

——. (1997). "The Role of the Book in *Tristia* 3.1." *Ramus* 26:57–79.

Nicoll, W.S.M. (1980). "Cupid, Apollo, and Daphne (Ovid, *Met.* 1.452ff.)." *Classical Quarterly* 30:174–82.

Nims, J.F. (ed.) (1965). *Ovid's Metamorphoses. The Arthur Golding Translation 1567.* New York.

Nisbet, R.G.M. (1982). "'Great and Lesser Bear' (Ovid, *Tristia* 4.3)." *Journal of Roman Studies* 72:49–56.

Nisbet, R.G.M. and M. Hubbard (eds.) (1970). *A Commentary on Horace: Odes Book 1.* Oxford.

Nischke, A. (1982). "Vom Mythos zum Emblem. Die Perseuserzählung in Ovids Metamorphosen (4.607–5.249)." *Der altsprachliche Unterricht* 25:76–87.

Offermanns, W. (1970). *Die Wirkung Ovids auf die literarische Sprache der lateinischen Liebesdichtung des 11. und 12. Jahrhunderts.* Beihefte zum Mittellateinischen Jahrbuch, 3. Wuppertal.

O'Hara, J.J. (1990). *Death and the Optimistic Prophecy in Vergil's Aeneid.* Princeton.

———. (1996a). "Sostratus *Suppl. Hell.* 733: A Lost, Possibly Catullan-Era Elegy on the Six Sex Changes of Teiresias." *Transactions of the American Philological Association* 126:173–219.

———. (1996b). "Vergil's Best Reader? Ovidian Commentary on Vergilian Etymological Wordplay." *Classical Journal* 91:255–76.

Oliensis, E. (1997). "Return to Sender: The Rhetoric of *Nomina* in Ovid's *Tristia.*" *Ramus* 26:172–93.

Oliver, R.P. (1945). "The First Edition of the *Amores.*" *Transactions of the American Philological Association* 76:191–215.

Otis, B. (1936). "The *Argumenta* of the So-called Lactantius." *Harvard Studies in Classical Philology* 47:131–63.

———. (1966; 2d ed. 1970). *Ovid as an Epic Poet.* Cambridge.

Otto, A. (1890). *Die Sprichwörter und sprichwörtlichen Redensarten der Römer.* Leipzig.

Owen, S.G. (ed.) (1889). *P. Ovidi Nasonis Tristium Libri V.* Oxford.

———. (1924). *P. Ovidi Nasonis Tristium Liber Secundus.* Oxford.

———. (1931). "Ovid's Use of the Simile." *Classical Review* 45:97–106.

Palmer, A. (ed.) (1898). *P. Ovidi Nasonis Heroides.* 2d ed. Oxford.

Palmer, L.R. (1954). *The Latin Language.* Oxford.

[Papathomopoulos] Παπαθωμόπουλος, Μ. (ed.) (1976). *Μαξίμου Πλανούδη Μετάφρασις τῶν Ὀβιδίου Ἐπιστολῶν.* (Πανεπιστήμιον Ἰωαννίνων Φιλοσοφικὴ Σχολή· Σειρὰ Πέλεια, 1.) Ioannina.

Parker, H.C. (1997). *Greek Gods in Italy in Ovid's Fasti.* Lewiston, NY.

Parker, H.N. (1992). "Love's Body Anatomized: The Ancient Erotic Handbooks and the Rhetoric of Sexuality." In Richlin: 90–111.

Parsons, P.J. (1988). "Eine neugefundene griechische Liebeselegie." *Museum Helveticum* 45:65–74.

Pasco-Pranger, M. (2000). "*Vates operosus*: Vatic Poetics and Antiquarianism in Ovid's *Fasti.*" *Classical World* 93:275–91.

Pasquali, G. (1951). "Arte allusiva." In his *Stravaganze quarte e supreme*, 11–20. Venice.

———. (1962). *Storia della tradizione e critica del testo.* 2d ed. Florence.

Perraud, L. (1983–84). "*Amatores Exclusi*: Apostrophe and Separation in the Pyramus and Thisbe Episode." *Classical Journal* 79:135–39.

Pearce, T.E.V. (1966). "The Enclosing Word Order in the Latin Hexameter." *Classical Quarterly* 16:140–71, 298–320.

Pease, A.S. (ed.) (1935). *Publi Vergili Maronis Aeneidos Liber Quartus.* Cambridge, Mass.

Perrot, J. (1955). "Observations sur les derives en -*men.* Mots en -*men* et mots en -*tus* chez Lucrèce." *Revue des Études Latines* 33:333–43.

Peterson, W. (ed.) (1891). *M. Fabi Quintiliani Institutionis Oratoriae Liber Decimus.* Oxford.

Phillips, C.R. (1992). "Roman Religion and Literary Studies of Ovid's *Fasti.*" *Arethusa* 25:55–80.

Pianezzola, E. (1972). "Conformismo e anticonformismo politico nell'Ars amatoria di Ovidio." *Quaderni dell'Istituto di Filologia latina dell'Università di Padova* 2:37–58.

———. (ed.) (1991). *Ovidio: L'arte di amare.* Milan.

Pighi, G.B. (1959). "La poesia delle 'Metamorfosi.'" In *Atti* 2:15–25.

Pinotti, P. (ed.) (1988). *Publio Ovidio Nasone. Remedia Amoris.* Bologna.

Platnauer, M. (1951). *Latin Elegiac Verse. A Study of the Metrical Usages of Tibullus, Propertius & Ovid.* Cambridge.

Pohlenz, M. (1913). *De Ovidi carminibus amatoriis*. Göttingen.

Porte, D. (1985). *L'Étiologie religieuse dans les Fastes d'Ovide*. Paris.

——. (1993). "Les Trois Mythologies des Fastes." In Graf: 142–57.

Pöschl, V. (1959). "Kephalos und Prokris in Ovids 'Metamorphosen.'" *Hermes* 87:328–43.

——. (1977). *Die Dichtkunst Virgils. Bild und Symbol in der Aeneis*. 3d ed. Berlin and New York.

Postgate, J.P. (1907–8). "Flaws in Classical Research." *Proceedings of the British Academy* 3:161–211.

——. (1916). "On the Trajection of Words or Hyperbaton." *Classical Review* 30:142–46.

Prince, G. (1982). *Narratology. The Form and Functioning of Narrative*. The Hague.

Pulbrook, R.M. (ed.) (1985). *P. Ovidii Nasonis Nux Elegia*. Maynooth.

Quinn, K. (1968). *Virgil's Aeneid. A Critical Description*. London.

Quint, D. (1993). *Epic and Empire. Politics and Generic Form from Virgil to Milton*. Princeton.

Quirin, W. (1930). *Die Kunst Ovids in der Darstellung des Verwandlungsaktes*. Diss. Giessen.

Rabel, R. (1981). "Vergil, Tops, and the Stoic View of Fate." *Classical Journal* 77:27–31.

Rahn, H. (1958). "Ovids elegische Epistel." *Antike und Abendland* 7:105–20.

Ramírez de Verger, A. (1999). "Figurae Veneris (Ov. *ars* 3,769–88)." In Schubert 1:237–43.

Rand, E.K. (1907). "The Chronology of Ovid's Early Works." *American Journal of Philology* 28:287–96.

——. (1963). *Ovid and His Influence*. New York.

Ransmayr, C. (1988). *Die letzte Welt*. Nördlingen.

——. (1990). *The Last World*. Trans. J.E. Woods. New York.

Rawson, E. (1985). *Intellectual Life in the Late Roman Republic*. Baltimore.

Reeve, M.D. (1973). "Notes on Ovid's *Heroides*." *Classical Quarterly* 23:324–38.

——. (1974). "Heinsius' Manuscripts of Ovid." *Rheinisches Museum für Philologie* 117:133–66.

——. (1976). "Heinsius' Manuscripts of Ovid: A Supplement." *Rheinisches Museum für Philologie* 119:65–78.

Reitz, C. (1999). "Zur Funktion der Katalog in Ovids Metamorphosen." in Schubert 1:359–72.

Reitzenstein, E. (1936). *Wirklichkeitsbild und Gefühlsentwicklung bei Properz*. Philolologus Suppl. 36. Leipzig.

Reynolds, L.D. and N.G. Wilson (1974; 3d ed. 1991). *Scribes and Scholars*. Oxford.

Richlin, A. (1992). "Reading Ovid's Rapes." In Richlin: 158–79.

Richmond, J.A. (ed.) (1962). *The Halieutica Ascribed to Ovid*. London.

——. (1976). "The Authorship of the Halieutica Ascribed to Ovid." *Philologus* 120:92–106.

——. (1981). "Doubtful Works Ascribed to Ovid." *Aufstieg und Niedergang der römischen Welt* 2.31.4:2744–83.

——. (1998). "The Relationship of Vindob. 277 and Paris. lat. 8071." *Philologus* 142:80–93.

Rieks, R. (1980). "Zum Aufbau von Ovids Metamorphosen." *Würzburger Jahrbücher für die Altertumswissenschaft* 6:85–103.

Robathan, D.M. (ed.) (1968). *The Pseudo-Ovidian De Vetula*. Amsterdam.

Robinson, M. (1999). "Salmacis and Hermaphroditus: When Two Become One (Ovid, *Met.* 4.285–388)." *Classical Quarterly* 49:212–23.

Robinson, O.F. (1992). *Ancient Rome: City Planning and Administration*. London and New York.

Romano, E. (1980). "*Amores* 1,8: L'elegia didattica e il genere dell' *Ars Amatoria*." *Orpheus* 1:269–92.

Rosati, G. (1981). "Il racconto dentro il racconto. Funzioni metanarrative nelle 'Metamorfosi' di Ovidio." In *Atti del Convegno internazionale "Letterature classiche e narratologia" (Selva di Fasano, 6–8 ottobre 1980)*, 297–309. Perugia.

——. (1983). *Narciso e Pigmalione: Illusione e spettacolo nelle Metamorfosi di Ovidio*. Florence.
——. (1985). *Ovidio: I Cosmetici delle Donne*. Venice.
——. (1989). *Publio Ovidio Nasone. Lettere di eroine*. Milan.
——. (1991). "Protesilao, Paride e l'amante elegiaco: un modello omerico in Ovidio." *Maia* 43:103–14.
——. (1994). "Il racconto del mondo." Introduction to G. Faranda Villa and R. Corti (eds.), *Ovidio, Metamorfosi*, 5–36. Milan.
——. (ed.) (1996a). *P. Ovidii Nasonis Heroidum Epistulae XVIII–XIX: Leander Heroni, Hero Leandro*. Florence.
——. (1996b). "Sabinus, the *Heroides* and the Poet-Nightingale. Some Observations on the Authenticity of the *Epistula Sapphus*." *Classical Quarterly* 46:207–16.
——. (1997). "Il bel ritroso e il rifiuto d'amore: un modello Callimacheo nelle *Metamorfosi*." In Papponetti: 167–80.
——. (1999). "Form in Motion: Weaving the Text in the *Metamorphoses*." In Hardie et al.: 240–53.
Rosenmeyer, P.A. (1997). "Ovid's *Heroides* and *Tristia*: Voices from Exile." *Ramus* 26:29–56.
Ross, D.O. (1969a). *Style and Tradition in Catullus*. Cambridge, Mass.
——. (1969b). "Nine Epigrams from Pompeii (*CIL* 4.4966–73)." *Yale Classical Studies* 21:125–42.
——. (1975). *Backgrounds to Augustan Poetry: Gallus, Elegy and Rome*. Cambridge.
Rouse, W.H.D. (1899). *Demonstrations in Latin Elegiac Verse*. Oxford.
Roy, B. and H. Shooner (eds.) (1996). "Arnulfi Aurelianensis «Glosule de Remediis amoris»." *The Journal of Medieval Latin* 6:135–96.
Rudd, N. (1976). "Ovid and the Augustan Myth." In his *Lines of Enquiry*, 1–31. Cambridge.
Rüpke, J. (1994). "Ovids Kalenderkommentar: Zur Gattung der libri fastorum." *Antike und Abendland* 40:125–36.
——. (1995). *Kalendar und Öffentlichkeit: Die Geschichte der Repräsentation und religiösen Qualifikation von Zeit in Rom*. Religionsgeschichtliche Versuche und Vorarbeiten 40. Berlin and New York.
Sabbadini, R. (1967a). *Le scoperte dei codici latini e greci ne' secoli XIV e XV*. New ed. by E. Garin. Biblioteca Storica del Rinascimento: Nuova Serie 4. Florence.
——. (1967b). *Le scoperte dei codici latini e greci ne' secoli XIV e XV: nuove ricerche col riassunto filologico dei due volume*. New ed. by E. Garin. Biblioteca Storica del Rinascimento: Nuova Serie 4**. Florence.
Sabot, A.F. (1981). "Les Heroides d' Ovide." *Aufstieg und Niedergang der römischen Welt* 2.31.4:2552–2636.
Salmon, E.T. (1967). *Samnium and the Samnites*. Cambridge.
Sandbach, F.H. (1940). Review of Cordier (1939). *Classical Review* 54:198–99.
Santini, C. (1973). "Toni e strutture nella rappresentazione delle divinità nei *Fasti*." *Giornale Italiano di Filologia* n.s. 4:41–62.
——. (1975). "Motivi astronomici e moduli didattici nei *Fasti* di Ovidio." *Giornale Italiano di Filologia* n.s. 6:1–26.
Schauenberg, K. (1960). *Perseus in der Kunst des Altertums*. Bonn.
Scheid, J. (1992). "Myth, Cult and Reality in Ovid's *Fasti*." *Proceedings of the Cambridge Philological Society* 38:118–31.
——. (1993). "Cultes, Mythes et Politique au Début de l'Empire." In Graf: 109–27.
Schilling, R. (ed.) (1992, 1993). *Ovide: Les Fastes*. 2d ed. 2 vols. Paris.
Schmidt, P.G. (1990). "The Quotation in Goliardic Poetry: The Feast of Fools and the Goliardic Strophe *cum auctoritate*." In Godman and Murray: 39–56.
Schmitzer, U. (1990). *Zeitgeschichte in Ovids Metamorphosen*. Beiträge zur Altertumskunde 4. Stuttgart.
Schuelper, S. (1979) "Ovid aus der Sicht des Balderich von Bourgueil, dargestellt anhand des Briefwechsels Florus-Ovid." *Mittellateinisches Jahrbuch* 15:93–118.

Scivoletto, N. (1976). *Musa Iocosa*. Rome.

Seaford, R. (ed.) (1996). *Euripides. Bacchae*. Warminster.

Segal, C.P. (1969). *Landscape in Ovid's Metamorphoses. A Study in the Transformation of a Literary Symbol*. Hermes Einzelschriften 23. Wiesbaden.

Seidensticker, B. (1982). "Die Wahl des Todes bei Sophokles." In J. de Romilly (ed.), *Sophocle*, 105–53. Fondation Hardt: Entretiens sur l'antiquité classique 29. Vandoeuvres-Geneva.

Shackleton Bailey, D.R. (1989). "More Corrections and Explanations of Martial." *American Journal of Philology* 110:131–50.

Sharrock, A. (1990). "*Alternae Voces*—Again." *Classical Quarterly* 40:570–71.

———. (1991). "Womanufacture." *Journal of Roman Studies* 81:36–49.

———. (1994a). *Seduction and Repetition in Ovid's Ars Amatoria 2*. Oxford.

———. (1994b). "Ovid and the Politics of Reading." *Materiali e discussioni per l'analisi dei testi classici* 33:97–122.

———. (1995). "The Drooping Rose: Elegiac Failure in *Amores* 3.7." *Ramus* 24:152–80.

Simon, E. (1967, 1968). *Ara Pacis Augustae*. Tübingen and Greenwich, Conn.

Skutsch, O. (ed.) (1985). *The Annals of Quintus Ennius*. Oxford.

Slater, D.A. (1927). *Towards a Text of the Metamorphosis* [sic] *of Ovid*. Oxford.

Smith, K.F. (ed.) (1913). *The Elegies of Albius Tibullus*. New York. [Repr. Darmstadt, 1964.]

Solalinde, A., L. Kasten, and V. Oelschläger (eds.) (1930–1961). *Alfonso X el Sabio. General Estoria*. 2 parts in 3 vols. Madrid.

Solodow, J.B. (1977). "Ovid's Ars Amatoria: The Lover as Cultural Ideal." *Wiener Studien* 90:106–27.

———. (1986). "*Raucae, tua cura, palumbes*: Study of a Poetic Word Order." *Harvard Studies in Classical Philology* 90:129–53.

———. (1988). *The World of Ovid's Metamorphoses*. Chapel Hill and London.

Southern, P. and K.R. Dixon (1996). *The Late Roman Army*. London.

Spoth, F. (1992). *Ovids Heroides als Elegien*. Munich.

Steer, G. (1983). "'Carmina Burana' in Südtirol. Zur Herkunft des clm 4660." *Zeitschrift für deutsches Altertum* 112:1–37.

Steinby, E.M. (ed.) (1993–2000). *Lexicon Topographicum Urbis Romae*. 6 vols. Rome.

Steiner, G. (1952). "The Text Tradition of the Ovidian Incunabula." *Transactions of the American Philological Association* 83:312–18.

Steudel, M. (1992). *Die Literaturparodie in Ovids Ars Amatoria*. Hildesheim.

Stok, F. (1991). "L'ambiguo Romolo dei *Fasti*." In Gallo and Nicastri: 183–212.

Stroh, W. (1968). "Ein mißbrauchtes Distichon Ovids." In von Albrecht and Zinn: 567–80.

———. (1969). *Ovid im Urteil der Nachwelt. Eine Testimoniensammlung*. Darmstadt.

———. (1979). "Ovids Liebeskunst und die Ehegesetze des Augustus." *Gymnasium* 86:323–52.

Sullivan, J.P. (1985). *Literature and Politics in the Age of Nero*. Ithaca and London.

Syme, R. (1978). *History in Ovid*. Oxford.

———. (1984). "The Crisis of 2 B.C." In his *Roman Papers* 3:912–36. Oxford.

Tafel, S. (1910). *Die Ueberlieferungsgeschichte von Ovids Carmina Amatoria verfolgt bis zum 11. Jahrhundert*. Diss. Munich. Tübingen.

Tarrant, R.J. (1981). "The Authenticity of the Letter of Sappho to Phaon (*Heroides* XV)." *Harvard Studies in Classical Philology* 85:133–53.

———. (1982). "Editing Ovid's *Metamorphoses*: Problems and Possibilities." *Classical Philology* 77:342–60.

———. (1983). "Ovid" and "Pseudo-Ovid." In L.D. Reynolds (ed.), *Texts and Transmission: A Survey of the Latin Classics*, 257–86. Oxford.

———. (1989). "Silver Threads among the Gold: a Problem in the Text of Ovid's *Metamorphoses*." *Illinois Classical Studies* 14:103–17.

——. (1995a). "The *Narrationes* of 'Lactantius' and the Transmission of Ovid's *Metamorphoses*." In Pecere and Reeve: 83–115.

——. (1995b). "The Silence of Cephalus: Text and Narrative Technique in Ovid, *Metamorphoses* 7.685ff." *Transactions of the American Philological Association* 125:99–111.

Tate, J. (1835). *Richmond Rules to Form the Ovidian Distich with Some Hints on the Transition to the Virgilian Hexameter*. London.

Thibault, J.C. (1964). *The Mystery of Ovid's Exile*. Berkeley and Los Angeles.

Thomamüller, K. (1968). "Doppelte Enallage (zu Ovid *Am.* 3.7.21f.)." *Rheinisches Museum* 111:189–90.

Thomas, E. (1969). "Ovid at the Races. *Amores*. III,2; *Ars amatoria*, I,135–64." In J. Bitauw (ed.), *Hommages à Marcel Renaud*, 1:710–24. Collection Latomus 101–3. Brussels.

Thomas, R.F. (1982). *Lands and Peoples in Roman Poetry. The Ethnographical Tradition*. Proceedings of the Cambridge Philological Society Supplementary Volume 7. Cambridge.

——. (1983). "Callimachus, the *Victoria Berenices*, and Roman Poetry." *Classical Quarterly* 33:92–113.

——. (1986). "Virgil's *Georgics* and the Art of Reference." *Harvard Studies in Classical Philology* 90:171–98.

——. (1990). Review of Hinds (1987a). *Classical Philology* 85:77–80.

——. (1993). "Callimachus Back in Rome." In Harder et al.: 197–215.

Tissol, G. (1993). "Ovid's Little *Aeneid* and the Thematic Integrity of the *Metamorphoses*." *Helios* 20:69–79.

——. (1997). *The Face of Nature. Wit, Narrative, and Cosmic Origins in Ovid's Metamorphoses*. Princeton.

Todorov, T. (1977). *The Poetics of Prose*. Trans. R. Howard. Ithaca.

Toohey, P. (1996). *Epic Lessons*. London.

Tracy, V.A. (1971). "The Authenticity of *Heroides* 16–21." *Classical Journal* 66:328–30.

Tränkle, H. (1960). *Die Sprachkunst des Properz und die Tradition der lateinischen Dichtersprache*. Hermes Einzelschriften 15. Wiesbaden.

——. (1963). "Elegisches in Ovids Metamorphosen." *Hermes* 91:459–76.

Traube, L. (1911; repr. 1965). *Einleitung in die lateinischen Philologie des Mittelalters*. Ed. F. Boll. Vorlesungen und Abhandlungen, 2. Munich.

Treggiari, S. (1996). "Social Status and Social Legislation." In A.K. Bowman, E. Champlain, and A. Lintott (eds.), *The Cambridge Ancient History*. 2d ed. Volume 10: *The Augustan Empire, 43 B.C.–A.D. 69*, 873–904. Cambridge.

Trevelyan, G.O. (1908; repr. 1923). *The Life and Letters of Lord Macaulay*. 2 vols. London.

Trickett, R. (1988). "The *Heroides* and the English Augustans." In C. Martindale (ed.), *Ovid Renewed*, 191–204. Cambridge.

Van Dam, H.-J. (ed.) (1984). *P. Papinius Statius. Silvae Book II*. Leiden.

Vandiver, E. (1999). "The Founding Mothers of Livy's Rome: The Sabine Women and Lucretia." In F. Titchener and R. Moorton (eds.), *The Eye Expanded: Life and the Arts in Greco-Roman Antiquity*, 206–32. Berkeley and Los Angeles.

Verdière, R. (1992). *Le Secret du Voltigeur d'Amour ou le Mystère de la Relégation d'Ovide*. Collection Latomus 218. Brussels.

Vessey, D.W.T.C. (1969). "Notes on Ovid, *Heroides* 9." *Classical Quarterly* 19:349–61.

——. (1973). *Statius and the Thebaid*. Cambridge.

——. (1981). "Atedius Melior's Tree: Statius, *Silvae* 2.3." *Classical Philology* 76:46–52.

Viarre, S. (1964). *L'image et la pensée dans les 'Métamorphoses' d'Ovide*. Publications de La Faculté des Lettres et Sciences Humaines de Paris, Série 'Recherches' 22. Paris.

Videau-Delibes, A. (1991). *Les Tristes d'Ovide et l'Élégie Romaine. Une Poétique de la Rupture*. Paris.

Vollgraff, W. (1909). *Nikander und Ovid I.* Groningen.

Vredeveld, H. (1987). "Pagan and Christian Echoes in the 'Ecloga Theoduli.' A Supplement." *Mittellateinisches Jahrbuch* 22:101–13.

Vries, S. de (1885). *Epistula Sapphus ad Phaonem apparatu critico instructa commentario illustrata et Ovidio vindicata.* Leiden.

Walbank, F.W. (ed.) (1957). *A Historical Commentary on Polybius,* vol. 1. Oxford.

Wallace-Hadrill, A. (1987). "Time for Augustus: Ovid, Augustus and the *Fasti.*" In M. Whitby, P. Hardie, and M. Whitby (eds.), *Homo Viator: Classical Essays for John Bramble,* 221–30. Bristol.

———. (1997). "*Mutatio morum*: The Idea of a Cultural Revolution." In T. Habinek and A. Schiesaro (eds.), *The Roman Cultural Revolution,* 3–22. Cambridge.

Walsh, P.G. (ed., trans.) (1993). *Love Lyrics from the Carmina Burana.* Chapel Hill.

Walther, H. (1969). *Initia carminum ac versuum Medii Aevi posterioris Latinorum.* 2d ed. Göttingen.

Washietl, J.A. (1883). *De similitudinibus imaginibusque Ovidianis.* Vienna.

Watson, L.C. (1991). *Arae: The Curse Poetry of Antiquity.* Leeds.

Watson, P. (1983a). "Mythological Exempla in Ovid's *Ars amatoria.*" *Classical Philology* 78: 117–26.

———. (1983b). "Ovid *Amores* ii.7 and 8: The Disingenuous Defence." *Wiener Studien* n.s. 17:91–103.

———. (1985). "Axelson Revisited: The Selection of Vocabulary in Latin Poetry." *Classical Quarterly* 35:430–48.

———. (2001). "Parody and Subversion in Ovid's *Medicamina Faciei Femineae.*" *Mnemosyne* 54:457–71.

Weinstock, S. (1971). *Divus Iulius.* Oxford.

West, D. (1969). "Multiple-Correspondence Similes in the *Aeneid.*" *Journal of Roman Studies* 59:40–49.

———. (1970). *Individual Voices. An Inaugural Lecture.* Newcastle upon Tyne.

Wetherbee, W. (1972). *Platonism and Poetry in the Twelfth Century.* Princeton.

Wheeler, A.L. (1910). "Propertius as Praeceptor Amoris." *Classical Philology* 5:28–40.

———. (1910–11). "Erotic Teaching in Roman Elegy and the Greek Sources." *Classical Philology* 5:440–50, 6:56–77.

———. (1925). "Topics from the Life of Ovid." *American Journal of Philology* 46:1–28.

Wheeler, S. (1995). "*Imago Mundi*: Another View of the Creation in Ovid's *Metamorphoses.*" *American Journal of Philology* 116:95–121.

———. (1999). *A Discourse of Wonders. Audience and Performance in Ovid's Metamorphoses.* Philadelphia.

———. (2000). *Narrative Dynamics in Ovid's Metamorphoses.* Classica Monacensia: Münchener Studien zur Klassischen Philologie 20. Tübingen.

———. (2002). "Ovid's *Metamorphoses* and Universal History." In Levene and Nelis: 163–90.

White, D.G. (1970). "Ovid, *Heroides* 16.45–6." *Harvard Studies in Classical Philology* 74:187–91.

White, P. (1988). "Julius Caesar in Augustan Rome." *Phoenix* 42:334–56.

———. (1992). "'Pompeius Macer' and Ovid." *Classical Quarterly* 42:210–18.

———. (1993). *Promised Verse: Poets in the Society of Augustan Rome.* Cambridge, Mass.

Whitta, J. (2002). "*Ille ego Naso*: Modoin of Autun and the *Renovatio* of Ovidian Poetry." *Latomus*: forthcoming.

Wiedemann, T. (1975). "The Political Background to Ovid's *Tristia* 2." *Classical Quarterly* 25:264–71.

Wilamowitz-Moellendorff, U. von (1924). *Hellenistische Dichtung in der Zeit des Kallimachos.* 2 vols. Berlin.

———. (1972). *Kleine Schriften VI. Philologiegeschichte Pädagogik und Verschiedenes.* Berlin.

Wilkins, E.G. (1932). "A Classification of the Similes of Ovid." *Classical Weekly* 25:73–79, 81–86.

Wilkinson, L.P. (1940). "The Augustan Rules for Dactylic Verse." *Classical Quarterly* 34:30–43.

——. (1955). *Ovid Recalled*. Cambridge.

——. (1958) "The World of the Metamorphoses." In Herescu: 231–44.

——. (1959). "The Language of Virgil and Horace." *Classical Quarterly* 9:181–92.

——. (1963). *Golden Latin Artistry*. Cambridge.

Williams, F. (ed.) (1978). *Callimachus, Hymn to Apollo*. Oxford.

——. (1981). "Augustus and Daphne: Ovid *Metamorphoses* 1,560–63 and Phylarchus *FGrH* 81 F 32 (b)." *Papers of the Liverpool Latin Seminar* 3:249–57.

Williams, G.D. (1991a). "Conversing after Sunset: A Callimachean Echo in Ovid's Exile Poetry." *Classical Quarterly* 41:169–77.

——. (1991b). "Vocal Variations and Narrative Complexity in Ovid's Vestalia: *Fasti* 6.249–468." *Ramus* 20:183–204.

——. (1992a). "Ovid's Canace: Dramatic Irony in *Heroides* 11." *Classical Quarterly* 42:201–9.

——. (1992b). "Representations of the Book-Roll in Latin Poetry: *Tr*. 1,1,3–14 and Related Texts." *Mnemosyne* 45:178–89.

——. (1994). *Banished Voices: Readings in Ovid's Exile Poetry*. Cambridge.

——. (1996). *The Curse of Exile: A Study of Ovid's Ibis*. Proceedings of the Cambridge Philological Society Supplementary Volume 19. Cambridge.

——. (1997). "Writing in the Mother-Tongue: Hermione and Helen in *Heroides* 8 (A Tomitan Approach)." *Ramus* 26:113–37.

Williams, G.W. (1968). *Tradition and Originality in Roman Poetry*. Oxford.

——. (1978). *Change and Decline: Roman Literature in the Early Empire*. Berkeley and Los Angeles.

Wills, J. (1990). "Callimachean Models for Ovid's 'Apollo-Daphne.'" *Materiali e discussioni per l'analisi dei testi classici* 24:143–56.

——. (1996). *Repetition in Latin Poetry. Figures of Allusion*. Oxford.

Winbolt, S.E. (1903). *Latin Hexameter Verse. An Aid to Composition*. London.

Winther, H. (1885). *De Fastis Verrii Flacci ab Ovidio adhibitis*. Berlin.

Wiseman, T.P. (1983). "The Wife and Children of Romulus." *Classical Quarterly* 33:445–52. [= *Roman Studies, Literary and Historical* (Liverpool, 1987): 285–90.]

——. (1984). *Catullus and his World: a Reappraisal*. Cambridge.

——. (1995a). *Remus: A Roman Myth*. Cambridge.

——. (1995b). "The God of the Lupercal." *Journal of Roman Studies* 85:1–22.

——. (1998). *Roman Drama and Roman History*. Exeter.

Wissowa, G. (1904). *Gesammelte Abhandlungen zur römischen Religions- und Stadtgeschichte*. Munich.

Worstbrock, F.J. (1963). *Elemente einer Poetik der Aeneis. Untersuchungen zum Gattungsstil Vergilianischer Epik*. Orbis antiquus 21. Munster.

Wyke, M. (1994). "Woman in the Mirror: The Rhetoric of Adornment in the Roman World." In L.J. Archer, S. Fischler, and M. Wyke (eds.), *Women in Ancient Societies: 'An Illusion of the Night'*, 134–51. London.

Wyss, B. (ed.) (1936). *Antimachi Colophonii Reliquiae*. Berlin. [Repr. Hildesheim, 1974.]

Zanker, P. (1968). *Forum Augustum: Das Bildprogramm*. Tübingen.

——. (1988). *The Power of Images in the Age of Augustus*. Trans. A. Shapiro. Ann Arbor.

Zetzel, J.E.G. (1981). *Latin Textual Criticism in Antiquity*. New York.

——. (1989). "*ROMANE, MEMENTO*: Justice and Judgment in *Aeneid* 6." *Transactions of the American Philological Association* 119:263–84.

Zeitlin, F.I. (1996). "Playing the Other." In her *Playing the Other*, 341–74. Chicago.

Zingerle, A. (1869–71). *Ovidius und sein Verhältniss zu den Vorgängern und gleichzeitigen römischen Dichtern*. 3 vols. Innsbruck.

Zissos, A. (1996). "Iliadic Echoes in Ovid's Phaethon (*Met.* 1.747–2.400)." *American Philological Association Abstracts* 127.

——. (1999). "The Rape of Proserpina in Ovid *Met.* 5.341–661: Internal Audience and Narrative Distortion." *Phoenix* 53:97–113.

Zissos, A. and I. Gildenhard (1999). "Problems of Time in *Metamorphoses* 2." In Hardie et al.: 31–47.

Zumwalt, N. (1977). "*Fama subversa*: Theme and Structure in Ovid *Metamorphoses* 12." *California Studies in Classical Antiquity* 10:209–22.

INDEX LOCORUM

GENERAL INDEX